The NEGRO PEOPLE
in AMERICAN
HISTORY

The NEGRO PEOPLE *in* AMERICAN HISTORY

William Z. Foster

INTERNATIONAL PUBLISHERS, NEW YORK

SBN (cloth) 7178–0275–2; (paperback) 7178–0276–0

Printed in the United States of America

CONTENTS

Preface

During the three-and-a-half centuries since the first English colonies were planted along the Atlantic Coast, the landowner and industrialist rulers of this country, to further their own greed, have committed many monstrous crimes against the growing American people. They barbarously stripped the Indians of their lands, broke up their social institutions, and slaughtered them. The rulers also relentlessly exploited the immigrant wage workers and their children, forcing them down into poverty and ignorance, mangling them in unprotected industries, and hurrying them off to premature graves. Time and again, these predatory vultures have cynically sent off the sons of the nation to reactionary wars, to be killed in the interest of the profit grabbers.

But the worst of all the crimes of expanding capitalism in this country has been the centuries-long outrage it has perpetrated, and continues to perpetrate, against the Negro people. To satisfy the greed of an arrogant landed aristocracy, the Negroes were stolen from their African homeland and compelled to submit, generation after generation, to a chattel slavery which was a measureless tragedy to them and a shame to our nation. And after the Negroes were emancipated, in the course of the great revolution of 1861-65, they were forced into a semi-slavery which still persists. During three generations of "freedom," the Negroes have been lynched, pillaged, Jim Crowed, and generally mistreated as being less than human, in order to fatten the profits of insatiable capitalist exploiters. The most shameful pages of American history are those dealing with the exploitation and oppression of the Negro masses.

The long and heroic struggle of the Negro people against the outrages to which they have been subjected is the greatest epic in our nation's history. This struggle, carried on in the face of heart-breaking difficulties, has brought the Negro people to real heights of heroism and splendid achievement. They have broken many shackles and won their way to the front lines of our national artistic, athletic, and intellectual endeavor; they have become a vital factor in industry and agriculture and in the American labor movement; they are a decisive force in our general political life, and their fight against gross injustice and oppression has become an issue of major importance in the growing worldwide struggle of the oppressed colonial peoples for national liberation. During the course of their long, bitter uphill struggle the American Negro people have welded themselves literally into a nation.

No people has ever had their history, their achievements, and their human qualities more brazenly belied and distorted than is the case of the Negroes in this country. The exploiters, whether Southern planters or Northern industrialists, have found it both necessary and profitable to demean and slander the Negro people in every conceivable way. They have done this with the aid of shoals of lackeys among historians, scientists, politicians, preachers, journalists, novelists, and others. Such forces of reaction have systematically pictured the Negroes as a people without traditions or history. They have belittled the Negroes' intelligence, morality, and fighting spirit, and with the grossest prostitution of science, they have sought to condemn the Negroes as biologically inferior to the whites.

During the past two or three decades, however, progressive historians and scientists, Negro and white, have been delivering devastating broadsides against this carefully built wall of racist prejudice and oppression. They are rapidly reconstructing the general history of the Negro people, here and in Africa, and in doing so, have established them scientifically as the peers, physically and intellectually, of any people in the world. In this great work of scientific clarification and struggle against white chauvinism and racism Marxist thinkers and writers, as we shall see, have performed a very important part.

The general purpose of the present book, written from the standpoint of Marxism-Leninism, is to outline the growth of the American Negro people in relation to the historical development of the American nation. Concretely, the book also aims to stimulate further the present struggle of the Negro people for the fullest freedom along with their white allies, to analyze the factors making for their historical growth into "a nation within a nation," and to indicate the main lines of the young nation's perspective of further social development.

The writer takes occasion herewith to express his appreciation to the many friends, too numerous to mention individually, who have cooperated actively in making this book possible. He also wishes to thank the numerous writers in this general field, upon whose works he has so freely drawn.

New York, December, 1953   WILLIAM Z. FOSTER

1. Africa

Africa is the second largest of the continents, 11,860,000 square miles in area. Lying mostly in the tropics, from 37° North to 35° South latitude, it is about 5,000 miles long and, at its broadest, 4,600 miles wide. Largely a great plateau, without tall mountain chains, it has an average elevation of 2,000 feet. The continent's four biggest rivers are the Nile in the North, the Congo and the Niger in the West, and the Zambesi in the Southeast. Rainfall varies widely, from as much as 369 inches yearly in parts of the Congo basin, to almost nothing in the great desert of the North, the Sahara, which is about as large as the United States.

The African continent, as yet only partly surveyed, is richly endowed with natural resources. It has huge known supplies of iron throughout, major coal fields in various regions, large petroleum areas, the richest gold and diamond mines in the world, and big deposits of uranium, copper, tin, zinc, chromium, and other strategic metals and chemicals.[1] Over $4 billion in precious stones and metals has been taken out of South Africa in 60 years. The continent also possesses enormous timber reserves, immense cattle-grazing areas, and vast stretches of farming land capable of a highly productive agriculture.

THE PEOPLE OF AFRICA

The population of Africa is estimated at about 200 million. Of the total, only about three percent are European, mostly located in South Africa and in the French and Italian colonial areas along the Mediterranean. The Africans are made up of several great ethnic groups—Hamitic, Libyan, Negro, Pygmy, Bushman, Hottentot and Bantu, all except the first group being Negroid. The Negroid groups make up three fourths of the total population. These peoples vary widely from each other physically: from the light colored Berbers of the North to the deep black Negroes of the Equatorial regions, and to the brown-hued peoples of South Africa; from the dwarfish Pygmies, who

15

average only about four and one half feet high, to the gigantic Watusi Negroes, magnificent human specimens, ranging over six feet and often reaching seven feet in height—the tallest people in the world. There is also a great linguistic profusion: the Sudanese languages and dialects number 264, and the Bantu 182, and there are a vast number of others.[2] Delafosse says that the "suppleness, richness and precision of these languages" astonish all those who study them.[3] Through the centuries there has been a profound intermingling of the many African peoples, physically and culturally, from one end of the continent to the other.

Darwin said, "Africa is the cradle of mankind." Of the present population, the people with the longest known history are the Pygmies, or Negrillos. They are closely related to the Bushmen. Apparently, at one time the Pygmies and Bushmen ranged over the greater portion of Africa, between the Sahara desert and the Zambesi River. But, beginning in some remote period, they have been gradually pushed back and largely exterminated by powerful rival Negroid peoples, first the Hottentots and then the Bantus. Whether these invaders came from South Africa or from across the sea via now vanished land bridges is one of the many unsolved problems of ethnology. In any event, the Pygmies have been greatly reduced in numbers and territory, until now they count but 80,000 people and inhabit only the more inaccessible areas.[4] The lighter colored native peoples of Northern Africa are probably of Asian and European origin.

AFRICAN CIVILIZATION

Contrary to the slanderers of the Negro peoples, who have tried to picture the Negroes as mere hordes of wild savages without influence upon the cultural advance of mankind, they have played a very prominent part in the development of world civilization. This is particularly true in North Africa. They were especially a big factor in evolving the civilization of ancient Egypt, a country which was largely Negro. As early as 2000 B.C. the Negro Ra Nahesi sat upon the Egyptian throne. Franklin says, "The blacks from Nubia had helped to construct the great sphinxes, pyramids, and public buildings of Egypt. They had helped to perfect the political organization of the country." [5] Du Bois says, "We conclude, therefore, that the Egyptians were Negroid and not only that, but by tradition they believed themselves descended not from the whites or the yellows, but from the black peoples of the South."[6] Herodotus says that the Egyptians of his time had dark skins and woolly hair.

Ethiopia (Abyssinia), a Negro land, was for centuries a place of culture in the world. About 741 B.C., Piankhi, an Ethiopian emperor, overran Egypt and made it a dependency of his country. At this time Northern Europe was in the lower stages of barbarism. It is said that Greek art received a decisive impulse from African civilization and centuries later African culture exerted a profound influence upon the intellectual development of Spain, Portugal, and Italy. It has often been asserted that "Negroes are responsible for European civilization, as Modern Europe really derives her civilization from Rome, Rome borrowed hers from Greece, and the Greek civilization rested on the arts and science of Negro Egypt."[7] J. H. Lawson says, "The culture that we call European owes as much to Africa as to Asia."[8]

In the central and southern areas of Africa, far isolated from the main stream of world cultural development, the more primitive Negro peoples had also made great progress by the time they came into active contact with the predatory white nations. In many parts of the continent they had built up "kingdoms" and "empires." Among these were Ghana, in West Africa—by 300 A.D. 44 kings had reigned there; Melle (Mandingoland), which succeeded Ghana around the seventh century, and became dominant in the twelfth—occupied about the same territory as present-day French West Africa; Songhay in the bend of the Niger, which was founded in the eighth century, and by 1500 was "easily the largest and most powerful state in the history of West Africa"; the Mossi states south of the Niger from 1300 on, and there were numerous others—Ashanti, Dahomey, Benin, Congo, Bushongo, Uganda, Monolapa, etc.

Many of these Negro regimes, especially those in or adjoining the Sudan, reached high levels of culture and organization. It is said that Negroes discovered the smelting of iron, a tremendous contribution to world civilization. Woodson says that the "Africans near the heart of the continent were the first to learn the use of the valuable metal."[9] These peoples had agricultural, hunting, and fishing economies, and they had domesticated animals—sheep, goats, and fowls. In the North they worked out an alphabet, something never accomplished by any primitive people in early Europe. They also developed the xylophone, violin, guitar, zither, harp, and flute. Their drum "telegraph" enabled them to send messages over long distances with great rapidity. The Berbers in North Africa, who are partly Negro, practiced surgery, even upon the brain.[10] In 1324, in Melle, or Mandingoland, the resplendent "emperor" Gonga-Mussa made a celebrated pilgrimage to Mecca, with 24,000 pounds of gold and an entourage of 62,000 persons. "When Gonga-Mussa died in 1332 Melle could boast of a political state as powerful and as well organized as any of that period."[11]

Modern students and travelers grow enthusiastic over the beautiful craftsmanship still being practiced among the African peoples, despite the havoc caused among them by the white invaders. They produce marvelous pottery, textiles, basketry, ivory carving, and fancy metal work. Woodson declares that "Their cutlery not only compares favorably with that of Sheffield, but even shows workmanship and inventive genius unexcelled in the modern world."[12] Delafosse, a noted French expert on Africa, remarks that the Negroes are past masters in the industrial arts, in working clay, wood, iron, copper, gold, leather, and textiles.[13] And "Professor Von Luschan considered the craftsmanship of Benin workers as equal to the best that was ever produced by Cellini."[14] *The Nation* says that the bronze and terra cotta beads from Nigeria stand as "artistic miracles rivaling the best in Greek sculpture," and *The Reporter* states that the African folk tales are as fine as those "that have come down from early Greece, from Asia, from medieval Europe."[15]

According to the standards used by the famous American scientist Lewis H. Morgan,[16] in analyzing the societies of the Iroquois, Aztecs, and other American Indians, the African Negroes, following the same general course of social evolution as other peoples throughout the world, varied in the degree of their culture from the savagery of the Pygmies and other remote tribes all the way to the high civilizations of the Negroid peoples of the Mediterranean area. Their achievements compared well with those of other primitive peoples in the world in corresponding stages of evolution. Du Bois says, "There can be no doubt but that the cultural level among the masses of Negroes in West Africa in the fifteenth century was higher than that of Northern Europe."[17] Montagu states that, "At the time when Caesar set foot in Britain the African Negro kingdoms and their people were from the cultural standpoint in an incomparably more advanced state of development than the Britons, upon whom they might well have looked as a primitive people."[18]

SOCIAL ORGANIZATION

As in the case of all other primitive peoples—in Asia, America, Europe, and Australia—the African Negroid peoples, prior to the advent of the white man, had social regimes based upon the family. Their various stages were the gens, the clan, the phratry, the tribe, and the confederation of tribes. This was the African expression of the once universal system of primitive communalism. Morgan's analysis of American Indian society could well serve as a general outline of the basic African tribal organization.

Land was held in common. Delafosse says that among the African tribes: "The ground, according to the native conception, does not belong to anybody, neither does it belong to all. . . . In fact the ground is a god that no one would think of appropriating to himself and still less of buying or selling."[19] Land occupation is based upon usage and the cultivator owns the product of his toil. "Under this system," says Delafosse, "no member of an African community is ever in want."

At the dawn of their known history the tribes in most of the lower parts of Africa were based upon the gens system and democratically elected their chieftains, in line with the universal customs of primitive communalism. Delafosse states that, "We are very far from the system of absolute monarchy which one is sometimes inclined to suppose exists in the Negro countries."[20] In the higher civilizations of the North, however, primitive communalism had largely broken down, and definite classes of land-owning exploiters and landless slaves had evolved. In many places certain clans had seized upon and made hereditary the right of rulership; they created "kings" and "emperors." This was also the general path of evolution followed by the great empires of antiquity—Sumeria, Assyria, Babylon, Greece, Rome, and others. Ignorant slave traders, explorers, and historical writers, meeting up with the Negroes of Central and South Africa, did as the Spanish explorers had done with the Indians in America: they tended wrongly to apply to them and their institutions terms and conceptions arbitrarily taken from their own institutions in Europe. Hence, every chief became a "king" or an "emperor" and every organized tribal area an "empire."

Adjacent to the Sahara, the population of North Africa is chiefly Moslem, some 65,000,000[21] and there are about 20,000,000 Christians throughout the continent; the religion of the remaining mass, about

115,000,000, is aboriginal African. The native religions are very complex. Du Bois describes them as the "universal animism or fetishism of primitive peoples, rising to polytheism and approaching monotheism."[22] Delafosse says, "they believe in the existence of souls of the same essence in all beings, those which are of inanimate appearance as well as those which are animate, the dead as well as the living." This belief leads to the creation of numerous gods and the development of a rudimentary mythology. Supposedly, one has both a body and a spirit. After his death, his spirit goes on living. The various tribes have a more or less well developed conception that the world was created by a supreme being.

Cannibalism, mostly of religious significance, existed in some primitive parts of Africa. Vilifiers of the Negro peoples have made much of this practice. The reality is that all over the world, cannibalism is to be found at certain lower stages of social development. Engels says that cannibalism was the universal primitive form of disposing of vanquished enemies.[23] In modern times cannibalism has existed in Polynesia, in Australia, and the more remote parts of Asia; in early America it was practiced as a religious rite by the Aztecs and by other Indian tribes. In Europe, in prehistoric times, cannibalism was also to be found. It is suggested that the custom in Northern Europe of drinking from human skulls harks back to ancient cannibalism.[24]

THE CONQUEST AND PARTITION OF AFRICA

Ancient Greece and Rome knew little of Africa—only of Egypt, Ethiopia, and the areas along the Mediterranean. The rest of the continent was a blank to them. In the seventh and eighth centuries the Arabs overran most of North Africa, conquering the country and making the peoples Moslem. It was not until the fifteenth century that daring Portuguese navigators sailed around the Cape of Good Hope, explored the coasts, and dotted them with tiny settlements. Then followed 400 years of the slave trade, with all the leading powers of Europe participating in it. Although the explorers of these states were daringly surveying the whole continent, the authority of the powers hardly reached beyond gun-range from their many coastal forts. Moon points out that "Before 1875 not one-tenth of this, the second largest continent, had been appropriated by the civilized nations of Europe."[25]

During the last quarter of the nineteenth century, however, the major capitalist countries of Europe passed into the stage of imperialism. They rapidly industrialized themselves, their monopoly interests became dominant, and the respective powers developed the most urgent drive for foreign markets, for supplies of strategic materials, and for capitalist investment abroad. This resulted in a wild rush to grab the less developed areas of the world as colonies. Consequently the world colonial possessions of the six biggest capitalist powers increased from 40 million square kilometers in 1876 to 60,500,000 in 1914, and the foreign investments of England, the leading capitalist power, soared from 3.6 billion francs in 1862 to 75-100 billion in 1914.[26]

By the end of the nineteenth century the imperialist powers had grabbed about 80 percent of Africa. The Negro peoples were robbed of their lands largely by the methods used previously in stripping the American Indians of their territories—direct seizure, corruption of chieftains, tricky treaties, and the like. The rape of Africa was accompanied by many fierce quarrels among the imperialist powers, which almost precipitated general wars several times. A big factor in causing World War I was the struggle among the powers over the division of Africa. Germany and Turkey were stripped of their African colonies as a result of their defeat in that war, their losses totaling over 1,500,000 square miles. Italy lost her African colonies in World War II, about 1,030,000 square miles.

The score today shows Great Britain and France respectively holding 3,018,000 and 4,283,000 square miles of Africa, or about one-third of the continent each, with Belgium, Portugal, and Spain having much of the remaining third. The "independent" nations of Africa—principally the Union of South Africa, Egypt, Ethiopia, Libya, and Liberia—comprise only about 20 percent of the total territory of the continent and 25 percent of its population. The imperialist conquest of Africa was one of the greatest land rapes in history, and it was carried out with the utmost cynicism and brutality, generally under the hypocritical pretense, typified by Kipling, that the Europeans were taking on "the white man's burden" of civilizing the "dark continent."

The imperialists, the various European powers, set up the most ferocious system of super-exploitation of the African peoples. Their plantations and mines were literally slaughterhouses, devouring the native workers. And imperialist rule was maintained by tyranny and violence. The best lands were taken from the indigenous peoples, and they were denied all real representation in government. They were denied every semblance of education, and drastic Jim Crow systems were established.

THE RESISTANCE OF THE AFRICAN PEOPLES

The Negro peoples, although hopelessly outgunned by the white invaders, made a heroic struggle to defend their homelands. They suffered from much the same handicaps as the American Indians in trying to counter the European invasion of their country. That is, there could be little or no common defense action by the many tribes and peoples who from time immemorial had been hostile to each other; there was much corruption among their chieftains, who often fell victim to the trickery and blandishments of the Europeans, and their primitive weapons could not withstand the up-to-date guns of the invaders. Besides, the weakening effects of 400 years of the slave trade had undermined the resistance of the native peoples.

Nevertheless, the Africans delivered many smashing blows against their oppressors. In the Sudan, in the early 1880's, the Negro warriors under the Mahdi, defeated and drove out the combined British and Egyptians, and it was not until 1898 that the British, under Kitchener, partially overcame them. In Ethiopia, under King Menelik, the people wiped out the Italian forces at the Battle of Adowa, in March 1896,[27] and maintained their country's independence. And in Morocco, France and Spain had to wage endless wars against the Riffs and other militant tribesmen of this region.

In mid-Africa, along the Gold Coast, the Ashantis, a highly developed people, valiantly defended their homes and lands. Between 1803 and 1874, they waged no less than six victorious wars against the British, and it was not until 1894 that the better-armed Europeans finally overwhelmed them.[28] In the Congo basin, the Belgians encountered fierce tribal resistance, and they established themselves there only after twenty years of bloody warfare and savage atrocities which shocked the world.

Farther south, the white invaders also met fierce opposition from the Hottentots and especially the Basuto peoples. Macmillan says that the first officially recognized Kaffir war was in 1778, the ninth and last in 1877, so that in effect the Cape frontier struggle was South Africa's Hundred Years War.[29] In South Africa the term "Kaffir" still remains one of hatred and contempt to white supremacists. Macmillan says that "The Metabeles under Moselekatze had to be driven out to the Northwest; the Basutos kept the Free State at war for many years—Sekukuni came near to causing the downfall of the Transvaal in the late '70s." The hard-fought wars between the Zulu and Bechuana tribes and the Boers kept the whole country aflame for 20 years. The Germans had to wage a desperate war to crush the Bantus, Hereros, and Hottentots. In the Boer-Basuto wars of the 1850's, Buell states, that the Free State proved no match for the Basutos, who, sheltered by mountain passes, even manufactured their own gunpowder.[30] Great Britain had to mobilize major forces to defeat Lobengula, chief of the Matabeles, during the early 1890's. Middleton says, "The name of Lobengula will go down to posterity with that of Boadicea, Caractacus, and the Athenians and Romans who died to protect their country from the invaders. The fiery spirit of the struggling Negro tribesmen was well illustrated by Lobengula who, returning 10,000 rifles formerly given to him by the British, somewhat unwisely declared that, "One Metabeles, with his *assagai* [light javelin], is a match for four Englishmen with machine guns."[31] By 1900 the power of the Basuto peoples was crushed and the British, Germans, and Dutch had stolen the vast bulk of their territory.[32]

The brave struggle of the peoples of Africa against the imperialist invaders is a great epic, whose recital awaits the hand of some inspired Marxist writer. These primitive peoples, like the American Indians, had no real solidarity among the many tribes and thus no possibility of making a successful stand, in the face of the better guns, higher techniques, and stronger organizations of the Europeans. But in our own day, these brave peoples have resumed their struggle against imperialist oppression with renewed strength; this time for national liberation, with modern solidarity, slogans, weapons, and methods, and with the growing support of the free Socialist and democratic peoples of the world. The prospect for them is one of inevitable and complete victory over their oppressors. Meanwhile the imperialist powers, especially the United States, strive desperately to maintain and extend their hold on the rich continent of Africa.

2. The International Slave Trade

Slavery has existed from time immemorial. It arises when primitive society reaches the point of productivity where it is more profitable to work a war prisoner than to kill him. Slavery was widely developed in Sumeria, Assyria, Babylonia, Greece, Rome, and other ancient empires, and it was to be found, too, in China, India, and among the American Aztecs and Incas. In many parts of Africa also there were slaves. African slavery was built mainly upon war prisoners and condemned criminals. The great Egyptian pyramids were built by slaves. Among the Negro peoples of Central and Southern Africa there was an indigenous slavery. Davies says of it, "The slaves have great liberty; their labor is light; they are considered as members of the family, can acquire and inherit property, own slaves themselves, and often purchase their freedom. This type of slavery is vastly different from the kind of bondage to which the Negroes were introduced, first by the Arabs and later by the European nations."[1]

The Arabs, who had conquered most of Northern Africa by the eighth century, instituted a wide slave trade in Negro women for their harems and of men to serve as soldiers and field laborers. The first Europeans to engage in the nefarious traffic were the Portuguese, in the middle of the fifteenth century. During this period the latter were exploring the coast of West Africa and establishing posts there. By 1452 the first African slaves arrived in Portugal, and twenty years later that country was importing up to 800 per year. The Spanish designated African slaves as *negros,* a word derived from the Latin term *niger,* meaning black and pronounced "neeger." Previously, the English had called Negroes "blackamoors" or "Ethiopians."

Early in the sixteenth century, the great demand from the new American continent for workers to cultivate the rapidly spreading plantations began to make itself felt. It was then that the slave trade took on the huge proportions that were to make it of decisive world

24

importance for three and a half centuries and to stigmatize it as the greatest mass crime of genocide ever perpetrated.

THE EUROPEAN POWERS AS SLAVE TRADERS

"The Popes as early as 1482," says La Farge[2], "had positively forbidden, under pain of excommunication, the reduction of Negroes born free to slavery, and also the purchasing of those who were thus reduced." But obviously these prohibitions were merely for the record. The Christian nations of Europe, Catholic and Protestant, blithely ignored them and went right ahead developing the slave trade. It was a highly profitable business, and the slavers concerned themselves not at all with its disastrous effects upon the millions of enslaved human beings. Of course, the Catholic popes never enforced their excommunication threats, neither against the Catholic slave-trading nations nor against the Catholic slave drivers on the American plantations. Indeed, Franklin says that the proposal of the famous Spanish bishop, Las Casas, in 1517, that each Spanish immigrant be permitted to have twelve Negro slaves, marked the formal opening of the slave trade to the New World.[3]

Portugal maintained a virtual monopoly of slaving throughout the fifteenth and sixteenth centuries. But it was followed into this bloody business by Holland, France, England, Spain, Denmark, Brandenburg, and the American colonies. These countries ferociously fought for control of the profitable trade. The slave trade was the direct cause of at least two wars and a factor in various other wars of the period. The whole business was also a mass of piracy and hijacking. By the early eighteenth century, England had defeated all other powers, and as the leading maritime state, it became the world's greatest slave trader.

The main single prize of the slave trade was the so-called Spanish *Asiento*—the contract for furnishing slaves to the Spanish colonies in America. The *Asiento* was held first by Portugal until the end of the sixteenth century; Holland got it in 1640; France grabbed it in 1701, and finally in 1713, the English, by the Treaty of Utrecht, seized the filthy prize. England held it for 33 years, until Spain took over the job herself.[4]

The English colonies got into the slave trade on their own account on a large scale at the end of the seventeenth century. Before this, the English colonial slave trade had been a monopoly of the Royal African Company; but in 1698 this monopoly was cancelled and permission for slaving given to any vessel flying the British flag, upon the payment of a ten percent tax. The shippers of New England thereupon rushed in and soon secured their full share of the slave trade, as we shall see later.[5]

The vast armies of Negro slaves, forcibly torn from their African homeland, were transported mainly to three great American plantation areas—Brazil, the West Indies, and the British North American colonies. Estimates of their numbers vary widely. It has been calculated that 12 million slaves were brought into Brazil alone prior to 1850, when the slave trade was halted.[6] Du Bois says that, "The British colonies between 1680 and 1786 imported over two million slaves."[7] Korngold declares that Santo Domingo itself got a million more.[8] It has been estimated that by 1860 about one million slaves had come into the United States, mostly via the West Indies, and at least another million or two went to the Spanish colonies of Central and South America. It has also been calculated that for every slave who reached the Americas, three or four other Negroes died—in slave wars in Africa, from hardships en route to the slave pens, and on shipboard. Thus, Africa was stripped of at least 60 million of its people because of the modern slave trade. The trade was also highly demoralizing to the tribal organization of Africa.

CAPITALISM AND THE SLAVE TRADE

Growing capitalism in Europe, particularly in England, profited hugely from the highly lucrative slave trade. Slave voyages produced usually from 100 to 1,000 percent profit. In the eighteenth century slaves cost about $50 in Africa and sold for up to $400 in the West Indies. Among the innumerable surviving profit-and-loss statements of the slave ships, is Captain Theodore Canot's report that on a typical trip his expenses were $39,980 and his net profit $41,438. He also reported that the British ship *Enterprise* cleared $24,430 on 392 slaves.[9] Slavers during this period figured that if they successfully evaded pirates, other types of sea marauders, the hazards of the sea, and they got through with one cargo of slaves out of three, they would become rich.

The English slave trade grew to enormous proportions during the eighteenth century. Liverpool was practically built upon slave trading, and most of its businessmen were engaged in the bloody traffic in one way or another. Donnan says that one-fourth of the ships sailing out of Liverpool were slavers. Thus, from January 5, 1798 to January 5, 1799, there were 150 Liverpool sailings, bringing 52,537 slaves from Africa to America.[10] Macinnes states that about 1800 there were "directly and indirectly," some 18,400 British seamen employed in the slave trade;[11] besides many thousands more of ship carpenters, riggers, sailmakers, ironmongers, rope makers, clerks, and others. Bristol, London, and other English ports were also heavily engaged in the slave trade. Industry throughout England was greatly stimulated by the production of textiles, metal wares, and other goods for which the slaves were bought in Africa.

Karl Marx points out that the profits of the murderous African slave trade were one of the major sources of primitive accumulation of British capitalism. From this trade were largely derived the resources which financed the Industrial Revolution in England. Marx says, "The discovery of gold and silver in America, the extirpation, enslavement, and entombment in mines of the aboriginal population, the beginning of the conquest and looting of the East Indies, the turning of Africa into a warren for the commercial hunting of black-skins, signalized the rosy dawn of the era of capitalist production. These idyllic proceedings are the chief momenta of primitive accumulation."[12] Referring to England during the later, American Civil War period, Marx shows the dependence of British industry upon slavery: "Slavery is an economic category like any other. . . . Direct slavery is just as much the pivot of bourgeois industry as machinery, credits, etc. Without slavery you have no cotton; without cotton you have no modern industry. It is slavery that has given the colonies their value; it is the colonies that have created world trade, and it is world trade that is the pre-condition of large-scale industry. Thus slavery is an economic category of the greatest importance."[13] By the same token, the slave trade also helped lay the basis of industry in New England.

For over two centuries, the aristocracy, businessmen, and clericals of England, almost unanimously gave their blessing to the horrible slave trade. At first they denied that Negroes were human, and later they hypocritically declared that by the slave trade they were saving the souls of the benighted Negro heathen. Sir John Hawkins, pioneer English slaver, a cold-blooded murderer of Negroes, and a favorite of Queen Elizabeth, set the tone of this hypocrisy in the mid-sixteenth century. Hawkins' slaver flagship was called the *Jesus,* and he bade his men "to love one another" and always to bear in mind the admonitions of the "Good Book." Not only British business, but also the

High Church, fattened on the bloody profits of the slave trade. As Marx says, "With the development of capitalist production during the manufacturing period, the public opinion of Europe had lost the last remnant of shame and conscience. The nations bragged cynically of every infamy that served them as a means of capitalist accumulation."[14]

METHODS OF ENSLAVEMENT

The modern slave trade, which lasted for a full 400 years, had as its main grounds for recruiting slaves the thickly populated areas along the west coast of Africa, some 4,000 miles in extent—from above Cape Verde in Senegal, in the North, to Angola, below the Congo River, in the South. The west coast was chosen for slaving chiefly because it is relatively near the Americas—South, Central, and North; it being only 1807 statute miles from Sierra Leone, on the western bulge of Africa, to Brazil, on the eastern bulge of South America. Few slaves were taken from the more remote east coast of Africa, and these came chiefly from Mozambique and Madagascar. The main stretch of slaving territory was called the Guinea Coast.

The English and American slavers frequented the middle sections of this coast, including Sierra Leone, the Niger Delta, and the Grain, Ivory, Gold, and Slave coasts, drawing their victims chiefly from these regions. Slaves sometimes made journeys to the slave ports from as far as 1,000 miles inland, but Herskovits believes that the bulk of them hailed from points not more than 200 to 300 miles from the coast.[15] The great net enmeshed slaves from many African peoples—from the Senegalese and Sudanese in the North to the Bantus and Hottentots in the South—including many of the tribal headmen who had been enslaved as prisoners in tribal wars. Among the major tribes which furnished slaves to the United States were the Foulahs, Coromantees, Eboes, and Angolese.

At the inception of the slave trade, Hawkins and other early slavers attempted to get cargoes of slaves simply by seizing them in the villages along the coasts; but the bitter resistance of the tribesmen soon taught these man-stealers that such methods were too costly in casualties. Consequently, while continuing to kidnap Negroes wherever favorable opportunities presented themselves, the slavers generally adopted the device of buying them from the tribal chieftains. To this end, the rival European slave-trading powers—mainly England, France,

Holland, and Portugal—dotted the west African coast with armed "factories" for collecting slaves. By the end of the eighteenth century there were 40 such "factories." For the slaves the traders paid varying sums in rum, muskets, gunpowder, linen, calico, copper, pewter utensils, knives, basins, brass kettles, beads, needles, scissors, and whatnot. In return the slave traders would accept only the youngest and healthiest Negroes. Women usually made up about one-third of a shipload of slaves. The various shipmasters iron-branded the slaves with the owners' initials.

Many tribal chieftains, especially those who had more or less become dictators in their tribes and were corrupted by the goods of the slave-traders, took part in seizing and selling members of their own and other tribes. Historically this was the way of the oppressor in America, Asia, Australia, and elsewhere to dupe and bribe primitive tribal leaders. "The usual procedure," says Franklin, "was to go to the chief of the tribe and to make arrangements with him to secure 'permission' to trade on his domain."[16] Besides furnishing slaves from among their own people—those who had already been enslaved for various crimes, the chiefs also made kidnaping raids and wars upon neighboring tribes. Such slave forays, stimulated by the European slave traders, ravaged large sections of Africa for generations. "The removal of the flower of African manhood left the continent impotent, stultified, and dazed."[17]

THE "MIDDLE PASSAGE"

Betrayed into European hands by corrupt tribal leaders, the seized slaves were tied together in coffles and marched long distances to the mouths of innumerable African rivers. The sick were left to die by the wayside. At the "factories" the slaves were jammed into the slave ships of the "civilized" Christian Europeans and borne away from their native land, they and their children, to work, presumably forever, like animals, for the sordid profit of their white masters.

European slave voyages were usually triangular; the first leg, from Europe to Africa, with trade goods for buying slaves; the second leg, to the West Indies, Brazil, or the United States with shiploads of slaves; and the final leg, back to Europe, with cargoes of slave-grown products from these colonial countries. These triangular voyages were also made by American slavers. The second phase of the three-sided voyage—carrying slaves to the Americas—was known as the "middle passage," a term which came to be infamous as one of the most dreadful ever formulated by man. The "middle passage," full of misery, torture, sickness, and death for the slaves, lasted from six to twenty weeks, depending upon the weather.

The most terrible aspect of the middle passage was the incredible crowding of the slave ships. The slaves, known as "black ivory," were literally packed in, like so many cases or barrels. Shackled, they were laid side-by-side, often with their legs doubled up and quite unable to change their position. Sometimes the height between decks was as little as 18 inches. Barbarous British law provided that each male slave be allowed a floor space of but six feet by one foot and four inches, with women and children spaced accordingly.[18] As one slave ship captain said, "They had not so much room as a man in his coffin."

Conditions in these crowded quarters were terrible, especially during rough weather, when the hatches were battened down. The heat was stifling in the tropical latitudes and many slaves died of suffocation. Sanitary conditions were indescribable. Slavers could be smelled several miles down the wind.

Usually, the slave ships were unbelievably small, the average British slaver of the eighteenth century being of but 100 tons burden, and the average American was still smaller, being a sloop of only 50 tons.[19] Some ocean-going American slavers were as small as 40 tons. The vessels were supposed to carry not more than two slaves per ton of the ship, which required terrible packing in; but they often doubled this ratio, actually piling the slaves on top of each other. Captain Canot states that two of the ships he had commanded, the *Estrella* of 120 tons, and the *Volador* of 125 tons, transported 480 and 747 slaves each.[20] In the American slaver *Pongas* 250 women, many of them pregnant, were squeezed into a compartment of 16 by 18 feet, and "the men were stowed in each other's laps, without an inch to move to right or left."[21]

Under such terrible conditions disease was rife among the slaves. Smallpox was the worst, the deaths from this plague sometimes running as high as 25 percent of the slaves and crews. Macinnes says that of the crews of 24 Bristol ships in 1784 (940 all told), 216 lost their lives in the slave trade. Many slaves went crazy. Ophthalmia, an eye disease, was another terror. On the French slaver *Le Rodeur*, in 1819, everybody aboard the ship, crew as well as slaves, went blind from the disease, and for many days the ship was sailed by blinded men. Eventually all but 39 of the slaves either wholly or partially recovered their sight. The 39 Negroes, blind and unsalable, but insured, were thrown overboard to enable the owners to collect the insurance.[22]

Rigid and brutal discipline was enforced on the slave ships. Slaves who dared to protest were lashed, had their heads or hands cut off, or were thrown to the sharks. When the ships ran short of food and water on unexpectedly long voyages, numbers of slaves were cast overboard. Smallpox cases were similarly treated. The skipper of the ship Zong, in 1784, threw 132 sick slaves overboard.[23] After the outlawing of the slave trade by England in 1807, slave captains, fearing capture, sometimes "got rid of the evidence" by jettisoning their whole cargoes of slaves. Hungry sharks ceaselessly trailed the slave ships.

Present-day detractors of the Negro people allege that the slaves submitted unprotestingly to these outrages. The truth is that some slaves strangled themselves, others jumped overboard, and the slaves generally seized upon every opportunity to revolt. The slave-ship captains had no illusions about their captives, and they took out "insurrection insurance" in England. Aboard ship, the captains took the most elaborate precautions against the dreaded slave mutinies. Dow says that the slaves "were ever on the watch to take advantage of the least negligence" on the part of the crew. Donnan cites a slaver captain who says, "They are fed twice a day, at ten in the morning and four in the evening, which is the time they are aptest to mutiny, being all upon deck; therefore, all that time, what of our men not employed in distributing their victuals to them, and settling them, stand to their arms; and some with lighted matches at the great guns that yawn upon them, loaded with partridge, till they have done and gone down to their kennels between decks."[24] Despite all such precautions, however, the slaves managed occasionally to rid themselves of their shackles and to attack the crews. Hence, every authentic report of slave-trading is replete with accounts of insurrections by slaves aboard ship. Harney Wish lists 55 known slave mutinies on English and American ships from 1700 to 1845, and this was probably only a fraction of the reality.[25]

3. Slavery in the American Colonies

Beginning in the early seventeenth century, the most urgent tasks of the English colonists along the North Atlantic Coast, after their first efforts to eke out an existence, were to secure for themselves broad stretches of the virgin land, to find crops that could be grown and would have ready markets in Europe, and to secure a working force to cultivate their fields. These tasks the landowners and merchants, who dominated colonial life, attacked with the vigor and ruthlessness characteristic of later American civilization, of which they were then unconsciously laying the foundations.

The land problem they solved by robbing the indigenous Indians of their farms and hunting grounds. They also wangled land grants from the British government, stole land from each other, and seized or "bought" the territories of adjoining countries—Spain, Holland, France, and England. The land-grabbing, which the early colonists set afoot, was to go on for over two and a half centuries, until their descendants had seized the whole vast continent, from the Atlantic to the Pacific.

To find the most practical crops presented a problem for the early settlers. It was especially necessary, for real success, to raise crops not competitive with those of England. The ruling class of that country, with its agricultural base, did not welcome the importation of farm products duplicating those from its own fields. The settlers in the Middle and Northern colonies, with a climate comparable to England's, never solved this problem; but those in the South—in Virginia, the Carolinas, and Georgia—with their warmer climates, did solve it. They developed as their non-competitive staples for export—tobacco, rice, and indigo. Upon this basis, the great American plantation system, with its chattel slavery was founded. Cotton and sugar became decisively important crops after the revolution of 1776.

Tobacco, a native Indian product, was first cultivated in Jamestown in 1612 by John Rolfe, husband of Pocahontas, five years after the establishment of the colony by the London Company of Gentleman Adventurers. From the start tobacco growing was a success, except for recurring gluts of overproduction, as it ordinarily found a ready market in England and elsewhere in Europe. The colonial tobacco plantations spread rapidly. "The streets and market places of Jamestown were planted with it."[1] Tobacco was "king." By 1664 Virginia and Maryland were producing 25 million pounds annually, and by 1770 Virginia was exporting 100,000,000 pounds per year. For about two centuries tobacco was the main money crop in the South.

Rice was brought in from Madagascar in 1694, and before long it was being cultivated widely in the low-lying lands of the "Rice coast" of the Carolinas, Georgia, and upper Florida.[2] Indigo was introduced from the West Indies in 1743, and soon became a paying crop.

Cotton was planted in Jamestown as early as 1621, but owing to the difficulty of cleaning out the seeds, for over a century it remained merely a garden plant. Wright states that "no exportations of this great staple of any consequences were made until the year of the Constitutional Convention—1787—when Charleston, South Carolina, sent 300 pounds to England."[3] It was not until after the invention of the cotton gin in 1793 that cotton began its spectacular development and in its turn became "king" of the plantation economy. As for sugar, Hawk says it was cultivated in Louisiana as early as 1751 by Jesuit priests from Santo Domingo, but it was not until 1795, when the problem of crystallizing the cane juice into sugar was solved, that the crop began to take on commercial importance.[4]

Significantly, the major American plantation crops, tobacco and cotton, flourish best in lower temperate zone areas, where world competition was least. Sugar cane, however, grows best in tropical areas, where there was vast competition from the West Indies, Brazil and the Far East. These facts explain why sugar culture was undertaken so late in the United States and almost exclusively in Louisiana.

THE PROBLEM OF A WORKING FORCE

In both North and South, the American colonists attacked with characteristic capitalist energy and greed the basic problem of providing the necessary manpower operating their expanding estates and plantations and harvesting the bonanza crops. Although they had in so many instances come to the American wilderness in protest against the tyrannies and injustices of Europe, they did not hesitate to enslave as workers whomever they could in the new country. The Indians were their first victims as slaves, mostly those who were captured in the frontier wars. During the sixteenth and eighteenth centuries there were Indian slaves in practically all the colonies. Thus, in South Carolina in 1709, of the total population of 9,580, some 1,400 were Indian slaves. But the Indians generally made poor slaves. They were difficult to enslave, the powerful tribes on the near-by frontiers resisting enslavement attempts and providing refuge for runaways, and they did not adapt themselves to high pressure farm work.

But if the colonists did not succeed in making effective slaves of the Indians, they had no hesitation whatever in reducing to bondage men, women, and children of their own color. They raided the crowded jails of England; Hawk states that up to the time of the American Revolution about 50,000 convicts were sent to Maryland and Virginia.[5] Political oppositionists were thrown into jail by the reigning tyrant— Roman Catholics, Quakers, and non-conformists of various brands— were shipped off to Barbados, Jamaica, and Virginia.[6] But the great majority of white bondsmen were "indentured servants." They were shipped in horrible immigrant ships. Large numbers of these bondsmen were to be found in all the English colonies, up to the American Revolution and after. Kirkland says that "As late as 1670 the number of white indentured servants in Virginia was three times that of the Negroes."[7]

The indentured servants, in return for the cost of their passage to America, and those serving as punishment for crimes, had to serve for several years as bond laborers. Generally, their "rights" as such were on a but little higher level than those of actual slaves. They could be flogged by their masters, sold to other masters, their service could be arbitrarily extended, and they could not marry without permission. "Some of these laborers, men and women, boys and girls alike, were lured on shipboard by kidnaping 'spirits' and borne to sea before they knew their destination and their fate. . . . Thousands were simply knocked down on the streets of English cities and dragged away by brutal bands which made a regular business of that nefarious traffic."[8] Conditions on the immigrant ships were terrible. According to Morris, "a mortality of more than fifty percent of the passengers was not an unusual experience on these 'white Guineamen'."[9] The indentured servants proved to be an inadequate source of labor power, however—their upkeep was relatively costly, they plotted with rebellious Negroes and Indians, they ran away to the frontiers and took land for themselves, and their general tenure as bondsmen was temporary and uncertain.

Especially in the South, with its expanding plantation system, the supply of Indian and white slaves was totally inadequate to meet the need. So the planters fell upon the African Negro as the best one to exploit and live on. He was adapted to tropical and semi-tropical climates, he came from cultures where agriculture was considerably developed, his dark color helped to single him out from the general population for special exploitation, and he was entitled to no rights under the law. He could be obtained in great numbers from Africa, where the tribal regimes were too weak politically and economically to defend them from seizure and enslavement.

But most important of all, quite isolated far from his native land, it was extremely difficult for him to revolt successfully. Therefore, like the Spanish, Portuguese, Dutch, and French before them, the English-American planters in the American South seized upon the Negro for their chattel slave. In future generations the Northern industrialists were to satisfy their vast demands for labor power by mass "voluntary" immigration from Europe; the planters their demands by forced immigration from Africa.

THE GROWTH OF NEGRO SLAVERY

The first Negro slaves to come to United States territory arrived with Lucas Vasquez de Ayllon, the Spaniard, who set up a colony at the mouth of the Peedee River in South Carolina, in 1526.[10] The Negroes rebelled, the colony failed, and the whites sailed away, leaving the Negroes behind, they thus becoming the first permanent immigrants to this country, pre-dating the Virginia settlers by almost a century.

In August 1619, a Dutch vessel, accompanied by a British warship, landed and sold "20 negers" in Jamestown. Slavery grew slowly at first; by 1650 there were still only 300 Negroes in Virginia, and not all of these were slaves. "But by 1671, Virginia had 2,000 slaves, and in 1715 almost one-third of the total population of 95,500 was in a state of lifelong bondage. Maryland's figures were not far behind."[11] By 1760 Negroes had come to outnumber the whites in South Carolina.[12]

The colder climate of the Northern colonies did not facilitate the wide extension there of the plantation system and Negro chattel slavery; they did not lend themselves then to the production of crops which had a strong world market during this whole period. "Chattel slavery did not become firmly established in the Northern states because there was no fertile soil for its existence. The labor of chattel slavery was not needed by industry and commerce. The capitalist system needed a different kind of slavery, namely, wage slavery—it required 'free' laborers."[13] Yet slaves, mostly house servants and farm hands, were to be found in all the Northern colonies. In Pennsylvania, William Penn and others held slaves and bondsmen. New Netherlands was founded in 1621 by one of the biggest slavery concerns of the time, the Dutch West Indies Company, and it established slavery locally from the start. From 1709 on there was a slave auction market in Wall Street. New England also had a number of Negro slaves. On the eve of the American Revolution, of a total of 659,446 people in New England, some 16,034 were Negroes,[14] at least three-fourths of whom were slaves.

In the lush sugar plantations of the West Indies and Brazil, slavery grew by leaps and bounds; at the end of the eighteenth century, in many areas, the Negro slaves outnumbered the whites by as much as twenty to one. No such tremendous growth of slavery took place, however, in the English colonies in this country—even in the plantation South—because cotton and sugar, the greatest of all slave crops to be, were not yet widely cultivated. Tobacco alone could not produce huge slave systems. On the eve of the Revolution in 1776, of the entire colonial population of some 3,500,000, approximately 500,000 were Negroes, nine-tenths of them slaves.

The English shipmasters reaped big profits from the expanding slave system in the colonies. So, too, did the hypocritical Puritan shippers of New England, especially after 1698 when Royal African Company's monopoly of the slave trade was liquidated. The first American slave-ship was the *Desire,* of Salem, Massachusetts. She was soon joined by scores of others. Rhode Island became the main slaving center. "The career of the town of Newport," says Phillips, "in fact was a small scale replica of Liverpool's."[15] "The Puritan colonies ranked as the greatest slave-carrying section in the New World," and the "slave trade developed into New England's greatest industry."[16] Profits on voyages ran to 100 percent and more. The usual trans-ocean trip followed a route from New England to Africa with rum and other goods to buy slaves, then to the West Indies with slaves, and finally back to New England with molasses for making rum. Newport alone had 22 distilleries to make rum for Africa. "That the slave trade was the very life of the colonies, had, by 1700, become an almost unquestioned axiom of British practical economics."[17]

The tinsel reputation of the capitalist families of New England thus has its roots in Negro slavery, exploitation and genocide, as had that of the aristocrats of the Old South. In the colonial slave trade was founded the alliance between Southern slaveholders and Northern merchants, which for generations was to pursue its reactionary course under different forms up to the Civil War of 1861-65, and traces of which linger even to our own days.

THE LEGALIZATION OF SLAVERY

Anglo-Saxon morality and law contained no specific justification of slavery, hence the status of the early Negro slaves in the colonies was dubious. In Virginia, for example, Negro slaves were treated at first as indentured servants, entitled to freedom after a specified period when they could take up land like other citizens. Moreover, baptism was held by some to be a bar against enslavement. Such limitations irked the planters, however, and soon the Church and State, obedient as ever to the will and interests of the ruling class, proceeded to institutionalize the chattel slavery of the Negro.

In 1661 the Virginia Assembly passed a law differentiating the status of Negroes from that of white indentured servants, making the former slaves for life. The other colonial assemblies took similar action, making legal in various forms the Negro slavery which was already largely a fact. Massachusetts legally recognized slavery in 1641; Connecticut in 1650; Rhode Island in 1652; New York in 1665; South Carolina in 1682; New Hampshire in 1714; North Carolina in 1715; Delaware in 1721; Georgia in 1749.[18] The utter brutality of this legalization of slavery was illustrated by a law in Maryland, which characteristically put Negroes in the same category with "working beasts, animals of any kind, stock, furniture, plate, books, and so forth."

Meanwhile, the colonies as a whole, including New England, were adopting slave codes for repression and control of the Negroes. These codes developed partly as an outgrowth of the old regulations for indentured servants and partly as an importation from the British West Indies. They elaborately regulated the habits, "rights," and duties of the slaves. The codes deprived the slaves of all civil, juridical, and marital status. Slaves could be flogged by their masters, fugitives had to be returned, rebels could be put to death, slaves were to be tried in special courts, and the children of mixed marriages between slave and free became slaves. In the West Indies and the Southern colonies, says Du Bois, "Crucifixion, burning, and starvation were legal modes of punishment for slaves."[19] Baptism did not bring about manumission, which in general was made very difficult. Virginia wrote the first of such slave codes.[20]

The slave codes and the whole slave regime in the English colonies, both in the West Indies and on the American continent, were the most severe in the entire American colonial world. The legal codes in the Spanish, Portuguese, and to some extent the French colonies, were somewhat less drastic than those of the English. They bore down on the slaves less heavily in respect to marriage, civil rights, punishment, education, property-holding, and especially manumission.

The churches, without exception, gave their moral blessing to the legal enslavement of the Negro. Only an occasional religious voice, usually that of a dissident Quaker, was raised against slavery. Of course, in the plantation South the church generally, was almost solidly pro-slavery from earliest colonial times. Nor was the church in the North appreciably better. In Pennsylvania, the hypocritical William Penn felt that slaves were more desirable than other servants, because "a man has them while they live."[21] Roger Williams of Rhode Island likewise condoned Negro slavery, as did other clerics. "The Puritans," says Greene, "justified slavery upon the highest spiritual grounds. Slavery, they maintained, was established by the law of God in Israel. . . . New Englanders looked upon the enslavement of the Indians and the Negroes as a sacred privilege Divine Providence was pleased to grant his chosen people." "What law is it," asked Cotton Mather, "that sets the baptized slaves at liberty? Not the law of Christianity." And Greene further remarks, "The Anglican church did not oppose slavery, and . . . many of its ministers were slave-holders."[22]

THE COLONIAL PLANTATION SYSTEM

In its colonial beginnings, the American plantation regime was a hybrid of three economic systems—ancient, medieval, and modern. The ancient element was its physical enslavement of the Negro; its feudalistic element was the network of primogeniture, entails, and quitrents (in the Southern colonies, New York, Pennsylvania, etc.) by which it held the plantation together within one family; and its capitalistic element was the fact that, in contrast to the slave regimes of antiquity, which were mostly subsistence economies producing mainly for the master's consumption, it produced tobacco and other commodities for sale in the world market from the outset. This triple aspect of slavery greatly complicated the general political problems at all stages, which the system presented during the decades between the war of 1776 and that of 1861. These peculiarities still haunt the United States, particularly in the continuing Jim Crow system and the special oppression of the Negro people.

Karl Marx characterizes the capitalist basis of the American slave system thusly: "In this case, the landowner and the owner of the instruments of production, and thus the direct exploiters of the laborers counted among these instruments of production, are one and the same person. Rent and profit likewise coincide then, there being no separation of the different forms of surplus value. The entire surplus labor of the workers, which is here represented by the surplus product, is extracted from them directly by the owner of all the instruments of production, to which the land and, under the original form of slavery, the producers themselves belong. When capitalist conceptions predominate, as they did upon the American plantations, this entire surplus value is regarded as profit."[23] "Those who carry on their own businesses with Negro slaves are capitalists."[24] The planter, especially in the later stages of the slavery system, was essentially a capitalist big farmer, despite the fact that he used slave labor.

In colonial times, slavery was essentially patriarchal, especially in the North, and those parts of the South where Negro labor could not be effectively exploited on the land. But the expansion of the world market for Southern staples—tobacco, rice, indigo, and especially the growth of the cotton industry in the first half of the nineteenth century, constituted a more severe regime of exploitation of the slaves. Marx states, "Whilst the cotton industry introduced child-slavery in England, it gave in the United States a stimulus to the transformation of the earlier, more or less patriarchal slavery, into a system of commercial exploitation."[25] The historic trend of the plantation system, from the foundation of the Jamestown Colony to the Civil War, was toward the adoption of more capitalistic methods of land tenure, labor exploitation, production for the world market, accounting and marketing.

The plantation-slave system produced its own marked type of class differentiation. At the top was the group of big landowners, whose holdings grew ever larger. Erik Bert shows that between 1626 and 1632, the average farm in Virginia was 160 acres in size and the largest 1,000 acres; whereas, by 1695-1700, the average had grown to 688 acres and the largest to 13,400 acres.[26] Similar trends were to be found in other plantation areas. The small farmers, many in number, were squeezed out onto the stony hills or into the barren pine woods. Industrialists were a negligible factor, and even the local merchants played a relatively small role, most of the planters buying their supplies directly from New York or London. Middle class groups—doctors, lawyers, writers, teachers, etc.—were few and far between. The white proletariat was also very small: nearly all the major work in the South, skilled and unskilled, was done by Negro slaves. Consequently urban communities were small, Southern centers being usually mere hamlets. In the South, in 1770, the only town with a population of over 8,000 was Charleston, South Carolina.

The plantation system also created differentiations among the slaves themselves. "Negroes who worked as domestics in the big house occupied a position of priority. . . . Next came the slaves who had developed special skills. As carpenters, coopers, blacksmiths and wheelwrights, Negroes acquired such a high degree of competence that they were frequently hired out, much to the dissatisfaction of competing white craftsmen and wage earners. Lastly came the field hands who lived in crude huts, were fed salt pork, and wore coarse clothing.[27] At most the house servants and mechanics were but little better off than the field hands.

By the end of the colonial period, there were a number of free Negroes, probably not more than 50,000. These had either bought themselves out of slavery (from part of the wages they had earned from their owners or on the side), had distinguished themselves for some act of great courage and been set free, or had been emancipated by the will of humane planters. The political status of the Negro freedmen was very precarious, especially in the South. Generally, their situation was only a step above that of the actual slaves. "The position of these people was an anomalous one. In the South all sorts of restrictive laws were placed upon them."[28] Usually, but not always, they could not vote, nor could they give testimony in court in cases involving white men. They could not marry whites and they had to be very circumspect in dealing with them. In Maryland and Georgia a freedman could be reduced to slavery merely for crossing over from a slave state or for marrying a slave, and there are many cases on record of free Negroes being kidnaped and sold into slavery.

SLAVE RESISTANCE

The slave system—with its man-stealing, barbaric slave coffles, flesh-branding, horrifying "middle passage," forced labor, religious fakery, cultivated ignorance, whips, fetters, and auction blocks, and the complete denial of all civil and human rights—was the most brutal of all forms of exploitation and founded upon force and tyranny. Consequently, the basic attitude of the slaves, with their human love of freedom, was one of passive and active resistance and of outright revolt. The truth of this statement is not vitiated by the fact that over large areas and for long periods, a semblance of full submission often reigned, largely a pretense, among the slaves. But the modern working class, the revolutionary enemy of capitalism, also has its passive periods as well as those filled with activity and general progress. To say, as many bourgeois writers have done, that the Negroes tamely submitted to the terrible subjugation of slavery, is an outrageous distortion of reality and a burning insult to the Negro people.

As the African record shows, at the outset the slaves fought bitterly against being kidnaped; on the slave ships, too, they were ready to mutiny at a moment's opportunity. They carried their struggle to the American plantations, where they and their children's children were supposed to serve forever in beast-like slavery. Herskovits says, "Contemporary accounts are so filled with stories of uprisings and other modes of revolt . . . that it is surprising that the conception of the compliant African ever developed."[29] The reason for this is, of course, that such slander was a definite part of the whole repressive mechanism of the slaveholders.

The resistance of the slaves was persistent and various. There are innumerable accounts of how slaves ran away, committed suicide, idled on the job, pretended illness, refused to bear children, burned plantations, killed tyrannical overseers and planters, and so on. The big mountain and swamp areas of all the slave colonies had their groups of "maroons" or runaway slaves. The slaves even conducted "strikes," difficult though the conditions were. That is, they would sometimes hide out in the surrounding swamps, forests, or neighboring plantations, letting their demands be made known to their masters.

They would carry on negotiations through friendly slaves on other plantations. Generally, however, facing impossible conditions, the slaves would grasp at more drastic weapons—flight or insurrection.

The highest form of resistance was the insurrection. Colonial records are replete with stories of these slave uprisings, most of which were finally suppressed by the most savage atrocities. Aptheker[30] lists scores of such slave plots and rebellions all over the country, including the North, during the American colonial period, from the first in South Carolina in 1526, right up to the outbreak of the Revolution of 1776; no doubt his long list could be extended.

An important slave struggle during colonial times was that in Stono, South Carolina, 1739, led by a slave named Cato. It spread terror over the whole countryside and was finally drowned in blood. Another important revolt took place in New York City, in 1712, for there were numerous slave revolts in the North, as well as in the South. The draconian measures used to repress this New York revolt illustrate the customary ferocity. "Twenty-one, then were executed and since the law of 1708 permitted any kind of punishment for this offense . . . some were burnt, others hanged, one broken on the wheel, and one hung alive in chains in the town." In more than one instance, Negroes, whites, and Indians were to be found in the same struggle against the common oppressor. Significantly, when the Indians almost wiped out the colony of Jamestown in 1622, they carefully avoided killing any Negroes. Practically every Indian tribe in the South had its contingent of runaway Negro slaves, welcomed into the tribal life.

Armed struggles by the slaves were by no means peculiar to the British colonies along the Atlantic Coast; they also occurred in every other colony—Spanish, Portuguese, French, and Dutch—throughout all the Americas. Du Bois presents what is only a partial list of the more important of these Negro slave revolts during the colonial period from 1522 on, including those in Santo Domingo, Mexico, Peru, Central America, Jamaica, Barbados, Brazil, Surinam, Cuba, St. Lucia, etc.[31] The two biggest of these uprisings were the revolt in Palmares, Brazil,[32] which lasted from 1630 to 1697, and the great revolution in Haiti, a world event of decisive importance,[33] and of which more later.

4. The Negro in the Revolution of 1776

The first American Revolution was a violent economic, political, and military collision between the young colonial capitalism striving to grow and acquire independence, and the dominant British capitalism, which sought to stifle and restrict it. Under King George III, the combination of landlords, merchants, and industrialists ruled England in accordance with the mercantile spirit of the times. They considered the colonies as merely so many appendages apparently designed by nature for the profit and glory of British exploiters— a supposition which sounds familiar enough in these days of ruthless imperialist exploitation of colonial peoples. British policy aimed specifically to prevent the growth of American industry and trade. The end result was the Revolution of 1776, in which the American merchant capitalists, landowners and slaveholders, with their allies among the masses of the people, broke the controls of the British masters and began their own independent course of national development.

CAUSES OF THE REVOLUTION

From the founding of the Virginia and Massachusetts colonies, British policy moved persistently to strangle independent American economic development. "Whether the king's authority was strong or weak, whether the party in power was Whig or Tory, British landlords and merchants worked increasingly to keep the colonies in leading strings."[1] The economic life of the colonies was confided to the tender care of the Council of Foreign Plantations in 1660, which became the Board of Trade in 1696. This body was responsible thenceforth for many crippling laws and regulations, such as the Navigation Acts of 1660-63, giving England a monopoly of the tobacco, rice, indigo, and dyewood trades; the Act of 1699, prohibiting the shipment of wool from one colony to another to protect the English woolgrowers; the Act of 1732, forbidding the export of American-made hats; the Act of 1733, designed to force the importation of sugar and molasses directly from the British West Indies, regardless of price; the Act of 1750, forbidding the construction of iron-works in the colonies; and the persistent wiping out of all colonial legislation and practices facilitating the growth of American commerce and industry. To put teeth into these restrictions, England governed the colonies through a whole set of corrupt Royal provincial governors and judges, appointed by the Crown and altogether beyond the control of the colonies.

It was one thing, however, for the "home country" to put crippling economic decrees on the books and quite a different matter to enforce them. For over a century, England had been waging a life-and-death struggle with other European powers to establish its control of the seas, and it was in no position to give very close attention to controlling its vigorous American colonies. Hence, by seizing upon every opportunity, the latter were able to extend their commerce, create some industrial beginnings, and to win a small measure of democracy in the various colonies. The Americans smuggled on a wide scale, traded with the enemy in times of war, and openly flouted many economic and political regulations that had been solemnly proclaimed by the bigwigs in London. These illicit economic operations "virtually became the foundation of northern mercantile capitalism."[2]

Upon the conclusion of the Seven Years' War in 1763, which definitely crippled the power of France in America and Europe, England decided upon a more drastic policy regarding her American colonies, which were fast getting out of hand, with their expanding commerce and budding industries. Many severe regulations followed— the restriction of western land speculation and the far-flung fur trade by the Treaty of 1763, which established a demarcation line along the Appalachian mountains; the Sugar Act of 1764, which hamstrung the big American slave trade and put a damper on widespread smuggling and piracy; the Stamp Act of 1765, which hit all commercial activity; and the Acts forbidding the colonial issuance of money; the Tea Act of 1773, etc. The British also sent troops to terrorize the colonial population.

The inevitable explosion followed. The American bourgeoisie (which now sends Communists to jail for long terms for even mentioning revolution), proceeded to take up arms against the oppressor, when its own vital class interests were menaced. Boldly enunciating the right of revolution, the Declaration of Independence of July 4, 1776, proclaimed to the world: "that all men are created equal, that they are endowed by their Creator with certain unalienable Rights, that among these are Life, Liberty, and the pursuit of Happiness. That to secure these rights, Governments are instituted among Men, deriving their just powers from the consent of the governed, that whenever any Form of Government becomes destructive of these ends, it is the Right of the People to alter or to abolish it, and institute new Government."

THE NEGRO IN THE REVOLUTION

The war declared by the Continental Congress lasted seven years and was indeed a difficult one to win. England was the strongest military power in the world and its army and navy towered above those of the colonies. The colonial industrial system was much the weaker, and the colonies were honeycombed with tories and traitors. Moreover, for all their fine words of revolt, the American merchants and planters were very hesitant to push their demand for national independence through to the logical end. These two groups, directly and through their respective political agents, led the Revolution officially. Of the 56 who signed the Declaration of Independence, eight were merchants, six were physicians, five were farmers, and 25 were lawyers.[3] Washington, Jefferson, Randolph, and many others were slaveholders. The Revolution could never have been carried through successfully had it not been for the heavy political pressure and militant fighting spirit of the small farmers, petty merchants, craftsmen, and laborers.

From the outset, the Negroes and slavery played an important part in the revolutionary struggle. Like the immature working class of the period, the Negroes, free and slave, realized more or less clearly that the Revolution offered them an opportunity to come forward with their own specific demands. It was no accident, therefore, that the first man to be killed in open struggle in the Revolution was a Negro, Crispus Attucks, who died in the Boston Massacre of March 5, 1770. Attucks, 47 years old, led a group of workers to the Old Brick Meeting House to protest against the British. Captain Preston and a file of British soldiers fired upon them, and the American Revolution had its first martyrs. Characteristically, they were all workers—Crispus Attucks, sailor; Samuel Gray, rope-maker; James Caldwell, sailor; Samuel

Maverick, joiner's apprentice; and Patrick Carr, leather worker.[4] A monument to Attucks and his comrades now stands on Boston Common.

Slaves also fled the plantations in great numbers during the Revolution. The British realized from the beginning of the struggle that the institution of slavery was a great weakness on the American side and sought to take advantage of this fact by calling upon the slaves to desert the plantations and go over to them. Lord Dunmore, British Governor of Virginia, in 1775 offered to free all slaves who would fight in his forces, and General Carlton thought this would crush the Revolution. Great Britain, however, fearing the effects on slavery in the West Indies, never completely adopted this policy. The Negroes who, far and wide, saw in the Revolution a good occasion to strike for their freedom, were not slow in hearkening to such opportunities.[5] During the Revolutionary War, although some slave conspiracies took place, most of the slaves' spirit of resistance expressed itself in wholesale flight from the American plantations to the British lines.

"Thomas Jefferson declared that in the one year of 1778 Virginia alone saw thirty thousand slaves flee from bondage, and we know that many more escaped both before and after that year. Georgians felt that 75 to 85 percent of their slaves, (who numbered about fifteen thousand in 1774), fled, and South Carolinians declared that of their total number of some one hundred and ten thousand slaves at the start of the Revolution, at least twenty-five thousand made good their escape . . . it appears to be conservative to say that from 1775 until 1783 some one hundred thousand slaves, (*i.e.*, about one out of every five), *succeeded* in escaping from slavery, though very often meeting their death or serfdom instead of freedom."[6]

This mass flight of slaves put the Southern planters in a real predicament. In general they supported the Revolution, among other reasons because they were head over heels in debt to England for imports. Hacker says that at the outbreak of the Revolution, of the total of about £5 million owed to England by the colonials, the planters owed some five-sixths. Jefferson said, "these debts had become hereditary so that the planters were a species of property annexed to certain mercantile houses in London."[7] When the planters took the great revolutionary plunge, they hoped to unload this burdensome debt, but the last thing they wanted was for the Revolution to free their slaves, the source of all their luxury and easy life.

The new revolutionary government shared the embarrassment of the planters at the untoward attitude of the British, who themselves had done so much to build up slavery in the American colonies. Voices were raised to use Negroes as soldiers in the Continental Army, but at first there was much opposition. Madison, among others, urged that slaves be freed and armed. In October 1775, Washington and his council of generals decided, however, to reject Negroes as soldiers, and a month later they issued instructions to this effect to recruiters. On January 6, 1776, under pressure of the British, Washington reversed himself and agreed that free Negroes could serve in the ranks.[8] Therefore Negroes were to be found among the armed forces of all thirteen colonies, sometimes in separate regiments and sometimes together with the whites. It is estimated that of the 300,000 soldiers and sailors who fought in the war, at least 5,000 were Negroes. Often Southern planters sent slaves, as their substitutes, into the army. Many slaves who fought were freed, the Government reimbursing their former masters $1000 for each slave. Others, to our people's disgrace, were re-enslaved.[9] Negro veterans, after the war, significantly increased the number of freed Negroes, North and South.

The Negro soldiers and sailors in the Revolutionary War acquitted themselves bravely and with honor. They took part in numerous key struggles—Concord, Lexington, Bunker Hill, Brandywine, Ticonderoga, Boonesboro, Fort Griswold, Eutaw, Yorktown, Saratoga, Trenton, Princeton, and many other places. They distinguished themselves especially in the battles of Long Island, Red Bank, Rhode Island, Savannah, and Monmouth.[10]

Speaking of the [Negro] troops who took part in the battle of Long Island a veteran, Dr. Harris, said: . . . "Three times in succession they were attacked with more desperate valor and fury by well-trained, disciplined troops and three times did they successfully repel the assault, and thus preserved our army from capture."[11] Among the outstanding Negro revolutionary fighters were Peter Salem, a hero of Bunker Hill; Salem Poore, who was commended to Congress by fourteen commanders for bravery at the battles of Savannah and Charleston; James Armistead, an astute Negro spy who fooled Lord Cornwallis and saved the army of Lafayette; Austin Dabney who, for his bravery in many battles, was honored by Georgia and the Federal Goverment, and Prince, the Negro soldier who captured the British General Richard Prescott. The heroic figure, Deborah Gannett, who fought through the war disguised as a man, is believed to have been a Negro.

THE REVOLUTION AND CHATTEL SLAVERY

Objectively, the Revolution of 1776 was faced with the abolition of chattel slavery as one of its central tasks. This was because the building of capitalism in the United States, which was the fundamental process being advanced by the Revolution, could not be achieved on the basis of a slave labor system. Capitalism requires wage-earning workers who, with at least bodily freedom, are able to fulfill the complex functions of capitalist production. Already at the time of the Revolution, the plantation-slave system, although a great boon to British capitalism, was a drag upon American industrial development, particularly in the South.

As the Revolution expanded, there was a considerable body of public sentiment pressing toward the abolition of the slavery cancer. First and most clear and resolute in this demand were the Negroes themselves, both slaves and freedmen, and they played an important part in the Revolution. Naturally, with their freedom at stake, they were outright Abolitionists. They were fighting against slavery, as we have seen, by mass flight to the British, by resistance on the plantations, and by petitioning the Congress for emancipation. Characteristic of the Negroes' pressure for freedom, a petition in 1779 to the New Hampshire state assembly, calling for the abolition of slavery, declared that "the God of Nature gave them life and freedom upon the terms of the most perfect equality with other men."[12] Another, directed to the General Assembly of Connecticut in 1779, asserted that "we are endowed with the same Faculties with our Masters," and demanded to know if it was "consistent with the present laws of the United States to hold so many thousands, of the Race of Adam, our common Father, in perpetual slavery."[13] At the time of the Revolution slavery was legal in twelve of the original thirteen states.

A body of anti-slavery sentiment had also long been growing up among the general public. A few of its many expressions were the following: in 1645, Richard Saltonstall of Massachusetts made an anti-slavery protest; in 1688, the Germantown Quakers protested against slavery; in 1700, Judge Samuel Sewell of Boston wrote his anti-slavery pamphlet, *The Selling of Joseph*; in 1714, a Pennsylvania Quaker published an anti-slavery tract, *The American Defense of the Golden Rule*; in 1716, the New Jersey Quakers condemned the slave trade; in 1729, *The Mystery of Inequity*, a repudiation of slavery, was published by Ralph Sandiford; in 1754, John Woolman issued an anti-slavery pamphlet, *Some Considerations on the Keeping of Negroes*; in 1750, Anthony Benezet, of Philadelphia, became an anti-slavery agitator and established a school for Negroes; in 1770, the Rev. Samuel Hopkins of Newport, Rhode Island, attacked slavery; and in 1773, Dr. Benjamin Rush, the famous surgeon, published an address in Philadelphia against slavery.[14] Thomas Pownall, Governor of Massachusetts, 1757-60, turned against slavery, advocated emancipation, and supported the equality of Negroes and whites.[15]

With the approach of the Revolution, in the midst of a general growth of the spirit of liberty, the anti-slavery sentiment grew and took on more concrete form. In Philadelphia, on April 14, 1775, there was formed the first local anti-slavery society in America, an organization which still exists. The leading spirit in this movement was Benjamin Franklin. State anti-slavery societies were formed as follows: 1785, New York; 1786, Rhode Island; 1788, Delaware; 1789, Maryland; 1790, Connecticut; 1791, Virginia; 1792, New Jersey and Pennsylvania. By 1792, there were anti-slavery societies with varying programs in practically all the states from New England to Georgia. The movement held a general convention in Philadelphia in 1794, with Joseph Bromfield, later to be Governor of New Jersey, presiding. Ten states were represented. The gathering condemned slavery and the slave trade, addressed Congress on the question, and proposed the holding of annual conventions.[16] Generally, in these movements free Negroes were active.

Many prominent political leaders of both North and South also mildly favored the abolition of slavery by one means or another. Often they themselves were slaveholders. They saw, in some measure at least, the contradiction between proclaiming, on the one hand, that "All men are created free and equal," and on the other, maintaining the barbaric system of Negro chattel slavery. Among those who spoke out, with varying emphasis, against slavery were Thomas Jefferson, Thomas Paine, John Adams, Patrick Henry, John Jay, Dr. Rush, and James Otis. Even the conservative George Washington, himself a slaveholder, said: "There is not a man living, who wishes more sincerely than I do, to see some plan adopted for the abolition of slavery."[17] Alexander Hamilton was secretary of the New York Abolition Society, and Lafayette asked him to propose his name for membership.[18] Benjamin Franklin was especially conscious of the need to destroy slavery. He argued that slave labor was expensive as compared with free wage labor, and he showed that slavery was a barrier to the growth of manufactures. He also challenged the theory that Negroes were inferior mentally to whites.[19]

At this time, the whole position of the slave system was unclear and uncertain. The opinion was widespread throughout the country, (even in the South, this being long before the spectacular development of cotton production) that slavery was obsolete and would soon die out of itself. But the sequel showed that the body of Southern slaveholders, together with their Northern merchant allies, had no such illusions.

MERCHANT-PLANTER DOMINATION

Lenin called the American War of 1776 "one of those great . . . really revolutionary wars of which there have been so few."[20] It was just that, and it dealt a mighty blow to feudal reaction and greatly stimulated democracy all over the world. The Revolution beginning in 1776 was a bourgeois revolution, with strong democratic currents within it. It unified the nation and established American national independence, freed the national market from English domination, and opened the way to the more rapid development of trade and industry: it largely abolished the feudal land tenure system, separated Church and State, and set up a Republican form of government. The Revolution also created objective conditions for the realization of considerable political rights by the farmers and artisans: its greatest weakness was that it did not abolish Negro chattel slavery.

The bulk of the fighting to win this great Revolution was done by the common people—the farmers, handicraftsmen, shopkeepers, and Negroes. They also furnished it with its revolutionary spirit, which carried the struggle to victory over the hesitations, confusions, and outright treacheries of the dominant merchants and planters. But when it came to drafting the basic law of the new republic at the Philadelphia Constitutional Convention, the representatives of the toiling masses were not there, nor was their cause defended. The Convention was entirely in the hands of the ruling classes, who had controlled the country during the Revolution.

Hacker thus describes the make-up of the Convention: "In February, 1787, Congress issued a call for a national convention to revise the Articles of Confederation. Fifty-five representatives from all the states but Rhode Island assembled at Philadelphia. Clearly, in terms of their personal interests and class loyalties, they spoke not for the underprivileged and oppressed, as did so many in the First and Second Continental Congresses, but only for the high-born and the affluent; not for the small farmers and traders and for town mechanics and laborers, but for security speculation, commerce, manufacturing, slave planting, land jobbing, and moneylending. Indeed, of the fifty-five, only two may be said to have had any sympathy with the aspirations of small-propertied men: the aged Benjamin Franklin of Pennsylvania and Luther Martin of Maryland. Jefferson at this time was in France. George Washington, himself a large slaveholder, presided over the proceedings; but if the thought of any single individual dominated there, it was Alexander Hamilton's."[21] He was the reactionary who said, "The people!—the people is a great beast."[22] Madison, however, was the main architect of the Constitution. The Constitutional Convention of 1787 held secret sessions and kept no public records.

The merchants and planters, in full control of the Constitutional Convention, proceeded to build a government that would consolidate all the victories of the Revolution in their own special class interests. They also undertook to prevent the toiling masses and the oppressed—farmers, workers, Negroes, Indians—from reaping any political gains from the Revolution. The business transacted by the Convention was a compromise of the interests of the two ruling classes at the expense of the masses. It was to take the latter many long years to realize in bitter struggle some of the democratic potentialities of the Revolution—the franchise, education, and the right for workers to organize; access to the land through a homestead law for the farmers; and, at long last, emancipation from chattel slavery for the Negro people.

As a substitute for the makeshift Articles of Confederation, the Convention constructed a semi-centralized national Constitution and government to enable the ruling classes to carry out effective policies at home and abroad. The latter clipped the states' rights economically, so that a national market would be built up—the central objective of the bourgeoisie in the Revolution. In the government they set up an elaborate system of checks and balances among the legislative, executive and judicial branches, in order to balk the democratic will of the people, which many of them sneered at as "mob rule." "Shays' Rebellion," which broke out in 1787, gave them a real democratic fight. The merchants and planters in the Convention created national armed forces with which to enforce their class objectives against both foreign and domestic foes. They developed a federal financial system of banks, tariffs, taxes, currency, and public debt. They established national control of the vast lands, opening up constantly before the new republic.* During the revolutionary period many big estates in the North were confiscated and broken up. But the plantation system in the South survived intact; it was even invigorated by being shorn of some of its feudalistic hangovers such as primogeniture, entails, and quitrents. It was only in the face of great resistance from the masses to its reactionary features that it was possible to have the new Constitution eventually ratified by the states.

SLAVERY WRITTEN INTO THE CONSTITUTION

The Indians, who then numbered about 750,000 certainly had a valid claim for favorable consideration, but they got less than nothing from the new Constitution. This document assumed that all territory, from the Atlantic to the east bank of the Mississippi, including huge sections still occupied entirely by Indians, belonged to the United States government. The creation of a strong Federal government, in fact, opened the way for even more vigorous land raids upon the Indians. The young government's policy toward the Indians was one of genocide, according to the slogan, "the only good Indian is a dead one."

The Constitution, worked out in Philadelphia by the merchants and planters in their own class interests, also gave no consideration to the specific rights and needs of the small farmers, shopkeepers, and workers, who formed the great majority of the four million people then living in the colonies. It was not until 1791, four years after the Constitutional Convention, that ten amendments—the Bill of Rights—were tacked onto the Constitution under mass pressure of the workers and farmers, and upon the initiative of James Madison and Thomas Jefferson. The general population, including the workers, were thereby accorded such minimum rights as freedom of speech and assembly, freedom of the press, freedom of worship, trial by jury, right of petition, and freedom from arbitrary search and arrest, and from compulsion to testify against themselves. It was to take many years of mass struggle, however, to translate even these formal paper rights into at least partial realities.

As for the Negro slaves, who numbered 697,624 in the 1790 census,

* Expressed in the Land Ordinance of 1785.

the Constitution operated to tighten their legal fetters, especially in the South. The new law of the land was based upon a tacit recognition of slavery and a perspective of its indefinite continuation. As the Fathers of the Republic in the majority saw things, the Negro slaves were only chattels and therefore subject primarily to the laws governing property. The authors of *The Federalist* boasted that "the Federal Constitution, therefore, decides with great propriety—the case of our slaves, when it views them in the mixed character of persons and property."[23]

In this convention, called to centralize the government, the slaveholders especially wanted a strong national fugitive slave law, and they got it. For the rest, they wanted mainly the issue of slavery left to the various states, and it was, In this respect their model was essentially the Articles of Confederation, under which the young republic had been working since 1779. Formally ignoring the question of slavery, the Articles by implication abandoned the matter to the individual states. Already, the slaveholders were beginning their historic fight under the banner of states' rights, which they continued and intensified to the great climax in the Civil War, and which still remains the basis of the white supremacists' fight against civil rights for the Negro people.

The "Abolitionists" in the convention did not venture to propose the ending of the slavery blight. The Beards say that[24] "the ethics of slavery itself was broached though at no time did it rise to the position of a leading issue." The Southern states fended off all real or pretended attacks upon the slave system. Earlier they had defeated Jefferson's attempt to include a clause in the Declaration of Independence, denouncing England's slavery policy and stating that George III had violated the "most sacred rights of life and liberty of a distant people, who never offended him, captivating them into slavery in another hemisphere, or to incur miserable death in their transportation thither." The arrogant slaveholders did not have too much trouble in preventing any anti-slavery wording from getting into the Constitution, especially since such men as Jefferson, Henry, and Paine were absent. Many Northern merchants, already allied with the South in the slave trade and in other shipping and banking business, lent their aid to the slavers' cause.

Three Constitutional clauses definitely recognized slavery, (although the word "slave" was carefully avoided throughout the Constitution):

"Article I, Section 2: Representatives and direct taxes shall be apportioned among the several States which may be included within this Union, according to their respective numbers, which shall be determined by adding to the whole number of the free persons, including those bound to service for a term of years, and excluding Indians not taxed, three-fifths of all other persons." The "all other persons" were the slaves, for whom the slaveholders got themselves three-fifths representation in Congress, although, of course, they denied the slave every semblance of representation. Thus the Negro slave was condemned as being less than a man—only three-fifths.

"Article I, Section 9:   The migration or importation of such persons as any of the States now existing shall think proper to admit, shall not be prohibited by the Congress prior to the year 1808, but a tax or duty may be imposed on such importation, not exceeding ten dollars for each person." This clause, which indirectly implied the abolition of the slave trade twenty years later, was largely the work of Virginia and North Carolina, which had a surplus of slaves on hand, and wanted the African slave trade ended.

"Article IV, Section 2:   No person held to service or labor in one State, under the laws thereof, escaping into another, shall, in consequence of any law or regulation therein, be discharged from such service or labor, but shall be delivered up on claim of the party to whom such service or labor may be due." This provision was a big concession to the slaveholders. It provided the basis for the shameful Fugitive Slave Law of 1793, the first in our national history. Of that law, McMaster says: "For fifty-seven years it remained unaltered and in force, and during those fifty-seven years caused more misery, more injustice, more outrageous violation of the rights of men, both black and white, than any other piece of legislation ever enacted in the United States."[25] This plan was superseded by the even more drastic Fugitive Slave Act of 1850.

The slaveholders were also largely instrumental in the adoption of Article I, Section 3, of the Constitution, which allows two senators to each of the states, large or small. The Southerners feared the growth of the population in the free states and they hoped, by the "two-each" rule, to control the Senate, or at least to neutralize it. The experience of the next two generations proved that in this hope they were not mistaken.

Although the slaveholders prevented the issue of slavery as such from coming squarely before the Constitutional Convention, definite cleavages between the Northern and Southern wings of the bourgeoisie developed in the sharp discussions around the fringe of the question. It was the beginning of the big political division between the supporters and the enemies of slavery. The astute Madison noted this fact, and forecast that slavery was the issue that one day would rend the Republic.

The Constitutional Convention did not solve the fundamental problem of abolishing chattel slavery, nor did it try to do so. By this failure, besides committing an enormous crime against the Negro people, the bourgeois Revolution of 1776 left a high barrier to the development of the national market and the expansion of industrialization. It also created in the Southern slavocracy a bitter class rival to the growing Northern industrialists, one which was long to contest their bid for national leadership and domination. But the abolition of slavery was imperative—a task conditioned by history for the growth of American capitalism—and it had to be carried through eventually, whatever the cost. Slavery was finally abolished, but only after the United States had been torn with political strife for two generations, and after a million people, civilian and military, had laid down their lives in a second great revolution.

5. The Abolition of Slavery in the North and Northwest

Of major importance to the Negro people in their struggle to free themselves was the abolition of slavery in the Northern and Northwestern states and territories during and after the great Revolution of 1776. This was an organic part of the big people's democratic movement, which began in the Revolution and had its first climax in the epic victory of the Jefferson forces in 1800.

At the end of the Revolution, the United States was overwhelmingly an agricultural country—even in 1800 only four percent of the people lived in cities of 8,000 population or over. Existing capital was invested in inland commerce, shipping, land, and slaves. Industrial production as such was carried on mainly by artisans working in small shops. Manufacture was hardly born yet. There were but the beginnings of iron and coal mining, iron-smelting, and textile making. Spinning and weaving were done mostly in homes. It was not until 1788 that the first real woolen mill was established in Hartford, Connecticut, and 1791, that Slater set up the pioneer cotton mill in Pawtucket, Rhode Island. The budding iron and coal industries, as yet very small in scope, operated on the basis of tiny plants. Lumbering, flour-milling, and shipbuilding were more developed, but also were worked in very small production units.

The decisive capitalist groupings in the new American bourgeois order were the big Northern merchants and the Southern slaveholders. The larger merchants combined in themselves the functions not only of merchandisers, but also of transporters and, to a large extent, bankers. In many cases, too, they were pioneers in manufacturing. The genuine wage-earning working class of the period was relatively small—consisting mostly of seamen, dockers, carters, day laborers, clerks in government and commerce, and agricultural laborers. Industrial development, however, was eventually to make real wage workers of the large numbers of carpenters, painters, blacksmiths, coopers, bakers, printers, etc., then working in small shops as artisans.

THE ATTEMPT AT COUNTER-REVOLUTION

The Revolution of 1776 was a bright beacon light to the oppressed peoples of the Americas and the world. It was an epoch-making victory for social progress and human freedom. But hardly had the difficult political and military struggle against England been won, when organized American reaction undertook to seize the newly-freed country and people and to exploit and dominate them ruthlessly. The richest merchants and wealthiest planters, North and South, set out essentially to create a United States in which they, acting jointly, would own the land and the industries and completely control the government. The Negroes would remain slaves permanently, and the white workers, deprived of the franchise and other civil rights, would be merely objects for unbridled capitalist exploitation. All this meant that the Revolution had entered a new and higher stage—from primarily a national struggle against England it was being transformed into a sharp class struggle on the domestic scene.

In the previous chapter we saw the counter-revolutionary merchant-planter alliance busily manipulating the Constitutional Convention of 1787 to serve its ends and later on formulating the infamous Fugitive Slave Act in 1793. All through the eight years of Washington's presidency, from 1789 to 1797, this two-class alliance of big merchants and planters continued its reactionary course. The counter-revolution, however, began to reach its climax in 1796 with the election as president of the Massachusetts lawyer, John Adams, who had been vice-president under Washington. Among the many reactionary steps taken under the Adams Administration was the passage of the notorious Alien and Sedition Acts of 1798. These laws were designed to terrorize the immigrant foreign-born and to rob the workers and farmers of such meager political rights as they then possessed. In the government's attempt to enforce this drastic legislation in the face of the widespread popular opposition, ten editors and others were thrown into jail for sedition. The merchant-planter combination constituted the Federalist Party, and its chief leader, Alexander Hamilton, spokesman of the merchants, arrogantly demanded a strong government entirely in the hands of the propertied classes.

The democratic masses of the people, fresh from their great revolutionary war victory over the English oppressor, promptly took up the cudgels against this internal big planter-merchant menace, which they knew of old. Their chief leader after 1790 was Thomas Jefferson, the author of the Declaration of Independence, who had just returned from a stay in Europe. Jefferson, himself a planter, was an agrarian democrat. He built the Republican-Democratic Party, forerunner of the present-day Democratic Party, as a combination of planters, small farmers of the North and South, western frontiersmen, and shopkeepers, artisans, and workers of the eastern cities. Although his policies did much to lay the foundation of American capitalism, Jefferson held the perspective of a society based primarily upon small farmers and artisans.

Jefferson, in tune with the Declaration of Independence (which was written in the home of a bricklayer), boldly proclaimed the people's right of revolution. Commenting upon Shays' Rebellion of 1786-7, which was directed against mortgages, foreclosures and persecution of debtors, he declared, "God forbid that we should ever be for twenty years without such a rebellion."[1] Jefferson fought against the powerful monarchist sentiment among reactionary political leaders; he opposed the notorious Jay Treaty with England, and also Hamilton's banking and other dangerous financial maneuvers. Jefferson was a friend of popular education and an opponent of slavery, although never resolutely attacking the latter question head on. He especially battled against the Alien and Sedition Acts. An important struggle in this period was the so-called Whiskey Rebellion of Pennsylvania farmers in 1794 against exorbitant taxes.

The development of the great French Revolution, from 1789 on, added much fire to the sharp American class struggle. The Hamiltonian Federalists denounced this Revolution and wanted to force the United States into war against France on the side of England; the Jeffersonians took an opposite course. As Parrington says, "The Federalists went with Great Britain and turned fiercely on the democratic movement, assailing it with increasing venom. The democrats, on the other hand, became French partisans, and denounced all aristocrats with true republican fervor, becoming more radical as French Jacobinism developed."[2] During this bitter struggle, the United States got its first real taste of red-baiting, the reactionaries wildly denouncing the Jeffersonians as Anarchists, Communists, atheists, destroyers of the home, and paid agents of revolutionary France.

But the vituperative attacks had little weight with the popular masses, who were then in an ascending revolutionary spirit. Consequently, in the elections of 1800 Jefferson won the presidency in one of the greatest popular demonstrations in the entire history of the

United States. The people would not allow themselves to be robbed of the democratic fruits of the Revolution.

Jefferson's Republican-Democratic victory was a victory for capitalism, as well as for democracy; and in these times, inasmuch as it was developing the social forces of production, capitalism was a progressive social system. Jefferson's cultivation of the poor farmers and small producers was the main means, indispensable at that time, to lay the broadest base under production in general, and also under American democracy. The policy of Hamilton and his Federalist camp, on the other hand, could only have resulted in the strengthening of reaction and of the existing feudal elements, the planters and their system of slavery. This would not have furthered industrialization, much less popular democracy.

THE NORTHERN STATES ABOLISH SLAVERY

The victory of the Jeffersonian people's forces was the result of a continuing fight from the time of the Revolution, and before. Although the democratic elements did not put the abolition of slavery into their program, they nevertheless tended to weaken that system by virtue of the fact that their program strengthened democracy in general. This struggle was a powerful, if not decisive, factor in developing the most important blow struck against the chattel slave system in the post-revolutionary period—namely, the abolition of slavery in the Northern and Northwestern states.

Although the Constitutional Convention of 1787 had protected and legalized the plantation-slavery system of the South, Abolitionist sentiment continued to grow among the people, especially in the states and territories of the North and Northwest. It was one of the major democratic currents released by the great American Revolution. Already during the revolutionary war this growing Abolitionist spirit began to manifest itself. In 1777, Vermont, although still not formally organized as a state, abolished slavery within its borders. Several other Northern states, during the war and in the post-war period, adopted legislation either cutting off the slave trade or beginning the gradual abolition of slavery, or both. In doing this the common method was for a state to set an age—usually 25 or 28—at which the children of slave mothers would become free and also then set later dates on which slavery was to be abolished altogether. Such legislation was adopted in 1780 by Massachusetts and Pennsylvania; in 1784 by

Rhode Island and Connecticut; in 1799 by New York, and in 1804 by New Jersey.[3] Within twenty years after the end of the war all the original states in the North had adopted legislation either restricting or abolishing slavery. In 1803, 1816, and 1818, Ohio, Indiana, and Illinois came into the Union as free states. Many cases of individual manumission of slaves also took place during this whole period.

A very important development in 1787 was the prohibition by a federal ordinance of slavery in the Northwest Territory—a region which contained the present-day states of Ohio, Indiana, Illinois, Michigan, Wisconsin, and part of Minnesota. In 1784, Thomas Jefferson had originally proposed the exclusion of slavery from the areas now constituting Tennessee, Kentucky, Alabama, and Mississippi, as well as those of the Northwest. If this proposal had carried, it would have dealt a mortal blow to the whole plantation-slave system, isolating it in the half-dozen Southern states along the Atlantic Coast. His bill was one of the most important legislative proposals ever made in the history of the United States. But it failed to pass in Congress, being defeated by one vote cast by a representative of a slave state.[4] When the Northwest Ordinance, written by Jefferson, which passed both Houses of Congress unanimously, finally went into effect in 1787, it abolished slavery only in the Northwest, in the territories, (later states), named above. Slavery in all the rest of the public domain was left as a matter of controversy. The Northwest Ordinance, which was to play an important role in the great anti-slavery struggle of later decades, provided in Article 6 that "There shall be neither slavery nor involuntary servitude in the said territory, otherwise than in the punishment of crimes, whereof the party shall have been duly convicted"—but fugitive slaves from slave states had to be returned.[5]

While this movement toward Negro emancipation was taking shape in the Northern and Northwestern states and territories, a reactionary counter-current, to strip free Negroes of the right to vote was appearing in many states, North as well as South. In the South, "in colonial times, the free Negro was excluded from the suffrage only in Georgia, South Carolina, and Virginia. In the Border states, Delaware disfranchised the Negro in 1792; Maryland in 1783 and 1810." "In the Southeast Florida disfranchised them in 1817; in the Southwest, Louisiana disfranchised them in 1812; Mississippi in 1817; Alabama in 1819; Missouri in 1821; Arkansas in 1836; Texas in 1845." In the North, Ohio disfranchised free Negroes in 1803; Connecticut in 1814; Indiana in 1816; Illinois in 1818; Michigan in 1837; Pennsylvania in 1838; Iowa in 1846; Wisconsin in 1848; New Jersey in 1847; Minnesota in 1858.[6] As long as the Negro freedmen were only a tiny minority, they were allowed to vote; but when their numbers increased, the franchise was taken from them. By the outbreak of the Civil War in 1861, free Negroes were barred from voting in almost every state in the Union. Thus, at a time when the white workers were progressively knocking out the property qualifications and winning the right to vote, the free Negroes were being systematically stripped of their franchise.

Usually the loss of the Negroes' franchise was accompanied by a general deprivation of basic civic rights. McMaster paints this picture of the Negro "freeman" in the North in the first decade of the century: "Nowhere did the black man have all the rights of the white. Here he could not vote; there he could not serve in the militia; nowhere was he summoned to be a juror. Race prejudice shut him out of a long line of trades and occupations, and condemned him to a state of gross ignorance. No carpenter, no blacksmith, wheelwright, mason, or shoemaker would take him as an apprentice; no shopkeeper would have him as a clerk. He was excluded from every hotel, inn, and tavern, and from every school save such as benevolent persons had established for the especial benefit of his race."[7]

THE EARLY GENERAL ANTI-SLAVERY MOVEMENT

The basic reason for the failure of slavery in the North and Northwest was because of the climatic factor which made it impossible to produce the chief world market crops of the slavery period—the plantation-slave system simply did not suit these areas. The Northern farmers were also adamant against the plantation system. The growing anti-slavery sentiment in the three decades after the Revolutionary War, fed by the widespread belief that slavery was gradually dying out, likewise helped to wipe out its remnants in the inhospitable places. Then, too, in many cases, Northern white mechanics, fearing the slave-mechanics as competitors, were inclined to support the abolition of slavery in their own states.[8] Throughout this whole period, however, the number of slaves nationally (nearly all in the South) continued to increase rapidly. In 1790, according to the first census, they numbered 697,624; in 1810, the third census put their number at 1,191,362.

The scattered local anti-slavery societies were quite alert during this period. In these movements, some of which dated back to the Revolution, Negro freedmen were very active. Their programs varied widely. But in the American Convention of Abolition Societies, held in 1804, delegates complained of flagging interest in the work. In 1809, the Pennsylvania Society, after 25 years of existence, made a similar complaint. Wilson thus sums up the type of activity of the latter organization, "It made special efforts against kidnaping, educated and secured homes for colored children. It examined laws respecting colored people, noted their defects, and prepared bills for the legislature. It memorialized Congress on the fugitive slave law and the slave trade. In 1818, it examined and condemned the colonization scheme then just being inaugurated. In 1819, it appointed a committee to watch the struggle for the admission of Missouri; and in 1820 it obtained from the Government a portion of the school fund for colored children. In the same year it memorialized the legislature for the total abolition of slavery in the community."[9]

During the decades immediately following the Revolution the Protestant churches, under the democratic mass pressure, yielded for a while in their support of slavery. Thus, the Methodists in 1784, the Baptists in 1789, and the Presbyterians in 1793, came out against the slave trade. The Methodists set the pace by declaring "that those who buy, sell, or give away slaves, except for the purpose to free them, shall be expelled immediately." These churches, however, all enforced a Jim Crow policy toward Negroes, free and slave, seating them in special pews in remote corners of the church. The Quakers had the best record of any sect regarding slavery, although many rich Quakers owned slaves throughout the colonial period. For a hundred years past, however, there had been strong voices in that church against slavery, and Quakers were active in every abolitionist movement. As early as 1773, the yearly Philadelphia meeting of Friends disowned Stephen Hopkins, Quaker signer of the Declaration of Independence, for refusing to dispose of his slaves.[10]

THE NEGRO PEOPLE STRIKE AT SLAVERY

Despite the weak, and temporary, concessions of the Protestant churches to the anti-slavery movement, the Negro people could not tolerate their disgusting Jim Crow practices, and even during the Revolution the free Negroes began to establish their own independent churches. The first Negro Baptist Church was formed in Augusta,

Georgia, "not later than 1775" by George Lisle and Andrew Bryan; and the first Methodist Episcopal Church, in Philadelphia in 1791 by Richard Allen and Absalom Jones.[11] Thenceforth the Negro Church took root, grew, and became an important part in the developing Negro people's movement.

These pioneer churches were the beginning of the separate national organization of the Negro people, which in our time has grown to such large significance. Negro schools also began to be established shortly after the Revolution. In 1787, the Philadelphia Free African Society, the forerunner of the present-day Negro insurance companies, was organized in Philadelphia.[12] Prince Hall, a well known Boston Negro who pioneered in Negro education, also founded Negro Masonry in 1787 in Massachusetts.

Negro freedmen were active initiators and participants in all the anti-slavery movements in these early stages of the historic struggle. They built Negro anti-slavery societies, sent petitions to the state legislatures, and Congress, circulated literature, and carried on a general anti-slavery agitation.[13]

During these post-war decades, the free Negroes were delivering blows against the hoary slave-masters' arguments that Negroes were inferior to whites. Despite the enormous handicaps from which they suffered, with the grossest discrimination of all kinds directed against them, many free Negroes were making outstanding achievements. Among the more prominent of these pioneers was Benjamin Banneker, a noted Negro mathematician, astronomer, and inventor. Born in Maryland on May 9, 1731, of a free mother and a slave father, Banneker early displayed his striking abilities. When only a youth, he built a unique clock. In 1791 he issued his first Almanac, which became a national institution. Banneker also helped to lay out the plans for the city of Washington.[14] Then there was Phyllis Wheatley of Long Island, New York. She was born in Senegal, Africa, and brought to America as a slave. She was educated and became a poet of intelligence and beauty, and her works, published from 1761 on, attracted international attention. Jupiter Hammon, "America's first Negro poet" also lived at this time. Vasma was another Negro of noted talent in this period. He was an outstanding fighter for Negro freedom, and in particular helped to link together the Abolitionist movements of England and the United States. Paul Cuffee, born a free man in Massachusetts, became prominent in the New England shipping industry, and was identified with the anti-slavery movement.

With such Negro figures in the public eye, many people began to question or to combat the current white supremacy theories. The 1795 convention of the Abolition societies, for example, proposed by Negro education to "confound the enemies of truth by evincing that the unhappy sons of Africa, in spite of the degrading influence of slavery, are in no wise inferior to the more fortunate inhabitants of Europe and America."[15] Thomas Jefferson, who equivocated on this question, finally came to recognize something of the potentialities of the Negro people, and Benjamin Franklin was a sturdy champion of the intellectual equality of Negroes and whites.

Meanwhile, the slaves on the plantations were dealing heavy blows against the slave system. Aptheker points to much slave unrest during these years.[16] The most important of the numerous insurrections of this period was that in Henrico County, Virginia, in 1800. It was led by Gabriel, a slave of Thomas H. Prosser. Gabriel was a giant of a man, six feet two in height, and his chief aid, Jack Bowler, was three inches taller. The rebellious slaves, some mounted, armed with clubs and home-made swords and bayonets, assembled for action on the night of August 30, not far from Richmond. But the meeting was disorganized by a sudden storm of hurricane force.

The slaveowners had been greatly frightened by word of the uprising, and before the rebels could reorganize their ranks, the hastily assembled militia fell upon them and dispersed them. Scores were arrested. Gabriel himself was seized on September 25, and he later died stoically, refusing to reveal details of the conspiracy. About 35 other Negroes were executed. The number of slaves involved in this uprising has been variously estimated at from 1,000 to 10,000. The uprising threw the whole South into a panic. Richmond was heavily occupied by troops and thereafter maintained a special guard against insurrections. Planters everywhere tightened up their terroristic controls over their slaves.

Another important insurrection took place ten years later, on January 9, 1811, near New Orleans, Louisiana. Several hundred slaves, led by Charles, the slave of a Mr. Andry, took part. Speedy action by the ever-watchful state troops, however, caught the movement at its inception and destroyed it. New Orleans was in a wild panic. Sixty-five of the rebels were executed, many of them with torture. Scores of other slaves disappeared, doubtlessly shot down in the woods. A significant feature of this insurrection was that the slaves, having heard of the liberation slogans of the French Revolution, had planned to spare Frenchmen known to oppose slavery. This incident illustrates a fact noted by many observers, that slaves, despite all efforts of the planters to keep them in deepest ignorance, often had a pretty good picture of what was happening in the world—information which was probably picked up from the table talk of the white masters. There is reason to conclude that the American, French, and Haitian revolutions had profound repercussions among the slaves on the Southern plantations of the United States.

THE REVOLUTION IN HAITI

During the last decade of the eighteenth century, a tremendous event, which inspired the Negro slaves in the United States and terrified their masters, was the great, successful revolution of the slaves in Haiti during the years 1790-1803. The Haitian Revolution was one of the most important fights for liberty in modern times, and it had world-wide repercussions.[17] It was a major influence in weakening slavery in the United States.

Haiti, a French colony, southeast of Cuba, was the richest of the West Indian "sugar islands." Half a century earlier, France had valued this possession above French Canada. Its exports compared favorably in value with those of the United States. In a total population of about 536,000, the Negro slaves and free Mulattoes outnumbered the white planters and their hangers-on by about 15 to one. The slaves were usually worked to death, one-ninth of them dying annually. The lush island, a hell for the slaves, was a tropical paradise for the aristocratic white French planters.

The Revolution in Haiti was directly related to the great French Revolution, which began in 1789. The Haitian Mulattoes and Negroes demanded that the principle of "Liberty, Equality, and Fraternity" apply to Haiti as well as France. And in order to make this demand stick, for a dozen years they waged one of the hardest-fought and bloodiest wars in the history of the Western Hemisphere.

In this war, François Dominique Toussaint L'Ouverture, born a slave in Haiti, came forward as a brilliant general. He overwhelmingly defeated the British, Spanish, and French forces. The British lost 40,000 soldiers in this struggle and the French still more. Napoleon, whose casualties were 70,000 men in the great Spanish campaign, lost 63,000 men in trying to hold onto the rich colony of Haiti. Toussaint was the first military leader to defeat Napoleon. The final result was that the rebellious slaves won completely, chased their erstwhile masters from the island, freed all the slaves, took away the planters' lands, and set up a republic which stands today. Toussaint was overcome only by being tricked into a peace conference, where he was seized and then transported to a French prison to die.

The revolutionary victory of the Negroes in Haiti served as a spearhead for the still broader national independence revolution, which, beginning in 1810, before it was finished, had swept all Latin America from Mexico to Chile, destroying the American colonial empires of Spain, Portugal and France. Besides freeing themselves, the Haitians gave money, arms, and ships to the patriot leader Sebastian Francisco Miranda in 1806, when he was trying to initiate the revolution in Venezuela. Toussaint, who is systematically ignored or played down by conservative bourgeois historians, stood head high with Simon Bolívar, José de San Martín, George Washington, Thomas Jefferson, and the other outstanding patriots, generals, and political leaders of the great American revolutions of that period.

The Haitian Revolution had profound repercussions in the American slave system. The slaves were given heart and the slaveholders frightened half to death. Among its other effects, it helped to speed the abolition of slavery in the Northern and Northwestern states. The Southern planters used every means to keep the news of the Revolution from their slaves and to prevent Haitian Negro sailors from making their way ashore in Southern ports. The planters were alarmed by scare reports that Toussaint was about to invade Florida (then held by Spain) with a big army of Negro revolutionists to touch off a general slave revolt in the United States. Korngold remarks that this was not such a fantastic project as might be imagined at first, because Toussaint had an army of some 55,000 veteran soldiers (the largest force George Washington ever commanded was only 20,000 men), and it might well have been possible to get an effective part of Toussaint's troops from Haiti to Florida.

The loss of Haiti by France also had consequences of world importance. For Napoleon had planned to build an empire in Louisiana, which stretched more than a thousand miles north and south and had fallen into his hands from Spain in 1800. To do this, he had to have Haiti as a base. But when that country was lost, Louisiana was of no further use to Napoleon and he was compelled to sell it to the United States in 1803. The American people have much for which to thank the Negro revolutionists in Haiti.

6. Suppression of the International Slave Trade

In 1807 the United States and Great Britain officially condemned the international slave trade and made its practice subject to severe penalties. The American law was passed on March 2, 1807, and went into effect on January 1, 1808; the British law was adopted by Parliament, received the royal assent, and became operative after May 1, 1807. The Danes had banned the slave traffic in their dominions in 1802 and the French forbade it in theirs on June 1, 1819.

The outlawing of the slave trade by England and the United States in the same year—1807—was not a joint action; but it was a close coincidence and not without an intimate interconnection. The simultaneous actions, taken only three weeks apart, put the two main culprits on record against the world traffic in human beings. But it was to take them many years to exterminate the bloody trade altogether. Slave-trading was not wiped out finally until slavery itself was abolished—in 1838 in the British West Indies, with compensation to the planters, and in 1863 in the United States, by revolution and confiscation.

THE FIGHT FOR THE AMERICAN ANTI-SLAVE TRADE LAW

The British legislation, with its sharp penalties, provided that ships could not clear from English ports for slaving, nor could they land slaves in any British possession after the law went into effect. The American Act to Prohibit the Importation of Slaves provided that "it should not be lawful to import or bring into the United States or the territories thereof from any foreign kingdom, place, or country, any negro, mulatto, or person of colour, as a slave, or to be held to service or labor."[1] Violators of the law were to forfeit their vessels, have their slaves freed, and pay a fine of $800 per slave. Both Britain and the United States pledged themselves to patrol the African coasts to stamp out the practice of slave-trading.

The strong anti-slavery trends that developed during the Revolution of 1776 exerted powerful influence against the infamous African slave trade. The extreme barbarities of this trade were a noxious offense to even the most elementary civilization. Many people who refused to take a stand against slavery as such, or even condoned slavery, were outspoken in their opposition to the international slave trade.

Morais points out that "In 1774 the Continental Congress proposed that the practice of importing slaves be stopped. A pledge was made not to rent ships to slave traders, or sell goods to those engaged in this traffic. . . . Various colonies and states acted individually toward the same end. As early as 1774, Rhode Island and Connecticut passed laws providing that all chattels brought within their respective provinces be freed. Delaware prohibited the importation of bondsmen in 1776."[2]

Sentiment against the slave trade was also widespread in the South during this period. There were two reasons for this. First, before the advent of the cotton gin, the plantation system was somewhat languishing. Second, and more specifically, some of the Southern states had a surplus of slaves and to protect slave prices, favored cutting off African competition from the American slave market. Bogart has this to say of the situation: "Except on the rice and indigo plantations of the Carolinas . . . the economic disadvantages of slave labor were so apparent that many prominent Southerners favored its early abolition. By 1796, Virginia, South Carolina, Georgia, North Carolina and Maryland, of the Southern states, had all forbidden the importation of slaves."[3] Mason of Virginia, himself a slaveholder and a supporter of slavery, condemned the slave trade as "diabolical in itself and disgraceful to mankind."[4]

The slaveholders, however, had built into the Constitution a strong barrier against federal anti-slave trade legislation. The reader will recall that the Constitutional Convention of 1787 wrote a clause into the Constitution making it impossible to abolish the slave trade before 1808. McMaster comments thus on this arrangement, "All Congress could do was, lay a tax of ten dollars on each imported slave, and forbid citizens of the United States, and subjects of other states, to fit out ships in the ports of the United States for the purpose of engaging in the African slave trade."[5] These steps were taken but were flagrantly violated by slave traders, who proceeded to sail American ships under the Spanish flag. Sometimes the slavers had several sets of ships' papers.

When the constitutional barrier period expired, President Jefferson hailed the expiration date in a message to Congress and proposed that appropriate anti-slave trade legislation be enacted. The law was finally passed after a long discussion and in the face of considerable Southern opposition. The aristocratic planters took special exception to the idea of slaves, who were confiscated in the illegal slave trade, being released in the South as freedmen. "Did the gentlemen suppose that the inhabitants of the slave states would suffer free negroes to live among them?" shouted one firebrand Representative. "Not one of them would be alive in a year."[6] Nevertheless, January 1, 1808 was set as the historic day when the United States would finally clean its hands of the shameful African slave trade.

THE ANTI-SLAVERY MOVEMENT IN ENGLAND

On June 22, 1772, on behalf of the whole English bench, Lord Mansfield ruled in the case of the American Negro slave Somerset, lately brought to England, that there was no basis in English law for slavery, and that when a slave set foot on the British Isles he automatically became free. This ruling set free 15,000 slaves on English soil. Although permitting Negro emancipation in Britain itself, the British bourgeoisie nonetheless continued for a generation to carry on vigorously the African-American slave trade, with its fabulous profits and prosperity for English capitalists and landlords.

A growing far-sighted force in bourgeois circles, however, began to challenge the wisdom of the slave trade for Britain, especially after 1780. The movement was headed by such outstanding figures as Lord William Wilberforce, Thomas Clarkson, George Thompson, and Granville Sharp. It was also supported from its earliest days by a galaxy of well-known economists, preachers, lawyers, poets, and politicians, including Adam Smith, Dr. Johnson, Dean Tucker, John Wesley, William Cowper, Alexander Pope, Daniel Defoe, and many others. From the time of George Fox in 1671, the Quakers were pioneers in the British anti-slavery movement, which had contact with the parallel trend in the United States.[7] The trade unions were a big factor in this movement. Agitation by the English Abolitionist group was primarily a humanitarian protest against the outrages against the Negroes. Like their colleagues in the United States, the English Abolitionists denounced the slave trade in all its horrors. But they did not come out against slavery as such until 1823.[8] The kernel of the argument used against the slave trade, however, was economic. In substance, the English Abolitionists contended that for Great Britain the rich African continent offered far greater economic opportunities than mere man-stealing, profitable though this was. So long as the slave trade lasted, keeping Africa in chaos and turmoil, substantial economic penetration and trade with its teeming peoples, they said, was out of the question. Real trade with Africa required abolishing the slave trade.

Year after year, for two decades after 1789, Wilberforce continued —to no avail—to introduce bills into Parliament calling for the abolition of the slave trade, while his collaborators carried on militant anti-slavery agitation among the English people. A network of anti-slavery societies was built up, and Cowper and others wrote poems against slavery.[9] But it was not until 1807, when the British rulers were convinced that support of the slave trade was economically a short-sighted policy, that they had Parliament declare for its abolition.

Significantly, immediately upon the official banning of the African slave trade, England began active preparations for widespread trade on the "dark continent." In 1807, the African Institution was founded, and it soon became an instrument of British economic penetration in Africa. During the next generation, British explorers and ivory hunters crisscrossed the continent, establishing small posts and preparing the way for trade development and the eventual seizure of most of South Africa by the British. (See Chapter 1.)

The adoption of the anti-slave trade law of 1807 did not mean that the British were ready to wipe out richly-paying slavery itself in Jamaica, Barbados, and the other West Indian sugar islands. An anti-slavery law was enacted in 1833 and enforced only in 1838, when chattel slavery had become uneconomic in view of England's developing policy of free trade and the pressure of British sugar producers in the Far East, who had no slaves themselves and would not tolerate the protected slave plantation system of the West Indies.

VIOLATIONS OF THE ANTI-SLAVE TRADE LAWS

With its eyes definitely fastened upon economic penetration of the African Continent, the British government made immediate and determined efforts after 1808 to wipe out the slave trade. Britain, formerly the number one slave-trader, now became the chief force in breaking up the traffic. English cruisers haunted the river ports all along the Guinea Coast looking for slavers, and they were generally a menace to these ships of prey. But with the American government it was quite a different matter. From the outset it made no real effort to enforce the law against slave-trading by American ships—and this for several important reasons. First, the government was pressed by a tremendous demand for slaves at home, stimulated by the rapidly-developing cotton production; second, it had no intention as yet of developing markets within Africa; and third, its New England slave-traders would not give up the bloody profits of the slave trade.

Instead of trying to extirpate the slave trade, cruisers sent by the United States to patrol the slave coasts of Africa actually protected and cultivated it. Many of the American commanders hailed from the slaveholding Southern states, and of course they would not lift a finger against the slavers. The fact was that slave ships of other nations, when pursued by the vigilant and aggressive British cruisers, often found safety by hoisting the United States colors. In 1820, in agreement with Great Britain, the United States—tongue-in-cheek—finally outlawed the slave trade as piracy, a crime which was supposed to carry the death penalty but generally did not.

Slave-trading, as it became more dangerous, also became more profitable. "A good hearty Negro costs but $120 or thereabouts, and brings from $300 to $400 in Cuba."[10] The whole problem of the illicit slave trade grew worse with the passage of the years. New York was the chief and unashamed home port and fitting-out place for slave ships, and Charleston, South Carolina, was the main port where the unhappy African victims were unloaded and sold into slavery. This outlaw slave trade continued right up to the Civil War, when the captured captain of a slave ship, Nathaniel P. Gordon, was convicted of piracy in New York and hanged on February 21, 1862. It has been estimated that half a million slaves were smuggled into the United States between 1808 and 1860. During this period, Americans dominated the slave trade throughout the hemisphere. Du Bois says that the slave trade "finally came to be carried on principally by United States capital, in United States ships, officered by United States citizens, and under the United States flag."[11]

As the outlaw slave trade grew, the slave ships became bigger and faster, dwarfing the tiny slavers of a century before. Many fast American clippers were put into the trade, to outrun the alert British cruisers. The speedy *Nightingale* of Salem, a ship of 1,000 tons burden, carried 2,000 slaves per trip. And the slaver clipper ship, *Flying Scud*, logged 449 miles in one day, or over 18 knots per hour—which is faster than many good steamers of today.[12] A wealthy man's yacht, the *Wanderer*, flying the colors of the New York Yacht Club, engaged in the lucrative traffic. During the last years of the slave trade, on the eve of the Civil War, even steamers began to get into slaving.

The "middle passage" between Africa and America, notorious for centuries, became still more frightful during the half century of the outlawed slave trade. The slaves were packed even more densely in the ships, terror discipline over them was much more rigorous, and disease took a more deadly toll. Even more horrible, more and more slave-traders would throw their slaves overboard to avoid capture and conviction by the British for slave-trading and piracy. During this period, "Thrice as great a number of Negroes as before, it was said, was exported from Africa, and two-thirds of these were murdered on the high seas."[13]

After the passage of the American anti-slave trading law of 1808, Abolitionist organization in this country slumped. "The national conventions ceased, meetings were no longer, or rarely held, and most of the societies died out. The first anti-slavery movement in the United States was no more."[14] This decline was mainly due to widespread illusions that the slave trade would halt and that this would finish off the whole slave system.

NEGROES AND THE WAR OF 1812

The War of 1812, fought during the administration of James Madison, was largely a follow-up of the War of 1776. England, the arrogant mistress of the seas, had never become reconciled to the loss of her invaluable American colonies, and had steadily pursued a policy designed to prevent the commercial and industrial development of the United States. War was the sure consequence of this course. Negroes played a part in the War of 1812. Had England won this war—and for a time the issue was in doubt—that country would undoubtedly have tried to re-establish her old colonial regime upon the wreckage of the United States. For the Americans, therefore, the War of 1812 was a just and defensive war.

The Americans, who were already distinctly expansionist, saw in this war a golden opportunity to carry through one of the major projects they had in mind, namely the absorption of Canada. During the War of 1776 too, this had been a central American objective. Article XI of the Articles of Confederation provided that "Canada, acceding to this confederation, and joining in the measures of the United States, shall be admitted into, and entitled to all the advantages of the Union." Hence, the Americans in the War of 1812 strove hard but unavailingly to take over Canada—an ambition which is still very much alive in our days of militant American imperialism.

One of the immediately provocative factors causing this war was the insistence by England that she had the right to search United States vessels on the high seas. This issue had a direct bearing upon the question of the illegal slave trade. Seeking to stamp out this harmful business, England demanded the right to search the ships of all nations. The United States, on the other hand, cultivating the slave trade, militantly opposed England's attempts to search her ships. On this matter, McMaster comments, "The persistent refusal of the United States to consent to search, in any form and in any degree, had made our flag the protector of every slaver bold enough to fly it."[15]

This unsavory fact is not emphasized, however, in United States history books. Significantly, at the same time, those shippers of New England, who had a dirty paw in the slave trade, were violently opposed to the War of 1812 and threatened secession on account of it. They were quite willing to run the risk of English search and seizure as part of the hazards of the rich slave trade. At the same time, they demagogically blamed the pro-slavery planters for the war.

An important event in connection with this war was the so-called Tecumseh Indian conspiracy. The able Shawnee chief, Tecumseh, convinced that only through a united stand could the Indian peoples successfully resist the ever-encroaching whites, undertook to build a great defensive Indian alliance along the frontier from Canada to the Gulf of Mexico. The brilliant plan was nipped in the bud, however, when General Harrison crushed and dispersed the Indian forces at the Battle of Tippecanoe, Indiana, in 1811. Several of the tribes in the South—Cherokees, Creeks, Seminoles, Tuscaroras, and others—later fought in loose alliance with the British against the Americans, their main enemies. At this time many runaway Negro slaves were living in fraternal harmony with these Indian tribes, and although the records are meager, they must have been active in the war.

Remembering the War of 1776, the British tried to get the slaves to join their armed forces in the War of 1812, promising freedom to all those who did. Apparently very few joined. Aptheker states that the war years were a period of minor slave insurrections and general unrest, but he could find only two that appeared to be directly connected in any way with the British.[16]

On the American side, says Redding, "Negroes were once again allowed to serve their country. Pennsylvania enlisted Negro troops. New York, having passed an enabling act granting freedom to all slaves who got their masters' permission to join, raised two regiments of colored soldiers. . . . The Negroes who bore arms for the United States acquitted themselves with valor. . . . After the battle of Lake Erie, even Captain Perry, who had objected to Negroes on his ship, praised the colored sailors."[17]

The greatest military achievement of the Negro soldiers in the war was in the hard-fought Battle of New Orleans, late in December 1814. Here the Negro troops, displaying great heroism against Pakenham's veterans of the Napoleonic wars, saved the day for the American cause. General Andrew Jackson, who was no special friend of the Negro people, paid a glowing tribute to his Negro soldiers. On the eve of the battle he said, "Through a mistaken policy, you have heretofore been deprived of a participation in the glorious struggle for national rights in which our country is engaged. This no longer shall exist. As sons of freedom, you are now called upon to defend our most inestimable blessing. As Americans, your country looks with confidence to her adopted children for a valorous support, as a faithful return for the advantages enjoyed under her mild and equitable government. As fathers, husbands and brothers, you are summoned to rally around the standard of the Eagle, to defend all which is dear in existence."[18]

Later, after the Battle of New Orleans, General Jackson also declared: "To the Men of Color—Soldiers! From the shores of Mobile I collected you to arms—I invited you to share in the perils and to divide the glory of your white country-men. I expected much from you; for I was not uninformed of those qualities which must render you so formidable to an invading foe. I knew that you could endure hunger and thirst, and all the hardships of war. I knew that you loved the land of your nativity, and that, like ourselves, you had to defend all that is most dear to man. But you surpass my hopes. I have found in you, united to these qualities, that noble enthusiasm which impels to great deeds. Soldiers! The President of the United States shall be informed of your conduct on the present occasion; and the voice of the Representatives of the American nation shall applaud your valor, as your General now praises your ardor. . . ."[19]

7. King Cotton and the "Irresistible Conflict"

While the events that we have been reciting had been taking place —the abolition of slavery in the North, the outlawing of the world slave trade, and the War of 1812—another development of tremendous importance was taking shape in the plantation-slave system. This was the improvement and extension of the cotton culture. The cultivation of this textile fiber was growing to a point where it would soon be decisive among American agricultural crops, with economic and political consequences of the most far-reaching importance to the South, the United States, and the world.

THE INVENTION OF THE COTTON GIN

The historic development of cotton culture began with the invention of the cotton gin by Eli Whitney in 1793. Prior to that time, as we pointed out in Chapter 3, the production of cotton was at a very low level; it was almost insignificant in the prevailing Southern economy. The plantation system rested mainly upon tobacco and, to a lesser extent, upon rice and indigo. Cotton was a negligible factor, and sugar cane was nothing at all until after 1800. The high value of cotton for textile manufacture had been well known for many centuries, but the trouble with it was in the technical difficulty of producing it.

The great unsolved problem, which for hundreds of years had stood in the way of the wide use of cotton, was the lack of an economical means of separating the cotton seed from the fiber. Traditionally, this process had always been done by hand, a most laborious anl expensive method even for slaves. Two varieties of the plant were used in the American cotton culture—the short staple and the long staple. Since a worker could clean only one pound of the short staple and ten of the long staple in a day, the cost of cotton goods was too high for their general use.[1] The production of cotton (only 2,000 tons of it being exported to England in 1770) was infinitesimal compared to the great potential demand.

The inventive drive which finally produced the cotton gin, or "engine," was closely tied up with the Industrial Revolution in England. During the latter half of the eighteenth century, tremendous strides were made in textile-manufacturing processes in that country. Between 1768 and 1784, Arkwright perfected the spinning mule, and Kay the flying shuttle. In 1769 Watt perfected the steam engine, and in 1785 it was brought into the factories and used to operate the new textile machinery. Under these circumstances, the cotton gin simply "had" to be invented in order to produce cheap cotton for the hungry textile market—and so it was. If ever there was an invention "demanded" by history, it was the cotton gin.

The aristocratic, arrogant, and conceited Southern planters, spent most of their time in cock-fighting, dueling, horse-racing, gambling, loafing, and general carousing. For generations past, they had been totally incapable of producing the relatively simple device necessary to separate the cotton seed from the cotton fiber. So the job was done by a Yankee mechanic, Eli Whitney, who was in Georgia at the time seeking a job as a school teacher. Once the problem was called to his attention, he solved it in a matter of only ten days.[2] Aptheker states that the first gin made in Mississippi was constructed on the basis of a crude drawing made by a skilled slave.[*3] With the new gin a slave could clean 150 pounds of cotton a day instead of one pound, and when steam was applied to the mechanism, he could clean 1,000 pounds. Meanwhile something typical happened: true to the dog-eat-dog nature of capitalism, the planters, who had been altogether unable to create the simple cotton gin, were quite willing to steal it—and this they did. Disregarding the patent laws, they lifted the new invention, using it on all sides. Whitney got very little money out of it. With the appearance of the gin, the great cotton industry was born.

THE EXPANSION OF COTTON PRODUCTION

Cotton-growing immediately felt the stimulating effect of the cotton gin and the ravenous new machinery in England. Production soared. In 1790, just before the invention of the gin, an estimated 3,000 bales, of 1,000 pounds each, were produced in this country. By 1815, the figure had run up to 209,000 bales, by 1840 to 1,348,000

* Slaves made many inventions, but were not allowed to take out patents; so the whites grabbed their creations.

bales, and by 1860 to 3,841,000, a 1,000 percent increase over 70 years. This swift increase was to go right on after the Civil War, reaching the enormous peak of 18,946,000 bales in 1937.[4] From 1866 [first reliable figures] the acreage of harvested cotton went up from 7,660,000 to 44,608,000 in 1926, its highest point.[5] By 1810, cotton had become the center of Southern agricultural production, superseding the erstwhile king, tobacco.

With the gin, cotton culture on a large scale began in South Carolina and Georgia, and by 1820 the states of the Old South [Georgia, South Carolina, North Carolina, and Virginia] were still producing one-half of all the cotton grown in the United States. But the industry was rapidly on the way West. Between 1824 and 1830 the Gulf states doubled their cotton production, and by 1835 they had passed the Atlantic states in output. By 1860 Mississippi, Alabama, and Louisiana alone were producing half the nation's cotton, and Virginia had lost its traditional economic and political position in the South. Under the pressure of the expanding market and the search for new lands to replace the exhausted lands in the East, the westward trek of the cotton industry has continued right down to our own days. Texas, Arizona, and California have now become major cotton-producing areas.

By 1859 cotton was the most important agricultural crop in the United States. At that time it furnished 61 percent of all American exports, 3,533,000 bales being exported in that year. It was the center of the whole economic, political, and cultural life of the South. Cotton had indeed become king, but a king who sat upon a very shaky throne.

The expansion of cotton production, with high profits and with the African slave trade partly closed, vastly increased the demand periodically torn with cyclical economic crises. As Aptheker points out, "this system was quite as subject to business cycles, or periods of so-called prosperity, depression, and panic, as any other system of private gain dependent on a world market."[6] Accordingly, the price of cotton fluctuated widely through the years, and it has always been the subject of endless stock gambling and speculation.

The explosive advance of the cotton plantation system wrought havoc among the small farmers of the South. They could not produce cotton successfully in competition with the larger planters, and they fell by the wayside in the struggle. Pushing ever onward, the big planters shoved the small farmers aside and grabbed all the best new land. The small farmers found themselves driven into the stony and unfertile mountains, or farther out on the frontier to fight Indians. In 1860, of one million people born in Georgia, 400,000 had been forced to emigrate elsewhere, and in South Carolina, of 470,000 native-born, 193,000 had left the state.[7] The ousted farmers became the "poor white trash"—the "hill-billies," "crackers," "clay-eaters," "sand-hillers," and "piney woods folk"—of the mountain areas all over the South. While the big planters reveled in luxury, based on the unpaid labor of armies of slaves, the poor whites, racked by pellagra, malaria, and hookworm, lived in misery and squalor that have rarely been equaled in human history. The slave system bore down heavily upon these white toiling masses.

Anti-slavery sentiment was strong among the Southern small farmers and poor whites, who made up the great bulk of the population and who had few or no slaves. They repeatedly developed resistance to the arrogant slavemasters; but they were deeply soaked in white supremacy prejudices, hatreds, and illusions, which tended to liquidate their anti-planter opposition. From these groups the planters drew most of their plantation overseers, "slave-breakers," and innumerable road patrol squads. Of the poor whites, Cairnes remarks: "The class is not peculiar to any one locality, but is the available outgrowth of Negro slavery wherever it has raised its head in modern times. It may be seen in the new state of Texas, as well as in the old settled districts of Virginia, the Carolinas, and Georgia, in the West India Islands no less than on the Continent."[8]

The Indians of the South also suffered heavily from the westward advance of the cotton planters and their slave system. The political tools of the planters ruthlessly robbed the Indians of their lands under every plausible pretext, and then proceeded, by hook or crook, to put these rich lands into the hands of the big planters. Redding comments, "In the dozen years preceding 1809, the savages had 'sold' 48,000,000 acres, not seldom when made drunk for the purpose."[9] Andrew Jackson was especially militant in clearing the Indians of Georgia, Alabama, Mississippi, Tennessee, and Florida from the path of the expanding plantation system. James states that after the defeat of the Creeks in 1814, "Jackson demanded 23,000,000 acres, or half of the ancient Creek domain. . . . In all the checkered narrative of our dealings with the Indian people, General Jackson's terms are unequaled for exorbitance."[10] Later, when he became president, Jackson finished the job on the Creeks, Cherokees, Seminoles, and others. He forced them off their Southern preserves altogether and across the Mississippi River in 1835; they were finally rounded up, stripped of their hunting grounds, and confined in concentration camps, known as Indian reservations. All this constitutes one of the most shameful and tragic episodes in American history. Of course, the big planters got the cream of the wide and fertile Southern lands so obligingly stolen from the Indians by the government. Jackson, in many respects, was a democrat; but he had a great blind spot where the Negroes and Indians were concerned.

THE RAPID GROWTH OF THE SLAVE SYSTEM

The invention of the cotton gin, resulting in the spectacular growth of cotton production especially after 1825, had a number of important economic, political, social, and even military consequences. The entire development of cotton culture solidified the foundation of the slave system. Cotton provided an incomparably broader and stronger basis for human bondage than the comparatively narrow cultivation of tobacco and such plantation crops as rice, indigo, and eventually sugar cane. Before 1790, many people, including large numbers of planters, had believed that slavery was limited in its scope and perspective, and that it would eventually pass away of itself. Now, after the turn of the century, it took on new strength and vigor. Cotton gave the slave system a fresh spirit of life. In earlier years the slave-masters had defended their "peculiar institution" somewhat shamefacedly. After the invention of the cotton gin they boldly and arrogantly supported it as a blessing to man (including the slaves) and ordained by God. The plantation-slave system launched upon an aggressive course designed to dominate and enslave the entire United States.

Increased cotton production raised the question of slavery from what had become essentially a sectional issue after the Revolution to a matter of profound national importance. "With the admission to statehood of Louisiana in 1812, Mississippi in 1817, and Alabama in 1819, the political and economic power of the 'cotton kingdom' became the predominant factor in our national life and remained so until it was destroyed by the Civil War."[11]

The wide expansion of cotton production before the Civil War sentenced the economy of the South to remain agricultural. King Cotton precluded a substantial growth of industry in its realm for several reasons. First, the plantation capitalists poured all the capital they could scrape together into land and slaves, the latter absorbing most of it; consequently, there was neither the capital nor the desire to build Southern industry. Second, the planters, who could not successfully use slaves in industrial production, acutely feared the effects of a "free" industrial proletariat upon their slaves, and this would have been the inevitable result of any substantial development of industry in the South. And third, the plantation-slave system repelled the immigrant workers then pouring into the United States, as these workers wanted no competition with slaves, and could not meet it.

"All the labor, all the capital, all the increase of population and wealth by immigration from more northern climates, all the accumulations of every trade, or business, or pursuit, were devoted to the one [cotton] cultivation."[12] For Southern slavery to live, industry must be kept out. The plantation-slave system devoured everything in its own monstrous growth.

The expansion of cotton production, with high profits and with the African slave trade partly closed, vastly increased the demand for slaves and tended also to raise their price, which rose from about $300 in 1800 to $1,500 or $2,000 at the outbreak of the Civil War. Slave prices also varied with the price of cotton. Besides loading Southern agriculture and industry with an impossible financial burden, rising slave prices also tended to check the process of manumission, which had previously been developing. It became far more difficult for slaves to buy themselves and their families free. With the demand for and high cost of cotton slaves, an outcry was raised for the legal resumption of the African slave trade, and there was gross, wholesale violation of the anti-slave trading laws on every hand.

Cotton growing was much more intensive than the slave production of other crops in colonial times. This fact resulted in much sharper exploitation of the Negro slaves and the institution of more brutal and rigid systems of control and domination. This, in turn, led to more insurrections and active forms of slave unrest and revolt. It also stimulated more militant types of Abolitionism among Negro freedom and their white allies. The growth of the fighting Abolitionist movement after the turn of the century was definitely linked with the rapid extension of the realm of King Cotton.

SOUTHERN PLANTERS VERSUS
NORTHERN INDUSTRIALISTS

The wide and swift development of the cotton industry sharpened and matured all the basic contradictions between the Southern plantation system, based on slave labor, and Northern industrialism, based upon "free" wage-earners. These fundamental and inevitable antagonisms enlisted eventually almost every section of the North—industrialists, many merchants, farmers, professionals, and workers. Consequently, when the Civil War finally broke out, they were lined up in a fighting alliance against the Southern slavocracy. Either the industrial North or the plantation South had to conquer.

The fundamental antagonism between the North and South originated in the fact that, due to the great expansion of cotton production, the whole South was largely separated from the national market. This was true not only with regard to Northern commodities but also capital investment. The Southern planters, who found their best customers for their cotton in England, tended in turn to buy a large percentage of the commodities they needed from that country. In fact, the South with its cotton came to develop a sort of colonial relationship with England, producing raw materials for that country and receiving manufactured goods in return—to the partial exclusion of commodities from the North. All this was intolerable to Northern businessmen. For it is a first principle of a national bourgeoisie, especially one as vigorous as that of the North, that it must have the fullest control over the whole national market in its entire territory. It took the Civil War to enable the Northern bourgeoisie to put this principle into effect in the South.

The contradictory interests of the Northern industrialists and the Southern planters over the control and regulation of the national market also expressed themselves in long, chronic, and ever-more bitter struggles over the question of the tariff. Ever since the Revolution of 1776, the Northern capitalists, who wished to safeguard the home market for themselves, had veered more and more toward a policy of protective tariffs. This was also the general position of the Northern workers and farmers at the time. On the other hand, once intensive cotton growing had really gotten under way, the Southern planters usually championed a low tariff, seeking to get the manufactured commodities of their key customer, England, as cheaply as possible. This head-on antagonism over the tariff created an issue which was to bedevil American politics for half a century and sharpen the struggle between the North and the South right up to the Civil War. In this struggle, the South managed to sew up a firm alliance with those large sections of Northern businessmen, bankers, and shippers who devoted their main attention to financing, transporting, and marketing the increasing cotton crop. The latter groups eventually became the basis of the Northern "Copperheads" of Civil War times.

Another major source of conflict was the fundamental question of which wing of the bourgeoisie, North or South, would control the disposition of the huge amounts of land either already in the hands of the Federal Government or about to be stolen from the Indians or weak neighbor governments. For instance, in the great Yazoo land frauds of 1795 the planters seized one-half of western Georgia—now Alabama and Mississippi. The planters' appetite for land was insatiable—they wanted to grab everything west to the Pacific Coast and south to Brazil, and they even eyed northern territories as potential slave plantations. On the other hand, inasmuch as the colder climate did not facilitate a slaving plantation system based on the production of cotton and other world market crops, the Northern bourgeoisie favored getting the land into the hands of free farmers. They wanted the government to hand over huge tracts of land to speculators, who would sell it at immense profits. As for the workers and other democratic groups in the North and West, they, too, wanted to build up a great body of free farmers, but by direct government land grants to actual settlers.

All these ever-sharpening contradictions between the Northern industrialists and the Southern planters and their respective allies naturally took on political forms. Initially the most acute form of this antagonism was the struggle to control politically the many new states which were coming into the Union as fast as they accumulated sufficient population. These state fights sometimes grew into miniature armed conflicts.

Uniting all these individual struggles was a still broader contest— for control of the presidency, Congress, the Supreme Court, and the nation as a whole. It was a life-and-death conflict for power between the industrial North and the plantation South that was developing during these decades. One or the other had to conquer. This was the basic meaning of the "irrepressible conflict." Its inevitable climax was revolution, the great Civil War of 1861-65.

8. The Missouri Compromise of 1820

At the time of the Constitutional Convention in 1787, as we have seen, certain internal collisions took place over the matter of slavery. But the issue was not yet clearly drawn nationally and the existence of slavery itself was not challenged. The congressional debates turned around secondary, though vital issues, among them the proposed Constitutional clauses on fugitive slaves and representation of slave states. In the great Jeffersonian victory of 1800, the slave question, though a basic issue, was also in the background. In the 1807 debate in Congress over the abolition of the world slave trade, growing friction was in evidence between the slavers and their opponents, but slavery itself was not assailed. The first real general political clash, where the issue of slavery was clearly raised as a national issue, was the big dispute within and around Congress which resulted in the so-called Missouri Compromise of 1820. This fight was a forecast of the tremendous struggle over slavery which was soon to rack the country and finally to plunge it into sanguinary civil war.

In 1820 the United States, then under the administration of James Monroe, was a nation of 9,638,453 people. Of these, 1,771,656 were Negroes, including 1,538,022 slaves and 233,634 freemen. The country, which had more than doubled its population since 1790, was developing rapidly. At the outbreak of the Revolution of 1776 its western frontiers had averaged only 255 miles from the Atlantic Coast, but now, with the absorption of Louisiana in 1803, they stretched westward 2,000 miles to the Rocky Mountains. The nation had recently emerged victoriously from the difficult War of 1812.

The national economy was expanding with speed. In the South the dynamic growth of the cotton culture was now well under way, in 1820 335,000 bales of cotton were produced as against only 3,000 bales a generation before. The commerce and industry of the North, as well as the free agriculture of the Middle West, were growing no less rapidly. The industries of Massachusetts were flourishing, and so were those of the other Atlantic Coast states in the North. Iron mills and coal mines were being established, and there were 250,000 textile spindles in operation—a 200 percent increase within ten years. The newly-contrived steamboats (1807) were already plying the rivers, and the first commercial line had been started on the Great Lakes in 1818. The Erie Canal was begun in 1817, and a network of canals and roads was spreading over the whole North. The West was growing so fast that six new states, one a year, joined the Union from 1816 to 1821. The complex and sharp political dispute, which climaxed in the Missouri Compromise of 1820, was an inevitable collision between two expanding, but inherently hostile systems of Northern industrialism and the Southern plantation system.

The class line-up in this sharp political fight was basically the same as during the big Republican-Federalist fight of 1796-1800—a reactionary combination of big Southern planters and Northern merchants arrayed against the rest of the nation. But the specific weight of the two classes in the combination had altered, the slogans of the movement were changed, and the leaders and issues with them. The slave question now stood out definitely as the central issue. In the earlier struggle the merchants were the leaders, but now the planters had clearly become the heads of the whole reactionary grouping and they were aggressively fighting to protect and extend slavery. As yet, the people's forces were essentially a continuation of the old Jeffersonian movement, but they too were fighting under new slogans and new leaders, essentially anti-slavery. The working class was more mature.

THE DEVELOPMENT OF THE STRUGGLE OVER SLAVERY

In 1820 the issues between the industrial North and the plantation South had not yet fully matured. Thus, on the question of the tariff, which was later to assume great importance, the South had not yet developed a free trade program. The tariff laws of 1816, 1818, and 1824, which contained protective features, were passed by Congress without serious planter opposition. It was not until 1828 that this issue ripened fully, the planters bitterly fighting and eventually slashing the protective tariff law of that year.[1] The conquest of the Southern market by the aggressive Northern bourgeoisie was also becoming more and more urgent, under the pressure of the North's expanding industries, merchant marine, and network of river steamboat lines, canals, and turnpikes. There was a similar contradiction about internal improvements. The North favored such developments while the

Southern plantation economy generally opposed them, although John C. Calhoun, the chief slavocrat leader, actually prepared a big program of such improvements in the rivers and harbors in 1817.[2] The homestead issue had not yet fully matured. Since the Revolution, the democratic forces had progressively cut down the size of minimum land areas that could be bought from the government from 640 acres in 1785, to 320 in 1800, 160 in 1804, and 80 acres in 1820. But the big mass demand for free government homesteads, which the planters stubbornly resisted, was yet to materialize.

The main issues around which the big struggle of 1820 took place, were states' rights in the question of slavery, and the admission of new states. The planters realized that, come what might, they had to make sure that the new states coming into the Union were committed to slavery beforehand. Otherwise, they would find themselves unable to control the Senate and the Federal government generally, although they had no hope of controlling the House, which was based on popular representation. The big question was free soil versus slave soil, with the industrialists and the democratic masses of the people on one side and the planters and their allies and agents on the other. As yet, however, the reactionaries had no definite party of their own; this was the "era of good feeling," and the Jeffersonian Democratic Party was the only major party in existence.

As things had stood at the close of the Revolution, the thirteen original states were about evenly divided on the slavery question. Although slavery was legal, in the North slaves were largely limited to service occupations. The real slave plantation states were Virginia, Maryland, Delaware, North Carolina, South Carolina, and Georgia.* Vermont joined the Union in 1791, as a free state, and this tipped the scales heavily against the slave group. However, Kentucky and Tennessee entered as slave states in 1792 and 1796, evening matters up again between the rival forces. About this time the question of representation in the Senate became doubly important because the Northern states were all on the way to abolishing slavery, as we have seen in Chapter 5.

Ohio, Indiana, and Illinois came in as free states in 1802, 1816, and 1818 respectively; but only after a severe struggle between the pro- and anti-slavery forces in each state. While presumably these

* The formal boundary line between the North and South was the so-called Mason and Dixon's line, at 39°, 43', 26", drawn between Maryland and Pennsylvania in 1763-67.

states, which did not carry on production of cotton, tobacco, and other world market crops, were beyond the boundaries of the plantation areas for climatic reasons, the slaveholders were not deterred by this fact. Already nursing the hope of spreading an intensive slave system far into the North, they made desperate efforts to control these three key states. So strong were the slavers in this whole region that Mc-Master remarks, "To all intents and purposes slavery was then as much a domestic institution of Illinois of 1820 as of Kentucky or Missouri."[3] The slaveholders, however, redressed the balance of power in the Senate with the uncontested admission of Louisiana in 1812, Mississippi in 1818, and Alabama in 1819 as slave states. Since the end of the Revolution the new states had alternated one slave and one free, until in 1820 there was an exact balance of forces in the Senate, 11 free and 11 slave states.

THE ISSUE OF MISSOURI STATEHOOD

The showdown came over Missouri. This was a section of the Louisiana Purchase of 1803. Louisiana then covered a vast stretch of territory extending northward from the mouth of the Mississippi on the Gulf of Mexico, indefinitely to the eventual Canadian border, and westward, also vaguely, to the Rocky Mountains. The slaveholders had been busily colonizing the Missouri section of this area, which had a population of 56,000 whites and 10,000 Negro slaves in 1818. The slavers' agents in Congress proposed that it be admitted as a slave state. This provoked an intense debate, which lasted two years.

The Missouri debate brought out the quarrel over the slave system as such much more clearly than the Constitutional Convention or any of the later controversies between the developing pro- and anti-slavery forces. Present were the elements of all the arguments, for and against, that were to appear in the raging discussions of the next forty years. In particular the debate sharply developed the issue of states' rights, and it also raised the fundamental matter of the role of slavery itself.

The slaveholders' position on states' rights was direct and definite; namely, that slavery was purely a state matter and that the Congress had no right to interfere. Each state, of course including Missouri, could do as it pleased about the question, permitting or prohibiting slavery as it saw fit. The slavery question, they claimed, could not be raised by the Federal Government when a territory, which had acquired sufficient population, applied for statehood. A hole in the Southerners' argument for states' rights, however, developed over the question of fugitive slaves. In this matter the slaveholders repudiated states' rights completely and demanded categorically that every state, under the Constitution and the Federal law of 1793, be unreservedly compelled to return all runaway slaves who should reach their borders.

The anti-slavery forces challenged the whole states' rights conception. They opposed the Southern contention that the Union was merely a loose alliance of fully sovereign states, each of which could do as it pleased and also had the right of secession. The Northerners stressed the imperative necessity that Congress regulate inter-state trade and take many other actions which undoubtedly tended to infringe upon the absolute sovereignty of each state. They especially insisted that the government had both the right and the duty to determine the vital issue of whether a newly-formed state should legalize slavery or not. Behind this general Northern argument was the sound conclusion that capitalism, in order to develop, required a relatively centralized state.

Although no proposals were made for a general abolition of slavery during the protracted debate over Missouri, nevertheless the merits of the slave system itself became deeply involved in the discussion. Under the stimulus of the developing cotton economy, the Southerners took a much bolder stand than before in defending their "peculiar institution" as one according with the divine will. But old-time arguments were still to be heard among them that slavery was "a necessary evil for which no plausible remedy had yet been found." Randolph of Virginia even "claimed that the greatest evil that had ever befallen him was being born a slaveholder, but he and all slaveholders must bear their heavy burden for the good of society and the black man."[4]

The anti-slavery forces defended wage labor as against slavery, as indispensable to industrial development. They also pointed out that slavery was inconsistent with the equalitarian principles of the Declaration of Independence. As white chauvinists they also conjured up the grave danger to white supremacy in building up a big Negro population as slavery was doing. They were especially sensitive to the fake arguments of the slaveholders that the Negro slave in the South was better off economically than the boss-driven, poverty-stricken wage slave in the factories of both New and old England.

THE MISSOURI COMPROMISE

Since they were not yet ready for an open break, the two sides to the big controversy had to find an accommodation for the difficulty. This they did. The architect of the ensuing compromise was Senator Henry Clay of Kentucky. In his early career Clay had been an active opponent of slavery. Essentially he represented the small slaveholders, free farmers, and petty business interests of Kentucky and other Border states. His political position, typical of the bourgeois politicians of the Border states, was to maneuver between the two hostile groups of Southern slaveholders and Northern industrial and business interests. His chief political achievements were several major compromises between the clashing Southern and Northern forces. While making concessions to the agressive big slaveholders, he also supported such industrialist measures as the tariff and the United States Bank. His general line was to conciliate slavery and to protect it from the blows of Northern industrialism.

The Missouri Compromise of 1820 was a glorified horse trade. It was based on three major proposals—the admission of Missouri as a slave state and of Maine as a free state, and the drawing of a demarcation line for slavery at 36° 30' north latitude. That is, while the state of Missouri was to be slave, all the rest of the territory of Louisiana above 36° 30' (the southern border of Missouri) should be free. The Missouri Enabling Act of March 6, 1820,[5] stated that in this area "slavery and involuntary servitude, otherwise than in the punishment of crimes, whereof the parties shall have been duly convicted, shall be, and is hereby, forever prohibited." One exception was that fugitive slaves had to be returned to their insistent owners in the slave states. The entire Southern delegation in both Houses of Congress voted for the 36°30' limit to slavery, an action which they regretted in later years.

The Missouri Compromise, typical of Clay's pro-slavery policies, was fundamentally a big concession to the aggressive plantation system. The slave system had to expand or die. By the Compromise the slaveholders took a huge bite out of what had been generally envisaged as non-plantation country. Naturally, the Compromise did not "settle" the struggle between the slaveholders and their Northern enemies, as was commonly believed at the time. Instead, as the sequel showed, it merely whetted the insatiable appetite of the slaveholders for boundless territorial expansion and political power. So the "irrepressible conflict" continued, soon becoming more acute and threatening than ever.

THE COLONIZATION MOVEMENT

An important development concerning Negroes in this period was the formation of the American Society for the Colonization of the Free People of Color of the United States, in Washington in the chamber of the House of Representatives on December 21, 1816. Its leading spirit was Robert Finley, a Presbyterian minister. The purpose of the organization was to transport free Negroes to Africa and to colonize them there. The scheme was Southern-inspired. The free Negroes were rapidly increasing in number—in 1790 they were 59,557, and in 1820, 233,634. Thus one of eight Negroes was free— and a thorn in the side of the Southern slaveholders. The freemen struggled against their own bad conditions, they gave leadership to rebellious slaves, and, indeed, their very presence was a stimulus to the slaves to fight for freedom. John Randolph stated the slaveholders' viewpoint: "It is a notorious fact that the existence of free negroes is looked upon by every slaveholder as one of the greatest sources of insecurity to slave property."[6] So it was decided to get rid of this menace by shipping the freemen off to Africa.

Among the many bourgeois dignitaries present at the founding meeting of the Colonization Society were Henry Clay, Francis Scott Key, author of "The Star-Spangled Banner," John Randolph of Roanoke, Hezekiah Niles of the famous Niles Register, and Judge Bushrod Washington, a relative of George Washington. In the society, "the president [Washington], was a Southern man; twelve of the seventeen vice-presidents were Southern men; and all of the twelve managers of the project were slaveholders."[7] Among the society's outstanding supporters were James Madison, James Monroe, Andrew Jackson, Daniel Webster, Dr. Lyman Beecher, James Marshall, and many others. Woodson thus states the general program of the society: "Each community was called upon to take steps to provide for the transplantation to Africa of all slaves who might be liberated at the will of the masters concerned or purchased for this purpose. The Negroes were not to be consulted in the matter."[8] Aptheker thus characterizes the society: "Its object was to transport free Negroes to Africa on the plea that they were incapable of serving useful lives in the United States, and the society informed slaveholders that the removal of free Negroes would make more secure the institution of slavery."[9] A dozen state legislatures endorsed the society, and it established groups in many parts of the country.

The formation of the society was the culmination of long agitation on the proposition, not only by slaveholders but by some freedmen among the Negroes. As early as 1713 Quaker Abolitionists were urging that freed Negroes be returned to Africa. Many democratic leaders during the Revolution also favored African colonization. Thomas Jefferson said, "Nothing is more to be wished than that the United States should thus undertake to make such an establishment on the coast of Africa."[10] His plan was general emancipation and deportation.[11] Numerous white anti-slavery leaders such as Benjamin Lundy, the pioneer Quaker Abolitionist, the Tappan brothers, Gerritt Smith, and others, similarly toyed with the idea. So did the fiery Garrison himself, but later, in 1832, he dealt the Colonization Society a deadly blow with his famous pamphlet, *Thoughts on African Colonization.*[12] The colonization plan in various forms, as we shall see, caused dissension in Negro ranks for decades. In fact, during this early period the concepts of emancipation and colonization were greatly confused. Thus, the famous English Abolitionists, Wilberforce, Clarkson, and Sharp, had already established a struggling colony of returned freed Negroes in Sierra Leone, Africa.

The colonization scheme was to persist for a long period. In later years Abraham Lincoln, among many others, was an ardent supporter. He said, "What I would desire would be a separation of the white and black races."[13] The notion also flourished in the Reconstruction period, with some Negro leaders supporting it. And decades later, Marcus Garvey, in harmony with the Ku Klux Klan, made colonization the basis of his program after World War I. Variations of this back-to-Africa theme were the basis of the numerous schemes, brought forward from time to time, for colonizing the free Negroes in other parts of the world—Haiti, Central America, Canada, and various sections of the United States. The masses of the Negro people, however, have always sturdily opposed colonization in foreign lands.

The most advanced groups among the free Negroes immediately took a firm stand against the American Colonization Society and its whole program. They proclaimed themselves Americans and announced their determination to stay in this country, come what might. Some Negro leaders, however—Paul Cuffee, the noted merchant, and J. B. Russwurm, graduate of Bowdoin College and the first Negro in the United States to get a college degree, and various others, who were not without a considerable Negro following—favored African colonization. Eventually, however, the Abolitionist movement, headed by William Lloyd Garrison and Frederick Douglass, sharply condemned the colonization plan and made ruthless war on the society and all its works. Thus the resolute position of most of the Negro people and their white allies against deportation, voluntary or compulsory, crippled the colonization movement and finally condemned it to failure. The society, in skeleton form, has existed until recent years.

Under the prodding of the slaveholders, the Federal Government promptly got behind the American Colonization Society. Congress, declaring for colonization, decided that the proposed colony must be in Africa, not in the United States. At first the idea was to get Great Britain to admit American Negroes to its colony of freedmen in Sierra Leone, but this plan was abandoned as impractical. Meanwhile, the running expenses of the Colonization Society were largely met out of the sale of slaves who had been seized and confiscated by the government in the illicit slave trade.

In 1819 Congress appropriated $100,000 to establish the new African colony. Some 43,000 square miles of land, between Sierra Leone and the French Ivory Coast, were secured, and in 1821 Liberia was founded, after much heart-breaking work by hardy Negro pioneers. Outstanding among these pioneers were Jehudi Ashman, Elijah Johnson, and Lett Cary.[14] The capital city was named Monrovia, after President Monroe. Despite many difficulties, Liberia managed to gain a foothold. It became independent in 1847, and was recognized in 1848 by France and in 1852 by England. The American slaveholders were against all Negro ambassadors, and it was not until 1862 that the United States accorded the country diplomatic recognition. Today Liberia, while nominally independent, is virtually an American dependency, dominated by Firestone, Republic Steel, and other corporations.

Despite all its backing from the Southern slaveholders and the United States government, the American Colonization Society never succeeded in convincing any considerable number of Negroes that, freed from slavery, they should return to Africa. Woodson thus sums up the scanty return of thirty years of the society's endeavors: "From 1820 to 1833 only 2,885 Negroes were sent out by the society. More than 2,700 of this number were taken from the slave states and about two-thirds of these slaves were manumitted on the condition of their emigrating. Of the 7,836 sent out of the United States by 1852, 2,720 were born free, 204 purchased their freedom, 3,868 were emancipated in view of removing them to Liberia, and 1,044 were liberated Africans sent out by the United States Government."[15] All of which evidences a great victory won by the Abolitionist movement—especially by the free Negroes—over the attempt of the slaveholders and their agents to deport them en masse.

9. The Early Negro Liberation Movement

The swift expansion of cotton production in the decades following the invention of the cotton gin (see Chapter 7), increased the exploitation of Negro slaves on the Southern plantations and sharpened the terror discipline under which they labored in bondage. During the same period and as a result of the same general causes (see Chapter 5) a strong reactionary movement took shape to strip free Negroes of their right to vote and to subject them to a more rigid Jim Crow system of segregation and discrimination. This disfranchising movement affected not only the South but also the North. This situation inevitably sharpened the Negro liberation struggle among the slaves in the South and among the free Negroes of both the South and the North.

The conditions of the free Negroes in the North were deplorable. As McMaster described their situation, they were "a despised, proscribed, and poverty-stricken class." By 1800, ghetto-like conditions had developed in Philadelphia, the principal Negro center in the North, and everywhere freemen were Jim Crowed and discriminated against in industry. The Northern Negro freemen, in the face of innumerable handicaps of persecution and prejudice, took up the cudgels of struggle against the intolerable conditions under which they were living. Their fight became more marked after about 1800, especially under the stimulus of such stirring events as the great Haitian Revolution and the Gabriel Prosser slave revolt of 1800.

THE NEGRO CONVENTION MOVEMENT

What immediately aroused the free Negroes to action, however, was the formation of the American Colonization Society in 1816 (see Chapter 8). With its program of mass deportation of free Negroes to Africa, this sinister movement was a deadly menace. It threatened to tear the freemen from their homes, such as they were, and to force them out of the country. At once Negroes in various parts of the

North and South met, protested, and denounced the colonization movement. An important meeting was held in Richmond, Virginia, in 1817. The free Negroes of that city emphatically insisted upon their right to live in the United States, the land of their birth, and they especially protested against being torn away from the mass of their brother folk who were still enchained in slavery.[1]

The sharp protest of the Negroes against mass deportation, which was the real objective of the Colonization Society and its slaveholder backers, was expressed when the free Negroes of the country came together in a local convention in Philadelphia, in January, 1817. Three thousand Negroes attended the meeting held at Bethel church. The convention roundly denounced the Colonization Society and its program, and proposed to extend this protest by holding meetings and establishing organizations in other centers. James Forten was elected president and Russel Parrot secretary.

The local conventions and meetings in Richmond and Philadelphia had national effects, and marked the beginning of organized Negro protest over the country. They were basic signs of the growing movement of national Negro liberation. As such, they were a very important milestone in the history of the Negro people of the United States.

The conventions of 1817 were the first steps in a long series of similar Negro gatherings, which bore a definite national character after 1830. The conventions, consisting ordinarily of from 50 to 100 delegates, usually took place each year, and they were often followed by state and local gatherings. With only occasional lapses, they continued up to the Civil War and into the Reconstruction period.[2] The principal national conventions prior to the Civil War were as follows: 1830, Philadelphia (the 40 delegates to which are known as "the 40 immortals"); 1831, 1832, and 1833, also Philadelphia; 1834, New York; 1835, 1936, 1937, Philadelphia; 1847, New York; 1848, Cleveland; 1853 and 1854, New York; 1856, Chatham, Canada. Especially between this date and the Civil War, there were many state Negro conventions.[3] Definite traces of this early convention movement are still to be found in the history of the Negro national organizations of our times.

The Negro convention movement had high political significance in the life of the Negro people of the United States. But like practically every other manifestation of struggle and achievement by Negroes, it has been almost completely ignored by white chauvinistic bourgeois historians. It is only in recent years, especially as a result of the work of Aptheker, Foner, Gross, and others, that its chief documents have been uncovered and its prime significance realized.

The national Negro conventions, which were usually followed by state and local gatherings, devoted special attention to fighting the American Colonization Society and its deportation scheme. This issue was, in fact, the main one which had called the movement into existence. Garrison was led to change his attitude toward colonization by what he heard at the 1831 Negro convention in Philadelphia.⁴ The convention movement, true to its role as national spokesman for the enslaved and oppressed Negro masses, broadened its program and took up many of the major problems confronting both free and slave Negroes. It fought against slavery and demanded unconditional emancipation; it advocated emigration of fugitive slaves to Canada, defended runaway slaves from slave-hunters, stimulated the struggle against Jim Crow, demanded the right to vote, advocated jobs and vocational schools for Negroes, and supported many other progressive causes. The convention of 1830 organized the American Society of Free Persons of Color, the pioneer national Negro political organization. The conventions co-operated freely with other anti-slavery and progressive movements. They played a big part in the Abolitionist struggle, and we shall come back to them later.

Among the outstanding figures in the Negro convention and Negro Abolitionist movement were Samuel E. Cornish, James Forten, Absalom Jones, Robert Purvis, Richard Allen, Randall C. Shepherd, James C. Morel, John Summersett, John Gloucester, Frederick A. Hinton, James McCune Smith, David Walker, Henry Highland Garnett, David Ruggles, Harriet Tubman, Sojourner Truth, William H. Day, J. C. Pennington, Martin R. Delany, Austin Steward, William Still, Charles L. Remond, William Wells Brown, William C. Nell, William Jones, T. S. White, Charles Lenox, Francis E. W. Harper, Henry Foster, Abraham D. Shadd, Lunsford Lane, Charles Gardner, Andrew Harris, David Nickens, James Bradley, and Samuel R. Ward.

In this big array of writers, lecturers, pamphleteers, and Underground Railway workers, the most outstanding figure, after the 1840's, was Frederick Douglass. Born a slave in Maryland about 1817 (his mother was a Negro and his father was white, presumably the owner of the plantation), Douglass escaped to the North in 1838. Becoming a wage worker and taking an active part in the Abolitionist movement, he speedily educated himself and developed into one of the most brilliant writers and orators our country has ever produced. He spoke all over the nation, exposing slavery and arousing the masses against it. As a tactician in the complicated problems facing the Abolitionist movement, Douglass was unexcelled. But characteristically, white historians have systematically played him down. Aptheker points out that McMaster, in his eight-volume *History of the People of the United States,* mentions Douglass only once and then misspells his name; the Beards do not refer to him at all in their two-volume *Rise of American Civilization,* and Parrington also ignores him in his three-volume work, *Main Currents of American Thought.*[5] Practically the same may be said of James Ford Rhodes' eight-volume *History of the United States, 1850-1906.* It is only now, especially owing to the work of writers like Du Bois, Foner, and Aptheker, that the full stature of this powerful leader is coming to be appreciated.[6]

The convention movement of the pre-Civil War period—plus the other distinctive Negro organizations and activities of the time—the Negro church, the Negro press, the Negro schools, the Negro fraternal societies, etc.—were the first beginnings of national sentiment and organization among the Negro people. They were looked upon by their initiators as racial organizations rather than as incipient national bodies. They lacked national maturity, but they were sure expressions of the forces that were to weld the Negro people increasingly into a national conciousness. For the sprouting Negro national tendencies, the great stimulating and unifying force was the all-absorbing fight against slavery by the Northern free Negroes and the Southern slaves.

THE PIONEER NEGRO PRESS

Together with the convention movement, in their fighting against the intolerable conditions to which they were subjected, the Negro people also built up a press of their own. This was another of the many trends toward a growing national spirit. The first Negro paper in the United States—*Freedom's Journal*—was founded on March 16, 1827, in New York City. It was later reorganized as *The Rights of All.* This paper appeared four years before the famous *Liberator* was first issued by Garrison. The editors of *Freedom's Journal* were Samuel E. Cornish and John B. Russwurm. The paper carried on a vigorous struggle against the American Colonization Society and also against the injustices experienced by the Negro people. Challenging the society's deportation program, Cornish declared in the name of the

Negro masses: "We are Americans. Many would rob us of the endeared name of Americans, a description more emphatically belonging to us than to five-sixths of this nation, and one we will never yield."[7] Thus early did American Negroes put forth their demand for the fullest rights of American citizenship, a demand which they have never since relinquished.

Freedom's Journal was the first of a long series of Negro papers. Detweiler says that 24 Negro journals were known to exist prior to the Civil War.[8] Many of them published under great difficulties, appeared irregularly, being hardly more than a series of pamphlets. Among the best known of these papers were the *African Sentinel, Mirror of Liberty, Elevator, Clarion, Genius of Freedom, Alienated American, Ram's Horn, National Watchman, Weekly Advocate, Colored American,* and the most famous of all, *The North Star*—later known as *Frederick Douglass' Paper.* There were numerous Negro pamphleteers, while other writers composed anti-slavery poems and songs.

THE EARLY NEGRO CHURCH

As we pointed out in Chapter 5, the two major sections of the present-day Negro church, the Baptists and the Methodists, were organized by free Negroes during the last quarter of the eighteenth century in a reaction against the Jim-Crowism of the white churches. In the people's conventions of the early nineteenth century, as in every other phase of the fight against slavery, the Negro churches played a very vital role. While not prohibiting them outright, the slaveholders generally kept a wary eye on them to observe what went on, and they kept a close watch on the many slave and free preachers.

On the plantations the formal church services for the slaves always had whites in attendance, to observe and control what went on. The slaves, however, frequently held their own services surreptitiously, choosing their own preachers, establishing picket lines to protect their gatherings, etc. Such church movements appear to have been the chief underground organization of the slaves on the plantations. These religious get-togethers the slaves used as favorable opportunities to discuss their grievances and, upon occasion, to organize insurrections.

Negro preachers, free and slave, often had a hand in slave insurrections. It was characteristic that after the Nat Turner insurrection of 1831, which frightened the whole slavocracy to its very bones, various Southern legislatures took steps to curtail the activities of the Negro churches and their preachers. In 1831, a law was passed in Virginia forbidding Negroes to preach, and in Maryland more than five Negroes were prohibited from meeting together, even in religious services. All this was a tribute to the revolutionary significance of the church in the Negro people's struggle against chattel slavery.

"WALKER'S APPEAL"

One of the major political-agitational achievements in the Negro people's struggle for emancipation of the slaves and for civil rights for the freedmen during the first third of the nineteenth century was the appearance, in 1829, of the famous pamphlet *Walker's Appeal*. It was written, published, and circulated by David Walker, a free Negro living in Boston. Walker was born in North Carolina, of a free mother and a slave father. He issued his pamphlet in the form of "four articles," and it appeared in several editions.

The *Appeal* was a ringing call to the slaves to fight for freedom. Walker openly advocated an armed revolt of the Negro slaves in the South. He insisted that this was the will of God, and boldly declared, "Let twelve good black men get armed for battle and they will kill and put to flight fifty whites. . . . If you commence make sure work, don't trifle, for they will not trifle with you. Kill or be killed. Had you rather not be killed than be a slave to a tyrant who takes the life of your wife and children? Look upon your wife and children and mother and answer God Almighty, and believe this that it is no more harm to kill a man who is trying to kill you than to take a drink of water when you are thirsty."[9]

Walker also asserted militantly the Negro demand for American nationality. "This country is our country; its liberties and privileges were purchased by the exertions and blood of our fathers, as much as by the exertions and blood of other men; the language of the people is our language; their education our education; the free institutions they love, we love; the soil to which they are wedded, we are wedded; their hopes are our hopes; their God is our God; we were born among them; our lot is to live among them, and be of them; when they die we will die, and where they are buried, there will we be buried also."[10]

Walker sent bundles of his pamphlet into the South. Slaves got some of them, and their masters learned of it. Always living in mortal dread of slave revolts, the slaveholders got a real fright from Walker's militant pamphlet. The mayor of Savannah secured a copy and sent it to the governor. The latter forwarded it to the Georgia legislature, which hurriedly passed panic laws to curb the danger. One new law imposed a quarantine of forty days on vessels having free Negroes aboard, all intercourse with such vessels by free Negroes was forbidden, and various other measures for more rigid controls over slaves were adopted. Other states also passed drastic anti-Negro legislation.

Stories conflict on what became of Walker. Redding asserts that, "disdainful of the South," he went to Richmond, Virginia, to distribute his pamphlet, was there arrested and never heard of afterward.[11] McMaster simply states that Walked died in June, 1830, but he does not state where or how.[12] And Aptheker speaks of "his mysterious death in 1830."[13] Copies of *Walker's Appeal* were found far and wide among slaves in the South, and it is believed by some that the famous Nat Turner, leader of the big insurrection of 1831, had heard of or read it.

THE RISING TIDE OF REVOLT

While the free Negroes, South as well as North, were carrying on their work of agitation and organization against slavery, often at the risk of their lives, the slaves themselves, on the plantations in the South, were also fighting. The thoroughly frightened slaveholders had by this time set up a state of semi-martial law to hold their increasingly rebellious slaves in check. Every master's house was a veritable arsenal, armed bodies patrolled the roads at night, and the slaves were constantly watched. But despite this organized terrorism, many individual and group revolts took place. Aptheker, the leading authority on this matter, lists scores of such actions during the first generation of the nineteenth century.[14] Hardly a year passed without one or more of these insurrections.

One of the most commonly used and effective weapons of slaves against their masters was flight. They simply ran away—to the latter's heavy loss and confusion. Du Bois says, "The most effective revolt of the Negro against slavery was not fighting, but running away."[15] Slaves used this flight weapon all over the Western Hemisphere—in the West Indies, in Central America, in Brazil, and in the American South. Such runaway slaves often grouped themselves in strongholds among the mountains and swamps, frequently in friendly collaboration with the Indians. Aptheker, who pioneered this field of study, says, "Evidence of the existence of very many such communities in various places and at various times, from 1672 to 1864, has been found."[16] The South had many groups of outlawed slaves or Maroons. Brawley remarks that "The Dismal Swamp in Virginia became a famous hiding place. A colony here defied owners right in the midst of a strong slave community. Soldiers never ventured into the colony, and bloodhounds sent thither did not return."[17] Swamps in many Southern states sheltered fugitive slaves.

THE BATTLE OF NEGRO FORT

Many encounters in various parts of the South took place between the slave-hunters and the runaway slaves. Florida was the scene of many struggles of this kind. The biggest and best-known of these clashes between runaway slaves and slave-hunters was the battle of Negro Fort on the Apalachicola River in Western Florida in 1816. Over a thousand runaway slaves from Georgia had gathered at this point and, as was usual in such circumstances, had made common cause with the Indians—the Creeks and Seminoles. McMaster says that they were commanded by chiefs and captains and had farms and grazing lands that stretched fifty miles up and down the Apalachicola River. The fort had once been a British post, although Spain still formally controlled Florida.

The United States, then moving to take over Florida from Spain (which it did in 1819), would not tolerate the Negro stronghold in its path of conquest. Therefore, General Andrew Jackson ordered his subordinates to "destroy it and restore the stolen negroes to . . . their rightful owners." Colonel Duncan Clinch, with the Fourth U.S. Infantry and a body of Seminole allies, undertook the task of conquering Negro Fort. The Negroes in the fort answered their demand for surrender by "hoisting of a red flag with the English Union Jack above it, and by a discharge of cannon." On July 27, 1816, however, the attack succeeded, after a ten days' siege, when a red-hot cannon shot fired by Clinch's forces found its way into the magazine of the fort and blew it up. "The roar, the shock, the scene that followed, may be imagined, but not described. Seven hundred barrels of gunpowder tore the earth, the fort, and all the wretched creatures in it to fragments. Two hundred and seventy men, women, and children died on the spot.

Of the sixty-four taken the greater number died soon after." The fort's leaders were the Negro Garcon and an unknown Choctaw chief.[18]

Before the advancing United States army, the runaway Negro slaves in Florida retreated into the Everglades. There they were able long to maintain themselves in the almost impenetrable swamps. Repeatedly the United States government, which sought a plausible pretext to crush the powerful Seminoles, demanded that they return the large numbers of Negro Maroons. This the Indians refused to do. Thus the question of runaway slaves played an important part in causing the two Seminole wars of 1817 and 1832. The latter war, the hardest fought in American Indian history, lasted seven years. The Indians and their Negro allies held off and repeatedly defeated the best United States regular troops; and in the end they themselves were only partially defeated. The brilliant leader of this great struggle was Osceola, who, Brawley says, had a Negro wife. He was cold-bloodedly assassinated by United States military forces, after having been lured to a peace conference.

THE DENMARK VESEY CONSPIRACY

As Aptheker points out, the decade from 1820 to 1830 was one of "sharply increased rebellious activities" on the part of the slaves. It reached two climaxes of struggle—that of 1822, led by Denmark Vesey, and that of 1831, led by Nat Turner. This decade was a period of severe economic depression in the South, which pressed severely upon the slaves and aroused their resistance. A big growth of anti-slavery sentiment throughout the northern part of the United States also had repercussions among the slaves in the South. The slaves, much more than is generally realized, knew about the current political campaigns at home and of revolutions in Europe, and these events stirred their spirit of resistance. Listing many revolts during this period, Aptheker says, "It is in such an atmosphere that the great unrest of the slaves of the United States for a dozen years after 1819 was displayed."[19]

Denmark Vesey, who organized the Charleston, South Carolina, insurrection of 1822, is said to have been born either in Africa or Haiti, and was supposed to have been in his middle fifties at the time of the conspiracy. Vesey arrived in Charleston at an uncertain date. In 1800, having won $1,500 in a lottery, he bought himself free.

He managed to educate himself, and spoke English and French. He worked in Charleston as a carpenter.

Obviously influenced by the Haitian Revolution, Vesey set about organizing an insurrection in South Carolina. He enlisted as his chief aides among the slaves Peter Poyas, Mingo Harth, Rollo Bennett, Ned Bennett, Monday Gill, and Gullah Jack. Vesey himself was said to be the only free Negro connected with the conspiracy. The recruiting was concentrated among the field workers; Vesey warned that house servants were untrustworthy. The well-conceived plan was to attack Charleston from half a dozen points simultaneously. The date set was a Sunday in July—Sunday was chosen because then the largest number of Negroes, on holiday bent, was to be found in Charleston, and July was selected because that was vacation season for the whites. Contacts were established with Negroes in Haiti. Work was begun to make pikes and bayonets, and it is estimated that some 10,000 slaves became directly involved. The stir of the insurrection spread far into the surrounding country.

Despite elaborate precautions, in May a slave betrayed the plot to his master. Arrests followed on May 30. Vesey, a strong natural leader, attempted to counter this blow by advancing the revolt date a month—to the middle of June. But the authorities, who had managed to secure information from additional informers, clamped down on the movement, arresting 131 Negroes, including Vesey.

Vesey defended himself in court with great skill against the revolt charges, but to no avail. From June through August, 35 slave rebels were hanged, he among them, and 43 more were banished. Four white men were also jailed for aiding the slaves' movement. Peter Poyas set the tone for the heroic deaths of the condemned slaves, saying to the others, "Do not open your lips. Die silent as you see me do."

The Vesey insurrection plot created panic far and wide among the slave masters. Thenceforth they took special measures to protect Charleston. They spared no means to keep out free Negroes who came into harbor on ships, especially those from the West Indies. They seized the Negroes on 41 ships, and their final release became a matter of international dispute. Drastic legislation was adopted to restrict the movements and activities of local slaves. One measure dissolved the newly-formed African Methodist Church which was supposed to have been an organizational center of the rebels. The Denmark Vesey plot was the best organized of any slave insurrectional movement in the history of such revolts in the United States.[20]

THE NAT TURNER INSURRECTION

In the years following the Denmark Vesey conspiracy of 1822 there were many lesser revolts of individual Negroes or of small groups of slaves in various parts of the South. These uprisings were the products of what Woodson calls "slavery at its worst"—that is, the wretched slave conditions under the increasing pressure of the new and expanding cotton economy. The growing slave discontent expressed itself most sharply in the Nat Turner insurrection, which took place in Southampton County, Virginia, in August 1831. Southampton was a big cotton producing center, and in 1830 the Negroes outnumbered the whites by 9,501 to 6,574.

Nat Turner, called "the Prophet," was born a slave in Virginia on October 2, 1800. He was owned by Joseph Travis of Southampton. From his early boyhood Turner was resolved to free his people. He managed to learn how to read. Of a strong religious turn of mind, he said that he saw visions and heard voices urging him on to the work of Negro liberation. Turner gradually built around himself a small body of confidants. His chief co-workers were Henry Porter, Mark Travis, Nelson Williams, Samuel Francis, and Jack Reese.

Unlike Vesey, Turner apparently had no elaborate plan of organization and campaign, evidently expecting that the great body of slaves would follow his lead in revolt. In line with the religiosity of the times and circumstances he awaited "a sign," and this, he understood, came in the form of the solar eclipse of February 12, 1831. Consequently, Turner and his co-workers set the following July 4 as the day to strike. But Turner was sick on that day and the plan could not be carried out. The rebels awaited another "sign," which they saw in the "greenish blue color" of the sun on August 13.

On August 21, the six slaves started their revolt. Their plan was to terrorize the country, and they undertook this by killing off such whites as they met, beginning with all the members of the family of Turner's master, Travis. Within 24 hours, 70 slaves joined the band of insurrectionists, and 61 whites were dead. Meanwhile, the panic-stricken whites in the neighborhood scattered and frantically called for help in all directions. Quickly, armed bands of whites, local militia, and Federal troops converged upon the district, murdering Negroes right and left. In the terror at least 120 slaves were killed and hundreds more were arrested. This broke the armed movement of the slaves and kept them from reaching the town of Jerusalem, where they aimed to capture stores of arms. Some 53 Negroes were arraigned; 16 of them, including three free Negroes, were executed. Many others got long prison sentences and other punishment.

Turner himself escaped for a time, hiding for six weeks in a fence corner of a field nearby before he was discovered. He was captured on October 30, 1831, convicted November 5 and hanged six days later. Turner died bravely. During his imprisonment he dictated a brief account of his life to a white reporter, who edited it.[21] Aptheker indicates some white participation in, or sympathy with the plotting of slaves in this period, although he doubts that any were involved in the Turner revolt.[22]

Turner's insurrection had profound repercussions throughout the South. Troops poured in "from Murphreesborough in North Carolina, from Norfolk, from Fortress Monroe, from the United States ships of war *Warren* and *Natchez*, and from Richmond."[23] The wildest excitement prevailed in North Carolina. Rumors flew about that Wilmington was burned, that half of its inhabitants were killed, and that the Negroes were on the march to capture Raleigh. According to McMaster, "The people of Fayetteville and Raleigh flew to arms, troops were hurried to Newburne. Plots that did not exist were next discovered in Delaware, and the people on the eastern shore of Maryland and the lower part of Delaware were so alarmed that expresses were sent off for arms and negroes arrested and examined."[24] Far and wide throughout the South ran similar rumors of impending doom for the whites at the hands of the aroused Negroes. "The Nat Turner insurrection shook slavery to its very foundations and cast somber shadows over all the slaveholding states."[25]

In several states the frightened legislatures—in Maryland, Delaware, North Carolina, Tennessee, Virginia, Georgia, Mississippi, Alabama, Missouri, Louisiana—adopted drastic measures to curb the rebellious spirit of the slaves. These regulations took the various forms of forbidding the movement of free Negroes into neighboring states, establishment of more stringent curfew laws for Negroes, adding penalties against teaching slaves or free Negroes how to read, applying more rigid Jim Crow laws against Negroes, restricting Negro religious meetings, and many other terroristic measures.[26] After 1831 and Nat Turner, the South became virtually an armed camp, with the guns pointed against the restless slaves. It was a situation ill conforming with the theories of those reactionaries who today claim that the Negroes accepted slavery submissively.

10. The American
Anti-Slavery Society

In previous chapters we have indicated four major currents in the developing anti-slavery movement in the United States. These were: 1. the abolition of slavery in the states of the North and Northwest; 2. the drive to abolish the world slave trade; 3. the fight of the Free Soilers, both within and without Congress, to prevent the spread of slavery into new states, which climaxed in the Missouri Compromise of 1820; 4. the growing Negro liberation movement, with its program of Negro conventions, civil rights, individual manumission, sabotage of plantation work, and armed insurrection.

Meanwhile, picking up from the slump in activity following passage of the anti-slave trading law in 1808, a widespread sentiment for the abolition of slavery had been growing all over the country, North and South. This phase of the anti-slavery movement achieved a major expression with the publication in Boston, on January 1, 1831, of the anti-slavery weekly, *The Liberator,* owned and edited by William Lloyd Garrison. The Abolitionist movement took on organized form nationally by the establishment of the New England Anti-Slavery Society in Boston in 1832 and with the formation of the American Anti-Slavery Society at Adelphia Hall, Philadelphia, on December 4, 1833. This meeting had to be protected by police from expected ruffian attacks. There were 67 delegates at the convention. Arthur Tappan was elected president and Elizur Wright secretary; headquarters were established in New York. The society set up the *National Anti-Slavery Standard* as its official organ. Thus was launched one of the most important mass movements in the history of the United States.

THE GROWTH OF THE ANTI-SLAVERY MOVEMENT

Numerous factors combined to produce the militant American Anti-Slavery Society at this time and to make it strong. Cotton production was rapidly expanding—it had gone up from 3,000 bales in 1790 to 732,000 in 1830—and with this growth came a broad extension of slavery. The conditions of the slaves were steadily worsening;

insurrections and other forms of slave protest and revolt were multiplying; a widespread Abolitionist spirit was developing among the
people, and the fight was sharpening in Congress to have the new
states coming into the Union bar slavery within their confines. Important events abroad were also operating to stimulate the anti-
slavery movement in the United States. Among these was the huge
Revolution of 1810-25 throughout the far-flung Spanish-American
colonies, from Mexico to Tierra del Fuego. This revolution had
unleashed a movement that gradually was freeing the slaves all over
this vast area. Also many slave insurrections were breaking out in
Brazil, Cuba, Martinique, Puerto Rico, Demerara, and elsewhere—
events which were not without repercussions in the United States.
Especially important, too, was the decision of England in 1833 to free
its slaves in the West Indies, a law which went into effect in 1838.
This step deeply influenced the American anti-slavery movement.
There were also bourgeois revolutions in a number of European
countries—Turkey, Greece, Italy, Spain, France, Belgium, Poland, and
elsewhere.[1] This was a period of revolutions. One of the basic developments accompanying this consolidation of world capitalism was the
emancipation of Negro chattel slaves. At this time it became definitely
a world movement.

Garrison, the founder of the American Anti-Slavery Society, was
recruited into the Abolitionist movement by the pioneer, Benjamin
Lundy. The latter, born in New Jersey, was raised in the anti-slavery
Quaker tradition. In 1817 he was a contributor to *The Philanthropist,*
a Quaker-run periodical devoted to "the cause of peace, temperance,
and anti-slavery." The following year Lundy and a fellow Quaker
founded *The Emancipator* in Jonesboro, East Tennessee, the first
exclusively anti-slavery journal in the United States. This paper later
became *The Genius of Emancipation,* also edited by Lundy. The
latter traveled ahorse and afoot through 24 states agitating against
slavery. In 1828, during a visit to Boston he met Garrison, then the
editor of a temperance paper, and won him to the cause of Negro
emancipation.

Garrison, descended from a pioneer family of New Brunswick,
Canada, was born in Newburyport, Massachusetts, in 1805. He was 23
years old when he became an Abolitionist. A printer and editor, a
trenchant writer and resolute fighter, Garrison devoted himself thenceforth to the emancipation struggle and lived to see the shackles
stricken off four million American Negro slaves. The appearance of

The Liberator, with the fiery Garrison at the helm, where he remained for 35 years, galvanized the weak and uncertain Abolitionist groups of the period into a powerful national movement of dynamic action. This marked the beginning of a generation-long campaign of penetrating analysis, aggressive exposure, and burning denunciation of the monstrous system of chattel slavery, without parallel in this or any other slaveholding country.

McMaster says that at the time *The Liberator* was founded there were 50 newspapers which opened their columns wholly or in some measure to the Abolitionist cause. Citing Birney, he also lists the following definitely anti-slavery journals in addition to those previously mentioned: *Abolition Intelligence* in 1822, in Kentucky; *The Edwardsville Spectator* in 1822 and *The Illinois Intelligence* in 1823, in Illinois; *The African Observer* in 1826, in Philadelphia; *The National Philanthropist* in 1826, in Boston; *Freedom's Journal* in 1827, in New York; *The Investigator* in 1827, in Providence; *The Free Press* in Bennington, Vermont; and *The Liberalist* in 1828, in New Orleans.[2]

Before the publication of *The Liberator,* there were also a number of general anti-slavery organizations in existence—as well as the Negro convention movement, which had at least 50 local groups. The 143 local anti-slavery societies held a convention in Baltimore in 1826 and another in the same city a year later. A convention was also held in 1828 in Washington, D.C.[3] The movement grew rapidly after the appearance of *The Liberator* and the establishment of the American Anti-Slavery Society.

MILITANT ABOLITIONISM

At its founding convention in Philadelphia, the American Anti-Slavery Society formulated its program in two main documents: its Constitution and its Declaration of Sentiments.[4] This program was far in advance of anything that had yet been produced by the general Abolitionist movement. It was fundamentally revolutionary, although Garrison was to prove incapable of developing all its revolutionary implications. Its central demand for the immediate, uncompensated liberation of the slaves, implying the overthrow of the dominant planter class, could not be, and was not, accomplished short of a revolution.

The society condemned slavery as both a sin and a crime, and

launched a militant crusade against it on this basis. Garrison struck
this clear Abolitionist note in the first number of *The Liberator*. He
declared, "Let Southern oppressors tremble—let their Northern apologists tremble—let all the enemies of the persecuted blacks tremble. . . .
Urge me not to use moderation in a cause like the present. I am in
earnest—I will not equivocate—I will not excuse—I will not retreat a
single inch—*and I will be heard*."[5] Despite many errors in policy,
Garrison lived up loyally to this militant pledge.

The society's constitution declared that, "Slavery is contrary to
the principles of natural justice, of our republican form of government, and of the Christian religion, and is destructive of the prosperity of the country, while it endangers the peace, union, and liberties
of the State." On this categorical basis, the society demanded "the
immediate abandonment" of slavery, declaring that "We maintain
that no compensation should be given to the planters emancipating
their slaves." It also stated, "We regard as delusive, cruel, and dangerous any scheme of expatriation which pretends to aid, either
directly or indirectly, in the emancipation of the slaves, or to be a
substitute for the immediate and total abolition of slavery." The
society was not the first body to call for immediate, non-compensated
emancipation, but its clarity and the great stress upon these conditions were vital.

Regarding political and social equality, the society stated its stand
as follows in its Declaration of Sentiments: "We further believe and
affirm—that all persons of color, who possess the qualifications which
are demanded of others, ought to be admitted forthwith to the enjoyment of the same privileges, and the exercise of the same prerogatives,
as others; and that the paths of preferment, of wealth, and of intelligence, should be opened as widely to them as to persons of a white
complexion." In its work, the society, as the sequel showed, was to put
little stress upon these specific equality questions, devoting its main
efforts to a general attack upon the system of slavery.

Although its objectives were not new in principle, the society's
forthright statement helped to clear up a number of illusions and
confusions which had hitherto plagued the anti-slavery movement.
Among such previous misconceptions were various schemes to confine
the anti-slavery movement simply to ameliorating the conditions of
the slaves, to bring about the emancipation of the slaves gradually,
instead of by a single act, to compensate the slaveholders for their
"losses" in freeing their slaves, as well as tendencies to consider the

deportation, or "colonization" program of the American Colonization Society as a constructive answer to slavery. Much of the success of the Anti-Slavery Society was due to its clarity and resolute insistence upon its no-compensation, no-repatriation points. Previously only the Negro wing of the anti-slavery movement (with some exceptions) had understood the elementary fact that the slaves had to be freed speedily and completely without slaveholder compensation or Negro expatriation. Dr. Hopkins of Newport, Rhode Island, said Frederick Douglass, advocated immediate emancipation long before Garrison was born.[6]

The American Anti-Slavery Society was very unclear, however, on the means of achieving the Negro emancipation which it had so definitely set as its goal. This was its basic weakness. Its program called upon the people to "remove slavery by moral and political action"; but later experience showed that it had confused ideas of what political action really meant. Throughout its existence, the society's essential work was confined to agitation, although the most militant and successful in American history. The society also tended to take on a sectarian and anarchistic anti-political trend. This even reached the point of proposals by Garrison to break up the American Union because of the pro-slavery clauses in the Constitution. Thus the society's chief weapon was moral suasion, not political action. In the tremendous work of awakening the American people to the horrors and damage of slavery, which it did with notable success despite its many errors, the society boldly attacked Church and State, both of which stood as barriers to Negro freedom.

In the field of political action further specific mistakes weakened the work of the society in its anti-slavery campaign. A serious one was that it bowed to the states' rights doctrine, the chief ideological argument of the slaveholders. Its constitution declared that the society "admits that each State, in which slavery already exists, has, by the Constitution of the United States, the exclusive right to *legislate* in regard to its abolition in said State," and it conceded to the Federal government only restricted powers, such as the right to abolish slavery only in the District of Columbia and the territories and to limit its extension into new states. This left virtually the whole slave system outside the control of the government. The weakness of this position is obvious, as the basic political task confronting the Abolitionist movement was precisely to have the Federal government stamp out slavery by surmounting the principle of states' rights. This was exactly what took place in the end, in the course of the Civil War.

Another major error of the Anti-Slavery Society was its overstress upon the power of educational agitation, of moral suasion. Some abolitionists even believed that the slaveholders as a class could be talked into voluntarily freeing their slaves, as indeed a few of them were. This exaggeration of the possibilities of agitation not only led to the minimizing of the importance of mass political action, but also to belittling or condemning the great weapon of the slaves—armed insurrection. On the latter question the society's constitution stated, "This Society will never, in any way, contenance the oppressed in vindicating their rights by resorting to physical force." This position led Garrison to condemn Walker's Appeal, Nat Turner's insurrection, and John Brown's revolt. In the long run, the force of events compelled the society to abandon its theories on states' rights, apoliticalism, and non-resistance, and to join with the rest of the anti-slavery forces in the great Civil War—but not without much confusion and heavy loss of effort all along the way to this culmination.

THE CLASS ROLE OF THE ABOLITIONIST MOVEMENT

During its period of active struggle the American Anti-Slavery Society drew in, along with its outstanding Negro supporters (see Chapter 9), a brilliant array of white leaders and workers. They displayed varying degrees of understanding, of loyalty to and activity in the Abolitionist cause. Among them were such noted names as Wendell Phillips, John Greenleaf Whittier, Ralph Waldo Emerson, Walt Whitman, Henry David Thoreau, Thomas Wentworth Higginson, Arthur and Lewis Tappan, Stephen S. Foster, Theodore Weld, Lucretia Mott, Angelina and Sarah Grimké, Lydia Maria Child, Abby Kelly Foster, Elijah Lovejoy, Henry Ward Beecher, William Goodell, Gerritt Smith, Elizur Wright, Levi Coffin, Samuel May, Beriah Green, Joshua Giddings, Lucy Stone, Mary Weston Chapman, Susan B. Anthony, Albert Brisbane, Theodore Parker, William Ellery Channing, Richard Henry Dana, Horace Greeley, Oliver Wendell Holmes, James Russell Lowell, James Fenimore Cooper, Henry Wadsworth Longfellow, and many others. Its roster of members and co-workers carried the brightest names in the American intellectual firmament. In the political field and not directly connected with the society were a host of other anti-slavery figures—Free-Soilers and Abolitionists—

including Thaddeus Stevens, Charles Sumner, Henry Wilson, Daniel Wilmot, Horace Mann, Dix, Hale, Niles, King, Palfrey, Seward, Root, Fremont. The best known white Southern Abolitionists were Benjamin Lundy, James G. Birney, Cassius M. Clay, and John G. Fee of Kentucky. Daniel Reeves Goodloe of North Carolina, Grimke sisters of South Carolina—and there were scores of others.[7]

The Abolition movement, of which the American Anti-Slavery Society was the main organization, was based on Negro-white cooperation, which it achieved to a high degree. The society not only gained hundreds of valiant fighters from its Negro affiliations but also the revolutionary impulse that was fundamental for the development of its fighting character. From the outset Negro intellectuals and Negro Abolitionists among workers were very prominent in the leadership and work of the society. They were the most consciously revolutionary elements in the organization. Foner says that, "Several Negroes were delegates at the founding Convention; three Negroes were among the sixty-two signers of the Declaration of Sentiments, and the Board of Managers included James G. Barbadoes of Massachusetts, Peter Williams of New York, and Robert Purvis, James M. Crummell, John B. Vashon, and Abraham D. Shadd of Pennsylvania."[8] Of the 450 subscribers to *The Liberator* in its first year, 400 were Negroes, and of 2,300 in 1834, no less than 1,300 were Negroes.[9] It was a regular procedure for Garrison and other white leaders of the Anti-Slavery Society to attend meetings of the Negro Convention movement, and vice versa. Towering among all the Abolitionist fighters, Negro and white, was Frederick Douglass, who was a vice-president of the Anti-Slavery Society.

Objectively, the historical task of the middle class Abolitionist intellectuals in the Anti-Slavery Society and elsewhere was to serve as the vanguard of the second democratic Revolution in the indispensable task of breaking the power of the Southern planters and thus opening the way to a fuller capitalist development in the United States. This required the emancipation of the slaves, the central task to which the Abolitionists militantly addressed themselves. The fact that the Abolitionists were the most radical section and vanguard of the Northern capitalist class is not contradicted by the reality that the great majority of them approached the anti-slavery struggle from a moral and humanitarian standpoint and had no inkling whatever of the class role they were playing in the development of the capitalist system.

Most of the outstanding Abolitionist leaders, both Negro and white, were petty bourgeois intellectuals. There were a few minor capitalists helping to lead the struggle, such as the Tappan brothers and Thaddeus Stevens; and there were even a few ex-slaveholders such as James G. Birney and the Grimke sisters. Mainly, however, the leaders came from the middle class—they were editors, preachers, doctors, lawyers, poets, novelists, and the like. Although belonging to the middle class and constituting its revolutionary left wing, these intellectuals were nevertheless acting as the ideologists of the entire bourgeoisie, and especially the Northern industrialists. They were engaged in a task vital for the development of the whole capitalist system. It was no mere coincidence that the Garrison movement was born in and always had its greatest strength in New England, then the heartland of American industrialism.

The Northern bourgeoisie who opposed the slave power, consisted principally of the growing body of industrialists and the shippers, merchants, and bankers who were not directly tied up with the Southern cotton and general trading business. They were, however, long unappreciative of the basic work of their revolutionary vanguard, the middle class Abolitionists. They harassed and persecuted the movement and its militants. Mobbing, tar and feathering, house-burning, rotten-egging, beating, jailing, and even lynching were everywhere the lot of the militant Abolitionists, not only in the South but also in the North. These attacks had their roots in the activity of definitely pro-slavery elements, but also in the then current opposition of the Northern capitalists to the emancipation of the Negro slaves. The capitalists' newsmen, preachers, and politicians shouted in chorus that to free the slaves would be contrary to the law of God, the cause of freedom, and the interest of mankind. Typically, "the merchants and lawyers of Boston feared abolition as a plague; they regarded abolition as an enemy to be fought with all weapons."[10]

This early rejection of Abolitionism merely indicates, however, that the Northern capitalists, still weak and unconsolidated, were, as yet, blind to the real course of history and to their true class interests. They were not yet prepared to have recourse to the revolutionary measure of slave emancipation proposed by their own ideological vanguard. It was not until 1863, with the Second American Revolution in full swing, that the Northern capitalists only partially reached the program of the advance-guard Abolitionists in the Emancipation Proclamation, a fundamental measure to win the war.

In this respect, the experience of the American and English Abolitionist movements was much alike. In England, too, in the face of rigid opposition, mainly of agriculturists but also of industrialists, a group of middle class intellectuals for 50 years carried on a resolute fight, first against the slave trade and then against slavery istelf. In both countries the large property owners generally dreaded this revolutionary consequence of abolition. For a long while the British capitalists did not see that Negro emancipation in the West Indies was in their most basic class interest, but finally, in 1833, after half a century under the pressure of the Haitian Revolution, the broad Latin American revolution, and the rising anti-slavery movement elsewhere, they abolished slavery, as the Americans did after an even greater delay.

THE MASS DEMOCRATIC SIGNIFICANCE OF ABOLITIONISM

It would be much too narrow, however, simply to define the Abolitionist movement as the most advanced section of the Northern industrial bourgeoisie and to let it go at that. It was much more complex. The fact is that the Abolitionist movement was the storm center of a whole series of mass democratic movements of Negroes, farmers, workers, and Negro and white women. These movements were stimulated by the Revolution of 1776, developed by the growth of bourgeois democracy, following the Jefferson-Jackson period of 1800-1837, and crystallized into a wide fighting alliance with the approach of the Second American Revolution, the Civil War of 1861. This is the broadest significance of the Abolitionist movement.

The heart of this whole network of democratic movements was the Negro people's fight for freedom. The national liberation struggle of the Negro people, ripening during the early days of the Republic, continues under new forms and issues down to the present time. The fight of the Negro people against slavery and Jim Crow discrimination, which we have already discussed at length, was the most revolutionary and urgent of all the developing people's movements of the time. It finally furnished the issues and became the amalgam and driving force uniting the great people's alliance that was to fight and win the Civil War.

If the Abolitionist intellectuals were the vanguard of the Northern bourgeoisie, the Negro wing of the movement had the specific quality of being the beginning of a national Negro liberation movement. That is, its basic objective was to free the Negro people from slavery and Jim Crow, and in so doing, it was also laying the basis for their future development as a nation. In this objective of general emancipation, the national interests of the Negro masses dovetailed with those of the Northern white bourgeoisie, inasmuch as Negro emancipation constituted a fundamental necessity for maximum capitalist development. The same principle applied to the other participating movements.

Another vital phase of the people's democratic struggles before the Civil War was the broad popular movement for land reform—that is, for free homesteads on public lands. This great movement, which we shall discuss later, ultimately threw mighty masses of farmers and workers into direct collision with the Southern planters over the distribution of the free government lands, and eventually over the existence of the slave system. It therewith became a cornerstone of the great people's anti-slavery alliance.

Still another of the many progressive mass struggles of the first half of the nineteenth century was the woman's rights movement. Women played a most important part in the Abolitionist movement from the outset, and the two movements had a strong spirit of cooperation. The names of the white women who fought for women's rights (whom we have already mentioned) are inseparably linked to the fight for emancipation. Just so, the names of the many Negro women fighters for Abolition—Harriet Tubman, Sojourner Truth, Frances Ellen Watkins Harper, Sarah Douglass, Mary Cary, Grace Mapps, Mary Bibb, Frances Coffin, and numerous others—cannot be separated from the great struggle for women's rights in general.

During the 1830's and '40's, utopian socialism grew considerably in the United States. A number of communistic colonies arose, established by followers of Robert Owen, Charles Fourier, and Etienne Cabet. These movements, especially the Fourierists of The Brook Farm colony, were generally sympathetic toward Negro emancipation. They constituted another, if minor, facet of the great democratic upsurge of the times.

The advent of Marxism on the American political scene in the early 1850's introduced another powerful democratic and revolutionary element into the general struggle for Negro emancipation. But of this, more later.

ORGANIZED LABOR AND ABOLITIONISM

The American trade union and labor party movement which was also related to the Abolitionist movement, was born in this pre-Civil War period of general democratic ferment, organization, and struggle. It fought for improved labor conditions, universal franchise, free and public education, abolition of debtors' prisons, etc. This basic movement, too, was destined to become an integral section of the vast people's alliance that broke the power of the Southern slavocracy and won the revolutionary Civil War. In 1833, however, when the American Anti-Slavery Society was founded, the labor movement was only in its swaddling clothes. Industry was just entering the factory stage, and the artisans were only then becoming real wage workers. In 1830 home production still outranked factory production by four to three.[11] Consequently, the young trade unions were by no means conscious of the white workers' fundamental interest in the emancipation of the Negro slaves. Current among their illusions were fears that freeing the Negroes would throw a flood of cheap labor on the market that would ruin their living standards. Often there were strikes against Negro freemen who were trying to establish their right to work in industry. At this time there were but very few trade unions in the South.

Nevertheless, already strong anti-slavery currents were in evidence among the workers. Schlueter quotes Thomas Wentworth Higginson, noted Abolitionist, to the effect that "The anti-slavery movement [of New England] was not strongest in the more educated classes, but was predominantly a people's movement, based upon the simplest human instincts and far stronger for a time in the factories and shoe-shops than in the pulpits and colleges."[12] Schlueter also points out that "The platform of one of the first political labor parties of New York contained a plank demanding the abolition of chattel slavery."[13] There are many similar examples among the earliest trade unions.

A strong factor, however, tended to drive a wedge between the Abolition and trade union movements. This was the strong anti-union bias of Garrison and other middle class Abolitionists. In the very first number of *The Liberator* Garrison roundly denounced the efforts of Boston workers in 1831 to form a party of workers and farmers in Massachusetts. He said: "An attempt has been made— it is still making—we regret to say—to inflame the minds of our working classes against the more opulent, and to persuade men that they are condemned and oppressed by a wealthy aristocracy. . . . It is in the highest degree criminal, therefore, to exasperate our mechanics to deeds of violence or to array them under a party banner."[14] Garrison maintained this hostility to trade unions until after the Civil War. Wendell Phillips, a co-worker of Garrison, however, later became very friendly to the labor movement. Shortly after the Civil War, speaking in Faneuil Hall, Boston, in support of the eight-hour day, he said that "the Anti-Slavery cause was only a portion of the great struggle between Capital and Labor."[15] In 1871 he became a member of the First International.

Other middle class Abolitionist intellectuals, here and abroad, took a definite pro-capitalist position. In England the petty-bourgeois Abolitionists had this slant. "The abolitionists," says Williams, "were not radicals. In their attitude to domestic problems they were reactionary. . . . Wilberforce was familiar with all that went on in the hold of a slave ship but ignored what went on at the bottom of a mineshaft."[16] "Wilberforce, whose goal for Negro liberty was only equalled by his enthusiasm for repressing insubordination in white workers."[17] We shall come back later to these matters of labor and the Abolitionist movement.

As the years passed the political struggle developed. Under the pressure of the great life-and-death battle between the Northern industrialists and Southern slavocracy all these popular movements— of Negroes, women, farmers, workers, Marxists—grew and came closer together in the basic political fight for the abolition of Negro slavery. Finally, they coalesced in the grand people's alliance, under the general hegemony of the Northern industrialists, which carried the Civil War to victory.

11. The Tariff, Texas and Mexico

The Compromise of 1820, which in reality was bold aggression on the part of the Southern slavocracy, did not "settle" the contradictions between the rival systems—the slave plantations in the South and industrialism in the North. Instead it provided but a brief respite. Soon the incompatible regimes were again at each other's throats. The generation from 1820 to 1850 was one of sharply rising struggle between the pro- and anti-slavery forces in the United States.

Both systems were expanding rapidly. In the South cotton production was blazing its triumphant way to the Mississippi River and on into Texas. In 1820, 335,000 bales were produced, and by 1850, the figure had gone up to 2,136,000 bales[1], or an increase of over 600 percent. The number of Southern slaves increased accordingly—the figure climbing from 1,538,022 in 1820 to 3,204,313 in 1850.[2] Of these, some two million worked in cotton.

An even more spectacular economic growth was taking place in the North. In 1820 the value of national manufactures (90 percent of which were in the North), was approximately $200 million; but by 1850 it had mounted to $1,019,106,616.[3] Textiles were growing rapidly, and so were iron, metal-manufacturing, shoe, lumbering, and various other industries. The railroads were expanding swiftly, and the lakes and rivers, especially in the North, were laced with steamboat lines. Farming, on the basis of small farms, was making tremendous headway in the North and Middle West. Immigration had soared from 8,385 in 1820 to 369,880 in 1850. During the same period the population of the United States went up from 9,638,463 to 21,191,876, with the North registering by far the greatest gains in both immigrants and population growth.

JACKSON, CALHOUN, WEBSTER, CLAY

The four outstanding bourgeois figures in the sharpening struggle of this crucial generation deserve a brief analysis. They were, namely, Andrew Jackson of Tennessee, John C. Calhoun of South Carolina,

Daniel Webster of Massachusetts, and Henry Clay of Kentucky. These men reflected the great conflicting class forces and struggles of the times.

General Jackson, long the leader of the Democratic-Republican Party, later the Democratic Party, was President from 1829 to 1837. He was a dynamic national figure from the time of the Battle of New Orleans in 1815, which he led, to his death in 1845. Jackson believed in bourgeois democracy, but a democracy of the Greek pattern, based upon slavery. A well-to-do cotton planter with a large number of slaves, Jackson especially represented the West. He defended the interests primarily of the lesser slaveholders, the small farmers and frontiersmen, and, to a certain extent, also the wage workers.

In his democracy Jackson had no place for Negroes except eternal slavery. The Indians, too, were outlaws with no tangible rights, as far as Jackson was concerned. He was the most militant Indian fighter in American history. He robbed the Cherokees, Creeks, Chickasaws, and Choctaws of 50 million acres of land in Georgia, Alabama, Mississippi, and Tennessee, and then drove these tribes out of their traditional homelands and across the Mississippi. Most of their rich lands fell into the hands of the big cotton planters. Jackson also tore Florida away from the Spanish and the Seminole Indians.

Jackson's democratic standing depends primarily upon his bitter and successful fight against the United States Bank, which was the financial instrument of Nicholas Biddle and other Northern bankers for monopolizing the banks, industries, and politics of the whole country. This historic fight, resulting in a great victory for democracy and capitalist progress, won Jackson an immense and loyal following among the farmers all over the country, among the professionals and small industrialists, and among the working class. During the Jackson regime, big advances were made in trade unionism, people's education, factory legislation, democratic state institutions, and the establishment of the franchise—for whites.

John C. Calhoun was the chief political leader and ideologist of the Southern planters through three decades after 1820. He died in 1850. Calhoun served as Secretary of War under President Monroe, as Vice-President during the first term of President Jackson, and as Secretary of State in 1844-45 under President Tyler. He was born of poor whites in the Carolina uplands; but he married a large plantation along with his wife. Thenceforth he identified his interests with those of the big planters and, as senator from South Carolina, he was for two decades their major spokesman in Congress. Cold, cynical, brilliant, Calhoun ruthlessly and unremittingly defended slavery. He equated Southern chattel slavery with Northern wage slavery, and defended the former as the less harsh. He arrogantly declared that wherever the flag was planted, there slavery should be also. Taking it for granted that the ruling class had to exploit a slave working class, he said, "There never has been a wealthy and civilized society in which a portion of the community did not in point of fact, live on the labor of the other."⁴ He was an ardent champion of unlimited states' rights on the question of slavery. Calhoun was the leader of the right wing of the Democratic Party—Jackson's party, until Jackson died and the planters soon took over the party altogether.

Daniel Webster was the most eloquent spokesman of Northern capitalism. His chief backing came from the shipping and manufacturing interests of New England. He was Congressman and later Senator from Massachusetts from 1823 to 1850 except for four years. He died in 1852. Webster's changing attitude in Congress represented the shifting relationships of the shipping and manufacturing interests in New England. Thus, he opposed the early tariff legislation because the shipping concerns, which were then dominant in capitalist circles, favored free trade. But in 1828, Webster was a militant high tariff man, signifying that the industrialists had become decisive in New England capitalistic circles. Webster opposed the spread of slavery into the Northern and Western states, but was against abolition. He said, "I regret that slavery exists in the Southern states, but it is clear and certain that Congress has no power over it."⁵ His attitude towards the Southern planters was one of conciliation. When he died, he had been thoroughly discredited among the New England Abolitionists for having supported the pro-slavery Compromise of 1850. He belonged to the Whig Party.

Henry Clay of Kentucky was, as we have seen in Chapter 8, the political sponsor of the futile Missouri Compromise of 1820, as well as several other compromises during the great struggle over slavery. His was a typical opportunist, Border state position. He attempted to maneuver between the opposing forces of Northern industrialism and the Southern plantation system. Together with Webster, Clay organized the Whig Party in 1834. Clay favored Northern industrialism by his support of the United States Bank, the darling project of the big Northern capitalists. Clay served a couple of terms as Secretary of State, and he was a prominent figure in Congress as Representative and Senator from Kentucky from 1809 to 1850. Like Webster, Clay died in 1852, frustrated in his burning ambition to be the Whig candidate for President in 1848.

THE "NULLIFICATION" FIGHT OVER THE TARIFF

For sixteen years following the Missouri Compromise of 1820, the bitter fight over the admission of new states into the Union was in abeyance. It was not until 1836 and 1837 that Arkansas and Michigan came in, the one slave and the other free. Again the race began to maintain the balance in the Senate. The pro- and anti-slavery forces clashed over many other issues, however, such as maneuvers to grab Cuba and Haiti as slave areas—attempts which were balked by vigilant Great Britain. Interesting were the instructions given by President Monroe to the American delegation to the first Pan-American conference held in Panama in 1826 which were to prevent the then revolutionary countries of Spanish America from taking any action condemning slavery. The first heavy clash in the United States between the two great opposing forces after 1820 however, came in 1832 over the question of the tariff.

As we have remarked earlier, since colonial days the Northern manufacturers had favored the tariff to protect their weak but growing industries from British competition. The Southern slaveholders, on the contrary, generally favored free trade, or at most tariff for revenue only, so that they could buy more cheaply the manufactured commodities they needed. This free trade policy kept down the prices not only of imports from England but also of those things which they bought in the North, which had to meet British prices. In the first four decades of the Republic, however, the situation was somewhat different—the big shippers of New England favored free trade, whereas the Southern slaveholders tended to go along with the Northern manufacturers in support of a moderate tariff for revenue. But with the great expansion of cotton in the South and industry in the North, the South became militantly free trade and the North aggressively protectionist. The first heavy battle over the tariff question came to a head in 1832.

In 1816 and 1824 the tariff had been raised without strong Southern opposition; but when it was given a still higher boost in 1828, the cotton planters went into battle against it—especially those of South Carolina. In general, the Southern states denounced the new law as "the tariff of abominations." John Randolph declared that if the tariff were not lowered, soon slaves would be looking for runaway masters, instead of vice versa. Calhoun pronounced the tariff unconstitutional, and Webster and Hayne held one of the most famous debates in American history upon the question, with the former supporting the high tariff and the latter opposing it. Talk of secession was rife all over the South. Under this strong pressure, the North made some concessions to the South in the tariff law of 1832.

But South Carolina was irreconcilable; it took the bit in its teeth and announced its doctrine of nullification. The South Carolina state convention adopted an ordinance "to nullify certain acts of the Congress of the United States, purporting to be laws, laying duties and imposts on the importation of foreign commodities."[6] This theory—that states could pick and choose among the Federal laws those which they would or would not obey—was an extreme form of the states' rights doctrine, next door to actual secession. The firebrands of South Carolina backed up their nullification theories with threats of armed action to prevent Federal enforcement of the tariff laws.

Jackson was President, and like most slaveholders at the time, was opposed to splitting the Union. He threatened to hang Calhoun if he tried this, declaring also that any attempts at secession would be met by use of the Federal Army. Jackson ruthlessly trampled upon the sacred states' rights dogma. In this crisis, Henry Clay came forward with another "compromise." He proposed, on the one hand, that the tariff should be cut back to the low 1816 level, as the planters demanded; but that this be done gradually over a period of ten years. The plan was adopted. This was a victory for the planters over the industrialists in one of their most sensitive areas—the tariff. From that time until the Civil War, the arrogant planters were able to keep a tight rein on the tariff rates, thereby developing one of the sharpest issues between the North and the South.

By using the threat of secession in this struggle the Southern planters got a taste of red meat. Thenceforth they used this threat as a regular weapon, notably the South Carolina "firebrands." "From 1832 to 1860 South Carolina was in effect not so much a part of the country as a dissatisfied ally, for the last thirteen years of the period only awaiting a favorable opportunity to dissolve the alliance."[7] It was South Carolina that finally led the great secession of 1860.

During this period of the tariff fight, the Northern bankers and industrialists suffered another defeat, in which the slaveholders played a prominent part. This came when Jackson knocked out the United States Bank in 1832 by refusing to recharter it when the existing charter expired. Jackson was heavily backed by the people. The defeat of this insolent attempt by the Northern capitalists to grab the entire banking system of the United States was fundamentally a victory for the democratic forces of the whole country. But it would not have occurred without the support given Jackson by many slaveholders, who also rejoiced in the discomfiture of their traditional Northern enemies.

THE SEIZURE OF TEXAS

By the mid-1830's, slavery was the decisive political issue in the United States. Under the pressure of rapidly expanding cotton production and stimulated by their triumph in the nullification fight of 1832, the Southern panters were now well on their way with their great offensive to dominate completely the entire United States, which was to culminate in their overwhelming defeat in the Civil War. One of the first fruits of this early offensive by the planters was the seizure of Texas from Mexico. This added further fuel to the already blazing fire between the Southern plantation system and Northern industrialism.

In 1821, the Spanish government, which then controlled Mexico, naively opened the door to American immigrants led by Stephen F. Austin. But on certain conditions—the newcomers were supposed to be Catholics, to have no slaves, to obey the colonial laws, to become Mexican citizens, and to recognize the sovereignty of Spain. The Americans, however, had been claiming the Texas area ever since the Louisiana Purchase in 1803, and they had no intention of conforming to the above conditions. Nor did they. The immigrants were mostly Protestants, they brought large numbers of slaves with them, they maintained their American citizenship, they flouted the laws of Spain and, after 1826, those of the new Mexican Republic. In particular they militantly disobeyed the Mexican law of 1829 which abolished chattel slavery. They were openly preparing to tear Texas away from Mexico.

After he became President in 1829, Jackson, who was an ardent expansionist, took an active hand in all this. He worked closely with his good friend Sam Houston, military leader of the Texans, undoubtedly with the set purpose of having the United States take over

Texas at the first favorable opportunity. Jackson's friendly biographer, James, says, "General Jackson closed his eyes to an extraordinary emigration of American 'settlers,' lugging guns rather than plough-shares."[8] In 1835 the armed struggle began over the Americans' refusal to pay taxes and abolish slavery, as the Mexican laws provided. On March 2, 1836, Texas declared its independence of Mexico. After hard fighting and savage massacres on both sides, Houston's Texan forces, because of Jackson's thinly-disguised help, defeated the Mexicans decisively at the Battle of San Jacinto on April 21, 1836, and captured the chief Mexican general, Santa Anna. This ended the war, and for nine years Texas was an "independent" republic.

Thus, the Southern slaveholders got hold of an immense new stretch of country, much of it adapted to slavery. Texas was 269,000 square miles in area, or more than five times as large as the state of New York. Small wonder that immediately after Texas set itself up as an independent government, the chief slaveholder leader, Calhoun of South Carolina, moved in Congress that it be admitted into the Union as a slave state. This brought on a strong fight, however; the Free Soil forces of the North and West bitterly opposing the absorption of such a vast area of new slave territory. The danger was all the greater because the Southerners openly hoped to break up Texas into several states, with, of course, a corresponding increase in their representation in the Senate. The annexation of Texas was a big issue in the presidential elections of 1844. James K. Polk, a Democrat, with active Jackson support, won on an annexationist platform. Consequently, Texas came in as a slave state the following year. This was another great victory for the aggressive Southern slaveholders. The Northern Free Soilers, however, had some small consolation in the admission of Iowa in 1846 as a free state, which thereby restored the balance between the rival forces in the Senate.

THE WAR WITH MEXICO

The Mexican War of 1846-48 was a direct result of the expansionist drive of the cotton plantation-slave system of the South. With their dogma of "Manifest Destiny," the arrogant slaveholders figured that they were on the way to building a great slave empire, which would dominate all of the United States, would take in the West Indies, and stretch away south into Brazil. The war was deliberately caused by President James K. Polk of North Carolina and other agents of the slaveholders, who were then dominating the government of the

United States. It was the biggest land steal and the most barbarously unjust war in the history of the United States and of the entire Western Hemisphere. Some planters, however, looked askance at this grandiose expansionism, fearing that it would overextend the cotton industry beyond the possibilities of the world market.

The war with Mexico was immediately precipitated over the question of Texas and California. The United States, as we have seen, had grabbed the vast area of Texas through a pseudo-revolution and an "independent" republic in 1836. The same strategy had been tried again—successfully—in seizing California from Mexico in 1845. This job was engineered by General John C. Frémont and Commodore Sloat. They staged a "revolution" and established the California Republic, with its Bear flag. The following year Congress declared California to be American territory, and in 1850, it was absorbed as a state. The original plan to seize California from Mexico was worked out by Jackson, but he had been unable to execute it.[9]

Meanwhile, to further its plans for a predatory war against Mexico, the Polk Administration opened negotiations with that country in 1845, offering to "buy" New Mexico and California. The Mexicans, however, outraged by the arrogant, expansionist policies of the United States, refused to sell. Thereupon President Polk ordered General Zachary Taylor to invade Mexico in July 1845, and war was formally declared on May 12, 1846. Although torn by internal struggles against counter-revolution within their young republic, the Mexican people resisted gallantly, but to no avail. General Winfield Scott occupied Mexico City in August 1847.

This reactionary war provoked widespread opposition in the United States. Many Whigs, among them young Abraham Lincoln, then a Congressman, outspokenly denounced the war as a cold-blooded slaughter organized by the Southern planters to expand their slave system. In Congress, Joshua R. Giddings boldly declared that it was "a war against an unoffending people, without adequate or just cause, for the purpose of conquest; with the design of extending slavery; in violation of the Constitution; against the dictates of justice, humanity, the sentiments of the age in which we live, and the precepts of the religion which we profess. I will lend it no aid, no support whatever."[10] The Abolitionist movement was generally unsparing in its denunciations of the Mexican War. Frederick Douglas declared it "a most disgraceful, cruel and iniquitous war," the work of "our slave-holding President."[11] And the young trade unions of the time also opposed the unpopular war. Lawson cites a characteristic action by a convention of New England workers in Lynn, Massachusetts, in 1846, which condemned the war and resolved not to support it.[12]

The Mexican War almost precipitated an armed struggle with Great Britain. After the break-away of the Latin American colonies from Spain in their big Revolution of 1810-25, Great Britain had never ceased maneuvering to absorb the young republics as its own colonies, or at least to establish a British sphere of interest and control over them. It was, therefore, very vigilant to combat growing United States influence throughout the western hemisphere. Great Britain dominated the first Pan-American conference in 1826; it stood on guard against the possibility of the United States taking over Cuba and Haiti; it opposed every step in the American conquest of Texas and California; and it tried hard to grab Texas for itself. Britain was also much in the mood to take up arms alongside Mexico when the United States attacked that nation, but it could not quite make up its mind to this drastic action, for it doubted that it could handle militarily its big and rapidly growing American rival.[13]

So the slaveholder expansionists had their way, beating down and circumventing both the domestic and the foreign opposition to their predatory Mexican War. On March 10, 1848, they forced Mexico to sign the Guadalupe Hidalgo pirate treaty, by which Mexico was compelled to cede to the United States, more than one-half of its entire territory, counting Texas, for the relatively small sum of $15 million. In 1853, by the Gadsden Purchase, the United States took away another important slice of Mexico for $10 million. This country thus seized from Mexico a vast area greater than France and Germany combined and rich with natural resources. It was later organized into the states of Texas, California, Arizona, New Mexico, Utah, Nevada, Colorado, and part of Wyoming.

All this constituted a big victory for the slaveholders, but it did not sate their voracious territorial appetite by any means. The Beards thus comment, "The Americans who favored annexing the whole of Mexico or at least holding all the territory in the North conquered by General Taylor, after some grumbling, accepted the gains of the settlement as the best that could be accomplished in the circumstances."[14] But this temporary planters' victory, instead of stifling, stimulated the ever-rising movement of revolt among the Negro slaves and the growth of Abolitionism throughout the North and West.

12. The Split in the Abolitionist Movement

Immediately upon the founding of *The Liberator* in 1831 and of the American Anti-Slavery Society in 1833, the Abolitionists developed strong and effective agitation against slavery. For a generation they turned their powerful battery of speakers and writers against the "peculiar institution" of the South, against attempts to extend it into free territory, against the South Carolina nullification movement, against the colonization scheme to deport free Negroes to Africa or elsewhere, against the seizure of Texas, and against the expansionist war against Mexico. Garrison, in *The Liberator*, poured out his fiery denunciation of slavery; so did the eloquent Wendell Phillips on the platform, and a myriad of lesser figures worked with a burning zeal to destroy slavery.

A most prominent figure in all this struggle was Frederick Douglass, who both wrote and spoke with unparalleled brilliance. One of the outstanding figures in American political history, Douglass was a power in every phase of the Abolitionist movement. Among the many famous Negro agitators of the period was Sojourner Truth, an ex-slave and a woman, who traveled up and down the country, setting audiences aflame with her powerful denunciations of slavery.

CONVENTIONS AND INSURRECTIONS

The Negro Convention movement, which functioned as part of the general Abolition struggle, worked closely in and with the Anti-Slavery Society. Its workers and leaders, as remarked earlier, were to be found in all the many fronts of the fight. A big event of theirs was the first appearance on December 7, 1837, of Frederick Douglass' paper, *The North Star*, later renamed *Frederick Douglass' Paper*. On the Southern plantations, the slaves reacted to worsening economic conditions and the developing national struggle against slavery by many revolts and conspiracies during these crucial years. Urbanization, economic depression, the general increase in the slave population

126

based on cotton expansion, and the hard-fought national election campaigns, all tended to awaken the slaves' consciousness and determination to fight.

Aptheker lists many slave revolts and conspiracies, large and small, in the period between Nat Turner's historic revolt in 1831 and the critical year of 1850.[1] The planters lived in great fear of slave uprisings, and all attempts were repressed with savage ferocity. Occasionally poor whites co-operated with the slaves in their desperate struggles and suffered harsh penalties therefor. Hangings, floggings, and jailings took place in many areas and the South became more and more like an armed camp. White Abolitionist leaders, mostly believers in "moral suasion," disclaimed responsibility for slave revolts (this was on the shoulders of the slaveholders), but without doubt there was a connection between their propaganda and these uprisings. Douglass and other Negro Abolitionist leaders, however, had a keener appreciation of the importance of slave insurrections in exposing and combatting the horrors, crimes, and unworkability of slavery. As a rule, they supported such actions more or less openly.

This fighting note was clearly sounded by Henry Highland Garnet, outstanding Negro Abolitionist, at a Negro convention in Buffalo in 1843. He said, "However much you and all of us may desire it, there is not much hope of redemption without the shedding of blood. If you must bleed, let it all come at once—rather die as freemen than live as slaves. . . . Awake, awake; millions of voices are calling you! Let your motto be resistance! resistance! resistance!"[2] Garnet proposed that the convention declare for a general strike of slaves, to be followed by a broad insurrection, but he was defeated by one vote.[3]

One of the best known of the many uprisings of this period was the mutiny of the Negroes aboard the Spanish slave-schooner *Amistad*, off Cuba in 1839. The slaves, led by one named Cinque, killed the captain and crew, sparing the two passengers aboard to act as navigators. They were supposed to head the vessel back to Africa. Instead the navigators tricked the mutineers, wandered around the North Atlantic for two months, and finally brought the *Amistad* to port on Long Island. The passengers claimed the Negroes as their slave property, but in the face of a strong campaign by the Abolitionists in which John Quincy Adams played a big part, the U.S. Supreme Court in 1841, found it necessary to rule against them and to free the slaves.[4] This vital and dramatic fight was a real victory over the slavocrats.

TERROR AGAINST THE ABOLITIONISTS

The Abolitionists worked in the face of violently antagonistic opposition largely organized by agents and friends of the Southern slavocracy. The Northern bourgeoisie was unwilling as yet to adopt the revolutionary course advocated by Abolitionists. Fighters against slavery were tarred and feathered, beaten, and jailed. "Many of them sacrificed property, home, and friendship, and even life itself for the slave."[5] It took political courage to be an active Abolitionist. Garrison himself was dragged through the streets of Boston on October 21, 1835, and narrowly escaped lynching; a group of women locked arms together and saved him from the mob. Douglass was repeatedly insulted, abused, Jim-Crowed, and threatened with death; George Thompson, who came from England, was mobbed and beaten; Whittier, Tappan, and other Abolitionist leaders were assaulted and their meetings broken up. Charles Sumner was attacked in the U.S. Senate and crippled by a South Carolina "fire-eater."

The anti-Abolitionist campaign was especially violent in the South. Vigilante committees operated in many communities; they slugged Abolitionists and lynched more than one of them. Consequently, the Southern sections of the Anti-Slavery Society were early broken up or driven underground. The Southern slaveholders brazenly offered "Rewards of $10,000, $50,000, and even $100,000 for the bodies or heads of prominent Abolitionists."[6] On the New York Stock Exchange a Southern sympathizer openly said he would give $5,000 for the head of Arthur Tappan.[7] The terrorism in the North came to a head on November 7, 1837, with the brutal lynching, in Alton, Illinois, of Elijah P. Lovejoy, prominent Abolitionist and editor of the *Illinois Observer*. His assassins were freed by the local authorities.

One measure by which the slaveholders tried to counter the effective agitation of the Abolitionists was a persistent effort to bar their printed material from the mails, whence some of it was reaching slaves in the South. Numerous proposals to this effect were made in Congress, including a recommendation by President Jackson on December 7, 1835, that it be made a Federal crime to send Abolitionist literature through mails. Strong mass resistance, in which John Quincy Adams was quite active, prevented Congress from taking this drastic action. The fight lasted 25 years, right up to 1860.[8] The slaveholders scored their point in the South, however, as in practice it was left up to the postmasters to choose what printed matter they would deliver.

This meant that no Abolitionist journals or pamphlets were thereafter delivered by mail in the South.

Another drastic method used by the slaveholders in Congress and in the various state legislatures was to deny Abolitionists the right of petition. From the founding of the Anti-Slavery Society the Abolitionists had persistently deluged the legislators with petitions against slavery. These were received at first, but in 1836 the House and Senate voted not to accept them.[9] This "gag rule," which lasted until 1845, was a denial of a fundamental constitutional right of the people. A special House resolution denied slaves the right to petition Congress.[10]

The Abolitionists of the United States and Britain worked in close co-operation, to their mutual benefit. In 1833, Garrison visited England, speaking all over that country against slavery. He linked up the American Abolitionist movement with the fight of the Irish, Poles, and other oppressed peoples for freedom. In 1834 George Thompson, the noted English Abolitionist, returned the visit and was long active in the United States. The Abolitionists made London the world center against slavery, holding a big world-wide anti-slavery conference there in 1840. Frederick Douglass visited England in 1845. With his brilliant oratory and statesmanlike conduct, he created a sensation.

Despite all opposition, the American Anti-Slavery Society grew rapidly, because its issue was definitely on the immediate agenda of history. It was not a loose, amorphous grouping, but a strongly defined organization, with a dues-paying membership and well-organized local and state branches. It possessed a discipline and was capable of clearly formulating policy and of carrying on concentrated national campaigns. During the society's first seven years, up until the split in 1840, it grew into a body of some 250,000. At that point it had at least 25 anti-slavery journals, its leading organs being *The Liberator*, and the *National Anti-Slavery Standard*. In 1836 the Society had 70 lecturers in the field. Foner tabulates its organizational growth, by local groups as follows: 1834, 60; 1835, 200; 1836, 527; 1838, 1,350; 1840, 2,000.[11] There were some 15 state branches. The membership was composed mainly of farmers, workers, and intellectuals. Negroes and women were very prominent in it. The American Anti-Slavery Society, which embraced the bulk of the Abolitionists of the United States, constituted an agitational and political force of great national weight.

THE UNDERGROUND RAILROAD

One of the most remarkable and effective means of struggle against slavery was the celebrated "Underground Railroad," or "U.G." This was one of the greatest achievements of the democratic forces in the history of the United States. The purpose of this organization was to help slaves to flee from Southern slavery into the North, usually to Canada. It operated in flagrant violation of the Fugitive Slave law. The U.G. had its "stations" (homes of sympathizers where the Negroes stayed in transit), "trains" (groups of fleeing slaves), and "conductors" (those who were leading the mass escapes). The first traces of this organized underground began to take shape among the Negroes and Quakers about 1800, but as early as 1642 slaveholders complained that whites were helping runaway slaves to escape.[12] By 1860, the U.G. had reached large proportions. The "President" of this revolutionary railroad to freedom was Levi Coffin, a Cincinnati Quaker.

"There were myriad routes, both in the East and the West, from the borders of Delaware, Maryland, Virginia, Kentucky, and Missouri north to Canada."[13] There was no safety for the runaways short of Canada, where the Fugitive Slave Act did not reach. The escaping slaves traveled at night, hiding by day in the barns, garrets, cellars, and secret compartments of the stations. Between 1830 and 1860 at least 60,000 slaves thus made their way to freedom. It is claimed that 9,000 passed through Philadelphia alone from 1831 to 1861.[14]

Most of these fugitives—those who did not go to Canada—gathered in the industrial centers of the North. In the true spirit of the pioneers, however, some found their way despite great difficulties to the Middle West and even the Far West. In Michigan, for example, the number of Negroes increased from 2,500 in 1850 to 6,700 in 1860. In California, as early as 1855, a Negro people's convention was held; there were some 6,000 Negroes in the state as a whole.

Histories of the Underground Railroad are full of accounts of the hardships experienced by the slaves in their flight. Especially in the South, they had only the North Star to guide them through the night across stubbly fields or through unknown woods. Many swam or log-forded all the rivers from the Gulf states to the Ohio. How many were recaptured by the gangs of slave-hunters or perished along the way will never be known.[15]

The main organizers and operators of the U.G. were free Negroes and Quakers. It is estimated that in 1860 Negroes made 500 trips from

Canada to the South to bring out slaves. With their faithful Abolitionist spirit and their farms scattered all through the Northern states, the Quakers were also indefatigable and efficient workers in the great cause. Some 3,211 persons, all told, have been identified as workers in the Underground, but there were many more.

Severe penalties were attached to helping fugitive slaves to escape. Some persons served long prison sentences for this work. The agents and conductors ran incredible risks. In the South, to be caught as a worker on the Underground was to invite a lynching bee. Captain William Bayliss, Abolitionist master of the *Keziah,* was convicted of violating the Fugitive Slave Act in Virginia; his ship was auctioned off, and he was sentenced to 40 years in jail. Not until Federal troops took Richmond in 1865 was he released.[16] Many U.G. agents in the South simply disappeared after they were apprehended.

Negro leaders of the U.G. were William Still in Philadelphia, David Ruggles in New York, Stephen Myers in Albany, Frederick Douglass in Rochester, Lewis Hayden in Boston, J. W. Loguen in Syracuse, Martin R. Delany in Pittsburgh, George De Baptist in Madison, Indiana, John Hatfield in Cincinnati, William Goodrich in York, Pennsylvania, Stephen Smith, William Whipper, and Thomas Bessich in Columbia, Pennsylvania, Daniel Ross and John Augusta in Morristown, Pennsylvania, Samuel Bond in Baltimore, Sam Nixon in Norfolk.[17] These were but a few of the Negro fighters, there were hundreds of others. Some of the workers brought out or helped large numbers, of slaves to freedom: among them Calvin Fairbank aided 2,700 to escape; Udney Hyde, 517; Josiah Henson, 200; Levi Coffin, 2,500; Thomas Garrett, 2,200.

Of the many brave fighters engaged in this heroic work, the most outstanding was the famous Harriet Tubman. Born a slave in Maryland in 1820, she fled North in 1849. Immediately afterward she took up the ultra-dangerous work of conductor on the Underground Railroad. During the next dozen years, until 1860, she made no less than 19 trips to the South, bringing out 300 slaves. She became a fabulous figure in the South; the slaves knew her far and wide as "Moses." The slaveholders posted a reward of $40,000 for her, dead or alive. She had incredible adventures on her many trips South. Thomas Wentworth Higgins, in his history of the Underground Railroad, calls Harriet Tubman "the greatest heroine of the age." She became known as "General Tubman" and deserves to rank among the first of all our political heroes. She lived to see her people freed, and for many years after the Civil War, she was an active fighter in the Negro people's movement. She outlived nearly every other Abolitionist leader. Harriet Tubman, beloved of her people, died on March 10, 1913, well on to 100 years old.[18]

THE WOMEN'S RIGHTS MOVEMENT

As we remarked earlier, there was a direct relationship between the Abolitionist movement and the other democratic and progressive movements that developed before the Civil War, including the trade union, women's suffrage, land reform, utopian socialism, Marxist Socialism, manhood suffrage, and public education movements. The connection between the Abolitionists and the fighters for women's rights was especially close. From the outset, women were in the front line of the fight against slavery. Indeed the women's movement largely grew out of the Abolition movement. "In the early Anti-Slavery conventions, the broad principles of human rights were so exhaustively discussed, justice, liberty, and equality so clearly taught, that the women who crowded to listen, readily learned the lesson of freedom for themselves and early began to take part in the debates and business affairs of all associations."[19] The training that the women got in the Abolitionist movement they put to good use in their own special fight.

Professor Charles Walker, in his book of that period, *Introduction to American Law,* paints a grim picture of the status of women: "At the marriage altar, the law divests her of all distinct individuality. Blackstone says, 'The very being or legal existence of the woman is suspended during marriage, or at least incorporated or consolidated into that of her husband.' Legally she ceases to exist, and becomes emphatically a new creature, and is ever after denied the dignity of a rational and accountable being. The husband is allowed to take possession of her estates, as the law has presumed her legally dead. All that she has becomes legally his, and he can collect and dispose of the profits of her labor without her consent, as he thinks fit, and she can own nothing, have nothing, which is not regarded by the law as belonging to her husband." The woman was, in fact, in bondage to the man, and she felt a deep political kinship with the Negro slave fighting for freedom.

In the vigorous women's movement of the 1830's and 1840's, the principal demands were for the right to vote and to share in all political offices, honors, and emoluments; for equal rights in universities and in the trades and professions; for complete equality in marriage, property, wages, children; for equal personal freedom; for the right to make contracts, to sue and be sued, and to testify in courts of justice. The women amended the Declaration of Independence to read, "All men and women are created equal."

The women's rights movement was conceived in the spirit of the famous Mary Wollstonecraft, British pioneer suffragist of the 1790's. It had to face sharp ridicule, denunciation, and opposition from organized reaction. Its leaders and fighters, including many Negro women, were nearly all active Abolitionists—Frances Wright, Lucretia Mott, Amelia Bloomer, Susan B. Anthony, May Cary, Grace Mapps, Margaret Fuller, etc. Many male Abolitionists, notably Garrison and Douglass, gave active support to the militant women's rights movement—a fact which was eventually to have important consequences for the Abolitionist movement in general. But at the founding convention of the Anti-Slavery Society in 1833, even these men did not ask the women Abolitionists present to sign the society's Declaration.[20]

DISSENSION IN THE AMERICAN ANTI-SLAVERY SOCIETY

Garrison was the major ideologist of the American Anti-Slavery Society. He laid out the Abolitionist program at the start of the organization in 1833, and then, as a rigid dogmatist and hard-bitten fighter, he proceeded to expound it ruthlessly. Inevitably, serious internal dissensions soon developed. These quarrels had to do mainly with three major questions: political action, religion, and women's rights. The consequent disruption led to a national split in 1840.

At the start of the society, Garrison had mildly advocated the use of the ballot; but more and more he came to rely simply on doctrines of moral suasion and passive resistance. He believed that slavery would be killed if the people were taught the injustice of it. He deprecated political action and especially the formation of an Abolitionist political party. Garrison renounced participation in the government, stating, "As every human government is upheld by physical strength, and its laws are enforced virtually at the point of the bayonet, we cannot hold any office which imposes upon its incumbent the obligation to compel men to do right, on pain of imprisonment or death. We, therefore, voluntarily exclude ourselves from every legislation and judicial body and repudiate all human politics, worldly honors, and stations of authority."[21]

With limitless invective, Garrison denounced the United States government. On the basis of the pro-slavery clauses in the Constitution, he called it "a covenant with death, and an agreement with hell." His major slogan of action was "No Union with Slaveholders." This led him eventually to the absurd position that the only way to free the slaves was by dissolving the Union itself—which was just what the slaveholders wanted. Garrison led the "Come-Outers" who wanted to quit the Union. At a Fourth of July meeting in New England, he dramatically burned the American flag, a copy of the Fugitive Slave Act, and a court order directing the return of runaway slaves. His anti-political line, of course, tended to and did isolate the Garrison wing in the Abolitionist movement from the big national struggle that other anti-slavery forces had long been conducting, specifically on a Free-Soil basis—notably the fight to prevent new territories from being brought into the Union as slave states.

Garrison and his followers were no less categorical in their denun- ciation of the churches for their shameless pro-slavery position. After the Revolution of 1776, when slavery was believed to be dying out of itself, most of the churches favored its liquidation. But when slavery took on great vigor and life with the great expansion of cotton pro- duction, the churches, North and South, retreated and took either a pro-slavery or an equivocal position. John Wesley, the great pioneer Methodist leader, had once called slavery "the sum of all villainies," but his followers had long since forgotten this. As Frederick Douglass says, "As went the Methodist Episcopal Church [which attacked the Abolitionists], so went the Baptist and Presbyterian Churches. They receded from their anti-slavery ground."[22]

At the first convention of the Anti-Slavery Society, one of the resolutions adopted proposed an investigation of which and how many preachers owned slaves. That such an investigation was much needed, Jennings makes clear: "Prominent leaders in church life, elders, deacons, presbyters, bishops, ministers, or whatever they might be called, as well as prominent women, bred slaves for the market."[23] The only church that was not thoroughly besmeared with the filth of slavery was the Friends, the Quakers. Thus, at the foundation of the Anti-Slavery Society, 37 of the 67 delegates were Quakers; the Quakers were the principal whites engaged in operating the Under- ground Railroad; and two Quaker boys were hanged along with John Brown.

A fervently religious man himself, Garrison scathingly denounced the mealy-mouthed preachers who supported or conciliated slavery. He went on to denounce the churches as a whole as "a great *Brotherhood of Thieves*" because they countenanced the worst of all thievery, man-stealing. The Anti-Slavery Society convention of 1840 formally condemned the whole body of the churches for their pro-slavery stand: "The church ought not to be regarded and treated as the Church of Christ, but as the foe of freedom, humanity, and pure religion, so long as it occupies its present position."[24] Wendell Phillips, then an ardent supporter of Garrison, summarized the anti-political, anti-church line of the society in an epitaph for himself in case he should die before Negro emancipation: "Here lies Wendell Phillips, infidel to a church that defended human slavery—traitor to a government that was only an organized conspiracy against the rights of men."[25] All of which brought thunder down upon the head of the Abolitionist movement from the conservative church figures, and also resentment from many religious Abolitionists.

Garrison's petty-bourgeois radical doctrines also caused acute dissensions in the Anti-Slavery Society itself. The opposition claimed that Garrison's anti-political stand was depriving the Abolitionist movement of its most powerful weapon, political action, and was alienating it from many potent allies in the political field. They also argued that the violent attacks upon the church by Garrison and others were tending to make an anti-religious sect of the Anti-Slavery Society. The opposition also would have nothing to do with supporting the women's rights movement, which, in the spirit of male supremacy, they held to be a great affront to all sense of womanly modesty and to public decency and propriety.

Behind the moot issues of women's rights, political action, and religion in the Anti-Slavery Society lay the deeper question of the use of armed force against the aggressive slaveholding oppressors. The insurrections of the slaves were in substance the practice of the people's right of revolution against intolerable persecution, against the systematic violence of the planters, which was perpetual and organic to the slavery system. Generally, the Negro Abolitionist leaders supported this right, though not always publicly. Garrison, however, with his ideas of non-resistance, repudiated any idea of force. He said that he could not conceive of a situation in which he would take up arms. In the second issue of *The Liberator* on January 8, 1831, he stated, "We do not preach rebellion—no, but submission and peace." This pacifist attitude led him to take a negative or deprecatory attitude toward contemporary Negro slave conspiracies or revolts. As the struggle sharpened between the forces of slavery and freedom, and as the country approached the great revolutionary crisis of the Civil War, the issue of the use of force, of the people's right of revolution, became more and more alive in the Anti-Slavery Society and the country as a whole.

THE SPLIT IN THE ANTI-SLAVERY FORCES

The internal struggle within the Abolitionist movement reached the breaking point at the national conventions of the American Anti-Slavery Society in 1839 and 1840. The immediate splitting issue was women's rights, but underlying this were the deeper questions of the society's attitude toward political action, religion, and armed force. The split began at the 1838 convention of the powerful New England Anti-Slavery Society. Following the leadership of Garrison, this body voted to seat a number of women delegates, whereupon a group of preachers walked out in protest. The following year, at the national convention of the society, the split widened and deepened over the same issue. The convention voted by 180 to 140 to allow all persons present, including women, to be seated as members. This brought forth a vigorous protest from 120 delegates, who declared that the society should be an organization made up only of men, and that admitting women would divert it from its basic purpose of Abolitionism.

The split culminated at the 1840 convention of the American Anti-Slavery Society in New York City, on May 17. The convention was a big one, with 1,008 delegates. Obviously a breach was inevitable. Factional strife was at fever pitch. The opposition, led by the Tappan brothers, Gerrit Smith, Elizur Wright, Myer Hall, and James G. Birney, had previously met in Albany on April 1, founded the Liberty Party, and nominated Birney for president. Again the decisive clash at the convention came over the woman question. By a vote of 557 to 451, Abby Kelly Foster was placed on the Business Committee. Then Lucretia Mott, Lydia Maria Child, and Maria Weston Chapman were elected to the Executive Committee. As a result a number of delegates walked out claiming that the action of the convention had virtually merged the Abolition and women's rights movements. That night, the dissenters met at the call of Lewis Tappan and formed the American and Foreign Anti-Slavery Society,[26] with Arthur Tappan as president, and James G. Birney and Henry B. Stanton as secretaries.

Now there were two national anti-slavery societies in the field, with mutual recriminations going on between them. Consequently, there was a great deal of confusion in the Abolitionist movement as a whole. The "old" organization, the Garrison body, was hard hit by the split; its national income dropped within a year from $47,000 to $7,000, and its membership fell from about 250,000 to but 70,000. It never recovered its previous strength. The organization continued, however, and remained an agitational power up to the Civil War. With the political elements gone from their ranks, Garrison and Phillips had a free field for their middle class ultra-radicalism. They made the main issue the extinction of slavery through the dissolution of the Federal Union. This policy, says Henry Wilson, facilitated the charge of reaction that the Abolitionists were all guilty of "disunity, atheism, revolution, and treason."

The "new" organization, headed by Tappan, never grew to the size and influence of the "old" society. Its leaders and members turned their attention chiefly to political action and had little need for such a propaganda organization as the "old" Anti-Slavery Society. The "new" society also lingered on to Civil War times, but had little size or strength. The real Abolitionist movement was expressing itself through new political organizations and movements.

Despite the initial confusion and disruption caused by the split in the American Anti-Slavery Society, the Abolitionist movement actually took a long step forward through this division. The main body of the movement moved from the program of pure (even if brilliant) propaganda to one of organized political action. Abolitionism reached new levels of effectiveness. From 1840 on, the Garrison wing tended toward sectarianism and isolation; whereas the political wing, led by the two Tappans, Douglass, Smith, Birney, and the rest, moved toward effective alliances with the other mass anti-slavery forces. This was the beginning of the historically necessary political junction between the Free Soilers and the Abolitionists, heading up to the Revolution of 1861-65.

NEGRO ABOLITIONISTS AND THE SPLIT

The split in the American Anti-Slavery Society naturally affected the Negro people's convention movement (see Chapter 9). This movement worked with and within the Anti-Slavery Society, for despite white persecutions, the Negro leaders understood that there were progressive white forces with whom they could and must work. The early Negro liberation movement split over the same questions which had disrupted the old society—women's rights, political action, the attitude toward the churches, and behind all this, the basic question of the use of armed force. In addition, the convention movement was further split over a special basic question of its own: namely, whether the Negro people should confine their activities to the general Abolitionist societies or should also build up definite Negro organizations, journals, and leadership.

Thus began the historic dispute over the question of separate organization for Negroes in their national struggle. The course of events was to prove that such organization was indispensable. The movement was to learn that it was one thing to be forced into segregation, and quite another to build a voluntary Negro organization. The Negro people's convention movement, in its full significance, like the Negro church and other independent Negro organizations, was marked evidence of the early beginnings of national consciousness among the Negro people—a trend which, in our day, is approaching fruition. The question of Negro migration to Africa, Central America, and the West Indies, always a matter of dispute, also became a serious splitting issue during the 1850's, as we shall see later.

With his characteristic sectarianism, Garrison was sharply opposed to separate Negro organizations, claiming that they were essentially Jim Crow and would isolate the Negroes from the struggle as a whole. He especially opposed Douglass' founding the Negro paper, *The North Star*. At the 1834 Negro people's convention the whole question of specific Negro organization was of major importance, and by 1836 the Negro movement had split over it. Thenceforth, there were two Negro national movements, each holding yearly conventions. The split-off group called itself the American Moral Reform Society and had the *National Reformer* as its organ. It generally accepted Garrison's line, whereas the original convention movement, with *The Colored American* as its chief journal, was anti-Garrison—with special stress upon the question of political action and the need for separate Negro organization.

The chief Garrison supporters in this early fight were William C. Nell, James G. Barbadoes, and William P. Powell, while the anti-Garrison faction was led by Samuel E. Cornish, Christopher Bush, and Charles B. Ray.[27] At the beginning of this struggle, before 1838, Frederick Douglass was still a slave in the South. For a time, after fleeing North and becoming active in the Abolitionist movement, he supported the Garrison-Phillips position, including opposition to separate Negro organizations. But before long, he took a position against sectarianism in all its forms and he passed over to the militant political action wing, where he became the outstanding leader. For this, Douglass was denounced as a renegade by the bitter Garrison. Nevertheless, Douglass always remained a warm friend of the old white battler for Negro emancipation.

At first Douglass accepted the basic Garrison demand for the dissolution of the Federal Union, but he soon came to see its folly. Years later, in the fight against the Dred Scott decision, Douglass said on this matter: "The dissolution of the Union would not give the North one single additional advantage over slavery to the people of the North, but would manifestly take from them many which they now certainly possess. Within the Union we have a firm basis of anti-slavery operation. National welfare, national prosperity, national reputation and honor, and national scrutiny; common rights, common duties, and common country, are so many bridges over which we can march to the destruction of slavery. To fling away these advantages because James Buchanan is President or Judge Taney gives a lying decision in favor of slavery, does not enter into my notion of common sense."[28]

Contrary to Garrison, Douglass declared that the Constitution was not fundamentally a pro-slavery document and that it was both possible and necessary for the Abolitionists to work within its framework. Among his many arguments to this effect, Douglass asserted: "The Constitution, in declaring that 'no person shall be deprived of liberty without due process of law' and that, 'the right of the people to be secure in their persons shall not be violated,' prohibits slavery."[29] He also asserted that Congress, under the Constitution, had the full right to enforce these provisions.

On the moot question of support for armed slave insurrection, Douglass at first opposed the militant H. H. Garnet at the Negro people's convention of 1843, when the latter said: "It is your solemn and imperative duty to use every means, both moral, intellectual, and physical that promises success."[30] But by 1847 Douglass had largely rid himself of Garrisonian ideas of non-resistance, and in 1849 he declared: "I should welcome the intelligence tomorrow, should it come, that the slaves had risen in the South, and that the sable arms which had been engaged in beautifying and adorning the South were engaged in spreading death and destruction there."[31] There was a gradual growth of militancy among both Negro and white Abolitionists.

Douglass also broke with Garrison's sectarianism on religion. Although highly critical of the church's pro-slavery position (he was frequently called an atheist by irate clericals), he refused to make religion as such the issue, as Garrison tended to do.

The fight among the Negro Abolitionists continued throughout the 1840's and early 1850's. The general trend of the movement was away from Garrisonian sectarianism and toward full participation in the broad and growing political fight against slavery. Experience demonstrated that so far as the separate Negro convention movement was concerned, political action had helped, not hindered the general fight for emancipation. The convention movement survived every attempt to hamper and destroy it, and it continued as a representative and effective force up to the Civil War and over into the Reconstruction period.[32]

13. The Compromise of 1850

The generation between the Compromise of 1820 and that of 1850 was one of swift national economic development and territorial expansion. Consequently, the collisions between the mutually contradictory systems of Southern plantations and Northern industrialism multiplied and grew ever sharper. Slavery became the all-decisive national political issue. In Chapter 11 we dealt in some detail with three of these major struggles of the period—the tariff nullification controversy of 1833, the battle over the seizure of Texas in 1836, and the acute controversy provoked by the predatory war against Mexico in 1846-48. Meanwhile, the two groups were constantly wrangling over the vital question of internal improvements, principally the Federal development of means of communication—rivers, harbors, and railroads. The plantation South generally opposed such improvements, while the industrial North and agricultural Northwest demanded them. By the 1850's, this contest was beginning to turn around the question of government construction of a transcontinental railroad.

THE WILMOT PROVISO

The key question of political power—the winning of new states for or against slavery—was in abeyance for most of the three decades between 1820 and 1850; the admission of Arkansas (slave) in 1836 and of Michigan (free) in 1837 was carried out without great friction. But the whole issue burst forth with more intense fury than ever in the later 1840's, when it came to admitting the enormous territories that had been stolen from Mexico. Between 1845 and 1850 five new states came into the Union: Florida, 1845 (slave); Texas, 1845 (slave); Iowa, 1846 (free); Wisconsin, 1846, (free); and California, 1850 (free). The battle over these states, especially California, directly precipitated the sharp crisis and the ensuing Compromise of 1850.

The great struggle began formally on August 6, 1846, when David Wilmot, a Democrat and Free Soil farmer from Pennsylvania, introduced in the House his famous "Wilmot Proviso." The Mexican War was then going on, and President Polk, anticipating a big land grab from Mexico, asked Congress to appropriate two million dollars to "pay" that country for territories that were about to be taken from her. The bill was sailing through the House, when Wilmot made his amendment to the effect that "as an express and fundamental condition to the acquisition of any territory from the Republic of Mexico . . . neither slavery nor involuntary servitude shall ever exist in any part of said territory, except for crime, whereof the party shall first be duly convicted."[1]

The heart of the question which Wilmot raised was this: Inasmuch as the expected new territories under Mexican law were free of slavery, therefore they should not be transmuted from free territory into slave states by the Congress. The slaveholders were aghast at Wilmot's amendment, because they had taken it more or less for granted that these territories—like Alabama, Louisiana, Mississippi, and Texas—would automatically come into the Union as slave states. After the Wilmot Proviso had twice passed in the House, they filibustered it to defeat in the Senate, and Polk's whole bill along with it.[2]

During the next decade, the supposedly rejected Wilmot Proviso was the storm center of the rapidly sharpening controversy over slavery. It was endorsed wholly or in principle by the Whig, Free Soil, and Liberty parties, and eventually also by the Republican party. The Abolitionists actively supported it, and the anti-slavery masses of the people rallied around it. The key phrases of the Wilmot Proviso had been taken word for word from the famous Northwest Ordinance of 1787 (see Chapter 5), and they were to be followed verbatim in the formulation of the thirteenth, anti-slavery Amendment to the United States Constitution in 1865.

THE NATIONAL DEBATE ON SLAVERY

When the Mexican War ended and the United States took away half of the territory of defeated Mexico, it was necessary to make some arrangements for government control in the newly acquired areas. Gold-seekers were streaming into California, and New Mexico already had 60,000 inhabitants. This need for state organization again put the issue of slavery squarely up to Congress. The big debate on the question, one of the most celebrated in the history of the United States, began in December 1849 at the opening of Congress.[3] In the meantime, after a bitter wrangle, Oregon was organized as a free territory in late 1848.

The slavocrats, as usual, knew quite well what they wanted from Congress—namely, to expand the slave system on all fronts. Their outstanding spokesman, the hoary old John C. Calhoun of South Carolina, presented their program with his customary clarity, bluntness, and arrogance. He demanded the extension of slavery into the conquered Mexican territories, California and New Mexico; he insisted that the North be rigidly required to return all fugitive slaves, and he demanded particularly that a stop be put to all Northern agitation for the emancipation of the slaves. Behind this position, upon which the Southern orators hammered, lurked the threat, often openly expressed, that if the Southern demands were not met a general secession of the slave states could be expected.

The main spokesman for the Northern anti-slavery forces was William H. Seward of New York. Senator Seward, Whig governor of New York in 1839-42, was an outstanding lawyer, who later became Secretary of State under Lincoln. It was he who coined the famous characterization of the North-South struggle—"the irrepressible conflict." Although by no means a militant Free Soiler, Seward and those who sided with him in the long and heated debate insisted that the former Mexican territories should not be surrendered to slavery, that the fugitive slave law could not be enforced, and that the agitation in the North against slavery was impossible to suppress.

The Abolitionist leaders—Douglass, Garrison, Phillips, and others—took an active part in the great debate among the broad masses, of course combating Calhoun's position. But practically none of the whites among them were members of Congress because of their early anti-political attitudes. The collision between the two great contending forces was head on, and the crisis deepened.

In this critical situation, Senator Henry Clay of Kentucky, author of the famous compromises of 1820 and 1833, came forward with another compromise proposal. Clay, who was a Whig, received the support of his Massachusetts Whig colleague, Senator Daniel Webster. On March 7, 1850, after the fight had been going on for a long time and he had said nothing, Webster suddenly made a speech favoring the Clay proposals. He assailed the Abolitionists, thereby dealing the decisive blow to his declining prestige among the anti-slavery forces. Clay and Webster, with their "compromise," spoke essentially in the name of those Northern bankers and merchants whose financial interests tied them to the cause of the cotton oligarchy of the South. This great battle was the last clash of the three biggest political figures of the period—Calhoun, Webster, and Clay—for within two years they were all dead.

THE COMPROMISE

Clay's compromise proposals, submitted as an omnibus bill, were adopted in a series of separate laws.[4] The first was the Texas and New Mexico Act of September 9, 1850. This law established more definitely the borders of Texas, but the heart of it was a payment of ten million dollars to that state, presumably for concessions made by it. In reality, the appropriation was a graft subsidy to the holders of nearly worthless Texas securities, many of whom sat in Congress. Greeley remarks on this matter: "Corruption, thinly disguised, haunted purlieus and stalked through the halls of the Capitol; and numbers, hitherto in needy circumstances, suddenly found themselves rich."[5] As for New Mexico, the Act provided that when this territory finally came into the Union, the decision on slavery was to be made by the state itself. This was a flat rejection of the Wilmot Proviso and a victory for the cherished Southern doctrine of states' rights.

In line with Clay's proposals, the Utah Act of September 9, 1850, provided that this territory, too, should decide for itself whether slavery was to be legal within its borders—another blow against the Wilmot Proviso and for states' rights. Supposedly to offset these big surrenders to the slaveholders, California, which during the gold rush had filled up with white settlers, was admitted as a free state on September 9, 1850. This was no real concession to the anti-slavery forces, however, as the slaveholders had no solid grip in California and popular sentiment was overwhelmingly against their infamous slave system.

An important section of the great "compromise" was the District of Columbia Act of September 20, 1850. While failing to do away with slavery in in the District, this law did abolish the slave trade there. Ever since the earliest fight against slavery, the Abolitionists had made it a central point of their program to demand the wiping out of slavery in the nation's capital. This was because the authority of the government regarding slavery was obvious and definite in that area and the major states-rights contention did not apply. For decades, however, the slaveholders managed to ward off every attack against slavery in the District, including the compromise settlement of 1850.

Georgia, at this time, openly threatened to secede if slavery were abolished in the District. Indeed, it was not until the Civil War that slavery was finally cleaned out in the District of Columbia, which for many years had stood as the very national symbol of slavery. And even up to our day, the tradition of slavery is so strong in Washington that the capital remains one of the worst Jim Crow cities in this country. John Pittman has aptly called it "the Jim Crow capital of the world."

In the so-called Compromise of 1850, the slaveholders won their most cherished victory with the passage of the Fugitive Slave Act of September 18. This act, which was far more stringent than the earlier law of 1793, was an attempt by the slaveholders to stop the big drain upon their plantation system caused by the wholesale flight of slaves to the North via the Underground Railroad. The law authorized the slaveholders to pursue runaways into other states, instructed all U.S. marshals to apprehend fugitive slaves, gave them the power to organize posses and mobilize all the help they might need, and imposed heavy fines upon all who in any way gave aid or shelter to fleeing slaves. The law was especially designed to break up the Underground Railroad.

To enforce this Act, the government sought to transform the people and the legal authorities of the Northern states into a vast police network, charged with the responsibility of returning to the South the large number of runaway slaves. The states were instructed to enforce the law firmly. The Act said, "All good citizens are hereby commanded to aid in the prompt and efficient execution of the law." Heavy fines and jail sentences were provided for all those who in any way opposed or hindered the application of this slave-hunting legislation.

As for the runaway slaves themselves, they were to have no say whatever in the matter, but were simply to be picked up by U.S. marshals and rushed off to the South. They were to be denied regular trials and also deprived of the right of habeas corpus. The Fugitive Slave Act specifically declared that "In no trial or hearing under this law shall the testimony of such alleged fugitives be admitted in evidence." This meant carrying the Southern slave codes into the North. The law was an invitation to slave-hunters to kidnap free Negroes in the free states and to hurry them to waiting slave-masters in the South. Significantly, the law anticipated forceful resistance to its enforcement. It gave the Federal marshals the authority to muster a sufficient number of armed deputies to overcome any force that might be arrayed against them. In reality, this barbarous law, which was meant as a basic prop for the slave system, aroused such widespread anti-slavery sentiment in the North, that it became a veritable disaster to the slaveholders' whole cause.

The Compromise of 1850 was, for the time being at least, a real victory for the Southern slave system. It reflected, on the one hand, the aggressive expansionism of the slaveholders and, on the other, the confusion and indecision still to be found in the ranks of the Northern anti-slavery forces. Of course, the "compromise" could not end the great quarrel that was tearing the nation asunder. Instead, it only served to stimulate the aggressiveness of the slaveholders and thus to hasten the country toward the great revolutionary crisis that was only ten years off.

REALIGNMENTS OF CLASS AND PARTY FORCES

During the three-quarters of a century between the Revolution of 1776 and the Compromise of 1850, there had been many fundamental developments in the national economy and, correspondingly, in the composition of social classes, the political alliances of these classes, and the character of the political parties of the United States. One of the major dynamic forces in all these changes was the ever-sharpening national controversy over Negro chattel slavery, with its profound economic and political implications. This issue was at the heart of the conflict in interest between the Southern plantation system and Northern industrialism.

Two alliances were in the making throughout this whole period. One was the growing alliance between the big Southern planters and the Northern bankers, merchants, and shippers directly involved in the handling of cotton and tobacco, who joined on a number of issues under various leaders and parties. The other was the gradual coming together into a political alliance of the Negro people, the farmers, the workers, the intellectuals, shopkeepers, merchants and the Northern industrialists—also under varying circumstances. These two great, hostile class groupings finally matured politically and clashed in the revolutionary Civil War.

After the end of the first Revolutionary War, as we pointed out in Chapter 4, there were for a time no definitely established political parties, but by 1796 two parties had crystallized politically. The

Federalist Party, under the leadership of Alexander Hamilton, represented principally the big merchants and big slaveholders; the Democratic-Republican Party, led by Thomas Jefferson, represented slaveholders, frontiersmen, small farmers, artisans, tradesmen, etc. The great
election clash of 1800, which Jefferson won, dealt the Federalist
Party a mortal blow, and by 1816 it had virtually disappeared as a
political factor.

The Democratic-Republican Party was the party of Jefferson,
Madison, Monroe, and Jackson. The latter renamed it the Democratic
Party, a title which it has retained ever since. It was essentially an
alliance between the agrarian West and the agrarian South. After
the dissolution of the Federalist Party, when for a time there was
only one party, the reactionary elements, planters and merchants,
functioned loosely as a sort of right-wing, independent faction within
the Democratic Party. But early in the Jackson administration, they
organized themselves into the National Republicans and also the
Anti-Masonic Party. During Jackson's big fight against the United
States Bank in 1832-36, Webster and Clay, Jackson's most vigorous
enemies, founded the Whig Party.

The Whig Party grew rapidly. It based itself upon the business
interests; but reactionaries of all stripes, including big planters,
gravitated toward it. The Beards aver that in 1850 three-fourths of
all slaves were owned by planters affiliated to the Whig Party.[6] The
party stood for moderate tariffs, internal improvements, the United
States Bank, industry in the South, and no serious interference with
the slave system. It favored the status quo and took a straddling
position. The Whigs elected William Henry Harrison to the presidency in 1840 and Zachary Taylor in 1848, as well as many members
of Congress from various states. Made up of contradictory class forces,
the party was torn with dissension over the great national issue of
slavery. By 1850 it was well on the way to dissolution. Its two great
leaders, Webster and Clay, who had fathered the pro-slavery compromises of 1820, 1833, and 1850, died in 1852, and the Whig Party
died with them.

Meanwhile, the slaveholders moved actively to take over the
Democratic Party, which still commanded broad support among the
Northern workers and Western frontiersmen and farmers. Presidents
Martin Van Buren (1837-41), James K. Polk (1845-49), Franklin
Pierce (1853-1857), and James Buchanan (1857-61) were all Demo-
crats, and the last three were increasingly tools of the big slaveholders.

THE LIBERTY PARTY

In 1840, an important new political party appeared on the national scene, born of the great struggle against slavery. This was the Liberty Party, headed by James G. Birney, a former slaveholder who had emancipated his slaves. This party resulted from the split in that year in the American Anti-Slavery Society between the pro- and anti-political factions (see Chapter 12). The Liberty Party ran Birney for President in 1840, when he polled 7,906 votes. In 1844, the party again nominated Birney, whose vote went up to 62,300. The Liberty Party platform demanded an end to slavery in the District of Columbia and opposed the expansion of slavery into the territories. It declared its opposition to slavery everywhere as "against natural rights." The party called for disobedience to the fugitive slave law of 1793. It spoke for the rights of labor, for free speech, and for the right of petition.[7]

The Liberty Party invited Negroes to join, and it elected to a minor office John M. Langston, the first known Negro candidate on the ticket of any political party. Frederick Douglass became a member of the party's national committee, and in 1853 he was the party's candidate for Secretary of State in New York. Many Negro leaders—Samuel Ringgold Ward, Henry H. Garnet, J. W. Loguen, William Wells Brown, and others—supported the party. A Negro people's convention, meeting in Buffalo in 1843, endorsed the Liberty Party,[8] and others followed suit.

The Liberty Party occupies a historic position in the long struggle for Negro emancipation. It was the first national political party to speak out boldly for the abolition of chattel slavery. It carried the emancipation question clearly onto the political field and thus constituted a long stride toward consolidating the Free Soil and Abolitionist movements. The small vote polled by the Liberty Party in no way indicated the vast extent of Abolitionist sentiment at the time; it merely showed that the anti-slavery masses were not prepared to break away from their traditional political moorings.

THE FREE SOIL PARTY

Except for a remnant, the Liberty Party merged into the Free Soil Party. The latter party was organized in Buffalo on August 9, 1848, through an amalgamation of Liberty Party Abolitionists, Free

Soil Whigs, and "Barnburners"—the Free Soil wing of the Democratic Party. As its presidential candidate the convention put up Martin Van Buren, who had been the Democratic President of the United States in 1837-41. The party, as its name signified, took as its main issue opposition to the extension of slavery into the territories. The party was organized before the Compromise of 1850, when the country was torn with controversy over the status—free or slave—of California and New Mexico. Basing itself upon the United States Constitution, the Buffalo convention denied that Congress had the power "to deprive any person of life, liberty, or property, without due legal process." It declared, "Congress has no more power to make a slave than to make a king; no more power to institute or establish Slavery than to institute or establish monarchy."[9] The party's motto was "Free Soil, Free Speech, Free Labor, Free Men." While nominally "Free Soil," the party was basically anti-slavery.

After a bitter election fight, the Free Soil Party candidates, Van Buren and Adams, polled 291,342 votes, or slightly more than ten percent of the total national vote cast. The Party elected five Congressmen. Zachary Taylor and Millard Fillmore, the Whig national candidates, won the election. The Free Soil Party also put up national candidates in the 1852 elections, with John P. Hale heading the ticket. This time it polled only 156,000 votes. Franklin Pierce, a Democratic tool of the planters, was elected. Historically, the Free Soil Party was the direct forerunner of the Republican Party, the party of the Second American Revolution.

Negro leaders and workers took an active part in the building and struggles of the Free Soil Party, which operated chiefly in the North. Frederick Douglass, by then the outstanding Negro leader, was present at the founding convention of the party and gave it his general support. He still retained his formal affiliation, however, with the fragment of the old Liberty Party that persisted as late as 1854. A militant Abolitionist, Douglass was highly critical of the limited program of the Free Soilers, which was primarily a fight against the extension of slavery. He said in *The North Star* of March 25, 1849: "The free soil movement has done, and is still doing much harm. It is standing in the way, blocking up the path, and cutting off supplies, from a higher and holier movement than it has ever aspired to be."[10] On the other hand, many Free Soilers, like Wilmot, differentiated themselves sharply and even bitterly from the Abolitionists and their revolutionary program of Negro emancipation.

Douglass by this time had broken completely with Garrison sectarianism and was now fully embarked upon his program of political action. The break was dramatized when Douglass launched *The North Star* in Rochester, New York, on December 3, 1847—a move which Garrison actively opposed. For Garrison's slogan, "No Union with Slaveholders," Douglass substituted his own, "No Union with Slavery." Garrison, with typical sectarian narrowness, never forgave Douglass for this political break and descended to the most scurrilous personal attacks against him. Gerrit Smith, Birney, and other political actionists supported Douglass; Wendell Phillips remained in the Garrison camp. Garrison's hatred of Douglass continued right up to the Civil War and beyond it. But, obviously, Douglass' more realistic position was justified by the course of historic political development.

STEVENS AND SUMNER

In 1852, death removed from the Senate those temporizers and pseudo-fighters against the slave system—Webster and Clay. At almost the same time, two new and highly significant figures appeared in Congress, men who were destined to play central roles in leading the great battle against slavery. They were Thaddeus Stevens of Pennsylvania and Charles Sumner of Massachusetts, resolute battlers in the struggle to destroy slavery outright. Their advent to leadership in Congress was quick, sharp, and definite. It signified a great advance on the part of the growing anti-slavery coalition of the North —from trying to live with slavery to a determination to root it out, from the Free Soil policy to the policy of Abolition. Stevens and Sumner belong with Lincoln, Douglass, Phillips, and Garrison, as the great leaders of the Second Revolution.

Thaddeus Stevens was born in Vermont in 1792. He was a cripple with a clubfoot, the son of a shoemaker.[11] As a lawyer who had become a small capitalist, he already had a long record of fighting in anti-slavery causes when he was elected to the House of Representatives in 1849. There he stayed until his death in 1868, save for the years 1853-59. Stevens was a militant fighter for Negro emancipation and full social equality—a man made of the steel-like qualities necessary for the hard revolutionary struggle ahead. He won leadership almost immediately upon his arrival in Congress with a famous speech in February 1850. Denouncing slavery, he defied the South to put into effect its constantly repeated threat of secession. "It marked the first appearance in Congress," says Woodley, "of a Northerner fearless enough to hurl back at the South its own challenge."[12] Stevens became more hated by the reactionaries than any man who ever held Congressional office in this country. Adams, the reactionary historian, has called him "perhaps the most despicable, malevolent, and morally deformed character who has ever risen to high power in America."[13] But he was beloved by the masses, and his reputation rises with the passage of the years. He stands in the very front rank of the greatest revolutionists of the United States.

Charles Sumner was born in Boston in 1811. A lawyer, he opposed the annexation of Texas, fought against the Mexican War, and strongly resisted the extension of slavery. In 1848 he was a Free Soil Party candidate for Congress. Elected to the United States Senate in 1851, he remained there until he died in 1874. Sumner was brilliant in debate, a hard-bitten fighter, and an ardent Abolitionist. Frederick Douglass called him the Wilberforce of the American anti-slavery cause. Sumner, like Stevens, was violently hated by the slaveholders. In 1856 one of their number, Brooks of South Carolina, made a cowardly attack upon him while he was unarmed and seriously crippled him. All through the Civil War and into the Reconstruction period, Sumner was the outstanding anti-slavery leader in the Senate.

14. American Slavery in the Mid-Nineteenth Century

After the Compromise of 1850 there was but a short respite in the national struggle over slavery until the rival groups again got at each other's throats. If this lull was more uneasy and shorter than the one following the Compromise of 1820, the basic contradictions between the contending class forces were fundamentally much more acute and therefore quicker to burst forth again into flame. Let us, in this interim period, take a further look at the system of human slavery which was the bone of contention in the ever-deepening national economic and political conflict.

History condemned American chattel slavery to death for three fundamental reasons: first, because it acted as an intolerable brake upon the free development of United States capitalism; second, because it was an archaic and inefficient system of agriculture and increasingly out of place in the modern capitalist United States; and third, because it was a complete denial of all human rights and constituted a threat to the welfare and freedom of the great mass of working people, white as well as Negro.

In our narrative so far, we have dealt chiefly with the first of these contradictions, namely, the conflict between the industrialists and the plantation owners over such elementary questions as the control of the national market, the tariff, the distribution of the land, and the political domination of the state and Federal governments. This struggle was eventually to reach such a pitch of violence and desperation that the forces of industrialism had to fight for their very lives against the encroachments of the plantation-slave system. As for the economic inefficiency of slavery, we shall deal with that contradiction when we analyze the two great economic and political forces arrayed against each other at the outbreak of the Civil War. Here, let us confine ourselves to examining the third basic contradiction: the human—or rather, inhuman—anti-democratic aspects of slavery.

BRUTAL EXPLOITATION

Hosts of writers, in the North as well as the South, now try to gloss over the horrors of slavery and to picture it as an easy-going system. They picture the slaves as well cared-for and even beloved of their masters, and living in indolent, irresponsible contentment. This concept, in fact, is widespread in conservative bourgeois circles, who appear to draw their ideas of slavery from the nostalgic songs of Stephen Foster. But the reality was quite different. Slavery was a murderously brutal system, the worst of all methods of human exploitation.

As Marx points out (see Chapter 3), the planters were landowner-capitalists and their objective was to wring all possible profits from the labor of their unwilling slaves. Especially on the larger plantations, they drove their slaves as hard as they could under this primitive system. Americans were notorious for over-working their slaves. "In the United States slaves on the large plantations began work at sunrise, and toiled to the crack of the whip . . . until sundown. . . . In Brazil conditions were generally easier for the slaves . . . we are told that at three in the afternoon, at least at Pernambuco, the heart of the sugar belt, work ceased, and the slave had the rest of the day to himself . . . Slaves in America welcomed Sundays and the days around Christmas as periods of rest and recreation. In Brazil not only did the slaves have Sundays and Christmas, but something like over thirty holidays on the Catholic calendar."[1] Even after the Portuguese stopped celebrating some of their religious holidays, these were still kept for the slaves.

Marx says, "In proportion as the export of cotton grew to be a vital interest of the slave states, overwork became a factor in the calculated and calculating system, so that in many places it was 'good business' to use up the Negroes' lives in seven years. No longer did the slave owner aim merely at getting a certain quantity of useful products out of the work of his slaves. He now wanted to extract surplus labor itself."[2] Although the American planters lacked the "efficiency methods" of today, they had many devices for getting the maximum amount of work out of their slaves. For one thing, on the larger plantations they used the gang system, by which the slaves were constantly under the observation of the drivers and overseers. They also had the task system—a notorious device for speeding the work; each slave, according to sex, age, and strength, was given a certain task

for his or her day's work, after which the worker was supposed to be
at leisure. The result of this was to hurry the slaves to increase
production.

The boss system, too, was contrived to wring the maximum
amount of work out of them. The immediate bosses of the slaves
were the field "drivers." These were Negro slaves; but they were
given small privileges for hurrying the work along in the face of the
studied go-slow methods of the field hands. The overseers, who were
whites and the working managers of the slaves, sometimes got regular
salaries—$200 to $600 or more per year—but generally they worked
on a crude bonus system. The more cotton they produced, the bigger
the wages they got. In tobacco, where the plantation units were
smaller, this driving method was not practical. Says Cairnes, in *The
Slave Power,* "It is a maxim of slave management in slave importing
countries that the most effective economy is that which takes out of
the human chattel in the shortest space of time, the utmost amount
of exertion it is capable of putting forth."[3]

Olmsted, who made a tour of the South just before the Civil War
and who was not an Abolitionist, quotes local opinion of a typical
cotton planter in the neighborhood: "He's got three plantations, and
he puts the hardest overseers he can get on them. He's all the time
buying 'n----s,' and they say around here that he works them to death.
. . . The overseers around here have to go armed; their life wouldn't
be safe if they didn't." Rhodes quotes an Alabama planter who said
that if the overseers make "plenty of cotton the owners never ask
how many 'n----s' they kill."[4]

On overseers' wages, which in some cases reached $2,000 annually,
Olmsted quotes a local comment: "A real devil of an overseer would
get almost any wages he'd ask; because if it was told around that such
a man made so many bales to the hand, everybody would be trying
to get him."[5] Phillips, an apologist of slavery, thus characterizes
overseers in general: "They were crude in manner, barely literate,
commonplace in capacity, capable only of ruling slaves by severity in
a rule-of-thumb routine."[6] All this helps to explain why the life span
of slaves was far shorter than that of whites, why seven to ten years
was their working period, and why old slaves were a comparative
rarity on the plantations. Patrick Henry once called overseers "the
most abject, degraded, and unprincipled race."

Many present-day apologists for slavery such as Gunnar Myrdal[7]
argue that, inasmuch as slaves were valuable property, the planters

had every reason to, and did, take good care of them—even as they took care of their farm animals. A fine thing, indeed, to compare the state of human beings to that of beasts on the farm. But even if slaves were as well cared for as farm animals, just what would this have meant? Faulkner comments as follows upon how farmers and planters in those days treated their animals: "Horses are in general, even valuable ones, worked to death and starved. They plow, cart, and ride them to death, at the same time they give little heed to their food. . . . This bad treatment extends to draft oxen, to their cows, sheep, and swine."[8]

Of course, there were some "good masters." But this was often a frail and dubious advantage to the slaves. Well known as "good masters" were George Washington, Thomas Jefferson, James Madison, and Andrew Jackson. But Washington, known in his time as a "scientific" farmer, was noted for his keen exploitation of his slaves.[9] Even the liberal Jefferson, who politically was against slavery, did not hesitate to sell a dozen of his 150 slaves in the open market when hard up for money.[10] Jackson, whom James calls "an ideal slave-owner," occasionally did some professional slave-trading, and he complained that he had to put in irons some refractory runaway slaves who apparently did not appreciate their "good master."[11] Madison, too, sold his slaves when short of money.[12]

SLAVE WORKING AND LIVING CONDITIONS

The working period of slaves was normally from sunup to sundown, six days a week. In midsummer this meant up at four A.M. and out in the fields until nine P.M. Not unusually, the last one out of the slaves' quarters in the morning felt the driver's lash. There were no laws to prevent the planters from working slaves as long and as hard as they pleased, and God help the slave who protested. Sundays were usually holidays, but at harvest time the masters could cancel these days off as they saw fit.

Apologists for slavery claim that the slaves were at least amply fed. But the record does not bear this out. Frederick Douglass, who worked for many years as a slave on a big plantation in Maryland, states that the monthly ration for a field hand was eight pounds of pickled pork (very poor quality), or its equivalent in fish, (also of bad quality), one bushel of Indian corn meal, and one pint of salt—with less for children, women, and the aged.[13] The house servants and the artisans got somewhat better food. On some plantations the slaves were allowed to eke out their meager rations by means of tiny gardens, with maybe a pig or chicken. Innumerable records of the plantation regimes bear out Douglass' account of the slaves' diet. McMaster cites a Louisiana planter who stated that the cost of feeding his slaves averaged $7.50 each per year, or a trifle over two cents a day.[14] A U.S. Treasury report, published in 1846, estimated at $30 the yearly cost of the upkeep of a slave.[15] Such figures tell their own tragic story. In cases where they were hired out by their masters by the day—a widespread practice in or near the cities—the slaves usually got a small share of their wages. This enabled some, by many years of rigid economy, eventually to buy themselves free.

The slaves were clothed no better than they were fed. Douglass reports that the slaves he worked with were allowed two tow-linen shirts and one pair of trousers for summer wear; and for winter, one pair of woolen trousers, a woolen jacket, and a pair of the coarsest shoes. A Federal Writers' Project essay, written in 1936 on the basis of interviewing several hundred ex-slaves in Virginia, paints this picture of the slaves' garb: "The usual dress for a man was canvas trousers and a cotton shirt with half elbow sleeves. Women wore a cotton 'shift' and a heavier dress over it. Children wore a simple 'tow' shirt, the discarded apparel of grown-ups, or a guano bag with armholes cut in the corners."[16] "All observers agree that the slaves who labored on the cotton and sugar plantations presented a ragged, unkempt, and dirty appearance."[17]

The slaves lived in more or less tumble-down huts. They had no beds, except those they could contrive for themselves. Like work animals, they were entitled to "medical treatment," but what this amounted to may be imagined. When the slaves grew old, they were generally allowed to remain as unwelcome guests on the plantations, but often they were "freed" and thrown upon the county authorities for sustenance. Kirkland estimates at $20 the total yearly cost of maintaining a slave.[18] This was less than convicts were allowed in jail, and not half of what was allowed at the time for the upkeep of non-working inmates in skinflint Northern poor houses.

The foregoing description, however, represents only the "rosy" side of the slaves' conditions, during the "prosperous" periods when the prices of cotton, tobacco, and sugar were high and times were good. But periodically, like the industrial system in the North, the Southern plantation system went through crises of overproduction, especially in cotton. Often, too, whole regions were stricken by drought. Unlike the Northern employers, the slaveholders could not throw their workers out on the streets, as they represented invested capital; so they allowed them to starve on the plantations. Aptheker describes devastating scenes of hunger, misery, and desolation among the slaves during such periods of economic dislocation and drought.[19] The stories of the "good care" given to the slaves during their periods of non-productivity are just so many fairy tales, concocted by the professional defenders of slavery.

A SOCIETY SUSTAINED BY THE LASH

"Violence was the essential element of slavery. From the first slave-hunt in Africa to the surrender of the Rebel army at Appomattox . . . violence was the law of its being."[20] Contrary to all the apologists for slavery, no people could voluntarily accept such barbarous exploitation and degradation as that inflicted upon the slaves. The slaves with normal aspirations for freedom, could and did think and plan and conspire and revolt. The planters understood this perfectly well and they enforced the enslavement of the Negroes with an elaborate system of repression and terror. This was true not only in the American South, but also in every slave country in the world.

Slavery in the United States, which was by far the most severe in the western hemisphere, involved the complete denial of all human and political rights to the slaves. Slaves were not persons, but property. They had no rights of family; they were married and divorced at the master's will; their families were dispersed whenever the master saw fit to sell slaves. Slaves worked under the lash with no say whatever as to their working hours, food, or living conditions. They were systematically kept illiterate; and generally, to teach a slave to read or write was a crime. Slaves could not acquire property, save to the extent that they had the master's permission. They had no right to defend themselves against the master's brutality, and slaves who raised their hands against a white man, no matter what the justification, were barbarously punished. They could not testify in court. The judges who tried them for crimes were slaveholders, and even though a thousand Negroes saw a white man kill a slave, their word was not taken against him. Slaves' oaths were not binding, and they could not use or make contracts. And, of course, they were stripped completely of every right to a voice in the government under which they lived.

"Justice" for slaves in the ante-bellum South was crude and brutal. There were a few laws on the books, allegedly designed to protect the slaves from extreme cruelty; but little attention was paid to them. For minor "crimes," slaves were arbitrarily punished by the masters themselves. For major offenses, usually a few neighbors were called in to form the court, or a special court was made up of local justices of the peace. One of the origins of lynching in the South may be traced to this whole informal, offhand system of "justice." These kangaroo courts could always be depended upon to deal summarily with Negroes brought before them, but even this speed did not always suit the whites. Sometimes they lynched slaves, as many accounts show. This was done to terrify the whole Negro community. Whites, too, were occasionally lynched in the pre-war South, and in the West and North as well. Aptheker reports the lynching of a slave in 1827,[21] and Phillips cites the case of a slave who was burned alive by a crowd of some 3,000 people in Sumter County, Alabama, in 1855.[22] Masters were reimbursed for slaves officially executed.

With variations here and there, the low legal status of the slaves was written into the slave codes, or special laws for Negroes, which existed in every Southern slave state in the Union. The codes were backed up by the lash, the branding iron, the fetter, the prison, the curfew, the "Negro breaker," the faggot, and the gallows. Semimilitary rule prevailed all over the pre-Civil War "sunny South," with its night road patrols and heavy military establishments. The vigilante-like regime was based on the principle that "every white man is a soldier." And behind all this stood the armed forces of the United States, to enforce slavery.

Wilson quotes from the slave code prevailing in Washington, the nation's capital, as late as 1862: "If a slave should be guilty of the seemingly small offense of rambling, going abroad in the night, and riding horses in the daytime without leave, he should be punished by whipping, cropping, and branding with the letter R." If a slave should strike a white man, he should be "cropped." A slave convicted of petit treason, arson, or murder should have "his right hand cut off, be hanged in the usual manner; the head severed from the body, the body divided into four quarters; the head and quarters set up in the most public places of the county." A person "stealing a slave, or being accessory thereto, and being convicted, or who shall obstinately or of malice stand mute, shall suffer death without benefit of clergy." Runaway slaves who refused to surrender and resisted, "it shall be lawful to shoot, kill and destroy"; and any one thus shooting and killing "shall be indemnified from any prosecution for such killing." The value of such slave shall be paid by "the treasurer of the province out of the public stock."[23]

THE NEGRO WOMAN SLAVE

Slavery was particularly harsh upon Negro women. They bore the responsibility of raising their families and working regularly in the fields, side by side with the men. They had no rights to their persons, as against the sex wishes of the masters. Frazier says that "there is sufficient evidence of widespread concubinage and even polygamy on the part of the white masters."[24] Phillips says that "The rape of a female slave was not a crime, but a mere trespass on the master's property."[25] And Olmsted states that in Virginia and other slave exporting states "women were regarded much the same as brood mares."[26] "Some masters," says Frazier, "with no regard for the preferences of their slaves, mated them as they did their stock. There were instances when Negro males were used as stallions."[27]

The slave woman, in view of the instability or absence of marriage, tended to become the head of the family. Aptheker says "During slavery there was no marriage *per se* and therefore whatever household existed revolved completely about the woman, and it was the female, not the male, who provided what little degree of stability existed for the pre-Civil War Southern Negro's home."[28] For the Negro woman to assume this family authority was facilitated by the fact of the high degree of honor and esteem in which she had been held in African tribal life. The authoritative position of the Negro slave woman also reflected itself in the organization of the master's household. This was almost always in control of a Negro woman housekeeper, with exceptional authority over all the other servants and over the rearing of the slaveholder's children. As for the Negroes' children, they were put to work in the fields almost as soon as they were able to toddle about.

Not unnaturally, Negro slave women also played important parts in the oft-recurring slave insurrections and other forms of slave resistance. Aptheker cites characteristic cases of this in Virginia, Mississippi, and elsewhere. Sojourner Truth and the celebrated fighter, Harriet Tubman, were true symbols of the brave Negro women of slavery times.

RELIGION AND SLAVERY

Marx says, "Religion is the opium of the people." Enlarging upon this elementary truth, Lenin remarks: "Religion is one of the forms of spiritual oppression which everywhere weighs upon the masses who are crushed by continuous toil for others, by poverty and loneliness. The helplessness of the exploited in their struggle against the exploiters inevitably generates a belief in a better life after death, even as the helplessness of the savage in his struggle with nature gives rise to a belief in gods, devils, miracles, etc. Religion teaches those who toil in poverty all their lives to be resigned and patient in this world, and consoles them with the hope of reward in heaven."[29]

Historically, during all the systems of human exploitation throughout the ages, religion has always been cultivated by the exploiters, along with ruthless violence, to hold their unwilling slaves in submission. This was true of the slaveholders in the South, as well as everywhere else where human masses have been held in subjection and robbed. The Southern slave-masters used religion in a double sense—as a justification of the slave system (of which more later) and to cultivate obedience among their slaves.

For this latter purpose they searched the scriptures for texts calling upon the believers to obey their masters, and such items were easy to find in the Bible. The Southern preachers spouted to the slaves about submission and found all possible excuse and justification for this worst form of tyranny and exploitation. In the early days of slavery, the business of Christianizing the slaves loomed as quite a problem—many planters had qualms about holding Christians in slavery. But, as we saw in Chapter 3, the masters soon overcame these first naive scruples and concluded that Christians, as well as any others, were quite fit for slavery. After this they made systematic use of religion and of all the churches as mainstays of the slave system. Birney called the churches "the bulwarks of American slavery."

Aptheker gives various examples of the types of sermons delivered to slaves by white preachers in the pre-Civil War decades. "We choose one that was popular among clergymen of the Protestant Episcopal Church in Maryland and Virginia during the eighteenth and nineteenth centuries. The slaves here are assured that God has willed that they occupy their lowly position. They are told that unless they perform their allotted tasks well they will suffer eternally in Hell. Specifically, they are warned that the Lord is greatly offended when they are saucy, impudent, stubborn, or sullen. Nor are they to alter their behavior if the owner is cross or mean or cruel; that is the Lord's concern, not theirs, and they are to leave the master's punishment to Him."[30]

According to Aptheker, the slaves managed to draw quite different lessons from the Bible and from what they knew of religion. "Their God had cursed man-stealers, had led slaves out of bondage, had promised the earth as an inheritance for the humble, had prophesied that the first would be last and the last would be first. Their God had created all men of one blood, and had manifested no preference among those into whom he had breathed life."[31]

The Protestant churches split eventually over the question of slavery, and established Northern and Southern branches. It was thus that the Methodist and Baptist churches split in 1844-45.[32] There was much anti-slavery sentiment in the Northern churches, but the dominant clerics remained openly hostile to Abolitionism. Just a few years before the Methodist and Baptist splits took place, says McMaster, "The Methodist Bishop of New Hampshire repudiated the Abolitionists; the American Bible Society declined to accept money from the American Anti-Slavery Society to be used to put Bibles in the hands of slaves, and the Baptists' General Tract Society of Philadelphia required its general agents to pledge themselves not to meddle with the question of slavery."[33] The Presbyterian and Protestant Episcopal churches, both of which had many slaveholders as members, did not split, North and South, until 1861. The Catholic Church remained intact all through the Civil War, a militant pro-slavery organization.

Some of the upper class Jews were not to be outdone by their Christian brethren when it came to profiting from slavery. Reverend Dr. David Einhorn, a Jewish Abolitionist of the time, disavowed "the great Rabbi of New York," who "to the delight of the Jewish slaveowners and stockholders," had "proclaimed the God of Israel as the God of slavery."[34] Obviously, the rabbi in question was affiliated with the big pro-Southern bankers and merchants of his city. Between 1717 and 1721, says Marcus, "Jewish slave traders were responsible for two of the largest slave cargoes to be brought into New York, in the first half of the eighteenth century."[35]

SLAVE BREEDING STATES

One of the most terrible aspects of slavery was the internal slave trade, which brought out many of the worst features of the whole rotten system. The domestic slave-trader, who was a sort of hatchet-man for the supposedly cultured planters, was generally looked down upon and ostracized by polite slaveholder society. The traders were bitterly hated by the Negroes. The sharp discredit ascribed to the profession actually benefited the slave-traders by reducing the competition among them. It was not too logical for the planters to condemn those who bought and sold slaves, while they glorified those who worked the slaves to death on the plantations or sang the praises of the slave system in Congress.

The great market for slaves during the four decades before the Civil War was in the rapidly growing cotton and sugar plantations of the Gulf states, and especially the cotton states. In 1840 two-thirds of all slaves were in the cotton states, and the percentage increased.[36] During this period, it is estimated that some 25,000 slaves were smuggled into the United States each year from the West Indies and Africa, in violation of the anti-slave trading laws. In 18 months of the years 1859-60, no less than 85 slave ships were reported to have fitted out in New York Harbor.[37] Meanwhile, there was a big campaign in the South for repeal of the anti-slave trading law. The "African Labor Supply Association" was formed in Mississippi, with J. B. D. De Bow (editor of *De Bow's Review*) as President, to cultivate the African slave trade.[38]

But these imported slaves by no means satisfied the voracious Southern demand for workers. Therefore, slaves were brought in large numbers from the older slave states, where cotton played a lesser role; that is, from Virginia, North Carolina, Maryland, Delaware, Kentucky, Missouri, and Tennessee. These became slave-breeding states, especially Virginia. Estimates of the number of slaves taken from these states to the deep South ran up to 100,000 a year. This traffic to the Gulf states was the rich field of the professional slave-traders, and provided an opposition to the reopening of the slave trade with Africa. They gathered up their slaves by purchase, stealing, or kidnaping. Slave-stealing was widespread in the South, and the penalty for it was frequently death. Kidnaping of free Negroes was also a common offense, but no serious penalties were attached to this practice. Most of the slave gangs were gathered together by buying slaves from "respectable" planters, who did not hesitate to sell their workers "down the river" when their financial interests were furthered thereby.

McMaster gives factual details of the barbarous slave auctions. "A common result," says he, "of the sale of slaves at auction or by dealers was the separation of husbands and wives, parents and children, the sale of very young children, and, at times, infants."[39] Du Bois points out that a Negro babe at birth was worth $200 to $300. One of the major slave-trading centers of the country was Washington, D.C. This traffic in human beings was a great tragedy in the life of the slaves.

By various means, the slaves were transported South—to the rice, sugar, and cotton plantations of the Gulf areas. Some went down the Ohio and Mississippi rivers by boat; others were taken by sea, along the coasts, in real slave ships; but most were driven overland on foot in the notorious slave "coffles." They were a common sight in the ante-bellum South—long trains of slaves, who had been torn from their families and friends, chained together and plodding along the roads, heading South to be worked to death by unknown masters. Such coffles, marching under the lash of the drivers and making about 25 miles a day, were blood kin to the original slave coffles in Africa. The casualties among the slaves were heavy under this brutal treatment. Coleman estimates a loss of about 25 percent in the first year of such forced migration.[40] This was American civilization in the mid-nineteenth century.

It was out of such barbarous exploitation and tyrannical oppression that the Southern slave-masters built their columned mansions and their luxurious existence. The slaveholders became petty dictators. As Redding points out, slavery "tended to inflate the ego of most planters beyond all reason; they became arrogant, strutting, quarrelsome knights; they issued commands; they made laws; they shouted their orders, they expected deference and self-abasement; they were choleric and easily insulted."[41] It was a hollow and corrupt life—with its absurd pretensions of democracy, its tawdry and paper-thin culture, and its make-believe of warm-hearted hospitality. Still in existence 75 years after the Declaration of Independence had pronounced all men "free and equal," chattel slavery was an outrage and a disgrace to the United States. The exploiter society erected upon it was as rotten and decadent as were its foundations set in human slavery.

15. Slave Revolts and Fugitive Slaves

The decade of 1850-1860 was one of rapidly sharpening struggle between the Southern planters and the Northern industrialists, and their respective allies. The conflicting class interests of the two great groups were irreconcilable. The Compromise of 1850, far from settling the elemental contest, stimulated and inflamed it. The struggle involved all areas and classes in the country and was indeed "the irrepressible conflict" that Seward called it. It was becoming swiftly more intense in all of its aspects—ideological, economic, political—and, during this stormy decade, it took on definitely a military character in some states. A great political crisis was in the making, and all roads were leading to the profound revolutionary collision of 1861.

SLAVE UNREST AND INSURRECTIONS

"The pre-Civil War decade," says Aptheker, "witnessed an increased straining by the Negro people against the degradation and oppression of their enslavement."[1] This took the usual forms used by rebellious slaves—mass flight, insurrections, arson on the plantations, and the like. The slaves sensed the growing tension in the country over the question of slavery, and they reacted to it in their own ways of discontent and struggle. Underlying this widespread slave unrest, and giving force and strength to it, was the fact that during the decade of 1850-1860 cotton production almost doubled, climbing up from 2,136,000 bales in 1850 to 3,841,000 bales in 1860.[2] With this went a correspondingly deeper exploitation of the slaves and worsening of their general conditions. The arrogance and political aggressiveness of the planters were also intensified. All this affected the slaves deeply.

Aptheker lists dozens of insurrectionary conspiracies and rebellious acts during this period.[3] They took place in all parts of the South. Often whites were involved and, in the Southwest, the Indians were allies of the slaves. The year 1856 was an especially high point in this wave of unrest. There were important slave movements in Louisiana, Florida, Arkansas, Georgia, South Carolina, Virginia, Kentucky, and Tennessee. In a plot in New Orleans in 1853, an estimated 2,500 slaves were involved. Dallas, Texas was burned in July 1860; slaves were blamed for it, and three of them—Sam, Cato, and Patrick—were executed.

The situation in Texas was typical. The Cherokee County *Enquirer* of January 12, 1857, said, "Servile insurrections seem to be the order of the day in this state."[4] Coleman says, "Throughout the Fall of 1856 a series of startling allegations regarding slave insurrections broke through the habitual reserve maintained on the topic by the Southern press. Wild rumors of an all-embracing slave plot, extending from Delaware to Texas, with its execution set for Christmas Day, spread through the slaveholding states."[5] In these movements, large numbers were arrested, hundreds were lashed and tortured, and at least 60 were killed.

The insurrectionary spirit also affected the considerable number of slaves who had been put to work in the various local industries in the South. In 1856, some 60 slaves employed in the Cumberland Iron Works in Tennessee were involved in a plot, which was exposed beforehand. For this projected revolt, 20 slaves were hanged, some by outright lynching. One slave was whipped to death in a vain effort to make him stoolpigeon on his co-workers. A white man was also hanged for complicity.[6]

The slave struggles were influenced by many factors. Often they were aided or led by the large number of freed Negroes that had gradually grown up in the South. They were facilitated, too, by the fact that many slaves were sent to the cities by their masters, where they worked as wage workers—laborers, carters, blacksmiths, cooks, etc. There they were able to gather a great deal of information about what was going on in the United States and the world. The slaves were undoubtedly affected, too, by news of the Negro convention movement and by the agitation of the Abolitionists, some of which reached them. Thus, in the 1856 elections, according to Lincoln himself, the slaves of Tennessee developed high hopes that John C. Frémont, the candidate of the newly-formed Republican Party, would free them if elected. When he lost the election, they "flashed into insurrection."[7] The slaves also reacted widely to John Brown's raid of October 16, 1859, when they finally learned about it. And all this was just a prelude to "the greatest slave insurrection of all" during the Civil War.

Many cases are on record of whites assisting the slaves in their conspiracies, revolts, and fights. Aptheker has listed many such instances, and so has Johnston. The latter, in a special article devoted to the cooperation of whites with Negro slaves, mentions among others the case of James Allen of Virginia. Allen, a white man, had helped a slave to run away. He was taken into the woods by a mob and commanded to tell where the slave had gone. When he refused, he was flogged so badly that he died—but without revealing the desired information.[8]

Under pressure of the sharpening struggle, not the least phase of which was the growing activity of the slaves, the Abolitionist movement was swiftly discarding its erstwhile illusions of non-resistance. By 1850, Douglass and other Negroes were almost unanimous in supporting the insurrectionist policy, and they and the white Abolitionists were ever more militant in meeting the arrogance of the slaveholders and their Northern agents. Biel thus describes the historical evolution of the Abolitionist movement in this respect: "Originally this aimed at gradual emancipation induced by moral suasion. Then came the demand for immediate liberation, but still only via moral suasion. Then followed a split into those favoring political action and those opposed. Finally, and most noticeable in this decade, there arose a body of direct activists whose idea was 'to carry the war into Africa.' "[9]

Today many plush-chair strategists, including some alleged friends of the Negro people, criticize the Negroes, saying that the slaves did not show enough rebellious reaction against the terrible system of bondage under which they lived. But such critics, besides deliberately ignoring the records of innumerable slave uprisings, also conveniently overlook the immense obstacles which stood in the way of slave revolts in the United States. Isolated, illiterate, terrorized, and living virtually in the midst of the armed camp of their enemies, it was extremely difficult for the slaves to organize uprisings. History shows that every such attempt in the United States failed utterly and its leaders were savagely executed. These deadly facts were quite well known to the slaves.

In organizing revolts, Negro slaves on the American plantations faced vastly greater difficulties than did the slaves in the Spanish, French, and Portuguese plantations in the West Indies, Brazil, and Central America. First, the slaves in these areas sometimes outnumbered the whites by as much as ten or twenty to one, which helped to overcome the whites' superior military equipment. But the slaves in the American South as a whole were usually in the minority, and in those localities where they did have a majority it was relatively small. Second, the Spanish, French, and Portuguese slaves lived under a disciplinary control far less severe and effective than that under which the American slaves had to exist; hence, they were in a much better position to move about and organize themselves for struggle. Third, the slaves in the Spanish, French, and Portuguese colonies faced governments much less strong and capable of mobilizing forces against them than was the case in the United States.

Under such extremely difficult conditions, slave revolts in the United States, by the very nature of things, were bound to be heroic acts of sheer desperation with little prospect of success. The Negro people of this country, therefore, may well be proud of the slaves who bravely led so many insurrections.

THE FIGHT AGAINST THE FUGITIVE SLAVE ACT

A weak spot in the Southern slave system, especially after 1800, was the flight of slaves to the North and freedom. Between that date and 1850, the slaves who made their way North over the Underground Railroad averaged about 2,000 a year. In the last decade before the Civil War, however, this exodus became a broad movement. This constituted a grave loss to the slaveholders. The possibility of winning freedom in this way spread wide waves of unrest among the great body of slaves. This was why the planters insisted so much upon the Fugitive Slave Act as part of the Compromise of 1850, and also why they made such a determined effort to enforce this infamous law.

During the decade in which the Fugitive Slave Act of 1850 was in force the planters were in a dominant position politically. They controlled the legislative, executive, and judicial branches of the Federal government. Presidents Zachary Taylor, Millard Fillmore, Franklin Pierce, and James Buchanan did the bidding of the slaveholders. With such controls, the planters were able to create a whole machinery of U.S. marshals, commissioners, deputies, etc., in the North and to set them all vigorously to bringing runaway slaves back to the South. The Fugitive Slave Act of 1793, which imposed only fines for violations, had been rendered virtually inoperative by strong resistance in the North, and the slaveowners, with their law of 1850, which imposed imprisonment, were determined that this would not happen again.

The new law was brutally enforced. Greeley says that, "In repeated instances, the first notice the alleged fugitive had of his peril was given him by a blow on the head, sometimes with a heavy club or stick of wood; and being thus knocked down, he was carried, bleeding and insensible before the facile commissioner, who made short work of identifying him, and earning his ten dollars by remanding him to Slavery."[10] Under the law, the commissioners received a ten-dollar fee if they condemned a Negro, but only five dollars if they set him free.

Such scenes were repeated all over the North. Many Negroes were slugged, and some shot and killed. Numerous freemen were also caught in the dragnet and hustled South into slavery. The attacked Negroes often resisted boldly, declaring that they would rather die than be returned to slavery. More than one slave-hunter was killed in futile efforts to seize Negroes. As a result of the vigorous slave-catching campaign, which enlisted many underworld elements in the North, Greeley says, "Within the first year of its existence, more persons probably were seized as fugitives than during the preceding sixty years."[11]

It was in this deadly situation that Frederick Douglass delivered his famous Fourth of July oration in Rochester, New York, in 1852. Eloquently, he pointed out that the Negro, free or slave, had no grounds for rejoicing in this national holiday, commemorating the foundation of the Republic, which was supposedly dedicated to the principle that all men are born free and equal. Douglass cried out: "What to the American slave is your Fourth of July? I answer, a day that reveals to him more than all other days of the year, the gross injustice and cruelty to which he is the constant victim. To him your celebration is a sham; your boasted liberty an unholy license; your national greatness, swelling vanity; your sounds of rejoicing are empty and heartless; your denunciations of tyrants, brass-fronted impudence; your shouts of liberty and equality, hollow mockery; your prayers and hymns, your sermons and thanksgivings, with all your religious parade and solemnity, are to him mere bombast, fraud, deception, impiety, and hypocrisy—a thin veil to cover up crimes which would disgrace a nation of savages. There is not a nation of the earth guilty of practices more shocking and bloody than are the people of these United States at this very hour."[12]

The Abolitionist movement immediately began an active struggle to halt the outrageous slave-catching campaign. Nor did it content itself with passing resolutions of protest, sending petitions to Washington, or hoping for relief in distant elections. Instead, in tune with the increasingly revolutionary spirit of the people, it had recourse to direct action. The Government was betraying the people by the monstrous slave-hunt; therefore the people would undertake by direct intervention, to prevent the application of the fugitive slave law. This determination brought about one of the most bitter political struggles in the history of the United States.

There were scores of cases where groups of citizens, taking the law into their own hands, interfered in the slave-catching business, beat up the slave-catchers, and released their victims. The first number of the *New York Times* on September 18, 1851, contains a typical account of how a number of Negroes in Christiana, Pennsylvania, along with white sympathizers, defended a free Negro, William Parker, from seizure by slave-catchers, who were aided by a U.S. marshal, killing two of them in the process. Vigilance committees of Negroes and whites were set up in many places to challenge the work of the slave-hunters to defend the Negroes and to fight the fugitive slave law. The battle was also carried into the courts. In one case, it cost the Government $22,000 to deport a Negro woman, Margaret Garner, to the South.

Boston was an especially strong center of opposition to the slave-hunters. Hardly was the new law on the books when the local Abolitionists freed Shadrach Jenkins from the authorities and sped him off to Canada. Three months later Thomas Sims, a fugitive, became the object of another rescue attempt. But this time the Abolitionists, including some of the most famous, failed, and Sims was taken back to Georgia, where he was publicly whipped and dramatically returned to slavery.

Another famous case was that of Anthony Burns, a fugitive slave from Virginia, who was seized in Boston by a marshal in the winter of 1853. The Abolitionists took up his cause, great meetings were held, and an unsuccessful attempt was made to rescue him by force from the courthouse. Thomas Wentworth Higginson was wounded in this bitter fight. The court decided that Burns had to be returned to Virginia. But as he was taken away, "The people draped their houses in mourning and hissed the procession that took Burns to his ship." This incident did more to crystallize Northern sentiment against slavery than any other except the exploit of John Brown, "and this was the last time that a fugitive slave was taken from Boston."[13] "It took 22 companies of state militia, four platoons of marines, a battalion of United States artillerymen, and the city's police force . . . to ensure the performance of this shameful act, the cost of which, to the Federal Government alone, came to $40,000."[14] There were similar cases in various other Northern cities.

The Abolitionists also carried their resistance into Congress and the state legislatures. In the Senate, while the subservient Webster was calling upon the people to obey and enforce the Fugitive Slave Act, his Abolitionist co-senator from Massachusetts, Charles Sumner, boldly declared that he would not support the hated law, and he bade the people to take a similar attitude.[15] During the next years, from 1854 on, a number of the states in the North adopted "Personal Liberty" laws, the plain purpose of which was to block the enforcement of the slave-catching Federal law. In so doing, the people of the North, with a rising revolutionary spirit, collided head-on with the planter-controlled Government, denying it the right to return fugitive slaves from the free states. This time the states' rights argument was on the other foot.

The Massachusetts Personal Liberty Act of May 21, 1855, for example, contained a whole row of provisions designed to obstruct the Fugitive Slave Act.[16] It made the identification of fugitives almost impossible, and gave them the rights of *habeas corpus* and trial by jury; kidnapers were heavily penalized; state officers were forbidden to issue fugitive slave warrants under the Federal fugitive slave acts of 1793 and 1850; lawyers acting in behalf of claimants of runaway slaves were to be disbarred; sheriffs, constables, and others who arrested runaway slaves were to be removed, fined, and imprisoned; the militia was not to be used to help the slave-catchers; and the jails were not to be used to hold captured runaway slaves or to imprison persons convicted under the Fugitive Slave Act.

In Wisconsin, in March 1854, a fugitive slave named Joshua Glover was seized, but was forcibly released by sympathizers. Sherman M. Booth, a local editor, was arrested and charged with helping in the rescue. But he was released on a writ of *habeas corpus* by a judge of the Wisconsin Supreme Court, on the ground that the Federal Fugitive Slave Act was unconstitutional. Booth was later convicted in the Federal District Court, in January 1855, but was again released by a Wisconsin court. Meanwhile, the state passed a Personal Liberty law, which challenged the right of the United States Supreme Court to interfere in the matter. In 1858, however, the Supreme Court, headed by the notorious Judge Taney, reversed the decision of the

Wisconsin Supreme Court in the Booth case; but its decision, too, remained unenforced.

With such militant tactics, the Abolitionists and their hosts of sympathizers eventually rendered the hated Fugitive Slave Act virtually inoperative. The bitter fight created anti-slavery spirit far and wide in the North. It made vast numbers of people realize that they had to fight for their most cherished freedoms against the arrogant Southern slaveholders. It was a basic preparation for the tremendous revolutionary struggle soon to begin.

In 1854, the insatiable planters made a bold effort to seize Cuba. They wanted to expand their plantation system to that island and to cut it up into two or more states, which would mean at least four more members of the Senate for them. Besides, they were afraid that Cuba might begin a slave revolution and become another Haiti. So they had a group of their American ambassadors in Europe issue a manifesto from Ostend, Belgium, in which they gave Spain the alternative of either selling the island to the United States for some $20 million or having it taken from her by force. But this time the slaveholders overstepped themselves. Their crude plan of aggression failed owing to the opposition of Great Britain and of a North that was already embittered by the Fugitive Slave and Kansas-Nebraska Acts.

THE NEGRO EMIGRATION MOVEMENT

With the violent application of the Fugitive Slave Act, particularly in the early 1850's, the situation of the 100,000 or more fugitive slaves then living in the North became chaotic. Their whole status of fancied security was challenged overnight. An exodus to Canada began at once. According to Woodson, "Within thirty-six hours thereafter forty Negroes left Massachusetts for Canada. The Negro population of Columbia, Pennsylvania, decreased from 943 to 437. A Negro settlement at Sandy Lake in the northwestern part of that State was broken up altogether. Every member of a Negro Methodist Church, eighty-two in number, including the pastor, fled from a town in New York to Canada."[17]

In the terror some Negro leaders, themselves fugitives from slavery, had to take cover, as fighters in many countries have often had to do under similar circumstances. Frederick Douglass stood his ground, although, also a fugitive, he was in imminent danger of being seized and sent South. He spoke at meetings over the country, collected funds, and housed and fed fugitives. To preserve his free status he bought himself out of slavery, paying his erstwhile master $716.96. But this was little protection against kidnapers. Douglass was criticized by sectarian Garrisonians for paying for his freedom; this, they argued, was in violation of the principle of "no compensation to the slave-holders" for freeing their slaves. But the more practical-minded Negro people had long before adopted the sensible policy of getting out of slavery any way they could—by purchase, by flight, by revolt. Douglass acted in this established Negro tradition. After all, few or none realized in those years that emancipation was so close at hand. As late as 1859, Ralph Waldo Emerson, an Abolitionist, said, "No living man will see the end of slavery."[18]

The vicious terror unleashed under the Fugitive Slave Act also generated a considerable sentiment among Negroes for migration to countries other than Canada. The great mass, however, remained firmly opposed to leaving this country. As pointed out in Chapter 8, there had long been a feeling among some Negroes that the answer to the barbarous oppression, of both freemen and slaves, was a migration to Africa or elsewhere abroad. Paul Cuffee and John B. Russwurm, very prominent Negro leaders, had supported this idea a generation before; but after some initial hesitation, the organized Negro move-ment, and the Abolitionist movement in general, actively opposed the plan—especially as it was put forth by the American Colonization Society after 1817. Frederick Douglass was a particularly vigorous opponent of emigration and colonization in all their forms. And H. H. Garnet expressed the dominant Negro opinion when he said: "America is my home, my country, and I have no other."

The new growth of emigration sentiment among Negroes mani-fested itself strongly at the Negro people's convention of 1852 in Cincinnati. This convention, however, condemned once more the American Colonization Society and favored Canada as the place where fugitive slaves should go if they found it impossible to live as free people in the United States. The Negro people's convention of 1853, held in Douglass' home city of Rochester, New York, also rejected the overseas emigration plan, although in some circles there was obviously a strong and growing sentiment for it. After this convention had adjourned, the minority called a pro-emigration convention, to be held in 1854. This convention was duly held and it recommended that studies of Negro emigration should be made, with reports to the next convention in 1856.

The Negro leaders of this emigration movement were Martin R. Delany, co-founder with Frederick Douglass of *The North Star,* who favored colonizing in Nigeria; James Whitefield, who preferred Central America; and James T. Holley, who believed that Haiti was the best place. Considerable activity was displayed in behalf of each of these plans. Early in 1861 a ship with 2,000 Negro emigrants aboard sailed from Philadelphia to Haiti. The outbreak of the Civil War, by profoundly changing the situation of the Negro people, put an end to these particular emigration projects, although others were to be launched later from time to time.

In the preparation of his plans for American Negro colonization in Africa, Delany sounded a sharp note of bourgeois national ideology, the clearest as yet of any American Negro leader. He said: "Every people should be the originators of their own designs, the projectors of their own schemes, and creators of the events that lead to their destiny —the consummation of their desires. Situated as we are, in the United States, many, and almost insurmountable obstacles present themselves. We are four-and-a-half millions in number, free and bond; six hundred thousand free, and three-and-a-half million bond. We have native hearts and virtues, just as other nations; which in their pristine purity are noble, potent, and worthy of example. We are a nation within a nation—as the Poles in Russia, the Hungarians in Austria; the Welsh, Irish, and Scotch in the British dominions."[19] This was giving definite expression, in a generalized form, to the spirit that had brought the Negro masses, free and slave, to think like an oppressed people and which was causing them to build their own national institutions —churches, newspapers, fraternal orders, and political organizations.

THE DRED SCOTT CASE

Meanwhile, in the tense national setting of the sharpening struggle over Kansas, the most famous political-legal case in the history of the United States—that of the Negro, Dred Scott—became a major issue. Scott had been held as a slave in Missouri by one Dr. Emerson, an army surgeon. In 1834 he was taken to Fort Snelling in free territory, and he remained there, on free soil, for four years, marrying and having two children. In 1838, Scott was returned to Missouri and again held as a slave. In 1842, he sued for his freedom on the ground that he had been liberated by his residence on the free soil of Illinois and Wisconsin. The case dragged on. Scott won in the lower court, but the Supreme Court of Missouri decided against him in 1852. He also lost in the U.S. Circuit Court, and then appealed to the United States Supreme Court.

Of the nine Justices seated on the Supreme Court, five were from the South. They seized upon the opportunity to strike a sweeping blow at the whole anti-slavery movement. In January 1857, Chief Justice Roger B. Taney delivered the majority opinion, with Judges McLean and Curtis dissenting. Taney declared that Scott was not a citizen, but a slave. He ruled that Negroes were inferior to whites, that they could be justly reduced to slavery for their own benefit, that they "had no rights which a white man was bound to respect," and that they were not, and could not become, part of the American people, even when accorded the right to vote.

Taney based these harsh conclusions upon the pro-slavery clauses in the United States Constitution (see Chapter 4). He argued that under the Constitution slaves were property, just like any other property, and that, consequently the Constitution permitted no distinction between them and property in general. Therefore, the slaveholder had the full right to take his slaves to any part of the country and to maintain ownership in them there, even as he could with any other form of property. Declared Judge Taney, "The Act of Congress which prohibited a citizen from holding and owning property of this kind in the territory of the United States north of the line therein mentioned, is not warranted by the Constitution, and is therefore void."[20]

Here was the logic of the slave system carried to the ultimate. At one blow, Taney not only reduced Negroes to the status of inferior beings destitute of all human rights, but wiped out the Compromises of 1820 and 1850, which prohibited slavery in the territories north of the 36° 30' line. The decision, in effect, made slavery national in scope. Slaves could now be legally bought and sold in New York and Boston, and slave ships could once more freely ply their infamous trade. Under the decision, slavery could not be abolished anywhere without first changing the U.S. Constitution. This overrode the hitherto cherished slaveholder doctrine of states' rights—that each state could make its own laws about slavery, but of course, in this case there was no protest from the South.

Politically, the Supreme Court's decision meant that the arrogant cotton planters, as part of their growing offensive against their Northern enemies, had deemed the time ripe to knock out every legal restriction on the slave system. The decision was received with bitter protest in the North. Various state legislatures adopted resolutions condemning it as a reactionary usurpation of power without binding force, and virtually calling upon the people to nullify it by disobeying it. According to the Beards, Abraham Lincoln urged that the President and the Congress ought to disregard Taney's opinion as a rule of law, that slavery ought to be abolished in the territories in spite of the doctrines announced by the Court,[21] and that the Court itself should be re-constituted by new appointments.

As usual, Frederick Douglass sounded the real note of the Abolitionists in opposition to the Dred Scott decision, in New York, May 11, 1857. Blasting the Supreme Court's infamous ruling and bidding the Abolitionists to be undismayed, he said, with splendid foresight: "The whole history of the anti-slavery movement is studded with proof that all measures devised and executed with a view to allay and diminish the anti-slavery agitation, have only served to increase, intensify, and embolden that agitation. . . . This very attempt to blot out forever the hopes of an enslaved people may be one necessary link in the chain of events preparatory to the downfall and complete overthrow of the whole slave system."[22] History was to justify Douglass' analysis fully and more quickly than even he could have imagined.

16. Bleeding Kansas and John Brown

The ten years just prior to the outbreak of the Civil War were a period of swiftly developing revolutionary crisis. One of the most important events, revolving around the Fugitive Slave Law and the Dred Scott case, was the bitter struggle over Kansas and Nebraska, which began in 1853 and lasted into the Civil War. This struggle brought to the pitch of local civil war the historic conflict between the aggressive Southern planters and the increasingly militant Northern industrialists and their allies. It was, in fact, the first skirmish of the great Civil War.

The struggle began with the introduction into Congress in 1853 of the so-called Kansas Bill, which was later amended into the Kansas-Nebraska Bill. The purpose of this bill was to organize into definite territories the vast stretch of country lying between Missouri and Utah (the summit of the Rocky Mountains), and extending north to Minnesota.

This immense area, mostly part of the Louisiana Purchase of 1803, was generally known as "the Platte country." It was inhabited almost exclusively by Indians, save for a few white trappers and traders. Between 1830 and 1840, many Eastern Indian tribes, robbed of their lands, had been driven across the Mississippi. The Federal government promised them undisputed control of this entire country, the home of the monster buffalo herds, "as long as grass should grow and rivers run." But now, only a few years later, these promises were being ignored and the Indians were about to be robbed of their last free home on a continent that had once been entirely theirs. The white expansionists had no qualms whatever about this greatest despoliation of the Indians. Besides unleashing a local civil war among the whites, the organization of the Kansas-Nebraska area also marked the beginning of a great war against the Plains tribes—a war which was to continue for 40 years and to end with the complete and final defeat of the Indian peoples—the last stage of a losing defense of their homelands for 275 years.

THE KANSAS-NEBRASKA BILL

The Kansas-Nebraska area, because of its cold winter climate, was not generally considered slave territory. But the Southern planters nevertheless wanted to control this rich agricultural country, because they were striving to legalize slavery all over the country, because they hoped to get the additional votes in the Senate from the new states in these territories, and because at this time they were nursing illusions that the slave system could be extended into cattle-grazing, general farming, and even industrial production. The railroad owners, who were willing to strike a bargain with the planters, also wanted the Kansas-Nebraska area opened up, to clear the way for the transcontinental railroad which they were already contemplating.

The historic Kansas-Nebraska Bill, designed to hand the area over to planter control, was chiefly the work of Senator Stephen A. Douglas of Illinois, chairman of the Senate Committee on Territories. Born in Brandon, Vermont, in 1813, Douglas was a lawyer who had grown wealthy from real estate speculation in Illinois. He was tied in with the railroad interests and, before his election to the House in 1843 and to the Senate in 1847, he had made a considerable reputation as an Illinois politician. Douglas was generally supposed to have drawn up the first outline of the Compromise of 1850, which Clay and Webster engineered through Congress. His political line was much the same as theirs, representing Northern capitalist interests conciliatory to slavery.

The Kansas-Nebraska Bill[1] provided that the question of slavery be left to the people of the two proposed territories to decide. This was Douglas' famous doctrine of "squatter sovereignty," which went beyond the planters' doctrine of states' rights by virtually prohibiting the abolition of slavery in the territories. The bill was a major part of the political offensive of the Southern slaveholders. Its principal effect was to liquidate the Compromise of 1820 and of 1850, by which Congress, exercising its admitted power, had supposedly excluded slavery from this entire area forever. Douglass, in fact, asserted that the Compromise of 1850 had abrogated that of 1820 and therewith left the question of slavery a moot one to be decided upon by the inhabitants of the new territories and states. The area involved—the heart of the continent—was 33,000 square miles larger than all the existing states in the Union put together including California.

The Kansas-Nebraska Bill was adopted on May 30, 1854, after

a bitter battle in Congress and throughout the country. It was passed in the Senate by a vote of 35 to 13, and in the House by 112 to 99. This action took place only three years before the notorious Dred Scott decision, discussed in the last chapter. The Scott decision denied Congress the right to legislate against slavery in any state or territory. Thus, it made slavery into a national institution, which could be altered or abolished only by a change in the Constitution. The effect of this decision was to hold constitutional the Kansas-Nebraska Act. No doubt, this was its real purpose rather than a simple decision as to the fate of the luckless slave, Dred Scott. The decision was designed to "settle" the slavery issue once and for all.

THE STRUGGLE AGAINST THE KANSAS-NEBRASKA BILL

The Kansas-Nebraska Bill provoked active opposition throughout the North. The alarm was sounded in a statement issued on January 19, 1854 (while the bill was pending), by a group of "Independent Democrats" in Congress (most of whom were Abolitionists), including Salmon P. Chase, Charles Sumner, J. R. Giddings, Benjamin F. Wade, Gerritt Smith, and Alexander De Witt. This committee warned the country that the passage of the bill would strike a deadly blow at the liberties of all the people, especially labor and the farmers. Militantly, the manifesto declared: "Even if overcome in the impending struggle, we shall not submit. We shall go home to our constituents, erect anew the standard of freedom, and call on the people to come to the rescue of the country from the domination of slavery."[2]

This appeal did not fall on deaf ears. During the next four and a half months, while the struggle over the bill went on in Congress, mass resentment rose swiftly in the North. In several places Senator Douglas was hanged in effigy. "In the North," says McMaster, "Douglas was hated with a bitterness which found no parallel in our history save in that felt for Benedict Arnold."[3] A number of state legislatures then in session condemned the Kansas-Nebraska Bill, and innumerable people's organizations went on record against it. "From mass meetings, from political conventions, from anti-slavery societies, churches, presbyteries, ministers, and clergymen of every denomination, from yearly meetings of the Friends . . . from men of all sorts and conditions, came to Congress hundreds of petitions, memorials, resolutions, remonstrances."[4] While the majority of Northern newspapers clearly opposed the bill, Douglas had powerful support in the pro-slavery press of the North.

At the heart of the popular agitation against this latest arrogant attack by the planters were the Abolitionists. They were to be found everywhere, stimulating the people's fighting spirit. Their effectiveness was all the greater inasmuch as this was also the time of the bitter struggle against the Fugitive Slave Act and the Dred Scott decision, dealt with in the previous chapter. The Negro people's convention movement was especially active during this crucial period. It held important national gatherings in 1852, 1853, 1854, and 1856, as well as innumerable state conventions. It was a real factor in arousing the toiling masses, Negro and white, to struggle. The weak trade union movement of the time, then fighting for its very existence, participated increasingly in the fight against the Kansas-Nebraska Bill.

Frederick Douglass was especially active in this historic struggle. With many of the other Negro leaders abroad or underground as a result of the terror set in motion by the Fugitive Slave Act, Douglass faced very heavy responsibilities of leadership. He spoke all over the country at big meetings, ran his paper, and took an active part in the current election campaigns. On the Kansas-Nebraska Bill, Douglass declared with his usual clarity and force, "The struggle is one for ascendancy. Slavery aims at absolute sway, and to banish liberty from the republic. It would drive out the school-master, and install the slave-driver, burn the school-house and erect the whipping post, prohibit the Holy Bible and establish the bloody code, dishonor free labor with its hope of reward, and establish slave-labor with its dread of the lash." Douglass sharply criticized the fight of the Free Soilers, which aimed essentially at maintaining the pro-slavery compromises of 1820 and 1850, holding slavery within specified boundaries, and he demanded instead an offensive against the entire slave system. "The ground should be distinctly taken that slavery has no rightful existence anywhere—that it is a system of lawless violence, and its multitudinous crimes and horrors should be spread out before the world with such terrible truth as to make the traffickers in human flesh tremble and call for rocks and mountains to fall on them."[5]

The passage of the Kansas-Nebraska Bill was a triumph for the South. It whetted the appetite of the planters for fresh assaults upon the forces of freedom in the North. There were many "fire-eaters" in the South, however, who considered the bill only a half measure and an infringement upon the sacred principle of states' rights. They did not concede to Congress even the right to tell the states or territories that they had the authority to establish slavery or not, as they saw fit. The "fire-eaters" wanted Congress to keep its hands off slavery completely, except in the case of their holy Fugitive Slave Act, which they insisted that the Federal government enforce with all its power. Actually, Stephen A. Douglas, who aspired to the presidency, lost so much prestige in the South over the Kansas-Nebraska Bill that he was defeated for the Democratic nomination for president in 1860.

CIVIL WAR IN KANSAS

The passage of the Kansas-Nebraska Act was an invitation to civil war, to a bitter struggle between the planters and the Abolitionist forces for control of the new territories. Nor was this struggle long in getting under way. The pro-slavery men planned to colonize Kansas and to leave Nebraska to the Free Soilers from the North. To this plan, however, the Free Soilers did not acquiesce—they decided also to fight for Kansas.

Although Kansas was not yet legally open to settlement, hundreds of settlers poured in from the South and pre-empted the most desirable land. But the anti-slavey forces in the North were not idle. They formed Kansas Emigrant Aid Societies in Massachusetts, New York, Ohio, Pennsylvania, and many other states. Frederick Douglass called for a mass emigration of Negroes to Kansas, although Negroes were not entitled to take up government land under the Jim Crow land law. "The country is swarming with emigrants," says McMaster. "Men on horseback, with cup and skillet, ham, flour, and coffee tied behind them, and axe on shoulder, are hurrying westward, companies with flags flying are staking out the prairies, trees are falling, tents are stretching, cabins are going up, and everybody is alive and awake. Hurrah for Kansas."[6] All this was in mid-1854.

By March 1855, there were 10,000 people in Kansas. The only political organizations existing were the Emigrant Aid Societies and the planters' "secret" societies. An effort was made to elect a territorial government, but the pro-slavery Missourians "came in organized bands with cannon, guns, pistols, and bowie knives . . . took possession of the polls, and went home declaring they had made Kansas a slave-holding Territory."[7] New elections were therefore ordered for May. Only the Free Soilers voted; the pro-slavery elements abstained. Under the condemnation of the pro-slavery Federal government, this new legislature soon collapsed. By this time the unorganized Kansas settlements were in a state of chaos. The local civil war was beginning.

The Free Soil supporters called a state convention at Topeka, which issued a state constitution. This they submitted to a popular vote, and a government was elected on this basis. Meanwhile, the pro-slavery elements called a meeting of their bogus legislature in Leavenworth. This body declared itself the legitimate government of Kansas, and the inveterate enemy of Abolitionism, Free Soilism, and all other "isms." Presiding over this rump legislature was Governor Shannon, an appointee of President Pierce, who was a tool of the Southern slaveholders. Now there were two local governments, both demanding Federal recognition. Pierce denounced the Free Soil Topeka government, recognized the pro-slavery one in Leavenworth instead, blamed the Emigrant Aid societies for all the troubles in Kansas, and pledged full support to the pro-slavery territorial government. Meanwhile, from various Southern states, armed bands came to Kansas, flaunting banners demanding "The Supremacy of the White Race."

On May 21, 1856, the town of Lawrence, a Free Soil stronghold, was sacked by a pro-slavery armed force. This act provoked far-reaching indignation throughout the North. Men, money, and arms were freely gathered to help the embattled Kansas Free Soilers. The tide of emigrants to Kansas swelled. Then John Brown, a settler in Osawatomie, Kansas, took a hand. On May 25 he and his five sons wiped out several of the opposition at Dutch Henry's Crossing. This was the beginning of Brown's extensive activities in the Kansas civil war. His action further inflamed the struggle and both sides now rushed to arms. "Bands of guerillas, drawn from both parties, traversed the country, burning, robbing, plundering, shooting."[8]

The Free Soilers were now definitely in the majority in Kansas; but in 1857 the pro-slavery elements, at a packed convention, were able to adopt the so-called Lecompton Constitution allowing slavery, by a vote counted as 6,266 for and 567 against. The following year, however, the territorial legislature held an election in which the Lecompton Constitution was rejected by 10,266 to 262, with the pro-slavery elements boycotting the election. Meanwhile, the guerrilla war went on. By 1859, however, the Free Soilers, by superior force, had secured a firm grip on the situation in Kansas. They elected a Free Soil territory legislature and executive. In February 1860 they demanded the admission of Kansas into the Union as a free state. But the Democratic Congress (President James Buchanan was another tool of the Southern planters) refused to accede to this demand. Upon Democratic insistence, Congress laid the Kansas application on the table just before it adjourned. It was not until January 29, 1861, with the secession of the slave states already a fact, that Kansas was finally admitted as a free state, the 34th state in the Union. This long and bitter fight for control of Kansas exerted an enormous influence in preparing and organizing the anti-slavery forces of the North for the great revolutionary struggle immediately before them.

JOHN BROWN'S RAID

John Brown was born in Torrington, Connecticut, in 1800. His ancestors, six generations before, had come over on the *Mayflower*. He was an intensely religious man. An ardent Abolitionist, Brown operated a station of the Underground Railroad in Richmond, Ohio, through which he helped many slaves to freedom. He and his sons took an active part in the civil war in Kansas, where they had gone to take up land and to help hold the territory as free soil. There he became known as Osawatomie Brown.

Seeking to strike a solid blow against the slave power, Brown in 1857 conceived the idea of making a raid into Southern slave territory for the purpose of freeing the slaves. He chose Harper's Ferry, Virginia (now in West Virginia) as the place to strike. This town of 5,000 inhabitants, 57 miles from Washington, was chosen because it was the site of a Federal arsenal, in which from 100,000 to 200,000 rifles were usually stored. Brown's precise plans were never made clear publicly. But the facts show that he believed his invasion would start a general struggle which would result in the overthrow of the slave power in the South. He looked very far beyond merely a local slave uprising. A highly intelligent man, as all who knew him agreed, Brown correctly judged the historic course of national events; but his strategy did not conform to the relation of forces. Yet his "war" was only a year and a half ahead of the real Civil War.

That Brown believed his movement would be the beginning of a general war against the slaveholders was borne out by the fact that, as part of his preparations he had written what he called a new United States Constitution. This plan he presented to a few chosen followers who were assembled in a Negro church in Chatham, Canada

West, on May 8, 1858. This document, entitled "Provisional Constitution and Ordinances for the People of the United States," was not intended as a substitute for the existing Constitution, but rather as an amendment to it. It was more of a set of regulations to be adopted in an expected civil war, and it named him Commander-in-Chief.[9]

Brown worked diligently to prepare for his raid. He went to New England to raise funds with which to buy arms, consulting many prominent Abolitionists about his general plan. After their bitter experiences with the Fugitive Slave law, the Dred Scott decision, and the civil war in Kansas, the anti-slavery elements were in a fighting mood. Old-time notions of non-resistance were very much on the wane. At this time, as Redding remarks, Garrison spoke to an Abolitionist rally in Boston and asked the crowd how many of them were non-resisters. The answer was one lonesome "I."[10] Many Abolitionists contributed money to Brown, but they, Douglass and others, considered his project impractical.

Under these circumstances of semi-publicity, Brown's insurrectionary plans could not long remain a secret, and they did not. Indeed, an unknown informant wrote to Secretary of War Floyd, telling him of the whole project and informing him that Harper's Ferry was the place chosen for the attack. But the Secretary considered the matter too fantastic to believe and did nothing about it. He never even notified the authorities at Harper's Ferry to be on the alert.

The attack was made on the night of Sunday, October 16, 1859. Brown and his tiny "army" of 22 men, five of them Negroes, (S. Green, O. P. Anderson, D. Newby, J. A. Copeland, and T. S. Leary), had previously established themselves on a small rented farm in Maryland, four miles from Harper's Ferry. There they had gradually assembled arms and perfected themselves in the details of their daring raid. The assault went off as scheduled: the little band of intrepid men occupied the bridge over the Potomac River, took charge of the Federal arsenal, and found themselves in control of the town. They seized as a prisoner Colonel L. W. Washington, who was in charge of the arsenal and the other local military establishments.

However, the Negroes did not flock to Brown's banner, as he had doubtless expected, nor did the local white population. This failure of the slaves to rise can not be ascribed to unresponsiveness among them; Brown's raid took place in a part of Virginia where slaves were relatively few, and these were mostly house servants. Moreover, Brown had put on no campaign whatever of preparatory agitation and organization among the masses. Consequently, in general, they knew nothing of his bold venture until it was all over.

While Brown and his followers held Harper's Ferry, the startled white leaders of the country around them swiftly awoke. Already on the night of October 16, local armed forces compelled the little army of liberation to take up a defensive position in a brick fire-house. On the morning of October 17, Brown's forces were surrounded by some 1,500 militiamen, gathered hastily from the neighboring towns. Bitter fighting ensued but the heroic insurrectionists could not be dislodged. In the evening, a body of troops arrived from Baltimore, commanded by Colonel Robert E. Lee and Lieutenant J. E. B. Stuart, both of whom were later to gain renown in the Civil War. Next morning, in overwhelming force, they attacked Brown's men in the fire-house and, after a bloody encounter, overcame and captured them. Of Brown's little liberation army, nine were dead, seven had escaped, and six, besides Brown, were prisoners, three of them wounded. In a typical lynch spirit, the militia mutilated the body of Newby, a Negro, one of Brown's men who had been killed. All of these stirring events were causing a profound national sensation.

THE HANGING OF JOHN BROWN

The "trial" of John Brown took place before Judge Parker in Charlestown, Virginia, only a week after the battle. It was a legal lynching; Brown was not given time even to get a competent lawyer or to assemble his witnesses. Seeing what was coming, he boldly demanded that the "trial" be dispensed with.[11] Brown was wounded and had to be carried into the courtroom on a stretcher. A farmers' jury, with slaveholders among them, found him guilty of treason, of inciting a slave insurrection, and of murder in the first degree. On October 31 he was sentenced to die.

After his arrest, John Brown did not make it clear just what his specific plans had been, beyond broad statements that he intended to free the slaves on a large scale, as he had done in Kansas. In an interview with the *Boston Traveler*,[12] in a statement issued while in jail,[13] and in his speech to the court before being sentenced, he confined himself somewhat to generalities. Evidently, he hoped to create a repetition of the struggle which had taken place in Kansas, in which he had played such a prominent part; but in reality he aimed at a much broader scale of operations.

Huge masses of people in the North at once applauded Brown's heroic action. A great wave of indignation swept over them at the semi-lynch execution of a man who was already on his way to becoming one of America's greatest people's heroes. Six of Brown's men were also executed. Large bodies of troops were held in readiness, presumably to guard against possible lynch mobs, but actually in fear of an expected attempt at rescue. According to Villard, "Greater precautions could hardly have been taken had a grave state of war existed."[14]

John Brown was hanged in Charlestown on December 2. It took 38 minutes before the tough old fighter, 60 years of age, was pronounced dead. Through it all he displayed a calm courage that won admiration from even his worst enemies. His death evoked widespread protests among the masses of the people. "In many cities in the North the day was marked by public ceremonies and expressions of sympathy and grief. Sympathy meetings were held at Philadelphia, Albany, Providence, Worcester, Boston, and Syracuse. Emerson, Thoreau, and other outstanding figures, spoke up for Brown. At all these places speeches were made and at some collections were taken up for the relief of the martyr's family. Elsewhere, as at Concord and Plymouth and New Bedford and Birmingham, sixty-three strokes were struck on the bells, and in some places, a hundred minute guns were fired."[15] Repercussions were also heard in Europe; Victor Hugo and many others paid tribute to John Brown.

Papers were allegedly found at Brown's farm rendezvous in Maryland, implicating a number of prominent Northern Abolitionists, including Frederick Douglass, Gerritt Smith, Frank Sanborn, G. L. Stearns, Harriet Tubman, and Thomas Wentworth Higginson. The planters' lynch government of Virginia particularly wanted to get Douglass into its clutches; but before he could be arrested he fled to Canada, and later went to England. Staying in Europe until May 1860, Douglass returned to the United States where he found a very different political situation.

The confirmed advocate of non-resistance, William Lloyd Garrison, felt the rising militant spirit of the masses. He declared: "I am prepared to say: 'Success to every slave insurrection at the South, and in every slave county.' And I do not see how I compromise or stain my profession in making that declaration. . . . Rather than see men wearing their chains in a cowardly and servile spirit, I would, as an advocate of peace, much rather see them breaking the head of the tyrant with their chains. Give me, as a non-resistant, Bunker Hill, and Lexington, and Concord, rather than the cowardice and servility of a Southern slave-plantation."[16]

The masses of the common people in the North, Negro and white, were quick to recognize in John Brown a true representative of their best hopes and interests. This was partly because of his superb courage under fire and on the scaffold, but more basically because his brave raid and his little liberation army were profoundly in tune with history. Brown became a veritable symbol of the revolutionary action that the whole people of the North would soon take to free the slaves and to smash the power of the arrogant planters of the South. It had a tremendous effect in uniting and inspiring the Abolitionist forces of the North and West. In only a short time immense Union armies, singing "John Brown's Body," were to begin their long and bloody march to victory over the slave power. John Brown is one of the most heroic and significant figures in American history.

17. The Formation of the Republican Party

The bitter struggles in the early 1850's between the broad pro- and anti-slavery forces, especially over the Fugitive Slave and Kansas-Nebraska acts, together with the mounting wave of slave revolts, inevitably produced a sharp realignment of political forces. As a result, the Republican Party was formed in 1854. This laid the basis of the great alliance of democratic forces under the leadership of the Northern industrialists, which was to fight through and win the Civil War, the Second American Revolution.[1]

At the time of the Compromise of 1850, there were two major political organizations, the Democratic and the Whig parties, and two smaller ones, the Free Soil and the Liberty parties (see Chapter 13). The pro-slavery Democratic Party was controlled by the Southern planters, in alliance with Northern banking and commercial interests. The Whig Party, the party of Webster and Clay, who originated the pro-slavery compromises of 1820 and 1850, was dominated by Northern capitalist interests in alliance with slaveholders of the South. The Free Soil Party, as its name implied, was opposed to the extension of slavery. The Liberty Party represented the political wing of the Abolitionist movement.

THE BREAK-UP OF THE WHIG PARTY

Franklin Pierce, a Democrat from New Hampshire and tool of the slaveholders, was elected president in the hard-fought election of 1852, over General Winfield Scott of the Whig Party. The Free Soil and Liberty parties polled very small opposition votes. The Whig Party, torn with dissension over the question of slavery, did not survive this defeat and it never put up another national ticket. It perished the same year that its two outstanding leaders, Webster and Clay, died. The Whig Party could not become the party of the Northern bourgeoisie in the revolutionary work ahead, so it had to die.

The collapse of the national Whig Party gave rise to the American, or the so-called Know-Nothing Party. This party had been founded

in New York State in 1843, principally by Northern pro-slavery elements.[2] It was a chauvinist, nativist party, which directed its main
blows at the flood of immigrants then beginning to pour into the
country (4,311,465 arrived between 1840 and 1850.) It was anti-
foreign-born, anti-Catholic, anti-Negro. It was also a secret organization, and in response to queries, its members would reply, "I know
nothing"—hence its nickname. The Know-Nothing Party grew rapidly
as the Whig Party disintegrated, and it became very active. In the
state and local elections of 1854 it swept Massachusetts and Delaware,
and almost carried New York. It sent 75 members to Congress and
had a million and a half followers.[3] In 1855, the party split over the
question of slavery. Its official, compromising policy on the issue was
essentially that of Webster and Clay, which the "fire-eating" Southern
wing would not tolerate. In the election of 1856, it candidate, Fillmore, polled a disappointing vote, which hastened the party's disintegration. Obviously too reactionary for the revolutionary purposes of
the industrialists, the American Party lingered on until 1860, leaving
a political stench behind it. Its historic role was to sabotage the
crystallization of the anti-slavery forces.

THE ORGANIZATION OF THE REPUBLICAN PARTY

The Republican Party was born out of the fierce struggle against
the Kansas-Nebraska Bill and Fugitive Slave Act. Neither the Democratic, Whig, nor American parties, the larger parties of the decade,
could become the political organization to carry on the anti-slavery
fight, and the Free Soil and Liberty parties were small and relatively
isolated. Hence, the people's demand for a new party arose. The
formation of the Republican Party was the result; it was spontaneous,
springing up all over the country.

The first definite steps toward forming the new party were taken
in Ripon, Wisconsin, in February 1854. There a local meeting was
held in response to a call issued by a Whig, a Free Soiler, and a
Democrat. The initiator was A. E. Bovay, formerly secretary-treasurer
of the National Industrial Congress, an early national organization of
trade unions. The passage of the Kansas-Nebraska bill in May 1854,
spurred the new party movement. In July of the same year a meeting
was called in Jackson, Michigan, to form a party in that state. After
this, sections of the new party grew in many states and localities.

Popular demand favored a new organization based upon the

Free Soil program; that is, opposing the further extension of slavery into the territories. By spontaneous consent rather than formal decision, the new party called itself the Republican Party. The name was taken from the party of Jefferson, who was called the original Free Soiler because of his anti-slavery provisions in the Northwest Ordinance of 1787.[4]

The Republican Party grew like a prairie fire. Within a year, by 1855, there were anti-Nebraska majorities in 15 states, and 15 anti-Nebraska Senators and 117 Representatives of the party in Congress. Whigs, Free Soilers, Abolitionists, Know-Nothings, and anti-Nebraska Democrats flocked to the new party. Prominent political leaders and outstanding newspapers came out in favor of it. The party had little strength in the South; however its quickly expanding forces were located almost exclusively in the North—both East and West.

The party held its first national convention in Pittsburgh in February 1856, and its nominating convention in Philadelphia, beginning on June 17, 1856. There it picked out as its presidential ticket General John C. Frémont and W. L. Dayton. Frémont was a well-known Abolitionist. "Among the delegates were such men as James G. Blaine, Charles Francis Adams, E. R. Hoar, David Wilmot, Thaddeus Stevens, Alfonso Taft, Joshua R. Giddings, Zachariah Chandler, Owen Lovejoy, John M. Palmer, and Samuel C. Pomeroy."[5] The platform opposed the repeal of the Missouri Compromise of 1820 and the extension of slavery into free territory; it favored the admission of Kansas as a free state and a program of national internal development, especially the building of a great continental railroad along a central route. The platform was a typical Free Soil document: it undertook to contain slavery within its existing borders, but did not attack the institution of slavery itself. Woodburne says the Republican Party "was organized primarily for the purpose of resisting the extension of American slavery."[6]

In the election of 1856 there were three major candidates: Buchanan, Democrat; Fillmore, American; and Frémont, Republican. It was a hard-fought election. Buchanan polled 1,838,169 votes; Frémont 1,341,264; and Fillmore, 874,534. Buchanan carried 19 states with 174 electoral votes, and Frémont, 11 states with 114 electoral votes. Frémont's states included Connecticut, Iowa, Maine, Massachusetts, Michigan, New Hampshire, New York, Ohio, Rhode Island, Vermont, and Wisconsin. He got a small vote in Maryland and Delaware, but had no organization in the other Southern slave states.

His big political success definitely established the Republican Party as a major party. At last the Northern bourgeoisie had in its hands the weapon with which to fight its Southern planter enemies. The party was a great coalition of several classes. We shall now proceed to analyze its composition.

THE NORTHERN CAPITALISTS

Most of the industrialists in the Northern and Western states, although they did not pioneer in founding the Republican Party, quickly moved in and took charge of it. They were in direct conflict with the planters on many questions, all of which came to sharp expression in the long Free Soil fight. The Republican Party was their party from the outset. Previously most of them had been members of the Whig Party, where they were a controlling influence; but obviously Abolitionists such as Joshua R. Giddings had no place in the same party with Toombs, the Southern "fire-eater." Many industrialists were also in the Democratic Party, where they formed a Free Soil minority. When the mass movement for the Republican Party got under way, the industrialists, in the main, had severed their Whig and Democratic connections and affiliated themselves with the new organization. Most of the Northern newspapers took the Republican line.

The *Chicago Tribune* was the principal Republican paper in the Midwest; but outstanding in this extensive Republican press was the *New York Tribune,* edited by Horace Greeley. Greeley founded the *Tribune* in 1841 as a Whig organ. It advocated trade unionism, a high tariff, women's rights, temperance, a homestead law, and Fourierist utopian socialism, and it also opposed the big capitalists. After 1850, Greeley joined in the fight against the compromise of that year, and particularly the Kansas-Nebraska Act. His paper was far and away the largest and most influencial in the entire country. Bayard Taylor said that in the rural districts of the West, the *Tribune* was next to the Bible in influence. Greeley at once became a power in the leading circles of the Republican Party.

Although the Northern industrialists—and with them large numbers of bankers, merchants, and railroad capitalists—generally supported the Republican Party and its program of "No More Slave States," powerful sections of the big Northern financiers, merchants, and shippers showed much less enthusiasm for that party. This was true also of the New England cotton manufacturers, who depended on the South for raw material. Especially hostile were many big financiers in the New York and Chicago areas. These groupings, affiliated with the Democratic Party, were connected with the South through trade and the financing and shipping of its huge cotton crop, which at this time constituted the largest part of all American exports.[7] New York City was, in fact, "the prolongation of the South." Its leading merchants had close social, political, and business relationships with the Southern planters, marrying into their families and buying into their plantations. One prominent New York banker owned a Southern plantation with 1,200 slaves. New England sold $60 million worth of goods to the South annually, and much political sympathy went with this good business.

New York's big business interests were so tied in with the slave economy that DeBow, the leading ideologist of slavery, could boast that without slavery, "the ships would rot at her docks, grass would grow in Wall Street and Broadway, and the glory of New York, like that of Babylon and Rome, would be numbered with the things of the past." The clique of pro-slavery New York bankers and merchants was a source of political poison all through the great struggle for Negro emancipation. "During the months from January 1859 to August 1860, it was conservatively estimated, close to 100 vessels left the city for the slave trade." The business-controlled city government fired a salute of 100 guns at the Battery when the Compromise of 1850 was enacted by Congress, and New York clergymen, submissive to the local business reactionaries, were especially notorious supporters of the Fugitive Slave Act and other pro-slavery measures. New York became the main nesting ground for the "Copperhead" traitors during the Civil War.

THE NEGRO PEOPLE

Although almost entirely without the right to vote, the more than four million Negroes, free and slave, who represented the social group with the greatest stake in the national struggle convulsing the country, became most active supporters of the Republican Party. Like many others, Frederick Douglass, their outstanding intellectual and political leader, had some hesitation about the Republican Party at first because of the Free Soil limitations of the new party's program and the opportunist character of many of those who flocked to its standard.

As late as April 25, 1856, Douglass still pledged his support to the Liberty Party, with its Abolitionist program. But in the issue of *Frederick Douglass' Paper* of August 15, 1856, immediately after the Republican nominating convention, he gave full backing to its candidates, Frémont and Dayton. Douglass had been nominated for vice-president at a convention of radical political Abolitionists on May 28 in Syracuse, but he dropped this and devoted himself to the Republican ticket, while criticizing its limitations. This was the practical course to take, and Douglass justified it by saying, "We have turned Whigs and Democrats into Republicans and we can turn Republicans into Abolitionists"[8]— a prophecy which was to come true sooner than he suspected.

Douglass' action in supporting the Republican ticket was another long stride away from the sectarianism which had been so harmful to the Abolitionists. The Negro convention movement soon followed his example. This was the beginning of the Negro people's support for the Republican Party, which was to last for over half a century.

THE MIDDLE CLASS

The broad white city middle class of the North—professionals, shopkeepers, small manufacturers, etc.—heavily supported the Republican Party. They favored the free soil, high tariff, and internal improvements policies of the growing party, all of which brought them into direct conflict with the Southern planters. They constituted one of the pillars of the new political party.

But the Garrison intellectuals in their American Anti-Slavery Society continued on their sectarian way. It was not until the war started that they finally joined up with the great anti-slavery coalition. In a lecture delivered in January 1855,[9] Frederick Douglass stated that the "old" organization had dwindled to the point where it had relatively few members, only two papers, and half a dozen lecturers in the field. The annual report for 1859, however, listed many prominent occasional speakers for the society, and gave $11,426.41 as its total national income.[10] As for the split-off "new" organization, the American and Foreign Anti-Slavery Society, this remained a sect, devoting itself mainly to cultivating Abolitionist sentiment among the churches.

The growing Abolitionist forces had left these two sects on the side in their march toward political action and a broad mass movement. The Liberty Party of 1840 and the Free Soil Party of 1848 were but two stages in this process of growth in program and organization. The evolution culminated in 1854 in the establishment of the Republican Party, which came, by the outbreak of the Civil War, to absorb all the anti-slavery forces, including those of the middle class.

THE FARMERS

The farmers of the North and West constituted a fundamental section of the great anti-slavery alliance which was crystallizing in the Republican Party. The farmers had been the backbone of the Jeffersonian and Jacksonian movements, which were primarily directed against combinations of big slaveholders and Northern bankers and merchants. In Jefferson's day, their organization was called the Democratic-Republican Party; later, after Jackson, it was renamed the Democratic Party. During the latter part of the 1840's, the big slaveholders began to take over the Democratic Party, which they soon had firmly in their grasp. This was a signal for the farmers to begin to break with that party.

The farmers collided with the big slaveholders on many issues. They wanted Federal-financed internal improvements and lots of them—roads, canals, railroads, and good harbors—which the planters did not. Looking toward the growth of industry and the national market, they were also inclined to favor the tariff, whereas the big planters were ardent free traders, for reasons we have already explained. Another important factor in the changed relations between the Southern planters and the farmers of the North and West was a change in the route for swiftly expanding exports, principally wheat to Europe. Formerly the farmers had sent goods for export down the Ohio, Missouri, and Mississippi rivers to New Orleans by river boat. The development of the Erie Canal and the railroads diverted commerce to the Northern route, through New York, Philadelphia, and Boston. This change in route broke the trading contacts of the Western and Northern farmers with the South and established a whole set of new trading relations with the North and East.

The biggest conflict between the Northern and Western farmers and the Southern slaveholders was over the question of land. The farmers fought for free farming against slave farming, against the virgin land becoming slave land. The farmers wanted free government land for homesteads, whereas the slaveholders undertook to grab all they could for their big plantations. The slaveholders' agents in Congress and in the presidency had repeatedly defeated farmer-backed homestead bills. Even as late as 1860 such a bill was vetoed by the pro-slavery President, Buchanan. It was not until 1862, with the Civil War in full blast, that a satisfactory homestead act was finally passed.

This contradiction between the farmers and slaveholders over the land received its highest political expression in the bitter struggles of the Free Soilers to prevent the slaveholders from grabbing the Western territories as slave states, and, with these territories, control of the Federal government. The farmers were on the firing line in all these hard-fought battles. It was the local civil war over Kansas and Nebraska that finally aligned the bulk of them with the great anti-slavery coalition taking shape in the Republican Party.

These farmer-planter antagonisms also involved the free farmers of the South, who were outrageously abused, robbed, and subjugated by the big planters. There was disaffection among the farmers in every Southern state; in some mountain areas it was strong enough to result in solid Republican sentiment and organization. In the Border states it eventually proved to be so powerful that it definitely influenced the outcome of the Civil War—probably averting the defeat of the North—by preventing the Border states from going over to the Confederacy.

THE WORKING CLASS

The interests of the workers also conflicted directly with those of the Southern planters in many respects. In the South the presence of slave labor not only ruined the wages of free labor, but also hindered the growth of industry and the working class. The workers in the North also felt in their wages the depressing effects of the impoverishment of the great body of Southern slaves, who outnumbered the wage workers of the nation. The opposition of the planters to the tariff, to internal improvements, and to a homestead law also injured the welfare of the workers. And the planters' attempts to seize control of the new states, and to strengthen their grip upon the Federal government, were likewise blows to the interests of the workers. The very existence of the slave system was a grave menace to the better living standards, education, and democracy for which the workers were struggling.

Consequently, contrary to the assertions of nearly the whole body of bourgeois historians—who are enemies of the labor movement—anti-slavery sentiment was always strong among the workers. This was especialy true of the workers in New England, the birthplace both of American industry and of Abolitionism. As early as 1832, women workers in Lowell, Massachusetts, cotton mills formed an anti-slavery society.[11] Schlueter says that "The mass of the organized workingmen of the Northeastern portion of the country remained hostile to slavery; they were among the most enthusiastic agitators in the Abolitionist cause."[12] Except the Negro people, of course. The local labor parties of the 1830's generally condemned chattel slavery, and workers were prominent in all the anti-slavery societies and movements before the Civil War. They developed into a basic sector of the great anti-slavery alliance which fought through that revolutionary war.

A number of elements tended, however, to keep the workers from participating in the anti-slavery movement. Among these were the following: The working class was just being born, as industry was then only passing from the handicraft stage to factory production, and class consciousness among the workers was relatively undeveloped; their trade unions were weak, and, save for sporadic local labor parties, the workers had no political organization. Consequently, the workers were without a class program which definitely identified their interests with those of the Negro people. This difficulty was increased by the fact, pointed out in Chapter 10, that Garrison and many other Abolitionist leaders had a strong anti-labor bias and deeply antagonized the otherwise friendly workers.

In addition, the young labor movement of the period was plagued by several illusions that tended to weaken it as an anti-slavery force. One of the worst was the stubborn notion that if the slaves were freed, this would release a flood of cheap labor that would ruin the wages of the workers. This was a crippling illusion, and everything was done to cultivate it by the reactionary pro-slavery forces throughout the North, not the least of which were the churches, Catholic and Protestant. The pro-slavery Democratic Party made this a major point in its campaigns up to and through the Civil War.

This widespread misconception overlooked all the depressing effects of slavery upon the wages of the free workers. In actual fact, the emancipation of the slaves was the great, indispensable step necessary for improving the economic conditions of all workers, as well as the slaves themselves. This principle Marx made clear in his famous terse formulation that "Labor cannot emancipate itself in the white skin where in the black it is branded."[13]

In general the fledgling trade unions of the pre-Civil War decades took a stand for the abolition of chattel slavery. In so doing, they usually declared themselves against all slavery, wage slavery as well as chattel slavery. Thus, in its constitution of 1845, the Industrial Congress proposed to establish "equality, liberty, and brotherhood among men of every race." Characteristically, a big labor mass meeting, held in New York on March 1, 1854, to oppose the Kansas-Nebraska bill, condemned slavery, both white and black.[14] Many labor organizations expressed themselves similarly against both types of exploitation.

While sound in principle, this demand for the abolition of both chattel and wage slavery inevitably led to much confusion. There were tendencies to put the fight for the abolition of wage slavery ahead of that for the abolition of chattel slavery. There were assertions that wage slavery was worse than chattel slavery, and also notions that the fight to do away with chattel slavery conflicted with the struggle of the wage workers to improve their economic conditions. As one worker put it in *The Liberator,* "They [the workingmen] do not hate chattel slavery less, but they hate wage slavery more."[15] There was a failure to realize clearly that the abolition of chattel slavery, which was an urgent necessity for the capitalist industrialists in their fight against the slavocracy, stood immediately upon the stage of history—to be realized in the great bourgeois-democratic revolution that was brewing. On the other hand, the abolition of wage slavery, due to be the center of an eventual, higher, Socialist revolution, was still generations beyond the political horizon.

Another element confusing the workers' struggle against chattel slavery was the question of land reform. All the trade unions of the time fought for free government homesteads, in the hope that much of the 1,500,000,000 acres of land then held by the government would pass into the hands of the workers. "Vote yourself a farm" was a potent slogan among the workers in the 1840's and 1850's. But this legitimate demand for land was grossly distorted by land reformers and utopians. Thus, George R. Evans, editor of the *Workingman's Advocate* and other workers' papers, and an influential labor leader, took the position that labor's complete emancipation was to be achieved only by the workers getting themselves government homesteads.

During the 1840's, the Evans land reformers were very active, and their ideas led to serious neglect of the fight for the abolition of Negro slavery. Herman Kriege, a pseudo-socialist who was very influential among the large numbers of German immigrants in the 1850's, actually opposed outright the abolition of chattel slavery as being detrimental to the wage workers. Kriege said he felt "constrained . . . to oppose abolition with all our might."[16] Wilhelm Weitling, another German leader, disdained abolitionism, and W. Banque even advocated support of slavery.

Despite all these confusions and difficulties, the workers did become a power in the broad political movement against slavery, especially with the development of the fight against the Fugitive Slave Act and the Kansas-Nebraska Bill in the 1850's. By and large, they escaped from the ideological influence of such opportunists as Evans, Kriege, Weitling, and Banque.[17] Primarily, they supported the stand of the Free Soilers and opposed the further extension of slavery. They especially saw the slaveholders as obstacles to their getting homesteads. Big workers' meetings, labor conventions, and demonstrations so expressed themselves at the time.[18] In general, the undeveloped working class followed the policy of the Northern industrialists regarding slavery: first, the fight for Free Soil and eventually for Abolition.

When the Republican Party was founded in 1854 trade unionists took an active part in it. Significantly, Bovay, its main initiator in Ripon, Wisconsin, had been a prominent New York labor leader. Many workers, however, were reluctant to quit the Democratic Party, with its Jacksonian traditions and its sympathy for foreign-born workers. They hesitated to join up with the Republican Party, which was tainted with Know-Nothingism and also led by their capitalist enemies, the industrialists. It took a good deal of understanding for the workers to realize that the fight against the planters was so important to themselves that it justified a united front at that time even with their traditional capitalist enemies.

Organized labor was active in the important election of 1856, generally supporting the Republican candidate, Frémont. The workers' slogans were "Free Soil, Free Labor, Frémont," and "We Won't Work for Ten Cents a Day." The extent of labor's participation may be gauged by the fact that, during the campaign, a great mass meeting of 25,000 was held in Pittsburgh. This big gathering denounced slavery, stated that "our interests as a class are seriously involved in the present political struggle," and that "we have laid aside minor differences in the face of the great danger." It warned that if the planters should extend their system over the territories, this would give them supreme power over the government, "and they will then extend it over us."[19] With the constant sharpening of the general struggle against slavery, the workers had become a basic power in the revolutionary anti-slavery alliance of the Republican Party by the crucial elections of 1860.

THE MARXISTS

During the early 1850's, a new force—Marxism—began to develop in the American labor movement. This was to play a basic part in the education and mobilization of the workers in the great struggle against chattel slavery. The first advocates of Marxism in this country were predominantly German immigrants, mostly workers. Outstanding among them was Joseph Weydemeyer;[20] among the many others were Friedrich Sorge, Adolf Douai, A. Jacobi, Herman Mayer, and Robert Rosa. Most of them were political refugees who had been close co-workers with Marx and Engels in the German Revolution of 1848. They soon became a power in winning to the anti-slavery cause the large bodies of German workers in such key centers as New York, Chicago, Cincinnati, St. Louis, and Milwaukee. The Germans formed one-fifth to one-third of the local population in these centers.[21]

Although Marxism, the science of economic, political, and social development, originated in Europe, it was, like all other sciences, fundamentally international in character; it provided the American workers with a scientific understanding of the course of American economic and political development; it explained the significance of the class struggle; it clarified the question of the recurring economic crises, which were so confusing to American workers. Marxism laid out a clear-cut program of combined trade union and political struggle, and it gave the workers a definite, ultimate perspective of a Socialist society, based upon the dictatorship of the proletariat—the rule of the working class and its allies. All this tended to raise the American labor movement to a much higher ideological and political level than before.

Even in those early days, the Marxists had to combat advocates of American exceptionalism, particularly among the land reformers, who maintained that the United States represented a new type of society, basically different from Europe. One of the biggest tasks of the Marxists then—as it still is—was to convince the workers that American society is fundamentally the same as capitalism in all other countries, and that it is subject to that system's laws of growth and decline. The Marxists also had to fight against the sectarian tendencies of many German workers, to hold themselves aloof from American labor organizations, and to concern themselves too exclusively with the developing class struggle in Germany.

The Marxists at once became leaders in the German workers' trade union movement and also in their political activities. Germans were a big political force—German immigration, mostly of workers and peasants, reaching the record figure of 200,000 yearly during the 1840's. Naturally, the Marxists early turned their attention to the question of slavery which was then becoming a burning national issue. Marx and Engels were Abolitionists, and so were their leading supporters in the United States.

Three great problems faced the American workers during the 1850's on the question of slavery. These were: (a) to understand that their economic interests dovetailed with the emancipation of the Negro slaves; (b) to grasp the fact that the abolition of slavery was absolutely indispensable to the further advance of democracy in the United States; and (c) to realize the need for building a great alliance of all the forces whose interests conflicted with those of the slave-holders.

Upon the foregoing propositions the Marxists' policies were essentially based. They combated and eventually broke the influence of the Krieges, Weitlings, and other pro-slavery oppositionists in the working class, and they did much to convince the workers that their class interests would be greatly advanced by the emancipation of the slaves. Not without some vacillations among their following, they conducted a widespread and effective campaign for Abolition, despite their small numbers. Adolph Douai issued an Abolitionist paper in San Antonio, Texas, from 1852 until 1855, when he had to flee for his life from a lynch mob. In Alabama, the Marxist Abolitionist, Herman Mayer, had a similar experience. Through the Communist Club of New York (organized in 1857) and similar groupings in the Middle West, Joseph Weydemeyer was an indomitable fighter against slavery. The Communist Club of Cleveland in 1851 resolved to "use all means which are adapted to abolish slavery, an institution which is wholly repugnant to the principles of true democracy."

In the light of Marx's teachings, the Communists understood that chattel slavery had to be abolished if the working class was to progress in the United States. They also understood the need for the workers to collaborate with all anti-slavery forces—even with the Northern industrialists, the exploiters of the workers. As early as 1848, Marx and Engels, in speaking of Germany in the celebrated *Communist Manifesto,* had made it clear that Communists fight "with the bourgeoisie whenever it acts in a revolutionary way."[22]

The Communists took an active part in building the Republican Party. They fought against the activities of the Know-Nothing elements in the organization; they strove to cultivate the influence of the workers within the new party. The American Workers' League, under Marxist leadership, was a considerable factor in winning trade unions to support the Republican Party. The Marxists were notably alert in fighting the Kansas-Nebraska Act and explaining its deadly threat to the workers. They strongly defended John Brown's raid at Harper's Ferry, refuting the arguments of those who wavered in the face of such revolutionary action. They were also very active in the vital election campaign of 1856. One of their most important actions in this struggle was the initiation of a conference, in February 1856, in Decatur, Illinois, of 25 newspaper editors, including the German-Americans. The aim of the conference was to unite all the anti-slavery forces for the coming elections. And in the 1860 election struggle, as we shall see, the Marxists were a very important factor.

18. The Ideological Struggle Against Slavery

The anti-slavery forces in the 1850's, confronting the aggression of the Southern slave power, had three elementary tasks, although they were but little realized at the time. These tasks were: (a) to build an organized political movement powerful enough to defeat the slaveholders; (b) to develop a revolutionary program with adequate mass support; and (c) to proceed with revolutionary action against the slaveholders. As history showed, these tasks, attacked more or less without a guiding theory, were eventually achieved. In Chapter 17, we saw how the first of these basic tasks was accomplished by the founding of the Republican Party. In the present chapter we shall deal with the second task—the development of a revolutionary political program, in preparation for the third and ultimate task of carrying through the revolutionary Civil War.

THE SLAVEHOLDERS' DEFENSE OF SLAVERY

American slavery throughout the Western Hemisphere was one of the greatest crimes in all history. The essence of the system was economic. For their own enrichment, the planters wanted the cheapest workers possible to work the plantations; hence, by force and violence they proceeded to enslave the Negroes. They seized them in Africa, kidnaped them to America, stripped them of every human right, and forced them under the lash to work all their lives in ignorance and deepest poverty. They did not dare, however, to allow the crime of slavery to stand forth in all its naked outrage; so the planters, from the outset, undertook to camouflage their criminality with every form of moral and legal justification.

Religion was the most potent of the planters' means to give a veneer of morality to their slave system. Their preachers were very facile in digging up texts from the Bible to justify slavery. The Negroes were made to appear as cursed of God and sentenced by Him to serve the whites obediently and for nothing all their lives. At first the slavers pretended that their purpose was to Christianize the Negroes; but they had to abandon this thin pretext when the slaves, expecting to get emancipation thereby, began to accept Christianity. For the Negroes the Christian religions were not gates to emancipation—but fetters to enslave them. To the religious sanction for slavery, the planters added other crude improvisations—that the Negroes were inferior mentally to the whites and born to be slaves; that under slavery Negroes were better off than they had been in their native Africa, and that slavery was the only means by which production could be carried on in the American sugar, tobacco, and cotton plantations.

In the late 1820's the Southern slaveholders greatly intensified their ideological defense of slavery. This was due primarily to the wide expansion of cotton production, which increased the planters' aggressiveness on every front. It was also largely in answer to the relentless and effective attacks of the Northern Abolitionists, which had sharply increased after the launching of Garrison's *Liberator* in 1831. The leading slavery politicians, led by Calhoun, pronounced slavery "a good, a positive good," and defended it on that basis. They reiterated their doctrine of states' rights, regarding the control of their peculiar institution. The preachers split off the Southern wings of the Protestant churches, the better to support slavery. "Economists" hastened to prove that slavery was a great progressive economic force, for without it there could be no general production in the South and no national industrial advance. "Historians" also proclaimed that the Negro people had never made any contributions to world cultural progress. "Ethnologists" alleged that the Negroes of Africa and elsewhere were hopelessly backward and primitive peoples, indeed not really human. And "biologists," upon the appearance of Darwin's great works on evolution, proceeded to distort them into classifying Negroes as mentally inferior peoples. There was a united ideological attack upon the Negro people by all the apologists of slavery, in the North as well as in the South.

COUNTERATTACK BY THE ABOLITIONISTS

The Abolitionists of the North, organized in the anti-slavery societies and the Negro people's convention movements, met the propaganda blasts of the slaveholders head-on with an even more intense offensive of their own. Never before or since has the United

States witnessed such a keen political-economic-social discussion. This great debate went on to the accompaniment of the thunderous political struggle around the Compromise of 1850, the Fugitive Slave Act, the Kansas-Nebraska Act, the Dred Scott decision, and John Brown's raid.

The Abolitionists attacked slavery from every angle. They smashed into the states' rights fallacy, and they contested the political claims of the South to leaderhip of the territories. The preachers among them cited Christian ethics and mustered religious texts to counter the pro-slavery Bible quotations of the Southerners. With his book, *The Impending Crisis,* Helper wrecked the propaganda of the Southern economists; and Stowe, with her *Uncle Tom's Cabin,* dealt a body smash to the hypocritical humanitarian pretenses of the planters. Garrison, Douglass, Phillips, and many others, battered away at slavery with sledge-hammer blows.

The center of the Abolitionists' case was a great humanitarian protest against the indignities and outrages perpetrated upon the Negro people. They fought for Negro emancipation and the granting of basic human rights to the slave—the right to own his own body, to have his own family, to own property, to have freedom of movement, to have a say in the determination of his economic status—rights which were so elementary that they were not even mentioned in the Constitution and the Bill of Rights.

The white Abolitionists, although fighting against Jim Crow in general, said little at this time specifically about the franchise, and about full social equality for Negroes. These demands, especially at this point, were left mostly to the Negro Abolitionists to fight for. Indeed, there was no little white chauvinism (white supremacy moods) among the white Abolitionists.[1] Thus, three of the most effective fighters against slavery during these stormy decades—Harriet Beecher Stowe, Abraham Lincoln, and the blatant anti-Negro Hinton Rowan Helper—were all advocates of Negro colonization abroad, a notoriously white supremacist scheme.

The apologists for slavery devoted their main attention to cultivating white chauvinism among the masses by stressing the "horrors" of political and social equality. To hear the white supremacists tell it, this would mean Negro domination, and they shouted then as they do now, "How would you like to have your sister marry a Negro?"

In this acute national polemic the Negro Abolitionist intellectuals played a very important part. They not only fought through the humanitarian, political, and economic case for Abolition; but they especially defended the Negro people in the fields of history, ethnology, and biology—something the white Abolitionists showed no great initiative in doing. In 1848, H. H. Garnet, a noted Negro Abolitionist, produced his pioneer history, *The Past and Present Condition, and the Destiny of the Colored Race;* and in 1851, there appeared W. C. Nell's pamphlet on the role of Negro soldiers in the wars of 1776 and 1812. Most important was the address delivered by Frederick Douglass at the Western Reserve College, on July 12, 1854, entitled "The Claims of the Negro Ethnologically Considered."[2] In this speech Douglass battled against the attempt of the pro-slavery pseudo-scientists "to read the Negro out of the human family." He demonstrated "the oneness of the human family" and the equality of the Negro with the Anglo-Saxon. Douglass also delved into African history, identifying the Negro people with the splendid cultural achievements of Egypt. In this great national anti-slavery debate were laid the foundations of the historical and cultural studies of the Negro people's past and present which have since been advanced by innumerable Negro scholars. All of this work by Douglass and others constituted a long stride in the developing national consciousness of the Negro people.

THE DEADLY PARALLEL

The furious debates of the 1850's over the question of slavery presented a rare spectacle of the two quarreling sectors of capitalism —the Southern planters, with their obsolete production system, and the Northern industrial capitalists, representing the interests of capitalism as a whole. They exposed and denounced each other's system of exploitation, and many true words were spoken in these mutual unveilings. Never, in any country, have the sinister workings of capitalism been so thoroughly aired from within.

The Southerners boldly defended their enslavement and exploitation of the Negroes. Their leader, Calhoun, who died in 1850, said that every society necessarily rested upon an exploited class, and that only on the basis of this arrangement were progress and civilization possible. Capital and labor were united in one person, the slave, he maintained; so in the South conflict between these elements could not take place. Social inequality was a law of nature, and the inferior

Negro was born to be a slave. Slavery, Calhoun contended, was the ideal form, not only for production, but also for democracy. He eulogized it as "the most safe and stable basis for free institutions in the world."[3]

Along these lines, the Southerners declared that the chattel slavery of the South was more humane, democratic, and effective than the wage slavery of the North. They also declared that the Negro slaves were better off than the miserably exploited white workers in the South. On March 4, 1858, Senator James H. Hammond sensationally expounded this general viewpoint in Congress. He told the industrialists of the North: "Your whole hireling class of manual laborers and 'operatives,' as you call them, are essentially slaves. The difference between us is, that our slaves are hired for life and well-compensated; there is no starvation, no begging, no want of employment among our people, and not too much employment either. Yours are hired by the day, not cared for, and scantily compensated which may be proved in the most painful manner at any hour, in any street, in any of your large towns. Why, you meet more beggars in one day, in any single street of the City of New York, than you would meet in a lifetime in the whole South."[4] Hammond and other Southern aristocrats, shedding crocodile tears over the Northern workers, went on at length to describe the awful poverty in all the industrial centers of the Northern United States and Great Britain. They especially denounced the industrialists because they had enslaved their racial equals, people of their own color; whereas the planters had put in bondage only those of an "alien, lower race." They did not, however, mention their own mulatto children, whom they were keeping in slavery.

The advanced Northern workers had an answer to all this Southern propaganda as they proposed to abolish chattel and wage slavery alike, since they considered both intolerable. But the Northern industrialists were highly embarrassed by the Southern uncovering of the terrible conditions prevailing among their workers. Henry Wilson, Abolitionist Senator from Massachusetts, replied to Senator Hammond and made the best of a bad job. He showed that whereas workers in an iron mill in New England were paid a dollar a day, workers in the South in the same occupation got only fifty cents, with other wage rates in proportion. As Schlueter remarks, "It was easy to convict the South Carolina Senator of misrepresenting the social conditions of the South, but it was difficult to refute his statement concerning capitalist development and its consequences for free workingmen."[5]

"UNCLE TOM'S CABIN"

One of the heaviest blows for the cause of Negro emancipation during this crucial period was struck by Harriet Beecher Stowe with her celebrated anti-slavery novel, *Uncle Tom's Cabin*. This great work was first published in serial form in *The National Era* in June 1851, and as a book in 1852. Mrs. Stowe had lived for eighteen years in Cincinnati, just across the Ohio River from the slave state of Kentucky. She knew the "peculiar institution" very well, especially as she had helped fleeing slaves along the Underground Railroad. She therefore got the basic truth about slavery into her famous book, and it shocked the United States and the world.[6]

Uncle Tom's Cabin was sensationally successful. This was because it appeared at a strategic moment in the slavery debate and went straight to the core of the great national issue. Within a year the book sold 300,000 copies, and eventually its sale ran up to several millions. The North was enthralled by the vivid story of the tragic life of Negro slaves. Mrs. Stowe's book was adapted for the stage, and for decades Uncle Tom shows were produced all over the country. The book also had a tremendous impact abroad. It was translated into German, Russian, Polish, Chinese, Bengalese, Finnish, Persian, French, Italian, and many other languages. Nearly 200,000 copies were sold in England the first year. Tolstoy, Hertzen, Heine, Dickens, George Sand, Macaulay, and other famous European writers hailed the book.

Uncle Tom's Cabin was a terrific blow at slavery, and the South was stunned by it. Lincoln referred to Mrs. Stowe as the little lady who started the Civil War. Pro-slavery writers furiously attacked the book as fantastically untrue; but Mrs. Stowe, in reply, was able to document it thoroughly from slave life, piling outrage upon outrage. She also produced the real Uncle Tom (Josiah Henson), Eliza, and Little Eva. In a vain effort to offset the tremendous effects of *Uncle Tom's Cabin,* Southern writers turned out a muddy flood of books, articles, and poems justifying slavery. Parrington states that within three years no less than 13 pro-slavery novels appeared in the South.

Mrs. Stowe's condemnation of slavery was brilliant, but her remedy for the evil was empty. She was essentially a non-resistant, Garrisonian Christian and she proposed that eventually the Negroes should be sent back to Africa. She said, "Let the Church of the North receive these poor sufferers in the spirit of Christ; receive them to the educating advantages of Christian Republican society and schools, until they have attained to somewhat of a moral and intellectual maturity, and then assist them in their passage to their shores [Africa], where they may put into practice the lessons they have learned in America."[7]

"THE IMPENDING CRISIS"

Another battering stroke against slavery was delivered in 1857 by Hinton Rowan Helper, with his book, *The Impending Crisis*.[8] Mrs. Stowe had attacked slavery from a humanitarian standpoint, but Helper assailed it on the economic side. Helper, hailing from North Carolina, had a "poor white" background. His text was, "To say nothing of the sin and shame of slavery, we believe it is a most expensive and unprofitable business." (p. 31). He defended the interests of the South in general against the narrow class interests of the planters.

Helper said that three-quarters of a century earlier the South, with rich resources, had begun an even race with the North, and now "we find her completely distanced, enervated, dejected, and dishonored." (p. 84). And the reason he gave for this disaster was the slave system. Helper showed that the North had incomparably more manufactures and capital, far greater value in farm lands, vastly more railroad mileage, and that New York State alone had more real and personal values than Virginia, North Carolina, Tennessee, Missouri, Arkansas, Florida, and Texas combined, with all their slaves counted in.

"All the free states are alike, and all the slave states are alike," said Helper. "In the former wealth, intelligence, power, progress and prosperity are the prominent characteristics; in the latter, poverty, ignorance, imbecility, inertia, and extravagance are the distinguishing features" (p. 110). The slave system benefits only a few big slaveholders, said he. As for the mass of poor whites, among whom he was raised, Helper stated: "Poverty, ignorance, and superstition are the three leading characteristics of the non-slaveholding whites of the South. Many of them grow up to the age of maturity and pass through life without ever owning so much as five dollars at any one time. Thousands of them, at an advanced age, are as ignorant of the common alphabet as if it never existed" (p. 381).

Helper was an "Abolitionist," but of a special type. He proposed to do away with slavery gradually. The slaveholders were to be reimbursed eventually from the great rise in land values which he foresaw after the abolition of slavery. A new and golden industrialism, on the Northern pattern, would spring up, and all would benefit. As for the freed slaves, they would be shipped away and colonized in Africa. Helper attacked the Negroes as competitors of the whites, and later on he opposed vital Reconstruction measures.

The Impending Crisis caused a great national sensation, second only to *Uncle Tom's Cabin*. Over three million copies of the book were sold. The Republicans made a veritable textbook of it and distributed 100,000 copies in the 1860 election campaign. Sixty-eight members of the Senate and House publicly backed it. Many thousands of copies were shipped to the South, which was dazed by the whole business. Southern postmasters refused to deliver the book to addressees, vigilante gangs gathered up all the copies they could find and made bonfires of them, and more than one unfortunate was manhandled for having the banned book in his possession.[9]

THE LINCOLN-DOUGLAS DEBATES

One of the most important segments of the national discussion of slavery was the great debate between Abraham Lincoln and Stephen A. Douglas in 1858. Lincoln and Douglas were the Republican and Democratic candidates, respectively, for Senator from Illinois. During their previous sharp informal polemic publicly, they agreed upon a series of joint discussions, which took place between August 21 and October 15 in Ottawa, Freeport, Jonesboro, Charleston, Galesburg, Quincy, and Alton, Illinois. The historic discussions attracted national attention, and they went far toward setting the stage ideologically and politically for the crucial presidential election of 1860.[10]

Lincoln was born in the backwoods of Kentucky in 1809. His father was a carpenter, and he himself was a laborer in his youth. He had no formal schooling, but he managed to teach himself enough law to be admitted to the Illinois bar. He served four times in the Illinois Legislature, and one term (1847-49) in the U.S. House of Representatives. In his early years Lincoln was a Whig, but in 1856 he joined the Republican Party and was an unsuccessful candidate for the party's vice-presidential nomination in that year. On June 16, 1858, he was chosen as the Republican nominee for U.S. Senator from Illinois. In accepting the nomination, Lincoln made his famous statement that "a house divided against itself cannot stand," and that "this government cannot endure permanently half slave and half free." Either one side or the other had to win decisively, he maintained. Lincoln looked upon slavery as a "sin," an "injustice," and a political danger, and he opposed its further spread. Later, in 1864, he said, "I am naturally anti-slavery. If slavery is not wrong, nothing is wrong. I cannot remember when I did not so think."[11] But Lincoln originally was not an Abolitionist. In his early career he sharply attacked the Abolitionists, and he once appeared as counselor for a Kentucky slaveholder seeking the return of a runaway slave.[12]

Douglas, a Chicago railroad attorney, whose political biography we have outlined briefly in Chapter 16, was a rich man and a conciliator of slavery. Along with Clay and Webster, he had been an architect of the pro-slavery Compromise of 1850. He was closely associated with the infamous Kansas-Nebraska law, which was based upon his states' rights principle of "Popular [squatter] Sovereignty." Officially the leading Illinois Democrat, Douglas was known as "the Little Giant," because of his small stature and keen intelligence.

The Lincoln-Douglas debates covered many phases of the slavery question. Lincoln said, "The real issue in this controversy . . . is the sentiment on the part of one class that looks upon the institution of slavery as a wrong, and of another class that does not look upon it as a wrong." He declared that the Republicans were in the former and the Democrats in the latter category. Lincoln claimed that when the Founding Fathers declared that all men were created equal, they included the Negro. Then, contradicting this liberal interpretation of the Constitution, Lincoln repeatedly assured his audiences that he did not advocate political and social equality for Negroes. In reply, Douglas gave slavery an implicit endorsement by failing to attack it. He denied flatly that Negroes were entitled to political equality under the Constitution, maintaining that to them were due only such rights and privileges as each state saw fit to accord them. A militant white supremacist, Douglas declared that "This government of ours is founded on the white basis, was made by the white man for the benefit of the white man, and is to be administered by white men in such wise as they see fit."

Lincoln declared that eventually slavery would have to be eliminated. He said that the Republicans "desire a policy that looks to a peaceful end of slavery at some time, as a wrong." But he added, "I have no purpose directly or indirectly, to interfere with the institution of slavery in the States where it exists." Lincoln favored amending the Fugitive Slave Act and then enforcing it. He supported the abolition of slavery in the District of Columbia, with compensation for the slaveholders. Douglas assailed Lincoln's "house divided" theory. He said that the idea of the eventual liquidation of slavery would inevitably involve interference with slavery in the slave states, as indeed it finally did. Douglas declared, "In my opinion our government can endure forever divided into free and slave states, as our fathers made it"—which was very poor prophecy.

At the center of the debates, reflecting the bitter national controversy over the Kansas and Dred Scott disputes, was the question of whether or not the government had the duty and the constitutional power either to legalize or to ban slavery in the territories. Lincoln took essentially the traditional Free Soil position. He insisted that the Dred Scott decision should be reversed and that Congress should specifically outlaw slavery in the territories as Federal-controlled areas. Otherwise, he said, slavery would develop there, with or without legal sanction. Kansas was a glaring proof of this. "One of the methods," said Lincoln, "of treating it [slavery] as a wrong is to make provision that it should grow no larger."

Douglas countered Lincoln's Free Soil proposals by presenting, with a lot of glittering demagogy, his theory of "Popular [squatter] Sovereignty"; which meant that the people in each territory should decide by popular vote whether or not they wanted slavery. On the surface, this sounded democratic, but Lincoln wrecked the whole proposition by pointing out that by the Dred Scott decision slavery had been legalized throughout the nation, and that, therefore, any local legislation to establish or disestablish it would be unconstitutional. Lincoln put Douglas, who was an aspirant for the Presidency, in a dilemma, either horn of which was disastrous for him. If he supported the right of Congress to decide upon slavery in the states and territories, he would surely lose much of his support in the South; and if he contended that Congress had no such right, but that it resided locally, he would cut into his Northern support. So he chose the first horn of the dilemma, with the result that he lost support in both the South and North.

Douglas was an excellent speaker and a brilliant debater, whereas the tall and ungainly Lincoln, although a convincing speaker, was slow in speech and possessed of a poor voice. The Democratic press howled that the Little Giant had made mincemeat of the backwoods Rail-Splitter, but the sequel showed otherwise. In the Illinois State Legislature (as the legislatures chose United States Senators in those years), Douglas was elected by a vote of 54 to 46. Lincoln would probably have won by a popular vote, however, as the Republicans carried the state for local offices. It turned out, in fact, that the victory in the great debate was Lincoln's. It cleared the way for him to secure the Republican presidential nomination in 1860; whereas Douglas thereby ruined his own chances of heading the Democratic ticket in that election.

19. The Presidential Election of 1860

Throughout the decade of 1850-60, there was a rising wave of political struggle between the Southern plantation system and the industrialists and democratic forces of the North. Cotton production was rapidly growing and with it the arrogance of the planters; industrial production was also expanding swiftly and the Northern industrialists were less and less disposed to yield to the insolent demands of the slaveholders. During this decade, as we have seen, the great collision had reached the pitch of local armed struggle, and at the end of the period the nation was standing upon the verge of revolution.

This crucial decade began with the ill-omened Compromise of 1850. Then followed in rapid succession such vital events as the Fugitive Slave Act of 1850, the publication of *Uncle Tom's Cabin* in 1851, the passage of the Kansas-Nebraska Act in 1854, the formation of the Republican Party in 1854, and its big success in the election of 1856, the Dred Scott decision in 1857, the publication of *The Impending Crisis* in 1857, and John Brown's raid in 1859. Intense, cumulative mass struggles developed around all these issues, and they were sharpened by the deep economic crisis which hit the country in 1857. The presidential elections of 1860 capped this series of struggles and brought the country to a revolutionary climax.

THE KNOW-NOTHING CONVENTION

The major political party conventions in the fateful year of 1860 took place during April and June. The remnants of the American, or Know-Nothing Party, held their convention in Baltimore on May 16, under the name of the Constitutional Union Party. The party nominated John Bell of Tennessee for president (defeating Sam Houston of Texas), and Edward Everett of Massachusetts for vice-president.

Since its foundation in 1843, the American Party had followed a narrowly chauvinistic policy, cultivating hatred of the foreign-born,

Catholics, Jews, and Negroes. In 1856, it stated its general line in the following paragraph of its platform: "Americans must rule America; and to this end native-born citizens should be selected for all State, Federal, and municipal offices of government employment, in preference to all others."[1] In 1860, however, what was left of the reactionary party adopted a platform devoted to general platitudes about patriotism. It ignored the burning question of slavery, as though it did not exist. This was the Know-Nothing Party's swan song; it was destroyed in the 1860 election.[2]

THE REPUBLICAN PARTY CONVENTION

The convention of the six-year-old Republican Party was held in Chicago, beginning on May 16, 1860. It was made up of 466 delegates from all the free states, plus Delaware, Maryland, Missouri, and Virginia. David Wilmot, of "Wilmot Proviso" fame, was chosen chairman. The party was a heterogeneous gathering of capitalists, merchants, intellectuals, farmers, and workers, with the capitalists in command. At that time there was very little separate organization among these classes—such as employers' associations, farmers' groups, and trade unions. Hence the revolutionary alliance was not a federation of these class forces, but a general mixture of them. Present at the convention were high tariff capitalists, Free Soil farmers, Whig intellectuals, and anti-slavery workers. The cement which bound them all together was the need for joint struggle against the common enemy, the Southern planters.

Although political opinion ranged wide among the delegates, the convention had no difficulty in agreeing upon a platform, which was unanimously adopted on the second day. The platform reiterated the principles of the Declaration of Independence and endorsed the proposition that "no person should be deprived of life, liberty, or property, without due process of law." On the basis of this, the convention denied "the authority of Congress, of a territorial legislature, or of any individuals to give legal existence to Slavery in any Territory of the United States." The party declared that "the normal condition of all the territory in the United States is that of freedom," and it expressed alarm at the new dogma—(Dred Scott decision)—which "carries slavery into any or all of the Territories of the United States." It specifically condemned the brutal attempts of the Pierce Administration to force slavery upon the beleaguered people of Kansas. The platform, essentially a Free Soil document, did not specifically attack slavery, or foresee its eventual extinction.

The convention endorsed the protective tariff, which was urged to secure liberal wages to workingmen, adequate prices to agriculture, and good profits to manufacturers. For the farmers, the platform called for a satisfactory homestead law; for the foreign-born, full protection of their civil and citizenship rights; and for the country in general, an active program of internal improvements, with special stress upon the building of a transcontinental railroad.[3]

There were three well-defined political trends in the convention. The left wing was made up of Abolitionists—whose leaders were Stevens, Sumner, Douglass, Birney, and others—and it strove to do away altogether with slavery; in the center was the Lincoln-Free Soil group, which criticized slavery and expected that it would die out some day; the right wing, gathered around men like Seward, wanted only to contain slavery, but not to attack it. The platform followed essentially the political line of the right wing. For the first 18 months of the Civil War, it was to become the general program of the Lincoln Administration.

THE NOMINATION OF LINCOLN

The real struggle in the convention came over the selection of the presidential candidate. The two principal aspirants for the nomination were William H. Seward of New York and Abraham Lincoln. In his earlier years, Seward had been an outspoken enemy of slavery, but by 1860 he was beginning to make big concessions to the slavocracy. He had bitterly denounced John Brown, and he tended more and more to yield to the insatiable demands of the planters. At the Chicago convention, the more conservative elements rallied around his candidacy. Lincoln, whose national reputation had soared as a result of his famous debate with Senator Douglas, had powerful support from the Western farmers and frontiersmen, the city workers, and the business interests.

The balloting took place on the third day of the convention. A simple majority only was needed to decide. The first ballot showed Seward with 173½ votes, and Lincoln with 102. The third ballot, however, gave Lincoln 231½ against 180 for Seward. Thereupon several states changed their votes, giving Lincoln the majority. This was a victory for the center and left-wing groups. Hannibal Hamlin of Maine got the nomination for vice-president.

The Marxists—Weydemeyer, Douai, and others—played an important part in the nomination of Lincoln. They were instrumental in preventing the placing in nomination of Frémont, which would have defeated Lincoln and given the victory to Seward. Prior to the convention, German workers in New York, Chicago, and elsewhere, among whom the Marxists were very influential, had also called upon the Republican convention to take a vigorous stand against slavery. Among their other activities was the well-known conference at the *Deutsches Haus* in Chicago. This was a broad conference, at which Douai was present and Weydemeyer represented the German workingmen's movement of Chicago. The conference submitted several resolutions to the Republican convention, urging that "they be applied in a sense most hostile to slavery."[4] The German and labor vote at the convention went strongly for Lincoln, who was favorably known among the workers, the farmers, and the foreign-born.

THE SPLIT IN THE DEMOCRATIC PARTY

The Democratic Party called its convention in Charleston, South Carolina, on April 23, 1860. Senator Douglas was the outstanding contender for the Democratic nomination. At the start, however, he ran into very heavy opposition from the Southern delegations. The latter took umbrage at Douglas' theory of "popular sovereignty," which he had dwelt upon at length in his big debates with Lincoln two years earlier. The Southerners, taking the bit between their teeth, were militantly on the offensive. They were heading toward secession, and they refused to accept Douglas' conception of states' rights. On the basis of the Dred Scott decision, they now claimed that slavery had become a national institution, that it was guaranteed as such by the Constitution, and that Congress had no right either to establish or abolish it.

This viewpoint was stated at the beginning of the convention by a Mr. Avery of North Carolina: "That the National Democracy of the United States hold these cardinal principles on the subject of Slavery in the Territories: First, that Congress has no power to abolish Slavery in the Territories; second, that the Territorial Legislature has no power to abolish Slavery in the Territories, nor any power to prohibit the introduction of slaves there, nor any power to destroy or impair the right of property in slaves by any legislation whatever."[5] Avery later elaborated his resolution to contain demands for the acquisition of Cuba and the faithful enforcement of the Fugitive Slave Act.

Although it had the backing of a majority of the Resolutions Committee, Avery's resolution was rejected by the convention. Thereupon the delegations of Mississippi, Louisiana, Florida, Texas, Alabama, Georgia and North Carolina—led by Alabama—withdrew from the convention. What was left of the convention proceeded to ballot for nominations, with Senator Douglas leading. But after 57 ballots, with no one receiving the necessary two-thirds vote, the convention recessed until June 18, to be re-opened in Baltimore.

After this debacle, the seceding Southern delegates assembled and adopted a platform, as outlined by Avery. Then they recessed to meet again in Richmond the second Monday in June. The regular Democratic convention re-assembled in Baltimore, and after a big wrangle, nominated as its presidential ticket Stephen A. Douglas of Illinois and Benjamin Fitzpatrick of Alabama. The seceders' convention also duly met in June and nominated as its candidates John C. Breckinridge of Kentucky and Joseph Lane of Oregon.[6]

The Democratic Party was now split down the middle, with two mutually hostile tickets in the field. In their platforms[7] both Democratic parties endorsed enforcement of the Fugitive Slave Act, the acquisition of Cuba, and the building of a railroad from the Mississippi to the Pacific Coast. As for the disputed question of the power of Congress and the territorial governments, over which the split had occurred, the Breckinridge seceders insisted that slavery was legal everywhere under the Constitution and that neither Congress nor the territorial governments could interfere with it. On the other hand, the Douglas regulars, while currently accepting the Supreme Court decision in the Dred Scott case, hoped for a new decision on the basis of their "Squatter Sovereignty" theory.

THE 1860 ELECTIONS

The election campaign reflected the coming secession of the Southern states. Breckinridge expressed thinly disguised support for secession. Douglas advocated union with no attack upon slavery, and Lincoln supported union and the containment of slavery within its present boundaries. The Republican Party had no ticket in ten of the Southern states. The Democrats had two sets of candidates in practically every state. None of the parties in the field proposed the abolition of slavery.

Lincoln actively sought the support of Northern businessmen and this effort did not go unheeded. As Faulkner says, "By stressing a protective tariff, free land for the settlers and a Pacific railroad, and reaffirming their opposition to the extension of slavery, the Republican platform held out a beckoning hand to the conservative business interests of the North-East."[8] In New York, however, where there was a notorious pro-slavery group in capitalist circles, anti-Lincoln sentiment was strong. The *Journal of Commerce* sneered that of the 53 banks in the city only five had endorsed Lincoln.[9] The Douglas-Breckinridge-Bell forces joined in a New York fusion ticket, and William B. Astor and other wealthy men are said to have spent $200,000 in an effort to prevent Lincoln from carrying New York State.[10] Nevertheless, Lincoln won the state by a majority of 50,000 votes.

Lincoln made a powerful appeal to the farmers of the North and West. But he ran into strong opposition in Ohio, Indiana, and Illinois. "Perhaps about 40 per cent of midwesterners in 1860 were of Southern blood."[11] The great mass of voters in these states had been pushed out of the slave states by expanding cotton production, which relentlessly squeeezed the small farmers into the mountains or out onto the frontier. These elements were violently anti-Negro, and were to cause the Lincoln Administration a world of trouble during the Civil War. Even so, Lincoln carried all three states.

The workers gave Lincoln heavy support. Weydemeyer and other Marxists were a big factor in educating the workers to back Lincoln. The bulk of the trade unions endorsed him. All unionists did not take this action, however; William C. Sylvis, the outstanding labor leader in this period, voted for Douglas. The Republican Party campaigned among the workers as the party of labor. Lincoln himself had been a worker, and although he was by no means an opponent of capitalism, he had shown great sympathy for workingmen. During the war this attitude of his was to be more clearly expressed in his defense of the workers' right to strike and especially in his famous statement that, "Labor is prior to, and independent of capital. Capital is only the fruit of labor and could never have existed if labor had not first existed. Labor is superior to capital, and deserves much the higher consideration."[12] The workers marched in torchlight processions all over the North and West. Foner states that "It is not an exaggeration to say that the Republican Party fought its way to victory in the campaign of 1860 as the party of free labor."[13]

The foreign-born, who in 1860 formed 47.62 per cent of the population in New York City, 50 per cent in Chicago, 59.66 per cent in St. Louis, etc., also gave strong support to Lincoln, particularly because of his anti-Know-Nothing record. This was especially the case among the Germans, where Marxist influence was strong. Carl Schurz was the outstanding German bourgeois pro-Lincoln leader. Of the 87 German language papers, 69 backed Lincoln. The German vote undoubtedly swung several doubtful states to Lincoln.

Most of the Abolitionists voted for Lincoln, save the small hard-core of sectarians around Garrison, who still clung to their non-political position. Frederick Douglass endorsed Lincoln's candidacy, although he sharply criticized the Republican Party because its inadequate platform failed to attack slavery, and especially because it did not demand the repeal of the infamous Fugitive Slave Act. Douglass said, "If the Republican Party shall arrest the spread of slavery . . . that party, though it may not abolish slavery, will not have existed in vain. . . . I sincerely hope for the triumph of that party over all the odds and ends of slavery combined against it."[14] And Wendell Phillips said with rare foresight, "The Republican Party have undertaken a problem, the solution of which will force them to our position."[15] As for most of the intellectuals who had long battled in the anti-slavery movement, they flocked to the Lincoln standard—Walt Whitman, John Greenleaf Whittier, Ralph Waldo Emerson, and scores of others. Lincoln's candidacy was the historical political juncture between the Free Soilers and the Abolitionists.

The campaign was the hardest fought in the history of the Republic. The Democrats—newspapers, employers, politicians—brought pressure upon the workers to terrorize them into voting against Lincoln. They threatened the workers with the loss of their jobs, with a labor market flooded with cheap Negro labor, with a great economic crisis, and with the violent break-up of the Federal Union. Nevertheless, the workers and other toilers voted for the Republican Party in far greater numbers than in previous elections. The party put out tremendous quantities of literature and held innumerable meetings. "Wide Awake" clubs marched in torchlight processions in many cities.[16]

The election resulted in victory for Lincoln. His total vote was 1,857,610 against 1,291,574 for Douglas, 850,082 for Breckinridge, and 646,124 for Bell. Lincoln carried all the free states except for New Jersey (where he got almost half the votes), with a total of 180 electoral votes; Breckinridge carried 11 Southern states, with 72 electoral votes; Bell carried Virginia, Kentucky, and Tennessee, with 39 electoral votes, and Douglas carried only Missouri and New Jersey, with 12 votes. In the 15 Southern states the popular vote was Breckinridge, 570,871; Bell, 515,973; Douglas, 163,525; and Lincoln 26,430. From these figures it can be seen that Lincoln, although he had secured a majority of electoral votes against the combined opposition (180 to 123), fell short of a majority of the total popular vote by 930,170.

The two Democratic factions together had polled more votes than Lincoln, and if they had had but one ticket, they would have undoubtedly won the election. But the South did not want Douglas enough to concentrate its full strength upon him; so he did not carry a single Southern state. He would have done far better as the Southern candidate in 1852 or 1856, but times were different now. The "fire-eaters" of the South, who had already decided upon secession, also could not utilize Douglas for this purpose. Although favoring slavery, he also stood for the maintenance of the Union, as he showed after Fort Sumter had been fired upon. The planters, however, were determined to wreck the Union and to pull as many states as possible with them into a new government based on slavery. The split in the Democratic Party was not, as many have said, the result of a blundering factional fight, but a carefully calculated step in a thoroughly planned scheme for Southern secession.

20. The Revolutionary Crisis of 1861

Lincoln's election was like an electric shock to the Southern slaveholders; and it galvanized them immediately into an energetic secession movement. As a class, they were dominated by a relatively few big planters—maximum 200,000—who knew what they wanted, had a solid command of the situation, and were determined to trample down all opposition. The time had come to put into practice the secession plans which had long been hatching.[1] In 1856 they had conspired to seize Washington if Frémont were elected, so they did not hesitate when Lincoln was elected in 1860. The planters' control of their forces was far more secure than that of their Northern enemies, who were but loosely united, had no uniform program, and were torn with confusion, indecision, and internal treachery.

The planters, in embarking upon secession, nursed the most ambitious plans. As Karl Marx wrote in the Vienna *Presse* of November 7, 1861: "With a peaceful cession of the contested territory to the Southern Confederacy, the North would surrender to the slave republic more than three-quarters of the entire territory of the United States. The North would lose the Gulf of Mexico altogether, the Atlantic Ocean from Pensacola Bay to Delaware Bay, and would even cut itself off from the Pacific Ocean. Missouri, Kansas, New Mexico, Arkansas, and Texas would draw California after them. Incapable of wresting the mouth of the Mississippi from the hands of the strong hostile slave republic in the South, the great agricultural states in the basin between the Rocky Mountains and the Alleghanies, in the valleys of the Mississippi, the Missouri, and the Ohio, would be compelled by their economic interests to secede from the North and enter the Southern Confederacy. These Northwestern states in their turn, would draw after them all the Northern states lying further east, with perhaps the exception of the states of New England, into the same vortex of secession. Thus there would, in fact, take place, not a dissolution of the Union, but a *reorganization* of it, a *reorganization, on the basis of slavery,* under the recognized control of the slaveholding oligarchy."[2] This plan, in essence, was openly proclaimed   by the slaveholders and, as Marx remarked, their new constitution provided a place for all the states of the Union.

"We will expand over Mexico," the secessionists cried, "over the isles of the sea, over the far-off Southern tropics, until we establish a Confederation of Republics, the greatest, the freest, the most powerful the world has ever seen."[3] Among their grandiose plans, the slaveholders were also resolved to make slaves of the white wage workers of the North. They boasted they would operate the mills of New England on a slave basis. Toombs, a Georgia fire-eater, declared that he "would call the roll of his slaves on Bunker Hill." Calhoun had pronounced slavery "a universal condition," and the slaveholders avowed that "the adoption of the chattel slavery principle in the Northern factory system would forever end the war between the employer and labor."[4]

The slaveholders planned to work all these miracles on the basis of the indispensability of cotton. They realized quite well the superiority of the North in man-power, industry, and wealth; but they believed this would all melt away before the magic strength of cotton. To get cotton, the North would supposedly be compelled within six months to sue for peace on the Confederacy's own terms.[5] They assumed, too, that England would make war on the United States, rather than allow its great textile industry to stand idle for want of cotton. Senator Hammond of South Carolina boasted that the South was as large as Great Britain, France, Austria, Prussia, and Spain together. "Is not that territory enough," said he, "to make an empire that shall rule the world?" . . . "You dare not make war on cotton. Cotton is King." He declared that if no cotton were produced for three years, "England would topple headlong and carry the whole civilized world with her, save the South."[6]

THE SECESSION MOVEMENT

On the basis of these grandiose plans and gross illusions, the big slaveholders of the South launched their secessionist movement. It was a revolt of the cotton planters. Their strategy was that of a quick offensive. This was quite in line with their aggressive policy of the past generation, including such actions as the seizure of Texas, the Mexican War, the Compromises of 1820 and 1850, the Fugitive Slave Act, the slashing of the tariff in 1857, the Kansas-Nebraska law, and the Dred Scott decision. These were but stages in the growing offensive of the cotton planters against their Northern enemies. So, immediately after Lincoln's election, they went energetically into action.

South Carolina, which had headed the 1832 nullification attempt at secession, again took the lead in 1860. Four days after the election, the secession movement began. The official state machinery was set in motion, the people were whipped up by flaming newspaper articles, liberty poles were set up, and the Marseillaise was sung in the streets. The masses were told that they were carrying through a people's revolution, and their action was compared to that of Massachusetts in 1776.[7] On December 20, the act of separation was accomplished by South Carolina. The other cotton states followed this lead. Within a month Florida, Georgia, Alabama, Mississippi, and Louisiana had also seceded. Texas, Virginia, North Carolina, Arkansas, and Tennessee went out in the next few months, making 11 states in all that quit the Union. Meanwhile, the Southerners hastily improvised military forces and took over nearly all the United States army posts and forts in the South, with the notable exception of Fort Sumter, in Charleston Harbor, which refused to surrender.

Aiming to confront Lincoln with an accomplished fact when he took office on March 4, 1861, the seceding states hastened to combine themselves into a new government. On February 4, the six states then out of the Union met in Montgomery, Alabama, adopted a provisional constitution for the "Confederated States of America," and elected Jefferson Davis and Alexander H. Stephens as provisional President and Vice-President. Davis, a wealthy Mississippi cotton planter, was Senator from Mississippi and had been Secretary of War under President Pierce from 1853 to 1857. The Constitution of the Confederacy was copied almost verbatim from that of the United States, except that it outlawed the protective tariff and legalized slavery throughout the country. It declared that "no . . . law denying or impairing the right of property in Negro slaves shall be passed."[8]

Meanwhile, President James Buchanan stood calmly aside and allowed all these events to happen without interference on his part. And so did the pro-slavery Democratic majorities in the Senate and House. In 1832, President Jackson had met South Carolina's threat to secede by mobilizing the army and threatening to hang Calhoun; but Buchanan was evidently a party to the present conspiracy, and did nothing. Knowing what was in the wind, he had previously rejected the advice of Chief of Staff, General Winfield Scott, to arm properly the garrisons in the South, and he had also allowed the core of the Federal Army to be shipped off to Texas, where it promptly surrendered when Texas seceded. When the general secession got under way, Buchanan gave it a green light by announcing on December 3, 1860, in his message to Congress that neither the President nor Congress had the power under the Constitution to coerce a seceding state.

The secession of the Southern states could never have been put through, however, had the matter been left to the people of these states to decide by referendum vote. The planters knew this and proceeded to force the break by terrorism and packed state conventions. Nevertheless, they encountered much heavy opposition, especially from the delegates of small farmers and poor whites from the mountain areas of the South. Aptheker says, "Secession was accomplished against the will of the vast majority of the Southern people."[9] Characteristically, in Tennessee, despite all coercion, 47,233 voted against and 103,399 voted for secession—East Tennessee cast a majority against secession, 33,000 to 14,500. In Georgia, in a hand-picked convention, the vote was 208 for secession and 89 against. In Louisiana, 20,448 voted for secession and 17,296 against. In Arkansas a majority voted in convention against secession, but they were slugged into line. Virginia at first voted against secession, and did not secede until the shooting war had begun. At that, when Virginia finally seceded, it lost by a popular uprising the whole western half of the state, which became the pro-Union West Virginia. The strong anti-secessionist feeling existing in many parts of the South was especially emphasized by the fact that the slaveholders were unable, with all their hooks and crooks, to dragoon the border slave states—Maryland, Delaware, Kentucky, and Missouri—into secession.[10] This constituted what, in the long run, turned out to be a decisive defeat for them. Secession from the Union was very far indeed from being the unanimous action in the South that the planters and their mouthpieces have tried to make it appear; on the contrary, it was forced through against the will of the people.

CONFUSED COUNSELS IN THE NORTH

When Abraham Lincoln took office on March 4, 1861, he found the country rent in two, with a rival government in full operation in the South. Still worse was the confusion in the North about how to meet the unprecedented situation. The Northern capitalist class was split, the labor movement was weak, the middle class wavered, and the Negro leaders, the clearest-sighted element in the situation, were not strong enough to give decisive leadership to the whole movement. The prospect of a civil war was dreadful, and many efforts were made to avert it. Immediately, a strong outcry arose in various Northern quarters, substantially agreeing with the Southern position that the states had the right under the Constitution to secede if they saw fit. Secession was further condoned on the grounds that it was revolutionary. This was a popular cry, as the people's right to revolution was still generally recognized in the United States at that time.

In line with their long-time program, Garrison and Phillips took the position that it was well for the free North to separate from the slave South. Three days after Lincoln's election, Horace Greeley, editor of the New York *Tribune* said, "If the cotton states shall decide that they can do better out of the Union than in it, we insist on letting them go in peace." The Chicago *Tribune* and other papers took a similar position. Most of the big merchants of New York, who were notoriously pro-slavery, favored peaceful secession; and Fernando Wood, the mayor of that city, came forward with a fantastic proposal that New York City should also secede and become a "free city." He called New York "the Empire city of the Confederacy."[11]

Many proposals were made to heal the widening breach between the North and the South. On December 18, Senator Crittenden of Kentucky proposed in a resolution in Congress, that slavery should be recognized south of the 36°30′ line and prohibited north of it, that Congress should have no power to abolish slavery in the present slave states, and that the Fugitive Slave Act must be strictly enforced, and that Congress could not abolish slavery in the District of Columbia while it existed in Maryland and Virginia.[12] Crittenden's proposal, which had the backing of many slaveholders, was defeated in the Senate by but one vote, with six Southern senators abstaining.

Another "peace proposal" was the convention called by Virginia (which had not yet seceded) in Washington, on February 4, 1861, a month before Lincoln took office. Twenty-two states were represented. The seven seceded Southern states did not send delegates, nor did Michigan, Wisconsin, Minnesota, California, and Oregon. No solid decision could be reached. Several resolutions were submitted to Congress by various groups of delegates, but nothing came of them.

Under Lincoln's prodding, Congress adopted an amendment to the Constitution that would have forever denied to Congress the right to abolish slavery in the states. On March 4, 1861, this dangerous proposal was sent out with Lincoln's approval for ratification by the states. Three of them had already endorsed it, when the rebels fired on Fort Sumter six weeks later and thus put an end to the proposal.[13]

There were many other less extensive attempts to patch up the internal split. In general, such proposals aided the South by sowing confusion and hesitation in the North. As for the planters, they were fully determined upon secession. They went right ahead consolidating their forces. They established the Confederacy, their representatives gave up their seats in Congress, and their generals and other officers resigned from the United States Army and began to build a Confederate army. Secession was an accomplished fact, and the decisive cotton planters had no interest in "peace" proposals. They figured that, with the master commodity—cotton—in their possession, they held the trump card. On this basis, they went ahead toward war.

Vice-President Stephens declared of the Confederacy, "Its foundations are laid, its cornerstone rests upon the great truth that the negro is not the equal of the white man; that slavery, subordination to the superior race, is his natural and normal condition." Walker, the rebel Secretary of War, announced that the Confederates would have control of Washington by May 1. Others, even more optimistic, planned to seize Washington immediately by attacks from without and within, and to prevent Lincoln from becoming President.

STATES' RIGHTS AND REVOLUTION

The defenders of the Union and Free Soil rejected the states' rights theory of the rebellious South, which was basically a cover-up for the slavery system. They asserted that the Union was permanent and indissoluble, and they denied the right of the states to quit it when they felt like doing so. States' rights, in their view, definitely fell short of the right of secession. This was a basically correct argument. For the right of self-determination, including the right of separation, belongs to nations, not to states or provinces of nations. The states' rights theory, defended by the slaveholders, was logically one of political atomization.

The Union men also repudiated the claim of the rebels that theirs was a people's revolution, that they were exercising the generally admitted right of revolution and were acting in the spirit of the great Revolution of 1776. Instead, Union supporters denounced secession as a treasonous rebellion and demanded that it be put down. In this they were correct. The cotton planters were not carrying through a revolution, but a counter-revolution. They were giving a striking example of Stalin's statement that "Rich experience . . . teaches that up to now not a single class has voluntarily made way for another class. There is no such precedent in world history."[14] Like all other reactionary classes when faced by a democratic advance of the masses which they cannot stem, the Southern planters had recourse to violence in an effort to maintain their position as exploiters. They tried to overthrow the government by force. There was indeed a revolution brewing in 1861, but it did not come from the Southern planters; it came from the Northern industrialists and their Negro, farmer, worker and middle class allies. Its spearpoint was directed against the rule of the planters and their system of chattel slavery. The first stage of this developing revolution was the election of Abraham Lincoln, and the revolution was fated soon to go into its second phase—military action against the planters' Confederacy.

LINCOLN'S POLICY

While the planters were pushing their new government to completion, firm voices in the North rejected the false "peace" moves and demanded that the government, patterning itself after Jackson in 1832, proceed vigorously against the rebels. These were the voices of the awakening industrialists, of the great revolutionary coalition of classes, now rapidly consolidating itself. Thaddeus Stevens, a small industrialist, denounced as moral treason the pacifist plan to "let the departing states go in peace," and he called for vigorous action against the seceders. Frederick Douglass, the great Negro leader, clearly expressed the rising spirit of resistance in the North and the war implications of the situation. Two months before Lincoln was inaugurated, he said, "The incoming President is elected to preside over the *United* States; and if any of them have been permitted, by the treachery and weakness of his predecessor, to break way from the Government, his business will be to bring them back, and see that the laws of the United States are duly extended over them and faithfully executed. . . . He is pledged to the maintenance of the Union; and if he has the *will* he will not lack the power to maintain it against all foes. . . . South Carolina must conquer the United States, or the United States must conquer South Carolina." He said that there must be more than windy resolutions to oppose the rebellion—"There must be swords, guns, powder, balls, and men behind them to use them."[15]

Lincoln had come to his inauguration in Washington in disguise, for in the wild turmoil a plot had been hatched to kill him. In his Inaugural Address,[16] Lincoln attempted to placate the South. He reiterated his previous statement that "I have no purpose, directly or indirectly to interfere with the institution of slavery in the States where it exists. I believe I have no lawful right to do so, and I have no inclination to do so." He also implied that he would enforce the Fugitive Slave Act. Lincoln, however, denied the right of secession of individual states, claimed by the Southern spokesmen. "No State," said he, "upon its own mere motion can lawfully get out of the Union." He stated that, therefore, "the laws of the Union [will] be faithfully executed in all the States." Following out this line, he said he would proceed to collect revenues, hold government property, and operate the mails in the seceded states, without in any way coercing them. The responsibility for civil war, should it come, he declared, would rest with the South.

In this speech Lincoln made his famous formulation of the people's right of revolution, but he did not recognize the secession of the South as an exercise of this right. He said: "This country, with its institutions, belongs to the people who inhabit it. Whenever they shall grow weary of the existing government, they can exercise their constitutional right of amending it, or their revolutionary right to dismember or overthrow it."

THE REBELS FIRE ON FORT SUMTER

The militant Free Soilers and Abolitionists in the North were disappointed at Lincoln's Inaugural Address. They considered it much too conciliatory to the South and to the institution of slavery. They were of the opinion that the militantly rebellious South would require far more rigorous handling than the gentler methods proposed by Lincoln. "This denial of all feeling against slavery, at such a time and in such circumstances," said Douglass, "is wholly discreditable to the head and heart of Mr. Lincoln. Aside from the inhuman coldness of the sentiment, it was a weak and inappropriate utterance to such an audience, since it could neither appease nor check the wild fury of the rebel Slave Power."[17]

As for the "fire-eating" rebels in the South, they took violent exception to Lincoln's inaugural speech. They denounced it as virtually a declaration of war. They let it be known that they were prepared to resist by force of arms any attempt of the Federal government to operate in the seceded states, no matter how limited this operation might be. They claimed that the Confederacy was now an independent nation, whose borders must not be violated on pain of war.

The inevitable clash came over the possession of Fort Sumter. This fort stood in Charleston harbor, dominating the whole area. Unlike many others in the South, it had refused to surrender to the seceders. The South Carolina planters considered it as a most irritating eyesore and were determined to reduce it at any cost. So they watched the fort closely, allowing nobody to go in or out without their consent. The fort was commanded by Major Robert Anderson, and the local rebel forces by General Beauregard.

By the time Lincoln was inaugurated, the fort's garrison was starving, and he sent men and provisions to relieve it. The Confederates seized upon this action as a provocation and they fired upon the fort, April 12, 1861. After 34 hours the fort surrendered.

This action caused tremendous excitement all over the country. At last the great conflict between the forces of freedom and slavery, which had been generating for half a century, had come to an open, armed clash. On April 15, Lincoln called for 75,000 volunteer militia, "in order to suppress such [rebellious] combinations, and to cause the laws to be duly executed." Hesitant Virginia, North Carolina, Tennessee, and Arkansas now joined the Confereracy, and the great Civil War was on.

The people of the North girded themselves for the fierce test of war. The masses were seized with intense patriotic fervor. The time for temporizing, for hopeless "peace" moves, was past. Now the arrogant planters had to be crushed. In this initial outburst of war spirit even the Copperhead* press was temporarily silenced. Few among the people even dreamed of the extent and horror of the awful struggle lying ahead.

* The term "copperhead," long one of opprobrium, was, at the outbreak of the war, applied to Northern sympathizers of the slave power.

21. The Relation of Forces North and South

The attack upon Fort Sumter, on April 12, 1861, launched the great revolutionary Civil War, which lasted almost exactly four years until April 9, 1865. It was one of the most significant and devastating wars of modern history up to that time. In their desperate effort to maintain human slavery and to establish their domination over the whole country, the Southern planters wracked the American people with the most deadly and ruinous war they had ever known. Before it was finally ended, 359,528 Northern soldiers, by official report, had been killed or died of disease; and by unofficial estimates, 133,-785 Confederate soldiers had similarly perished.[1] Nor do these figures take into account the many more soldiers who were badly wounded and crippled and the huge number of civilians who died as a result of the war.

THE NORTH'S SUPERIOR WAR POTENTIAL

In this fratricidal struggle, the North possessed by far the greater potential strength in nearly every respect. There were then 23 states, embracing about three-fourths of the country's territory, on the side of the Union, and only 11 seceding states in the Confederacy. In the North there were about 23,000,000 people, and in the South but 9,000,000, of whom 4,000,000 were slaves. During the conflict, the North was able to muster 2,898,000 enlisted men in the army and navy, but the most the Confederacy could put into uniform was 1,300,000. The Beards estimate that "on the basis of men and terms of service, the ratio of the contending forces was about three to two."[2]

Besides its greater territory, population, and armed forces, the North also had other advantages over the South. Three-fourths of all banking capital was located in the North, since this was the home of all the big banking concerns of the period. The amount of capital invested in industry was, percentage-wise, likewise favorable to the North—the ratio was about two to one. It is estimated that at the beginning of the Civil War the South owed the North about $400,000,000.

In industry the South faced a serious handicap in comparison with the North. Jennings thus sums up the situation: The 11 states which in 1861 composed the Confederacy had about 15 percent of the manufacturing establishments of the country as a whole, 9.5 percent of its capital invested in industry, 8.5 percent of the industrial wage workers, 7.5 percent of the national wage bill, and a little over 8 percent of the total national industrial production.[3] The South, with one-third of the nation's railroad mileage, had practically no merchant marine, and produced only one-seventh as much machinery as the North. Only 3 percent of the total iron mined, 8 percent of bituminous coal mining, as well as 15 percent of the cotton mills were in the South.

These figures show that a relatively heavy industrial concentration existed in the North. During the decade 1850-60, rapid industrial progress was made in the country as a whole; the number of factories went up from 123,025 to 140,433, the capital invested from $533,245,-000 to $1,009,856,000, and the value of products from one billion to almost two billion dollars.[4] But the proportion of this development in the South decreased steadily. "The eleven future Confederate states produced in the year ending June 30, 1860, 8.8 percent of the total manufactures of the United States, as against almost 13 percent in 1830."[5]

Southern economists and statesmen in the pre-war decades, who realized the serious backwardness of the South in industrial development and scented a possible war ahead, made a number of efforts to improve the situation. The planters did not want industry on the basis of free workers, so some of them undertook to create it with slave labor. In the fifty years prior to the outbreak of the Civil War, a dozen conventions were held in the South, looking to the encouragement of industry. The Macon and Montgomery cotton conventions in 1851-52 proposed the construction of cotton mills, to be operated by slaves, in the cotton counties of the South. At one such gathering, held in Charleston, South Carolina, in April, 1854, a resolution was adopted which stated that "experiments have fully proven that slave labor can be profitably employed in manufacturing establishments."[6] Slaves were also used to some extent in quarrying, mining, lumber, textiles, tobacco, and on the railroads—but with little success. One iron works, however, was capitalized at $700,000 and employed 700 slaves. Slavery could be applied to agriculture and also to various handicrafts, but it was not adapted to intensive industrial production.

The South in 1861 was in a somewhat better position regarding agriculture. Aside from the great cash crop, cotton, which was the most valuable crop produced in the United States, the South, including the Border states, with one-fourth of the nation's territory and one-third of its population, turned out or possessed one-sixth of its wheat, one-third of its corn, four-fifths of its peas, nine-tenths of its sweet potatoes, one-half of its tobacco, one-fourth of its horses, two-thirds of its mules, two-fifths of its oxen, about one-third of the other farm animals.[7] Much of the non-cotton crops, however, were raised in the Border states which did not go with the Confederacy.

The degree to which the South was dependent economically upon the North (not to mention England) was illustrated by the following lament made to the citizens of Tuscaloosa, Alabama, in 1851: "At present the North fattens and grows rich upon the South. . . . Our slaves are clothed with Northern manufactured goods, have Northern hats and shoes, work with Northern hoes, ploughs, and other implements, are chastized with a Northern-made instrument, are working for Northern more than Southern profit. The slave-holder dresses in Northern goods, rides in a Northern saddle . . . patronizes Northern newspapers, drinks Northern liquors, reads Northern books, spends his money at Northern watering places. . . . In Northern vessels his products are carried to market, his cotton is ginned with Northern gins, his sugar is crushed and preserved by Northern machinery; his rivers are navigated by Northern steamboats, his mails are carried in Northern stages, his negroes are fed with Northern bacon, beef, flour and corn; his land is cleared with a Northern axe, and a Yankee clock sits upon his mantel-piece; his floor is swept with a Northern broom, and is covered with a Northern carpet; and his wife dresses herself in a Northern looking-glass . . . his son is educated at a Northern college, his daughter receives the finishing polish at a Northern seminary; his doctor graduates at a Northern medical college, his schools are supplied with Northern teachers, and he is furnished with Northern inventions and notions."[8]

THE ARCHAIC PLANTATION-SLAVERY SYSTEM

The biggest handicap of the South in the Civil War was its obsolete methods of production, especially in its use of labor power. In Chapter 14, we have indicated that history condemned the slave system to death, not only because it stood in the way of American capitalist development and constituted a deadly menace to the freedom of all the people, but also because in itself slavery was a highly inefficient system.

The low productivity of slave labor was the basic cause of the inefficiency of the slave system. In considering the type of working force needed by the capitalist system of production, Adam Smith, the pioneer economist of capitalism in its youth, said in 1776, "the work done by freemen becomes cheaper in the end than that performed by slaves."[9] Karl Marx also indicated the inefficiency of slave labor for capitalist production, maintaining that slaves habitually sabotage their work. "Hence the principle, universally applied in this method of production, only to employ the rudest and heaviest implements and such as are difficult to damage owing to their sheer clumsiness."[10] Innumerable American economists support these conclusions by Smith and Marx. Bogart says, "Since his labor was forced, the slave gave it reluctantly; he put as little strength and earnestness into his work as was compatible with safety from flogging. . . . Only the heaviest and simplest tools could be used, improved implements and machinery and fine livestock could not be entrusted to the slaves on account of their wasteful and indifferent destruction of capital."[11] And Wesley remarks that "Four Virginia slaves could not accomplish in agriculture what one ordinary free farm laborer could do in New Jersey."[12]

The slave system was also extremely wasteful of capital. The slaveholder was obliged to put all of the capital he could scrape up into slaves, who were highly priced. As De Bow remarks, the Southern planter used his capital to make "more cotton, to buy more negroes, to raise more cotton, to buy more negroes," and so on and on.[13] Wright says that on the eve of the Civil War for example, the capital investment needed to operate a 100 acre farm in Ohio by free labor was $6,000, whereas, in slave Kentucky across the river, $20,000 was needed.[14] The slave system left no available capital with which to build industry in the South, or even to finance the handling of the cotton crop—the planters were dependent for this upon the capitalists of Great Britain and the Northern states. The waste of the plantation system was also shown by the total failure to use improved agricultural methods and fertilizers. Bogart remarks that the great resources of the South—iron, coal, water, etc.—remained undeveloped, and the exhausted, uncultivated land far exceeded the cultivated.[15] With these wasteful methods, the plantation system, as Marx said, had to expand or die.

Besides fettering agriculture and industry, the reactionary plantation system also put a brake upon the development of culture in general. The so-called high culture of the slave South was just a myth concocted by the beneficiaries and advocates of that system. Thus, the handful of third-rate intellectuals in the pre-war South was altogether insignificant in comparison with the bright galaxy of writers and poets of New England during the same period. Cole remarks that "Cultured Charleston produced little creative literature; its social set looked askance even at William G. Simms."[16] This intellectual stultification also extended to the field of invention. Practically all the great American inventions of the period, in industry and agriculture, originated in the Northern states. The only major Southern invention during the plantation slave regime was the cotton gin, and that was created by a Northern mechanic.

The plantation-slave system concentrated the wealth it created in the pockets of the larger slaveholders. The great majority of the Southern population, the slaves and the poor whites, lived at the lowest possible levels of deprivation. Slaveholding was centralized in the hands of a relatively small group. About 4,000,000 whites owned no slaves whatever. The total number of slaveholders, as officially reported, was but 325,514. Of these 174,602 held one to 5 slaves; 60,765 from 5 to 10 slaves; 54,595 from 10 to 20 slaves; 29,733 from 20 to 50 slaves; 6,196 from 50 to 100 slaves; 1,479 from 100 to 200 slaves; 187 from 200 to 300, and 67 from 300 to 1000 or more.[17]

Actually, the total number of slaveholders was smaller than these figures would indicate; for the government counted two or three times those slaveholders who owned slaves in more than one county or state. Karl Marx declared that an "oligarchy of three hundred thousand slaveholders" ruled the South.[18] These, in turn, were dominated by the small number of big slaveholders. This clique was responsible for the dreadful Civil War in its desperate effort to maintain the outrageous slave system and to extend it over the whole United States.

The plantation system, at the outbreak of the War, was in a basically unhealthy economic condition. In 1800 the value of all the yearly products of the 893,041 slaves amounted to $14,385,000, or $16.10 per slave; by 1850 the figure had risen to a total value of $165,084,517 for the 3,200,000 slaves, or $51.90 per slave. At first glance, this looks like a profitable situation; but the increase in the value of the output per slave during this period was canceled for most planters by the tremendous increase in the price of slaves, which had gone up from about $150 in 1808 to $2,000 and even $4,000, on the eve of the Civil War. "At these prices," says Simons, "only the largest plantations, working the slaves in the most effective manner upon the richest lands, raising the most profitable crops, could survive. Internally the chattel slave system was devouring itself; externally it was being strangled for lack of room to expand."[19]

There are still those, even among Northern writers, who maintain that slavery was a progressive system and constituted the only way that vitally important Southern agriculture, especially the production of cotton, could have been developed. It is an accepted fact, of course, that in ancient times—in the Egyptian, Assyrian, Greek, Roman and other empires—slavery was progressive. Engels says: "It was slavery that first made possible the division of labor between agriculture and industry on a considerable scale, and along with this, the flower of the ancient world, Hellenism. Without slavery no Greek state, no Greek art and science . . . the introduction of slavery under the conditions of that time was a great step forward."[20] Mark it that Engels uses the phrase "of that time." In the United States of the eighteenth and nineteenth centuries, chattel slavery was only a reactionary capitalist atavism.

Marx stresses the enormous importance of cotton production, then operated on the basis of Negro slavery, in the development of British and American industry. He says: "Direct slavery is just as much the pivot of bourgeois industry as machinery, credits, etc. Without slavery you would have no cotton; without cotton you would have no modern industry. It is slavery that has given the colonies their value; it is the colonies that have produced world trade, and it is world trade that is the pre-condition of large-scale industry. Thus slavery is an economic category of the greatest importance. . . . Without slavery, North America, the most progressive of countries, would be transformed into a patriarchal country."[21]

This does not mean, however, that in the modern United States, as in ancient Greece, slavery was the only possible means of carrying on large-scale agriculture. The fact is that during the same period, industrial as well as agricultural production was much greater on the basis of "free" labor. The same could have been achieved in the South, if the planters had not had at hand the opportunity to make chattel slaves of the Negroes. The sequel showed that after the slavery system had been abolished by the Civil War, cotton was eventually produced far more extensively and efficiently by wage labor and tenants than had ever been done by bondsmen under chattel slavery. The so-called progressive slave system, as Helper points out so devastatingly in his book *The Impending Crisis*, just about ruined the South economically and culturally. What made the Civil War a progressive war was precisely that it wiped out the reactionary economic system of slavery.

As for the pro-slavery assertions that slavery was voluntarily accepted by the Negro slaves, this false slander has received its death blow from modern progressive Negro and white writers, especially Du Bois and Aptheker. The latter has tabulated at least 250 cases of known slave conspiracies and insurrections, not to mention innumerable other disaffections and struggles for freedom.[22]

Although cotton production went up from 1,976,198 to 2,469,093 bales in the two decades prior to the Civil War, the plantation system was in a developing crisis. This crisis was being caused by the cumulative effects of the decreasing fertility of the land, the primitive methods of production, the practical shutting off of the African slave trade, the decreasing possibility for expanding the cotton area, the rising wave of slave revolts, the rapidly increasing price of slaves, the sharpening conflicts with the Northern industrialists, the intensification of the class struggle in the South, and the growing colonial-like dependence of the South upon the North and Great Britain. These difficult conditions were greatly accentuated by the severe economic crisis of 1857; the connection between this developing crisis of the plantation system and the firing upon Fort Sumter being direct, immediate, and compelling.

WHY THE CIVIL WAR LASTED SO LONG

When the Civil War began both sides believed it would be relatively short. The South was certain that the magic power of cotton, plus the boasted superiority of its generals, would quickly force the North to surrender. The North was equally sure that the far better equipped North could readily dispose of the South. Thus, Lincoln at first called for only 75,000 troops for a three-month period.

But these hopes for a short war were doomed to disappointment. The war lasted four long, dreadful years, with gigantic casualties and property losses. The North did not collapse as the South expected; it managed to fight along without its regular supply of cotton. And England, although on the verge of hostilities a couple of times, did not go to war with the North in order to reestablish its supply of the precious white fiber. To the amazement of the North, the South, with its industry and agriculture largely collapsed, was able to withstand for four years the bigger, better-equipped, and no less brave armies of the North. Indeed, as late as 1864, three years after the struggle began, the fate of the Union was still in jeopardy.

How was it then that the South, handicapped by its dilapidated, reactionary, medieval slave system, was able to stand off for so long the modern, progressive, capitalist North, and to threaten the very life of the Union, despite the North's vast superiority in population, size of army, industry, wealth, and organization? The answer to this key question lies in the different attitudes toward the war of the ruling classes in the two warring sections of the country. In the South the big cotton planters were unified and in command of their situation. They knew what they wanted—full control of the national government and unlimited recognition and expansion of the slave system. They threw in everything they had to reach their clear but impossible goal. They kept the slaves under substantial control by added terrorism. The poor whites complained that it was "a rich man's war and a poor man's fight" but the planters kept them pretty much in line by direct pressure and by white supremacist demagogy about "Negro domination." The planters were very well aware that the fate of slavery was at stake in the war, and on this basis they fought.

In the North, however, the situation was very different. The ruling capitalist class was confused and divided over its objective in the war. On the defensive, attacked by the aggressive slavocracy, it did not understand either the revolutionary nature of the situation or what to do about it. The capitalists were split into several groups, including those who wanted to abolish slavery outright, those who strove to keep it within specified bounds, and those who openly sympathized with the pro-slavery objectives of the planters. The industrialists were only winning hegemony over the merchants and vacillating middle class elements. The working class was, of course, too immature to take the political leadership. The political divisions in the ruling class weakened the war potential of the North and almost cost it the war. The history of the Civil War is largely a recital of the complex struggle to overcome these internal confusions on policy and to whip out a united program—which had to be revolutionary in content—capable of defeating the militant planter South.

22. War and Revolution

The Civil War was a revolution, the second in United States history. It was a bourgeois-democratic revolution. Lenin, in estimating it, spoke of "the greatest, world-historic progressive and revolutionary significance of the American Civil War of 1861-65."[1]

The Civil War was a revolution, because it brought about "a transference of power from one class to another."[2] Prior to the war, the planters had dominated the Federal Government. Up to 1856, the South had furnished 11 of the 16 presidents, and most of the others were Northern tools of the slaveholders. The Beards remark that from Jackson's time to the Civil War, the Democratic Party, the party of the slaveholders, had controlled the Presidency and the Senate for 24 years, the Supreme Court 26 years, and the House 22 years.[3] The war drastically changed this situation, putting the Northern industrialists firmly in the political saddle. The war also substituted one social system for another by knocking out chattel slavery and, despite its introduction of semi-serf sharecropping, eventually opening up channels for the introduction of capitalist industry and the wage system into the South.

The war was a bourgeois revolution, because the economic and political changes it brought about did not go beyond the scope of the capitalist system. The general effect of the war was to clear away barriers in the path of capitalism and to stimulate that system into tremendous expansion. Both South and North, it largely broke the fetters that the slave system had fastened upon capitalist development.

The war was also a democratic revolution, because it led to many important democratic developments. The most important of these were the emancipation of the slaves and the enfranchisement of the Negro people; the enactment of the Homestead law in 1862, which cleared the way for small farmers to get some of the government-held land; and the creation of a political climate in which the trade union movement could make great strides. Marx said on this latter aspect, "As the American War of Independence initiated a new era of ascendency for the middle classes, so the American anti-slavery war will do for the working classes."[4]

238

THE LINCOLN PROGRAM

For the Northern bourgeoisie to win the war and carry out the Revolution successfully, a number of elementary tasks had to be accomplished. Among these were the creation of a trustworthy administration that knew where it was going and was determined to get there, the building up of a reliable force of military officers, the emancipation and arming of the slaves, the suppression of treason and of the Copperhead anti-war and pro-slavery forces in the North, and the prosecution of a vigorous, all-out war against the South. To do these things, the government heads had to have at least a general understanding of the revolution that was taking place and also of their tasks in the situation.

The Lincoln government, in its early stages, neither understood nor met this situation. Its initial policy was essentially that of Free Soil—the containing of slavery within its specified limits. Especially at the start, Lincoln did not grasp the fact that he was heading a revolutionary struggle, the heart of which was the abolition of the slave system. This misunderstanding showed in his initial policies, and he put it into writing in his famous letter of August 22, 1862, to Horace Greeley, editor of the *New York Tribune,* in which he laid down the policy of his government. "I would save the Union. I would save it in the shortest way under the Constitution. The sooner the national authority can be restored, the nearer the Union will be 'the Union as it was.' If there be those who would not save the Union unless they would at the same time destroy slavery, I do not agree with them. My paramount object in this struggle is to save the Union, and it is not either to save or destroy slavery. If I could save the Union without freeing any slave, I would do it; if I could save it by freeing all the slaves, I would do it; if I could save it by freeing some and leaving others alone, I would also do that. What I do about slavery and the colored race, I do because I believe it would help to save the Union, and what I forbear, I forbear because I do not believe it would help to save the Union."

This letter of Lincoln's did not express the revolutionary nature of the situation and of the basic task in hand. The "restoration of the Union as it was" before the rebellion was historically impossible. Neither the planters nor the industrialists, even if they wanted to, could go back to a situation which, by the logic of its inner contradictions, had culminated in the great war. Karl Marx saw this elementary fact crystal clear. Writing in the Vienna *Presse,* November 7, 1861, he said: "The struggle has broken out because the two systems can no longer live peacefully side by side on the North American continent. It can only be ended by the victory of one system or the other."[5]

Lincoln's demand for the restoration of the Union itself was basically correct, since this was a fundamental requirement of the national bourgeoisie, of which he was the political leader. But in his famous Greeley letter he failed to realize that the Union could be restored only upon a new and revolutionary basis. The question of freeing the slaves was not a maybe-yes, maybe-no matter, as Lincoln here puts it, but an imperative necessity, upon which the fate of the war and the Union depended. Indeed, even as he was writing his letter to Greeley, Lincoln, under pressure of stern military necessity, was preparing to issue the Emancipation Proclamation. The need of the Revolution imperatively demanded that the Government pass beyond the traditional policy of Free Soil and adopt the revolutionary policy of Abolition.

It was in line with the general conception expressed in his letter to Greeley in 1862, that President Lincoln had organized his administration over a year before and since carried on the war. He operated on the basis of a "national unity" that included many dubious elements. In forming his cabinet he rigidly excluded Abolitionists and loaded it up with many men (Seward, Blair, Welles, and others) who had no thought of fighting to do away with slavery. In building his army leadership, he followed a similar line. Of the 110 brigadier generals, 80 were Democrats; the armies of the East and West were commanded by the Democratic generals, McClellan and Halleck. Such a situation was an invitation to military disaster. Lincoln also temporized with the insistent up-cropping of the question of slavery as a war issue; he did not crack down on the bands of profiteers who were shamelessly cheating the government and robbing the people; he did not bring drastic pressure to bear upon the resurgent treason in the North; and he took altogether too much dictation from the "Union-with-Slavery" politicians of the Border states, appeasing them "in order to keep them from going over to the Confederacy."

Lincoln's weakness and confusion were basically those of the Northern bourgeoisie, whom he represented, and of his own petty bourgeois origin and affiliations. But there was no other class mature and revolutionary enough to take over the leadership of the revolution. The working class was much too young and undeveloped for this historic task. Lincoln was essentially a centrist, but he had, however, the special quality, when pressed by the masses and by direct military necessity, to adopt various indispensable fighting policies, enough with which to win the war. Marx said of him, "President Lincoln never ventures a step forward before the tide of circumstances and the call of general public opinion forbids further delay. But once 'Old Abe' has convinced himself that such a turning-point has been reached, he then surprises friend and foe alike by a sudden operation executed as noiselessly as possible."[6]

REVOLUTIONARY POLICIES AND LEADERSHIP

The Civil War had to be—and was—won by the application of revolutionary policies. These came almost exclusively from the left, from outside the official ranks of the Lincoln Administration and often against the President's stubborn opposition. Marx himself was highly critical of Lincoln's slow and conservative policies. He said they have "smitten the Union government with incurable weakness since the beginning of the war, driven it to half measures, forced it to dissemble away the principle of the war and to spare the foe's most vulnerable spot, the root of the evil—*slavery itself.*"[7]

Frederick Engels, like many another of the time, was irked by Lincoln's maddening slowness in developing an effective policy, and he wrote thus to Marx in July 1862: "If the North does not proceed forthwith in revolutionary fashion, it will get an ungodly hiding and deserve it—and it looks like it." For this he was chided by Marx, who said that "In the end, the North will make war seriously, adopt revolutionary methods, and throw over the domination of the Border state statesmen."[8] And so it turned out.

The struggle of the Radicals* and Abolitionists against Lincoln, for a more revolutionary policy, continued all through the war. The left-wing pressure was a decisive factor in the Northern victory. These groups furnished the revolutionary leadership without which the defeat of the slave Confederacy would have been impossible. The Radicals, in general, had no formal organization. They functioned in their particular spheres without very close organizational connections.

* The term "Radical," first used against them by enemy elements, was proudly adopted by the anti-slavery forces.

Among the several elements on the left were the Negro people themselves. They were the most definitely revolutionary of any of the groups or classes in the Civil War period. This was true of both the slaves in the South and of the freemen and women in the North. There were several basic planks in their general program, as formulated in the North, including: *(a)* the emancipation of the slaves; *(b)* the arming of the Negro slaves and freedmen; *(c)* the enfranchisement of the Negro people; *(d)* the abolition of Jim Crow and social inequality; and *(e)* the redistribution of the land in the South.

These were the national liberation demands of the Negro people at the time. They had great revolutionary significance, aiming straight at the heart of the Confederacy. The degree of revolutionary content in the Federal Government's policy was always measured by the extent to which it adopted and was enforcing the national demands of the Negro people. The sequel showed that the Government never really made the Negro people's demands it own. It always considered them as something alien, to be picked up or dropped as political or military expediency dictated, to be used as a sharp instrument of struggle in the war when nothing else sufficed.

The great spokesman of the Negro people in this Revolution was Frederick Douglass. He hailed the war as an indication that the people were finally coming to grips with slavery. He realized the revolutionary character of the war, and understood fully that the demands of the Negro people, especially the emancipation of the slaves, were the master key to winning the war. Contradicting Lincoln's slogan that the war was being fought simply to restore the Union "as it was," Douglass said that it "is a war for and against slavery; and that it can never be effectually put down till one or the other of these vital forces is destroyed."[9] With splendid foresight, Douglass was ever pointing out to the government the decisive next steps in the war.

The political expression segment of the revolutionary Left in Congress was the Radical group led by Stevens in the House and Sumner in the Senate. They were the spokesmen of the Northern industrialists, and also were more or less conscious that they were dealing with a revolutionary situation. They also sensed the revolutionary sharpness of the Negro people's demands directed against the Southern slavocracy. Speaking of his program to give land to the emancipated slaves, Stevens, the outstanding Radical leader, said: "They say it is revolution. No doubt it would work a radical reorganization in Southern institutions, habits, and manners."[10] As early as December 1861, Stevens and Sumner, realizing the inadequacy of Lincoln's policies to win the war, set up in the Senate and House the Joint Committee on the Conduct of the War.[11] Thenceforth, this Joint Committee virtually became the left center and leadership of the war, constantly pressing Lincoln with revolutionary proposals and legislation. During the War and Reconstruction period, the Committee was able to rally a majority of both Houses of Congress for most of its policies. The Radicals had behind them the bulk of the workers, farmers, middle class, the Negro people, and many, if not most, of the industrialists.

The Garrison Abolitionists, mainly urban middle class elements, were also an important element in the wartime left bloc. When war was declared, Garrison, forsaking his old-time policy of non-resistance, declared, "There is not a drop of blood in my veins, both as an Abolitionist and a peace man, that does not flow with the Northern tide of sentiment."[12] Wendell Phillips took a similar stand. Thenceforth, the two men and their group pressured the Government for a militant policy, with special stress on the Negro people's demands for emancipation. With the outbreak of war, the voice of the Abolitionists became a real power in the land. The old American Anti-Slavery Society was inert, however, and in November 1861 the Abolitionist forces formed the Emancipation League. This brought Garrison and Douglass together again, after a split of many years. Horace Greeley, with some deviations, followed the general war line of the Abolitionists.

A most important group of the left were the Marxists, especially Karl Marx himself. During the first two crucial years of the war, Marx sent many articles from Europe to the *New York Tribune*. In this paper and the Vienna *Presse* he made a penetrating analysis of the great conflict, pointing out its fundamental characteristics and indicating the revolutionary path that it must take to achieve an anti-slavery victory. The *Tribune* was the most important paper and had the largest circulation in the United States and wielded tremendous popular influence. Marx's articles were probably read by Douglass, Stevens, Sumner, Garrison, and other Radical leaders. Engels also played an important part through his correspondence with Marx. He had participated in the German uprising of 1848, was a military expert, and closely followed American military developments. He advocated the march through Georgia to cut the Confederacy in half, two years before it actually took place. The Marxist groups of this country also played an important role in the war—but more about this in a later chapter.

THE RADICALS AND THE WAR

The war situation of the North remained very dangerous during the first two years of the struggle. The bulk of both armies sawed back and forth in Virginia, inflicting terrific losses upon each other; but neither was able to realize their respective slogans of "On to Richmond" and "On to Washington." The North could not yet make effective use of its enormous superiority in men and material. Instead, it suffered staggering military disasters. Bull Run, the Seven Days Battles, Manassas Junction, and Fredericksburg in Virginia were heavy defeats for the North, and in the West the fierce fighting was indecisive.

McClellan, the Democratic commander-in-chief, was not trying to win the war for the North. The treacherous Copperhead opposition was boldly sabotaging the war, and the international situation was ominous, with war clouds gathering between Great Britain and the United States. Clearly Lincoln's conservative war policy was bankrupt. It was necessary to adopt a more revolutionary line, and this began with the emancipation of the slaves at the end of 1862. This basic action, which marked the political turning point of the war and was soon to be followed by its military turning point, took place only after a long and hard struggle by the Radical forces against the weak line of the Lincoln Administration.

From the outset the Radicals, both in Congress and outside, condemned and fought against the conservative make-up of the Lincoln cabinet, which Ben Wade characterized as "a disgraceful surrender to the South." But Lincoln tenaciously supported the conservatives, as necessary to his conception of national unity. He had no place in his official family for such rugged Abolitionists as Stevens, Douglass, Phillips, and Sumner. Only in a real crisis, like that before the election of 1864, were the latter able to break one or two Conservatives loose from the cabinet, such as the notorious pro-slavery Montgomery Blair, who had voted against the Emancipation Proclamation.

The Radicals also battled to clean out the Copperhead influence among the Union generals. When the war began most of the big-name military men—Lee, Jackson, Forrest, Stuart, Johnston, and others

—quit the U.S. Army and went with the Confederacy, and Lincoln filled their places with new generals, chiefly Democrats of dubious political reliability. Of these, Grant and Sherman eventually became great military leaders, but most of the others were a dead loss—especially McClellan, "the little Napoleon," who in 1864 became the presidential candidate of the Copperheads. Marx said of him, "McClellan has incontrovertibly proved that he is a military incompetent."[13] And he also said of him, "Next to a great defeat he feared most a great victory."

McClellan, commander of all the Union armies, had to have odds of two or three to one in his favor before he would move militarily, with the result that he paralyzed the striking power of the Union forces. He was the special protégé of the New York *Herald,* organ of the New York Copperheads. The Radicals waged war against him in Congress, but Lincoln kept him in chief command despite the great demand to withdraw him. Finally, on September 17, 1862, McClellan was relieved of his main command, to the great rejoicing of the Radicals. This crucial change occurred when Lincoln, prodded by the Radicals, was in process of issuing the "Preliminary" Emancipation Proclamation, and there was a direct connection between the two events. They were both emergency measures for winning the war.

The Radicals also fought against the influence of reactionary Border statesmen in the Lincoln cabinet and generally in his administration. Wilson calls these the "men who loved both the Union and slavery."[14] They exerted a crippling influence throughout the war. To keep the Border slave states—Delaware, Maryland, Kentucky, and Missouri—from joining the Confederacy was a necessary and major objective of Northern war strategy. The fact that these states did not secede in the first burst of excitement over the firing upon Fort Sumter showed that the South could not swing them in the face of the overwhelming local mass anti-secessionist sentiment. Thenceforth, the job was to occupy them militarily and to repress the Copperhead tendency vigorously. This was the line proposed by the Radicals; but Lincoln greatly overestimated the danger of the secession of these states and followed a policy of appeasing their proslavery leaders. The result was that his policy was weakened in every department, whether it related to military operations, to arming the Negroes, to freeing the slaves, or whatever. Throughout most of the war, the so-called Border statesmen, despite Radical opposition, hamstrung the North, to the serious detriment of its military strength.

The enlistment of Negroes into the Union army was another issue on which all the Radical-Abolitionist forces exerted heavy pressure. This met with opposition from Lincoln, who feared that it would afford the Border statesmen an excuse to secede. From the beginning of the war, Frederick Douglass had demanded that Negroes be recruited, and one of the most eloquent documents of the whole period was his famous, "Men of Color, To Arms."[15] Karl Marx saw the importance of this issue. Writing to Engels, he stated, correctly enough, that "A single Negro regiment would have a remarkable effect on Southern nerves."[16] It was not until August 1862, however, that Negroes were officially accepted as fighters in the Union forces.[17] This meant the addition of powerful forces to the armies of the North.

Then came the task of trying to compel the Confederacy to recognize the slaves captured with arms as prisoners of war. But success in this was only partial. On December 23, 1862, President Jefferson Davis of the Confederacy ordered that "all . . . slaves captured in arms be at once delivered over to the executive authorities of the respective states to which they belong, to be dealt with according to the laws of said States."[18] Davis at the same time ordered that all captured white officers of Negro regiments were to be shot. Later, under Northern pressure, these savage orders were formally rescinded. The fact was, however, that most of the ex-slaves taken in battle were either returned to slavery or executed.[19]

WAR PROFITEERS

In every war that has ever been fought by the United States the capitalists have reaped a golden harvest of profits. While the soldiers are dying in the field, exploiters use every conceivable device for cheating the government and robbing the people. No matter how grave the crisis or how basic the issue, they never fail to sacrifice the national interest upon the altar of their insatiable greed. This was especially true during the Civil War, when the fate of the nation trembled in the balance. Some of the greatest American fortunes— Morgan, Vanderbilt, Gould, Field, Rockefeller, and others—were founded during this crucial period. These capitalists, of course, were careful not to go to the front, buying substitutes to take their places in the draft.

Since there were no price controls, the profiteers screwed up the prices of necessities to record levels. Pauperization spread among the toiling masses. Banks charged the government fabulous rates of interest, and in general made 20, often 50, and sometimes 100 percent on loans.[20] The railroads doubled their rates for transporting troops and munitions, and during the war they wangled 23,000,000 acres of government land from Congress "for railroad building." The robbery by the munitions-makers was without precedent. "So tremendous was the graft in connection with contracts for military supplies," says Simons "that most historians draw back in horror when they have lifted but a corner of the thick blanket of concealment that those who profited by the plunder have drawn over the mess."[21]

One of the innumerable crooked deals of the period was put across by young J. P. Morgan. He bought up a lot of condemned United States army rifles at $2.00, sold them to the government at $15.00, bought them in again at $3.50 when the government recondemned them, and once more got rid of them to the military buyers at $22.00. "These carbines were still so defective that they would shoot off the thumbs of soldiers using them."[22] This deal netted Morgan $109,912 and helped establish his fortune.

Many capitalists openly traded with the enemy while the war was going on. Cotton was selling at 10 cents a pound in the South and brought 50 cents in New England. Soon, on the basis of "permits," a flood of cotton was pouring into the North and a lot of crooks were getting rich. Actually bullets and powder also went into the South under purchased "permits." Senator Ten Eyck of New Jersey protested in Congress that this bloody traffic was prolonging the war. He said, "I am greatly afraid that in some quarters the movements of our armies have been conducted more with a view to carry on trade . . . than to strike down the rebels."[23]

Myers describes the situation thus: "They loaded upon the government, at ten times the cost of manufacture, quantities of munitions . . . so frequently worthless that they often had to be thrown away after their purchase. They supplied shoddy uniforms and blankets and wretched shoes; food of so deleterious a quality that it was a fertile cause of epidemics of fever and numberless deaths; they impressed, by force of corruption, worn out, disintegrating hulks into service as army and navy transports. Not a single possibility of profit was there in which the most glaring frauds were not committed."[24]

23. The Emancipation of the Slaves

Once the war began, the whole political struggle of the Radicals and the Abolitionists in general, centered upon getting the Lincoln Administration to pronounce the emancipation of the slaves. This proposal they put forward most emphatically as necessary from democratic, political, and military standpoints. For the abolition of slavery would strike a deadly blow at the very heart of the Southern Confederacy. But the realization of this demand for emancipation required a fundamental change in the war policy of the Lincoln Administration. It would mean that the policy of the North could no longer be "The Union, with or without slavery," as Lincoln put it; henceforth it would have to be "The Union, on the basis of the destruction of chattel slavery." Lincoln hesitated long before he finally accepted this new and revolutionary policy. To bring about this change in policy was the key political struggle of the Abolitionist forces during the early Civil War period.

MASS PRESSURES FOR EMANCIPATION

Hardly had the great war started when the Negro question thrust itself forward in the most imperative fashion like the basic revolutionary issue that it was. Nor was it to be stifled or shoved aside by the Lincoln Administration, which refused to recognize its fundamental importance and to accord it due weight. The question of freeing the slaves continued to press more and more strongly to the fore, until finally it reached its climax in the Emancipation Proclamation.

The outbreak of the war was accompanied by many slave revolts and a wholesale flight of slaves to the Union lines. Davie says, "The greatest and most successful slave revolt—a sort of general strike against slavery—occurred during the War between the States, which provided an exceptional opportunity for flight and which was aided and abetted by the Union Government and army . . . The cry,

'Yankees Coming!' was a signal for a wholesale exodus of slaves to the enemy."[1] This is an effective answer to those slanderers who claim that the Negroes were content as slaves.

The mass influx of fugitive slaves into the army camps and the military occupation of plantation territory by the Union forces put the emancipation question squarely up to President Lincoln. But as the Lincoln government had no established policy on what to do with the large number of ex-slaves who suddenly found themselves behind the Union lines, the generals undertook to meet the situation in the field as an urgent military problem. General Ben Butler, at Fortress Monroe, Virginia, took a step toward the solution in July 1861 by declaring slave fugitives to be "contraband of war," which meant, in reality, that thenceforth they were free and could not be returned to their former masters.[2] Shortly afterward, in August, General John C. Frémont, Commander of the Western Department at St. Louis, Missouri, took a long stride further by confiscating the property and emancipating the slaves of the rebel slaveholders in his district.[3] In South Carolina, in May 1862, General David Hunter not only freed the slaves in his locality, but also formed and armed a regiment of them.[4] Several other commanders followed similar methods.

All the Yankee generals were not so progressive, however. Some, like General Halleck in Missouri, refused point-blank to let runaway slaves come behind their lines, and others even permitted slaveholders to take back fugitives. The Democratic General McClellan, who had forbidden his soldiers to sing "John Brown's Body," promised to put down relentlessly any slave insurrection that might occur.[5] The Abolitionists denounced these reactionary generals, and the fiery Stevens said of them: "We have put a sword into one hand of our generals and shackles into the other."[6]

President Lincoln, faced by the growing importance of abolition as a military question in the field, was compelled to take a stand. Yielding to his usual fear that any action against slavery would alienate the Border states and drive them into the arms of the Confederacy, he ignored the pro-slavery attitudes of such generals as Halleck, Mc-Cook, Hooker, and McClellan, and reversed the anti-slavery actions of Hunter, Doubleday, McDowell, and Frémont. In fact, in November 1861, Lincoln removed Frémont from his Western command. The Radicals sharply criticized these actions of the President.

THE EMANCIPATION MOVEMENT IN CONGRESS

Meanwhile, in Congress, significant steps were being taken toward the emancipation of the slaves. On August 6, 1861, the first Confiscation Act was passed. This law provided that all slaves who were used by the rebels to prosecute the war were henceforth free. Lincoln reluctantly signed this law, fearing even this partial attack upon slavery would push the Border states into secession. He said that he would use his own discretion in applying the Act, and, in fact, he practically ignored it.

The next step was taken on March 31, 1862, when President Lincoln signed a bill, passed by Congress, which prohibited the army and navy from returning fugitive slaves to slaveholder claimants. Any officer violating the law would "be discharged from service, and would be forever ineligible to any appointment in the military or naval service of the United States."[7] This ended the shameful practice by Northern generals of returning Negroes to slavery, and it also stimulated the flight of slaves to the Northern lines.

On April 16 of the same year, Congress took another important action and freed the 3,000 slaves in the District of Columbia; but a clause was included in the law providing $300 compensation to the slaveholders for each slave set free. Despite its compensation feature, this Act was welcomed by the Abolitionists. Douglass hailed it as "the first great step towards that righteousness which exalts a nation." One of the key demands of the anti-slavery forces since the days of the 1776 Revolution—the wiping out of slavery in the nation's capital —was thus finally won.

On June 19, 1862, as a result of growing Abolitionist pressure, Lincoln signed an act of Congress prohibiting slavery in all the territories of the United States. This action, pledged in the Republican Party platforms of 1856 and 1860, brought the realization of another objective for which the anti-slavery movement had fought since Jefferson's early effort in 1784.

A month later, on July 17, Lincoln signed another Confiscation Act, which went far beyond the previous one, of the year before. But Lincoln first softened it up under threat of a veto, declaring that in its original version it would force the Border states out of the Union. This law, as summarized by Rhodes, proposed to seize all the estates and property, money, stocks, credits, and effects of all military and civil officers of the Southern Confederacy, likewise the property of all those engaged in armed rebellion against the United States, or aiding or abetting such rebellion. It freed forever, the slaves of those rebels convicted of treason or rebellion and also the rebel-owned slaves who took refuge behind the Union lines. It also authorized the President to employ Negroes as soldiers and provided for the colonization of "persons of African race made free."[8] "On paper," says Williams, "this act set free more slaves than did Lincoln's later emancipation proclamation."[9]

In line with developing anti-slavery sentiment in the country and Congress, two further important steps were taken by the U.S. Government. One was the formulation of a treaty with Great Britain finally to suppress the slave trade by granting the mutual right of search of each other's ships at sea. The other action was the diplomatic recognition of the Negro republics of Haiti and Liberia. The Southerners had long blocked this step on the ground that they "did not want any black ambassadors in Washington."

LINCOLN'S PLAN FOR COMPENSATED EMANCIPATION

Pressed by the unfavorable military situation for the North and the rising mass demand for Negro emancipation, President Lincoln felt constrained to add to his central issue of restoring the Federal Union, the burning, unavoidable question of freeing the Negro slaves. The matter could not possibly be longer avoided; so he worked out a program with three main points to solve this problem. First, the slaves were to be emancipated gradually; second, the slaveholders were to be compensated for the loss of their valuable property; and third, the Negro people, as an alien group, were to be transported from the United States to Africa or elsewhere. There were very many in Congress and throughout the North who agreed with Lincoln's general ideas.

During the latter part of 1861 and the early months of 1862 Lincoln devoted much attention to this program to meet the problem of slavery. In his message to Congress, on March 6, 1862, the President proposed "that the United States ought to cooperate with any State which may adopt gradual abolishment of slavery, giving to such State pecuniary aid, to be used by such State, in its discretion, to compensate for the inconveniences, public and private, produced by such change of system."[10] Lincoln was also responsible for the compensation clause in the law emancipating the slaves in the District of

Columbia. This was in line with his action long before, in 1849, when, as a Congressman, he had introduced a bill proposing gradual, compensated emancipation in the District.

Lincoln did not write his compensation provision into the final Emancipation Proclamation; but in his message to Congress, on December 1, 1862, one month before the Proclamation was to go into effect, he proposed that, "Every State wherein slavery now exists which shall abolish the same therein at any time or times before the first day of January, A.D. 1900, shall receive compensation from the United States. . . ."[11] Interestingly, this passage shows that Lincoln contemplated the existence of slavery until at least the end of the nineteenth century.

But the slaveholders never took to Lincoln's plans for the voluntary abolition of slavery, with compensation. It is significant that no state—either on the border or in the deep South, either during the war or afterward—ever applied for compensation for the loss of their slaves, as they might have done under the law of March 6, 1862. Lincoln tried hard to get the Border states to agree to emancipation on this basis, but without success. It was figured out at the time that it would cost the Union Government only $173,000,000 dollars to pay for all the slaves, at $400 each, in the slave states of Delaware, Maryland, Kentucky, Missouri, and the District of Columbia.[12] In February, 1863, after the Emancipation Proclamation had become effective, a proposal to compensate the slaveholders in the foregoing states at the rate of $300 per slave was defeated in Congress, although it had Lincoln's backing.

President Lincoln attached great importance to the third point of his program: that the freed slaves should be colonized, that is, deported to Africa, the West Indies, or South America. He held that the Negro was an inferior being and could not live on a basis of equality with the white man.

This belief Lincoln made very clear on numerous occasions. In his fourth debate with Stephen A. Douglas, on September 18, 1858, he said: "I am not nor ever have been, in favor of bringing about in any way the social and political equality of the white and black races—that I am not, nor ever have been, in favor of making voters or jurors of Negroes, nor of qualifying them to hold office nor to intimacy with white people; and I will say in addition to this that there is a physical difference between the white and black races which I believe forbids the two living together on terms of social and political equality. And inasmuch as they cannot so live, while they do remain together there must be the position of the superior and inferior, and I as much as any other man am in favor of having the superior position assigned to the white race."[13] Better then that the Negro should emigrate. Lincoln had Congress appropriate $600,000 for this purpose, and he commissioned a body to investigate colonization prospects in Haiti and Cuba. He was responsible for setting up a Haitian bureau of immigration, with James Redpath as agent. Arrangements were made for monthly sailings from Boston, New York and Philadelphia.[14] Some 1,500 Negro immigrants were actually sent out, but the plan finally collapsed.

In August, 1862, when speaking to a delegation of free Negroes in the White House—the first who had ever interviewed an American president—Lincoln urged upon the group a policy of foreign colonization. He said, "Your race suffers greatly, many of them, by living among us, while ours suffers from your presence."[15] There was strong Negro resentment at this. Indignant, Frederick Douglass declared: "Mr. Lincoln assumes the language and arguments of an itinerant colonization lecturer, showing all his inconsistencies, his pride of race and blood, his contempt for Negroes and his canting hypocrisy."[16] Bryce put in very few words the futility of the whole scheme of colonization. "There are two fatal objections to the plan of exporting the Southern Negroes to Africa. One is that they will not go; the other that the whites cannot afford to have them go."[17]

Lincoln's three-point plan to solve the slave question was impossible, as history was soon to prove dramatically. It was unworkable to emancipate the slaves gradually—this had to be done at one blow. It was impossible to compensate the slaveholders for their slaves—confiscation had to be applied. And it was simply unthinkable to deport the millions of Negroes—they were resolved to remain in the United States. In short, what was needed and what was finally put into practice, was the revolutionary program of the left wing, the Abolitionists—Douglass, Stevens, Garrison, Phillips, Tubman, and, abroad, Marx and Engels—namely: immediate general emancipation, without compensation and without colonization. Abraham Lincoln was soon to give definite acknowledgment of this historic reality by issuing his immortal pronouncement freeing the slaves.

THE EMANCIPATION PROCLAMATION

Toward the middle of 1862, the pressure for emancipation became irresistible. The freeing of the slaves grew imperative in order to break down the economic system of the South, to provide the United States with a fresh source of soldiers, to raise the prestige of the Union cause among the democratic masses of Europe, and to give a solid backbone to the war. In a letter to Engels on August 7, 1862, Marx remarked, "The North itself has turned the slaves into a military force on the side of the Southerners, instead of turning it against them. The South leaves productive labor to the slaves and could therefore put its whole fighting strength in the field without disturbance. . . . The long and short of the business seems to me to be that a war of this kind must be conducted on revolutionary lines, while the Yankees have so far been trying to conduct it constitutionally."[18] Above all, the liberation of the slaves was indispensable to the North from the military standpoint. In taking this step, Lincoln said that it was "a fit and necessary war measure."

Therefore, on July 22, 1862, Lincoln read to his cabinet the first draft of his great document, the Emancipation Proclamation. There was some opposition, but the plan generally was accepted. Seward, the equivocating Secretary of State, proposed, however, that in view of the low state of the Union's military fortunes it would be well to withhold the proclamation until some important military victory had been won. Lincoln agreed with this. So the proclamation was withheld until after the Union success in the Battle of Antietam on September 17, 1862. Five days later, on September 22, Lincoln made known to the world his fateful pronouncement, eventually freeing four million slaves.

The heart of the Emancipation Proclamation reads: "That on the 1st day of January, A.D., 1863, all persons held as slaves within any State, or designated part of a State the people whereof shall then be in rebellion against the United States shall be then, thenceforth, and forever free; and the executive government of the United States, including the military and naval authority thereof, will recognize and maintain the freedom of such persons and will do no act or acts to repress such persons, or any of them, in any efforts they may make for their actual freedom."[19]

The Proclamation went on that "such persons of suitable condition will be received into the armed services of the United States to garrison forts, positions, stations, and other places, and to man vessels of all sorts in said service." And Lincoln concluded, "Upon this act, sincerely believed to be an act of justice, warranted by the Constitution upon military necessity, I invoke the considerate judgment of mankind and the gracious favor of Almighty God."

In making this historic pronouncement Lincoln took a high place among the great of the world. In the Proclamation he had to disregard his theories of gradual, compensated emancipation. History had decided that this great question was to be settled in a revolutionary way, and so it was. Later, "in 1864, in explaining the Emancipation Proclamation and his decision to recruit Negro soldiers into the Union Army, Lincoln declared, 'I claim not to have controlled events, but confess plainly that events have controlled me.'"[20]

In addition to its vast political and military importance, the Proclamation constituted a great victory for the Radicals and Abolitionists. The action signified that the Northern bourgeoisie, faced by the harsh imperative of military need and pressed by its Negro, worker, farmer, and city middle class allies, had grasped the revolutionary weapon of slave emancipation on the basis of confiscation.

As events were to demonstrate, the Northern capitalists did not support this basic demand of the Negro people on the grounds of its inherent justice and long range democratic benefit to the great body of the American people. They did not even regard it as a permanent buttress to capitalism, but primarily as a war measure against the Southern planters. Nor was the Proclamation a guarantee that henceforth the war was to be waged on a revolutionary basis, and that the left wing could now rest content and easy. On the contrary, the immediate future was to confront the Left with even more difficult struggles to develop a revolutionary policy for the government.

Unlike the bulk of the Northern capitalists, who considered the revolutionary demands of the Negro people purely from the standpoint of expediency, to be pressed or discarded as the situation dictated, the Abolitionists genuinely accepted these demands and fought for them on a democratic basis. This was true of the demands for emancipation, the right to bear arms, and the right to vote; but Abolitionist support of the Negro demands for land and for social equality was only scattered. Thaddeus Stevens was outstanding among these white Abolitionists in fully accepting and militantly supporting the whole program of the Negro people.

CONSEQUENCES OF THE PROCLAMATION

The free Negroes of the North joyously welcomed Lincoln's Emancipation Proclamation and as word of it filtered into the ranks of the slaves on the Southern plantations, their joy was unconfined. The great event swelled their mass flight to the Union lines and it encouraged them to new revolts and conspiracies. Frederick Douglass, the eloquent spokesmen of the whole Negro people, declared, "We shout for joy that we live to record this righteous decree: *Abraham Lincoln, President of the United States, commander-in-chief of the army and navy, in his own peculiar, cautious, forbearing, and hesitating way, slow, but we hope sure, has while the loyal heart was near breaking with despair, proclaimed and declared: That on the First of January, in the Year of Our Lord, One Thousand Eight Hundred and Sixty Three, All Persons Held as Slaves Within any State or Designated Part of a State, the People Whereof Shall Then be in Rebellion Against the United States, Shall be Thenceforth and Forever Free.'* Free Forever, Oh! long-enslaved millions, whose cries have so vexed the air and sky, suffer on a few days more in sorrow, the hour of your deliverance draws nigh."[21]

The Radicals hailed the great victory; but they also saw many dangers in the situation. First and most urgent, if the slave states should surrender, or accept Lincoln's terms for emancipation with compensation before January 1, 1863, the emancipation order might not go into effect. Then there was the alarming fact that the Proclamation applied only to rebel territory. It did not free the 800,000 slaves in the Border States, or the large numbers in those parts of Virginia and Louisiana occupied by Federal forces. It was obvious, too, that Lincoln was still nursing hopes for his scheme of gradual, compensated emancipation, a plan which might have delayed the freeing of the slaves for a full generation. The Negro people and their allies spent an anxious three months waiting for January 1, 1863. In Boston and other Northern cities, watch meetings were held on the night of December 31, and they burst forth into joyous celebrations when the fateful moment arrived and the Proclamation went into effect.

The Emancipation Proclamation was welcomed by the Republican press and the popular masses all over the North. Trade unions, Negro conventions, and farmers' organizations poured out their endorsements to Lincoln. The Copperhead Democratic opposition, however, wildly assailed freedom for the Negroes. They denounced the Proclamation as unconstitutional and Lincoln as a dictator; and they warned the workers that a flood of low-paid ex-slaves would ruin their wage standards.

The Proclamation was bitterly condemned in the South. Among other organizations, the churches vied with each other in attacking it. Wilson states that "In the Spring of 1863 all the leading religious bodies of the South united in an 'Address to Christians Throughout the World,' in which they said: 'The recent Proclamation of the President of the United States, seeking the emancipation of the slaves of the South, is in our judgment, occasion of solemn protest on the part of the people of God.' "[22]

In the interim period before the Proclamation went into effect, the mid-term elections of 1862 were held. The Republicans suffered considerable losses; the Democratic representation increased from 44 to 75 in the House, with similar results in state and local elections. Lincoln boldly replied to the election setback by dismissing General McClellan on November 5, the day after the elections. Enemies of the Negro people blamed the Republican defeat upon emancipation; but in reality it was primarily caused by the difficult war situation, by the rapid rise in the cost of living, and by the widespread lack of confidence in the Lincoln Administration. The ensuing elections of 1864 and 1866, when emancipation was well understood and in full effect, resulted as we shall see, in resounding victories for the Radicals and Abolitionists.

LINCOLN AND THE BRITISH WORKERS

The Emancipation Proclamation had important effects in strengthening the diplomatic situation of the United States in European countries, especially England. The British ruling capitalists—industrialists, bankers, and landowners—hated the North and wanted the South to win the war. They bought Confederate bonds, gave diplomatic recognition to the Confederacy, and built warships for the South. They did all this because they wanted to conserve their supplies of cotton for their flourishing textile industry and to enjoy free trade relations with their good customers, the planters. They wanted the United States to remain agricultural. They looked askance at the industrial progress being made in the United States, and would have been glad to see their vigorous young trade rival torn in two and rendered impotent by a Confederate victory. They judiciously ignored the fact that Great Britain was supposed to be the world's principal antagonist of chattel slavery.

During the Civil War repeated diplomatic crises arose between the Northern states and Great Britain. The most serious one occurred in November 1861, when United States authorities aboard the warship *San Jacinto* took off the British steamship *Trent* two Confederate emissaries to Great Britain, James M. Mason and John Slidell. The British protested violently against this action as an infraction of their national sovereignty. The Confederates openly hoped that the affair would bring on the expected war between the North and Great Britain; but after a critical period of negotiations, in which war clouds loomed, the crisis was averted by releasing Mason and Slidell, with apologies to the British. Various other wartime conflicts with Britain were similarly circumvented. The British ruling classes could not make up their minds finally to go to war with the United States. They wanted Southern cotton, but they also wanted Northern wheat as much, if not more. Moreover, they also did not want to lose their heavy capital investments in the United States. They were making big profits at home producing war munitions, and they were busily grabbing the international trade formerly carried on by the vigorous American merchant marine. Besides all these detriments to war, they had to face powerful anti-slavery, pro-Northern sentiment in the militant British working class.

From the early days of the British Abolitionist movement (see Chapter 6), the workers of the British Isles had been active opponents of slavery. Hence, when the American Civil War broke out, they immediately ranged themselves on the side of the North—although they suffered severe hardships and heavy unemployment because of the shut-down of the big textile industry for want of cotton. The great influence of Marx and Engels in England was a large factor in stimulating this pro-North attitude. They continually appealed to the British workers, explaining the true cause of the Civil War and the meaning of the liberation struggle. Frederick Douglass and other Abolitionist leaders who visited England were also a big factor in this. Pro-North sentiment was further strengthened by Lincoln's promulgation of the Emancipation Proclamation. The workers of Manchester expressed the true opinion of the British working class when, on December 31, 1862, they wrote a letter to President Lincoln, congratulating him upon his freeing the American chattel slaves.

Lincoln replied on January 19, characterizing the anti-slavery attitude of the British workers in the face of economic hardships as "an instance of sublime Christian heroism which has not been surpassed in any age or in any country."[23]

Had Great Britain declared war upon the United States during the Civil War this might well have been disastrous for the Union cause. And if Britain did not do this, the main reason therefor, as Marx indicated, was out of fear of its own workers and their allies among the British people. Marx said, "It was not the wisdom of the ruling classes, but the heroic resistance to their criminal folly by the working classes of England that saved the West of Europe from plunging headlong into an infamous crusade for the perpetuation and propagation of slavery on the other side of the Atlantic."[24] The inability of the British ruling class to force England into a war with the United States was one of the greatest disasters for the Confederate cause.

The French ruling class also wanted a victory of the Confederacy, and they plotted constantly with British reactionaries, with the general idea in mind of a British-French war against the United States. It was in 1864, during the Civil War, that Napoleon III, with the connivance of England, defied the Monroe Doctrine and the United States, invaded Mexico, and placed his puppet, Maximilian, upon the throne. The Mexican people, however, under the leadership of Juarez, overthrew Maximilian and executed him. A basic reason why the French rulers, like the British reactionaries, were unable to develop armed intervention against the United States, was the powerful anti-slavery sentiment and resistance of the French working class.[25]

24. The Overthrow of the Confederacy

The political high point of the Civil War came in January 1863, when the Emancipation Proclamation went into force. This meant that the North moved from a position of a confused defensive to that of a revolutionary offensive. The military turning point of the war came six months later on July 3, 1863, with the Union victories at Gettysburg, where there were over 23,000 killed, wounded, and missing, and on July 4th at Vicksburg, another wholesale slaughter. Both of these victories were of the greatest strategic importance to the Northern cause. The capture of Vicksburg by General Grant opened up the Mississippi to the Union forces, and Lee's defeat by General Meade at Gettysburg turned back the most daring and threatening Confederate offensive of the entire war. In his drive into Pennsylvania, General Lee aimed immediately at the capture of Harrisburg, Philadelphia, and New York, and ultimately, with the help of the treacherous Copperhead forces, at the demoralization and probable collapse of the whole North.

Although Vicksburg and Gettysburg were shattering blows to the Confederacy, the slave power was able to fight on desperately for another 21 months and, as late as the middle of 1864, to jeopardize the very life of the Union. Meanwhile, as the bloody struggle wore tragically on, the North experienced serious difficulties and struggles behind its fighting lines.

THE DRAFT RIOTS IN NEW YORK

During the first two years, on the Union side, the war was fought on a volunteer basis. But as the tremendous scope of the struggle became evident, compulsory service had to be put into effect on May 3, 1863. By a strange lapse of democracy and common sense, a clause was put into the draft (and also into that of the Confederacy), under which a man could escape military service by paying $300 bounty for a substitute. This let the rich evade entirely war service, and they took full advantage of their opportunities. The Copperhead anti-war elements, seeking every means to hamper the

260

war, opposed the draft and they concentrated their fire especially against the outrageous bounty provision. Consequently, there was mass resistance to the draft in various parts of the North. This was even more the case in the Confederate South, where open anti-draft riots occurred in many places, and there was a widespread disaffection during the war. Numerous peace organizations were active. Guerilla fighting took place in many areas. Aptheker says that in the South, "a civil war against the Confederacy simultaneously raged" (*Daily Worker*, August 19, 1953). Southern armies lost 110,000 deserters, and tens of thousands of white Southerners also volunteered for and fought with the Union Army, including whole regiments from Mississippi, Louisiana, and Alabama, not to mention Kentucky, Maryland, Tennessee, and other Southern states.

The most serious disturbance in the North occurred in the big riots of New York City in July, 1863. New York had long been the center of active pro-slavery agitation. This had as its base the big banking and commercial firms, which were closely tied up to the slaveholders. All through the war, these groupings carried on a vigorous fight against the Lincoln Administration and against the war itself. They were seconded by many clericals who were also very largely pro-Southern in their sympathies. The combined Copperhead forces, who were in close touch with Confederate war leaders, as later investigation showed, carried on an open and violent campaign to sabotage the war. "Governor Horatio Seymour of New York, Democrat, said in a speech on July 4, 1863: 'Remember this: that the bloody and treasonable and revolutionary doctrine of public necessity can be proclaimed by a mob as well as by a government.' "[1] This was only nine days before the big riot began.

The disturbances started when the draft drawings began in the city on July 13. Mobs destroyed the recruiting stations, set fire to an armory, attacked the *Tribune* and prominent Republicans, burned a Negro orphan asylum, and generally created chaos throughout the city. The mobs directed their fury especially against the Negroes, assailing them wherever found. Many were murdered. The riots lasted four days. It is calculated that some 1,000 people were killed and wounded, mostly by police and soldiers. The disturbances were put down by Federal troops, brought in from neighboring forts.

This great riot, fomented by treasonable capitalists, was largely carried out by underworld elements. But many workers, animated by anti-Negro sentiments, took an active part in it. After the riots had subsided, trade unions held a large number of mass meetings at which they condemned the disturbances but also the $300 bounty exemption clause and capitalist wartime profiteering.[2]

THE VALLANDIGHAM CONSPIRACIES

The Civil War had to be fought on two fronts—on the Southern battlefields and against the Copperheads in the North. The latter were strong and brazen. In 1862, Lincoln said he feared treason at home more than he did the enemy at the front. Early in 1863, Congress authorized Lincoln to suspend the writ of *habeas corpus* and to suppress the back-of-the-line traitors. Accordingly, many of them were arrested, and their newspapers were banned. Supreme Court Justice Taney declared that Lincoln had no constitutional right to take such action, but "Lincoln put the opinion of the learned Justice in a pigeonhole,"[3] as the Beards say. The President defended this policy, saying, "Must I shoot a simple-minded soldier boy who deserts, while I must not touch a hair of the head of the wily agitator who induces him to desert?"[4]

The strong anti-war spirit in many localities reflected the split in the ranks of the bourgeoisie over the war, and its chief organized expression was in the Democratic Party. The Middle West with a large percentage of its population born in the South, was fertile soil for the Copperheads. Cyrus McCormick, the big reaper manufacturer, who was born in Virginia, was a heavy backer of the Democratic Party, and its outstanding political leader was C. L. Vallandigham. Others were John A. Logan, D. W. Voorhees, J. C. Robinson, and W. A. Richardson. Vallandigham, whose French Huguenot forebears had come to Virginia in 1690, was a prominent Ohio Democrat and a member of the House of Representatives from 1858 to 1863. He was an extreme advocate of states' rights and a fanatical supporter of slavery.

Vallandigham, who was involved immediately before the outbreak of the war in the Mid-west plot to establish a Northwest Confederacy, constantly agitated violently against the war. In fighting the serious Copperhead menace in the Midwest, General Burnside arrested Vallandigham, courtmartialed and jailed him.[5] Lincoln, however, changed his sentence to banishment behind the Confederate lines.

The Copperhead leader was not so easily disposed of, however. He made his way back from the South to Canada and then, in 1864, to the Middle West, where he resumed his poisonous activities. With the war going badly in Virginia and the masses of the people war-weary, Vallandigham, along with a Captain Hines, organized a conspiracy to create a general anti-war revolt. Their line was peace at any price. They established the Sons of Liberty, of which Vallandigham was Supreme Commander. This organization, one of several powerful pro-Southern secret organizations in the North, is said to have numbered some 200,000 members. They armed themselves and drilled.

The conspiracy centered in Illinois, where the Democratic-controlled legislature condemned the Emancipation Proclamation on January 27, 1863. Indiana took a similar stand. The general plan of revolt was to release the large number of Confederate prisoners held in nearby camps and to seize the local government. It is said that 10,000 Confederates were actually imported from the South to help organize the revolt. It was the old scheme of the Northwest Confederacy resurrected. The plot failed, owing to the adverse political situation, to important Northern military victories, and to internal disruption among the Copperhead leaders. The Sons of Liberty were disbanded, many leaders were arrested, and the rest fled. All eventually escaped heavy punishment because of pardons given them later on by President Johnson.

THE BEGINNINGS OF RECONSTRUCTION

From the early days of the war—with the flight of the slaves to the Union lines and the capture of rebel states by the Northern armies—the question of Southern Reconstruction began to loom as a big and vital matter. The most urgent aspect of the problem—feeding, clothing, housing, and medically caring for the masses of freed slaves—at first was left pretty much to the army commanders, the state authorities, and to Northern charitable organizations, which had early sent their representatives into the field. It was not until March 1865 that the Government took a real hand in the situation and established the Freedmen's Bureau or, more properly, the Bureau of Refugees, Freedmen, and Abandoned Lands. This body was set up for one year, and it had the multiple tasks of relief work for refugees, regulation of Negro labor contracts, administration of justice in matters relating to Negroes, management of abandoned and confiscated lands, and organization of schools for Negroes. Its chief was General O. O. Howard; its main office was in Washington, with state branches.

Setting up this relief body caused no serious political difficulties, but it was a very different matter when it came to establishing governments in the states won back from the Confederacy and reconstructing their relationship with the Federal Government. Lincoln stated his general Reconstruction program in his message to Congress on December 8, 1863, and he then applied it in Louisiana, Tennessee, and Arkansas.[6] His plan was based upon two assumptions—first, that the rebel states, by seceding, had not gone out of the Union, and second, that the matter of Reconstruction was one to be handled by presidential action. As his solution of the problem, Lincoln proposed that when one-tenth of the number of voters at the last election before secession took a specified oath, they could reorganize the respective state governments in state conventions. Only a limited number of higher Confederate political and military officials were denied the right to vote and hold office. Property rights were to be restored, except in slaves.

Certain bad features stood out in the Lincoln plan. First, the Negroes were to be denied the right to vote (although he had earlier advocated a limited suffrage). Also, with the rebels' property rights restored, the Negroes' chances of getting the planters' lands were nil. Almost automatically, the planters would come back to political control. The whole Reconstruction process would be carried on by the President as executive business, to the complete disregard of Congress. In short, the revolution, save for the formal abolition of slavery, would be lost.

Lincoln's Reconstruction plan provoked immediate and sharp opposition in Congress, which resulted in the passage of the Wade-Davis bill on July 8, 1864. Based upon the principles of the Sumner resolution of February 11, 1862, this bill maintained that the Southern states, by their secession, had virtually committed suicide, and that the matter of their reconstruction as states rested solely with Congress. The bill placed severe restrictions regarding the right of ex-rebels to vote and hold office; it provided for provisional governors in the rebellious territories, specifically prohibited slavery, and demanded the repudiation of war debts by the states. But the Wade-Davis bill, like Lincoln's plan, did not provide the franchise for the freed Negroes.

Lincoln vetoed the bill, which caused a bitter dispute in Congress and the issuance of the Wade-Davis manifesto. This document bitterly assailed Lincoln as a dictator, stating that "a more studied outrage

on the legislative authority of the people has never been perpetrated."
It declared that the authority of Congress is paramount and must be
respected, and that the President "must confine himself to his
executive duties—to obey and execute, not make the laws."[7] The
historic struggle between the legislative and executive branches for
control of the Reconstruction program was on, and behind it was
the fight of the left forces to consolidate the real gains made by the
revolution.

The freed Negroes in the North were dismayed by the fact that
in the Reconstruction plans of both Lincoln and the Congress the
former slaves were denied the right to vote. Frederick Douglass protested against this outrage time and again without avail. The great
war went on and the ex-slaves got no vote. In the revolution, so far,
the Negro people had achieved substantially if not fully, two of their
revolutionary demands—emancipation from slavery and the right to
bear arms. The third basic demand which they were to achieve, the
right to vote, had to wait until the revolution had reached a higher
stage, which was not to be long in coming.

THE PRESIDENTIAL ELECTION OF 1864

The crucial election campaign of 1864 opened with dismal prospects for the North. The military situation was discouraging. The
great war, with its mass slaughter, was wearing on from year to year,
with apparently no end or decision in sight. The fierce battles of the
Wilderness and Cold Harbor in the Spring seemed inconclusive.
Actually, by this time, the South, drained of manpower and resources,
was on the downgrade; but this fact had not yet made itself felt on
the battlefield. The people were weary of the terrible war. On August
9 Greeley wrote to Lincoln, "I know that nine-tenths of the whole
American people, North and South, are anxious for peace—peace on
almost any terms—and utterly sick of human slaughter and devasta-
tion."[8]

The political situation was equally unpromising. The Democrats,
with a powerful organization, were busily exploiting the war weari-
ness of the people, bitterly condemning every step of the
administration, and clamoring for peace at any price. To make
matters worse, the Republican forces were split wide open in internal
dispute. The Radicals were strongly in opposition to Lincoln, because
his Reconstruction plan was ultra-conservative and dictatorial, he

clung to unreliable Democratic generals, and he kept pro-slavery reactionaries in his cabinet—all of which could hand the final victory over to the planters. Many were threatening not to support him for a second term as president. As late as September 27, Wendell Phillips wrote to Elizabeth Cady Stanton, "He would 'cut off both hands' before he would do anything to aid Lincoln's election."[9]

The first national political convention of 1864 was held in Cleveland on May 31 by the Radical Republicans, who had no definite party organization. The convention nominated as its presidential and vice-presidential candidates, General John C. Frémont and General John Cochrane. Among its fourteen planks, the platform called for an active prosecution of the war, the Constitutional prohibition of slavery, direct election of the president for one term only, the handling of the Reconstruction problem by Congress alone, and most significant, "that the confiscation of the lands of the rebels and their distrubution among the soldiers and actual settlers, is a measure of justice."

The Union National Convention (as the Republican Party designated itself in this campaign) assembled in Baltimore on June 7. The most significant planks in the platform were full support of the war, unconditional surrender of the rebels, a Constitutional amendment banning slavery, endorsement of Lincoln's policies, condemnation of refusal by rebels to recognize ex-slaves as prisoners-of-war, encouragement of immigration, construction of a railroad to the Pacific Coast, and support of the Monroe Doctrine. Abraham Lincoln was unanimously nominated for President and Andrew Johnson for Vice-President. Thus there were two Republican tickets in the field.

The Democratic Party held its national convention in Chicago, beginning on August 29. This was the convention of the Copperhead forces; and the Order of American Knights, Sons of Liberty, and other disloyal organizations were strongly represented. The platform was written by the notorious C. L. Vallandigham. It was based upon "peace at any price." It called for the immediate unconditional cessation of hostilities and the calling of a general convention of the states to consider the re-establishment of the Union "as it was." It condemned all interference by the Federal Government in the states not at war; by implication it left the returned Southern states full power to organize themselves as they saw fit. The platform ignored altogether the question of slavery. The convention picked out as its national candidates General George B. McClellan (who had been removed from his command by Lincoln) and G. H. Pendleton, of Ohio.[10]

A fourth important national convention in 1864 was that of the Negro people in Syracuse, New York, on October 2. This was the first such convention in almost a decade. Present at Syracuse were 140 delegates from 18 states, including seven slave states. Frederick Douglass was elected president of the convention, and made the principal speech. The convention formed the Equal Rights League and strongly demanded the franchise for Negro men. It warned that slavery, although scotched, was not dead. It sharply criticized the Lincoln Administration for its errors, weaknesses, and wrong policies; but it correctly saw that Lincoln's candidacy had to be supported. Douglass offered to take the stump for Lincoln, but the Lincoln leaders, fearing white chauvinist reaction, refused the offer.[11]

LINCOLN'S RE-ELECTION

The split in the Republican ranks loomed as a deadly menace. If it persisted, obviously Lincoln would be defeated and the pro-Copperhead McClellan would be elected. Urgent efforts were made, therefore, to unite the forces of the Left, then mostly assembled behind the candidacy of Frémont. Finally, this was accomplished by securing promises from Lincoln that he would give less consideration to the pro-slavery Border state politicians and would make concessions to the Radicals in the selection of military commanders. Most important, Lincoln agreed to remove from his cabinet the notorious reactionary Montgomery Blair—a concession which the Radicals hailed as a real victory.[12] The Radicals also liked the fact that early in 1864, Lincoln had put Grant at the head of all the Union armies. On this basis, the Left and Center patched up their differences, and on September 22 Frémont withdrew his candidacy. But the most urgent question—whether Congress or the President was to lead in reconstructing the South—was left unresolved.

The agreement between Lincoln and the Radicals was not, as some have since said, a choice of the "lesser evil" by the latter. Up to the time of the split, Lincoln had headed the joint group of revolutionary forces; and despite his many weaknesses and errors, the movement was making progress under his leadership—with heavy pressure from the Radicals. The election promised that this progress would be accelerated. On the other hand, McClellan represented the counter-revolution and a victory for him would have resulted in a decisive defeat for the whole war and revolution. He had to be defeated at all costs, and no agreement with him was conceivable. The Radicals, with excellent judgment, made a politically sound decision in backing Lincoln.

The campaign was conducted in a rapidly improving political and military situation for the revolutionary Northern forces. There was a better spirit of unity among the Republicans. The trade unions were very active for Lincoln, and to facilitate their election work they set up the Workingmen's Democratic-Republican Association. As for the Democrats, they were torn with factionalism and defeatism. Their discomfiture became a panic with the fall of Atlanta on September 2, as General Sherman drove relentlessly across Georgia to the sea. The Confederacy was obviously in a bad way militarily, and the North's hopes for victory soared. They were to be fully realized in the spring of 1865. Nevertheless, the Democrats made a dangerously strong showing in the elections.

The results gave Lincoln 2,213,665 votes and McClellan 1,802,237, or a popular majority of 411,428 for Lincoln.[13] Lincoln secured 212 electoral votes to McClellan's 21. McClellan carried only Kentucky, New Jersey, and Delaware, with Lincoln getting all the rest. The vote was close in many states, and a key shift of 60,000 to McClellan would have changed the national outcome. In the new Congress the Republican representation went up from 106 to 143, and the Democratic down from 77 to 41.

THE VICTORIOUS END OF THE WAR

The Confederacy was defeated by the North on the basis of its greater manpower and superior industrial strength, and by the revolutionary strength of its political program. In its decisive aspects, the war consisted of four major stategical offensives which, taken together, smashed the Confederacy.

The first of these offensives was the military and political occupation by the Northern forces of the Border states—Delaware, Maryland, Kentucky, and Missouri. These states were very important. As Marx said in October 1862: "Whoever gets them dominates the Union."[14] By the end of that year, the North had basically eliminated the danger of Border-state defection, although Lincoln never seemed to realize this fact right up to the end of the war. By securing control of the Border states, the North therewith halted the explosive expansionism of the Confederacy and sentenced it to the narrow geographical limits within which it was finally beaten to earth.

The second big and successful offensive of the North was the freeing of the Mississippi River. This was begun by General Grant in February 1862, with his victory at Fort Donelson, Tennessee. It was continued by General Butler and Admiral Farragut with the capture of New Orleans in April 1862, and completed by General Grant in July 1863, with the capture of Vicksburg, Mississippi. These decisive victories opened the great river artery to the Union forces and also cut off the key states of Texas, Arkansas, and Louisiana from direct contact with the rest of the Confederacy.

The third great decisive offensive by the Union armies was the drive through Georgia by General Sherman. This started from Chattanooga, Tennessee, in May 1864, swept the Confederate armies of General Hood before it, captured Atlanta in September, and reached the sea at Savannah in December. The drive constituted an overwhelming disaster for the rebellion, as it again cut the Confederacy in two.

The fourth decisive offensive was the knockout blow, delivered by the Army of the Potomac under General Grant. On March 8, 1864, Grant was commissioned as lieutenant-general of all the United States armies, a title previously held only by General George Washington. In April, the drive on Richmond, the last of several bloody attempts to capture that city, got under way, with General Robert E. Lee as the opposing commander. During the next few months of that deadly summer the rival armies fought many bloody engagements—the Wilderness, Spottsylvania, Cold Harbor, and others. The drive was reopened in the spring, and on April 3, after desperate struggle, Richmond fell to the Union forces, Negro troops being the first to enter the city. On April 9, 1865, at Appomattox Court House, Virginia, General Lee handed his sword to General Grant and the great war was over. The slave power was broken.

THE ASSASSINATION OF LINCOLN

On April 14, 1865, Abraham Lincoln was assassinated by John Wilkes Booth at the Ford Theatre in Washington, D. C. The President was viewing the play, *Our American Cousins*. Booth, who had managed to worm his way into the box where Lincoln was sitting, crept up and shot him behind the ear. This was at about 10:30 P.M. Lincoln lingered on, unconscious, until he died at 7:22 next morning. At the time of the attack upon Lincoln, an assassin also tried to kill Secretary of State Seward with a knife, severely, but not mortally wounding him. Lincoln's assassination came as a grievous shock to the United States and the world.

After shooting Lincoln, Booth leaped to the stage, cried, *"Sic semper tyrannis.* The South is avenged,"* and disappeared through the back door to a horse provided for his escape. In the wild commotion he managed to get away. A reward of $100,000 was posted for his arrest and lesser rewards for his accomplices. On April 26, after a hysterical search, Booth was located in a barn near Bowling Green, Kentucky. He was shot while trying to escape from the burning structure. For years the legend persisted that, in reality, Booth was never actually caught.

Abraham Lincoln, murdered at the very moment of victory by the anti-slavery forces, was one of the greatest American bourgeois revolutionists. At the unveiling of the Lincoln monument in Washington, D. C., on April 14, 1876, eleven years after Lincoln's assassination, Frederick Douglass, paid a noble tribute to the Great Emancipator. Pointing out that Lincoln was primarily "the white man's President, entirely devoted to the welfare of white men," he remarked, "though the Union was more to him than our freedom or our future, under his wise and beneficent rule, we saw ourselves gradually lifted from the depths of slavery to the heights of liberty and manhood."[15]

Despite all his hesitations and his under-estimation of the Negro people, Lincoln headed the great coalition which carried the nation successfully through its life-and-death struggle with the planters. He was instrumental in smashing the greatest obstacle that stood in the way of national progress, the Southern slave power. He led in preserving the unity of the country, in clearing the path for a rapid industrial development, in laying the groundwork for a further growth of the labor movement. The greatest act of his life, the thing that placed him forever among the ranks of political immortals, was his issuance of the Emancipation Proclamation, the historic document which struck the shackles from four million Negro chattel slaves.

25. The Negro People in the Civil War

Besides being at the political center of the Civil War, the Negro people also took a decisive part in winning that great struggle. They served on all fronts. At the outbreak of the war (see Chapter 23), Negro slaves carried out many insurrectionary movements on the plantations and mass flights to the Union lines. During the war about 500,000 slaves fled the plantations. This disrupted food production in the Confederate states and it compelled the rebel leaders to divert many of their troops to guard duty at home in order to tighten the intimidation of the slaves throughout the South. But the greatest war services of the Negro people were in and in connection with the armed forces. Here they became an indispensable factor to victory.

Before the war Negroes had been recruited into the Navy but not the Army. As soon as the war began Douglass and other Abolitionists, including Karl Marx in the New York *Tribune,* strongly advocated the use of Negroes as soldiers, as a step that would be demoralizing to the South. There was, however, strong white chauvinist objection to this in the North. The Federal law of July 17, 1862, authorized the enlistment of Negroes, but it was not until the Emancipation Proclamation went into effect on January 1, 1863, that recruiting of Negroes into the armed forces really became a national policy. However, a number of previous important steps had been taken in this general direction, notably by Generals Hunter and Butler in Louisiana in 1862, in organizing Negro regiments, and by General Chetlain in Tennessee at about the same time. Governor Spryer of Rhode Island urged Negroes to enlist. The powerful voice of Frederick Douglass was heard throughout the land, insisting upon the right of Negroes to bear arms and calling upon his people to fight. Woodson states that before the end of 1862, there were four Negro regiments in the military service of the United States.[1] By the law of February 24, 1864, the draft was applied to Negroes.

By the end of the war there had been a total of 186,207 men in the Negro military organizations, (7,122 officers and 178,975 enlisted men), of whom 123,156 were in the service when peace was re-established. These figures do not include several thousand Negroes known to have served in "white" regiments, nor the large numbers employed in digging trenches and building fortifications. The latter were said to have numbered at least 250,000. All told there were 160 Negro regiments (140 infantry, 7 cavalry, 13 artillery), as well as 11 separate companies and batteries. The Secretary of the Navy reported that there were some 29,511 Negroes in the naval branches of the service.[2]

After the Emancipation Proclamation, Negro enlistments followed rapidly. Where slaves in the Border states were recruited, the slaveholders were recompensed. The Negro people responded enthusiastically to the opportunity to strike a real blow for their freedom. Among the volunteers were the two sons of Frederick Douglass. But the Negroes in the service had to face great discrimination. At first, they were paid as laborers, not as soldiers, at lower rates than the whites—ten dollars per month as against $13; they got less in bounties and there was a studied effort on the part of many white officers to confine them to back-of-the-lines garrison work and fatigue duty. Such rank discrimination caused much discontent among the Negro soldiers. Woodson says "Sergeant William Walker was shot by order of court martial because he had his company stack arms before the captain's tent in protest that the government had failed to comply with its contract. The Fifty-fourth and Fifty-fifth of Massachusetts refused to receive their pay until it had been made equal to that of the whites."[3] Pay was equalized by the government on January 1, 1864.

The Negro soldiers were organized in separate regiments. Generally their officers were white. During the war, however, some 75 Negroes managed to receive commissions as lesser officers. Some of the best known of these were Lieutenant Colonel W. N. Read of the First North Carolina Volunteers, Captain H. Ford Douglass of the Kansas Corps, Major Martin R. Delany and Captain O. S. B. Wall of the 104th Regiment, and Lieutenant Colonel A. T. Augusta of the U. S. C. T., Seventh Regiment. Among the best known of the white officers of Negro troops were Colonel R. G. Shaw, Colonel N. P. Hallawell, and Colonel Thomas Wentworth Higginson.

The famous Massachusetts regiment, "like most of the regiments to be raised under state auspices," says Quarles, "came from every walk of Negro life. Of the total of 980 recruits, 287 had been slaves. Five hundred and fifty were listed as pure blacks, and 430 were of 'mixed blood.' Nearly 500 could read and over 300 could both read and write.

Forty-six trades and occupations were represented, although farming, with 596, comprised more than all the others combined. The birthplaces of the men covered twenty-five states, the District of Columbia, Canada, and Africa." One soldier, Nicolas Said, a tribal leader from Central Africa, "spoke and wrote English, French, German, and Italian, while there is no doubt that he is master of Kanouri (his vernacular), Mandra, Arabic, Turkish, and Russian." (Benjamin Quarles, *The Negro in the Civil War*, p. 185, Boston, 1953.)

The Confederacy was never able to use Negroes as soldiers, although its need for manpower was urgent and the project was frequently discussed among the military leaders. Unlike their modern apologists, the slaveholders had no illusions that the Negroes liked slavery and would defend it. Under heavy guard, slaves were, however, used for the digging of trenches and the like. On March 13, 1865, in its great extremity, the Confederacy finally decided in desperation that Negroes should be tried as soldiers; but nothing came of it.[4] Stories that Negro troops were used by the rebels upon one or two occasions are altogether without confirmation. It has been well said by Aptheker that no Negro ever fired a shot in defense of the Confederacy.[5]

NEGRO TROOPS AT THE FRONT

In the North military necessity prevailed over white supremacist prejudices, and the Negro troops were sent to the front line to risk their lives in defense of freedom together with the whites. Of course, they acquitted themselves with splendid courage, as anyone even remotely acquainted with Negro history could have easily foretold. But their bravery in action came as a surprise to many whites, who believed the ability to meet the supreme test of battle was reserved only to men with white skins. The white chauvinists of Civil War times were astonished at the superb bravery of the Negroes on the field of battle, as their likes of today are amazed at the splendid fighting qualities now being exhibited by the non-white revolutionary soldiers of China, Korea, Indo-China, and other Asian countries.

Negro troops took part in some 198 battles and important skirmishes during the Civil War.[6] Among the more notable of these engagements were those at Port Hudson, Fort Wagner, Fort Pillow, Walton Bluff, Honey Hill, South Mountain, Olustee, Milliken's Bend, Doby River, Petersburg, and many other parts of the South. The white commanders were unbounded in their praise of the way the Negro soldiers bore themselves under fire. General Rufus Saxton, speaking of the campaign in Georgia, stated that they fought with the most determined bravery. Colonel Thomas Wentworth Higginson believed "it would have been madness to attempt with the bravest white troops what he successfuly accomplished with black." General Banks said of the Negro soldiers at the battle of Port Hudson, "Their conduct was heroic; no troops could be more determined or more daring." And Brawley tells of the brave Negro color-sergeant, Anselmas Plancancoes, in the same battle, who said, before a shell blew off his head, "Colonel, I will bring back these colors to you in honor, or report to God the reason why."[7]

The great courage the Negro soldiers displayed in the face of the possibility of being butchered or returned to slavery if they were captured (see Chapter 22). Several Southern massacres of Negro soldiers took place. On April 13, 1864, Fort Pillow, Mississippi, about 50 miles from Memphis, was recaptured by heavier Confederate forces under General Forrest. There 262 of the 557 Northern troops seized were Negroes. After the fort fell, 300 soldiers were massacred on the spot, most of them Negroes. The white troops fighting alongside of the Negroes were from Tennessee, which especially enraged Forrest.

Negroes also did a major service to the North by acting as spies behind the Confederate lines. The heroic Harriet Tubman, of Underground Railroad fame, was very active in this superlatively dangerous work. With their keen knowledge of local conditions, slaves were of invaluable assistance in this respect; they were the main source of information to the Union armies on what was going on behind the rebel lines. They were the eyes and ears of the Northern forces. One of the most spectacular acts of daring and heroism during the whole war was the capture of the rebel steamer *Planter* in Charleston harbor, by Robert Smalls, a Negro pilot.[8]

The Negro soldiers paid heavily in casualties for their war activities. Aptheker calculates, on the basis of official reports, that about 39,200 Negro servicemen, of whom some 3,200 were sailors, died from wounds and disease. He says that "the ratio of mortal casualties among the United States Colored Troops was 47.06 per thousand greater than that of the United States Volunteer Troops from the twenty-four loyal states. . . . The mortality rate among the United States Colored Troops in the Civil War was 35 per cent greater than that among other troops, notwithstanding the fact that the former were not enrolled until some eighteen months after the fighting began.[9]

The armed Negro fighters for freedom were an important factor in winning the great Civil War. This is attested by Abraham Lincoln himself. When urged in 1864, to give up the use of Negro troops, Lincoln declared, "Take from us and give to the enemy the hundred and thirty, forty, or fifty thousand colored persons now serving us as soldiers, seamen, and laborers, and we cannot longer maintain the contest."[10]

FREDERICK DOUGLASS, NEGRO POLITICAL LEADER

Besides their important role within the Union forces and behind the Confederate lines, the Negro people also made a vital political contribution to winning the war. It was they who developed two key demands for victory in the war—the emancipation of the slaves and the recruiting of Negroes as soldiers—and pushed these demands clearly and persistently with the slow-moving Lincoln Administration. And in their striving for liberation they produced a major political revolutionary figure in Frederick Douglass. He was not only the outstanding spokesman of the Negro people; he was also an unexcelled leader of the whole American nation.

Douglass, who had fled as a youth from slavery in 1838, was a mature political leader by 1850. From then on, more clearly and consistently than any American of the times, he explained what was happening in the United States and what was needed to be done about it. He saw from the outset that the abolition of slavery was the key political issue, and with his eloquent voice and powerful pen, he drove home this fact to the American people. He swept aside every befogging hypocrisy and paralyzing compromise. In 1864 with his usual great clarity, he expressed his idea of what was involved in the war: "No war but an Abolition war; no peace but an Abolition peace; liberty for all, chains for none; the black man a soldier in war, a laborer in peace; a voter at the South as well as at the North; America his permanent home, and all Americans his fellow-countrymen. Such, fellow citizens, is my idea of the mission of the war."[11] Virtually no white American political leaders of the time had anywhere near as clear a picture of the revolutionary tasks of the Civil War and the Reconstruction period in regard to the complex question of the Negro people.

Although Douglass had great prestige among the Negro people and enjoyed a wide reputation with the general public as a speaker and Abolitionist fighter, he was vastly underestimated and played down as a leader by his white contemporaries. This brilliant leader, who was qualified for any political office in the country, should have held an honored post in the top circles of the revolutionary government; but because he was a Negro he was shoved aside, while political nobodies and reactionary whites were given high positions.

Once it looked as though Douglass was about to be entrusted with important government work. He had visited Lincoln late in 1863, and a plan was worked out between them for him to take charge of the recruiting of Negroes for the war. On the basis of an agreement with Secretary of War Stanton, Douglass closed down his monthly paper, which had carried on the Abolition fight for 16 years, and prepared to take up his new duties. But Stanton welshed on the plan—it was much too daring to place a Negro in charge of such important work. In January 1870, Douglass launched another paper, the *New Era,* later known as the *New National Era.*

The Lincoln Administration was never willing to provide an important post for Douglass; even when he proposed to take the stump for Lincoln in the crucial campaign of 1864 his offer was rejected. During the Johnson and Grant administrations, proposals were considered to make Douglass the head of the Freedmen's Bureau and to designate him as Minister to Haiti, but the plans fell through.*
It remained for the administration of Rutherford B. Hayes, in 1877, to give Douglass a post, but one so small as to be an insult to such a capable man—United States Marshal for the District of Columbia. Even this minor appointment, says Douglass, "provoked something like a scream—I will not say a *yell*—of popular displeasure."[12] Backing down before the clamor of the white chauvinists, Hayes refused to reappoint Douglass as marshal when his term ran out, but he made him instead Recorder of Deeds in Washington. This insignificant job was the best that the Jim Crow United States had to offer this brilliant Negro statesman. But Douglass, despite all the gross Jim Crow persecution to which he was subjected throughout his political life, nevertheless succeeded in writing his name high in the ranks of American revolutionary leaders.

* Years later, in 1889, President Harrison appointed Douglass Minister to Haiti at which post he stayed two years.

THE WORKERS ON THE EVE OF THE WAR

When the Civil War began, the trade union movement, still very young and weak, found itself in a most difficult position. The main forces of the unions had been scattered by the economic crisis of 1857. By 1859 they were just pulling themselves together again, when once more they were largely broken up as a result of the economic dislocation caused by the outbreak of the war, with its initial wide unemployment.

Most of the unions supported Lincoln in the election of 1860, and they shared his viewpoint that the way to handle the slavery issue was to contain it within specified areas. They were alarmed at the growing prospect of war, and they spoke out actively against it. Their general position over the years in the developing struggle with the planters, we have dealt with in Chapters 10 and 17. The attitude of the unions on the eve of the war was expressed at the convention which they held in Philadelphia, beginning February 21, 1861, just as the secession crisis was developing.

This convention, attended by delegates from eight industrial states, worked out a general program. It picked William H. Sylvis, president of the National Iron Molders Union, as its general secretary, and it elected a Committee of Thirty-four, one for each of the existing states. The main purpose of the convention was to fight against the approaching war. The delegates attacked not only the secessionists and employers, but also the Abolitionists. Foner thus sums up the resolutions of the convention: "They (1) endorsed the Crittenden Compromise, (2) announced devotion to the Union and opposition to all traitors, North or South, (3) attacked secession as dangerous and repugnant to all workingmen, (4) warned politicians that the workers were determined to replace them with men from the shops and factories, (5) condemned a policy of coercion which would lead to civil war, (6) called for the repeal of the 'personal liberty' laws in several Northern states which were aimed at preventing the return of fugitive slaves to the South, and (7) urged the organization of state associations of workingmen in each of the thirty-four states."[13]

The Committee of Thirty-four called meetings and anti-war demonstrations in a number of cities, carrying on agitation along the line adopted at the national convention. The Southern trade unions quite generally took a stand against the growing secession movement.

The national convention was to meet again on July 4, 1861; but with war breaking out in the meantime, the convention never took place and the Committee of Thirty-four fell to pieces.

The labor movement of the early Civil War period was much too youthful and politically immature to map out a clear-sighted working class policy. The Communists of the period, Weydemeyer and others, were not strong enough to infuse the unions with their abolitionism. Consequently the labor movement was unable to set forth definitely the interests of the working class in the complex situation, much less give leadership to the revolutionary war as a whole. Hence, in the armed struggle, it mainly followed the lead of the bourgeoisie. As we have remarked earlier, there was a deep-seated hatred among the masses for chattel slavery, and the workers had always been well represented in all the struggles of previous generations against the spread of slavery and for Negro emancipation. In general, however, in the initial stages of the war, the great body of trade unionists did not see beyond the Lincoln Free Soil illusion that the problem of slavery could be solved by restricting the slave system to specified areas. They did not understand that the abolition of slavery was fundamental to the advance of all labor.

A big reason for the workers' failure to understand the slavery question better and to realize the revolutionary nature of the struggle was the fact that they were still, in considerable numbers, under the influence of the Democratic Party. This party, the party of Jefferson and Jackson, had for years been the traditional party of the workers; but it had long since fallen under the domination of the big planters and was working to save the slave system.

THE WORKERS IN THE WAR

Once the war began, Copperhead reactionary elements tried hard to turn the workers against it on the basis of the rising cost of living, the undemocratic character of conscription, and the workers' fear of a great flood of cheap Negro labor from the former slave states. They had influence among the undeveloped sections of the workers in Eastern commercial centers, and the draft riots in New York (see Chapter 24) showed that such propaganda was not without some effect. But, in the main, the workers stood firm and made a decisive contribution to winning the war.

When Fort Sumter was fired upon and the war began, the workers responded vigorously. In many cases, trade unions joined the army in a body. Schlueter recalls a Philadelphia local union which did this, recording in the minutes of its last meeting: "It having been resolved to enlist with Uncle Sam for the war, this union stands adjourned until the Union is safe or we are whipped."[14] The Painters Union of Brooklyn enlisted in a body. "The Mechanics' Phalanx of Lowell, led by Captain James N. Horse, a carpenter, won a $100 prize for being the first organization ready for camp."[15] Gould, an outstanding authority, estimates that of all those who enlisted 38 percent were workers.[16] Foreign-born workers—German, French, Polish, Irish—vied with the native-born all over the North and West in their patriotic fervor. The workers were a powerful foundation in the great coalition which fought the Civil War.

The employers' response to Lincoln's call for arms was very different. The great bulk of them, while the workers and farmers were hurrying to the front, refused to volunteer, and when the draft came, they paid the $300 price for a substitute and stayed at home to garner the rich profit pickings from the war. Powderly, head of the later-to-be Knights of Labor, says: "It is true that men from other walks of life enlisted and did good service in the Union cause, but the great bulk of the army was made up of workingmen. While the workingmen were enlisting in the service of their country, the bankers and owners of gold were working their way into Congress. . . . A speaker on the floor of the House of Representatives said, after looking around him, 'I see the representatives of eighty banks sitting as members of this house.' "[17]

After a temporary economic breakdown at the start of the war, industry in the North took a tremendous surge ahead, under pressure of the great need for munitions and other production for the army. Schlueter says, "Under the fructifying rain of millions . . . spent in liquidating army and navy contracts and supplies, industry on a large scale began to develop and consolidate by leaps and bounds. Mass production of the articles required by the army resulted in transforming all workshops into factories."[18] Without strong unions and unprotected by government price controls, the workers suffered heavy losses in their living standards. Commons says that from 1860 to 1864 prices of necessities went up 70 percent, while wages increased only 30 percent.[19]

Under these conditions of acute labor shortage and swiftly rising prices, trade unionism flourished. Local unions and city centrals sprang up in many crafts and localities. National unions were organized, either shortly before or during the war, among the iron molders, machinists and blacksmiths, steel workers, carpenters, painters, locomotive engineers, bricklayers, printers, tailors, shoe workers, etc. By 1865 the trade unions had an estimated membership of 150,000. In 1864, upon the initiative of Louisville trade unionists, a serious effort was made to form a national labor federation. On September 21 of that year, a convention met in Louisville and formed the International Industrial Assembly of North America. This organization died aborning, however, as the national trade union leaders did not like the idea of its having the general local trades assembly form as the basic unit.

Many strikes took place during the war. Sylvis deplored the necessity for wartime strikes, but Todes says that, "Throughout the years 1863 and 1864 more strikes occurred than had yet been seen in all the previous years in American history."[20] Many of the Northern army generals met these strikes with open strikebreaking. The printers of St. Louis appealed to Lincoln in one such case, reminding him that he had once said, "Thank God we have a system where there can be a strike." Usually, however, Lincoln left his generals a pretty free hand in such matters.

For the working class the revolutionary Civil War brought many important benefits. First of all was the emancipation of the slaves, since slavery had been a terrible obstacle to all economic and political advance by all workers. The revolution also gave a great stimulus to the movement for the eight-hour day, which, as Marx says, "ran with express speed from the Atlantic to the Pacific, from New England to California."[21] Of vital importance, the Civil War, which was a bourgeois-democratic revolution, put the trade union movement upon a more firm and stable basis. Before the war, the organizations of labor had been weak and temporary; but during the war they took on a new vitality, strength, and permanence. In the fire of the revolution, the labor movement advanced to a new higher level.

THE MARXISTS IN THE WAR

The Marxists, known at that time as Communists, understood the revolutionary significance of the Civil War. Under the ideological influence of Marx himself, they realized that in the great struggle much more was involved than the preservation of the Union or even the emancipation of the four million slaves. They understood that the existence of bourgeois democracy itself was at stake; that the United States was facing the alternative of either advancing to new and higher planes of democracy and industrial development, or sinking into a slavery that would eventually involve white as well as Negro workers. They gave everything they had to the winning of the war. Although as yet few in numbers, they were not without important, and even decisive influence.

The Communist Club and other Marxist political groups sent the bulk of their members into the Union Army. The Marxists were also instrumental in getting many trade unions to take an active stand in support of the war. They were especially influential in stirring the organizations of the foreign-born, notably the Germans, into action. Within a week after Lincoln's first call for volunteers, the New York Turners (German athletic societies) had organized a full regiment. The Missouri Turners recruited three regiments. Similar activities were carried on in Cincinnati, Chicago, St. Louis, Milwaukee, and other German centers. The Communists were the most active fighters against every form of defeatism and Copperhead influence among the workers.

Many of the Marxists had had military experience in Europe, and they used this to good effect in the Civil War. Joseph Weydemeyer, formerly an artillery officer in the Prussian army, raised a regiment, became its colonel, and was put in command in the key St. Louis military district. "August Willich, a close friend of Karl Marx, rose to the rank of colonel and in 1862 became a brigadier general. Robert Rosa, who had been an officer in the Prussian army before he became a member of the Communist Club of New York, was major of the Forty-Fifth Regiment of New York. Fritz Jacobi enlisted as a private, and attained a lieutenancy commission before he died on the field of Fredericksburg."[22] Lincoln welcomed the valuable co-operation of the Marxists.

The Communists distinguished themselves on many fronts during the war. Their most significant military achievement, however, was in helping save Missouri for the Union cause. This was a strategic Border state, and its loss would have been a major disaster to the North. The decisive forces in holding it were the Germans of St. Louis, among whom Weydemeyer and other Communists wielded powerful influence.[23]

Ideologically, the Communists were a strengthening force. Their Marxist understanding placed them in advance of the Radicals in political thinking. They not only demanded the emancipation of the slaves and the recruiting of Negro soldiers, but they worked to build the trade union movement in this favorable opportunity and to increase its influence on the broad coalition under Lincoln. One of their notable achievements in this respect was the important help they gave in the withdrawal of Frémont's candidacy against Lincoln during the pre-election fight of 1864 (see Chapter 24). Had this independent ticket been kept in the field, Lincoln would have surely been defeated—with disastrous consequences for the war. Weydemeyer was one of the clear-sighted Communists who saw this great danger and who were influential in getting Frémont to withdraw. The Communists were also a moving influence in building the Workingmen's Democratic-Republican Association, a strong force during the 1864 election.

The greatest of all services of the Marxists to the Civil War were the writings of Karl Marx in the New York *Tribune* and especially in the European press. These we have commented upon in passing. Marx had a clear picture of what was happening in the war—more so than any American political leader. Undoubtedly his articles, some of which Greeley's paper ran as editorials, exerted a real influence upon the thinking of the Radical Republicans, if not upon Lincoln himself. Lenin has high praise for Marx's writing during this revolutionary war.

INTERNATIONAL LABOR SOLIDARITY

During the long pre-war struggle against the slavocrats and also during the four bitter war years, the workers of Western Europe, and especially England, where the influence of Marxism was powerful, were loyal friends of the Negroes and Abolitionists in the United States. Undoubtedly, they prevented Great Britain from joining the Confederacy in its attempt to destroy the Union. In September 1864, in London, the advanced workers of Europe founded the International Workingmen's Association, known later as the First International. Its leading figure was Karl Marx. The International multiplied its activities all over Europe in support of the struggle against slavery in the United States.

When Abraham Lincoln was re-elected in 1864, the I.W.A. sent him a letter of greeting, congratulating him upon his victory.[24] The letter, written by Marx, stated: "From the commencement of the titanic American strife the workingmen of Europe felt instinctively that the Star Spangled Banner carried the destiny of their class." It also pointed out: "While the workingmen, the true political power of the North, allowed slavery to defile their own republic, while before the Negro, mastered and sold without his concurrence, they boasted it the highest prerogative of the white-skinned laborer to sell himself and to choose his own master, they were unable to attain the true freedom of labor, or to support their European brethren in this struggle for emancipation; but this barrier to progress has been swept off by the red sea of civil war." Lincoln, through the American Legation in London, sent the I.W.A. a warm note of appreciation for this letter.

On May 13, 1865, upon learning of the assassination of President Lincoln, the General Council of the I.W.A. sent a letter to President Johnson, expressing the European workers' sorrow at this tragic loss. This letter, also written by Marx, expressed appreciation of Lincoln as "a man, neither to be browbeaten by adversity, nor intoxicated by success, inflexibly pressing on to his great goal, never compromising it by blind haste, slowly maturing his steps, never retracing them.... Such indeed was the modesty of this great and good man, that the world only discovered him a hero after he had fallen a martyr."[25]

26. Problems of Post-War Reconstruction

The end of the Civil War marked the close of one stage in the revolution and the beginning of another. The revolution as a whole had three stages. In the first, during the pre-war decades, the issues were shaped and the revolutionary forces gathered. The second was the military phase, the four years of the war. And the third phase, just beginning, was that of Reconstruction after the war's ravages.

The post-war task of Reconstruction was huge and unique. No country had ever faced a comparable problem. It was fundamentally necessary to reconstruct the broken and shattered state governments of the Confederacy and realign them within the Union; to take care of the urgent needs and to start the great mass of liberated slaves on a new economic and political life; to break up the plantation system (the agrarian revolution) and to reorganize the economy of the South upon a new, more modern capitalist basis. The accomplishment of these revolutionary tasks depended upon the second one: to what degree the elementary problem of the freedmen was solved. The future of the nation, especially of the South, was at stake in the Reconstruction problem.

THE CONDITIONS OF THE FREED SLAVES

It is little realized now what an enormous change in status emancipation meant for the great masses of slaves. They were suddenly catapulted out of the generations-old system of chattel slavery, and although they became for the most part sharecroppers, this deep change, with its limited type of freedom and its manifold new problems, called for profound alterations in outlook, habits, and way of living on the part of the ex-slaves. Never in modern times has any people been confronted with such an immense problem of social readjustment.

The slaves, upon being liberated, literally had to rebuild themselves anew from the ground up. They did not even have names suitable for freedmen, and generally they had to adopt new ones. The slave code conceptions of marriage, forced upon them over long years by the planters, had to be replaced by new conceptions of the family relationship. They had to learn new ways of speaking to one another and to other people in place of the special manners and customs of slavery. The whole concept of being bodily free and able to go where they pleased was startlingly new to them, for under slavery they had been virtual prisoners on the plantations; unable to leave their homes without getting the master's permission.

The freed slaves had almost no property and they had little understanding of this whole basic institution. They owned no homes, no land, no farm animals, no implements, and hardly any of the field workers even possessed clothes fit to wear among freedmen. They had but a limited knowledge of money and wages, and only a few understood such problems as the marketing of crops. Their living conditions, such as they were, had been determined by the planters, the only labor discipline they had known was that of the lash, and they had very little contact with the law as such. Politics, so far as the slaves were concerned, also had been almost a closed world. They were about 96 percent illiterate, and had only a very indefinite understanding of the political situation at home and abroad. They had no experience whatever in voting or in political organization.

It was under such great handicaps that the freed slaves started out upon their new life of "freedom." The great accomplishments they made during the very difficult years of the Reconstruction period were a striking testimonial to their intelligence and adaptability. Their achievements were all the greater because, supported for the most part by only half-hearted white friends, they had to confront the still powerful class of cotton planters, who were resolved to keep them in bondage and exploitation at any cost.

REVOLUTIONARY TASKS

The specific revolutionary tasks confronting the Federal Government after the military defeat of the Southern cotton planters in the war may be summed up as follows: (a) the creation of a vast relief organization to take care of the immediate economic needs of the freed slaves; (b) the confiscation of the estates of the planters and their distribution to the Negroes and poor whites; (c) the granting of full economic, political, educational, and social equality to the Negroes; (d) the concession of land and full political rights to the poor whites; (e) the reorganization of the political life of the defeated secessionist states in such fashion as to insure political control by the Negro and white democratic masses and to make impossible the return to political power of the counter-revolutionary class of planters.

These revolutionary measures were necessary, not only to insure livable conditions for the masses of freed slaves and also for the impoverished whites all over the South. They were also basically needed for the further progress of American capitalism itself, particularly in the South. They were essential to the liquidation of the plantation slave system, which, for so many decades, had been a drag upon the industrialization and democracy of the whole country. The sequel showed (as we shall see) that these tasks of Reconstruction were not fully realized. And the consequence of this failure to complete the revolution was, besides keeping the Negroes still enslaved and the poor whites in deep deprivation, to slow up the development of capitalism in the South. The effects of this retardation are still very much in evidence at the present time.

A few of the white Radical leaders, but by no means all, had some idea of the essentially revolutionary tasks confronting them—notably the indomitable Thaddeus Stevens, the outstanding Radical in the House. During this period Stevens was a consistent fighter for the vote, the land, and social equality for the Negro people. As early as 1865, while speaking in his home town of Lancaster, Pennsylvania, and demanding that the land be taken from the planters and given to the ex-slaves, Stevens remarked: "They say it is revolution, and no doubt it would work a radical reorganization in Southern institutions, habits, and manners."[1]

But the clearest program among the Radicals was that of the Negro leaders, Douglass, Langston, Purvis, Garnett, Martin, Wier, and others. For years they had been demanding emancipation, the franchise, full social equality, and land for the slaves—which was the heart of the program necessary to the full bourgeois democratic potentialities of the revolution. These demands were supported by the Negro people, who reiterated them again and again in their state and national conventions. Thus, the important convention held in Nashville, Tennessee, in August 1865, demanded that Negroes be given full rights as citizens and that Tennessee's representatives be barred from Congress unless the state recognized equal Negro rights. The North Carolina Negro Convention, in Raleigh, in September 1865, approved the Thirteenth Amendment, recognition of Liberia and Haiti, cash wages for labor, free education for Negro children, and repeal of the Black Codes, and endorsed the Radical Republicans. The South Carolina Convention, in Charleston, in November 1865, demanded the repeal of the Black Codes, the right to serve on juries and to testify in court, the right to vote, the right to the land in the Sea Islands, the right to bear arms, full civil liberties, and free schools. The Georgia convention of the Negro people in Augusta, in January 1866, formulated a whole series of demands of the same general type.[2] This broad movement indicated that the Negroes understood the essential needs and opportunities of the Reconstruction period. It was a splendid testimonial to the political capacity of a people just emerging from over two centuries of slavery.

In Chapter 23 we saw how the Northern bourgeoisie, in its fight against its Southern cotton-planter rivals, seized upon and made use of the revolutionary liberation demands of the Negro people only when it was constrained to do so under the pressure of necessity. This was the case with the demands that the slaves be freed and that Negroes be used as soldiers in the war—propositions which were put into effect by the Lincoln Administration only because they were indispensable for winning the war. The same thing was true during the Reconstruction period regarding such vital Negro demands as the vote, civil liberties, education, and the land. The Northern bourgeoisie made use of them only to the extent dictated by its most urgent needs, casting these demands aside when they no longer served its class interests. At all times, the bourgeoisie of the North considered the Negro people and their demands as strictly expendable.

THE REPUBLICAN PARTY

The multi-class war alliance in the North, of which the political expression was the Republican Party, faced up to the new tasks of Reconstruction with a considerably different internal composition from that at the beginning of the Civil War. The industrialists, who were dominant in the combination, had greatly extended in size and strength during the war. Their influence had grown vastly with the enormous expansion of industry. They were prospering in all directions. They had raised the tariff from 19 percent to 47 percent; they were building what became the Union Pacific Railroad; they had passed the National Bank Act and were constructing a whole new banking system; they had stolen an empire of land from the government; they were reaping fabulous profits, were rapidly building industry, and they had full control of the Federal government.

The working class had also greatly expanded and matured during the war. It was acquiring a new consciousness and fighting spirit, and was laying the foundations of a permanent trade union movement. It was also developing an independent political policy, which was soon to cut it loose altogether from the Republican Party and to direct its main struggle against the rising, arrogant industrialists.

The Negro people, always a vital element in the historic struggle against the planters, had greatly increased their strength during the war. The emancipation of the slaves, even though it was succeeded by semi-serf sharecropping, was an enormous victory, and the splendid fighting record of Negro soldiers had done much to liquidate the thick clouds of anti-Negro prejudice that plagued the country. The free Negroes, who in 1860 numbered 488,070, about one-half of whom were in the South, were especially active during Reconstruction. In the long, hard anti-slavery struggle, the Negro people had not only gained tremendously in their organizable political strength, but they had clarified their program, improved their organizations, and built up qualified leadership. They were to be a strong revolutionary factor during the Reconstruction period, and were long to remain loyal supporters of the Republican Party.

The farmers' allegiance to the Republican Party was strengthened by the passage of the Homestead Act in 1862. They also shared in much of the initial "prosperity"—especially high prices for food stuffs —during the Civil War period. But it was not long until they, too, began to break with the Republican Party and to move into the Granger, Greenback, and Populist movements. As for the city middle classes—small businessmen, professionals, etc.—they were a major base of the Republican Party as it went into the crucial Reconstruction period, which was to last roughly from 1865 to 1876.

With the victorious end of the war, the Republican Party also gained important white allies in the South. These were the remnants of the middle class Whigs in the urban centers, and the small farmers and the rural poor. In general, these groups had been opposed to secession; they were more or less crowded into the war by pressure from the big cotton planters and their tools. These new Republican allies played a very significant role in Southern Reconstruction, as we shall see. But their Achilles Heel as a political force was white chauvinism. They generally held themselves to be superior to the

Negroes, and wanted neither to work nor to fraternize with them. Thus, they were usually an easy prey to the big planters, with their eternal cry about "Negro domination."

The Republican Party had two broad, well-marked factions or wings. The left—the Radical Republican wing—was led by Charles Sumner, Frederick Douglass, Thaddeus Stevens, General Benjamin Butler, Zachariah Chandler, Ben Wade, E. M. Stanton, Joshua R. Giddings, Olive P. Martin, John P. Hale, Horace Greeley, and others. Although they were often confused about the road ahead, their general purpose was to complete the revolution by thoroughly defeating the cotton planters, establishing Republican leadership in the South, and giving the Negro people at least certain elementary political rights. The right wing of the party, following the mottoes, "Let Us Have Peace" and "Go Easy With the South," took the position that the struggle was virtually over with the military defeat of the South. They were in favor of soft terms for the planters and a minimum of rights to the Negro people. Their line led to maintaining the Southern planters in power. They were headed, in varying degrees, and in later situations, by men such as Fessenden, Sherman, the Blairs, Trumbull, Seward, Curtis, Fowler, Stewart, Grimes, Moorehead, Conkling, Blaine, and others, most of whom had at some time been Radicals.

DISSOLUTION OF THE AMERICAN ANTI-SLAVERY SOCIETY

By the beginning of Reconstruction, the old Garrison-Phillips group in the Anti-Slavery Society had ceased to be the decisive factor in the revolutionary struggle. Garrison and other old-time Abolitionists had immense prestige among the people; but the anti-slavery struggle had found new leaders and new organizations. Now the real political movement was centered in such groupings as the Republican Party, the Joint Committee on Reconstruction in Congress, the Freedmen's Bureau, the Union Leagues, the Negro conventions, the trade unions, and the Equal Rights League.

Garrison discontinued *The Liberator* at the end of 1865, after 35 years of uninterrupted publication and struggle.[3] The Anti-Slavery Society split at that time, Garrison and Phillips severed their life-long association in their dispute over whether or not the organization should be dissolved. Garrison favored dissolution, while Phillips, Douglass, Purvis, and others opposed it. Garrison was defeated, 118 to 48, whereupon he resigned. Wendell Phillips was elected president, and he continued along with great activity. It was formally dissolved on April 19, 1870, with elaborate ceremony, many old-time Abolitionists being present at its demise.

Underlying the liquidation of the society was the failure to appreciate the revolutionary struggle that still remained to win the Negro people full equality. This was due in no small measure to the prevalence of white supremacist notions (white chauvinism) even in the ranks of the Abolitionists. Aptheker says many of them adopted a patronizing attitude and "thought of the Negro as not quite human, or as childish, stupid, meek"[4]—corrosive ideas that Douglass and other Negro leaders fought persistently.

In 1866, the Abolitionists and women suffragists—Susan B. Anthony and others—formed the American Equal Rights Association to fight for the vote for Negroes and women and for civil liberties in general. But at the third convention of this organization, in 1869, the women suffragists, who were discontented at the heavy stress on the Negro right to vote and little emphasis upon the franchise for women, dissolved the Association and launched a women's rights organization.

THE DEMOCRATIC PARTY

Although formally split into two nominally independent parties, North and South, the Democratic Party survived the Civil War. The Southern section, arms-in-hand, did its best to overthrow the Federal Government by military action; while the Northern section opposed the war by every conceivable means—through defeatist propaganda, financial sabotage, opposition to enlistment, anti-draft riots, plots for armed insurrection, and attempts to upset the Union government in elections. Its general line was "peace at any price," although the members divided themselves into "peace" Democrats and "war" Democrats. Northern leaders of the Party, who were in close contact with their confrères on the opposite side of the battle lines, were such men as Clarence L. Vallandigham, Fernando Wood, Horatio Seymour, George E. Pugh, George W. Morgan, G. H. Pendleton, Cyrus McCormick, and General George B. McClellan. The strength of this Democratic fifth column in the North was strikingly demonstrated by its strong showing in the national elections of 1862 and 1864.

The Democratic Party was based on the historic alliance of the big planters, mainly in cotton, with the extensive Northern mercantile interests tied in with Southern trade. They had a miscellaneous following from other classes in the North. This was essentially the reactionary planter-merchant combination which, throughout the decades, had formulated the Constitution in the 1787 convention (without the Bill of Rights), fought Jefferson in 1798-1800 over the Alien and Sedition Acts, combated Jackson in the 1830's over the Bank, and warred against Lincoln during 1861-65 over slavery. This reactionary bloc also fought all through the Reconstruction period; and in the Republican-Dixiecrat alliance, it still constitutes the basis of reaction in our own time, except that nowadays the big Northern industrialists are wholly dominant in the reactionary combination.

As soon as the Civil War came to an end, the two wings or segments of the Democratic Party, North and South, sewed themselves together again and began to function as one organization. The party's major objective in the Reconstruction years was to save the Southern planters from the penalties or hardships being placed upon them by the victorious North. Although completely defeated on the field of battle and with their economy in ruins, the planters still retained a great deal of economic and political strength. They had the powerful national Democratic Party in their hands, and they had come out of the war with the plantation system as such practically intact. Cotton production was down by two million bales in 1866 (less than half of what it was in 1859), but the price that year was three times the pre-war price. It was not until 1876 that cotton production again reached its 1859 level. The cotton planters' program was to retain political power in the South in the shake-up that was beginning and to keep the Negroes in an oppression and exploitation as near as possible to the conditions of chattel slavery. To these ignoble ends, the Democratic Party bent its chief efforts during the Reconstruction years. And but little camouflage was used in the process. Its leaders, especially in the South, boldly raised the cry of "white supremacy" and fought on that basis.

PRESIDENT ANDREW JOHNSON'S
REACTIONARY PROGRAM

Andrew Johnson, vice-president, became president of the United States automatically after the assassination of Abraham Lincoln on April 14, 1865. He was born in Raleigh, North Carolina, in 1808; but he spent most of his life in East Tennessee. There he lived in a non-slave-holding community. He came from a working class family, being apprenticed as a boy to a tailor. Successively Johnson held elective posts as alderman, mayor, member of the state legislature, member of the U.S. House of Representatives, and senator from Tennessee. In the mid-1850's he supported a proposition for a homestead law for farmers. Although endorsing slavery as an institution, Johnson actively opposed secession, as many Border state leaders did. He became a war Democrat. In 1862 Lincoln appointed him as military governor of Tennessee (which had seceded) and commissioned him to set up a loyal state government. This he succeeded in doing. It gave him great prestige, and in 1864, with Lincoln's blessing, he was nominated and elected vice-president on the Republican ticket. But he never became a member of the Republican Party.

While in the Senate, Johnson had worked closely with the Radicals. He was a member of the Joint Committee for the Conduct of the War, co-operated with the Radicals Wade and Chandler, fought against McClellan and the big planters, and demanded of Lincoln that the heads of the Confederacy be executed.[5] On June 9, 1864, in Nashville, Tennessee, he declared that "the great plantations . . . must be seized and divided into small farms, and sold to honest industrious men."[6] Upon the death of Lincoln, the Radicals were sure that Johnson would make a good president and one who would carry out their general conceptions of Southern Reconstruction.

But, once president, Johnson made a sudden about-face. Within three months he was in open conflict with the Radicals. The new president maintained that the Southern states had never been out of the Union; that the authority to reconstruct the South resided with the president, and not with Congress; and that there must be "easy" terms for the rebelling states in order to heal the war's wounds as soon as possible.

Superficially this looked like Lincoln's Reconstruction program, and Johnson so presented it to Congress and the people. There was, however, a fundamental difference between the two men and their roles. During his regime as president, Lincoln made many serious political errors and his Reconstruction program was one of the worst of them; but he also had the capacity, under the pressure of the developing revolution, to rectify his errors and to adopt correct policies. Thus he was able to stand at the head of the government of the revolution. For example, on the question of the franchise, by 1865 he had proposed that all "literate" Negroes and those who had served in the Union Army be given the right to vote—about half a million, all told. Lincoln's record during the war years makes it possible to assume that he might well have gotten around to a correct policy on Southern Reconstruction.

With Johnson, however, the situation was quite different. In his break with the Radicals he acted the part of a renegade and became the leader of the main forces of reaction, the cotton planters. Thenceforth, he made every effort to put into effect the program of the planters, which was designed to save them from the fury of the revolutionary storm. It was precisely in this role that Johnson was understood and dealt with, both by his friends, the planters, and by his enemies, the Radicals. President Andrew Johnson's place in American history is that of the chief leader of the counter-revolution during the early Reconstruction period.

27. Congress Versus the President

Upon assuming the office of president after the murder of Abraham Lincoln, Andrew Johnson immediately launched his drive for Southern Reconstruction. On May 29, 1865, only six weeks after Lincoln's assassination, he took the first step with his Amnesty Proclamation.[1] Under this agreement, all persons who had participated directly or indirectly in the rebellion, save certain groups, would have all their rights and properties (except the ownership of slaves) restored to them upon taking a loyalty pledge. The list of those not amnestied included members of the Confederate government; deserters to the Confederacy from the U.S. judiciary, military, Congressional, or civilian posts; those who had abused Negro war prisoners; graduates of West Point and Annapolis academies; governors of Southern secessionist states; naval raiders; and all those with yearly incomes of $20,000 or more who had participated in the rebellion. This list banned only a relatively small group of former rebels.

THE PRESIDENTIAL RECONSTRUCTION PLAN

On June 30, 1866, President Johnson proclaimed his plan for reconstructing the state governments in a communication addressed to the establishment of a provisional government in South Carolina.[2] Under this project a state convention was to be called by an appointed provisional governor, with delegates elected from those citizens who came within the provisions of the amnesty directive of May 29 and who had taken the loyalty oath. The state convention thus held was required to adopt certain measures, the chief of which were repeal the Secession Ordinance of 1861, abolition of slavery by specific provision, and reputiation of the state's Confederate war debts. This done, state officials could be elected and national representatives sent to Congress. Thereupon the Federal government would resume its normal functions in the state and the state in question would be in good standing in the Union. The whole plan was tied in with the Lincolnian theory that the secessionist states had never in reality been out of the Union.

A major fact stood out clearly in Johnson's scheme—Negroes were not to be extended the right to vote. The whole plan was aimed at restoring the ex-slaveholders to political power at once. This was what Johnson intended and also what happened in fact. As early as July 15, 1865, Engels wrote of this situation to Marx: "If things go on like this, in six months all the old villains of secession will be sitting in Congress in Washington."[3]

The planters fell in step immediately with Johnson's Reconstruction program. Between May 29 and July 13, 1865, the president issued seven Reconstruction proclamations to the rebel states, which promptly held state conventions and elected governments. It was all a sort of holiday occasion for the slaveholders, who, under this convenient arrangement, saw themselves sailing right back into power with the Negroes safely under control. In various Southern state conventions, many delegates sat in Confederate uniforms. They quickly met the soft conditions laid down by Johnson. Thus seven "Johnson states" were soon added to the already existing four "Lincoln states" as "reconstructed."

While thus "reconstructing" themselves, eight Southern states worked out Black Codes (and the rest developed similar procedures) to establish planter domination and exploitation of the newly-freed slaves. While not identical, they all ran along similar lines. Civil liberties were severely restricted. The ex-slaves, of course, had no votes and could not serve on juries. They were prohibited marriage with whites. They were denied the commonly-practiced right of bearing arms. Their right to own land was restricted. They could not act as preachers without a liscence. They were prohibited from intruding unasked among whites. Any white man could arrest a Negro. Elaborate work regulations were prescribed. Negro workers were known as "servants" and employers as "masters." Working hours on the farm were from sunup to sunset. Infraction of labor discipline brought fines. Negroes who left before the expiration of their labor contracts could be arrested and returned with all costs charged against them. The masters could whip workers under 18 years of age, and older workers by judicial order. Mississippi even rejected a resolution prohibiting slavery.

These Black Codes were obviously adapted from the old slave codes. Particularly severe vagrancy laws were passed. When freedom came at the end of the war, great numbers of slaves considered that the very symbol of freedom was to quit the home plantation and go elsewhere to work. Consequently, many freedmen went about the country, relocating themselves, or seeking to reunite scattered families. The Black Codes made a special point of ending this mobility. Workers absent from their place of work were fined at the rate of two dollars a day, or double their actual "wages." They were required to go to bed "at a reasonable time." And those who ran away from their jobs could be arrested, sentenced, and hired out to other employers—the beginning of the notorious vagrancy-peonage system in the South. The general idea was to tie the Negro workers to the plantations virtually as prisoners, much as was done under slavery.[4]

When Congress met on December 5, whole sets of senators and representatives presented themselves from all the erstwhile secessionist Southern states except Texas to claim their seats in the national legislature. The arrogance of the planters may be realized from the fact that among the new representatives of the Southern cotton kings were Alexander Stephens, vice-president of the Confederacy, four Confederate generals, five Confederate colonels, six Confederate cabinet officers, and 58 Confederate Congressmen.[5]

Johnson had done his utmost for the Southern cotton planters. He had cooked up the reactionary state governments that had brought this amazing delegation of ex-Rebel officers and representatives to the doors of Congress. But there his power ended; for the question of seating the new delegates rested entirely within the jurisdiction of Congress itself. At this point Johnson's Reconstruction program struck a fatal snag.

Meanwhile, in 1865, the freed slaves, alarmed by the growth of reaction in the South, developed a powerful political movement in Georgia, Tennessee, North Carolina, South Carolina, Louisiana, and elsewhere against the Black Codes and the newly "reconstructed" state governments. They held people's conventions all over the South, protesting the dangerous situation. This was the first general political movement they had ever conducted, and it touched off the great struggle against this dangerous grab for power by the resurgent cotton planters.

THE CONGRESSIONAL COMMITTEE OF FIFTEEN

In setting up out-of-hand a whole group of new governments in the secession states, President Johnson's *coup d'état* created a real problem for the Northern bourgeoisie and its Radical Republican representatives in Congress. They were confronted with the immediate perspective of seeing the planters again in full control of the South, of a vastly strengthened Democratic Party, of a resumption of the pre-war struggle for power between the planters and the industrialists; with the threat that the planters might again be able to take control of the Federal Government. If Johnson's counter-revolutionary plan went through, there was the gravest danger that the hard-won fruits of the revolution would be partly or wholly lost.

Bourgeois leaders in the North were not slow to grasp the basic significance of the dangerous situation confronting them. *The Nation* of January 11, 1866, remarked: "Viewed as a practical matter, what would be the effect upon Government securities of the immediate admission to Congress of 58 Southern Representatives and 22 Senators, nearly all of whom could be counted on as determined repudiationists?"[6] More clearly, the keen-witted fighter, Thaddeus Stevens, warned that under the Johnson set-up the Southern states would "send a solid rebel representative delegation to Congress, and cast a solid rebel electoral vote. They, with their kindred copperheads of the North, would always elect the President and control Congress."[7] Stevens said that the unreconstructed rebels "will at the very first election take possession of the White House and the halls of Congress."[8]

This was an intolerable perspective. With his sharp realization of the true bourgeois class interests, Stevens proceeded promptly to forestall Johnson. On December 2, three days before Congress convened, the Republican caucus met and, under Stevens' prodding adopted a Reconstruction program. This had four phases: (a) to claim the whole question of Reconstruction as the exclusive business of Congress; (b) to regard the steps taken by the president as only provisional; (c) to have each House postpone consideration of the admission of members from Southern states; (d) to elect a Joint Committee of Fifteen by the Senate and House (six senators and nine representatives) to inquire into the condition of the former Confederate states.[9]

Stevens presented this project in the House and it passed by a vote of 129 to 35, with 18 not voting. The Senate then took up the proposition and also passed it. On this basis both branches of Congress indefinitely suspended the seating of all delegates from the "reconstructed" Southern states.

The Joint Committee of Fifteen was duly constituted on December 26, 1865. The chairman was the conservative Republican, Senator W. P. Fessenden of Maine, a friend of President Johnson. There were three war Democrats on the committee, and also such dubious Radical senators as Bingham, Conkling, and Boutwell. The Senate considered Sumner too radical on the Negro question, so it left him off. The real leader and mainspring of the committee was the indomitable revolutionist, Thaddeus Stevens of Pennsylvania.

Ostensibly, the role of the Joint Committee of Fifteen was merely to assert the legitimate authority of Congress in the Reconstruction program, as against dictatorial usurpation of power by the president. In this respect, it was akin to the Joint Committee on the Conduct of the War during Lincoln's presidency. But its real significance went much further. It was to constitute the national revolutionary center in Congress in opposition to the national counter-revolutionary center in the White House. From the moment of its birth there began a life-and-death struggle between Congress and the president.

ISSUES OF THE VOTE AND THE LAND

In their fight against the Southern cotton planters, the Northern industrialist bourgeoisie and its democratic allies in the war—Negroes, workers, farmers, urban middle classes—had seen fit up to the time of Johnson's counter-revolutionary Reconstruction program to use two of the revolutionary demands of the Negro people—namely, the emancipation of the slaves and the right of the Negroes to serve as soldiers in the war. These demands, however, the dominant bourgeoisie advanced not in any spirit of social community with the oppressed Negro people, but through imperative necessity; they were powerful and indispensable weapons against the planters. On the other hand, men like Garrison, Phillips, Sumner, and Stevens had a genuine sense of solidarity with the Negro masses.

At the opening of Congress in December 1865, the Republicans gave official sanction to Negro emancipation by endorsing the Thirteenth Amendment, which was duly ratified by the states in the North and West on December 18, 1865. This historic amendment reads, "Neither slavery nor involuntary servitude, except as a punishment for crime whereof the party shall have been duly convicted, shall exist in the United States, or any place subject to their jurisdiction."[10] These words, based on Jefferson's anti-slavery Northwest Ordinance of 1787 and the Wilmot Proviso of 1850, were finally written into the basic law of the land. Ratification of the Thirteenth Amendment thenceforth became a condition for the re-admission of the rebel states into the Union.

At the beginning of post-war Reconstruction the situation made it imperative for the Northern bourgeoisie to use two further revolutionary demands of the Negro people. One was the establishment of the right of Negroes to vote and to hold office. This was indispensable if the political control of the Southern states was to be kept out of the hands of the cotton planters. To assure this, it was necessary to build up political co-operation among the Negroes and the Southern poor whites, farmers, and city middle classes. Working together, they would constitute majorities in the various states. This was politically feasible; the Negroes formed about 40 percent of the Southern population, and their potential allies among the whites made up a large majority of the white section of the population.

Stevens clearly grasped the major potentialities of a Negro-poor-white-middle-class coalition, and he set out consciously to achieve it. He stated the policy thus in Congress: "I am now confining my argument to Negro suffrage in the rebel states . . . The white Union men are in a great minority in each one of those states. With them the blacks would act in a body; and it is believed that in each of the said states, except one, the two united would form a majority, control the states and protect themselves. . . . It would assure the ascendancy of the Union [Republican] Party. Do you avow the party purpose?, exclaims some horror-stricken demagogue. I do. For I believe, on my conscience, that on the continued ascendancy of that party depends the safety of this great nation. . . . If this policy is not followed," warned Stevens, "you will be the perpetual vassals of the free-trade, irritated, revengeful South."[11]

AS TO THE CONFISCATION OF THE PLANTERS' LANDS

The second revolutionary demand of the Negro people that had to be applied in the Southern Reconstruction crisis was the confiscation of the estates of the big cotton planters and their parceling out among the Negro ex-slaves and the Southern poor whites. As later events showed, the Northern bourgeoisie came to realize the enormous significance to itself (if not to the Negro people) of granting the franchise to Negroes, but it never even attempted to realize the key Negro demand for the seizure and partitioning of the big Southern plantations. Therein lies the basic reason for the eventual victory of the counter-revolution in the South.

With his usual revolutionary clear-headedness, Thaddeus Stevens saw from the outset the fundamental importance of the land question. He realized that without land the Negroes would remain in practical bondage to the planters. As early as September 1865, Stevens, in a speech in Lancaster, Pennsylvania, outlined a plan for confiscating the planters' lands. In March 1867, he introduced a bill in the House to this effect. Stevens stated, in short, that 70,000 people in the South —the big planters—owned 394 million acres of land, besides the 71 million acres owned in farms of less than 200 acres. He would permit the small landowners to hold their farms undisturbed, but the lands of the big planters should be taken over by the Government. The approximately one million families of the Negro ex-slaves would be given farms of 40 acres and $50 each, and the balance of the confiscated land would be sold off at the rate of $10 per acre. The funds thus raised should be used to pay off the national debt, which had been enormously swollen by the war.[12] Stevens hoped in this manner to turn about two billion dollars into the national treasury.

The main weakness of Stevens' land plan (as of the revolutionary movement in general) was that it did not give adequate consideration to the Southern poor whites. They were landless and land-hungry, and they were much too poor to buy land in the post-war period, no matter how cheap it might be. Even the most advanced Radical leaders did not realize that the hoped-for Negro-poor-white political coalition could not be built successfully, except on the basis of the revolutionary confiscation of the planters' estates and their redistribution, free, to both the ex-slaves and the poor whites. But this was not done.

Stevens could not get the support of the Joint Congressional Committee of Fifteen for his plan, and the whole project died aborning. In support of his proposition, Stevens declared, "Congress is bound to provide for them [the ex-slaves] until they can take care of themselves. If we do not furnish them with homesteads, and hedge them around with protective laws; if we leave them to the legislation of their late masters, we had better have left them in bondage."[13]

Stevens' plan for confiscating and partitioning the planters' estates was rational and practical. (The French, in their Revolution, had confiscated the land of the big landholders, and when the Russian Bolsheviks took power in 1917, they also solved the land question in a revolutionary way by confiscating 400 million acres at one blow from the big landholders, or more than Stevens contemplated.) He planned to break up the plantations and establish a body of Negro and white small farmers in the South. But obviously, the Northern industrialists were in no such revolutionary mood. They did not feel compelled to confiscate the land; presumably Negro enfranchisement would suffice to defeat the planters. In their eyes bourgeois property, even that of an enemy class, was sacred; hence during the Reconstruction Period they did nothing whatsoever to take the land from the big planters and get it into the hands of the real cultivators, Negroes and poor whites.

The Confiscation Act of 1862, authorizing the seizure of the lands and other properties of rebels, had given the president great power to confiscate the estates of the big planters. It was also, in fact, a promise of land for the ex-slaves, and was so understood by them; but this power was never seriously used by Lincoln, Johnson, or Grant. The government's real land policy was expressed in the law of March 3, 1865, creating the Freedmen's Bureau. This act provided that the Bureau should rent, but not give to freedmen such lands as might be designated to its care by the government. From the outset the government was resolved not to give free land to the freed slaves. Actually, speculators got most of the lands confiscated by the government and most of the property thrown upon the market because of non-payment of taxes by the planters.

Stevens' land demands constituted a legitimate capitalist program. They did not go beyond the bounds of a bourgeois-democratic revolution. If his program failed, the chief reason—in addition to the opposition of the main body of the bourgeoisie—was that the capitalist leaders of the democratic forces did not understand it and gave it little or no support. The Western farmers were also not interested; nor were the heads of the young trade union movement or the city middle class.

Even outstanding Negro leaders did not rise to the height of Stevens' program. Foner says that Frederick Douglass, for example, "did not call for the confiscation and division of the landed estates in the South. But he did urge Congress to enact legislation enabling the Negro masses to purchase land on easy terms."[14] To this end Douglass proposed the formation of a "National Land and Loan Company," to be initiated by Congress and capitalized at one million dollars. But the plan failed, pushed aside by conservative Republican leaders.

THE NEGRO PEOPLE'S FIGHT FOR LAND

Unlike the more circumspect Radical leaders, Negro and white, the ex-slaves wanted the land, believed they were entitled to it, and were resolved to get it. They logically reasoned that they had been freed from the planters' bondage and that the land would have to be freed likewise. Innumerable writers report that the belief prevailed almost universally among the freedmen that the government was going to give each family "40 acres and a mule." So deep and widespread was this conviction that swindlers were able to take advantage of it, selling among Negroes special red, white, and blue pegs with which to stake out their expected lands.[15] There was a general belief that the land distribution would take place on Christmas Day, 1865. and there was fear in government circles of an insurrection should no free land be forthcoming.[16]

The ex-slaves did more than hope for land. In many cases they moved in, divided up abandoned plantations, shared out the stored cotton, tools, and mules, and began to cultivate the land. The Negro regiments were especially insistent that land be allotted to the freedmen. The ex-slaves refused to give up the seized lands to the returning planters, but it was the definite policy of the government that they do so. As Allen says, "With the insolence of revolution the untutored ex-slaves were proving themselves far better educated in the needs of the epoch than their Northern allies. In many instances they took possession of the land dangerously near the field of battle, risking their liberty and even their lives."[17]

In the face of local reaction, government opposition, and lack of support from the Radical Republicans, the freedmen did manage to get hold of some important chunks of land. Notable was the case of the 10,000-acre plantation of Jefferson Davis, president of the Confederacy, in Mississippi. General Dana, under the protection of a Negro regiment, allotted it to them as a home colony. "In a number of home colonies the Negroes set up a form of self-government and in some places worked the land on a cooperative basis."[18]

The most extensive bloc of land secured by the freedmen, however, was on the Sea Islands, off the Coast of South Carolina and Georgia. There General Sherman opened up the Sea Islands to the freedmen, allotting each family 40 acres. He took this action under pressure of the enormous local mass of freed slaves, at the instigation of a body of Negro leaders from Savannah,[19] and with the sanction of

Washington. Eventually 40,000 families occupied the cotton and rice plantations as far as 30 miles inland. As Allen remarks, the Sea Islands then became "the most advanced outpost of the Revolution." But the government welshed on General Sherman's order and later spared no effort to oust the Negro farmers and to return the land to the planters.[20] The freedmen resisted so stoutly, however, that even as late as 1890 they still owned some 60 percent of the land originally given them.

During the war the government gave 23 million acres of land as subsidies to the railroads, but it had none for the freedmen. The government's reactionary policy, in denying free land to the ex-slaves and protecting the ownership of the former slaveholders, set the pattern for the future regime in the South. It preserved the plantation system and forced the Negroes and poor whites into the categories of sharecroppers and laborers. Very few of them were ever able to buy land, although many bankrupt plantations were on sale after the Civil War. Thus, the basis was laid for turning the South into a horror prison for the Negro people and for preserving the planters as a reactionary political force, both of which have continued to plague the country right down to the present day. Allen hits the nail squarely on the head when he says: "When the bourgeoisie lent a deaf ear to the cry for land, the fate of the Revolution was already sealed."[21]

28. The Impeachment of President Johnson

To grant the freedmen the ballot was imperative for the Northern bourgeoisie. It was the only way they could control the South and make sure of their control of the Federal government. Thus, the lowly ex-slaves suddenly became a decisive national political force. This was indeed a far cry from their previous condition of chattel slavery but a year or two before. Karl Marx, in 1865, warned of the dangers of denying citizenship to the Negroes. He said, "Declare your fellow-citizens from this day forth free and equal, without any reserve. If you refuse them citizen's rights, while you exact from them citizen's duties, you will sooner or later face a new struggle which will once more drench your country in blood."[1]

But the bourgeoisie proceeded reluctantly to enfranchise the Negro freedmen. They were very hesitant to use this revolutionary weapon. In his last public address on April 11, 1865, Lincoln had made serious qualifications on this subject: "It is also unsatisfactory to some that the election franchise is not given to the colored man. I would prefer that it were now conferred on the very intelligent, and on those who serve our cause as soldiers."[2] Andrew Johnson pretended to follow this line, a forerunner of later literacy tests for Negro voters. It also had the support of even such an advanced fighter as William Lloyd Garrison.

There was outright and determined opposition to giving even this limited form of suffrage to the Negroes in the South. At the close of the war, Congress was opposed to full enfranchisement, and so, too, was the Joint Congressional Committee. Of the Northern states, only five had full Negro suffrage—a fact that the Southerners made much of in the long and bitter fight over the question. But needs must when the devil drives. Votes in the hands of the ex-slaves—Republican votes—were indispensable. Not for the Negro's sake, but in the basic interests of Northern capitalism. The big Southern delegations of Democratic ex-rebels, waiting at the doors to be seated in Congress, were sufficient warning. Whatever the odds, suffrage had to be granted to the Negro. Charles Sumner, Wendell

Phillips, Thaddeus Stevens, and of course, Frederick Douglass and all the Negro leaders showed the way in this historic fight.

THE FOURTEENTH AMENDMENT

On February 19, 1866, Congress adopted a bill extending the life of the Freedmen's Bureau by two years and enlarging its powers of control over and assistance to the great masses of destitute ex-slaves. This greatly displeased President Johnson, who, as the representative of the cotton planters, wanted to keep the freed Negroes as helpless as possible under the pressure of their former masters. So he vetoed the bill. This enraged Congress, and on July 16, a supplementary Freedmen's Bureau Act was passed over Johnson's veto. Thus, the growing feud between Congress and the president became an open struggle.

The next stage in this conflict came over the Civil Rights Act. This bill, passed by Congress on March 13, 1866, undertook to secure full citizenship to all persons born in the United States (excluding non-taxed Indians), without regard to race or color, or to "any previous condition of slavery or involuntary servitude." The law presumably gave Negroes the right to vote without specifically saying so. Naturally, it aroused the ire of President Johnson, who vetoed it. But Congress repassed it, and it became the law of the land on April 9. The rift between the legislative and executive branches of the government became deeper.

The big fight over the Constitutional right of Negroes to vote—leading up to the adoption of the Fourteenth Amendment—began on December 26, 1865, when Thaddeus Stevens brought in a proposition to base state representation in Congress on the number of voters. This opened up a big struggle, which soon developed into a fight for and against Negro suffrage. Every reactionary in the country, with President Johnson in the lead, strove militantly to prevent the formulation of a Constitutional amendment guaranteeing Negroes the right to vote. It was not until June 1866, after an interminable battle in the Joint Committee of Fifteen and in both Houses, that the amendment finally passed Congress and was submitted to the states for ratification. On July 28, 1868, it became part of the national Constitution.

The Fourteenth Amendment was a compromise; Sumner, Stevens, and the others being unable to get through a specific guarantee of the

Negroes' right to vote. The first part of the amendment confers the rights of citizenship upon all persons born or naturalized in the United States, and forbids any state from infringing upon the rights of these citizens "without due process of law." This section presumably made citizens of the ex-slaves, but the second section threw the question in doubt. For it provided that the Congressional representation of states which deny male citizens the right to vote should be cut. The clear implication was that states could refuse Negroes the franchise, but if they did, their representation in Congress would be reduced accordingly. In the practice, however, the Fourteenth Amendment came to be applied as enfranchising the freedmen.

THE CONGRESSIONAL ELECTIONS OF 1866

The 1866 elections were decisively important. The central political issue was whether or not the Southern states, as reconstructed by President Johnson, should be represented in Congress. This debate inevitably brought clearly before the country the question of Negro suffrage, with all the Radicals strongly supporting it. Johnson made a hard fight; he attempted to set up a new party by splitting the Republicans and also by stumping the North, but both ventures misfired.

The elections were conducted in a spirit of rising alarm in the North over what was happening in the South. The ultra-reactionary character of the reconstructed state governments, with their Black Codes and rejection of the Fourteenth Amendment, told its own story. Reports of 1,000 murders of Negroes in various parts of the South were pointed up by the sanguinary massacres in Memphis on May 3, Charleston on June 24, and New Orleans on July 30, 1866. Johnson added to the blazing fire by announcing that the war was ended and by issuing a general amnesty proclamation on July 4. He exempted all but the top secessionist officials of war guilt. As Dr. Du Bois remarks, "Industry and trade were convinced that they could not trust the white South. Therefore, the more extreme ideas which Stevens had advocated, were allowed to be broadcast."[3] That is, the Northern bourgeoisie had decided that the only way they could control the rebellious South was by granting the vote to Negroes.

The election resulted in a ringing victory for the Radicals. The South, in the hands of the planters, voted Democratic, and so did the Border states of Maryland, Delaware, and Kentucky; while all the

Northern and Western states gave heavy majorities to the Republicans. The results were as follows: in the House, 143 Republicans and 49 Democrats; in the Senate, 42 Republicans and 11 Democrats. The Radicals, now often called the Jacobins, won a sweeping victory.

Instead of seeing the handwriting on the wall in this Radical success, the Southern planters proceeded to provoke the situation further by rejecting with overwhelming votes in all the Southern states the Fourteenth Amendment, which granted the franchise to Negroes. The Border states took similar action. By 1868 all the Northern states had ratified the Amendment. Later on, however, New Jersey, Ohio, and Arizona, with Democratic administrations, tried to rescind this action.

Meanwhile, the Supreme Court, which in American history has an almost unbroken record of reaction, stepped in with three pro-planter decisions. It declared that neither the president nor Congress had the right to try citizens by courts martial, that it was unconstitutional to demand loyalty oaths of the ex-rebels, and generally disapproved of the Reconstruction of the Southern state governments.[4]

The decisions of the Supreme Court, which were meant to halt the revolution, greatly antagonized the Radicals. Stevens said of the first of them, which condemned the suspension of *habeas corpus:* "That decision, although in terms perhaps not as infamous as the Dred Scott decision, is yet far more dangerous in its operation upon the lives and liberties of the loyal men of this country." "There was talk of impeaching the Judges," says Rhodes. Even the conservative Republican, Senator John A. Bingham of Ohio, proposed that if the High Court did not halt its interference, to "sweep away at once their appellate jurisdiction on all cases," and if that did not suffice, to bring about "the abolition of the tribunal itself"[5] through a Constitutional amendment. All this militancy had a salutary effect upon the Supreme Court, which, during the upswing of the revolution, henceforth tended to keep its hands off Congressional acts.

THE REVOLUTION IN FULL SWING

Under these tense conditions, Congress began its fateful sessions on January 3, 1867. The Radicals were now definitely in control. The combination of the rejection of the Fourteenth Amendment in the South, the reactionary decisions of the Supreme Court, the murderous assaults upon the Negro people in the South, Johnson's amnesty proclamation and his generally arrogant attitude resulted in a deep-going change of opinion in the North in favor of a sharp program of Southern Reconstruction, based on Negro suffrage. The Radicals—Sumner, Stevens, Chandler, Wilson, Wade, Boutwell, and others—were not slow in responding to this clear popular mandate.

On the first day of the session, Stevens called up his bill on Reconstruction. This resulted, on March 2, 1867, in the passage by Congress of the first Reconstruction Act. This law, outlining the general Reconstruction program of the Radicals, declared that no legal state governments existed in 10 Southern states (Tennessee had endorsed the Fourteenth Amendment and been readmitted). The law provided that the South should be divided into five military districts, each headed by a general. Then, on the basis of universal suffrage including the Negroes, disfranchisement of the leaders of the Confederacy and specific endorsement of the Fourteenth Amendment, provisional state governments should be elected.[6]

To the applause of the ex-slaveholders, including General Robert E. Lee, President Johnson vetoed this proposition, pronouncing it unconstitutional and dictatorial. Thereupon Congress passed it over his veto. The Southern Democratic leaders, realizing that they had an ally in the Supreme Court, tried to get that body to pass upon the constitutionality of the new law; but the High Court, badly burned by its recent decisions, refused to act, biding its time for a more favorable occasion to knife the revolution.

During the next nine days, March 2-11, Congress passed three more Reconstruction acts, making more precise the general line laid down in the first law. All these were duly vetoed by the President and then passed over his head. Congress also enacted the Tenure of Office Act on March 2, 1867; the purpose of this was to prevent Johnson from arbitrarily removing officials confirmed by the Senate and favorable to the Radicals. This law, too, was vetoed by Johnson and passed by Congress over his veto.

The process of reconstructing the Southern state governments got under way during the latter part of 1867. By January 1868, all the Southern states except Texas had adopted constitutions based upon the Fourteenth Amendment and universal Negro suffrage, and had set up provisional governments. The Radicals in Congress had enacted other important measures, including the establishment of Negro suffrage in Washington, D. C., on June 7, 1867, and legislation, late in 1867, crippling the power of the Supreme Court to interfere between the President and Congress. Because of economic and financial difficulties, the elections of 1867 gave the Radicals a setback; but undiscouraged by this, they pressed on with their Reconstruction program. The revolutionary Congress was ruling the country, with the reactionary executive and judicial branches under its control.

JOHNSON'S PUTSCHIST POLICIES

Instead of being stayed by his rebukes at the hands of the electorate and Congress, President Johnson redoubled his efforts on behalf of the Southern cotton planters. With his executive power, he sabotaged Congressional Reconstruction in the South. In particular, he aimed to get control of the generals who were to be in charge of the new provisional state goverments. To this end he shifted Generals Sheridan and Sickles, sympathizers with the Radicals, from the South to the North. Then, taking the bull by the horns, he fired Secretary of War Edwin M. Stanton from his cabinet. Stanton, who was a member of Lincoln's cabinet, had supported the line of the Radicals and was an eyesore to Johnson. This brought about a sharp crisis, with Stanton refusing to leave his office and threatening to use force against anyone trying to dislodge him.

Meanwhile, President Johnson refused to bring Jefferson Davis to trial, although he had been in jail since May 22, 1865. This man, whom even President Johnson had denounced for responsibility in the assassination of Lincoln, who was personally responsible for the terrible conditions of war prisoners in Libby, Andersonville, and other prisons, and who had issued orders to reduce Negro war prisoners to slavery and shoot their white officers, was finally turned loose by Johnson on Christmas Day, 1868, in a broad amnesty order.

Johnson's policies of active resistance to Congress were part of a dangerous pattern. Undoubtedly, the President was carefully scheming for an armed revolt to put down the Radicals and to assure the power to his Southern Democratic friends. He even went so far as to begin to store military arms in strategic places in the South. It was because Stanton refused to be a party to this game that Johnson fired him. But Johnson was unable to organize the *coup d'état* he obviously had in mind, because his potential allies had just been crushed in a great war and could not rally.

THE IMPEACHMENT OF PRESIDENT JOHNSON

The Radicals resolved to put a stop to Johnson's sabotage by impeaching him. Proceedings to this end were started in December 1866, but hesitation developed in the Joint Committee of Fifteen and also in the House and Senate. It was not until February 16, 1868, that the impeachment proceedings, upon the motion of Thaddeus Stevens, got under way in the House. Though shattered in health, Stevens delivered a powerful attack upon the president, demanding his removal from office. It was a bold revolutionary act. The Committee on Reconstruction agreed with Stevens, and on February 22, the House voted to impeach Johnson, 126 to 47. This was a great victory for the Radicals.

Stevens headed the House Committee which presented the charges to the Senate, where, under the Constitution, Johnson had to be tried. They accused him of "high crimes and misdemeanors in office." The House Committee presented 11 articles of impeachment, the substance of which was that the president, in removing Secretary Stanton, had willfully violated the Tenure-of-Office Act and that, in denying the authority of Congress, he had repeatedly and violently assailed it and its members.[7]

The trial began in the Senate on March 30 and was presided over by Chief Justice Chase of the Supreme Court. Bingham, Boutwell, Wilson, Butler, Williams, Stevens, and Logan presented the case for the House, and Stanberry, Curtis, Ewarts, Nelson, and Groesbeck defended the president. The trial, brilliantly argued, lasted until May 16. The vote was 35 for guilty and 19 for not guilty. Johnson was, therefore, condemned by a big majority, but this was not enough. Inasmuch as the Constitution requires a two-thirds vote by the Senate in such impeachment cases, the chief justice pronounced the president acquitted. Reaction was strong enough to save him by one vote.[8]

Decisive votes in acquitting President Johnson were those of Senators Fessenden, Grimes, Ross, and Trumbull. All these men had presumably been Radicals, but in the crisis they turned tail. This ended them politically. President Johnson was saved, but the proceedings dealt him a heavy blow, from which he never recovered. It wiped out his hopes for a second term as president, and it killed his scheme for organizing an armed revolt against Congress. For the remaining months of his presidency Johnson preserved a sort of armed neutrality toward Congress. As for his chief antagonist, the valiant revolutionary battler, Thaddeus Stevens, who, old and sick, had to be carried into the Senate to make the fight—he soon died on August 11 at the age of 76. In Stevens, the Radical cause lost its most powerful leader, and the Negro people a real friend and ally. Even in his death, Stevens struck a blow against white chauvinism, insisting that he be interred in a "mixed" cemetery, rather than a Jim Crow white burial place.[9]

29. The Revolution in the South

General Ulysses S. Grant was elected President in the fall of 1868. He was born in 1822, was a graduate of West Point, had served in the Mexican War, and was a failure in farming and small business until the Civil War offered him an opportunity to resume his career as a soldier. A very capable officer, Grant showed great talent in the winning of Forts Henry and Donelson in Kentucky and Tennessee in 1862. The capture of Vicksburg on July 4, 1863, split the Confederacy and opened up the Mississippi River, and this brought Grant's promotion, early in 1864, to commander of all the Union armies. Grant then proceeded to chew up Lee's forces in Virginia and to end the war. He was hailed as the military leader who won the Civil War.

Before the war Grant had been a Democrat. His political convictions in 1868, as Johnson was going out, were a matter of speculation. Immensely popular, he could have had the nomination from either party. He was unanimously chosen by the Republicans. While no Radical of the Stevens type, Grant nevertheless went along (with diminishing enthusiasm) with the Radical program—that being the main line of the Northern industrial bourgeoisie and its allies during his two terms in office.

The Republican platform for the election of 1868 strongly endorsed the Congressional plan of Reconstruction, including Negro enfranchisement. The Democratic platform, however, denounced Congress as having "dissolved the Union" and "subjected ten states in time of peace to military despotism and Negro supremacy," as well as having inflicted "barbarous martial law" upon the whole country. Grant won the election, with a popular vote of 3,012,833 and 214 electoral votes, against 2,703,249 and 80 electoral votes for his Democratic opponent, Horatio Seymour.

The big job before the Radical Republican leaders after their election victory of 1866 was to reorganize the former secessionist states and bring their representatives back into Congress. To this end, beginning in March 1867, conventions were held in the Southern states. These conventions, based upon the right of the Negro to vote and upon an endorsement of the Fourteenth Amendment, elected state governments and also senators and representatives to Congress. By July 1868, seven states had been so reorganized—North Carolina, South Carolina, Georgia, Alabama, Florida, Louisiana, and Arkansas. Tennessee had come back into the Union in 1866, and the remaining three states of the former Confederate war alliance—Texas, Mississippi, and Virginia—were reorganized in January 1870, and their delegates were seated in the Congress.

THE NEW SOUTHERN DEMOCRACY

In 1866 began a decade of the broadest democratic experience for the South, the like of which it has never known before or since. It was a period that has been almost universally denounced by white historians as "Negro domination" and "brutal, corrupt, and inefficient." This is part of the general campaign to discredit the Negro and all his works. Such denunciations are the expressions of white supremacists, frenzied at the progress of the Negro people; and of reactionaries, anxious to expunge every trace of revolution from the pages of American history. In reality, the Reconstruction period from 1867 to 1876 was an era of which the Negro people and their white allies may well be proud. It is only during the past quarter of a century that this vital period has been scientifically evaluated by progressive and Marxist Negro and white writers, such as Allen, Du Bois, Haywood, Aptheker, Foner, Taylor, Mann, and others.[1]

In the South, at the beginning of Reconstruction, some 700,000 Negroes and 660,000 whites were registered—of the whites of voting age, 100,000 were disfranchised because of their part in the war and could not register and 100,000 more, for the same reason, were disqualified from holding office. The Negroes in South Carolina formed about 60 percent of the population; in Mississippi, 55 percent; in Louisiana, 50 percent; in Florida, 47 percent; in Alabama, 45 percent; in Georgia, 44 percent; in Virginia, 41 percent; in North Carolina, 37 percent; in Arkansas, 27 percent; in Tennessee, 27 percent; and in Texas, 25 percent.

Du Bois gives the following figures for the delegates to the constitutional conventions of 1867-68, chosen by this electorate in the ten Southern states (Tennessee not included):[2]

State	Negro	White	Total	Percent Negro
South Carolina	76	48	124	61
Louisiana	49	49	98	50
Florida	18	27	45	40
Virginia	25	80	105	24
Georgia	33	137	170	19
Mississippi	17	83	100	17
Alabama	18	90	108	17
Arkansas	8	58	66	12
North Carolina	15	118	133	11
Texas	9	81	90	10

In the state governments that were set up, "the Negroes," says Allen, "did not hold the dominant position . . . even in those states where they formed the majority of the electorate." In South Carolina, Mississippi, and Louisiana, where the Negro population was the largest, about half of the representation in the lower houses was made up of Negroes, but in each case the Senate and major state offices remained in the hands of the whites. In the other Southern states Negro representation was proportionately even less. In all states, the judiciary remained almost entirely in the hands of the whites. In South Carolina, Mississippi, and Louisiana, Negroes were elected Lieutenant Governor; and in the latter state, Lieutenant Governor P.B.S. Pinchback served as governor during an interim period of 43 days. But elsewhere they did not reach these positions.

Among the delegates sent to the Federal Congress, Negro representation was even more skimpy. Du Bois elaborates the following list of Negro members of Congress during the Reconstruction period from 1869 to 1876:[3] Senators Hiram R. Revels, Mississippi (1870-71), and Blanche K. Bruce, Mississippi (1875-81); and Congressmen as follows: Jefferson P. Long, Georgia (1869-71); Joseph H. Rainey, South Carolina (1871-79); Robert C. DeLarge, South Carolina (1871-73); Robert Brown Elliott, South Carolina (1871-75); Benjamin S. Turner, Alabama (1871-73); Josiah T. Walls, Florida (1873-77); Alonzo J. Ransier, South Carolina (1871-73); James T. Rapier, Alabama (1873-75); Richard H. Cain, South Carolina (1873-75, 1877-79); John R. Lynch, Mississippi (1873-77, 1881-83); Charles E. Nash, Louisiana (1875-77); John A. Hyman, North Carolina (1875-77); Jere Haralson, Alabama (1875-77); Robert Smalls, South Carolina (1875-79, 1881-87).

Under these circumstances, it is ridiculous to rant that "Black Parliaments" and "Negro domination" prevailed during the Reconstruction period. Actually, the Negroes got only a small percentage of the local, state, and Federal posts—and those of less importance—than their numbers entitled them to. Allen remarks, "If fuller democracy had been won, there would have been a much higher proportion of Negroes in the state bodies and in Congress, and they would have held most of the governmental positions in a number of Southern states."[4] However, "To the Bourbons the participation of the Negro in government, even to the smallest degree, was already 'Negro Domination.' "[5] It was a great historic moment when Hiram R. Revels of Mississippi, on February 25, 1870, took the seat in the Senate that had been vacated by Jefferson Davis; but to the planter white supremacists of the South it was a world-shaking outrage.

The charge that the democratic Southern governments of the Reconstruction period were "fantastically corrupt and wasteful" will also not stand the light of objective examination of the real situation. It is a fact, of course, that the debts of the Southern states went up during the Reconstruction period—about $100 million for all eleven. But this was primarily due to the development of schools, care for the sick and aged, and public improvements, which had been altogether neglected during the long regime of the so-called enlightened planters.

There were also some financial irregularities—unavoidable in the turbulent revolutionary situation. But it is nonsense to single out these minor thieveries for special condemnation during a period when the Federal Government and the Northern states were reeking with graft and corruption of all sorts. It came with ill grace for the heroes of the Tweed ring in New York, of the Credit Mobilier robbery, of the innumerable corruption scandals in Washington, of the wholesale despoliation of government lands, and of the other capitalist monster villainies of the period to point the finger of accusation at the few minor pilferers in the Reconstruction state governments of the South. But, as always, any stick will do to beat the Negro.

ACHIEVEMENTS OF THE STATE RECONSTRUCTION GOVERNMENTS

The Northern bourgeoisie maintained a firm control of the course of the revolution in the South. They dominated not only the Federal Government, but also the army, the economic life, and other key aspects of the situation. The revolutionary Negro people and their white Southern allies, therefore, worked within the confines of this general control of the victorious Northern industrialists. They never had the situation fully under their control.

The state programs of the Reconstruction governments in the South did not go beyond the framework of the capitalist system. But with their policies of far-reaching reforms, they were the sharp cutting edge of the bourgeois democratic revolution. In this sense, it is because of their revolutionary character that reactionaries of all stripes hate them so bitterly and seek, even down to this day, to discredit them. Their sterling revolutionary quality, however, was unmistakable in their legislative record. The Reconstruction state constitutions and legislatures swept away the rubbish of reactionary laws that had been accumulating for decades under the rule of the big planters.

The Reconstruction conventions and legislatures wrote a large body of constructive provisions into the constitutions and laws of the Southern states. Among the more important measures thus enacted were those providing for universal manhood suffrage; equality of civil rights; the construction of a public school system, with admission of Negroes to all educational institutions; granting of new rights to women (divorce, the right to hold property, etc.); a system of relief for the aged; a more democratic tax system, with added taxes upon the rich; aid to the railroads, etc. Other important measures abolished the Black Codes, old slave laws, and Jim Crow practices; imprisonment for debt and the use of whipping posts, stocks, and other barbarous punishments; the peonage system on plantations; property qualifications for voting; discrimination against Jews; and reduced the roster of capital crimes from twenty or more to two or three. The reapportionment of state representation was made according to population instead of property, with disfranchisement of those who had voted for secession.[6]

The weakest spot in this political work of the reconstructionists was the question of the land, the failure to push through the agrarian phase of the revolution. The Negro legislators understood pretty generally that what was basically needed was the confiscation of the planters' estates, especially those in cotton, and their division among the ex-slaves and poor whites. But Federal government policy strongly opposed this course, and inasmuch as the land was basically a national problem, these factors restrained the respective state legislatures from taking decisive action on the question. But the Southern legislatures during this period constantly rang with Negro cries for the land.

No states in the Union had ever contained on their books such a body of progressive legislation as prevailed in the Reconstruction states of the South. A striking testimonial to the high quality of these laws was the fact that even after democracy was crushed in the South after 1876, many of these laws remained in force for years. The planters were unable to eliminate them in the face of Negro and poor white opposition. Thus, in Virginia the Reconstruction constitution lasted for 32 years; in South Carolina 27 years; in Mississippi 22 years; in Florida 17 years, etc. And much of the specific state legislation of the Reconstruction period is still on the books.[7] These legislative achievements were all the more remarkable because many of the men who wrote them were former illiterate slaves, totally without political experience.

Hacker thus sums up Southern Reconstruction. "These Reconstruction governments erected public school systems. They democratized local and county units. They gave fair representation in state legislatures to the back country districts. They tried to free the judiciary from the executive. They established more equitable tax structures. They created public social services—eleemosynary institutions for the blind, insane, orphaned. With state funds they began to build railroads."[8] All of these achievements were sufficient reason why the white supremacist reactionaries should strive to destroy these governments and to discredit them in history.

"SCALAWAGS" AND "CARPETBAGGERS"

In the Reconstruction of the state governments and the establishment of a semblance of democracy in the South, the Negro ex-slaves had two major allies locally. These were, first, a large section of the Southern whites, and, second, the body of Northerners—officials and others—who had come into the South with the Northern armies or in connection with specific Federal Reconstruction tasks in the erstwhile Confederate states. The planters and their agents promptly dubbed these two categories of allies, "scalawags" and "carpetbaggers." And they gave to these terms a built-in slander and hostility that have hardly been equaled in American history. The "scalawag" was made the symbol of everything disreputable and treasonous—he was beneath contempt—and the "carpetbagger" was a fly-by-night opportunist, liar, crook, and exploiter. So fierce was the planter denunciation of these two groups that they have been so stereotyped in American bourgeois history.

Actually the "scalawag" was a Southern Republican and the "carpetbagger" a Northern Republican in the South. The "scalawags" were mainly members of the Southern middle class and poor whites, who together made up about three-fourths of the total white population in the South. With nothing to gain from slavery, they had resisted secession in the upland regions and piny woods all over the South. Among them generally, but particularly the independent farmers and the city small business men, there was a strong Whig tradition. The Whigs, be it remembered, in pre-war decades had controlled large sections of the South. They were the precursors of Republicanism, The "scalawags'" ranks contained many former Whig judges, political officials, some of whom, however, sabotaged Reconstruction. Lynch lists among other prominent "scalawags," ex-Governors Orr of South Carolina, Parsons of Alabama, Reynolds of Texas, Brown of Georgia, and Hahn of Louisiana.[9] Because they had dared to oppose the big aristocratic planters, especially in alliance with the Negroes and often at the risk of their lives, such men were excoriated as few other political groups have been in American life.*

The "carpetbaggers," on the other hand, were Northerners—officials in the Freedmen's Bureau, workers in the various social service agencies that went into the South at the close of the war to assist in educating and organizing the great mass of freed slaves, Northern free Negroes who had come South to help their people, members of various government Reconstruction agencies, officers and soldiers who had fought in the Union armies and decided to remain in the South, petty Northern capitalists seeking fields for investment and business, and doctors, nurses, teachers, etc. At most, they numbered only a few thousands. In contrast to the fantastic propaganda of the planters, they actually had every right as American citizens to vote and to a full participation in the political life of the South after they had satisfied the residence qualifications.

It was this combination of Negroes, local whites, and Northern Republicans in the South that led the Reconstruction governments all over the South during the years after 1867-68. The Negroes especially were in close alliance with the "carpetbaggers," whom they knew mainly as men who had either fought arms in hand to free them, or

* Albert R. Parsons, one of the Haymarket (1886) victims, was a "scalawag."

as government workers who were seeking to educate them and to protect and raise their living standards. The "carpetbaggers," who probably made up, on the average, 10 percent of the Reconstruction legislatures, were chiefly sent there by Negro voters in the Black Belt counties. The poor whites and middle class allies of the Negroes usually picked representatives from their own ranks. Often, between the poor whites and "carpetbaggers" there were strained relations, even hostility.

There were, of course, many opportunistic and disreputable persons among the "carpetbaggers"; but generally they supported a broad coalition struggle with the Negroes to establish bourgeois democracy in the South. The "scalawags," as it turned out, were much less reliable allies of the Negroes. Full of white supremacist illusions to the effect that they were superior to the Negroes, they were all too susceptible to the "Negro domination" slogans of the big planters. The breakdown of the Negro-white coalition in the South, with its eventual victory for the planters, came primarily through the defection of the poor whites from the democratic alliance.

THE BEGINNINGS OF NEGRO ORGANIZATION IN THE SOUTH

With the armed liberation of the Southern states from big planter control, the ex-slaves, totally inexperienced in political activity, were faced with the most urgent need for leadership and organization. The first to tackle the gigantic task were Negroes who had previously been free, especially those from the North who had been able to acquire considerable political knowledge and experience. Their earliest major move was to organize the Negro convention movement in the South. Consequently, even as early as the latter part of 1865, broad mass conventions were held in nearly all of the Southern states. These took up the cudgels at once against the resurgent planters, who, under the stimulus of President Johnson, were then setting up plantation-controlled governments, writing Black Codes, and developing terroristic domination over the South. The ex-slaves were doubly spurred into action by the dread that they were about to be re-enslaved, which the planters would have been only too glad to do, had it not been for vigorous democratic opposition of the Negroes and poor whites.

In the early stages, the Negro churches also played a very important part in the efforts of the freed slaves to meet their problems, including organized resistance against the planters. The preachers were usually the only—even partially—educated Negroes in the Southern communities, and many of them responded to the pressing demand of the newly freed Negroes for leadership and organization. This largely explains why there were so many preachers in the Republican state governments of the Reconstruction period. Characteristically, Bishop Turner of Georgia said that, besides his religious work, "I have put more men in the field, made more speeches, organized more union leagues, political associations, clubs, and have written more political documents . . . than any other man in the state."[10]

An important Negro political organization set up to meet Reconstruction problems was the National Equal Rights League. This was formed at the Negro convention in Syracuse, New York, in 1864. It held a couple of national conventions, set up numerous state branches, and carried on much political activity, North and South. Frederick Douglass was a moving spirit in it, and J. M. Langston was its president. In its broad program, the Equal Rights League demanded full emancipation and the franchise for Negro men.[11] The organization did not last long, however, as it tended to duplicate the work of the Freedmen's Bureau and especially that of the Union Leagues. At the 1869 Negro people's convention in Washington, D.C., an effort was made to revive the Equal Rights League, but the resolution was tabled lest the Equal Rights League compete with the Union League.[12]

The Freedmen's Bureau (see Chapter 24) also provided very considerable protection and help to the ex-slaves. Du Bois says that the Bureau "made laws, executed them and interpreted them; it . . . maintained and used military force."[13] It was bitterly hated and fought by the planters. The Bureau found work for great numbers of Negroes, although its $10-a-month wage scale for field hands was only a cut above former slave living conditions. It supervised the working out of "wage contracts," such as they were, between the planters and the the workers. It undertook to secure justice for Negroes in the courts and blocked the application of the Black Codes. General Howard estimated that every year the Bureau handled at least 100,000 complaints of all sorts. "At times," he said, "one was inclined to believe that the whole white population was engaged in a war of extermination against the blacks."[14] The Bureau operated 46 hospitals, with 5,292 beds, and it issued 15 million rations to the famished Negroes. The Freedmen's Bureau received total Federal funds of about $18 million;

and it existed from 1865 to 1872. Poor whites shared in many of these benefits.

THE MOVEMENT FOR EDUCATION

One of the most striking features of the Reconstruction period was the tremendous hunger of the ex-slaves for education. "As a general rule," says Donald, "the adults were as eager to learn as the children, and the reading or spelling book was the almost invariable companion of the freedmen when they were off duty."[15] Many educators reported that they found a keener desire to learn among the Negro children of the Reconstruction South than among white children in the North.

Many institutions undertook to meet the educational needs of the ex-slaves. The Negro churches of the North were the first in the field. Many other groups also participated, among them such as the American Missionary Association, Boston Education Society, Freedmen's Relief Association of New York, Port Royal Society of Philadelphia, etc. In 1866 these agencies combined in the American Freedmen's Union Commission. Numerous schools and colleges were set up. The Federal government also took a hand in the work; the Freedmen's Bureau either founded or heavily subsidized many of the early Negro colleges—Howard, Fisk, Atlanta, etc. The extensive Negro educational system of today was born during the Reconstruction years.

The Negro press, a big factor in this mass educational work, grew very rapidly during this period. In 1865, in Augusta, Georgia, there appeared *The Colored American,* the first Negro newspaper ever published in the South. Shortly afterward the first Negro daily paper, *The Tribune,* which reached a circulation of 10,000, was founded in New Orleans. Local weekly papers sprang up in various localities. The first national conference of Negro newspaper editors was held in Cincinnati in 1875.

THE UNION LEAGUES

The most important organizations of and for Negroes during the Reconstruction period were the Union (or Loyal) Leagues. They were in substance the basic units of the Republican Party in the South. The Negro people used them as their main mass revolutionary organizations to resist the attacks of the counter-revolution and put their own program into effect. Allen likens them to the Jacobin clubs during the French Revolution. The Republican Party also had its regular state organizations.

The Union League movement began in Pekin, Illinois, in September 1862, when the first council was formed to fight local disloyalists. There was a critical situation in the Middlewest, a notorious Copperhead stronghold. The Knights of the Golden Circle, one of many pro-slavery organizations, alone had 350,000 members. The new loyalist organization, named the Union League, set out to destroy this organized treachery. It grew like wildfire. By 1864, it had 175,000 members in Illinois, and within a year it had spread to 18 states in the North. Powerful Leagues made up of Radical intellectuals and industrialists, sprang up in New York, Philadelphia, Boston, and other cities.* Among the New York League's members were such prominent figures as John Jay, A. T. Stewart, F. H. Delano, A. Van Rensselaer Hamilton Fish, J. A. Roosevelt, Otis D. Swan, etc. The state and local leagues combined in the Union League of America, with headquarters in Washington, D.C. There were women's auxiliaries. The president of the National Council was J. M. Edmunds.

The Union Leagues stood for unconditional support of the Union government. The National Council stated its purposes as follows: "To preserve liberty and the Union of the United States of America; to maintain the constitution thereof and the supremacy of its laws; to sustain the government and assist in putting down its enemies; to thwart the designs of traitors and disloyalists, and to protect, strengthen, and defend all loyal men, without regard to sect, condition, or party."

The Leagues, which generally supported the line of the Radicals in Congress, were active and aggressive. They fought the Copperhead disloyalists head on. The Philadelphia League, for example, distributed some five million pieces of agitational literature during 1865-68. The Leagues in the North were undoubtedly responsible for the defeat of the Copperhead candidate, General McClellan, in the crucial elections of 1864.

From 1863 on, the Union Leagues followed the victorious Union armies into the South. They spread rapidly among the poorer whites in the upland regions, among the traditional Union-minded. Allen estimates that in 1866 probably one-third of these mountain people

---

* The Union Leagues in New York and Philadelphia still exist—but they are Republican millionaire clubs, ultra-reactionary and careful to hide any trace of their revolutionary origins.

were affiliated to the Leagues.[16] The local Leagues had a strong discipline with an elaborate ritual. Whites were in one local, Negroes in another.

By the middle of 1865, the Southern Negroes began pouring into the organization. At this time Chief Justice Chase, then in the South, wrote that "everywhere throughout the country colored citizens are organizing Leagues." Franklin states that South Carolina in 1867 had 88 local Leagues, with almost every adult Negro in the state enrolled.[17] Fleming estimates that in 1865 40 percent of the whites in northern Alabama were League members.[18] In North Carolina, it was said that "every Negro who could vote at the approaching election was an enthusiastic member of the League."[19] In Virginia there were said to be 800 councils or Leagues. And so it was all over the South. All told in the Southern states there were an estimated 500,000 members.

The South—the whole country—was amazed at the splendid organization and discipline shown in the building of the Union Leagues by the erstwhile slaves, who were quite destitute of previous political experience. Planters complained that when "meetings of the local Leagues were being held the field hands would drop everything to attend." The Leagues, working in close co-operation with the Freedmen's Bureau field staff and with other Reconstruction organizations, did an enormous amount of political educational work among the ex-slaves and poor whites.

With counter-revolutionary zeal, the cotton planters delivered heavy attacks against the Leagues, attempting to break them up with armed violence. Consequently, the Leagues frequently armed themselves, formed rifle clubs and militia bodies, and took all possible measures to protect the personal safety of their members, their organizations and meetings, and their right to vote. Although the records are incomplete on the subject, it is known that in many parts of the South during the early Reconstruction years there were many bodies of armed Negro militia. Sometimes these were given financial aid and official standing by the state governments.[20] Undoubtedly, without the Union Leagues, the planters would have been able to take over again immediately at the end of the Civil War and to maintain their domination. But for these organizations the Reconstruction governments could never have been made to function. Allen calls the Leagues "the heart of the Revolution."

The Union League movement lasted, all told, about 10 years. The

Northern wing of the movement began to disintegrate with the end of the war; with the victory of the Union armies, the peril from the disloyalists did not loom so acutely. In the Southern section of the movement, the poor whites, with their customary weakness on the false issue of Negro domination, lost much of their taste for the Leagues during the latter sixties, when they saw them being used to such good effect by the Negroes. As for the Negro Union Leagues, these were largely crushed in open struggle with the Ku Klux Klan; as a rule, they played no further important political part after about 1873-74.

30. The Struggle Against Counter-Revolution

The refusal of Congress to seat the senators and representatives of the governments of the secessionist states, reorganized by Presidents Lincoln and Johnson, was a heavy blow to the planters; but quickly reorienting themselves, the latter sought to get control of the situation by breaking up the political alliance of their enemies. They gave a perfect demonstration of the fact that defeated classes never give up the struggle until they have been politically destroyed as a class, with all economic controls torn out of their hands.

THE ATTACK UPON THE NEGRO-WHITE COALITION

The cotton planters acted upon the time-tested principle of exploiting classes—to divide and rule. They set out to liquidate the coalition between the freedmen and the poor whites by cajoling or forcing the Negroes out of it. While instigating a terrorist campaign against the Negroes all over the South, at the same time they started a systematic campaign of soft-soaping them. They tried to convince the ex-slaves that, in reality, the aristocratic planter whites were the Negroes' best friends, that the poor whites had always been their enemies, and especially that the "carpetbaggers" were "foreign intruders from the North" who only wanted to rob them.

This hypocrisy they pushed to ludicrous extremes. Hardboiled big planters and Confederate generals made speeches all over the South, telling what valuable citizens the Negroes were and how much the planters wanted them to prosper. Most leading Southern newspapers took the same honeyed line. The Richmond *Examiner,* for example, declared in 1867 that "the Southern people desire to see a fair trial of the Negro's capacity for self-government, and, most assuredly, every interest of the South urges her to desire also a successful issue of the experiment." Indeed, the Negroes might yet prove to be "industrious, intelligent, and upright citizens."[1] The planters even invited Negroes to attend political meetings of the Democratic Party.

The Negroes, however, were not to be caught by such paternalistic nonsense. They actively built and supported the Republican Party and co-operated loyally with their white allies. In so doing, they developed a discipline and solidarity that would do credit to the most experienced trade unionists. They ostracized those Negroes (and there were many) who were fooled by the planters. They refused to associate with them and often expelled them from the churches. Donald says that "voting the party ticket was for them a sort of religion. . . . In short, among the freedmen Republican politics and religion were practically the same."[2]

The cotton planters had much better success among the white members of the democratic coalition that controlled most of the new Reconstruction state governments in the South. Their great weapon here was an appeal to white supremacy prejudices. Many whites fought loyally side by side with the Negroes; but the history of the Reconstruction years is filled with the confusion and disintegration sown in the ranks of the whites by the poisonous white chauvinist agitation of the planters and their agents.

Typical of this virulent propaganda, carried on all over the South, was an editorial in the *Independent Monitor*. "Let every man at the South," it calls, "through whose veins the unalloyed Caucasian blood courses, who is not a vile adventurer or carpetbagger, forthwith align himself in the rapidly increasing ranks of his species, so that we may the sooner overwhelmingly crush, with one mighty blow, the preposterous wicked dogma of Negro equality."[3] Such papers, and they existed all over the South, freely advocated the massacre of rebellious Negroes.

THE KU KLUX KLAN

Basing themselves on violent white supremacist agitation and activities, the pseudo-genteel planter aristocrats proceeded to set up a reign of terror throughout the South and to drown the revolution in the blood of the Negroes. This they were finally able to do with the connivance of Northern reactionaries. All this organized murder was carried out under hypocritical slogans of the defense of white womanhood, the family, law and order, religion, patriotism, and civilization. Decades before Hitler was born, the Southern cotton planters worked out in detail the whole technique of organized racist demagogy and terrorism. The evil flower of such endeavors was the hooded Klan.

The Klan embodied the organized violence of the planters and their allies against the Negroes and their white allies. It was the extra-legal arm of the counter-revolution, designed to prevent the Negroes and poor whites from exercising their legal political rights. It was the chief means used by the planters in the reconquest of the South. The Klan had as its forerunners the patrols (the "pattyrollers") of slavery times, which nightly covered the roads of the South, flogging slaves, conducting midnight raids upon the slaves' quarters, and generally terrorizing the whole Negro community.

The Ku Klux Klan was formed in 1865 in Pulaski, Tennessee. At the outset, it was just one more of the numerous anti-Negro terroristic groups which infested the South, among them the Knights of the White Camelia, Knights of the White Rose, Pale Faces, Red Jackets, Knights of the Black Cross, White Brotherhood, Constitutional Guards, etc.[4] But the KKK got the backing of the planters, and it soon spread throughout the South. All other murder bands were also popularly known as "the Klan." It was organized chiefly by ex-Confederate army officers, but many poor whites belonged to it. Its Grand Wizard was General Bedford Forrest, of Civil War reputation.

In its statutes, the Klan opposed Negro equality, "both social and political," demanded "a white man's government in this country," insisted upon pre-war states' rights for the South, condemned the Republican Party, the Union Leagues, and the Grand Army of the Republic. It professed to advocate "Chivalry, Humanity, Mercy, and Patriotism" and to protect "the innocent and the defenseless." It was a secret order, with a weird ritual and a set of fantastic titles for its officials—Grand Wizard, Grand Dragon, Grand Titan, the Six Furies, Grand Giant, Grand Goblin, Grand Cyclops, Grand Magi, etc. Loyalty to the K.K.K. was violently enforced; its constitution provided that "Any member who shall reveal or betray the secrets of this Order, shall suffer the extreme penalty of the law."[5]

The Klan perpetrated barbarities all over the South. Its main efforts were directed toward breaking up the Union Leagues. Endless cases of its organized murder of Negroes were reported. "In 1871, fifty-three murders were attributed to the Klan in one county in Florida. In Vicksburg, Mississippi, and its environs, two hundred Negroes were killed in a week before the city election of 1874. In the next year, President Grant informed the Senate that 'a butchery of citizens was committed [on April thirteenth] at Colfax (Louisiana) which in blood-thirstiness and barbarity is hardly surpassed by any acts of savage warfare.' "[6] The fight of the Klan was aided by the fact that Confederate soldiers at the end of the war, were allowed to keep their small arms, whereas discharged Northern Negro soldiers had to give up theirs.

Du Bois thus characterizes Klan activities typical of the situation during Reconstruction days in the South: "Organized clubs of masked, armed men, formed as recommended by the Central Democratic committee, rode through the country at night, marking their course by the whipping, shooting, wounding, maiming, mutilation, and murder of women, children, and defenseless men, whose houses were forcibly entered while they slept, and, as their inmates fled, the pistol, the rifle, the knife, and the rope were employed to do their horrid work. Crimes like these, testified to by scores of witnesses, were the means employed in Louisiana to elect a President of the United States."[7] Uncounted thousands of Negroes and many poor whites were thus victimized. The Negroes made bitter resistance to the terror.[8]

During the early 1870's the Federal government banned the Ku Klux Klan, and officially it was supposed to have been dissolved. Actually, it just went underground and continued its activities unabated. The Klan operated all through the Reconstruction period. In fact, in later years it became a permanent feature of Southern life —in various forms, such as the White Caps, Night Riders, etc.—and has lasted right down to our own times. Such terrorist gangs, from pre-Civil War days, have always been a major weapon of the Southern ruling class in their attempt to hold the Negro people in subjection.

WEAK POLICIES OF THE GRANT ADMINISTRATION

General Grant, upon taking office in March 1869, faced a South in which the cotton planters and their allies had launched virtual K.K.K. civil wars in the various states in order to regain political power. For the president to realize the Congressional program of Reconstruction, which the Republican Party had supported in the 1868 elections, his administration had to follow a vigorous policy of advancing its program and suppressing the lawless counter-revolution. But no such energetic policy was forthcoming. The Northern bourgeoisie, facing new internal enemies and problems in the North and West, was displaying less and less interest in revolutionizing the South, and this changing mood expressed itself in the weakening policies of the Grant Administration, especially in its second four years.

To maintain the Negroes' right to vote—the heart of Republican control of the South—the Grant Administration among other measures formulated and sponsored the Fifteenth Constitutional Amend-men. This amendment, enacted on March 30, 1870, states: "The right of citizens . . . to vote shall not be denied or abridged by the United States or by any State on account of race, color, or previous condition of servitude. . . ." Congress also passed the Enforcement Acts of May 31, 1870, and of February 28, 1871.[9] These laws penalized interference with the right of citizens to vote and to practice other civil liberties; authorized the use of the army to enforce these rights, and gave the Federal courts and officers the right of control over the registration and voting in Congressional districts. Another law enacted on April 20, 1871,[10] was specifically directed against the Ku Klux Klan. It was designed to implement the dormant Civil Rights Act of 1866, and it gave the president wide powers to take action against the bands of terrorists and conspirators which were rampant all over the South.

At this time, the reactionary guerrilla bands had thrown the South into turmoil. As a result, it would have required a vigorous application of armed force by the government to translate the Enforce-ment legislation into reality. The arming of the Negroes was also indispensable. But these policies were not forthcoming from the executive branches. Grant used the army upon only a few occasions, and, though he moved against the planter political gangsters by arrest-ing several hundreds of them, convictions were rare. His half-hearted measures were quite inadequate. The total number of Federal troops in the South at the time did not exceed 20,000 men, or less than 2,000 per state. The Negro local militia, which never had real backing from the national administration, was much too weak to be a decisive force in the bitter struggle for power. All Negro troops had been withdrawn from the South by 1866.

Congress also did not help matters when, in May 1872, it passed a general Amnesty Act. This law reduced the number of former Confederate leaders barred from holding political office to only about 300 to 500. It was interpreted all over the South as a sign of weakness, and it did in fact indicate the new moods of conciliation growing in Republican ranks.

To make matters worse, the Republican Party suffered serious internal splits in both the North and the South. At the heart of this breach was the Southern question—what was to be done about Recon-struction. In the South, the issue turned concretely around the prob-lem of the status of the Negro. The poor whites and the new middle class that was springing up after the war were definitely influenced by the white supremacy agitation of the planters, their murder campaign against the Negroes, and their violent denunciation of the "carpetbaggers" and the Radical Reconstruction governments.

The result was deep internal disruptions in the Republican Party in every Southern state. This tended to divide the Negroes from their white allies. The Republican Party in the South became more and more a party of Negroes and white officeholders. "In 1873 the *Montgomery Daily Advertiser*, the leading Democratic paper of Alabama, could triumphantly point out that Alabama had 98,000 colored citizens and 90,000 Republicans, Texas 51,575 Negroes and 51,846 Republicans, South Carolina 85,475 Negro citizens and 85,071 Republicans, Louisiana 86,913 Negro voters and about the same number of Republicans."[11] Under these circumstances—with the Negroes largely deserted by their main allies, North and South—reaction marched from victory to victory in the South.

THE 1872 PRESIDENTIAL ELECTIONS

The split in the Republican Party was evident on a national scale in the elections of 1872. A so-called liberal reform movement had been growing up in the party. This was an expression of disgust at the corruption connected with the Grant Administration and also opposition even to the mild reconstruction policies Grant was following in the South. This somewhat expressed the confused opposition of the farmers and other middle strata on a national scale to the new rulers, to the railroad and other steals of national resources, and the return of large sections of labor to the Democratic Party. These opposition elements subordinated the needs of Reconstruction and of the Negro to other problems. The leader of this movement was Carl Schurz, and, after 1870, it began to take on organized form in Missouri. Behind the movement's liberal facade was the backing of big Northern capitalist interests. A powerful battery of newspapers supported the split movement in the 1872 elections, including the *Chicago Tribune, Cincinnati Commercial, Springfield Republican, The Nation, New York Evening Post, Louisville Courier-Journal,* and to a lesser extent, the *New York World* and *Tribune.*[12]

The "liberal" Republicans met in convention in Cincinnati, on May 1, 1872, to adopt a platform and to nominate candidates. Their platform, after tipping its hat to the Thirteenth, Fourteenth, and Fifteenth Amendments, declared, "We demand the immediate and absolute removal of all disabilities imposed on account of the Rebellion, which was finally subdued seven years ago, believing that universal amnesty will result in complete pacification in all sections of the country."[13] This would have meant complete abandonment of the revolution in the South, and surrender of the Negro minority there to the organized violence of the arrogant planters. It foreshadowed the line that the Northern bourgeoisie as a whole was to adopt four years later. The man chosen as the candidate to put this counter-revolutionary program before the American people was none other than Horace Greeley, erratic editor of the *New York Tribune* and one-time Abolitionist. The new organization called itself the Liberal Republican Party.

The regular Republican Party met in Philadelphia on June 5, with the Radicals still in control. The platform endorsed the general course of the Grant Administration, including its policies in the South, and proposed their continuation. Grant, who was still popular among the masses despite all his failings, was unanimously chosen to head the Republican ticket. In going into the campaign he also undoubtedly had the support of the main body of the Northern capitalists.

The Democratic Party assembled in Baltimore on July 9. Former slaveholders and Confederate leaders were there in force. The reactionary Democratic leaders were quick to grasp the opportunity presented to them by the split in the Republican Party. By a vote of 670 to 62, the convention accepted the platform of the Liberal Republican Party, and by 686 to 46, it endorsed the candidacy of Mr. Greeley. Thus, this former fighter (of a sort) for Negro rights became the standard bearer for Southern Bourbon reaction.

The bitterly fought election campaign of 1872 also split the ranks of the old time Abolitionists. Senator Charles Sumner, who for many years had fought gallantly for and with the Negro people, found himself, at the end of his career (he died on March 11, 1874), supporting Greeley, the mouthpiece of the planters. George M. Julian, Lyman Trumbull, and other erstwhile Abolitionists followed the same line. But William Lloyd Garrison and Wendell Phillips fought Greeley and supported Grant. So, with great militancy, did Frederick Douglass, who campaigned energetically for Grant, in both North and South. At the Negro people's convention, in New Orleans in April 1872, Douglass was a decisive force in keeping the Negro masses from being affected by the demagogy of Greeley, Sumner, Julian, and other former Abolitionists. He helped to swing the Negro vote almost solidly behind the Republican ticket. During this campaign Douglass was nominated for vice-president on the Equal Rights Party ticket (organized by a faction in the International Workingmen's Association), but he ignored this.

Organized labor played no important part in the Grant-Greeley struggle. The National Labor Union was then striking out toward independent working class political action in the shape of a labor party. The organization held a political convention in Columbus, Ohio, February 21, 1872, and nominated Judge John Davis of Illinois for President. "The platform of the National Labor Union was adopted as the platform of the National Labor and Reform party."[14] Nothing came of the nomination, however, as Davis supported Greeley.

Grant won the election by a popular vote of 3,597,132 against 2,834,125 for Greeley. The latter carried only Georgia, Kentucky, Maryland, Missouri, Tennessee, and Texas, with a total of 66 electoral votes. Grant got all the other states, with 272 electoral votes. The new Senate contained 49 Republicans, 5 Liberal Republicans, and 19 Democrats; the House, 195 Republicans, 4 Liberals, and 88 Democrats.[15]

REACTION SEIZES THE SOUTHERN STATES

Southern reaction, based upon the big cotton planters, waged a long, complex, and bitter struggle to capture the state governments in the South from the people's forces. This process the reactionaries called the "redemption" or the "restoration." Only the barest outline of it can be given here. But the ruthless attack by the counter-revolutionary forces, the unstable character of the Negro-poor white coalition, and the diminishing revolutionary energy in the national Republican Party combined to put the Southern reactionaries back in the saddle. The average duration of the Southern Radical governments was three-and-one-half years; nowhere did they last more than a decade.

The early Johnsonian Reconstruction governments (later dissolved) started the counter-revolution. Tennessee was the first state readmitted to the Union in 1867, and also the first to be captured by reaction. Negro representation in the legislature never exceeded a handful, and it was not long until the Democrats were able to take over. Virginia, which elected the conservative wing of the Republicans in 1869, had never really been under Radical control—

General Schofield, a pro-Southern reactionary, saw to that. After a bloody struggle, North Carolina was captured by the K.K.K. forces in 1870. Georgia, with Republican ranks split on the race issue, elected a Democratic governor in 1872. Extreme terror kept the Negroes from the polls in Texas in 1872, and the state passed to the control of the Democrats. During a reign of terror in 1874, Alabama "elected" a Democratic governor and also a Democratic majority in the state legislature. Arkansas, with two rival governments, was a scene of chaos from 1872 to 1874, when President Grant recognized the "Conservative Republicans"; as a result, the Democrats elected the legislature and the Governor. Through violence and terrorism, Mississippi went Democratic in 1875 in an election which President Grant characterized as unworthy of savages. In Florida, the Democrats, after a long and confused struggle, rewon control in 1876.[16] When Rutherford Hayes was elected in November 1876, only two Southern states—South Carolina and Lousiana—were left within Radical Republican control. These states were both scenes of civil wars for years. They were handed over to the counter-revolution by the shameful Hayes sell-out of 1877.

The Negroes, and those white allies who stood with them, made a gallant, if futile fight against advancing reaction. In each state there was violence. Dual state governments existed in several instances. The reactionary process was heightened by the severe economic crisis of 1873. Woodson says of the local struggles, "Some of the clashes became almost as serious as the battles of the Civil War."[17] Du Bois states that between 1868 and 1871 there were 371 cases of political violence in Alabama, including 35 murders; and during the next three years the situation got much worse. In Louisiana, in one month, 297 persons were slain in the parishes adjacent to New Orleans. In a riot in Memphis, Tennessee, in 1866, 24 unarmed Negroes were killed. As for the situation in North Carolina, Judge Albion W. Tourgee said, "Of the slain there were enough to furnish forth a battlefield and all from these three classes, the Negro, the scalawag and the carpetbagger . . . the wounded in this silent warfare were more thousands than those who groaned upon the slopes of Gettysburg."[18] Du Bois says, "Armed guerrilla warfare killed thousands of Negroes."[19] The odds were hopeless, and the struggle was a gradually losing one.

As late as March 1, 1875, Congress passed the Civil Rights Act, which was designed to put an end to the whole Jim Crow system of discrimination, North and South. It called for "full and equal enjoyment of the accommodations, advantages, facilities, and privileges of inns, public conveyances on land or water, theatres, and other places of public amusement . . . alike to citizens of every race and color, regardless of any previous condition of servitude."[20] The law provided fines up to $1,000 and imprisonment of not less than 30 days for violations. But this was a last-hour shot into the water. The law was not enforced and was eventually killed by the reactionary Supreme Court. With the victory of reaction in the South, the Jim Crow system, in the coming period, was not to get better but infinitely worse.

31. The Hayes Betrayal of 1877

In the last chapter, we indicated the growing reluctance of the Republican Party to support the revolutionary demands of the Negro people and insist upon a democratic regime in the South. During the eight years of the Grant Administration, there was an increasing tendency in Northern capitalist ranks to conciliate the ex-slaveholders and to adopt a more and more apathetic attitude toward the revolutionary program of the Radicals. It was basically this trend that in 1872 produced the national Republican split and the independent candidacy of Horace Greeley. At the very beginning of the administration of President Hayes, in 1877, this new attitude was to come to fruition in an agreement with the Southern reactionaries, among whom the cotton planters were dominant, that put an end to the revolution in the South.

THE HAYES-TILDEN ELECTION STRUGGLE

Rutherford B. Hayes of Ohio, the Republican candidate for president in 1876, was a lawyer who had risen to the rank of major-general in the Civil War. During his one term in Congress, in 1865-67, he fully supported the program of the Radicals on Reconstruction, and later he backed the Grant Administration. Samuel J. Tilden, the Democratic standard-bearer, was a New York lawyer, a "war Democrat."

The election campaign of 1876 was very sharp. The lines were drawn pretty much as in the previous presidential campaign. The Southern question was the main bone of contention, with Tilden demanding "full autonomy for the South"—meaning the restored power of the planters—and Hayes ostensibly promising to continue the general line of the Grant Administration. The Republicans, as usual, "waved the bloody shirt," that is, they relived the horrors of the war and the terror of the ex-slaveholders during Reconstruction, while the Democrats deplored the "excesses" of "carpetbag government" in the South. The economic paralysis of the 1873 crisis and the big graft scandals during the Grant Administration, worked heavily against the Republicans. The "liberal" split of 1872 was healed, but it seriously weakened the Republican Party.

The national vote was as follows, according to the eventual Republican count[1]: for Tilden 4,285,992 votes, and for Hayes 4,033,768, or a popular majority of 252,224 for the Democratic candidate. Tilden, therefore, claimed the victory, with 203 electoral votes for himself, against 166 for Hayes. The Republicans, however, contested this claim, challenging the returns from four states—South Carolina, Florida, Louisiana, and Oregon. Undoubtedly there had been big frauds in the South, with large numbers of Negroes—Republicans—, kept away from the polls by terror. The Republican challenge left the undisputed vote of Tilden at 184 and Hayes at 166—or one short of the needed majority for Tilden in the electoral college, with the votes of four states contested.

THE SELL-OUT

This situation created great tension and excitement throughout the country. To resolve the deadlock, Congress set up a commission of 15—5 from the Senate, 5 from the House, and 5 from the Supreme Court. The party line-up in the commission was 8 Republicans and 7 Democrats, and the vote went 8 to 7 all along. The commission accorded all the disputed votes to Hayes, who was thereupon declared elected. The crisis lasted for three months, and Democratic wrath exploded at the outcome. Henry Watterson of Kentucky called for an army of 100,000 to march on Washington to install Tilden as President. But the excitement died down on the basis of an agreement between Hayes and Southern Democratic leaders, and Tilden faded out of the political picture.

The Hayes-Tilden agreement consisted of a cynical sell-out of the Negro people. The bargain was made in a series of conferences, February 26-27, 1877, just before Hayes took office. Hayes promised liberal appropriations for Southern internal improvements and the passage of the Texas Pacific Railroad bill; but the key to the agreement was the surrender to the Democrats of political control of the state governments of South Carolina and Louisiana, which the Republicans still held. These terms were contained in a letter from Stanley Matthews and Charles Foster, speaking for Hayes, to the Democratic leaders in Congress.[2] The letter pledged Hayes to carry out the bargain, the substance of which was to abandon the South to the tender mercies of the white supremacists. It was a very profitable bargain for the Southerners and they accepted it—they were in no position to make an armed fight for the presidency, as the Democratic hotheads were demanding.

Hayes set the final stamp of approval upon this brutal betrayal of the Negro people by withdrawing the Federal troops from South Carolina and Louisiana in April 1877.[3] In this raw deal, Hayes never consulted the leaders of the Negro people. He considered the Negroes, who were loyal supporters of the Republican Party, to be strictly expendable and he proceeded on that basis. It was a cold-blooded sell-out that was to cause boundless misery and hardships to the Negro people and gravely handicap the fight for American democracy over many decades. Engels, in a letter to Karl Marx (May 23, 1862), forecast this eventual union of the "bourgeois" planters with the Northern industrialists to quell popular insurrections in the South.[4]

CAPITALIST GAINS IN THE REVOLUTION

The Northern bourgeoisie, who were beginning to develop monopoly capitalism, betrayed the Negro people by making a bargain with Southern reaction, because they had accomplished their major objectives through the revolution. That is, they had preserved the Union and smashed the menace of the cotton planters, thus forever removing them as a dangerous obstacle in their economic and political path. With this done, they had no further concern about the Negro people, except to make sure that they were kept in a position where the Northerners themselves could participate in their super-exploitation.

First by the revolution, the capitalists of the North, increasingly monopolist, had quite established their control of the Federal government. Prior to the Civil War, in the 72 years between Washington and Lincoln, the South had held the presidency for 50 years, and provided 20 of the 35 Supreme Court justices and 13 of the 23 Speakers of the House.[5] After the war, the political picture was radically changed. Since Johnson, no president has been a Southerner. President Wilson (1913-21), although born in Virginia, actually hailed from New Jersey, and President Eisenhower (1953-), Texas-born, has been almost altogether a resident of the West and North. During these decades the cotton industry vastly expanded—from 4,491,000 bales in 1860 to 15,694,000 bales in 1911; but never again were the once arrogant cotton masters able to challenge the victorious Northern capitalists. The illusion of "King Cotton" was liquidated. As part of their control of the Federal government, the Yankee capitalists proceeded to domesticate in their service not only the Republican Party, but the Democratic Party as well. They both became primarily Northern capitalist parties; henceforth, no matter which one carried the elections, Northern capitalist interests were safeguarded.

Second, by the revolution, the Northern industrialists also accomplished their basic economic objectives. After the war they were able freely to jack up the tariff, cultivate internal improvements, and consolidate into monopolies. They also won access to the raw materials and markets of the South. They ousted British influence in the South and took full command themselves. Parrington says that, after the Civil War, "an ambitious industrialism stood on the threshold of a continental expansion that was to transfer sovereignty in America from a landed and mercantile aristocracy to the capable hands of a new race of captains of industry."[6] Indeed, by 1877 this transformation had already been basically accomplished.

NEW CLASS ALIGNMENTS IN THE SOUTH

The fundamental reason why the Northern capitalists abandoned the Second American Revolution was that it had already provided them with the results they wanted. Moreover, the revolution had laid the basis for new economic developments and new class alignments in the South. Consequently, the Northern capitalists could enter into alliance with their erstwhile political enemies in the South. The substance of these new Southern developments was the rise of a new middle class and the beginning of a capitalist class. This brought about a relative decline in the dominating influence of the planters—cotton, sugar, tobacco, and rice. This general trend, which became marked after the Civil War, was to continue until, in our own times, not the planters but the financial-industrial capitalist interests control the South.

Simkins describes the earliest beginnings of this class differentiation. In the post war, "The breakup of the plantation into small [renting—W.Z.F.] units created much small trade and a consequent demand for small credit. This was met by the creation of the crossroads store and the commercial villages and towns with stores and banks. These new institutions were owned by an emergent economic group, the storekeepers. . . . The storekeepers were often also bankers, planters, church deacons, and sometimes state senators."[7] Allen points out that "In South Carolina, for example, there were only 16 places rated as towns in 1860, while the census of 1880 listed 110 towns and centers while another authority placed the number of towns and trading centers at 493."[8]

These tendencies laying the basis for trade and industry in the South were stimulated by Northern capitalist penetration during the 10 years of the Reconstruction period. To a greater extent than is realized, the "carpetbaggers" were direct agents of Northern capitalism and builders of industrialism in the South. Many of them stayed on after the Reconstruction period and became prominent Southern capitalists. Woodward has especially stressed this situation. "Some surprising naturalizations of Yankee capital into Confederate citizenship were effected," he says.[9] He cites as an example the well-known large-scale Louisiana Lottery. There were many other concerns. To stimulate the industrialization of the hitherto almost completely agricultural South, was one of the basic results of the Second American Revolution.

Woodward says of the "Redeemers" (those who led in overthrowing the Radical Reconstruction state governments): "In the main they were of middle class, industrial, capitalist outlook, with little but a nominal connection with the old planter regime. . . . Like the Redeemers of sister states, those of South Carolina, definitely allied themselves with the business interests—with the factory owners, railroad men, and merchants of Charleston, Columbia, and other cities." He adds, "As a rule, however, the planter and industrialist Redeemers were able to compose their differences amicably and to rule by coalition."[10] These tendencies toward industrialization fitted right in with the efforts of De Bow and others, who had tried in vain, in the 1850's, to begin a big movement for building industry in the slave South.

Allen correctly remarks, however, that, "Industry in the South developed very slowly during the Reconstruction period."[11] The existing political turmoil did not facilitate penetration by Northern capital. There was a revolutionary way to liquidate this turmoil—by repressing the counter-revolution, by building the Negroes up into an independent, small-farm-owning class, and by systematically cultivating industrialization. But the Northern bourgeoisie in the 1877 Hayes agreement, chose a different, reactionary route, betraying the

Negro people and coming to a settlement with its erstwhile cotton-planter enemy and the budding Southern middle class. After this betrayal, as we shall see later on, some indusrialization of the South was pushed vigorously by the Northern capitalists.

NEW ENEMIES OF THE NORTHERN CAPITALISTS

Still another major factor causing the Northern capitalists to adopt the treacherous Hayes agreement of 1877 was the fact that the great democratic alliance, which had waged the long struggle against slavery and won the Civil War had fallen to pieces at the end of the war. New class alignments took place on a major scale in the North.

The Northern bourgeoisie in the post-war period found itself confronting a dangerous array of powerful new enemies—workers, farmers, and middle classes—in upheaval throughout the North and West against the new and ruthless capitalist exploitation.

The workers in the North—and to some extent in the South—who had grown rapidly in numbers, were building a strong trade union movement, were beginning independent political action, and were taking up the cudgels against the rapacious industrialists, their erstwhile allies in the Civil War. During the two decades following the end of the Reconstruction period, they were to wage some of the hardest-fought strikes in the whole history of the American labor movement. The farmers in the West, rebelling against intolerable exaction from the railroads, the bankers, and other exploiters, were also approaching their broad and lengthy series of struggles—under the banners of the Grangers, Greenbackers, and Populists. Similarly, the middle class in the Northern cities was strongly agitating against the trusts, which were destroying the small manufacturer and business-man. By the end of the Reconstruction period, these movements, already under way, were gradually spreading into the South.

Foner thus analyzes the situation in the North: "Militant strikes, unemployment demonstrations, and the growth of independent political action heralded the fact that the class struggle was sharpening. Frightened by the popular upheaval, the masters of capital began to look with favor at the prospects of an alliance with reactionary elements in the South. Together they could build a solid front against the people's movements. Assured by the Southern conservatives that the status of the tariff, the national banks, and the national debt would not be disturbed, Northern capitalists no longer hesitated.

Once the popular governments in the South were overthrown and control restored to the old oligarchy, they reasoned, the way would be cleared for capitalist expansion below the Mason-Dixon line without the risk of social unrest and continued upheaval."[12]

Hence, the Hayes betrayal of 1877. The Southern planters and their budding local capitalist allies were restored to a measure of power in the states. This was done at the expense of the Negro people, faithful supporters of the Republican Party. They were finally bartered off by the callous Republican national leaders into a new form of enslavement—sharecropping-peonage—which, in fact, had been developing ever since the end of the war. The poor whites were also victims of this sell-out. As for the Northern workers and farmers who, potentially, could have prevented this great betrayal, their fighting attention was directed elsewhere. In the class struggle, they did not realize the fundamental importance for themselves of defending and protecting the rights and welfare of their natural allies, the oppressed Negro people.

THE REVOLUTION AND THE NEGRO PEOPLE

The revolution, despite its final betrayal, brought basic advantages to the Negro people, achieving some of their major demands. Most important of all, it freed them from the terrible, centuries-old bondage of chattel slavery. It also won for them the legal right to vote, the right to education and to bear arms in the national defense. During the long struggle against the Southern planters, the Negro people, by their fine fighting qualities, had vastly increased their standing among the people at large. Through the Civil Rights Acts they had also made at least a dent in the monstrous official Jim Crow system. For them, the greatest shortcoming of the revolution was its failure to win the land for them—a struggle which the Northern bourgeoisie was unwilling to join. In the coming post-Reconstruction period of heavy reaction, in the long oppressive political night, the Negroes were doomed to lose many of their revolutionary gains, especially the franchise and representation in government, and other traces of social rights which they had achieved.

The history of the Negro people in the United States is the history of a developing nation. In the long pre-war struggle against slavery and during the Civil War and the Reconstruction period, the Negro people made great progress in national growth. They unified themselves—the free and unfree—upon a higher social level; they built their convention movement on a much broader basis than before. They acquired new fighting allies in the white workers and the farmers. They greatly expanded the Negro churches; they established new Negro newspapers, notably Douglass' *New National Era* and the *Colored American*. They cultivated many strong leaders and a world of intense political experience. They founded several Negro colleges and a host of schools. Budding Negro culture was strengthened by such works as *The Black Man* by W. W. Brown, published in 1863, his *The Negro in the American Revolution* in 1867 and *The Rising Sun* in 1874; Miss Keckley's *Behind the Scenes* in 1868; W. Still's *The Underground Railroad* in 1872, etc.[13]

Class differentiation among the Negro people began to speed up, with the increasing development of a proletariat and small farmers, and with the beginnings of a city petty bourgeoisie. One of the basic reasons for the defeat of the revolution in the South had been precisely the lack of a strong working class, an established body of independent farmers, and a vigorous urban middle class, among the whites as well as among the Negroes—in other words, the lack of a characteristic class structure of capitalist society. These classes would have provided a strong alliance in the struggle against the planters.

In the drive ahead of the Negro people, they made an unfortunate venture into business during this period, the Freedmen's Savings and Trust Company of Washington, D. C. This bank was authorized by Congress in August 1865, but was not an official government institution. It grew rapidly, and by 1872 it had 34 branches all over the South, with $19,952,647 in deposits, nearly all from poor Negroes. Badly managed by its officials, mainly white, the bank got into difficulties. The panic of 1873 made its troubles disastrous. Frederick Douglass became its president in March 1874, and put in considerable of his own money in an attempt, through his great prestige, to save it. But on June 28, 1874, the institution had to close its doors. Eventually the depositors got about 50 cents on the dollar. Douglass' paper, *The New National Era,* died three months after the bank crashed. The Negro people were moved to undertake this banking venture because of the outrageous way in which they were Jim Crowed in white banking institutions.

The Hayes sell-out of 1877 confronted the Negro people with a grave policy crisis. The Republican Party, to which they were affiliated all through the revolutionary period, had cynically betrayed them.

Thenceforth, that party had nothing to offer the Negro masses, except forcing them down into the worst oppression and exploitation at the hands of the Southern planters and the Northern capitalists. Their twenty-year alliance with the Republican Party had become a deadly trap for the Negro people. Now, in order to defend their interests, it was imperative that they seek out new allies against their enemies. These needed allies could be found only among the white workers and the small farmers, who, North and South, were displaying a high degree of militancy and progressivism in the decades after the Civil War.

The Negro people realized this need in considerable measure. In the post-war decades, they showed strong tendencies to sever their connections with the Republican Party and to establish co-operative relations with the young, fighting trade unions and the farmer movements of the period. In the complex situation the Negro leadership, including Frederick Douglass, did not understand fully the crisis confronting the Negro people, or what to do about it. Nor, it may be remarked, did the official leaders of the trade unions and the white farmers, who were being drawn into the Democratic Party or shunted aside by Greenbackism, grasp the counter-revolutionary significance of the Hayes-Tilden sell-out. The same was also largely true of the American Marxists, who concerned themselves in the post-war period almost exclusively with the workers in the North and West.

From about 1850 to 1875—during the years of the pre-war decades, through the war, and in the Reconstruction period—Frederick Douglass had provided the Negro people with splendid political leadership. But in the new political situation which opened up after 1877 he could not grasp the significance of the changed class realignments in the United States; hence he was unable further to point the correct fighting line for his bitterly harassed people. He had said in 1872, "The Republican Party is the ship; all else is the sea." This expressed essentially a correct position for the Negro people in view of the burning struggle in the South, and the record of the Republican Party in the great struggle over slavery. But Douglass continued to act on this principle long after the Republican Party had ceased to have any constructive meaning for the Negro people.

In line with this wrong policy, Douglass did not, at the critical moment, raise his voice against the Hayes sell-out. It was unfortunate, too, that this great leader accepted a position as U.S. Marshal in Washington from the reactionary Hayes Administration. Douglass' failure, in common with that of the white leaders of the workers, to grasp the new problems of the post-Reconstruction period was exemplified by his inability to seize definitely upon trade unionism as a necessary instrument of the Negro people. On May 7, 1874, in a feature editorial in his paper, *The New National Era*, he even spoke of "The Folly, Tyranny, and Wickedness of Labor Unions." It is a fact however, that Douglass never ceased to petition and to urge the trade unions of his day to grasp the hands of their black brothers in labor. The chauvinism of the white trade union leaders of the time—closing the doors of the unions to Negro workers—and their growing affiliation to the Democratic Party were the decisive factors in driving a wedge between the trade unions and the Negro people's movement.

For three-quarters of a century the bitter struggle for supremacy went on between the Southern planters and the Northern industrialists and their democratic allies. This finally culminated in the great Civil War and the turbulent Reconstruction period. Throughout all these decades, the Negro question was the central, decisive, national political issue. The Hayes bargain of 1877, however, radically changed this situation by formally ending the historic all-out struggle between the planters and industrialists and thereby pushing the Negro question into a minor category as an active political issue. It is only in our own day that this great question, as befits its tremendous importance, has again thrust itself politically to the forefront. Now, again, the Negro is able to sway national presidential elections and to influence the international relations of the United States.

32. The National Labor Union and the Negro

With the rapid expansion of industry, the growth of the working class, and the big rise in the cost of living during the Civil War, the trade unions in the North and West grew and flourished (see Chapter 25). Invigorated and maturing, the labor movement quickly understood that the scattered local unions of pre-war days could not meet the growing combinations of capital. There had to be national workers' organizations, both for the individual trades and for the labor movement as a whole. A number of national unions were formed during the war, and an attempt was made in 1864 to unite them into a general federation of labor, the International Industrial Assembly; but this organization was still-born. On August 26, 1866, the trade unions, pressed by the urgent need for unity, came together in Baltimore and formed the National Labor Union.

THE NATIONAL LABOR UNION

The founding convention of the National Labor Union was made up of 68 delegates, representing 43 local unions, 11 trade assemblies, four eight-hour leagues, one national, and one international union. These bodies comprised, all told, some 60,000 members, mostly from Northern and Eastern cities. Several other national unions sent observers. The moving spirit behind the organization was the well-known William H. Sylvis, president of the iron-molders union; but it was not until 1868 that he became the official head of the general organization.[1]

All the way across the front of the convention hall stretched a banner—"Welcome to the Sons of Toil from the North, South, East, and West." The new organization had an elaborate program of labor reforms, which it proposed to accomplish by combined trade union and independent political action. Its program, as outlined in the 1868 convention, declared that "Even now a slavery exists in our land worse than ever existed under the old slave system. The center of the slave power no longer exists south of Mason's and Dixon's line. It has been transferred to Wall Street; its vitality is to be found in our huge national bank swindle, and a false monetary system. The war abolished the right of property in man, but it did not abolish slavery. This movement we are now engaged in is the great anti-slavery movement, and we must push on the work of emancipation until slavery is abolished in every corner of our country. Our objective point is a new monetary system, a system that will take from a few men the power to control the money, and give to the people a cheap, secure, and abundant currency. This done and the people will be free. Then will come such a social revolution as the world has never witnessed."[2] Already the new organization was afflicted with the Greenbackism which was largely responsible for its downfall.

During the six years of its life, the N.L.U. carried on many important struggles. It was militant in organizing the unorganized, in waging strikes, in fighting for the eight-hour day, in defending the interests of the unemployed. It also pioneered in the fight for women in industry, being the world's first labor organization to demand for women equal pay for equal work. The organization campaigned against child labor, for improved housing conditions, for workers' education, and for co-operative workshops. It put central stress upon independent political action by the working class. The N.L.U. marked the highest point of achievment thus far reached by the working class, and it left a deep impress upon the entire labor movement for decades to come.

Many old-time middle class Abolitionists hailed the young labor movement. Wendell Phillips greeted it enthusiastically, pointing out the organic connection between the fight of the white workers for better conditions and the struggle of the Negro slaves for emancipation. William Lloyd Garrison, who had been extremely antagonistic toward the trade unions a generation before, in 1866 wrote to Ira Steward, of the eight-hour day movement fame: "The same principle that has led me to abhor and oppose the unequalled oppression of the black laborers of the South, instinctively leads me to feel an interest in whatever is proposed to be done to improve the conditions and abridge the toil of the white laborer of the North."[3]

THE NATIONAL LABOR UNION AND RECONSTRUCTION

The N.L.U. was born at the outset of the Reconstruction period, but Sylvis, Trevellick, and others among its leaders did not understand the basic revolutionary significance of the vast struggle between the Northern Radicals and the Southern planters. They had realized the great significance of defeating the Confederates in the war and of freeing the Negro slaves; but they did not grasp the elementary fact that in order to smash the deadly reactionary power of the planters, they had to make sure that the Negroes were truly freed by helping them to win the land, the right to vote, and social equality. Instead of keeping the Southern planters too, under fire, during the Reconstruction period, these labor leaders turned all their guns upon their traditional enemies, the Northern industrialists and left the Negroes in the South pretty much to fend for themselves.

The N.L.U. had no Reconstruction program for the South. Practically no attention was paid to the fight for the right of the Negroes to vote, and none at all to their struggle for the land. Sylvis, the most advanced of the N.L.U. leaders, denounced the Freedmen's Bureau as "a stupendous fraud." He proposed instead "to loan the planters a few millions of dollars at a reasonable rate of interest . . . $20,000,000 loaned in this manner," he said, "would have done more to 'reconstruct' the South than a thousand millions spent upon the Freedmen's Bureau."[4] The first convention of the N.L.U. endorsed the policy of President Johnson which was for "a speedy restoration of the South" at the expense of the Negro people, and ultimately, also, of the white workers in the North.[5]

Although Sylvis and his co-workers in the leadership of the N.L.U. had little conception of the revolutionary meaning of Southern Reconstruction and its profound significance to the working class, they did appreciate the problems of Negro workers in industry. At its first convention, the N.L.U. paid great attention to this question; and just prior to its second convention, in 1867, it issued an address to workingmen in general: "Negroes are four million strong and a greater proportion of them labor with their hands than can be counted from among the same number of any other people on earth. Can we afford to reject their proffered cooperation and make them enemies? By committing such an act of folly we would inflict greater injury upon the cause of labor reform than the combined efforts of capital could accomplish."[6]

But these understanding words were not backed up by equally intelligent practice. The N.L.U. convention of 1866 spoke out well on Negro-white solidarity, and that of 1867 appointed a committee on the matter; but that of 1868 ignored the question. The convention of

1869 finally got around to appointing a committee to organize Negro workers. There were nine Negro delegates at this convention, "the first Negro representatives in organized labor." The convention resolved that the National Labor Union would know "no north, south, east, west, neither color nor sex on the question of the rights of labor." But only a scattering of practical work was done about the matter of organizing Negro workers.[7]

THE COLORED NATIONAL LABOR UNION

Meanwhile, the Negro workers were organizing themselves and striking to improve their conditions. They built separate Negro unions, just as they had learned from bitter experience that they had to have their own churches, people's conventions, newspapers, and other national Negro institutions. They were not building a rival, dual organization to that of the whites, however, as their movement was permeated with a spirit of friendly collaboration with white workers. This Negro trade union movement was part of the broad forward-driving tendency of the Negro people during the Reconstruction period.

Economic conditions were very bad for the freedmen in the South. Negro agricultural workers got $60 per year, or less, out of which they had to feed, clothe, and house their families.[8] Under these hard conditions trade union organization was imperative. In pre-Civil War times there had been various beginnings of Negro labor organization, such as The American League of Colored Laborers (New York, 1850), and at many of the ante-bellum Negro people's conventions the question of improving the workers' economic conditions was taken up. But the solid movement for labor organization did not get well under way until after the war. Foner says, "In 1867, a wave of strikes swept the South."[9] In many of these strikes there was active cooperation between Negro and white workers.

The first national expression of the growing Negro trade union movement was the convention held in 1869 in Union League Hall, Washington, D. C. Twenty-three states were represented. This convention, preceded by various state gatherings of Negro workers, was called by the Maryland State Convention of Negro Workers. In these pioneer days of trade unionism, the line of demarcation between the labor union and the political party was not clearly understood. Fifteen years later, the Knights of Labor still had many employers, farmers, and professionals in its ranks. Hence, characteristically, many Negro political leaders, such as Douglass, Garnet, Day, Langston, and others, were present at the Washington convention. Wesley remarks, "There were preachers, bishops, politicians, and local leaders of every walk of life in attendance."[10]

The convention bore many of the features of the traditional Negro people's convention movement, but it was radically different in the sharp stress that it placed upon trade unionism. Working class delegates were in the majority. Among the organizations they represented, mostly in the South, were those of the blacksmiths, caulkers, longshoremen, bricklayers, brick-makers, iron molders, waiters, tinners, carpenters, stove-makers, machinists, sail-makers, carters, printers, and other craftsmen. The convention established the Colored National Labor Union, with a constitution closely following that of the National Labor Union. Isaac Myers, a Baltimore caulker, was elected president, and W. U. Saunders, secretary. The organization established the *National Era* as its paper and set up a Bureau of Labor, with headquarters in Washington.

In opening the 1869 convention, Myers stated, "We desire union with the white laboreres for a common interest." This was the keynote throughout. The delegates voted affiliation to the National Labor Union. In line with the Reconstruction demands of the Negro people, the convention program placed heavy stress upon the question of getting land. It pointed out that there were 46,344,059 acres in the public domain in the South and urged that Negro settlers be given 40 acres apiece. It set as its goal "the ownership of your own homestead." The program further proposed the organization of trade unions with both Negro and white members, the eight-hour day, the establishment of co-operative workers' shops to prevent Negro workers from being squeezed out of industry, and woman suffrage. It endorsed the National Freedmen's Bank and building and loan associations, and the direct election of the U.S. president. It condemned attempts to revive the American Colonization Society, with its program for deporting the Negroes, it voted to send Sella Martin as its delegate to the convention of the International Workingmen's Association to be held in Paris the following year. The convention supported the Republican Party.[11]

Following the 1869 convention, a vigorous campaign was initiated to realize the objectives of the organization. Isaac Myers spoke in many cities, stressing the need for collaboration of Negro and white workers. In the South he had at least twice as many Negro listeners as white. In Washington, on April 11, 1870, he "told an audience of Negro workers that unless they organized, they would soon be ousted from the skilled trades and left as 'servants, the sweepers of shavings, the scrapers of pitch, and carriers of mortar',"—a prophetic statement. Later, in Norfolk, advocating joint Negro-white labor unions, Myers said that the day had passed "for the establishment of organizations based upon color. We are organized for the interest of the working-man, white and colored, and to do this, let the officers be composed of both white and colored men."[12] All this gave an impetus to trade union organization among Negro workers. Negro people's conventions in Tennessee, Texas, Alabama, Missouri, and Georgia, during 1870-71, all stressed the need for trade union organization.[13]

STRAINED RELATIONS BETWEEN THE N.L.U. AND THE C.N.L.U.

Meanwhile, the National Labor Union was making but little progress in organizing Negro workers into its affiliated unions. This was due primarily to the lack of understanding of the specific problems of the Negro people on the part of the leaders of the N.L.U. White chauvinism also played its part. The situation reached a head at the 1870 convention of the National Labor Union in a discussion on granting the privilege of addressing the convention to J. M. Langston, a well-known Negro Radical Republican leader. After an acrimonious political debate Langston was denied the floor by a vote of 29 to 23 on the ground that he, a Republican politician, had tried to tie the C.N.L.U. to the tail of the Republican Party,[14] and was aiming to do the same thing with the N.L.U. P. B. S. Pinchback, Negro governor of Louisiana, was also refused the floor for the same reason. Although this convention condemned by resolution all discrimination on account of race, color, nationality, or previous condition of servitude, the Negro delegates were affronted by the rough, short-sighted treatment which they had been accorded. Negro-white trade union unity had received a setback.

The National Labor Union at its height in 1869 numbered some 600,000 members, but by 1871 it was far in its decline. Only 22 delegates, mostly agrarian reformers, attended the convention that year. The sudden decay of the N.L.U. can be ascribed to several basic causes—the inclusion in its ranks of numerous preachers, lawyers, and other non-working class groups, its lack of centralized organization and a solid financial system, its addiction to cheap-money fallacies and agrarian panaceas, and its failure to establish strong working co-operation with Negro workers. As early as 1870, Friedrich A. Sorge, a prominent Marxist, wrote to Karl Marx that "The National Labor Union, which had such brilliant prospects in the beginning of its career, was poisoned by Greenbackism and is slowly but surely dying."[15] By 1872, the once-promising N.L.U. was dead.

The Colored National Labor Union carried on much agitational and organizational work in the South. It also led some minor wage movements. But in the fire of the great struggle over Southern Reconstruction, the C.N.L.U. lost most of the trade union aspects of its program. It moved still further toward becoming a purely political organization and an appendage of the Republican Party by electing Frederick Douglass president, and Bishop Loguen first vice-president. The C.N.L.U. carried on Republican political activities after that, but by 1874 it had perished as an organization.

PROBLEMS OF NEGRO-WHITE SOLIDARITY

There was much good will between the National Labor Union and the Colored National Labor Union, and if they could not establish closer working unity between Negro and white workers, this was due to their failure to overcome a number of serious obstacles. Chief among these was the N.L.U. failure to combat the employers' Jim Crow policies in industry. The white workers tended to oust Negro workers from the skilled trades, to refuse to work with them in the shops, and to bar them from the trade unions. This white chauvinist trend which was to wreak such havoc in the labor movement in later decades, was already manifest among unions in the N.L.U., despite the educational work of such men as Sylvis. The call for the founding convention of the Colored National Labor Union in 1869 said: "In the greater part of the United States colored men are excluded from workshops on account of their color."[16]

This deplorable situation was painfully dramatized in 1869-70 by the case of Lewis H. Douglass, the son of Frederick Douglass. The younger Douglass had secured a job at the Government Printing Office, but the printers' union would not allow him to become a union member. The pretext was that he had once worked for less than the union scale, but the real reason was that he was a Negro. Repeated appeals to the head of the International Typographical Union failed to rectify the injustice. This shameful incident contributed to Frederick Douglass' unfriendly attitude toward trade unionism and to that of many Negro workers as well.

Besides failing to cleanse their ranks of such white chauvinist practices, the National Labor Union did not understand the special nature of the Negro problem. Instead of giving active support to the basic demands of the Negro people in the Reconstruction of the South—for land, the vote, and equal rights—they tried to divert the attention of the Negroes away from their elementary demands and toward such issues as Greenbackism, currency reform and the like, in which the Negroes had little or no interest. This lack of realism among white N.L.U. leaders worked against the establishment of solid co-operation between Negro and white trade unionists.

A major bone of contention between these two groups was related to the general question of political action. The National Labor Union leaders, who were highly antagonistic to the Republican Party—the party of the employers—after the war, insisted that the Negroes break their connections with that party and join in building the Labor Reform Party.[17] But this was asking the impossible. At that time, from 1866 to 1872, the Radical Republicans were fighting vigorously for the establishment of democracy in the South, including basic rights for the Negroes; hence, it was unrealistic to expect the Negroes to split with them. However, Douglass himself was very near-sighted when he declared in 1872 that "The Republican Party is the true workingman's party of the country." At the same time, the Colored National Labor Union was correct in stating of the Republican Party that "To that party we are indebted for the Thirteenth, Fourteenth, and Fifteenth Amendments, the homestead law, the eight-hour law, and an improved educational system."[18]

Under these circumstances, it was idle for the white union leaders to expect the Negro leaders to break with the Republican Party. After Hayes's betrayal of 1877, however, such a policy would have been more practical. But insistence upon it in 1866-72 merely antagonized the Negroes and drove a wedge between them and the white trade unionists. It would have been far more realistic for the white N.L.U. leaders to work out a joint program with the Negroes, farmers, and Radical Republicans to enforce a genuine Reconstruction in the South as part of a national democratic program. Such a course would have been in the interests of the white workers as well as those of the Negroes.

THE MARXISTS AND THE NEGRO TRADE UNIONISTS

During the Reconstruction period, when the widespread development of the trade union movement took place in the North, the Marxists had small scattered groups in the major Northern cities—New York, Chicago, Philadelphia, Milwaukee, Cincinnati, St. Louis, etc.—especially in the centers most heavily populated with German immigrant workers. In 1864, the International Workingmen's Association was founded in London, England, and shortly after the Civil War, the Marxists began to build the I.W.A. in the United States. Section One was formed in New York in 1869, as an amalgamation of the German General Workers Club and the Communist Club of New York, with Friedrich A. Sorge as secretary. Other groups developed rapidly; by 1872 the I.W.A. had 30 sections and 5,000 members over the country as a whole.

Despite their relatively small numbers, the Marxists played an important role during the Civil War and post-war periods in the formation of the new local and national trade unions and in their consolidation into the National Labor Union. Unfortunately, Joseph Weydemeyer, the outstanding Marxist leader who had done so much to bring a national federation of labor into being, died of cholera in St. Louis on the very day that organization opened its founding convention in Baltimore.

The Marxists built unions, led strikes, organized demonstrations of the unemployed, and taught the elements of Marxism to the workers. As defenders of the principle of the unity of all workers, regardless of color, sex, or nationality, the Marxists systematically strove to bring the Negroes in industry into the trade unions and to establish their rights as workers in industry. They were largely responsible for the friendly attitude of many N.L.U. leaders toward the Negroes; but they were not sufficiently strong (nor did they understand the problem clearly enough) to eliminate the white chauvinist practices in the N.L.U. organizations.

The Marxists of the Reconstruction period also joined hands with the Negro workers in fighting for various political demands. The Social Party of New York was amongst the first organizations of the post-war period to highlight the struggle for equal rights for the Negro people. Its platform, presented at a mass meeting in January 1868, contained two planks demanding the repeal of all discriminatory laws and the right of all citizens to run for public office, regardless of race, color, or national origin.[19]

The Marxists of the period did not, however, have a rounded-out Reconstruction program, especially in relation to the Negroes in the South. In the letter of the I.W.A. addressed to the people of the United States, September 25, 1865, Karl Marx warned of the grave danger if full citizens' rights were not accorded to the newly freed Negroes. But the American Marxists failed to grasp the profound political significance of this clear lead. They failed to understand that after the emancipation of the slaves by the war, the Negro problem continued to be a special and very urgent one. They tended to look upon it simply as a general working class question. This weakness was to plague the labor movement for half a century after the Civil War, until the appearance of the present-day Communist Party upon the political scene.

There were few Negro Marxists in the Reconstruction years. None of the outstanding Negro Abolitionist leaders became Socialists. Douglass himself, to the end of his life, incorrectly hoped to work out the complete emancipation of the Negro people within the framework of the capitalist system. There were good co-operative relations, however, between Negro organizations and the Marxist forces. Allen points out that in 1869 Section One of the I.W.A. furnished a hall to a Negro trade union, which was unable to get one elsewhere; and that it was responsible for the admission of the local Negro unions in New York to the Workingmen's Union, the city central labor council. The I.W.A. also had a great deal to do with the participation of Negro unions in the great eight-hour-day parade in September 1871. And shortly afterward, a company of Negro militia, the Skidmore Guard took part in a New York demonstration called by the I.W.A. sections to protest the execution of the leading Parisian Communards.[20] These acts of solidarity took place in a city which only a few years before, in 1863, had been the scene of the terrible anti-draft riots. New York was also the place where, in the same year, it was impossible to get a band to head the 54th Massachusetts Negro Regiment on its way through the city, until the local Union League volunteered to lead the march. Other acts of solidarity which cemented a friendship between Negro workers and the Marxists took place in many cities of the North and West. In 1875, the Labor Party of Illinois, led by I.W.A. groups, presented demands to the Mayor of Chicago, protesting against discrimination in unemployment relief on account of color.[21]

33. The New South
Peonage and Terrorism

During the two decades following the Civil War, the so-called New South took definite shape. This was the regime of the dominant counter-revolution. But the once omnipotent cotton planters no longer ruled alone. Now they had to share the power with the rising Southern middle classes, and they were under the overlordship of the triumphant Northern industrialists and bankers. The reactionary New South, in its beginnings, was visible in the Reconstruction governments set up first under Lincoln, and later by Johnson; it came to maturity in the years immediately following the Hayes betrayal of 1877—after the revolutionary interlude of Reconstruction.

The reactionary New South represented white supremacy in full flower. It was based upon the deepest exploitation, persecution, and ostracism of the Negro people. It was a heaven for the exploiters, but a hell for the dark-skinned toiling masses, a misery, too, for the poor whites. The New South based its social relationships upon the barbarous Black Codes of the early Reconstruction period and upon the old-time slave codes. It constituted the nearest approach to chattel slavery possible under the national political circumstances.

It had been the tragic history of emancipated slaves, during the past century and throughout the western hemisphere—whether Indians or Negroes—that they did not pass from the status of slavery to that of free farmers and workers, but rather to one form of peonage or another. This occurred because of the economic weakness of the freed slaves, who were generally pressed by their ex-owners into new forms of servitude. So it was with the ex-slaves in the New South, with its organized agricultural, industrial, and political peonage. Characterizing the so-called New South, Lenin says: "The economic survivals of slavery differ in no way from similar survivals of feudalism; and in the formerly slave-owning South of the United States these survivals are very strong to this day."[1] And again he says, "Segregated, hidebound, a stifling atmosphere, a sort of prison for the 'emancipated' Negroes—this is what the American South is like."[2]

THE SHARECROPPING SYSTEM

In the early post-Civil War period, the Southern planters, with their slave system abolished, faced the necessity of devising a new method of labor exploitation in agriculture. This they did by organizing the system of peonage known as sharecropping (much akin to types of tenancy found in colonial Asia), which they enforced by terrorism. At first there was some show of developing wage labor on the plantations; but this was soon superseded by the intensive cultivation of various forms of tenancy, of which sharecropping is the dominant type. By its failure to give land to the Negroes and poor whites either through the confiscation of the planters' estates or through opening up the public domain in the South and also by the policies and practices of the Freedmen's Bureau, the Federal government definitely helped the planters to establish the infamous sharecropping system.

After the Civil War there was a big drop in the price of plantation lands. Jennings says that "Plantations which had sold for $100,000 to $150,000 before the war fell in value to $6,000 to $10,000."[3] But few of the poor whites, and fewer still of the even poorer Negroes, were able to buy any of them. Although a considerable amount of the plantation system was whittled away, in the main it stayed intact. For the vast majority of both Negroes and poor whites, the only way they could work the land they so much wanted was by renting it from the planters—mostly by sharecropping.

Governmental statistics for this period show a wide growth of small farm units, leaving the incorrect implication that this meant the break-up of the plantation system. Statistics for this period are highly unreliable, but properly interpreted, they do show trends. On the basis of contemporary figures, Coman gives the average size of farms throughout the South as follows: 1860—335.4 acres; 1870—214.2 acres; 1880—153.4 acres; and 1890—139.7 acres.[4] Using the same government statistics, Coulter indicates the growth of small farms in the South from 1860 to 1880, as follows: Alabama, from 55,000 to 136,000 farms; Mississippi, from 43,000 to 102,000; Texas, from 43,000 to 174,000; etc.[5] Henry states that the number of farms of 1,000 acres or more decreased, in Georgia, from 902 in 1860 to 419 in 1870; in Virginia, from 641 to 317; in Alabama, from 696 to 306, etc.[6] Actually, what was happening was not the development of a large number of small farms, as these figures would imply, but the growth of a system of tenancy, with each tenant-holding counted as a separate farm by the government census-takers.

The planters developed two systems of tenancy, each with variations. There were cash tenancy and sharecropping. The tenant system in general had various economic advantages for the planters over the old system of chattel slavery. For one thing, the planters no longer had to make an enormous capital outlay for slaves; moreover, under the new system, their cash expense of overseeing the work was very simple and inexpensive—the poverty-driven tenants became their own taskmasters. The planters learned, by various devices, to utilize the tenant system to squeeze the last drop of blood out of their workers.

The cash tenants, the minority, were akin to tenants elsewhere in the United States. They usually owned their own farm animals and implements, provided necessary fertilizer, and paid all or part cash rent for the land. They owned the crops which they produced. The sharecroppers, the vast majority, for the most part owned nothing. They were "furnished" by the planters with land, seed, tools, animals, fertilizer, and even food for their families—in return for which the planters took as their share from one-third to two-thirds of the crop. From that time to this, sharecropping has been the dominant form of production in Southern agriculture, especially cotton.

Sharecropping is a particularly vicious system of exploitation. The planter is able to rob the sharecropper almost at will. He charges usurious rates, up to 50 percent or more, on the "furnishings" which he provides, and he ruthlessly bilks the sharecropper in the sale of the cotton which he has produced. The sharecropper who is landless and owns little or nothing, instead of receiving cash wages as an agricultural worker, theoretically at least gets a share of the crop. He is a semi-feudal tenant. The planter, by his organized robbing devices, keeps the sharecroppers, Negro and white, permanently in debt to him and pressed down to the lowest possible standard of living. Sharecropping is bare subsistence farming, and altogether bad. It impoverishes the workers, depletes the soil, and prevents progress in farming techniques. The general result of sharecropping in the South has been to produce a more devastating poverty than any ever known in any other part of the agricultural United States. Lenin calls sharecropping semi-slavery, and says the farmers "are mainly semi-feudal or . . . semi-slave share tenants."[7]

CHANGED CLASS RELATIONS

Besides transforming the erstwhile Negro slaves and many poor whites into virtual peons, the reorganization of Southern agriculture after the Civil War also brought about other major shifts in class relationships. For one thing, there grew up a class of usurious merchants and bankers, who not only robbed the cash tenants, sharecroppers, and day laborers through high prices and interest rates on the basis of crop liens, but also managed by various credit devices to grab much of the plantation land—that is, where the merchant and the planter were not the same person. The widespread shifts in plantation ownership brought about by these practices are indicated by Woodward, who says that "At least half of the planters after 1870 were either Northern men or organized in corporations and financed by banks."[8] He cites an estimate, made in 1881 by the head of the Cotton Planters Convention, that "not one-third of the cotton plantations of the Mississippi Valley were 'owned by the men who held them at the end of the war.' "[9] These shifts in ownership were one of the main reasons why Henry Watterson, writing in 1880, could say, in commenting upon the planter-leaders of the Confederacy, that "not one of them remains upon the stage of active political life."[10]

Another very important element in the changed class relationships, brought about by the post-war reorganization of Southern agriculture, was the large-scale entry of whites into actual cotton production, some as small farmers but most as tenants and sharecroppers. This tendency was greatly accentuated by the widespread post-war expansion of cotton production. The extent of cotton expansion is shown by government figures: In 1866, 1,948,000 bales of cotton were produced on 7,666,000 acres; but by 1885, the figures had jumped up to 6,369,000 bales on 17,922,000 acres.[11] On the question of participation by whites in this extended cotton production, Hawk says, "In the ante-bellum period, the ratio of Negroes to whites employed in producing cotton was eight to one. Since the Civil War there has been a great shift in the labor force of the Cotton Belt. In 1876, nearly 40 percent of the cotton crop was produced by white farmers; in 1910, 67 percent."[12] The great increase of whites in cotton production occurred mainly in non-plantation areas—North Alabama, parts of Georgia, etc.—and in the new Western cotton lands which were never under the plantation system. In the main cotton plantation areas of the Black Belt, however, the great majority of producers are Negro sharecroppers and tenants to this day. The extensive entry of whites into cotton production was to have important political consequences in the Negro-white solidarity during the big Populist movement of the 1890's.

SUPER-EXPLOITATION IN INDUSTRY

The post-war years in the South, as we have indicated in Chapter 31, also witnessed the beginnings of a substantial industrial growth, based primarily upon the processing of raw materials. This was especially evident after the 1877 betrayal and the liquidation of the big economic crisis of 1873-78 when Northern capital began to penetrate the South on a rapidly increasing scale. This industrialization and the semi-slave conditions accompanying it were prominent features of the reactionary New South, which was taking shape between 1865 and 1885.

The major investment of Northern capital in the South during this period was in railroads. In 1870 all the Southern states east of the Mississippi had but 10,609 miles of railroad, whereas, by 1890, the figure had gone up to 27,655 miles. During the decade from 1880 to 1890, railroad expansion in the South was 108.6 percent against an average national increase of 86.5 percent. Northern capital also went heavily into lumber, buying up vast stretches of timber land and greatly expanding the sawmills. In the years from 1880 to 1900, the value of the output of the Southern lumber industry expanded ten times over. In this period, too, began the development of the South's rich coal and iron deposits. Birmingham started to produce steel in 1879, and by the late 1880's the South was turning out more iron than the whole nation had done before the Civil War. There was also a rapid expansion of cotton manufacturing, which laid the basis for the swift growth in the years 1880-1900—an increase from 161 mills to 400.[13] The Southern tobacco manufacturing industry also spurted ahead during these years.

The capitalists depended largely upon the Negroes to operate these new industries, with the notable exception of textile, which was a "white" industry. They were paid wages two-thirds to one-half those paid for similar work in the North. Wesley says that "In the majority of the Southern states the actual money paid to the freed Negro of 1867 was less than that which was paid to the [master of the] hired slaves of 1860."[14] Most of the skilled, better-paid jobs went to the whites, although this policy was not as fully developed as it was to become in later years. The working period ran from 60 to 84 hours per week; and, of course, the totally unorganized Negro workers had absolutely nothing to say about fixing the wages they got or the conditions under which they worked. The South was indeed a paradise for the exploiters of labor.

Of the many semi-feudal methods of exploiting Southern labor, especially the Negroes, one of the worst was the contracting out of prisoners. Workers would be arrested for trivial offenses (real or imagined), given long sentences, and then hired out to employers, to be exploited at will. Woodward remarks that "The system quickly became a large-scale and sinister business. Leases of ten, twenty, and thirty years were granted by legislatures to powerful politicians, Northern syndicates, mining corporations, and individual planters.... The degradation and brutality produced by this system would be incredible but for the amount of evidence from official sources. . . . For the Southern convict-lease system a modern scholar can 'find parallel only in the persecutions of the Middle Ages or in the prison camps of Nazi Germany.' "[15] Du Bois declares that "Hundreds of Southern fortunes have been amassed by this enslavement of criminals."[16]

POLITICAL TERRORISM

The capitalists and planters in the New South enforced their barbarous system of exploitation by a network of terroristic measures. These also hit the white workers, but the brunt of them, as usual, fell upon the Negroes. Bert correctly states that "the sharecropping system was fastened on the Negro people by terror and massacre."[17] The same was essentially true of the other savage methods of exploitation widely employed all over the South.

One of the most deadly forms of terrorism was the night riders. The Ku Klux Klan was officially dissolved in the 1870's, but this was only a pretense. Actually, this terroristic organization under various names went right on intimidating and killing Negro agricultural workers and sharecroppers. Appeals to the law against such murder gangs only brought more vicious attacks upon those who dared to protest. Such night-riding gangs of assassins have always been a basic feature of the reactionary South from the days of the night patrols in slavery times down to the present. They are closely related to the lynch mobs that have played such an atrocious part in the South. Until 1885, no reliable statistics were kept on the number of Negroes who were lynched, but even during the earliest post-war period this savagery was highly developed.

A major objective of the exploiters in the counter-revolutionary New South was to rob the Negroes of their newly won right to vote. Usually this was done by sheer terrorism—the Negroes who dared to go to the polls did so at the risk of a severe beating, if not at the cost of their lives. Besides, all sorts of trickery were used to disfranchise them. Buck paints this picture of the period: "Polling places were set up at points remote from colored communities. Ferries between the black districts and the voting booths went 'out of repair' on election day. Grim-visaged white men carrying arms sauntered through the streets or stood near the polling booths. In districts where the blacks greatly outnumbered the whites, election officials permitted members of the superior race to 'stuff the ballot box,' and manipulated the count without fear of censure. Fantastic gerrymanders were devised to nullify Negro strength. The payment of poll taxes . . . was made a requirement for voting. Some states confused the ignorant by enacting multiple ballot box laws which required the voter to place correctly his votes for various candidates in eight or more separate boxes. The bolder members of the colored race met threats of violence and . . . physical punishment. When the black man succeeded in passing through this maze of restrictions and cast his vote there was no assurance that it would be counted."[18] It was not, however, until a somewhat later period, a decade afterward, that the Southern states began to disfranchise the Negroes formally by law.

Despite these terroristic conditions, the Negro people fought desperately to keep their right to vote and met with some success. A notable example was the control of Virginia from 1879 to 1883 by a Negro-Radical coalition.[19] Aptheker says, "It will surprise many to learn that during the post-Reconstruction period—that is, from 1877 to 1901—there were 11 Negroes elected to Congress. They were: from Mississippi, Blanche K. Bruce and John R. Lynch; from South Carolina, Richard H. Cain, James H. Rainey, Robert Smalls, Thomas E. Miller, and George W. Murray; from North Carolina, James E. O'Hara, Henry P. Chatham and George H. White; from Virginia, John M. Langston." Aptheker also points out that during this terroristic period Negroes served in the House and Senate of all Southern legislatures, and that there were many Negroes holding office in Southern communities.[20] Blackburn says that in North Carolina in 1898, "there were nearly 300 Negro magistrates and, taking the state at large, there were nearly 1,000 Negroes holding office."[21] And Tindall lists as Negro members of the South Carolina legislature, from 1878 to 1900, 13 senators (Republicans) and 62 representatives (41 Republicans, 21 Democrats).[22] George H. White, who served from 1897 to 1901, was the last Negro congressman from the South from that day to this. Congress remained lily-white for a generation, until Oscar DePriest of Illinois was elected in 1928, the first Negro congressman from the North.

Women played a very important part in the struggle of the Negro people during the terrible decades of oppression following the Reconstruction period. Aptheker indicates these activities.[23] In 1878, under the leadership of Mary Jane Nelson, the Committee of Five Hundred Women was formed, and fought for the economic, political, and social equality for all Negroes, both men and women. In 1896, as an outgrowth of the many activities of Negro women, the National Association of Colored Women was organized under the leadership of Mary Church Terrell and Josephine S. Yates among others. This body, which played an important part in the formation of the Niagara Movement in 1905, still exists, the oldest, save the churches, of Negro national organizations.

THE ATTACK UPON THE NEGROES' SOCIAL RIGHTS

In the ultra-reactionary New South, the major labor exploiters—Southern planters and Northern capitalists—made a special point of stripping the Negro people of every semblance of social rights that they had won as a result of the revolution. This legalization of "white supremacy" has always been a central purpose of Southern capitalist life. During slavery times there were the slave codes, which denied the slaves the most elementary human rights. After the abolition of chattel slavery, these were succeeded by the infamous "Black Codes," written into the laws of the Southern states reconstructed during or immediately after the war, first upon the Lincoln, and then upon the Johnson plans of reorganization. These Black Codes were officially knocked out under the Reconstruction program of the Radical Republicans; but with the development of their counter-revolution, the planters and their allies successfully replaced them with the Jim

Crow system, which is only the Black Codes under another name.

The Jim Crow system, which has long remained a shocking national disgrace and an outrage to the whole civilized world, forces the Negroes into barbarous conditions of segregation and social inferiority in respect to marriage, education, residence, travel, work, hotels, theaters, etc. These barbaric regulations were written once more into the laws of the Southern states after the reactionaries took the control away from the Negro-white Radical Republican alliance. The United States Supreme Court, true to its reactionary history, helped in the Jim Crowing of the South by declaring in 1883, that the Civil Rights law of 1875 was unconstitutional.

Carl Schurz, noted German-American Republican leader, painted the following picture of the New South, which is still valid today: "Men who are honorable in their dealings with their white neighbors, will cheat a Negro without feeling a single twinge of their honor. To kill a Negro, they do not deem murder; to debauch a Negro woman, they do not think fornication; to take the property away from a Negro, they do not consider robbery . . . they still have an ingrained feeling that the blacks at large belong to the whites at large."[24]

THE WESTERN MIGRATION MOVEMENT OF 1879-80

The Negro people and their diminishing white allies fought against the encroachments of reaction in the South. In previous chapters we have described the bitter fight to keep the reconstructed state governments out of the hands of the counter-revolutionary planters and their political friends. Through their conventions, Union Leagues, and elementary trade unions, the Negro people tried to stem the adverse political tide; but it was a losing fight, especially after the Hayes sell-out of 1877. From then on, the counter-revolution picked up speed on all fronts.

The desperate situation of the Negro people in the South after 1877 caused a regrowth of migration sentiment among them. This desire to flee the South, the scene of so much misery for them, has recurred time and again in Negro history. Thus, there were the mass flight North of the slaves before and during the Civil War, the participation of numerous Negroes in the emigration schemes of the American Colonization Society, the Martin Delany migration movement during the late 1850's, the long migration in the South itself from the plantations to the cities, the numerous projects to colonize

Negroes in Canada, Cuba and in various states of the Union, and, in our own day, the Back-to-Africa movement of Marcus Garvey.

A characteristic example of Negro migration during these hard times was the Liberian movement of 1877 in South Carolina. Agitation sprang up to get Negroes to go to Liberia, away from the local hell. The old-time Negro Abolitionist and migrationist, Martin R. Delany, took a hand in it. Hundreds of families signed up to go. The Liberia Exodus Joint Stock Steamship Company was organized and the bark *Azor* was bought for $6,000. The vessel made one trip to Africa in 1878 with 206 emigrants. But the plan eventually collapsed, and the intended emigrants pointed their course toward the ever-alluring West, to Kansas.[25]

The most important example was the Negro migration to Kansas in 1879, the so-called Negro Exodus. Well known for his part in this movement was Benjamin Singleton, who had been a runaway slave. The trend took on a mass character in several Southern states. Wesley estimates that 98,000 Negroes expressed their willingness to migrate West.[26] The main emigration took place in the summer of 1879. Estimates of the actual number of migrants to Kansas vary from 6,000 to 25,000. In 1860 there were only 627 Negroes in Kansas, but in 1880 there were 43,104.[27] The migrants were known as "Exodusters." The Negroes ran into heavy difficulties in Kansas. They were met by hostile white mobs, their poor effects burned, etc. The planters in the South were alarmed at the movement, and in December 1879, the U.S. Senate held a hearing on it.[28] The movement died out after 1880.

The migration movement caused a big stir in leading Negro circles. Negro conventions in New Orleans, in April 1879, and in Nashville, in May 1879, discussed it. Northern Negro leaders were divided on the issue. Frederick Douglass took a sharp stand against the Exodus, urging the Negroes to stand firm in the South and to fight matters out there.[29]

After World War I, a later and much greater migration of Negroes from South to North was to have profound national effects on the position of the whole Negro people. Nevertheless, especially in Douglass' time, the overwhelming mass of the people remained in the New South, despite all the terrible conditions of existence, and there fought to improve their status.

34. Knights of Labor and American Federation of Labor

The American economy, freed from the fetters of chattel slavery, made tremendous progress during the period from 1860 to 1900. National wealth increased from approximately $16 billion to $88 billion. The total capital invested in industry and transportation rose from $1,111,000,000 in 1859 to $8,975,000,000 in 1899, and the value of manufactured products from $1,885,862,000 to $13,000,194,900. The monopolization of industry made tremendous strides. During the same period, the number of wage earners increased from 1,311,246 to 5,306,143.[1] In 1860 the United States was the fourth industrial power in the world; in 1894, it became the first. The South experienced a considerable, but minor measure of this industrial expansion. During the years 1880-1900 the capital invested there rose from $329,752,408 to $1,402,000,000, and the number of industrial workers from 369,000 to 983,000.[2] National agriculture also made huge output gains, with great improvement of its techniques in the process. In 1859, yearly agricultural production amounted to one billion dollars; in 1899 to $4.9 billion.[3] In 1890, non-agricultural production in the United States outstripped that of agriculture in value;[4] except in the South, which remained predominantly agricultural.

THE STATUS OF THE WORKERS AND THE NEGRO PEOPLE

The population of the United States increased from 31,513,514 in 1860 to 76,094,134 in 1900. A dozen new states came into the Union during this period. The Negro population, in the same years, rose from 4,441,830 to 8,833,994. Deducting from the total population figure the 14 million immigrants who came into the country from 1860 to 1900 and also the number of Negro inhabitants, we find that the native white population increased about 95 percent. The increase in the Negro population, despite all its hardships, amounted also to approximately 95 percent. In 1860, about 4,097,111 Negroes lived in the South (mainly working in agriculture) and 344,029 in the other states. In 1900, of a total of 8,833,994 Negroes, 911,025 (chiefly proletarians) lived in the North and West. The South, at the beginning of the century, thus remained overwhelmingly the homeland of the Negro people.

The industrial development of the United States following the Civil War brought worsened conditions in the economic status of the workers in factory and field, particularly the Negroes. The big capitalists and landowners grabbed the bulk of the new wealth created. The Rockefellers, Carnegies, Hills, Morgans, Vanderbilts, Stanfords, *et al.* built for themselves gigantic fortunes without parallel in the history of the world. But the workers toiled along at wages barely enough to keep body and soul together, in work places almost totally without safety protection, for ten to fourteen hours daily, with long periods of unemployment, and under the arbitrary dictation of employers who were totally devoid of any sense of human or social responsibility. All these adverse conditions bore down with double severity upon the Negroes, the oppressed of the oppressed.

Statistics on living standards of the workers during this period have little value, since they are very sketchy as well as "doctored" to show conditions more favorable than they actually were. During the so-called "good times" of these 40 years, the bulk of the workers lived in poverty. Samuel Gompers said of the "prosperous" year of 1883, that "the wage of workingmen is less now than it was in 1870."[5] The slums of New York and other big cities were the worst in the Western world. In the periods of economic crisis, the condition of the workers—who were totally without social insurance, beggared description. Vast masses of the unemployed roamed the country homeless, or eked out a miserable existence on bread lines in the cities. Conditions were especially desperate during the severe economic crises of 1873-78 and 1893-96. Worst of all were the conditions of Negro workers, who got the lowest wages and were the first to lose their jobs.

NEGRO AND WHITE WORKERS

During the period from the end of the Civil War to 1900, the workers fought a desperate battle against pauperization and carried on some of the hardest strikes and other struggles in the history of the

American labor movement. Among others were the "long strike" of the coal miners in 1875, the national railroad strike in 1877, the national eight-hour-day strike in 1886, the historic Homestead steel strike in 1892, the bitter strikes of the western metal miners (led by William D. Haywood and Vincent St. John) in the 1890's, the great strike of soft coal miners in 1893, Debs' American Railway Union strike in 1894, and the famous Coxey's army march of the unemployed to Washington in 1894.

Inevitably the Negro worker, especially in the North, found himself involved in this maelstrom of class struggle. In the railroad, coal, and other strikes of these crucial decades, the Negro played an important part. Briefly stated, the employers' program for him was to bar him from the more skilled trades, to pay him less wages than whites for equal work, to use his lower wage rates to batter down the higher wage scales of the whites, to keep him out of the unions, to employ him as a strikebreaker, and to utilize him generally to break the unity of the workers and weaken their organized strength.

In harmony with true working class interests, the proletarian trend of the Negro industrial worker, however, was to fight against these reactionary policies, to strike up unity with the white workers in the trade unions, and to hold up his end in the class struggle. This was his line in his pioneer organization—The Colored National Labor Union and in general during succeeding decades. Unfortunately, however, there were white chauvinist prejudices among the white workers and their leaders to bar the Negro from the unions, to keep him out of the skilled trades, and to force him into the role of strikebreaker if he wanted to work in industry—all of which errors dovetailed neatly with the employers' plans for the Negro in industry. Early American labor history is replete with the tragic experience of white workers striking to bar Negroes from skilled jobs and unions. Wesley lists 50 such strikes against Negro workers between 1882 and 1900.[6] On more than one occasion white workers also broke the strikes of Negro workers.

THE NEGRO WORKERS AND THE KNIGHTS OF LABOR

The National Labor Union, as we saw in Chapter 32, made a considerable effort to fight against the employer-cultivated Negro-white split in the trade union movement, but with only limited success. The N.L.U. was succeeded by the Knights of Labor, which was formed in

Philadelphia, in December 1869, by a handful of garment workers. It began to expand in 1871, and by 1877 it had 15 state and district assemblies. It extended into Canada. In 1886, at its peak, the K. of L. had some 600,000 members, making it then the largest labor organization in the world. After that date it declined, however, and by the mid 1890's it was virtually extinct. The founder of this very important labor organization was Uriah S. Stephens, an old-time Abolitionist and cofighter with Frederick Douglass and William Lloyd Garrison.

The K. of L., like the N.L.U. before it, aimed at uniting not merely a fringe of skilled crafts, but the whole working class. It proposed to organize all workers without regard to race, sex, or craft. The organization, stating that "labor created all value," proposed as its goal "to establish cooperative institutions such as will tend to supersede the wage system by the introduction of a cooperative industrial system." Its motto was, "An Injury to One Is the Concern of All." Its organization was based upon local mixed assemblies of various crafts, and also district and national assemblies. In some cases, the latter bodies took on much of the shape of national industrial unions. The organization had an elaborate ritual, and until 1878 it was a secret body. This practice of secrecy—to escape the bitter anti-union persecution of the times—was adopted by many other young trade unions.

Marxist Socialists played an important part in the Knights of Labor and they were the source of many of its progressive policies and much of its record of militant struggle. They were especially responsible for the order's friendly attitude toward Negro workers. A number of K. of L. leaders were Socialists. Even Terence V. Powderly, Grand Master Workman from 1879 to 1893 and ultimately very conservative, once belonged to the Socialist Labor Party. Also influential in the K. of L. were the Lassalleans, whose base was chiefly among the German workers. They were an off-shoot of the General Association of German Workers, founded by Ferdinand Lassalle in Germany in 1863. Pseudo-Socialists, they put forward state-subsidized workers' co-operatives as their goal. They condemned trade unions as useless and concentrated on opportunist electoral action; they were the originators of various harmful tendencies in the K. of L.

The K. of L. paid much attention to the organization of Negro workers. But it never adopted a solid policy of seeing to it that Negroes had the full right to work in all industries and crafts—the heart of the industrial question for Negro workers. Nor did the organization have any kind of constructive program for the Klan-terrorized South. Nevertheless, it generally welcomed Negro workers and many of them held official posts. At the height of the order's strength, in 1886, it had an estimated 60,000 to 90,000 Negroes in its ranks. Not until this day has the A.F. of L. achieved such a high percentage of Negro members. Moreover, ten percent of the members of the K. of L. were women.

Negro workers enthusiastically joined the K. of L., especially in the terror-ridden South of the post-Reconstruction period. Frederick Douglass and some other prominent Negro leaders, however, did not share this pro-trade union position. But the Negro press, hitherto distrustful, generally urged Negro workers to join the order. The national official organ of the Knights highly praised the Negroes as union members, saying: "The testimony is that for fidelity to their obligations, strict attendance in all meetings, prompt payment of dues, good conduct, and all that goes to make good members and good citizens, they are not excelled by any other class of man of the Order."[7]

Wesley reports labor parades in New Orleans in 1883, 1884, and 1885, in which white and Negro workers marched together, and he says that there were seven assemblies in Richmond, Virginia.[8] In a detailed study of the matter, Foner tells of many Negro-white organizations and activities of the K. of L. in the South. In Louisville, Kentucky, over 6,000 Negroes and whites marched in a parade; in Baltimore, Maryland, in 1886, 25,000 Negroes and whites marched; and in Dallas, Texas, a similar parade took place, with two Negroes addressing the throng. A local paper remarked, "This is the first time such a thing has happened in Texas."[9] Throughout the North, Negroes also played an important role in the K. of L. local and district assemblies—there were an estimated 3,000 Negroes in the New York local organization.

The policy of the K. of L., as stated by Powderly, its chief leader, was to organize Negroes and whites either in single unions or separately, as the local workers decided. Foner remarks "that both forms of organization prevailed widely. There were mixed local assemblies, not only in the North, but also in many Southern states. It was reported in 1885 that there were hundreds of colored assemblies in the South."[10] In the South, however, the white workers frequently excluded Negroes, a practice which the K. of L. leaders could not, or at least did not, eradicate. There were a number of paid Negro organizers in the field.

An interesting example of the role of the Negro in the K. of L. occurred at the meeting of the General Assembly (national convention) of the order in October 1886. The convention was held in Richmond, Virginia, obviously to stress the importance of organizing the South. There were a number of Negro delegates (an estimated 18), among them Frank J. Ferrell of the famous left-wing District Assembly No. 49 of New York City. The hotel at which the delegates were stopping attempted to Jim Crow Ferrell, whereupon the whole delegation moved to another place. A theater which discriminated against Negro delegates was boycotted. Then, in the face of threatened lynch mob violence, the convention decided to have Ferrell introduce Governor Fitzhugh Lee, a notorious Negro-baiter, who was slated to speak. This was a bit too daring for the conservative Powderly and he managed to wangle through a "compromise," by which Ferrell would introduce him and then he would introduce the governor—and this plan was followed. Under pressure of the local white chauvinist clamor, Powderly wrote a weasel-worded article in the Richmond *Dispatch,* assuring the local reactionaries that "No labor advocate seeks to interfere with the social relations of the races in the South, for it is the industrial, not the race question, we endeavor to solve."[11]

Despite the white chauvinist attitude of many of its officials, the Knights of Labor represented the highest stage of Negro-white unity yet achieved by the workers, as well as the most effective stand of the working class against the offensive of the employers. The organization began to decline after 1886 from a variety of causes. Among these were the destructive influence of the large influx of non-working class elements—farmers, professionals, etc.—who came into the order; tendencies of the leadership to play down and even betray strikes and other militant working class actions; trends toward purely opportunist political activities; disruptive activities by Most and other anarchists, and involvement of the organization in the prevailing "cheap money" quackeries. Especially destructive was the hostility of the rival national craft unions, which were strongly opposed to the organization form of the order. By 1895, after 10 years of its greatest activity, the K. of L. was no longer the key labor organization of the working class.

THE AMERICAN FEDERATION OF LABOR

The A.F. of L. was formed in Pittsburgh, Pennsylvania, on November 15, 1881. One hundred seven delegates attended the convention, about 60 from organizations of the Knights of Labor and 40 from six independent national trade unions. The new national center was called the Federation of Organized Trades and Labor Unions of the United States of America and Canada. Leading among its founders were Adolph Strasser, Samuel Gompers, Peter J. McGuire, and Frank K. Foster, all members of the K. of L. At the second convention Gompers became president of the A.F. of L., a position which he held continuously, except for the year 1894-95, until he died on December 13, 1924, 42 years later. Gompers was an immigrant Jewish cigar-maker, born in London. In December 1886, at its convention in Columbus, Ohio, the organization changed its name to the American Federation of Labor.[12]

The A.F. of L. was based upon craft unionism, as opposed to the mixed mass organization of the K. of L. It represented the coming together of the national craft unions, which had been gradually organizing themselves since the 1850's. At first there was no apparent clash between the two national organizations, but by 1886 they were at loggerheads. In its early years the A.F. of L. was a militant organization, and it outmaneuvered the K. of L. by taking over the leadership of the successful national eight-hour-day strike of 350,000 workers in 1886. This strike had been called by the K. of L. and then abandoned by its leader, Powderly. From this time on, the A.F. of L. was in the ascendant and the K. of L. in decline.

The advent of the A.F. of L. greatly worsened the attitude of organized labor toward the Negro worker. The National Labor Union and the Knights of Labor, being broad class organizations and aiming at the unionization of the whole body of the workers, had taken the position that the Negro workers had to be organized. But the American Federation of Labor, although in its earlier stages it showed some solidarity with Negroes in industry, generally cultivated the interests of individual skilled or semi-skilled crafts, and ignored and even worked against the organization of Negro workers. Traditionally, the unions of skilled workers in the main opposed Negroes entering or working in the crafts; hence they also barred them, in practice or by constitutional provisions, from joining the unions. This was the policy of many pioneer national trade unions—the Sons of Vulcan (Blacksmiths), the Typographical Union, the Railroad Brotherhoods, the Bricklayers, Carpenters, and others. Despite exceptions in the case of some of their unions, the N.L.U. and K. of L., as essentially class organizations, stressed the solidarity of all workers, including the Negroes. Despite contrary policies by many of its affiliates, the A.F. of L., based upon craft organization, put the accent upon white chauvinsm and the exclusion of the Negro from the skilled trades and the labor movement.

The A.F. of L. has always claimed to represent the whole working class; in reality, however, it has cultivated the interests of the labor aristocracy at the expense of the great mass of the workers. For many years it crassly ignored and sabotaged the interests of women workers, the youth, the unskilled, the foreign-born, and above all, the Negro workers. The crafts even betrayed each other upon numberless occasions; over the years hundreds of strikes have been lost because one group of craft unions in a given industry remained at work while the others were on strike.

These divisive craft policies, especially with regard to Negro workers, played right into the hands of the employers. They constituted the great tragedy of the labor movement for half a century, down to the birth of the C.I.O. in 1935. It cannot be assumed that these policies of betrayal were merely incidental to the cultivation of craft interests by the union leaders and were unwanted by them. On the contrary, the Gompersite leaders were cunning enough to know what they were doing. They constituted the most corrupt leadership in the history of world trade unionism, great numbers of them being barefaced crooks. They sold "strike insurance," robbed union treasuries, allied themselves with the underworld, took money from corrupt politicians, and made agreements with the bosses to keep the unskilled out of the unions. In line with this corruption, they also deliberately and knowingly sold out the interests of Negro workers (along with those of the women, youth, foreign-born, and unskilled) for such advantages as they could wangle for themselves and, secondarily, for their crafts. They were precisely what De Leon called them, "labor lieutenants of capital in the ranks of the working class," and they committed their working class treason consciously.

DEVELOPMENT OF THE ANTI-NEGRO POLICY OF THE A.F. OF L.

In its early years the A.F. of L., in the tradition of the N.L.U. and K. of L. and under the pressure of the Socialists in its ranks, was not altogether unfriendly toward the Negro. Its leaders called for the organization of all workers, regardless of "creed, color, sex, race, or nationality." A number of its unions, notably the miners and long-shoremen, accepted Negroes as full members. As an illustration of the prevailing early spirit, in Birmingham, Alabama, in 1885, says Wesley, "the delegates refused to take part in a banquet because there were three Negro delegates who had not been invited. . . . In the same year the Cigar Makers International Union left a hotel because the Treasurer, who was a Negro, was given a place for his meals outside of the regular dining room."[13] The A.F. of L. also refused to admit the International Association of Machinists, organized in 1888, because it drew the color line in its constitution.

But with the passage of the years and the growth of monopoly capitalist pressures, and the increasing corruption of its leadership, the A.F. of L. gradually gave up its early tolerant attitude toward Negroes. Many of its affiliated national unions either wrote anti-Negro clauses into their constitutions or followed, in reality, the nefarious practice of keeping Negroes out of skilled positions and barring them from the unions. The original ban of the A.F. of L. against Jim Crow unions fell into abeyance, and in its 1900 convention the Federation bowed to the white supremacists by endorsing a plan to organize Negroes into separate organizations. In effect, this action meant abandoning the Negro workers.

The independent railroad unions of engineers, firemen, conductors, brakemen, and switchmen all became Jim Crow in their policies toward Negro workers. Even the militant American Railway Union, headed by Eugene V. Debs, adopted a lily-white membership clause in its constitution, reading: "Any white person of good character employed in the railway service is eligible to membership."[14]

The A.F. of L., for purposes of the record, continued to express its desire to organize the Negro workers in industry.[15] But it never made serious efforts to do so. This was clearly illustrated by a study of the status of Negro trade unionists, made by Professor W. E. B. Du Bois at Atlanta University in 1902. The figures, not fully complete, show a total of 32,400 Negro members or less than three percent of the total A.F. of L. membership of one million at the time. Compare this with the 10 to 15 percent of Negroes in the K. of L. 15 years earlier. The United Mine Workers had 20,000 of the Negro A.F. of L. workers, the International Longshoremen's Association had 6,000, and 1,000 were members of the Brotherhood of Carpenters and Join-ers.[16] This bad situation was not even partially overcome for many decades; indeed, it tended to grow worse for a long time, as we shall see in later chapters.

Although he made an elaborate pretense of cooperation with the Negro workers, in reality Samuel Gompers furthered white chauvinst tendencies in the Federation. In 1910, when accused of weeding the Negro out of the labor movement, he replied by stating that, because the Negroes were only half a century out of slavery, "It could not be expected that, as a rule, they would have the same conception of their rights and duties as other men of labor have in America."[17] This white chauvinst insult to Negro workers was indeed a far cry from the high praise bestowed upon them earlier as unionists by the leaders of the N.L.U. and K. of L. In his later years, Gompers wrote a fat two-volume autobiography; but, characteristically, he did not find it necessary to make even the most cursory examination of the bitter hardships and problems of Negro workers.

The anti-Negro policy of the white labor aristocrats in the A.F. of L. not only resulted in a great injustice against the Negro workers, but it also worked serious harm to the whole labor movement. It gave aid and comfort to the Ku Klux Klan terrorists in the South. It also played into the hands of the employers who were striving to isolate the Negroes as a body of workers, in order to subject them to super-exploitation and to use them as an instrument for beating down the wages of all workers and splitting the working class in economic and political struggle.

By refusing the Negroes access to skilled jobs in industry and to membership in the unions, the white chauvinist leaders of the A.F. of L. thereby drove a wedge between the labor movement and the Negro people. It tended to force Negro workers (and Negro intellectuals) to the conclusion that if they wanted skilled work (any work in fact) in industry, their only way to get it was by acting as strikebreakers, as the employers wanted them to do. And in fact, this sometimes happened, both in these early days of the labor movement and in later years, although labor records of this period contain many examples of Negro workers striking side by side with whites.[18] In line with the almost universal attempts of conservative writers to slander the Negro people, the matter of Negro strikebreaking, however, has been grossly overstated. The fact is that for every Negro who took a striker's job there were dozens of white strikebreakers. Often the latter were union men turned into scabs because of the treacherous policies of the Gompersite misleadership.

THE DEATH OF FREDERICK DOUGLASS

In 1895, the Negro people were saddened by the death of their greatest leader, Frederick Douglass. He died of heart failure on February 20th, at his home in Cedar Hill, near Washington. He was 78 years of age. Apparently in good health, Douglass had spoken at a meeting of the National Council of Women for woman's rights and suffrage: but upon his return home he collapsed and died without recovering consciousness.

Douglass' passing evoked widespread expressions of condolence and appreciation of his life's work. All over the country the Negro people mourned him. The legislature of North Carolina adjourned in his honor, and the legislatures of Indiana, Illinois, Massachusetts, and New York adopted resolutions of respect. Telegrams of sympathy poured in from many parts of the world. America had lost one of its greatest leaders and revolutionary fighters.

From 1877 on, after the Hayes betrayal of the Negro people, Douglass' work was mostly agitational. His powerful voice and matchless eloquence were in constant protest against the outrages perpetrated upon his people. Devoted to the once revolutionary Republican Party, Douglass failed to understand the Negroes' role in the growing trade unions and in the new political movements of the times—Socialist and labor parties, the Populist Party, etc. He failed also to realize that the Negro people had come to face a much more powerful and malignant enemy than even the cotton planters—namely, American monopoly capitalism and imperialism, the chief political expression of which was the Republican Party. Douglass' greatest achievements came in organizing the pre-war Abolitionist struggle, in helping to win the Civil War, and in the fight of the Reconstruction period. During those 25 years of tremendous revolutionary struggle, Douglass wrote his name high and imperishably upon the scroll of American history.

35. The Negro and the
Populist Movement

During the years following the Civil War capitalist industry expanded rapidly and consolidated into trusts. Here was monopoly capitalism—American imperialism—in the making. This development confronted the workers, and farmers, and most of all, the Negroes with many new hardships and urgent problems. For the workers generally it meant intensified exploitation in work places devoid of health and accident provisions, low wages and long hours, and ruthless subordination to the dictation of the employers. For the small farmers, Negro and white, it meant robbery through excessive railroad rates, high prices for everything they had to buy and low prices for what they had to sell, usurious interest rates on mortgages, and a quick growth of tenancy. In 1880, 25 percent of the land nationally was cultivated by tenants; and by 1900, the percentage had risen to 35.[1]

In these decades the toilers of factory and farm militantly resisted this stepped-up capitalist exploitation and oppression. As we have seen in the previous chapters, the workers' main fight was along trade union lines. It resulted in many bitter strikes and the successive formation of the National Labor Union, the Colored National Labor Union, the Knights of Labor, and the American Federation of Labor. The workers were not yet fully caught in the trap of the two-party system, and they organized many local labor parties and independent political movements. Among these may be noted the campaign of Henry George for mayor of New York in 1886. There were similar movements in Pennsylvania, Wisconsin, and elsewhere.

Although in the main the Negroes still supported the Republican Party, many of them took a vigorous part in these movements in Northern cities. For example, a workers' convention of 400 delegates in Chicago nominated William Bruce, a Negro barber, who polled 28,000 votes for the legislature.[2] In the South, as described in previous chapters, the Negroes were also active in progressive political movements, in alliance with the Radical Republicans.

THE GRANGER AND GREENBACK MOVEMENTS

The main resistance of the small farmers during these decades was essentially political. It produced such national movements as the Grangers, the Greenbackers, and the Populists in the 1870's, 1880's, and 1890's. The organized workers gave substantial support to these basically farmers' movements, and Negro farmers played a considerable part in some of them.

The Granger movement was based upon the Patrons of Husbandry, founded in 1867. It grew rapidly during the 1873 economic crisis and reached its peak in 1875, after which it quickly disintegrated. The movement won a majority in several state legislatures in the Middle West. It was instrumental in setting maximum rates for railroads and in generally advancing the plan of government control of the railroads. The Grangers also gave a big stimulus to farmers' cooperatives. Centered in the Middle West, this movement had only minor repercussions in the South, when the Negroes played some role in it.

The much bigger Greenback movement was largely an outgrowth of the Grangers. It was organized into a party in 1875 and put up Peter Cooper as its candidate for president in 1876. The main stress of the party was upon a large printing of paper money—hence the name Greenback. The farmers vainly believed that cheap money would relieve them of their heavy debt burdens. Cooper polled 81,737 votes. In 1878 many local labor parties and trade unions allied themselves with the farmers and helped establish the National Greenback Labor Party. This party, which included labor demands in its program, polled 1,050,000 votes in the Congressional elections of 1878 and sent 15 members to Congress. In 1880, the party nominated General J. B. Weaver for president, but disintegration had set in within the organization and he polled but 300,000 votes. This low vote killed the party, but the Grange continued on.

Although mainly a movement of Middle Western farmers, the Greenback-Labor Party had considerable strength in the South. It had an important following in Alabama, Arkansas, North Carolina, and Mississippi, and in Kentucky it was strong enough to "give the Democrats a scare." In Texas, where the party claimed to have 482 Greenback clubs, it polled 55,000 votes for governor in 1878, and elected 10 state legislators and one congressman.[3] Negro voters were a considerable factor in these Southern movements, and they participated to some extent in the Greenback movement in the North. In the main, however, Negro voters supported their wartime ally, the Republican Party.

THE NATIONAL FARMERS ALLIANCE

By far the most important in this succession of farmer-labor movements was the People's Party, or the Populist movement, which ran its main course during the 1880's and 1890's. It grew out of the Farmers Alliances, which sprang up all over the country. These were to be found in New York, Wisconsin, Kansas, Texas, Louisiana, and many other states. According to Anna Rochester "These organizations grew until they included more than half of the farmers in the entire country."[4] Known by various names in the several parts of the United States, the state Alliances gradually crystallized into two general groups, North and South—called respectively the Northern Alliance and the Southern Alliance. The latter was the strongest section of the entire Alliance movement. Together with its affiliate, the Colored Farmers National Alliance and Cooperative Union, it numbered at its peak about three million members, of which some 1,250,000 were in the Negro organization.

The Southern Farmers Alliance (white) had its earliest beginnings about 1875 in Texas. It arose out of the struggle of the frontier farmers against foreign-owned land syndicates and the cattle kings.[5] It led a precarious existence during the next decade; but in the middle eighties, under the leadership of Dr. C. W. Macune, it began to grow. Organizers were sent to Alabama, Mississippi, Tennessee, Arkansas, Florida, the Carolinas, Kentucky, and Missouri. Many local farmers' organizations joined, notably the Agricultural Wheel of Arkansas, which had branches in various Southern states. The Southern Alliance, with branches all over the South, opened up national headquarters in Washington and issued its official journal, *The National Economist,* in March 1889. "In 1891 the Southern Alliance was reputed to have in the field 35,000 official lecturers."[6] It had 195 local papers.

The Southern Alliance admitted to membership small farmers, farm laborers, country mechanics, school teachers, doctors, preachers, and editors of agricultural papers. It explicitly excluded bankers, railroad officials, lawyers, real estate dealers, cotton buyers, storekeepers, and, usually, big landowners. The bulk of its members were small farmers in the upland areas. In its constitution it drew the color line against Negroes, restricting its membership to whites. Everywhere it developed friendly co-operative relations with the local trade union movement.

Meanwhile, in the West and North, the Farmers Alliance movement was also growing and consolidating itself. In October 1880, a Farmers Transportation Conference was held in Chicago, with several hundred delegates. "Shortly afterwards several state Alliances were organized, including Texas, New York, Illinois, Michigan, Wisconsin, Minnesota, Iowa, and Kansas. By 1882 a National Farmers Alliance, based on these Northern state organizations, could claim some 2,000 local groups, with a total membership of 100,000 farmers."[7] By 1890, the Alliance movement in the North and West counted up to a million members. The Northern Alliance, unlike the secret, white supremacist Southern Alliance, maintained an open organization and freely admitted Negroes to membership. The two organizations grew up largely distinct from each other. Negroes were active in the Populist movement in Kansas especially.

THE COLORED NATIONAL FARMERS ALLIANCE

From the outset, the Southern planters looked with hatred and alarm upon the growth of the Southern Farmers Alliance. They saw in it not only a challenge to their despotic rule; but they dreaded that despite the Alliance's lily-white clause, it would lead to common political action between the poorer white farmers and sharecroppers and the Negroes. Nor were their fears without basis; for the Alliance leaders in the South were quick to understand that they could accomplish nothing politically without the election support of the Negroes. Therefore, they definitely favored Negro-white co-operation on the political field. The misfortune was that this general conception could not have prevailed among these whites during the Reconstruction years, when the Negroes and their Republican allies were fighting so desperately to build some elements of democracy in the South. But the common action that the main body of small white farmers had refused to take then, they were now ready for under the heavy pressure of the rapacious landowners, the railroads, and other oppressive trusts. Therefore, the white Southern Alliance favored and helped organize the Negro farmers and farm workers, seeking as best it could, however, to control the Negro organization.

The Colored National Farmers Alliance and Cooperative Union was launched in Houston, Texas, in December 1886. It at once won wide support from among the Negro agricultural masses. Hicks says, "Members poured into the Colored Alliance in prodigious numbers."[8] In 1888, the national organization was formed, and by 1891, says Hicks, it had 1,250,000 members, including 300,000 women and 150,-000 youths. By this time there were members in all the Southern states and 11 state organizations had been chartered. The organization headquarters was in Galveston, Texas.

The specified purpose of the Alliance was "To elevate the colored people of the United States, by teaching them to love their country and their homes; to care more earnestly for the helpless and sick and destitute; to labor more earnestly in agricultural pursuits; to become better farmers and laborers, and less wasteful in their method of living; to be more obedient to the civil law; to become better citizens, and truer husbands and wives."[9] Presumably this conservative moralistic statement of principles, which jibed ill with the militant activities of the organization, was written by its white founder and "Superintendent," the Reverend R. M. Humphrey, a Baptist preacher from Texas.

Those whose business it is to belittle the Negro people picture the Colored Farmers National Alliance as having been a passive tool of the white organization. Actually the Alliance possessed much of the militancy of the Union Leagues of the Reconstruction period. Woodward significantly remarks that "there is considerable evidence of independence among the Negroes."[10] And Abramowitz says that, "Contrary to the general assumption that the Colored Alliance was a mere appendage of the Southern Alliance, there were serious differences between the two organizations, particularly over the issue of the Lodge Bill or Force Bill as it was known in the South."[11] One of the many other manifestations of the independent spirit of the Negro organization was its calling of a cotton-pickers' strike for a wage increase throughout the South in 1891. This movement, however, was broken by Colonel Leonidas L. Polk, president of the Southern (white) Alliance, who condemned it as "one section of the organization striking against another."[12]

The Negro press, North as well as South, took a lively interest in Populism, generally endorsing the movement. The rising young Negro leader, W. E. B. Du Bois, favored the movement. Among the outstanding Negro leaders in the Colored National Farmers Alliance and the Populist movement were: Norris Wright Cuney, J. B. Gaynor, Henry Jenkins, and Henry Jennings of Texas; E. A. Richardson, Anthony Wilson, and Anton Graves of Georgia; W. A. Grant, of South Carolina; George C. White of North Carolina; William Warwick of Virginia; and Benjamin F. Foster of Kansas.[13] These men worked in peril of their lives, developing Negro-white political co-operation in this vital movement, in the face of the reigning terror of the monopolists and planters during the 1890's.

NEGRO AND WHITE COOPERATION

During the years of its greatest activities the Southern Farmers Alliance developed very considerable political co-operation between its white and Negro supporters. This existed all over the South, and has never been equalled until this day. In the main, the Alliance developed no specific program for Negroes, on the assumption that their basic demands were met by its general farmer program for regulation of railroad rates, building farmers' co-operatives, cheap money, decreases in taxes, government ownership of the means of transportation, etc. Nevertheless, especially in its practice, the white Alliance was a distinct force in defense of Negro rights. Indeed, many of the leaders of the Alliance, although definitely white chauvinist in their outlook, had to express some spirit of co-operation. During many generations of bitter exploitation and oppression, the Negroes developed justifiable suspicions of all whites; nevertheless, as experience shows, they were always ready to extend the hand of friendship to those whites willing to fight side-by-side with them for joint objectives.

Thomas E. Watson of North Carolina, prominent Alliance leader, said (in his constructive days), "The accident of color can make no difference in the interests of farmers, croppers, and laborers."[14] Ben Tillman of Georgia declared for Negro-white co-operation, and in tune with the general trend of the Populist movement, the 1892 platform of the People's Party of Alabama declared. "We favor the protection of the colored race in their legal rights and should afford them encouragement and aid in the attainment of a higher civilization and citizenship."[15]

The very nature of the policy of the Southern Alliance, to win its demands through political action, involved a measure of defense of the Negroes' right to vote. In the post-Reconstruction period this right was, as will be recalled, under very heavy attack from the Klan elements, organized by the big planters and their Northern industrialist allies. Something of the situation in this respect was illustrated by the attitude of Colonel A. M. Waddell, who declared, "You're an Anglo-Saxon. . . . Go to the polls tomorrow and if you find the Negro voting tell him to leave the polls and if he refuses, kill him, shoot him down in his tracks."[16]

On the question of other rights of the Negroes, Woodward remarks, "In their platforms Southern Populists denounced lynch law and the convict-lease and called for the defense of the Negro's political rights. Populist officers saw to it that Negroes received such recognition as summons for jury service which they had long been denied. . . . Picnics, barbecues, and camp meetings were arranged for black Populists, and both races were welcome at party rallies and speeches, blacks to one side, whites to the other. One of the most effective Negro Populists was J. B. Gaynor of Calvert, Texas, a man of commanding ability and energy, who renounced Republicanism and with a corps of Negro assistants, set out to convert his people to Populism."[17] Southern Alliance influence was a positive force against lynching during this period.

An important phase of the Negro-white co-operation in the Southern Alliance was a certain recognition of the rights of Negroes to political representation—a thing foreign to the conception of the barbarous ruling class in the South. Something of the new spirit was expressed by the chairman of the first Populist convention in Texas, in 1891, when he said: "I am in favor of giving the colored man full representation. He is a citizen just as much as we are, and the party that acts on that fact will gain the colored vote of the South." The convention elected two Negroes to the State Executive Committee of the party.

Woodward remarks on this new solidarity: "Populists of other Southern states followed the example of Texas, electing Negroes to their Councils and giving them a voice in the party organization. Negroes were also elected as delegates to the National Conventions of the party. At the St. Louis convention in February, 1892, William Warwick, a colored delegate from Virginia, was placed in nomination for the assistant secretary of the body. A white delegate from Georgia moved that the nomination be made unanimous, adding: 'I wish to say that we can stand that down in Georgia.' The question was put, and there was 'a great aye' from the delegates, including over two hundred Southern whites—one 'no' from an Alabama delegate."[18]

At the important national convention of the Alliance, held in Ocalo, Florida, in December 1890, Negro delegates were present from all over the South, representing the Colored National Farmers Alliance, which held a convention simultaneously. Also during the unsuccessful conferences to amalgamate the Southern and Northern Alliances in St. Louis, in December 1889, the Southerners, in the name of unity, agreed to strike the word "white" from their constitution and also to seat Negroes in the Supreme Council of the new organization.[19] In January 1891, in Washington, Negro delegates from the Colored National Farmers Alliance sat in conference with the Knights of Labor, the Farmers Mutual Benefit Association, and other organizations, and formed the Confederation of Industrial Organizations.[20] And at the St. Louis Conference of 1892, Negro delegates were allowed 97 seats out of a total of 702. In many cases, too, Populists supported Negro candidates in elections. These Negro-white co-operative movements among the Alliance men and Populists were inadequate; but at least they demonstrated the feasibility of such working together by the two forces. They were miles ahead of the chauvinist, exclusionist policies in effect half a century later in many Northern Gompers-minded trade unions.

STATE VICTORIES OF THE ALLIANCES

In the Middle West, during the 1880's, the Alliance movement made real headway and scored many local victories. Altogether it was a period of active farmer-labor discontent. It was also the time of Edward Bellamy's *Looking Backward* and Henry George's *Progress and Poverty*. It was the period of the great national eight-hour strike in 1886, and of the legal murder of the Haymarket victims in Chicago as a result of that historic strike. Labor parties and farmer parties sprang up; and in 1887, in Cincinnati, a National Union Labor Party (mainly a farmers' party) was organized, which put up a national presidential ticket for the 1888 elections. In most of the states the Alliance worked closely with the Knights of Labor and local A. F. of L. unions.

In the elections of 1890 the Northern Alliance scored many state victories. Alliance men controlled both houses in Nebraska, and their majority in the lower house in Kansas was large enough to control a joint session of the legislature. Two Alliance senators were sent to

Washington, one from Kansas and one from South Dakota. Eight congressmen went from Kansas, Nebraska, and Minnesota. Big Alliance votes were registered in nearly all Middle West states.[21]

In the South, the Alliance men, in its early stages, worked almost exclusively through the Democratic Party, in many places nominating and electing Democratic candidates. Thus they won sweeping victories in the 1880 elections. South Carolina elected Ben Tillman governor and sent J. L. McIrby to the Senate. Georgia made a sweep of the state offices and elected Tom Watson to Congress. Texas and Tennessee elected pro-Alliance governors. In nearly all the other Southern states large blocs of delegates were elected to the state legislatures. Of the 332 congressmen elected nationally, some 50 were either Alliance men or friendly to the Alliance. Negroes were a decisive factor in all the Southern elections, and their work was carried on in the face of much physical violence and a ferocious campaign for "white supremacy."

Three of the most outstanding Alliance figures in the South were Governor (later, Senator) Benjamin R. Tillman of South Carolina, Governor James S. Hogg of Texas, and Representative (later Senator) Thomas E. Watson of Georgia. They based their activities principally upon the small white farmers and the Negroes. In the early upswing of the Alliance movement, they scoffed at the bogey of "white supremacy," made fiery attacks on the big planters, and expressed solidarity with the oppressed Negro masses. Unstable petty bourgeois elements, however, they all wound up as the most vicious of Negro baiters.[22] They were incapable of supporting the unity of the white workers and farmers and Negro people. "Pitchfork" Tillman, a rabid white chauvinist, later declared, "The whites have absolute control of the government and we intend at any hazard to maintain it."[23] And for years Watson yelled about "the *hideous, ominous, national menace* of Negro domination."[24]

THE PEOPLE'S PARTY

The great national united front of farmers, workers, and city middle classes—in which the Colored National Farmers Alliance was a prominent factor—crystallized into the People's Party, in St. Louis, February 22, 1892. In the early stages of the Alliance movement in the South, the Negroes generally supported the Republican Party while the whites worked through the Democratic Party. Later on, disillusioned with the Republican Party, which became increasingly lily-white, Negro Alliance members voted almost unanimously at the Cincinnati (1891) and St. Louis (1892) conventions for the establishment of a national third party. However, Frederick Douglass, then in his declining years, remained with the Republican Party.

The new "Populist" party included the Northern and Southern Farmers Alliances, the Knights of Labor, the United Mine Workers, and various other unions and progressive groupings. The Gompersite A. F. of L. remained aloof from the movement. The party held its nominating convention in Omaha on July 4, 1892, and picked as its standard-bearers the Union general, James B. Weaver, for president, and the Confederate general, James G. Field, for vice-president. This was to symbolize a new Northern-Southern unity. The convention worked out a platform calling chiefly for an ample supply of cheap currency through the "sub-treasury plan" of the Southern Alliance and the free coinage of silver; for government ownership and operation of railroads, telegraphs, and telephones; and for the break-up of the land monopoly of the railroads and other corporations through the reclamation of their lands by the government.[25]

The campaign was hotly waged, with women taking an active part in it. The famous Mary E. Lease of Kansas struck its militant keynote when she declared, "What you farmers need to do is raise less corn and more hell!" Among the campaign's most prominent Northern leaders were Senator William A. Pfeffer and Representative "Sockless" Jerry Simpson of Kansas, Ignatius Donnelly of Minnesota, and Judge W. V. Allen of Nebraska. In the South the election fight was especially bitter, 15 Negroes being murdered in Georgia alone.[26]

General Weaver polled 1,027,379 votes in the November elections, carrying Kansas, Colorado, Idaho, and Nevada. Populist governors were elected in Colorado, Kansas, North Dakota, and Wyoming. In 1893, there were 345 People's Party representatives sitting in 19 state legislatures. In the South, although a strong showing was made in Alabama and other states, the new party did not mobilize all the Alliance support, which hitherto had functioned through the Democratic Party. Tom Watson failed to be elected governor in Georgia.

The presidential winner in the election was Grover Cleveland, a "gold Democrat" of New York. He was the first Democrat to be elected president since James Buchanan in 1856, 36 years before. Although a Democrat, Cleveland was entirely under the control of Wall Street. The Democratic Party had ceased to be simply a planter-controlled Southern party, and had become the agent of Northern big capital.

The deep economic crisis of 1893, bringing poverty and hunger to millions of workers and farmers, gave a big impetus to the new People's Party; and in the elections of 1894, it polled a total of 1,523,-979 votes. In this campaign Debs declared himself a Populist. The great strength of the Populist movement in the South is indicated by the following percentages of the states' votes it polled in 1894: Alabama, 47.64; Florida, 20.68; Georgia, 44.46; Louisiana (1896) 43.68; Arkansas, 19.31; Kentucky (1895), 4.73; Mississippi (1895), 26.99; Missouri, 8.45; North Carolina, 53.78; South Carolina, 30.43; Tennessee, 9.93; Texas, 36.13; Virginia, 28.20.[27] At least 50 percent of these votes were cast by Negroes.

In 1896, the People's Party leaders made a disastrous alliance with the Democratic Party, behind the candidacies of William Jennings Bryan for president and Tom Watson for vice-president. Bryan failed to be elected, and the national vote of the People's Party in the campaign amounted to only about 200,000. By 1900, the People's Party had passed from the scene; and in the main, the Farmers Alliances, Northern and Southern, vanished along with it. In the South the planters and monopolists were especially determined to break up the Negro-white unity in the Populist movement. The terrorism conducted by them and their frenzied white supremacy demagogy against "Negro domination" was a sharply disintegrating factor. Nationally the big and promising Populist movement had been steered upon the rocks of capitalist control by the corrupt leaders of the Democratic Party.

36. Imperialism and Negro Disfranchisement

Lenin has defined imperialism as the final stage of capitalism, displaying five basic qualities: *(a)* the growth of great industrial and financial monopolies which dominate the life of the nation; *(b)* the merger of the industrial and financial trusts, with bank capital dominant; *(c)* the export of capital to foreign lands; *(d)* **the systematic** division of the world's markets among the big capitalist powers; and *(e)* the completion of the division of the world's territories among the imperialist powers.[1] These are the essential imperialist qualities of all the great capitalist powers—Great Britain, Germany, Japan, France, Italy, and the United States.

THE DEVELOPMENT OF AMERICAN IMPERIALISM

American imperialism began definitely to take shape from about 1880 on, and by 1900 it was well developed. As we have seen in Chapter 34, American industry made tremendous progress between .1860 and 1900. This was the concrete realization of the revolutionary victory of the Northern industrialists in the Civil War. Capital invested mounted by 450 percent, the value of manufactures climbed 500 percent, the length of the railroad mileage increased by 500 percent, profits soared as never before in history, and the total national wealth went up some 400 percent. Meanwhile the number of workers increased by 325 percent and the population by 150 percent.

Together with this great post-Civil War growth of the nation's economy went a rapid process of monopolization, of trust-building, especially after 1880. Consequently, by 1900, according to Moody, there were in the United States 445 large industrial, franchise and transportation trusts, with a total capitalization of over $20 billion.[2] The billion-dollar United States Steel Corporation was organized in 1901, and there were already in existence six huge railroad monopoly groups, each with a capital of from one to two and one-quarter billion dollars.

In the process of trustifying, the great industrial network had largely fallen under the control of a few huge banking-industrial-transportation concerns—finance capitalists; namely, Morgan, Rockefeller, Mellon, Vanderbilt, Kuhn-Loeb, and others. These wealthy capitalist overlords had also come to dominate the national government. Their first marked advance onto the world scene as militant imperialists, aiming at the conquest and robbing of colonial peoples, was during the Spanish-American War of 1898. In this war (deliberately provoked by imperialist Washington), the militant young United States stripped decrepit old Spain of the Philippines, Cuba, and Puerto Rico—the last remnants of its once vast American and Asian colonial empire.

INTENSIFIED EXPLOITATION OF THE WORKERS

In the enlarged, monopolistic industries, and in the big railroad systems that grew so rapidly after the Civil War, the employers introduced intensified methods of exploitation and oppression that were new and terrible in the life of the American working class. If successful, the general lines upon which they were proceeding would have produced a sort of peonage as the status of the workers. The latter were driven on the job as never before; and the shops and railroads, destitute of safety precautions, became veritable slaughter houses. Literally millions of workers were needlessly killed or crippled in industry.

The workers also, in a sense quite new to them, were powerless as individuals in the face of the powerful employers. Organization was imperative. But every effort they made to unite into unions was met with iron repression, the workers' ranks were filled with spies, and armies of professional gunmen and strikebreakers became an established institution. Meanwhile, the employers built strong labor-fighting associations of their own. Where all this tended was made evident in the "company towns," which began to take shape about this period. In these towns the companies owned and dominated everything—the town sites, the industries, the workers' homes, the stores, the banks, the newspapers, the churches, and the town officials—while the workers, completely devoid of trade unions and political organization, lived under a regime of gunman terrorism.

The pattern that the new monopolists sought to introduce among the workers of the soil was closely akin to the special American type of serfdom that they were trying to fasten upon the industrial workers. Their general aim was to take away the farms and reduce the farmers to a state of tenancy, not much better than that of the Southern sharecroppers. Their means to this end was a monopolistic control of freight rates, credit rates, and the prices of all those commodities that the poorer farmer had to buy or sell. On every side, the farmers were confronted by ruthless monopolies which strove to suck them dry.

During this period, the monopolists began to enforce their exploitation of the workers and farmers by a ruthless control and use of the government—federal, state, and local—in a way that was something new in American life. With the growth of the monopolies, there was also an increase in government corruption, to a degree also hitherto unknown. The big capitalists bought legislators "like fish in a barrel," and they freely used the courts against the workers and farmers. The breaking of strikes by court injunctions and the use of troops had already become commonplace by 1900. The city middle classes—storekeepers, small manufacturers, and professionals—also felt increasingly the crushing pressures of the growing monopolies, of developing imperialism.

During this period, particularly between 1880 and 1900, the monopolists began to develop a new and deadly weapon against the rebellious toiling masses. This was corruption of the top leaders of the trade unions, especially those of the skilled workers, and the utilization of these leaders to defeat the struggles of the working class as a whole. These misleaders of the workers were the "labor lieutenants of capital." By 1900 the Gompersite leaders of the A. F. of L. and the Railroad Brotherhoods were thoroughly recruited into the service of the big bosses; and they had sunk to depths of strikebreaking, personal corruption, and general reaction quite unknown in any other labor movement in the world. They had become a definite force to break strikes, to prevent the organization of the unskilled, women, and foreign-born workers, to maintain the Jim Crow barriers against Negro workers, to prevent the growth of a labor party, and to fight against Socialism and the development of class consciousness among the workers. The top union leaders, to this day, play this same essential role of helpers to the monopolists and imperialists. They are part of the general mechanism of Wall Street imperialism.

The workers and farmers of the period of 1865-1900 met the new exploitation and oppression of monopoly capital, as we have seen in previous chapters, with a whole series of bitter strikes and political struggles. Their main blows were directed against the trusts. Among the most important of the great achievements of these times were the building of the National Labor Union, the Knights of Labor, the American Federation of Labor, and the Socialist Labor Party; the waging of such historic strikes as those of the railroad workers in 1877 and 1894, and the several big coal and metal miners' strikes; the historic steel strike of 1892; and the carrying on of the major political movements of Grangers, Greenbackers, and Populists all through this generation of militant class struggle. These political movements generally took the form of broad anti-monopoly united fronts of workers, Negro people, farmers, and city middle classes, which were historical forerunners of the present-day policy of the people's front against monopoly capital.

MONOPOLY-IMPERIALISM IN THE SOUTH

Of course, the Negro people, who were located overwhelmingly in the South, did not escape the intensified exploitation and oppression characteristic of the growth of monopoly capitalism during the decades before 1900. On the contrary, they were the worst of all its victims. Kuczynski says, "If we compare the material conditions of the Negro workers at the end of the nineteenth century with those existing just before the Civil War, the change was very small indeed."[3] But before we deal concretely with this situation, let us glance briefly at the growth of monopoly capital in the South.

In Chapter 33, we indicated the development of Southern industry —railroads, steel, coal and iron mining, lumber, textiles, tobacco, and other branches—during the decades after the Civil War, and more especially in the years following 1880. These new and expanded Southern industries were established chiefly under the ownership and control of Northern monopoly capital. Taking over the Louisville and Nashville Railroad and greatly expanding it, was one of the earliest major invasions of the South by Northern big capital. During the economic crisis of 1873-78, that road passed into the control of Jay Gould, August Belmont, Thomas Fortune Ryan, and Jacob Schiff.[4] Russell Sage and other Northern capitalists at this time were also busily grabbing control of railroads in the South. In 1893, J. P. Morgan created the Southern Railroad out of the remains of the Richmond and West Point Terminal Railroad; and within ten years he controlled 10,000 miles of the most important Southern railroad mileage. In 1907 Morgan also took over the Tennessee Coal, Iron, and Railroad Company.[5] Meanwhile, other big Northern capitalists bought or stole their way into the lumber, coal, textile, and other Southern industries. By 1900, Wall Street capitalists, with a billion dollars invested in the South, dominated not only the economy of that area, but also its political life.

The South, being an organic part of the economic, political, and social structure of the United States, could not, of course, become a colony of Wall Street; but the Northern monopolists in many respects treated it as such. They achieved hegemony over the Southern industrialists; they subordinated the economic life of the South to the needs of the Northern economy; they practiced absentee ownership, sucking profits out of the South on a semi-colonial basis; they built up railroad differentials (much on the principle of tariffs) against the South; and they subjected the Southern workers, Negro and white, agricultural and industrial, to super-exploitation, much as they were then doing in their newly acquired real colonies—Cuba, Puerto Rico, and the Philippines. The Negroes especially suffered this super-exploitation. The Northern monopolists exploited them in the most brutal manner, treating them as an oppressed nation, entitled to no economic or political rights that they were bound to respect.[6]

The relations between the erstwhile rulers of the South (principally the cotton planters) and its new imperialist masters, the Wall Street monopolists, were essentially those of major and minor partners in an ultra-reactionary coalition. Perlo thus pictures the connections and policies of these allied forces: "Their economic course was to prevent the Negro people from getting the land, to preserve the plantation system in a new set-up in which Northern bankers, merchants, and manufacturers derived the lion's share of the profits from its operation, with the Southern landowners as junior partners and overseers."[7]

THE MONOPOLISTS' ATTACK UPON NEGRO RIGHTS

The domination of the post-Civil War South by the Wall Street monopolists and imperialists worsened the condition of the Negroes in every respect. There was then—and still remains—an unholy combination of reactionary exploiters. The planters, long-time robbers and murderers of the Negro people, had acquired worthy senior partners in the Northern monopolists, who were responsible for the serf-like conditions prevailing in the Northern company towns. Together, the planters and monopolists constituted a strong and virulent counter-revolution in the South.

The monopolists, it is true, did not invent the infamous peonage system of sharecropping; but they gave it their heartiest backing and have been active proponents of it ever since. The terrible outrage of lynching Negroes became more widespread and frightful with the advent of the big Wall Street capitalists in the South. And why not? The ruthless Northern exploiters, who could callously condone the needless slaughter of huge numbers of workers in the Northern industries would certainly never draw the line at the lynching of Negroes in the South. They cynically realized that lynching was necessary to terrorize the Negroes to work for lower wages. Lynching paid off in bigger dividends for Northern stockholders. During the time in question, Perlo remarks, "In a thirteen-year period there were almost two thousand recorded lynchings,"[8] most of them carried out under conditions of brutality that would shame the torturers in the Middle Ages. And these shocking figures on lynching do not include the infinitely larger number of Negroes individually murdered by gun-toting bullies, supporters of white supremacy in the South.

The development of imperialism, of monopolist-planter control in the South, notably after the Hayes-Tilden sell-out of 1877, also resulted in a vicious attack upon the already meager civil rights of the Negroes—in a great strengthening of the Jim Crow system. There is a long history of social discrimination against Negroes in the South (and in the North, too, for that matter), running back to colonial times; but heretofore it was mainly a matter of rigidly enforced custom. As Tindall says of South Carolina, "There was no basis in law for segregation."[9]

But after Wall Street imperialism became dominant in the South, Jim Crow was written into law to an unprecedented degree. Tennessee adopted the first Jim Crow law in 1875, with other states soon following suit. Buck says, "The educational system was revised to make obligatory separate schools and colleges. Separation extended into the churches where mixed congregations became a thing of the past . . . 'Jim Crow' cars became universal on Southern Railways. Negroes were barred from admittance to hotels, inns, restaurants, and amusement places which catered to white people. Street cars had separate sections reserved for whites and blacks."[10]

After the Civil War, the U.S. Supreme Court was notoriously an organ of Northern big business. In 1893, by wiping out the Civil Rights Act of 1875 as unconstitutional (see Chapter 30), it gave powerful legal sanction to the Jim Crow movement all over the South. Throughout the country Negroes met and protested at this outrage—but in vain.

NEGRO DISFRANCHISEMENT

After the Hayes betrayal of 1877 Southern reaction set out in earnest to strip the Negro of his second greatest achievement in the revolution, the right to vote. (His first achievement, of course, was emancipation.) All over the South a violent campaign of white supremacy was carried out to alienate the poor whites from their natural allies, the Negro people. Armed terror was used to keep Negroes away from the polling places; Negroes were required to vote in separate ballot boxes, and their votes were disregarded in the counting. Many other devices were used to eliminate the Negro vote. Nevertheless, the Negro people fought back heroically and managed to remain a real political force throughout the South.

It was during these decades of the rise of American imperialism ·that there were born, despite bitter persecution, well-known Negro newspapers, including the *Savannah Tribune* (1875), *Chicago Conservator* (1878), *California Eagle* (1879), *Indianapolis World* (1880), *Washington Bee* (1882), *Cleveland Gazette* (1884), *Philadelphia Tribune* (1884), *Baltimore Afro-American* (1892), *New York Age* (1895), *Norfolk Journal and Guide* (1899), *Chicago Defender* (1905), *Pittsburgh Courier* (1910), and others. Illustrative of the general difficulties of Southern Negro editors and of the fighting spirit of Negro women, Ida B. Wells-Barnett, Negro woman editor of the *Memphis Free Press*, went to work each day with a gun strapped on each hip to protect herself against the Ku Klux Klan which had made attempts to destroy her press and to run her out of the state. Mrs. Well-Barnett was especially effective, with her writings, speeches, and other activities, in making a national issue of Negro lynching. Aptheker says that she had more to do with "carrying forward the anti-lynching crusade than any other person."[11]

Hence, the planter-Northern monopolist exploiters resolved to disfranchise the Negro outright. They were moved to take this drastic step particularly because of the widespread Negro-white co-operation during the big Alliance-Populist movement of the 1880's and 1890's. This movement convinced the Southern rulers that even their virulent white chauvinist propaganda and Klan methods of violence were not enough to cancel out the Negroes as a powerful political force. Hence, they had to be stripped of the vote by law. This, it was hoped, would put a final stop to the dreaded Negro-poor white political co-operation.

Mississippi set the pace in the disfranchisement movement. In 1890, at a constitutional convention, it adopted a poll tax and a literacy test as requirements for voters. Henceforth no one was allowed to register for voting unless he produced his tax receipt and could read and interpret any clause of the Federal Constitution submitted to him. Illiterate white voters, who were legion, were "given considera-tion" by the registrars; but the Negroes were barred wholesale on the flimsiest of pretexts. This was the infamous "Mississippi Plan." It was soon applied in other Southern states.

South Carolina disfranchised Negro voters by a poll tax and a literacy test in 1895. Then came Louisiana in 1898, North Carolina in 1900, Virginia and Alabama in 1901, Georgia in 1907, and Okla-homa in 1910. Tennessee, Texas, Florida, and Arkansas also adopted poll taxes, property laws, and other disfranchising schemes. There were many variations in the plans. Louisiana in particular varied the pattern with its so-called "grandfather clause," by which any person was exempt from the literacy test who had voted before January 1, 1867, or who was the son or grandson of one who had then been a legal voter. This provision eliminated all the Negroes from the voting lists, but automatically left all the whites. In practice, the Four-teenth and Fifteenth Amendments were nullified.

In Louisiana, as a result of the new plan, the registration of Negro voters fell from 130,344 in 1897 to 5,320 in 1900. In Mississippi, "Roughly one Negro in seventeen and two whites in three were there-fore qualified to vote provided they paid the poll tax—and kept the receipt! By this means a potential electorate of 257,305 was reduced to an actual electorate of 26,742 and a Negro majority of 37,105 was converted into a white majority of 58,512."[12] In 1900 the total vote in Virginia was 264,240, but in 1904 it had declined to 130,544. The Negro vote was similarly decimated in all other Southern states. Between 1892 and 1902, the decline in the average vote for congress-men fell off 60 per cent in Alabama, 69 percent in Mississippi, 80 percent in Louisiana, 34 percent in North Carolina, 69 percent in

Florida, 75 percent in Arkansas, 50 percent in Tennessee, and 80 percent in Georgia.

"Before the twentieth century was a decade old," says Buck, "the constitutional disfranchisement of the Negro was a fact throughout the South."[13] Great masses of poor whites were also stripped of the vote. The Negroes fought as best they could against this new assault, but they were able to accomplish little in the face of the prevailing terror. The American Federation of Labor, itself saturated with Jim Crow practices, paid no attention to their plight and gave them no assistance. And their erstwhile poor white allies in the South, demoralized by the collapse of the Populist movement, also provided little help. Consequently, the Negroes in the South were reduced practically to the status of non-citizens.

THE SOLID SOUTH

The "Solid South," as it came to be known in political life, was consolidated after the Hayes sell-out of the Negro people in 1877. This one party—Democratic Party—rule, based upon the oppression, disfranchisement, and super-exploitation of the Negro people, is the legitimate political descendant of the pro-slaver wartime Confederacy. The Solid South has been maintained by virulent white chauvinist propaganda to terrorize the poor whites into line, and by legal and extra-legal violence to intimidate the Negroes. It is the product of planter-Northern monopolist rule. Both of these groups have always had a strong community of interest in developing a cheap source of labor supply among the Negroes (and among the poor whites). During the two full generations of its existence, the Solid South has been dented politically only twice: first, in the 1928 election, when Herbert Hoover carried seven Southern states on the basis of an awakened religious prejudice against the Catholic candidate for president, Alfred E. Smith; and second, in the election of 1952, when General Eisenhower carried the states of Texas, Virginia, Tennessee, and Florida against Adlai Stevenson.

The Southern wing of the Republican Party, the chief political representative of Northern big business, bears a historical responsibility for maintaining the Solid South. Its branches in the South have served traditionally more as a machine for controlling Federal patronage jobs in the South than for electing candidates. Like the Democratic Party, it is saturated with white supremacist poison. As early as 1890, the lily-white Republicans were purging the party of Negroes, their one-time revolutionary allies. "The fact is," wrote Ray Stannard Baker in 1908, "the Republican Party, as now constituted in the South, is even a more restricted white oligarchy than the Democratic Party."[14]

From the time of its inception, the Solid South has been a reactionary force in American politics, a cancer eating at the vitals of our national democracy. Every reactionary movement finds a powerful base in the South. The New South—the Solid South—has ever been the home of the most crushing poverty and oppression. To this day, one of the decisive tasks of the progressive movement, in fighting the plantation system, is to destroy the unholy alliance between the big planters of the South and the big monopolists of the North, who jointly maintain the Solid South.

37. The Socialists and the Negro People

During the formative decades of Marxism in the United States, roughly from the early 1850's onward, the Marxists (or Communists, as they were then called, and, later, Socialists) took an active interest in the welfare and struggles of the Negro people. They fought for the organization and well-being of all the toiling masses, without regard to color, race, or sex; they took an active part in the pre-war Abolitionist fight. They distinguished themselves during the war as bold fighters against the rebellious slaveholders, and after the war they were a strong force in bringing the Negroes into the young trade union movement. The last dozen years of this activity were carried out under the general leadership of the International Workingmen's Association (I.W.A.), led by Karl Marx. Because of internal dissension, however, this historic organization crumbled during the middle 1870's, and the American Marxists had to reorganize their forces.

THE SOCIALIST LABOR PARTY

The Socialist Labor Party was established in Philadelphia, July 19-22, 1876, just a few days after the I.W.A. had been dissolved in that city. The new party was a combination of Marxists, led by Friedrich A. Sorge and Otto Weydemeyer, the son of Joseph Weydemeyer, and Lassalleans, headed by Adolph Strasser, A. Gabriel, and P. J. Mc-Guire. The Marxists, with their ultimate goal of a Socialist society, aimed to approach this end by revolutionary propaganda and militant daily trade union and political action. On the other hand, the Lassalleans, while calling themselves Socialists, played down trade union action and strove for the establishment of state-financed producers' co-operatives. The Lassalleans were the political forebears of the later right-opportunist Socialists, while the Marxists were the forerunners of the present-day Communists. The first 15 years of S.L.P. history were marked by a bitter internal struggle between the Lassalleans and Marxists, which the latter eventually won.

On the Negro question, the S.L.P. inherited both the strength and weaknesses of the old I.W.A. The Marxists were very active in the great trade union struggles and in most of the broad worker-farmer political movements of the period—at least up until the middle 1890's. In all these spheres of activity they extended the hand of friendly comradeship to Negroes. They had great influence in the Knights of Labor and the young American Federation of Labor, and they exerted it on the side of admitting the Negro into the trade unions on the basis of full equality of membership. But they were not organizationally or politically strong enough to purge the K. of L. and especially the A. F. of L. of their crass white-chauvinist policies of excluding Negro workers from the trade unions.

At this time, the basic political weakness of the Marxist Socialists on the Negro question was their failure to recognize it as a special problem. They simply assumed that the Negro was a wage worker, and that, therefore, his problems were those of the working class in general. As a result of this oversimplification, they largely ignored such crucial problems of the Negroes as the peonage of sharecropping, the Jim Crow system, and the savagery of lynching. Yet the quarter century when the S.L.P. was the party of Marxist Socialism— 1876-1900—was one in which the Negro people in the South were conducting the most desperate struggle against the efforts of the planters and Northern monopolists to strip them of the vote and to enslave them generally.

The tragic fact is that the Party gave the Negro people in the South little if any aid in their bitter struggle against extreme reaction. Engels foresaw the Negro workers as part of a general labor party, but he did not develop the matter.[1] The Party had few or no Southern members, put forward no Negro demands as such, and concerned itself but seldom with what was going on in the South. While this gross neglect of the vitally important struggle of the Negro people was to be basically explained by the S.L.P.'s ignorance of the special nature of the Negro question, it was also due to the political immaturity of the Marxists in the Party, and to its failure to deal effectively with many problems of the class struggle—farmers, colonies, etc. But unquestionably it was also largely because of conscious or unconscious white chauvinism in the Party. This chauvinism was generally expressed by a lack of sympathy and solidarity with the doubly oppressed Negro people; but it often burst forth in the grossest forms of discrimination and prejudice. Undoubtedly, had it been whites rather than Negroes who were being so barbarously outraged in the South, the Party would have paid vastly more attention to the matter.

DE LEON AND THE NEGRO

In 1890-91, the Socialist Labor Party came under the leadership of Daniel De Leon. Thenceforth, for 25 years, his ideological domination of the organization was complete. He also acquired tremendous theoretical influence over the whole left wing, including that section which later became the Socialist Party. A brilliant writer, De Leon was a combination of Anarcho-Syndicalist, dual unionist, and abstract, dogmatic sectarian. Among his many theoretical shortcomings was a total failure to grasp the special significance of the Negro question. Indeed, it was De Leon who first definitely formulated the mistaken conception, which had prevailed vaguely in the labor movement since the foundation of the National Labor Union, that the Negro question was a class question and nothing else. He simply ignored the fact that at least 75 percent of the Negroes in the South were not wage workers, but tenants and sharecroppers.

De Leon wrote very voluminously, but in all his books, pamphlets, and newspaper articles there was no systematic treatment of the Negro question. He obviously considered the whole matter of no great importance, although, at the time he was most active, Negroes were being lynched in the South at the rate of two or more a week under conditions of savagery unequaled in the civilized world. It is significant that long after his death, De Leon's S.L.P. biographers never even mentioned the Negro question in writing the story of his life and work.[2]

In one of his very rare passages about Negroes, De Leon thus expounded his conclusion that they had no special problems in the class struggle. "In no economic respect, is he different from his fellow wage slaves of other races; yet by reason of his race, which long was identified with serfdom, the rays of the Social question reached his mind through such broken prisms that they are refracted into all the colors of the rainbow, preventing him from appreciating the white light of the question." And again: "Once on the path of progress, the Negro cannot long remain out of the Socialist camp. Well may the Socialist camp make ready to receive this division of the army of the proletariat that has been wandering in the wilderness since 1865."[3]

De Leon thus castigated the Negro, instead of criticizing the Party for not putting up a fight against lynching, sharecropping, and the Jim Crow system. Believing that all immediate demands were "banana peels under the feet of the workers," he was willing to let the scourge of Jim Crow and lynching take care of itself until Socialism arrived. De Leon's underestimation of the Negro question as such was strikingly illustrated in 1909-10 in a polemic he carried on in the *Daily People* with the unspeakable Negro-baiter, Tom Watson of Georgia. Instead of flaying Watson for the outrageous suppression and butchering of Negroes by K.K.K. bandits, of whom Watson was an ardent defender, De Leon ignored the Negro question altogether and indulged in a long harangue with Watson about general Marxist principles—surplus value, the class struggle, and the like. He did, however, find occasion to make an insulting reference to the Negro to the effect that "Mr. Watson and his 'n——s' have their hands in each other's wool."[4] Attitudes and ideas such as De Leon's did much to drive a wedge of misunderstanding between the Negro people and the advanced white workers.

THE PROGRAM OF THE SOCIALIST PARTY

The Socialist Party was established on July 29, 1901, in Indianapolis, with the amalgamation of the Social Democratic Party, led by Eugene V. Debs and Victor L. Berger, and a group of seceders from the Socialist Labor Party, led by Morris Hillquit. The new party was formed in opposition to the sectarianism of the De Leon leadership of the S.L.P. De Leon, with his rigid, abstract, and dogmatic conceptions of Marxism, had largely separated the Party from the strikes of the trade unions, from the broad labor-farmer political movements, and, of course (although few white members remarked this), from the struggles of the Negro people. In general the S.L.P. had failed signally in developing the policy of broad mass economic and political struggle made imperative for the working class by the rise of monopoly and imperialism; hence, the Marxists had to create a new and better party.

The newly formed S.P. broke with the S.L.P. nonsense that the only demand to be put forth by the working class was the overthrow of the capitalist system. It worked out a whole program of immediate demands as the basis for the workers' daily struggles. This was a big step forward, even though later on the middle class opportunists in the Party, in so far as they could, were to concentrate the whole attention of the Party upon these immediate demands, to the exclusion of revolutionary Socialist agitation.

The Socialist Party, from the outset, was poisoned with the seeds of reformism and was led by petty bourgeois opportunists. It could not, therefore, develop the militant policies of mass struggle demanded of it by the period of imperialism, into which it was born. It naturally was not interested in a revolutionary alliance between the workers and the Negro people, directed against the Southern planters and the monopolists.

Noticeably absent from the new Party's program, consequently, were specific demands for the Negro people—particularly in opposition to the terrible conditions prevailing in the South. The program said nothing of this intolerable situation, or what to do about it, although at the time the South was the scene of ghastly lynchings, K.K.K. terrorism, and counter-revolution. In this respect, there prevailed, implicitly if not explicitly, the theory that the Negroes were only a division of the working class and that, consequently, the general demands for the workers would also meet their needs. Three Negro delegates were present at the founding convention, however; and at the insistence of one of them, William Costley of San Francisco,[5] a special resolution on the Negro question was reluctantly adopted.

This resolution expressed sympathy with the Negroes in their hard situation but without directly mentioning Jim Crow or lynching. It completely identified the situation of the Negroes with that of the white workers in general and proposed Socialism as the solution. The resolution concluded with the resolve, "that we, the American Socialist Party, invite the Negro to membership and fellowship with us in the world movement for economic emancipation by which equal liberty and opportunity shall be secured to every man and fraternity become the order of the world."[6]

Thus, the new Socialist Party went on record to the effect that nothing in the specific situation of the Negroes was different enough from the general problems of the white workers to require that special demands be raised in their behalf. The Party saw the need to put forward immediate demands for workers, farmers, women, and children, and upon many single issues—but it believed that the bitter plight of the Negroes called for no immediate action. Twenty-eight years later the Socialist theoretician, James Oneal, was still arguing that "There is no color line in exploiting the workers," despite a world of evidence to the effect that Negroes are subjected to special, intensified, terroristic forms of super-exploitation based on their Negro nationality.[7] The 1901 resolution implied that no fight was to be made against the barbarous suppression and exploitation of the Negro people, as such; and so it turned out in the Party's practice.

The 1901 resolution laid down the basic line of the Socialist Party on the Negro question. "This," says Kipnis, "was the only resolution for Negro rights ever passed by a national Socialist body from 1901, through 1912." The 1904 convention of the Party did nothing further on the question, nor did the succeeding conventions of 1908 and 1912. And the S.P. Platform of 1916 did not even mention the words "Negro" and "lynching." It was not until World War I—with the ensuing Russian Revolution, the appearance of the Communist Party on the political scene, and the circulation in the United States of the writings of Lenin—that the S.P., as a Party, began to bestir itself on the Negro question, and then only feebly.

Belatedly, in 1920, the S.P. began to see the Negro question as a "race" problem. It demanded that Congress enforce the Thirteenth, Fourteenth, and Fifteenth Amendments and that Negroes be accorded "full civil, political, industrial and educational rights." The *New Leader*, June 21, 1930, expressed a widespread opinion in the Socialist Party as follows: "Almost all the Southerners believe in segregating the Negro and depriving him of the social and political rights that whites enjoy. The Southern Socialists must adjust their tactics to this state of affairs. It is certain that there will never be a thriving movement in the South unless it is conducted in Southern style."[8] As late as its 1932 convention, the S.P. rejected a motion demanding "full social equality for Negroes" and endorsed instead a slippery formulation in favor of "the enforcement of Constitutional guarantees of economic, political and legal equality for the Negroes."[9]

DEBS AND THE NEGRO

Eugene V. Debs, the outstanding mass leader of the Socialist Party, held the same general opinion on the Negro question as De Leon of the S.L.P.; namely, that it was a class question and nothing more. He was adamant in fighting against any attempt to work out demands to meet the special problems of the Negro. He wrote several articles to stress this position; in 1903, he stated his general conception as follows: "For capitalism the negro question is a grave one and will grow more threatening as the contradictions and complications of capitalist society multiply, but this need not worry us. Let them settle the negro question in their way, if they can. We have nothing to do with it, for it is their fight. We have simply to open the eyes of as many negroes as we can and do battle for emancipation from wage slavery, and when the working class have triumphed in the class struggle and stand forth economic as well as political free men, the race problem will disappear."[10]

With characteristic oversimplification, Debs maintained that the class struggle is colorless. The capitalists, white, black and other shades, are on one side, and the workers, white, black and other shades are on the other side. And, "We have nothing special to offer the Negro and we cannot make separate appeals to all the races. The Socialist Party is the Party of the whole working class regardless of color."[11] The matter of social equality, Debs dismissed as an individual question with which the Party could not concern itself. He said, "Social equality . . . forsooth . . . is pure fraud and serves to mask the real issue, which is not *social* equality, but *economic freedom.*"[12] He endorsed the fact that "The Socialist platform has not a word in reference to social equality."[13] Debs considered that even the innocuous resolution of 1901 on the Negro question constituted too much of a special Negro program, and he repeatedly urged its repeal.

In 1902, Charles H. Vail wrote a pamphlet (the only S.P. pamphlet on the Negro question for 19 years to follow) endorsing the line of the 1901 resolution. His main argument ran, "The changed conditions transformed the negro into a wage slave, identifying the negro problem with the labor problem as a whole, the solution of which is the abolition of wage slavery and the emancipation of both black and white from the servitude to capitalist masters. . . . Socialism is the only remedy."[14] He proposed no fight against lynching or the other specifically Negro problems.

Attempts to raise the Negro question as such in the Party were actively condemned and fought as opportunism. Max Hayes, a prominent Socialist trade union leader, said of the situation: "It is well that the Socialist Party has taken a firm stand on the so-called Negro question, and that Eugene V. Debs, G. A. Hoehn, A. M. Simons, and other writers and speakers have delivered sledge-hammer blows through the *International Socialist Review* and other Party publications along this line. There is no doubt that a surreptitious attempt is being made to make an 'issue' of the unfortunate race hatred that is being engendered in different parts of the country, just as the politicians have played the North against the South and Protestants against the Catholics in the past to obscure the economic problems that press for solution."[15] Whatever small part Socialists took in the struggle of the Negro people from time to time was as individuals, not as an organized Party.

THE LEFT WING AND THE NEGRO QUESTION

During this early period, the left wing of the Socialist Party, which was eventually to develop into the Communist Party, was very confused on the Negro question. This was to be clearly seen not only in the writings and speeches of Debs, the outstanding left-center leader, but from the fact that his incorrect line was generally followed by the S.P. left wing. The left definitely failed to understand the special nature of the Negro question and to realize that, with proper policies, the Negro people could be mobilized as a powerful ally of the working class and the poorer farmers.

Although never making the Negro question a matter of basic issue, left-wing Socialists in the trade unions always took the position that the Negro workers had to be admitted into the unions as full and equal members. Debs, in his later years, spoke out vigorously against the Jim Crow system, and William D. Haywood, at the founding convention of the Industrial Workers of the World in Chicago, in June 1905, denounced the A. F. of L.'s failure to organize the Negro workers.[16] In a series of bitterly fought strikes in the lumber woods of western Louisiana and eastern Texas, during 1911-12, the I.W.W. united several thousand Negroes in the same union with the whites, trampling upon the local Jim Crow codes in the process.[17] The I.W.W. also made considerable progress in organizing Negro longshoremen in Philadelphia. Its principal Negro leader was Benjamin H. Fletcher.

Despite its support for the organization of Negro workers, the S.P. left wing never made a real issue of the general Negro question in the Party. It fought the opportunist right-wing leadership of the Party for two decades in an ascending battle over many issues; but the Negro question was not among them. The left fought against the right's opportunist conception of Socialism, against its overstress on immediate demands and sabotage of Marxist education, against the domination of the Party by petty-bourgeois intellectuals, against the S.P. leaders' collaboration with the corrupt Gompers A. F. of L. machine, for industrial unionism, for the organization of the unorganized, against its pro-war policies, and for a consistent, militant policy in the struggle.

But the left did not fight for a militant struggle against lynching, Jim Crow, and against all the other bitter oppression to which the Negro people were subjected, not only in the South, but also to a large extent in the North. The left wing never evolved a program of demands for the Negro people which they could have fought to get the Socialist Party to accept. In the Haywood-Bohn program of 1912,[18] which largely expressed the left's general policies at that time, the Negro question was not mentioned; nor was it dealt with by the left wing in its fight against the right wing at the famous Socialist Party convention of that year. Not even in the big split of August 31, 1919, out of which came the Communist Party, did the Negro question appear as an important issue. The American left did not approach an understanding of the Negro question basically until its members began to read Lenin after the Russian Revolution began. Historically, one of the most marked ideological weaknesses of the left wing was its slowness in grasping the political importance of the special significance of the Negro question in the United States.

During the pre-World War I years of the Socialist Party, however, there were isolated voices in and close to the Party which demanded, although confusedly, that the Party work out demands for the Negro people and interest itself in their long and bitter struggle. Clarence Darrow in 1901 definitely defended the cause of the Negroes and criticized the trade unions and the Socialists for not fighting against the specific evils bearing down upon this oppressed people. He condemned the non-political program of Booker T. Washington.[19] I. M. Rubinow also wrote many articles in the *Review,* during 1908-10, urging that the Party seriously take up the Negro question. Rubinow in 1912 made sharp criticisms of the Party's neglect of the Negro question. But such critics were quite unable to correct the Party's line.

In 1913 Dr. Du Bois wrote a very sharp article, criticizing the white chauvinist attitude of the Socialist Party towards the Negro, saying: "No recent convention of Socialists has dared to face fairly the Negro problem and make a straightforward declaration that they regard Negroes as men in the same sense that other men are. . . . The general attitude of the thinking members of the party has been this: We must not turn aside from the great objects of Socialism to take up the issue of the American Negroes, let the question wait; when the objects of Socialism are achieved, this problem will be solved along with other problems."[20]

WHITE CHAUVINISM IN THE SOCIALIST PARTY

The Socialist Party's gross neglect of fighting with and for the Negro people, while basically caused by the opportunist orientation of the Party in general, also had in it strong elements of a deep-seated white chauvinism, particularly in the petty-bourgeois leadership. Even the left wing was not exempt from this corroding political disease. White chauvinism largely explains why the working personnel of the Party's papers, its officers, and organizing staffs were all lily-white; why Hillquit, Laidler, and other Party writers could produce several fat histories of the Party in theory and practice and never even mention the Negro;[21] why, save to a certain extent in Oklahoma and Texas, the Party had almost no organization or activity in the South, and why, in what little organization there was, "whites and blacks belonged to different branches."[22]

Often white chauvinism in the Party assumed the most open and disgusting forms. Thus Victor Berger, outstanding Party leader, said in his paper, the *Social Democratic Herald,* in May 1902: "There can be no doubt that the negroes and mulattoes constitute a lower race."[23] William Noyes outdid even this example of bourgeois ideology in the Party. In a whole tirade of similar filth, he stated, "Physically the negroes are as a race repulsive to us. Their features are the opposite of what we call beautiful. This includes, not their facial features alone, but the shape of their heads and hands and feet, and general slovenliness of carriage. The odor, even of the cleanest of them, differs perceptibly from ours. In a word, they seem like a caricature and mockery of our ideas of the 'human form divine.' An intimate knowledge of negroes still further enables one to sympathize with the common dislike of them."[24] And worse yet, such outrageous trash, appearing in a leading Party organ, went unchallenged. In the same anti-Negro spirit, A. M. Simons' widely circulated book, *Social Forces in American History,* repeats all the chauvinist slanders against the Negroes—that they did not fight for their freedom, that they did not demand the right to vote, that the Reconstruction governments were a maze of corruption and mismanagement, etc., etc.

The white chauvinism of the right-wing leadership of the S.P. came to particularly blatant expression in the adoption of a resolution offered by Hillquit at the 1910 congress of the Party. By clear implication, this called for the exclusion of the Chinese and other Asians from the United States.[25] The left wing, led by Haywood, made a bitter fight against this resolution, and also against a right-wing resolution presented by Berger and Untermann which proposed the "unconditional exclusion of Chinese, Japanese, Koreans, and Hindus." The Negro question as such did not come up in the discussion. The debate fairly reeked with gross white supremacy prejudices. Ernest Untermann declared: "We would be false to our Socialist agitation if we insisted first on doing away with race prejudice."[26]

An earlier shocking example of white chauvinism in the S.P. leadership occurred in 1902, when the International Socialist Bureau questioned the American Socialist Party about its policy on lynching. This brought forth a virtual apology for lynching as unavoidable in the brutal capitalist conditions prevailing in the South. The S.P. reply said, "The Socialist Party points out the fact that nothing less than the abolition of the capitalist system and the substitution of the Socialist system can provide conditions under which the hunger maniacs, kleptomaniacs, sexual maniacs and all other offensive and now-lynchable human degenerates will cease to be begotten or produced."[27]

With such white chauvinist conceptions and practices, the Socialist Party could not and did not become the party of the Negro people. That remained for the Communist Party.

38. Tuskegee and Niagara

Booker T. Washington, founder of the Tuskegee movement, was born a slave in Franklin County, Virginia a few years before the outbreak of the Civil War—the precise date is not known. He entered Hampton Institute in 1872, at about the age of 16. There, from General S. C. Armstrong, its president, he absorbed a belief in the great importance of vocational education. In 1881 he took charge of a small school in Tuskegee, Alabama, and began to put his theories into effect. Highly intelligent and a first-rate organizer, in four years' time Washington transformed the little shack school, with its handful of students, into a thriving institution of a dozen buildings and 300 students—Tuskegee Normal and Industrial Institute. It now has some 3,000 students, and many other colleges are associated with it.

THE TUSKEGEE PROGRAM

Washington concentrated, first of all, upon teaching farming and the handicrafts—bricklaying, carpentry, blacksmithing, and the like. He played down the importance of history, mathematics, and science for Negro students, and emphasized the practical skills and the virtues of patience and perseverance. He heavily stressed the importance of acquiring property. His general theory was that Negroes possessing these requisites were bound to prosper in the community, irrespective of all obstacles. The characteristic motto of the class of 1886 at Tuskegee was, "There is plenty of room at the top." Washington stated his philosophy thus: "The individual who can do something that the world wants done, will in the end make his way, regardless of his race."[1]

The second phase of Washington's program, which was the sum of it all, was the cultivation of Negro business institutions. This developed somewhat later in his career, and he organized the National Negro Business League in 1900, and became its first president. Dr. Du Bois, then a strong advocate of the potentialities of Negro business, was also very active in the League's formation. The purposes of this organization were "to give encouragement to the people to stand together, to build up individuals in various connections and to show

408

to the world the capabilities and possibilities of the race."[2] The organization still exists, but of this more anon.

The third phase of Washington's program was a complete playing down of political action and of a perspective for his people. His general idea was that the Negro people should make no serious assault upon existing political injustices, that they could get more from the ruling planters and industrialists by catering to them than by fighting them. Consequently, he discouraged all political activity, and made no sustained fight against the crying evils of Jim Crow, disfranchisement, and lynching, much less against capitalism itself. In his public speeches he only occasionally mentioned the outrages against his people.[3] He sought to adjust the Negro people to segregation, as indicated by his famous statement that, as between Negroes and whites, "In all things that are purely social we can be as separate as the fingers, yet one as the hand in all things essential to mutual progress."[4] He accepted the poll tax and literacy test requirements for voting, insisting only that these measures be applied fairly to both whites and Negroes. He was opposed to the urbanization of the Negro, and also the perennial panaceas of colonization, migration, and amalgamation. He not only condemned Jim Crow practices in labor unions, but he was an inveterate enemy of trade unionism, calling it "that form of slavery which prevents a man from selling his labor to whom he pleases on account of his color."[5] And he opposed "revolutionary action" and Socialism.

THE ATLANTA "COMPROMISE"

Booker T. Washington attracted national attention to himself and his program by a speech he delivered at the Atlanta Cotton Exposition on September 18, 1895. In this obsequious speech, Washington called upon his people to "cast down your buckets where you are." This symbol he drew from the story of a water-famished ship's crew off the shores of South America, who, casting their buckets into the sea, came up with the fresh water of the Amazon River, where they had thought all was salt water. Consequently, the Negro people should make the best of the situation confronting them and, by implication, not run after will-o'-the-wisps of migration and political demands. He called upon the rulers of the South also to "cast down their buckets" into the rich labor source offered by the Negro people, instead of wasting their efforts to attract white immigrants from Europe.

In return, Washington pledged that if this was done, the Negro people would prove loyal servitors to the master class. He said, "While doing this you can be sure in the future, as you have been in the past, that you and your families will be surrounded by the most patient, faithful, law-abiding, and unresentful people that the world has seen. As we have proved our loyalty to you in the past, in nursing your children, watching by the sick-beds of your mothers and fathers, and often following them with tear-dimmed eyes to their graves, so in the future, in our humble way, we shall stand by you with a devotion that no foreigner can approach, ready to lay down our lives, if need be, in defense of yours, interlacing our industrial, commercial, civil, and religious life with yours in a way that shall make the interests of both races one."[6] The speaker deplored the "mistakes" of Negro fighters in the past in seeking seats in Congress and the state legislatures, and he declared that "The wisest among my race understand that the agitation of questions of social equality is the extremest folly." He said nothing of the terrible outrages suffered by his people—during 1895, when this speech was delivered, 113 Negroes were lynched in the South.

W. E. B. Du Bois later characterized Washington's speech as "the Atlanta Compromise." It proposed to give up the whole militant line which the Negro people followed for generations. The speech was delivered seven months after the death of that great fighter for Negro rights, Frederick Douglass. Booker T. Washington's speech, in fact his whole program, was an offer to provide the industrialist and planter rulers of the South with a trained and obedient Negro working force for maximum exploitation. Without unions, without political organizations, without white allies among the workers and farmers, and without an orientation toward struggle, they would have been helpless in the grip of capitalist exploitation. Washington's conception of each one working his way ahead in competition with the rest, was in general more fitting for the times of Jefferson than that of the trusts. It was essentially a program of strikebreaking and submission. Booker T. Washington was much akin to the labor misleader, Samuel Gompers, who came forward at the same time.

Washington's program, coming when it did, was demoralizing to the Negro people. During the 1890's, at the time of this Negro leader's rise to influence, the Southern planter-Northern monopolist dictators, fighting against the Negro-white farmer unity in the Populist Movement, were disfranchising the Negro people in state conventions all over the South and were busily writing the Jim Crow system into state laws. Moreover, lynching was at its high point. Du Bois says that at this crucial time the effect of Washington's speech was, instead of condemning the exploiters, to put "the chief onus for his condition upon the Negro himself."[7] Washington's program disarmed the Negro people in the face of the offensive of their powerful and implacable exploiter enemies and fitted right into the plans of American imperialism in the South.

WASHINGTON'S GLORIFICATION

Naturally enough, Washington's Atlanta speech was hailed by capitalist spokesmen in the North as well as the South. The Negro-hating Southern capitalists saw in it and in his program generally the perfect answer to their age-long insoluble problem of holding down the Negro people to be mercilessly robbed. The Northern monopolists, with mounting investments in the South, hoped on the basis of the Tuskegee program, with the help of able Negro leaders, to create not only a subservient Negro working force in the South, but also a reliable body of strikebreakers for use in the North.

Seldom has the United States seen such a spectacular rise in capitalist popularity as that which attended Booker T. Washington in the years following his Atlanta speech. He was received and lionized everywhere in bourgeois circles. He became the personal friend and close associate of many multimillionaires, including such figures as H. H. Rogers of Standard Oil, William H. Baldwin, Jr., vice-president of the Southern Railway, Collis P. Huntingdon, builder of Newport News, and other exploiters of Southern Negro labor. He was the guest of Andrew Carnegie at Skibo Castle.[8] He dined at the White House with Theodore Roosevelt and he became the arbiter of all federal appointments relating to Negroes. Donations poured into Tuskegee from big bourgeois sources, Carnegie giving $600,000.

Washington received honorary degrees from Harvard in 1896 and Dartmouth in 1901. He went abroad and was received and made much of by Queen Victoria of England and by a long list of blue-blood notables. Of Washington's social conquests, Woodward aptly remarks, "The man who abjured 'social equality' in the South moved in circles of the elite in the North and aristocracy abroad that were opened to extremely few Southern whites. The man who disparaged the importance of political power for his race came to exercise political power such as few if any Southern white men of his time enjoyed."[9] Redding thus bluntly characterizes the famous Negro's role: "White America had raised this man up because he espoused a policy which was intended to keep the Negro docile and dumb in regard to civil, social, and political rights and privileges."[10]

Despite growing opposition, Washington also acquired a dominating position in Negro circles. To a marked degree, he was able to translate the friendship of the capitalists into terms of concrete Negro leadership. The *New York World,* says Redding, "called him the 'Negro Moses.' . . . He was the umpire in all important appointments of Negroes; the channel through which philanthropy flowed, or did not flow, to Negro institutions; the creator and destroyer of careers; the maker and breaker of men. . . . . He created what has been called the 'Tuskegee machine,' and with petulant pride kept it running in high gear for a dozen years."[11]

THE NATIONAL SIGNIFICANCE
OF BOOKER T. WASHINGTON

During the historical development of the Negro people, one of its basic trends toward nationhood was the gradual crystallization away from the general mass of slaves and into the characteristic class structure of capitalist society. This tendency was to be remarked from the earliest colonial times and it continued through the period of slavery. Even at the outset of the slave system, there was a free Negro proletariat—however small—and also the beginnings of a petty bourgeoisie, small storekeepers and the like. There were, likewise, a few small farmers and even some slaveholders. These early class differentiations became more marked after the Revolution of 1776.

The U. S. Census of 1830 says that there were 3,777 Negro masters of slaves in the United States—often these slaves were wives, children, and other relatives, where laws forbade manumission. Cyprian Ricaud of Louisiana, however, owned 91 slaves, and a Negro planter in North Carolina was said to possess 200.[12] John Jones of Charleston had $40,000, and Thomy Lafoon of New Orleans, $500,000. James Forten, a sail-maker of Philadelphia had amassed $100,000 in 1832; Robert Purvis, likewise of Pennsylvania, was a well-to-do man, and so was Paul Cuffee of Boston.[13] Stephen Smith of Columbia, Pennsylvania, was said to own $500,000.[14] In the pre-war period there were many small Negro stores and other businesses, especially in the Southern states. These included barber shops, livery stables, tailor and cooking establishments, ale-houses, etc. Harris says that "In personal service enterprises the free Negroes had practically no competition in the South."[15]

After the Civil War this class differentiation among the Negro people was further speeded up. By 1890 there were some 120,000 Negro farm owners and several times as many farm wage earners. There was also a growing body of Negro workers in industry. The bulk of the Negroes in the South, however, remained sharecroppers. The ranks of the Negro middle classes were growing; shopkeepers and small industrialists multiplied, and so did the professional classes. During this period, the Negro people, despite their immense handicaps, produced some inventors—notably Elijah McCoy, lubrication expert; Robert Rillieux, inventor of the vacuum pan used in refining sugar; Granville T. Woods, inventor of many electrical devices; Jan E. Matzeliger, creator of revolutionary shoe machinery; and others.[16] Negro intellectuals turned out an increasing volume of literature; and despite the terror, the Negro press grew rapidly in the South. In 1883, G. W. Williams wrote his important *History of the Negro Race in America,* and during the next decade, Chesnutt, Dunbar, Langston, Du Bois, Alexander and others began to write. A number of important Negro financial institutions also arose. Aside from the ill-fated Freedmen's Savings and Trust Company (see Chapter 31), Negro banks were organized in Washington in 1888 and in Birmingham in 1890. Between 1899 and 1905, 28 such banks were established.[17]

Booker T. Washington was a vigorous spokesman of this developing nationalism among the Negro people, although, characteristically, he understood it and spoke of it in terms not of Negro nationality, but of Negro race. He definitely cultivated the class differentiation necessary for the growth of Negro nationhood. He laid great stress upon the building up of a strong body of free Negro farmers, taking the position that the Negroes were essentially an agricultural people. With his intensive program of vocational education, he also cultivated the growth of an industrial proletariat, although he put more weight upon handicraft than upon modern industry. Washington also strove to subordinate the national consciousness of the Negro people to his system of bourgeois nationalism. Dearest to his heart was the encouragement of Negro business institutions of all sorts. Here he showed the bourgeois that was in him. His goal of nationalism was expressed by the National Negro Business League.

Harry Haywood correctly characterizes Washington when he says: "Here definitely was the voice of the embryonic Negro middle class, which, though staggered by the shock of the Hayes-Tilden sell-out, was again desperately striving to reform its scattered ranks and break through to a place in the sun. Booker T. Washington's philosophy became its rallying point. Considering the times, the program of the sage of Tuskegee was by no means wholly negative. . . . The inherent fallacy in the Washington doctrine was its counterposing of the Negro's participation in politics to his economic rehabilitation."[18] This meant, in substance, denying his people a perspective of independence, stifling their expanding nationhood, condemning them to a position of subordination to the worst exploiters, reducing them to a category of second-class citizens, and therewith, in sum, also defeating his own project of economic advance for the Negro people.

Washington's program of creating a body of trained, obedient, non-rebellious workers dovetailed fully with the interests of the big planter-industrialist exploiters, which is why they hailed it so enthusiastically. Thus, willingly or unwillingly, Washington became a tool of American imperialism for the exploitation of the Negro people, much as Gompers did for the exploitation of the working class in general. The history of oppressed peoples is full of leaders of the Washington and Gompers types, who want to keep the people subordinate to the ruling class.

The heart of the anti-Negro element in Washington's program was his systematic opposition to political education for Negroes. Like the planters and industrialists, to whom he so assiduously catered, Washington realized that political education was highly revolutionary for his people; that the more they came to understand the horrible conditions of enslavement and oppression under which they lived, the more they would rebel against them. He rightly looked upon the Negro intellectuals of the times as essentially revolutionary; hence, he did nothing to enhance their numbers or influence. Quite the contrary. From his standpoint he was correct; for it was from the ranks of the intellectuals that the decisive challenge to his political system finally came.

THE RISING TIDE OF OPPOSITION

From the time of Booker T. Washington's Atlanta Speech in 1895, there was a sharp and rising Negro opposition to his program of organized surrender to the big planter and industrialist exploiters. It was imperative that struggle be carried on against the burning plagues of lynching, race riots, disfranchisement, and Jim Crow, to which the Negro people were being increasingly subjected. Some of the earlier expressions of this developing revolt against Tuskegeeism were the short-lived National Association of Colored Men, formed in 1896 by R. T. Greener, D. A. Straker, J. Dickinson and others; the American Negro Academy, formed in 1897, by A. Crummell, W. E. B. Du Bois, F. J. Grimke, Kelly Miller, and others, which stressed higher education; and the National Association of Colored Women formed in 1896. Especially important was the Afro-American Council, organized in 1899, which demanded an end to lynching and the enforcement of the Thirteenth, Fourteenth and Fifteenth Amendments. The organization existed for several years.[19]

An important manifestation of the rising spirit of national consciousness among the Negro people was the development of anti-imperialist spirit among them at the time of the Spanish-American War and afterward (1898-1901). Negro troops played an important part in this war. Redding says, "There is no doubt that in the battle of San Juan the Negro cavalry turned a defeat into victory and saved the honor and the hides of Teddy Roosevelt's Rough Riders."[20] Alert Negro leaders such as Du Bois, however, correctly condemned the war as imperialist aggression. In the revolutionary spirit of Frederick Douglass 60 years before in Europe, the most conscious leaders of the Negro people identified the interests of their people with those of the struggling colonial peoples all over the world. They spoke primarily, in fact if not in words, as the representatives of the oppressed American Negro nation.

Du Bois, together with considerable sections of the Negro press, actively supported the Anti-Imperialist League of the time. This body, formed in Chicago, on October 17, 1899, condemned the war in the Philippines as "an unjust," imperialist war. It denounced "the slaughter of the Filipinos as a needless horror." The platform said, "We deny that the obligation of all citizens to support their government in times of grave national peril applies to the present situation."[21] On November 17, 1899, the *American Citizen,* a Negro paper in Kansas City, Kansas, expressed a widespread Negro view in stating that imperialist "expansion means extension of race hate and cruelty, barbarous lynchings and gross injustice to dark people."[22] *The Broad Ax,* of September 30, 1899, called for the formation of a "National Negro Anti-Expansionist, Anti-Imperialist, Anti-Trust, Anti-Lynching League."[23]

DU BOIS AND THE NIAGARA MOVEMENT

The anti-Booker T. Washington trend became definite and concrete with the appearance of the Boston *Guardian,* a Negro journal founded in 1901, and edited by Monroe Trotter and George Forbes. This group bitterly denounced Washington for his capitulation policies and initiated a fight for Negro rights. Soon the group was joined by William Edward Burghart Du Bois, a brilliant Negro scholar and fighter, who soon became the group's leader. Dr. Du Bois was born in Great Barrington, Massachusetts, in 1868. He came of free Negro and Huguenot ancestry and was educated at Fisk, Harvard, and Berlin universities. He taught English, French, German and Greek.

While teaching at Atlanta University, Du Bois had for several years been developing a position of sharp opposition to the program of Booker T. Washington. This he crystallized in his *Souls of Black Folk,* published in 1903. This series of essays criticized Washington's playing down of higher education and concentration of Negro attention upon "a gospel of Work and Money." Du Bois also came forward at this time with his theory of the "Talented Tenth"—the idea that the Negro petty-bourgeois intellectuals had to be cultivated and relied upon as the natural leaders of the Negro people. This theory guided his activities for many years. It was not until 1952, on the basis of decades of rough experience with opportunist middle class elements and a growing realization that the reliable leading force among the Negro people is the Negro proletariat, that Du Bois gave up his theory of the "Talented Tenth."[24]

The Niagara Movement was organized by the Boston *Guardian* group in Fort Erie, in Canada, just across from Buffalo, July 11-14, 1905. Du Bois, F. L. McGhee, C. C. Bentley, W. M. Trotter, J. Max Baker, and 25 others took part in the convention. Fittingly, the meeting was held at a famous terminus of the Underground Railroad of slavery times. Niagara's "Declaration of Principles" was a ringing protest against the many outrages perpetrated against the Negro people and it called on the Negro masses to rally to fight against them. It militantly demanded the right to vote, full education, court justice and service on juries, equal treatment in the armed forces, health facilities, abolition of Jim Crow, and the enforcement of the Thirteenth, Fourteenth, and Fifteenth Amendments. It protested against the "unchristian" attitude of the churches toward

Negroes, and it condemned the policies of the employers and trade unions excluding Negroes from industries and unions. It elected Dr. Du Bois and Reverend J. M. Waldron as general secretary and treasurer respectively.[25]

The Niagara Movement continued its activities for about four years. It held meetings in various parts of the country, popularizing its general program. It set up a Junior Niagara Movement and also a women's section, together with a legal department to organize the fight for civil rights. It fought a number of Jim Crow cases in court. In 1906, the Niagara Movement held its convention at Harper's Ferry, West Virginia, scene of John Brown's historic raid. At this time Du Bois made a ringing declaration of the Niagara policy: "We will not be satisfied to take one jot or tittle less than our full manhood rights. We claim for ourselves every single right that belongs to a freeborn American, political, civil, and social; and until we get these rights we will never cease to protest and assail the ears of America. The battle we wage is not for ourselves alone, but for all true Americans."[26]

THE ROLE OF NIAGARA

The formation of the Niagara Movement marked a turning point in the history of the Negro people. It was both a revolt against the stifling reactionary bureaucracy of Booker T. Washington and the beginning of a more militant policy of struggle against the Jim Crowers and lynchers. The new movement could and did progress only in the face of Washington's opposition. Redding says, the chief of Tuskegee, "with the help of influencial friends, tried to destroy both Du Bois and his position."[27] Among other measures, Washington practically bought up several of the most influential Negro papers. But the new movement was not to be stopped.

From a programmatic standpoint this whole development can be summarized as follows: The Niagara movement largely agreed with Washington on the need for the propagation of vocational education; going much further, it demanded full educational rights for Negroes especially in areas of culture and the humanities. The Niagarans joined with Washington in the furtherance of Negro business organization; indeed, on the latter point, Du Bois, with his great stress upon the possibilities of a Negro economy, outdid Washington in some respects. The main point of divergence between the movements, however—and this was decisive—was where Washington preached humility and submission for the Negro people, Du Bois and his followers advocated a course of militant struggle. They gave their people a new dignity, a new hope, and a new perspective. It was a renaissance of the Negro struggle for freedom. As Haywood says, "The banner of revolt was unfurled, and the modern Negro liberation movement was born."[28] It was a long stride ahead in the national growth of the Negro people. In developing the fighting position of the Niagara movement in opposition to Washington's surrender line, Dr. Du Bois proved himself to be one of the greatest of Negro spokesmen.

The new and brilliant leader of the Negro people, Du Bois, for at least a generation largely shaped the main line of struggle along which the Negro people have made splendid progress. And even now, in his middle eighties, this fine leader stands in the front rank of the fighters of the Negro people. Throughout the years, Dr. Du Bois, despite political shortcomings which we have indicated in passing, has carried forward the fighting tradition of Frederick Douglass, of whom he was the political heir. For decades, many of the very best fighters and thinkers produced by the American Negro people have been actively grouped around Du Bois.

Booker T. Washington died in November 1915, at the age of about 60. Du Bois says that this exceptional leader reached the height of his career during 1899-1906; but to the last he retained immense personal prestige[29] and power. Redding thus sums up Washington: "After all, Washington was the white South's man. The white South had made him, raised him up as the savior of its conscience, and when he died the South wept. . . . the North was less stricken in its grief and clearer in its judgment. . . . 'In stern justice,' wrote Du Bois with general Negro approbation, 'we must lay on the soul of this man a heavy responsibility for the consummation of Negro disfranchisement, the decline of the Negro college and public school and the firmer establishment of color caste in this land.' "[30]

39. Formation of the N. A. A. C. P.

The years between the turn of the century and the outbreak of World War I were a period of severe struggle for the working class and the Negro people. Monopoly capital was pursuing its ruthless course, seizing the natural wealth of the country, rapidly expanding the industrial system, reaping unprecedented profits, and submitting the workers of field and factory to ever sharper exploitation. This was the period of the economic crises of 1907 and 1913, a widespread expansion of the "open shop," the extension of company unionism, and gunman rule in the company towns. American imperialism was also rampant in Latin America—in Mexico, Nicaragua, Honduras, Venezuela, Cuba, etc. The trusts had acquired complete control of the Federal government, North and South. The National Industrial Relations Commission created by Congress in 1912 and appointed by President Wilson, declared that "The final control of American industry rests, therefore, in the hands of a small number of wealthy and powerful financiers."[1]

The Negro people, as always, suffered the most in these years of deprivation, oppression, and struggle. The Industrial Relations Commission pointed out that in the Southwest (typical of the whole South), in predominantly Negro agricultural areas, tenancy in 1910 ranged up to 53 percent in Texas and 54 percent in Oklahoma. "Furthermore, over 80 percent of the tenants are regularly in debt to the stores from which they secure their supplies, and pay exorbitantly for this credit." Credit rates run from 20 to 60 percent. The Commission warned of "acute civil disturbances" if conditions were not remedied.[2]

POGROMS, LYNCHINGS, MURDERS

On the eve of "the war to make the world safe for democracy" of 1917-18, the Negro people suffered from the most acute forms of exploitation and terror. They were shamelessly robbed as sharecroppers; they were stripped of the right to vote; they were systematically insulted by Jim Crow; they were barred from industry, and when they did get jobs they had to work for half of what a white man got in the North for similar work; they were crowded into the filthy ghettos; they were thrown into jails and onto the medieval chain gangs by the thousands for the most trivial offenses, real or imaginary. And over their whole life hung the constant menace of sudden, brutal death from their oppressors.

In this period, many cities were afflicted with pogroms against the Negroes. These were called "race riots"; but in actuality they were deliberately planned, organized attacks against the Negro people by armed white thugs in the service of the planter-monopolist reaction. One of the worst pogroms ocurred in Wilmington, North Carolina, in 1898. "Nine Negroes massacred outright; a score wounded and hunted like partridges on the mountain; one man, brave enough to fight against such odds, who would be hailed as a hero anywhere else, was given the privilege of running the gauntlet up a broad street, where he sank ankle-deep in the sand, while crowds of men lined the sidewalks and riddled him with a pint of bullets as he ran bleeding past their doors."[3]

In August 1900, a mob raged through the streets of New York, beating Negroes. In 1906, in Atlanta, Georgia, a riot lasted four days, with several Negroes and whites killed. In the same year there took place in Brownsville, Texas, the "riot" in which a Negro company of the 25th Regiment defended themselves successfully against a group of white ruffians. Springfield, Ohio, had two "race riots" within a few years, and Greensburg, Indiana, was the scene of another at about the same time. But the worst one was in Springfield, Illinois, in Lincoln's town, in August, 1908. This, says Franklin, "shook the entire country"—mainly because the Negroes got the best of the struggle. The final account showed two Negroes and four white men killed, with a couple of hundred arrested.[4] Any pretext was sufficient to send a band of armed murderers storming into the Negro quarters of the cities and towns. And, tragically, poor white farmers and workers often took a hand in these dreadful enterprises.

These were the years, too, of a great number of lynchings. Between 1900 and 1914 there were recorded no less than 1079 Negroes brutally murdered by armed mobs.[5] They were hanged, burned, shot, slashed to pieces, and dragged to death behind automobiles. No ferocity was too terrible for lynch mobs in their murder lust. Men, women, and children met this terrible fate, usually upon the slightest pretext. O course, no lynchers were ever punished for their terrible deeds. The lynchings were usually carried out with the full knowledge and consent, and sometimes with the actual participation, of the local authorities.

Dr. Du Bois cites as typical the burning to death of Jesse Washington in the town of Waco, Texas, in 1916, before a crowd of thousands: "While the fire was being prepared of boxes, the naked boy was stabbed and the chain put over the tree. He tried to get away, but could not. He reached up to grab the chain and they cut off his fingers. The big man struck the boy on the back of the neck with a knife just as they were pulling him up on a tree. Mr. ——— thought that was practically the death blow. He was lowered several times by means of the chain around his neck. Someone said they would estimate the boy had about twenty-five stab wounds, each one of them death-dealing."[6] No one was prosecuted for any of these outrages.

Just prior to the outbreak of World War I, such savage scenes of torture were taking place at the rate of about two a week in the South. Defenders of lynching argue that this terrible weapon was used only against rapists. But the facts show that about three-fourths of the Negroes lynched were murdered on other pretexts often of the flimsiest sort; and they also show that usually the alleged rape lynch cases were based upon sheer fraud.

Lynchings commonly took place in small country places, whereas the race riots ordinarily occurred in larger towns and cities. Lynchings were directed against the alleged crime of some individual Negro, or small group of Negroes; but the big city race riots were usually, although not always, provoked over issues of jobs, housing, use of parks, beaches, gang fights, etc., and they were aimed at the Negro people in general. They were organized, wholesale lynchings. In these pogroms, the North proved itself as viciously anti-Negro as the South. Lynching has always had the tacit, if not the active support of the bourgeois elements in the Southern communities. Thus, Myrdal says, "With but rare exceptions, preachers and local religious leaders have not come out against lynching."[7]

Together with pogroms and lynching, the Southern reactionaries have always used individual terror to intimidate the Negro people. That is, armed white men, sure of immunity from prosecution, shoot down unarmed Negroes for even the slightest offense to their tender white supremacist susceptibilities. Many more Negroes have been murdered in this way than by all the mob lynchings and pogroms combined. In the American tradition much has been said about the gunman of the West, but he was a mild figure compared to the innumerable cold-blooded gun-toters who have stalked—and continue to stalk—the highways and byways of the "Sunny South."

THE FOUNDING OF THE N. A. A. C. P.

This was a period of intense struggle, of the rapid organizational growth and ideological development of the toiling masses. The A. F. of L. membership climbed up from 600,000 in 1900 to 2,000,000 in 1914, with new unions being established in many crafts and industries. The Socialist movement also expanded rapidly. The Socialist Party increased from but 10,000 members in 1900 to a high point of 120,000 in 1912. Although woman suffrage was yet to come, the S. P. received 897,001 votes in the national election of that year. This was likewise the period of the foundation and historic struggles of the I.W.W. The Syndicalist League of North America was also born during this period, in 1912.

In tune with the rising spirit of struggle of the working class, the Negro people also made great strides toward organization strength and ideological clarity. They dealt increasing blows against their many vicious enemies. Their main achievement in this respect was the creation of the N.A.A.C.P.

The National Association for the Advancment of Colored People was organized on May 30, 1909, in New York City, as the National Negro Committee. It was formed in response to a call sent out on Lincoln's hundredth birthday anniversary by 55 prominent liberals and Socialists, Negro and white.[8] Among the Negro signers of the call were William L. Bulkley, a New York school principal; Mrs. Ida B. Wells-Barnett of Chicago; Dr. Du Bois of Atlanta; Reverend Francis J. Grimké, Bishop Alexander Walters, and Dr. J. Milton Waldron of Washington. Among the white liberals signing the call were Professor John Dewey, Jane Addams, William Dean Howells, Rabbi Emil G. Hirsch, Reverend John Haynes Holmes, Dr. Henry Moskowitz, Dr. Charles E. Parkhurst, Louis Wald, Mary E. Woolley, and Susan P. Wharton. There were also several white Socialists among the signers, including William English Walling, Charles Edward Russell, J. G. Phelps Stokes, Mary E. Dreier, Florence Kelly, and Mary W. Ovington.

The organization crystallized under its present name at its second national conference, in May 1910. Moorfield Storey, who had been

Charles Sumner's secretary and a leader in the Anti-Imperialist League, was chosen president, Frances Blascoer, executive secretary, and W. E. B. Du Bois, director of publicity and research. In November 1910, *The Crisis,* a monthly, was established as the official organ, with Du Bois as editor. Headquarters were in New York.

Meanwhile, there were numerous Equal Rights Leagues operating in various states. These worked in the tradition of the Equal Rights League of the Civil War and Reconstruction periods. W. M. Trotter, the militant Boston Negro leader, who looked askance at the liberal whites dominating the N.A.A.C.P., furthered this movement. It was soon absorbed, however, by the N.A.A.C.P.

The basis of the new N.A.A.C.P. was the rising wave of resistance among the Negro people, earlier expressed by the Niagara Movement, which the N.A.A.C.P. absorbed. The immediate impulse for its formation was given by the race riot in Springfield, Illinois, the home of Abraham Lincoln, in August 1908. W. E. Walling, himself a Southerner, was in Springfield at the time. He was so outraged by the unprovoked attack upon the Negroes that he wrote an article in *The Independent,* of September 3, bitterly condemning the "riot" and calling for action to prevent the recurrence of such barbarities. This article led directly to the founding of the N.A.A.C.P.

THE PROGRAM OF ACTION

The N.A.A.C.P. endorsed the political line pioneered by the Niagara Movement. It condemned Jim Crow and lynching, and all other forms of Negro oppression. It stood committed to the principle of social equality. "The original purpose of the association was to uplift the Negro men and women of this country by securing for them the complete enjoyment of their rights as citizens, justice in the courts, and equal opportunity in every economic, social, and political endeavor in the United States."[9] The program, however, was not so clear-cut, nor the organization so aggressive as the Niagara Movement which preceded it.

The militant Du Bois thus stated his conception of the movement, after the lynching of a Negro in Coatesville, Pennsylvania, in 1911, "Let every Black American gird up his loins. The great day is coming. We have crawled and pleaded for justice and we have been cheerfully spit upon and murdered and burned. We will not endure it forever. If we are to die, in God's name let us perish like men and not like bales of hay."[10]

The national composition of the N.A.A.C.P. differed from that of the Niagara Movement, the latter being a Negro organization, whereas the N.A.A.C.P. united Negro and white. Both were middle class in their leadership, and the N.A.A.C.P. remains so to the present day. The liberal whites were predominant at the start and for a long time afterward. Du Bois was the only Negro among the original executive officers. Haywood thus describes the set-up: "It was the pattern of white ruling-class paternalism which, as time went on, was to cast an ever-deepening shadow over the developing Negro liberation movement, throttling its self-assertiveness and its independen initiative, placing before it limited objectives and dulling the sharp edge of the sword of Negro protest."[11]

The N.A.A.C.P. carried on many campaigns against lynching and Jim Crow in the years before and during World War I. It combated segregation laws in Winston-Salem, Atlanta, Richmond, Roanoke, Louisville, and other cities. In 1912, it was instrumental in having the Southern Railway reverse its decision henceforth to employ only white workers in skilled trades. By 1914, the organization had spread into many Northern states; it had some 9,000 members in 50 branches, among them four in colleges. At the outbreak of the war, the circulation of *The Crisis* was about 20,000 copies.

In the beginning, the wealthy Northern white philanthropists who were interesting themselves in the Negro people, looked askance at the N.A.A.C.P.. They preferred such crippling activities as those cultivated by Booker T. Washington at Tuskegee. Later on, however, the organization, by its increasingly conservative course, was able to win the support of these people, including such figures as Mrs. Cyrus H. McCormick and Harvey Firestone. The continual intervention of big capitalists, notorious exploiters of labor, in movements designed to better the status of the Negro people has been characteristic since the end of the Civil War. Their influence on Negro leaders has always been a corrupting one and has served to tone down their radicalism. This paternalistic concern over the welfare of the Negro is explained by the capitalists' basic interest in cultivating the Negro workers as a convenient force for exploitation. The direct influence and participation of big capitalists—the Morgans, Rockefellers, Carnegies, Rosenwalds, and the like—in the organizations of the Negro people has always been, and continues to be a major handicap in the Negro's upward fight.

THE NATIONAL URBAN LEAGUE

The establishment and early political activities of the N.A.A.C.P. caused great concern among conservative Negro leaders of the Booker T. Washington type and also among their wealthy white friends. They feared the Negro people being lead astray, toward struggle and Socialism. One of the most important consequences of their growing alarm was the formation of the National League on Urban Conditions among Negroes in 1911. This body was an amalgamation of the New York Committee for Improving Industrial Conditions of Negroes and the National League for the Protection of Colored Women. Its first national chairman was Mrs. William H. Baldwin, wife of a big railroad magnate, and its field secretary Eugene Knickle Jones. It had much the same general composition as the N.A.A.C.P., with white liberals in control. At its founding conference, Mrs. Baldwin stated the general purposes of the organization as follows: "Let us work together not as colored people nor as white people for the narrow benefit of any group alone, but together as American citizens for the common good of our common city, our common country."[12]

Acting along the line laid down by Booker T. Washington, the National Urban League eschewed politics and devoted itself to questions bearing directly upon the economic welfare of the Negro masses. By mutual agreement it left to the N.A.A.C.P. the fight for civil rights, while it concerned itself with economic questions. The League was and remains a social service organization, devoting itself to placing Negroes in jobs and to the creation of better housing, school facilities, public playgrounds, health clinics, etc., in Negro communities. It has always been a conservative influence among the Negro people, with its non-political attitude, bureaucratic control and conservative outlook. Unlike the N.A.A.C.P., the Urban League made no effort to build itself into a broad mass organization.

In 1913, the League's board of directors was expanded to include such Negro and white liberals and social workers as Booker T. Washington, James Dillard, Charles D. Hillis, and Kelly Miller. With the backing of Washington and his eventual successor at Tuskegee, R. R. Moton, the Urban League had from the outset philanthropic backing of the big capitalists that, for a time at least, was withheld from the more radical N.A.A.C.P.

THE NEGRO WORKERS AND TRADE UNIONISM

Although during the 14-year period in question (1900-1914), the trade unions grew rapidly, they made no appreciable progress in their attitude toward the ever-increasing number of Negro industrial wage workers. The unions maintained their anti-Negro practices. Many of them formally excluded Negroes from their ranks; others excluded them in actuality, but without constitutional provisions to this effect. All of the unions, even those that admitted Negroes to membership, discriminated against them with regard to job promotion, union leadership, etc. In many cases the unions were active in driving the Negroes out of occupations that had been theirs for generations. It was most rare, too, for a Negro to be elected to any important union post; few unions had Negroes on their national executive boards, and, as for the Executive Council of the A.F. of L., it has never included a Negro—to this very day.

The A.F. of L. not only refused to see that the individual trade unions dropped their lily-white clauses and Jim Crow practices, conceded the Negro worker the right to work in industry, and gave him the protection on the job to which every worker was entitled; but it also ignored the major evils which bore down so heavily upon the Negro people as a whole. One may search in vain the records of the A.F. of L. and Railroad Brotherhoods in the pre-World War I years to find some trace of protest against the horror of lynching, Jim Crow, race riots, and the disfranchisement of the Negro voter. Significantly, no names of labor leaders appeared on the call to found the N.A.A.C.P. This negative attitude of the A.F. of L. and Railroad Brotherhood leaders was not mere neglect of the Negro; it was an outright white chauvinist betrayal of his interests. The unions' discrimination against Negroes and the failure of the top labor leaders to support the fight of the Negro people against their exploiters and persecutors lent definite aid and comfort to the Southern Negro-baiters and lynchers.

In view of the anti-Negro policies of the A.F. of L. and Railroad Brotherhoods, it is not surprising that the Negro intelligentsia developed a strong anti-trade union bias. Frederick Douglass, as we have seen, took a position against labor unionism. So did Booker T. Washington, who especially expressed an elaborate anti-union position supposedly in behalf of the Negro people. W. E. B. Du Bois also looked with disfavor upon trade unions during the early period we are discussing. This trend was to be found among many Negro leaders down to the days of Marcus Garvey, and beyond.

Before World War I, the N.A.A.C.P. carried on no campaign for the unionization of Negroes; and as for the more conservative Urban League, it was distinctly anti-union. In fact, it has often been charged with engaging in active strikebreaking activities. Frank R. Crosswaith, prominent Negro Socialist leader, later remarked, "The Urban League was established 25 years ago with the idea of getting jobs for Negroes by sending them often to act as strikebreakers. . . . The League was supplied with cash by wealthy white employers."[13]

The Negro worker, however, has never expressed the sharp anti-trade union attitudes which understandably, characterized the intellectual leaders for so long. Although on occasion, in the face of crass betrayal by the unions, the Negro has acted as a strike-breaker (and so have white workers on a vastly larger scale), he has always proved a willing recruit for the unions; and once admitted, he has shown himself to be a good member and fighter. He demonstrated this by his participation in the old National Labor Union and the Knights of Labor, by his long struggle to get into the A.F. of L. unions, and by his militant role in innumerable strikes where he was recognized as a union man. In our own day, he has no superior as a trade union-ist. It was not the Negro intellectual who taught the Negro worker the value of trade unionism, but the other way around. The Negro worker's instinct and interest as a wage worker made him fight his way into the unions, despite the crassest chauvinism of the white union leadership and some very poor advice from Negro intellectuals. In many cases, the latter openly told the Negro worker that the only way he could break through white chauvinist barriers and get into industry was by acting as a strikebreaker.[14]

THE NEGRO IN POLITICS

Between 1900 and 1914, the Negro people shared to a considerable extent the awakening of the working class on the question of political action. Traditionally, they had supported the Republican Party; for this, after all, was the party of Lincoln and of emancipation, and, as such, it had a tremendous prestige among the Negro people for a long period. The Hayes-Tilden sell-out of 1877 dealt a heavy blow to this loyalty, and the Populist movement of the 1890's, in which the Negroes of the South participated extensively, opened new per-

spectives of independent political action. Many Negroes, including
Dr. Du Bois, supported William J. Bryan. In March 1904, the Na-
tional Liberty Party was formed chiefly of Negroes, and it nominated
G. E. Taylor for president,[15] but it did not last beyond this election.

Theodore Roosevelt widely solicited the votes of the Negro people
in the North during the Bull Moose election campaign of 1912. In
that year Roosevelt, standard bearer of the United States Steel Corporation, split the Republican Party in an effort to dominate it. He
organized the Progressive Party, with himself and Burton K. Wheeler
as the national candidates. Roosevelt made many promises of fair treatment for Negroes; but they were suspicious of him because, while
president, he had forced the dishonorable disbanding of three Negro
companies of the 25th Regiment for having defended themselves
against the attacks of white ruffians in Brownsville, Texas. He gave
many other examples of a crass white chauvinism. The Negroes'
enthusiasm for Roosevelt was especially dampened by the Progressive
Party convention in 1912. There the N.A.A.C.P. presented a plank
calling for "the repeal of unfair discriminatory laws and the complete
enfranchisement of the Negro." Roosevelt made no opposition to
the Southern delegates when they rejected this from the platform,
nor when they barred a number of Negro delegates.[16] It has been
estimated that in 1912 about 100,000 Northern Negroes voted for
Woodrow Wilson, the Democratic candidate. The "progressivism" of
both Roosevelt and Wilson was lily-white. In 1892, there were 120
Negro delegates at the national convention of the Republican Party,
but in 1920 there were only 27—indicating the decline of that party
as the party of the Negro people.[17]

The mood and situation of the Negro people during the period
of 1900-1914 offered the Socialist Party a splendid opportunity to gain
a strong following among them. However, because of the opportunist
orientation of that Party and the white chauvinism prevailing in the
opportunist petty-bourgeois leadership (see Chapter 37), it completely
missed its chance. Throughout this era of bitter hardships for the
Negro masses, the Socialist Party leadership, like that of the A.F. of L.,
ignored their problems. Occasional articles appeared in the Socialist
press, complaining about the terrible conditions in the South; but
the party never felt called upon to do anything about them, except
to bid the Negroes (who had no franchise) to vote for Socialism.

At this time the S. P. group was strong in the A.F. of L. In 1912,
Max Hayes, the Socialist candidate for A.F. of L. president polled

5,073 votes against 11,974 for Gompers. But the Socialists never challenged the Jim Crow policies of the Gompers bureaucracy. Indeed, they tolerated the Jim Crow exclusion policy in some of the unions they directly controlled, notably the machinists. There were, it is true, several prominent Socialists among the founders of the N.A.A.C.P.; but they acted more in the spirit of liberals (which their support of World War I demonstrated them to be) than as Socialist Party members. There were no trade unionists among this group. Characteristically, they never even made the slightest fight to get the Socialist Party to endorse the N.A.A.C.P. or to support its Negro rights program. Consequently, few Negroes became Socialists. Dr. Du Bois joined the Party in 1911; but sinking no roots in its infertile soil, he quit it in 1912.

The year 1913, the fiftieth anniversary of the Emancipation Proclamation, was one of jubilee for the Negro people, and celebrations were held all over the South. It was a time of stock-taking on the progress that had been made in the acquisition of farms, businesses, and capital; in the liquidation of illiteracy, the production of literary works, and the creation of a body of Negro teachers, doctors, lawyers, scientists, and other professionals; in the building of the press and the growth of other Negro organizations and institutions. In all these fields notable progress was registered in the face of heart-breaking oppression and difficulties. But a vast mountain of work lay ahead. The main thing shown was that the young Negro nation was on the march ideologically and politically, readying itself for the big struggles and movements before it.

40. World War I
and the Negro

World War I had profound and lasting effects upon the Negro people economically, politically, and ideologically, as the ensuing years were to demonstrate. The great and bloody war began on July 28, 1914, and ended on November 11, 1918. It developed as a war between two great alliances of capitalist states—Great Britain, France, Russia, Italy, and the United States on one side, and Germany, Austria-Hungary, and Turkey, on the other. All the other principal powers eventually became involved. Before peace arrived, the war cost the lives of 10 million soldiers and innumerable civilians, the wounding of 21 million more, and the destruction of $338 billion in wealth.

It was an imperialist war, brought about by the insatiable greed of the various capitalist powers for more markets, more supplies of raw materials, more strategic points to control, more colonies, and more peoples to exploit. The United States was plunged into the war by the Wilson Administration. President Wilson, realizing the strong anti-war sentiment among the masses, had made the preservation of peace the center of his campaign for re-election in 1916. He was duly returned to the White House on the basis that "He Kept Us Out of War." But only a month after taking office, on April 6, 1917, the president cynically declared war on Germany, and the American people found themselves in the slaughter—the war in Europe then being two and a half years old. The early policy of Wall Street big business had been to let the European powers slash themselves to pieces in the war, while it got rich on munitions production. But this ruthless policy exhausted itself. Early in 1917, there was grave danger that rising German imperialism might win the war. This would have been disastrous to the imperialist interests of the United States; so despite the peace will of the people, Wall Street pushed the country into the war.

The great masses of the American people were opposed to entering the war—a fact which did not stay the hands of the imperialist war-makers. The top Gompersite leaders in the A.F. of L., true to their role as lickspittles of big business, promptly came out for the war. The main opposition to the war was led by the Socialist Party; that is, by the left wing, headed by Eugene V. Debs, Charles E. Ruthenberg, and others. The right wing and center of the Party veered more and more toward the Gompers pro-war position.

MASS ATTITUDES TOWARD THE WAR

The Negro people shared the peace sentiments of the American masses as a whole. In a letter of April 19, 1917, President Wilson professed amazement that "many of the members of the colored race were not enthusiastic in their support of the government in this crisis." Wilson, who during the war upheld Jim Crowism in the armed forces and after the war stirred not a finger against the raging lynch terror, tried to win the Negroes by jingoistic demagogy. He said, "With thousands of young sons in the camps and in France, out of this conflict you must expect nothing less than the enjoyment of full citizenship rights—the same as are enjoyed by every other citizen."[1]

The sharpest anti-war spirit among the Negro people was expressed by left-wing Negro Socialists gathered about *The Messenger* in New York. Despite its failure—in fact its refusal—to raise demands for relief of the specific grievances of the Negro people, the Socialist Party had nevertheless managed to attract a handful of Negroes, mostly intellectuals, who were interested in its advocacy of Socialism. They formed a Party branch in Harlem and, in 1917, they issued *The Messenger,* a monthly magazine. Among the leaders in this movement were A. Philip Randolph, Chandler Owen, Richard B. Moore, and Cyril Briggs. At first, in tune with the line of the left wing of the Party, the paper was actively opposed to the war. But once the war got under way, a split occurred in the leadership, and *The Messenger,* now controlled by Randolph, supported the war. It said, "Making the world safe for democracy is a big task. But since the President has announced the purpose of the war, we are willing and anxious to do our part."[2]

In general, the Negro press endorsed the war, once it began, but with many misgivings and demands. *The Crisis*, organ of the N.A.A.C.P., first condemned the war as an imperialist war caused by the rivalry of capitalist powers seeking to exploit "the darker and backward peoples for purposes of selfish gain." Nevertheless, it later declared, "We earnestly believe that the greatest hope for ultimate democracy, with no adventitious barriers of race and color, lies on the side of the Allies."

At the same time *The Crisis* came forward with a program of wartime demands for Negroes: "*(1)* The right to serve our country on the battlefield and to receive training for such service; *(2)* the right of our best men to lead troops of their own race in battle, and to receive officers' training in preparation for such leadership; *(3)* the immediate stoppage of lynching; *(4)* the right to vote for both men and women; *(5)* universal and free common school training; *(6)* the abolition of Jim Crow cars; *(7)* the repeal of Jim Crow laws; *(8)* equal civil rights in all public institutions and movements."[3] These demands were practically all ignored by the government.

THE NEGRO IN THE WAR

In World War I the Negro soldier was shamefully and flagrantly Jim Crowed in every conceivable manner; and President Wilson, a Virginia man, never raised a finger to stop the outrage. Although forming but 10 percent of the population, the Negro people furnished 13 percent of the soldiers. Of 2,290,525 Negroes registered in the draft, 367,000 were accepted, and 200,000 were sent overseas. Their rate of acceptance was 31 percent, against 26 percent for whites.

The Negro soldiers were segregated in Jim Crow regiments with white officers. Only after a bitter struggle by Negro leaders was a Negro officers' training camp set up at Fort Des Moines. The Negro officer graduates, however, were given the cold shoulder by white officers and generally ostracized. Many top white officers did not hesitate in their reports to slander Negro officers as inefficient. When the war ended, the highest ranking Negro officers were three colonels and two lieutenant colonels.[4]

As they had amply demonstrated during the Revolutionary War, the War of 1812, and the Civil War, Negro soldiers were courageous fighters, but the white supremacists at the head of the American armed forces dared to demean the Negro troops by delegating them mainly to the Service of Supply. Woodson says that "Not less than three-fourths of the 200,000 of the Negroes sent to France were reduced to day laborers."[5] In these occupations they were subjected to every insult. "Abusive language, kicks, cuffs, and injurious blows were the order of the day in dealing with Negroes impressed into this branch of the service." In the Navy Negroes were accepted only as messmen and officers' orderlies, and there was no place at all for them in the Army Air Force and the Coast Guard. The Y.M.C.A. and other organizations Jim Crowed the Negro soldiers.

The Negro troops who were given a chance to fight acquitted themselves with honor. Brawley says, "Negro soldiers fought with distinction in the Argonne Forest, in the Vosges Mountains, in the Champagne sector, and at Metz, often winning the highest praise from their commanders. Entire regiments were cited for valor and decorated with the Croix de Guerre—the 369th, the 371st, and the 372nd, and groups of officers and men of the 365th, the 366th, and the 368th, the 370th, and the first battalion of the 367th were also decorated." The French, with whom some Negro troops were intermingled, were tireless in praising them for their efficiency and bravery. Colonel William Hayward, an American officer not blinded by white chauvinism, said of his Negro troops, "There is no better soldier material in the world."[6]

The top brass of the U. S. Army were greatly alarmed that the Negro soldiers would be "set a bad example" by the democratic way the French people treated them. Hence, General Ervin issued his notorious Order Number 40, in which he ordered Negroes in the service not to associate with French women—an order which both Negro officers and soldiers freely violated. Negroes were also formally prohibited from attending French dances and otherwise Jim Crowed. General Pershing's headquarters capped the climax by sending out an infamous instruction, entitled *Secret Information Concerning Black American Troops,* which repeated the grossest white supremacist slander and warned the French not to associate with the "degenerate," "rapist" American Negro soldiers.[7]

Similar Jim Crow practices were directed against Negro troops in the United States. They were refused rooms in hotels, denied entrance to restaurants, theaters, and social organizations, and in the South they were openly insulted in the street. The Negro soldiers deeply resented these outrages, and they had many clashes with white ruffians. The most serious of these collisions took place in Houston, Texas, in August 1917. In retaliation for a typical brutal assault upon two local Negroes, the Negro troops, in conflict with the local whites, killed 18 of them. For this 19 Negro soldiers were hanged, 41 sentenced to prison for life, and four were given shorter terms. The Houston affair signalized to the whole country the fighting spirit of the Negro people.

To add insult to injury, President Woodrow Wilson yielded to

threats by K.K.K. elements that the American Negro soldiers returning from France and expecting social equality would be treated with
lynch violence. He sent to France Dr. Robert Russa Moton, Booker
T. Washington's successor at Tuskegee, to issue certain warnings to
these troops. Woodson says, "Dr. Moton bluntly told the Negro
soldiers that on their return home they must not expect in the
United States the democracy they had experienced in France, that
they must remain content with the same status they had before
experiencing democracy abroad. This message infuriated the Negro
soldiers. . . . Some of the soldiers talked of doing Dr. Moton bodily
injury, but the discipline of the Army prevented any such development."[8]

This was the shameful way in which American Negroes, "fighting
to make the world safe for democracy," were mistreated and abused
by the government in World War I. And the double tragedy of the
situation was that the American Federation of Labor and the Socialist
Party, in line with their traditional policy of ignoring the grievances
of the Negro people, made no fight whatever to insure more democratic consideration for the Negro soldiers. They failed to join with
the Negro people in their militant protests at such outrageous discrimination.

TO THE VICTORS BELONG THE SPOILS

The Anglo-French-American bloc won the war, which in truth
meant that, from a capitalist standpoint, the United States was the
the principal gainer. The capitalists flourished as never before, but
the workers' living standards sank. "There were," say the Beards,
"42,554 millionaires in America at the close of the war."[9] The richest
2 percent held 60 percent of the national wealth, and the poorest 65
percent held only 5 percent of it.[10] Most of the other capitalist countries received wounds in the war from which they never fully recovered; but the United States, undamaged by the war, emerged stronger
than ever. It became by far the most powerful of all the capitalist
countries and grew into the main creditor nation. The strong imperialist position of the United States was indicated by the rapid growth
of its capital investments abroad, which advanced from $2.5 billion
in 1914 to $9 billion in 1919 and to $19 billion in 1924.[11]

The victorious Allied powers signed a robbers' peace at Versailles,
France, on January 10, 1920. Although all the capitalist countries
were guilty of having started the war, the victors proceeded in true

imperialist fashion to strip the vanquished states of their colonies and part of their home territories. They also loaded them down with immense reparations obligations. Thus the peace-makers helped to lay the basis for World War II. At Versailles the League of Nations was formed upon the initiative of President Wilson. Influenced by "isolationists," however, the United States never became a member of the League, but exerted its decisive influence from the outside.

A very significant event was the holding of an international conference of Negroes, under the leadership of Dr. Du Bois, in Paris at the time of the Peace Conference. Fifty-seven delegates attended, including 16 American Negroes, 20 West Indians, and 12 Africans. The conference set minimum demands for democratic treatment of Negroes in various parts of the world; but the imperialist treaty-makers cynically ignored these proposals. The importance of this Pan-African Conference was that it emphasized the solidarity of American Negroes with the oppressed colonial peoples, and especially that it expressed the national sentiments of the American Negro people. Through the medium of this conference led by Du Bois, the Negro people, acting as a nation and placing their grievances before the international organization, set a precedent which was to be followed in later years upon several occasions—by the Garvey movement in 1921, the National Negro Congress in 1946, the N.A.A.C.P. in 1947, and the Civil Rights Congress in 1951.

THE RUSSIAN REVOLUTION

World War I caused irreparable damage to the world capitalist system. It marked the beginning of the general crisis of capitalism, the systematic decay of that hitherto dominant order of society. On November 7, 1917, the workers and peasants of Russia, under the guidance of Lenin and Stalin, the leaders of the Communist Party (Bolsheviks) rose in armed rebellion, struck down the landlord-capitalist regime and established the Soviet government, the first workers' Socialist Republic. Thus they put an end forever to the slavery and tyranny which had for centuries cursed Russia, and started the people on their way to building a free Socialist system.

The Russian Revolution not only smashed the tsarist-capitalist regime in Russia, but it also dealt a deadly blow to the world capitalist system as a whole. Imperialism had broken at its weakest link—Russia —and as a result the capitalist exploiters lost one-sixth of the world's surface. They tried in vain, during the next decades, to retrieve this disastrous loss by armed intervention, blockade, and diplomatic isolation of the Soviet Republic. During 1918-21, a dozen capitalist nations, including the United States, sought by force to overthrow the young Socialist government, but their armies were all defeated and driven out of the Soviet Union.

All the criminal capitalist assaults upon the right of the Soviet people to set up their own form of government failed completely. The Soviet masses went ahead building their country, from a backward tyrant-infested agricultural land into a highly industrialized country, the most democratic and most powerful in the world, which it is today. But the capitalists have never relinquished their insane determination to reconquer the U.S.S.R. and to seize its vast territory, about three times as large as the United States. Hitler tried this job in World War II, and it was fatal to him and his fascist clique. Now Wall Street is organizing its world forces for another attempt which, if actually put into operation, can only land them in a greater disaster than that which befell the Nazi invaders of the U.S.S.R.

The Russian Revolution had a tremendous impact upon the oppressed classes and peoples of the whole world. It was the first bright ray of sunlight in the long night of tyranny and exploitation in which they had suffered for ages. The glad response of the masses was also true, in a large measure, of the workers in the United States. Despite continued and unscrupulous efforts by opportunist A.F. of L. and Socialist Party leaders to slander and misrepresent it, millions of workers in this country sensed the U.S.S.R. to be their democratic champion. The Negro people especially reacted favorably. They were doubly impressed because of the Soviet Union's policy of equality among the various nationalities living within its borders and also because of its demonstrated friendship toward the colonial peoples of the world.

Article 123 of the Constitution of the Soviet Union declares: "Equal rights for citizens of the U.S.S.R., irrespective of their nationality or race, in all spheres of economic, state, cultural, social and political life, shall be an irrevocable law." And the enforcing clause states that "Any direct or indirect restriction of these rights, or conversely, any establishment of direct or indirect privileges for citizens on account of their race or nationality, as well as any advocacy of racial or national exclusiveness or hatred and contempt, is punishable by law."[12]

The Messenger of June 1919 expressed the most militant pro-Soviet attitude thus: "The Soviet Government proceeds apace. It bids fair to sweep the whole world. The sooner the better." During the many years since then, the Negro people have been deluged by an ocean of anti-Communist propaganda, but still they have a warm feeling for the U.S.S.R. After his visit to the U.S.S.R. in 1928, Dr. Du Bois said: "Never in my life have I been so stirred as by what I saw during two months in Russia."[13] Twenty years later, in the midst of anti-Soviet hysteria, *The Negro Year Book* of 1947 made this objective analysis: "The complete equality of all races is an integral element in the beliefs and attitudes fostered by the Government of the Soviet Union. Over 170 different nationalities of many varied racial stocks live within the borders of the Union of Soviet Socialist Republics, and consistent and energetic efforts have been made to improve the economic and social position of each group and to encourage cultural self-expression. This approach to the problem of nationality and race is unique among the nations of the world." And Frazier remarked in 1949, "The absence of racial prejudice and discrimination in Russia has had a tremendous influence on the American Negro."[14] And Paul Robeson says, "I am and always will be, a firm and true friend of the Soviet Union and of the beloved Soviet peoples."[15] The Soviet example of ethnical democracy has had a far more powerful effect upon the American Negro people than is generally realized.

THE GREAT MIGRATION NORTHWARD

Meanwhile, during World War I, the Southern Negroes migrated North in tremendous numbers. The war, of course, created an enormous demand for workers. This was triply acute, because the war demand for munitions and supplies of all sorts was so great, because the war drew so many millions of workers out of the labor force and into the armed forces, and because the German submarine menace had almost completely halted European immigration into the United States. In this situation, the Negroes in the South constituted a great reserve of labor power, and they proceeded northward in masses to fill the vacuum in the labor market. Northern employers encouraged this movement, sending many labor recruiters into the South.

This Northern migration far exceeded any other migration in Negro history, including the escape of Negro runaway slaves throughout the ante-bellum days, the movements to Africa and the West

Indies during the pre-Civil War decade, and the famous "Exodus" to Kansas in the late 1870's. It is estimated that, between 1915 and 1918, no less than 500,000 Negroes trekked North, hoping to get away from the hellish conditions of exploitation and oppression in the South. The migrants came from all over the South. The local exploiters were gravely alarmed at the loss of so many valuable workers. Immigrant agents, seeking Negro workers, were intimidated and required to pay high fees, and a big propaganda campaign was unfolded to induce the Negroes to "stay home." Characteristic Klan terrorist methods were also used to deter migrants. "White citizens of many towns threatened Negroes, while the white press urged Negroes to remain in the South. Homes were without servants, farms were without laborers, churches were empty, and houses were deserted."[16]

Arriving in the North, the Negroes flocked into the main industrial centers. They found jobs in the war industries but, as always, at the hardest and poorest-paid labor. Large numbers got work in the meat packing industry, and many others went into steel, coal, and automobile production. It is also estimated that about 27,000 worked at ship-building, and some 150,000 Negroes were employed on the railroads, with about 150,000 more in other forms of transportation and communication. Large numbers of Negro women found jobs in various industries.

In the so-called good times of the 1920's another strong Negro migration northward took place, stimulated by atrocious conditions in the South. During 1923 some 500,000 Negroes came North. Allen estimates that between 1910 and 1930, 1,070,000 Negroes came from the Black Belt alone to the North. The general result of these World War I and post-war migrations was a strengthening of the Negro proletariat.[17]

The N.A.A.C.P, Urban League, Tuskegee, and other Negro groups attempted in 1918 to get the A.F. of L. convention to regularize the entry of these new Negro workers into the industries and the unions. The convention unanimously endorsed their letter, but, characteristically, nothing came of it.[18] At the 1919, 1920, and 1921 conventions of the A.F. of L. similar resolutions were adopted at the insistence of Negro delegates, but the A.F. of L. leaders remained wedded to their traditional Jim Crow policy of excluding Negroes from the better jobs and labor organizations.

The white chauvinist attitude of the top leaders of labor led to unfortunate relations between white and Negro workers in the industrial localities. It is estimated that 30,000 Negroes were brought in as strikebreakers during the great steel strike that began in September 1919. This was a heavy blow, but it was not, as has been said, the main cause for the loss of this vital strike. The decisive reason was the treacherous refusal of the Gompersite craft union leaders to support the broad industrial strike, a betrayal which caused a large-scale return to work by the white skilled workers. Gompersite white chauvinism also contributed to the numerous race riots of the period.

The northward migration during World War I and the post-war period, however, had many important and favorable consequences for the Negro people. Most important of all, it greatly increased the strength of the Negro proletariat, which was of vital consequence to the advance of the Negro people; it increased the Negro intelligentsia; it gave a big stimulus to Negro culture; it strengthened the Negro press, (Brawley estimates that in 1920 there were 500 Negro papers of all kinds). All other Negro institutions grew correspondingly, the thriving N.A.A.C.P. in 1920 reported a membership of 100,000,[19] and during the next years it continued to expand. The migration gave the Negro people a new militancy and an invigorated sense of dignity and power. The migration had another most important result. Because strong Negro centers were built up in New York, Chicago, Cleveland, Philadelphia, St. Louis, etc., (the Negro population increasing by 50 to 600 percent in these cities), the Negro people eventually found themselves in a decisive political situation in New York State, Illinois, New Jersey, Ohio, Michigan, Pennsylvania, and Missouri.[20]

THE POST-WAR OFFENSIVE OF CAPITALIST REACTION

Hardly had the war ended when the monopolists opened a bitter offensive against the trade unions, to strip the workers of what gains they had won in the war years. During 1919-22, great defensive strikes raged in steel, meat-packing, coal, building, maritime, lumber, printing, clothing, and various other industries. Practically every trade union had to fight for its life in the face of the vicious open shop drive of the employers. The bosses were giving the workers a taste of what they meant during the war by "making the world safe for democracy." During four years over 10 million workers went on strike—by far the largest number in American history. The situation was made all the more difficult for the workers by the outbreak of the economic crisis of 1920-21, during which wages were slashed and 5,750,000 workers were unemployed. The Department of Justice also launched a fierce attack against the newly formed Communist Party, throwing thousands into jail.

The Gompersite A.F. of L. and Railroad Brotherhood leaders, bosom pals of the bosses during the war, were demoralized by this great attack on the unions. Their only policy was to run for cover, to save their own unions, if they could, at the cost of the rest. Craft union scabbing was widespread. Consequently, although the workers fought desperately, the labor movement suffered its most serious setback. The A.F. of L. dropped in membership from 4,160,348 in 1920 to 2,926,462 in 1923.

The Negro people had to face the heaviest attack during this great storm of the employers' offensive. The South was overrun by the K.K.K., which during the period reached an estimated national membership of five million. Terror stalked through the whole Southland. The special targets of the armed white ruffians were the returned Negro soldiers. The lynchers tried to burn out of the Negro veterans' minds any notions of social equality they might have learned in France. "There were floggings, branding with acid, tarrings and featherings, hangings and burnings . . . More than 70 Negroes were lynched during the first year of the post-war period. Ten Negro soldiers, several still in their uniforms, were lynched. . . . Fourteen Negroes were burned publicly, eleven of whom were burned alive."[21] During the war, from 1915 to 1918, some 199 Negroes were lynched; and in the post-war years, 1919-22, 239 more died at the hands of lynch mobs.[22] These figures do not include the great number of individual shootings of Negroes. And for all these brutal crimes, not one white man was punished by the law.

Conditions for the Negroes were not much better in the North. Because of the failure of the labor movement to meet squarely the problem of insuring the Negroes free access to jobs, unions, housing, schools, and recreational facilities, great tension had developed between Negroes and whites. This was fanned into race riots by boss-inspired hoodlums. Scores of such outbreaks took place in various parts of the country, largely in the North. In the summer and fall of 1919, there were 25 race conflicts of the bitterest character. The Negroes fought back in all these struggles, and casualties were heavy on both sides.

The first major race riot of the war period was in East St. Louis in 1917. An estimated 40 Negroes and an unknown number of whites were killed. In July 1919, a wild struggle broke out in Longview, Texas, provoked by white thugs, in which several whites and Negroes were shot and beaten to death. A week later Washington, the nation's Jim Crow capital, was the scene of a bloody race riot. It was precipitated by drunken soldiers, sailors, and marines, who undertook to shoot up the Negro quarter. But the Negroes fired back, defeating the police who were helping the white mob. For three days the city was in turmoil. No reliable report was ever made of the casualties. Other serious clashes occurred in Knoxville, Tulsa, Omaha, and Elaine, Arkansas. In the latter riot, provoked by the planters to prevent the sharecroppers from organizing a union, it has been estimated that five whites and 100 Negroes were killed. Twelve Negroes were sentenced to death and 67 to long prison terms.[23]

An especially fierce and bloody struggle took place in Chicago, beginning on July 27, 1919. The battle started when a young Negro swimmer was stoned and drowned at a lake beach by white bathers who objected to his presence. This incident touched off the explosive tension and soon fighting spread all over the southern part of the city. The great riot lasted 13 days. State troopers and armies of Chicago police and deputies were strung around the entire Negro district on the South Side. The whole city was wild with excitement, and near chaos prevailed. Final official reports, obviously too low, showed that 38 persons were killed, including 15 whites and 23 Negroes; 520 were injured, 178 of whom were whites and 342 Negroes. Hundreds of workers' homes, mostly those of Negroes, were destroyed by bombings and fires.

This great riot was directly instigated by agents of the meat packers, who wanted to use it to destroy the newly formed union in their plants. The city and state authorities co-operated with the bosses, the police and troops were used more to intimidate the Negroes than to restrain the white mobs. Through urgent measures to maintain Negro-white worker unity, the Stockyards Labor Council and the Chicago Federation of Labor prevented the situation from getting out of hand altogether; but of this more later.

In all these bloody local battles the fact stood out sharp and clear that the Negroes were prepared to defend themselves, arms in hand, against the organized white pogromists. This militant fighting spirit was but one of the many expressions of the growing national activity of the Negro people.

41. The Garvey Movement

The Universal Negro Improvement Association (U.N.I.A.), was organized in Jamaica by Marcus Moses Garvey, who spread it to the United States. Garvey was born in Jamaica, British West Indies in 1867. He was a printer, and at 18 was managing a print shop. Extremely intelligent, Garvey quickly interested himself in the problems of the Negro people. "I was not made to be whipped," he declared. He read the writings of Booker T. Washington and was deeply influenced by them. Washington invited him to come to the United States, but the Tuskegee leader died in 1915, before Garvey finally got here. In 1914 Garvey established the U.N.I.A. in Jamaica and traveled widely in the West Indies to popularize it. But he had no great success until after he arrived in the United States, on March 23, 1916. At this time a substantial immigration of Negroes was beginning to come into the United States from various parts of the West Indies—Cuba, Puerto Rico, Haiti, Jamaica, Trinidad, etc. These West Indians, with a long tradition of struggle behind them, have ever since played an important part in the cultural life and political struggles of the Negro people.

The U.N.I.A. took root immediately on American soil and flourished like a green bay tree. The organization established headquarters in New York. Garvey was its secretary general and *The Negro World* its official organ. This paper quickly became the largest Negro journal in the world. By 1919, the U.N.I.A. had 30 branches in various parts of the country. By 1921, according to W. B. Yearwood, assistant secretary general, the organization had 418 chartered divisions, with 422 more in formation but not yet chartered. In the same year Garvey claimed four million members throughout the world, with two million in the United States. Negro opponents of Garvey ridiculed these claims and produced widely differing and often drastically lower membership figures. William Pickens claimed he did not have 1,000,-000 enrolled,[1] and W. A. Domingo of the *Messenger* group said that, on the basis of official U.N.I.A. financial reports for the year following September 1920, the actual paid-up membership was only 17,784 members.[2] W. E. B. Du Bois, in 1923, also put the dues-paying figure as low as 18,000.[3]

Whatever the actual paid-up membership of his U.N.I.A. may have been, the incontestable fact is that Garvey had a tremendous following among the Negro people. His movement was based on the migrants from the South; it was led by the petty bourgeoisie, and it consisted mainly of workers. Garvey moved the Negro millions as never since Reconstruction days and the Populist period. Garvey's militant program and spectacular organizing methods had a tremendous attracting power for the harassed Negro people in this country, both North and South. The movement also exerted a considerable influence throughout the world. Everywhere that masses of Negroes lived, Garvey's name was familiar; and to the U.N.I.A. conventions came delegates from Africa, the West Indies, and Central America. The British and French governments took active exception to Garvey's activities in their African colonies, by barring Garvey's agents and intervening against him with the United States government.[4]

The growth of the U.N.I.A. was without parallel in Negro history. The basis for its great expansion in the United States was to be found in the severe conditions of exploitation and oppression under which the Negro masses suffered. This was a time, as we have seen, of hard economic conditions in the South, of mass migration, of brutal lynchings and race riots, and of K.K.K. terrorism. Behind the ensuing Negro discontent were also the tremendous employers' offensive and the workers' defensive struggle of the period. Especially pronounced were the influence of the great Russian Revolution, with its stirring slogans of national and social equality, and also the international revolutionary spirit of the working class in Europe. Negative causes for the success of the movement were the failure of the conservatively led N.A.A.C.P. and Urban League to give militant leadership to the embattled Negro people, and the widespread white chauvinism in the A.F. of L., Socialist Party, farmers' organizations, etc. Garveyism came as a flash of hope to the doubly exploited and oppressed Negro masses. Its militancy fitted in with the indomitable fighting spirit of the Negro people during the bitter years following World War I.

A white commentator thus describes the enthusiasm behind Garvey's leadership: "The bands of black peasant folk flock to Garvey. They worship him. They feel he is saying the things which they would utter were they articulate. They swarm to hear his fiery rhetoric. They pour their money into his coffers. They stand by him through thick and thin. They idolize him as if he were a black Demosthenes."[5] Negro women took an active part in the whole movement.

THE GARVEY PROGRAM

The first national convention of the U.N.I.A. was held in New York. This gathering worked out the basic program of the organization, consisting of a Preamble and a Declaration of Rights in 54 articles.[6] This program was couched in militant, fighting terms, and was both national and international in character. The Preamble declared that "The European nations have parcelled out among themselves and taken possession of nearly all the continent of Africa, and the natives are compelled to surrender their land to thieves and are treated in most instances like slaves." Strong protest was also made against the barbarous conditions of life of the Negroes in the West Indies and other colonial areas. But the heaviest fire was directed against the oppression of the Negro people in the United States. The Preamble denounced lynching, Jim Crow, race riots, discrimination in jobs and wage rates, inadequate education, denial of the right to vote, lack of justice in the courts, and the general state of terrorism under which the American Negro people were compelled to live.

The Declaration of Rights demanded in detail redress of the innumerable burning grievances of the Negroes in various parts of the world. It demanded the liquidation of every form of segregation and Jim Crow; it boldly called upon Negroes to disregard all discriminatory laws and to use every available means to defend themselves from such oppression; it urged them not to pay taxes to governments in which they were not represented; it protested the compulsory enlistment of Negroes; and it advised the Negro peoples of Africa to violate the laws which deprived them of their lands.

The political center of the Declaration of Rights was in points 13 and 15, which declared: "We believe in the freedom of Africa for the Negro people of the world, and by the principle of Europe for the Europeans, and Asia for the Asiatics, we also demand Africa for the Africans at home and abroad." And, "We strongly condemn the cupidity of those nations of the world who, by open aggression or secret schemes, have seized the territories and inexhaustible material wealth of Africa, and we place on record our most solemn determination to reclaim the treasures and possessions of the vast continent of our forefathers."

In support of this general line, all Negroes were declared free citizens of Africa, and the right of self-determination for all peoples was endorsed as a general principle. Specifically, the demand was made for the right of self-determination for Negroes, "wheresoever they form a community among themselves." Such communities "should be given the right to elect their own representatives to represent them in legislatures, courts of law, or such institutions as may exercise control over that particular community." The Declaration insisted upon the right of the Negro people to full recognition internationally, and it condemned the League of Nations "as being null and void so far as the Negro is concerned, in that it seeks to deprive the Negroes of their liberty."

BACK TO AFRICA

The central political slogan of the Garvey movement was "Back to Africa." Garvey held that it was impossible for Negroes to get justice in countries where they formed a minority, and that they must migrate to Africa, their traditional homeland. He cultivated this plan with all the skill of a great master of mass agitation. In this respect he has hardly been excelled by any agitator in American history. In the early, militant stages of his movement, he understood profoundly how to appeal to the oppressed and insulted Negro people and give them a new sense of national pride, dignity, hope, and power. He went beyond mere verbal propaganda, actually setting up in the United States a miniature replica of the governmental regime that he hoped to create in Africa. In 1921, he organized the Empire of Africa with himself as head and also set up "armed forces," with which eventually to clear Africa of white invaders.

"The West Indian Garvey," sums up Haywood, "proposed for the regenerated Africa a governmental structure which was an amalgam of British feudal forms and the structure of American secret societies. He ruled with the aid of a Potentate and a Supreme Deputy Potentate, a nobility including Knights of the Nile, Knights of Distinguished Service, the Order of Ethiopia, the Dukes of Nigeria and Uganda. A flag of 'Black, Red, and Green' was adopted as the national colors—'Black for the Race,' 'Red for their Blood,' and 'Green for their Hopes.' He set up a skeleton of the army of the future Negro state, founding the Universal African Legion, the Universal Black Cross Nurses, the Universal African Motor Corps, the Black Eagle Flying Corps, equipping them with uniforms and selecting their officers."[7] Garvey adopted a Negro national anthem. He conducted his movement with a maximum of spectacular parades, demonstrations, and the other fanfare of revivalist techniques, all carried out with most intense Messianic zeal.

The Back-to-Africa movement undoubtedly exerted a strong pull upon the Negro people. It expressed their traditional longing for land and freedom, and it dovetailed with historic tendencies among the Negro people to migrate out of the South—to Africa, to the West Indies, to Canada, to the West, to the North—anywhere to escape from the purgatory of the Southern planters. But the Negro people were realistic enough, even during the high thrills and excitement of the Garvey movement, to realize that, at most, comparatively few of them could ever reach Africa, at least within a measurable time.

A most important factor that accounted for the great upswing of the Garvey movement during its early stages was its aggressive protest against the wrongs inflicted upon the Negro people and its ringing demand for their redress. This fitted right in with the rising militancy of the Negro people during these crucial post-war years of offensive by the employers and struggle by the masses. This was the time of the "New Negro," as expressed in *The Messenger, The Crusader, The Challenge, The New Emancipator,* and other fighting journals and books of the period. The "New Negro," as conceived by *The Messenger,* was one who was quite willing to die, if need be, in defense of himself, his family, and his political rights. He stood for "absolute social equality, education, physical action in self-defense, freedom of speech, press and assembly, and the right of Russia to self-determination."[8] Garveyism flourished in its initial militancy and expanded in the midst of this growing spirit of struggle.

DISASTROUS BUSINESS VENTURES

Translating his burning nationalist evangelism into deeds, Garvey proceeded to prepare for the actual transportation of his people to Africa. He set out to organize a line of steamers, manned by Negroes, which would ply between Africa and the Americas. To this end, with his customary fiery zeal, in 1919 he incorporated the Black Cross Navigation and Trading Company, to be capitalized at $10 million under the laws of New Jersey, and set up the Black Star Line of steamships. From his enthusiastic followers he collected up to a million dollars, mostly by selling stock. No white person was allowed to purchase shares. The company finally bought a couple of small ships, the *General G. W. Goethals* (renamed the *Booker T. Washing-*

ton), and the *Yarmouth.* It had contracted for three others, the *Kana-wha* (to be the *Antonio Maceo), Shadyside,* and *Orion* (to be called the *Phyllis Wheatley).* Actually, a few voyages were made to Europe and Africa, but at catastrophic losses. The Black Star Line collapsed and the whole enterprise went into liquidation on April 1, 1922.

These business ventures were most unfortunate for Garvey and the U.N.I.A. How much Garvey was responsible for the welter of corruption that developed in the organization is problematical. The probability is that he, personally, was financially honest, but he was surrounded by a number of crooks and incompetents who flocked into the company when the money began to pour in. They voted themselves high salaries as officials of the company and played fast and loose with its assets. The steamer *Yarmouth,* carrying a cargo of whiskey, lost the fabulous sum of $300,000 on one voyage. Garvey was a very great political agitator; but he obviously knew little of the complexities of business and less of the wiles of business thieves. He kept no real books or accounts and published no financial reports. It was finally estimated by the courts that the general loss on the whole venture amounted to some $688,515.

The government, which conveniently ignored lynchers and ex-ploiters of Negroes, sanctimoniously held Garvey responsible and, in January, 1922, indicted him for fraudulent use of the United States mails. Garvey fought back, charging that he had been victimized by his enemies, especially the N.A.A.C.P. and the British and American governments, all exceedingly hostile to the U.N.I.A. He accused his trial judge, Julian W. Mack, of being a member of and contributor to the N.A.A.C.P.[9] He was found guilty, sentenced to five years in prison, and sent to Atlanta Federal penitentiary in 1925. There he served two years, after which, pardoned by President Coolidge in 1927, he was deported to Jamaica. For several years thereafter he was active politically in the West Indies, but not too successfully. He eventually made his way to London, England, where he died in obscurity in 1940.[10]

THE POLITICAL DECAY OF GARVEYISM

While the financial debacle of the Black Star Line was in the making, the U.N.I.A. itself was going through a process of political decay. Garvey was gradually shedding his early radicalism, and taking on a conservatism which amounted to a surrender of the Negro people into the hands of their worst enemies on a national and international scale. Garvey tended more and more toward the supplicating line of his friend, Booker T. Washington. The political degeneration of the Garvey movement was directly related to the subsiding of the great post-war struggle of the workers in this country and also to the temporary lull in the profound revolutionary movement which shook Europe in the early years after World War I. Garvey took the line of surrender characteristic of Social-Democratic and national reformists. This collided with the basic interests of the harassed Negro masses, and his movement proceeded to fade away. Its decline set in early in 1921.

Garvey dropped his demands for Negro rights and concentrated everything upon his utopian plan of a mass return to Africa. Benjamin J. Davis, Jr., later stated that "Garvey would surrender the fight for the complete freedom of the Negro in America, and in other lands which they helped to build, for the fantastic dream of a trek to Africa."[11] Indeed, although denying it, Garvey actually became an enemy of all struggle for Negro rights in the United States. He sharply opposed trade unions (which had long Jim Crowed Negroes), and warned the Negro "to be careful of the traps and pitfalls of white trade unionism. . . . It seems strange and a paradox, but the only convenient friend the Negro worker or laborer has, in America, at the present time, is the white capitalist. . . . If the Negro takes my advice he will organize by himself and always keep his scale of wages a little lower than the whites until he is able to become . . . his own employer." Garvey also stated that "Capitalism is necessary to the progress of the world, and those who unreasonably and wantonly oppose or fight against it are enemies to human advancement."[12]

Garvey deprecated all struggles for social equality for Negroes. He said "Let foolish Negro agitators and so-called reformers, encouraged by deceptive and unthinking white associates, stop preaching and advocating the doctrine of social equality."[13] As Robert Minor put it, "By a process of elimination, all demands which were offensive to the ruling class were dropped one by one and the organization settled down to a policy of disclaiming any rights for the Negro people in the United States."[14] Instead of his early threats to refuse to obey segregation laws and to oust the imperialists from Africa, Garvey later put out the slogan, "The Negro must be loyal to all the flags under which he lives."[15] From holding a friendly attitude toward the U.S.S.R., Garvey became a militant Soviet hater.

The U.N.I.A. degenerated into a mass deportation movement, hardly to be distinguished from the old reactionary American Colonization Society, launched in 1817 (see Chapter 8). Garvey appealed to the white chauvinism of the ruling class with his offer to settle the Negro question by getting rid of the Negroes altogether, by shipping them off to Africa. He visited Colonel Simmons, Imperial Grand Wizard of the Ku Klux Klan,[16] invited him to speak at the U.N.I.A. convention and praised the K.K.K. publicly. He also negotiated with various anti-Negro Southern senators and congressmen for co-operation. Du Bois charged that Garvey had plans afoot to get the Klan to finance the Black Star Line and that "the Klan sent out circulars defending Garvey and declaring that the opposition to him was from the Catholic Church."[17] Characteristically, in April 1938, when Senator Bilbo of Mississippi introduced a bill to deport 13,000,000 Negroes to Africa, Garvey's wife supported it.[18]

After Garvey's imprisonment, the U.N.I.A., a prey to internal disruption and outside pressure, rapidly declined. Factionally split, remnants of it still exist, however.[19] The movement gave birth to a series of minor groupings, such as the 49th State Movement, the Peace Movement for Ethiopia, and others.

NEGRO OPPONENTS OF GARVEY

Garvey and his U.N.I.A. constituted a definite threat to the established leadership of the Negro people, as represented by the N.A.A.C.P., the Urban League, and the leading Negro journals. Garvey's movement not only menaced their policies. It also strove to destroy the whole groundwork of these organizations by turning the Negro people's attention to Africa and, if possible, by transporting masses of them there. Consequently, the leaders of the established Negro bodies generally met Garvey's offensive with a strong counterattack. Garvey made few attempts to conciliate these enemies; instead he called them "opportunists, liars, thieves, traitors, and bastards."[20] He especially attacked the Mulattoes among them, declaring that they were not Negroes.

W. E. B. Du Bois, the influential editor of *The Crisis*, chief organ of the N.A.A.C.P., characterized Garvey as "a sincere, hard-working idealist," but also, "a stubborn, domineering leader of the mass." Later, when Garvey had developed his spectacular financial ventures and conservative policies Du Bois said of him: "He is not attacking white prejudice, he is grovelling before it and applauding it; his only attack is on men of his own race who are striving for freedom."[21] But this attack was mild compared with the blasts coming from other Negro leaders. The A. Philip Randolph group, who initially were members of the U.N.I.A., were especially violent, denouncing Garvey in every key. Eight of them went so shamefully far as to write a letter to U. S. Attorney General Dougherty, on January 19, 1922, demanding that Garvey be deported and that his "vicious movement be extirpated." They assailed Garvey with every insult, even regarding his physical appearance.[22]

The Communist Party, then newly established, took a critical, although friendly attitude toward the Garvey movement. Robert Minor called the U.N.I.A. "the most important mass phenomenon to be found in the sphere of Negro activities since reconstruction days. In a thousand sleepy villages today, tens of thousands of suffering and oppressed Negro laborers are meeting together and talking about their wrongs."[23] The Communist Party, which opposed the Back-to-Africa slogan, sent a letter to the 1924 convention of the U.N.I.A., criticizing mistakes of the organization and pledging support to the general liberation fight of the Negro people. The letter, signed by Charles E. Ruthenberg and William Z. Foster, thus stated the Party line: "We stand for driving the imperialist powers out of Africa and for the right of self-determination of the peoples of Africa. In taking this stand, we point out that it need not and must not involve a surrender of the Negroes' rights and equality in America or any other land."[24]

GARVEYISM: NEGRO NATIONALISM

The U.N.I.A. was a Negro bourgeois nationalist movement, a sort of Negro Zionism; and Garvey was a bourgeois nationalist leader. Garvey talked mainly in terms of "race"; but the whole import of his movement was in the spirit of a Negro "nation." Often, in fact, Garvey did speak in definitely national terms. This was the meaning of his whole concept of an African empire with a nobility, an army, and state trappings. Garvey said, "The Negro must have a country and a nation of his own."[25] He declared also that the 400 million Negroes "are determined to solve our own problems by redeeming our Motherland Africa from the hands of alien exploiters, and found there a government, a nation of our own, strong enough to lend protection to the members of our race scattered all over the world."[26] Garvey was speaking as a nationalist, too, when he said, "This is the Negro's job —that of remodelling our present civilization."[27] His glorification of Negro history had the same nationalist content. And it was in the same spirit that Garvey declared that the Negro people proposed to "take a leaf out of the book of George Washington."

Garvey's was the voice of the Negro petty bourgeoisie, seeking to secure the leadership of the Negro people by subordinating their national feelings and needs to class interests. It was trying to develop commercially, industrially, and politically. This was the significance of the whole string of co-operative enterprises—grocery stores, laundries, restaurants, hotels, printing plants, and, above all, the Black Star Line—which his movement built up. Planning to create a great Negro state in an industrialized Africa, Garvey was obviously speaking not merely in the vague, indefinable terms of "race," but in concrete and definite concepts of bourgeois nationalism. What he had in mind for Africa was some kind of replica of capitalist society in the United States.

Authorities on the Negro question are generally agreed that Garvey was an outspoken Negro nationalist. Haywood correctly sums up the Garvey movement as follows: "The huge movement led by Garvey cannot be explained purely by the personality of its leader. Yes, Garvey did have 'something,' and that 'something,' stripped of all the fantastic and bombastic trappings which marked the movement, was a deep feeling for the intrinsic national character of the Negro problem."[28]

42. The Communist Party
and the Negro Question

The collapse of the reformist Second Socialist International at the outbreak of the first world war, and the postwar revolutionary upheaval, led to the formation of the Communist International on March 2, 1919. This historic event was to have far-reaching consequences for the struggle of the Negro people in the United States, as well as in all other parts of the world. The establishment of the Communist International (sometimes also referred to as the Third International) marked the consolidation of the left Socialist parties and groups of the world, and at the same time it expressed a great rise in their theoretical levels, under the influence of the Russian Revolution and the writings of Lenin.

Many of the new Communist parties were born out of the left wings of the various Socialist parties. This was also the case in the United States where, ever since the Socialist Party was founded in 1900-01, a left wing had been taking shape within it. This situation led to a more or less continuous left-wing struggle against the right wing over many issues, and it resulted in serious splits in 1909 and 1912. The long struggle came to the breaking point in 1919 over basic questions of the Party's stand on World War I and its attitude toward the Russian Revolution and the Communist International. The left wing, constituting a large majority of the Party, opposed the war, supported the Revolution, and favored affiliation to the Communist International, all of which was anathema to the opportunist right wing S. P. leadership.

The split in the S. P. came at the end of August 1919, when the Communist Party was born in Chicago. It took the shape of two Communist parties, as the movement had not yet clarified itself theoretically and organizationally. The two parties were forced "underground" under fierce impact of the mass arrests organized by U.S. Attorney-General Palmer at the end of 1919, in which several thousand workers were slugged and jailed by the F.B.I. It was not until December 23-26, 1921, at a national convention held in New York, that the Party, now unified, was able to begin freely to exercise its constitutional rights as an open political party. Its name then was the Workers Party. The chief Communist leader through these stormy developments was Charles E. Ruthenberg of Cleveland, a long-time fighter in the left wing of the Socialist Party.

LENIN AND THE COLONIAL PEOPLES

One of the revolutionary qualities of the Communist International was its great concern from the beginning for the struggles and the welfare of the oppressed peoples of the world, especially in the colonial and semi-colonial areas. Its predecessor, the Second International, led by opportunist Social-Democrats, had almost completely disregarded and betrayed the interests of these peoples. In this respect, as in many others, that organization reflected the imperialist interests of the capitalists. With characteristic cynicism, a Dutch delegate said at the Stuttgart Congress in 1907, "If we were to take machinery to the savages of Central Africa, what would they do with it? Perhaps they would perform a dance around it or add another god to the great number they already have."[1]

The Second International was primarily a European organization. On the other hand, the Communist International, breaking sharply with this whole approach to the question of Socialism, was truly a world organization. It attached major importance to the conditions and the national liberation struggles of the races and peoples in Asia, Africa, Latin America, and all oppressed areas. This marked a revolutionary development of basic significance in the world fight for democracy and Socialism.

The attention paid by the Communist International to the oppressed peoples of the world was based upon the theoretical analyses of Lenin. Over many years and in innumerable writings, the great master of Marxism had pointed out the fundamental facts that the colonial system was a foundation of capitalism; that the oppressed peoples were super-exploited by the imperialists; that these peoples were rebellious against colonialism and were struggling to free and develop themselves as nations; and that, in their fight against the capitalists, the workers of the industrial countries had basic political interests in common with the agricultural peoples of the colonies. He showed that the breakdown of the colonial system would deal a mortal blow to world capitalism. Lenin thus laid down the alliance between the world's industrial workers and the oppressed peoples of the colonial and semi-colonial lands as an indispensable requirement for the victory of international Socialism.

"The intensification of national oppression under imperialism," says Lenin, "makes it necessary for Social Democracy not to renounce what the bourgeoisie describes as the 'utopian' struggle for the freedom of nations to secede, but, on the contrary, to take more advantage than ever before of conflicts arising also on this ground for the purpose of rousing mass action and revolutionary attacks upon the bourgeoisie."[2] Lenin thus became the political parent of the great anti-imperialist revolutions which are now tearing the world capitalist system to pieces. Lenin formulated his revolutionary theories on the relation between the struggles of the workers and the oppressed colonial peoples in his celebrated Colonial Theses, which he presented at the Second Congress of the Communist International in July-August 1920.[3]

LENIN AND THE COMMUNIST PARTY OF THE UNITED STATES

The American Communist Party got its eventual scientific understanding of the Negro question in the United States from the writings and personal counsel of Lenin. This was one of the many basic services to the American labor movement rendered by the Communist International, but it was not to be realized until 1929. As we have seen in Chapter 37, the Socialist Party and the Socialist Labor Party before it (much as the A.F. of L.) had held to the erroneous theory that there was nothing special about the Negro question, that it was simply a part of the general problem of the working class. This led to almost complete passivity regarding the distinct and terrible grievances of the Negro people—lynching, Jim Crow, disfranchisement, and all the rest. At the time, the left wing, which finally developed into the Communist Party, did not clearly challenge this white chauvinist, opportunist position of the Socialist Party and the Socialist Labor Party. Of course, left wingers—William D. Haywood and others —insisted upon the right of Negroes to belong to trade unions; but they never developed a program of distinct demands and struggle for and with the Negro people as such. This program, in theory and practice, uniting the struggle of the working class and the Negro people, had to be learned in later years from the Communist International and Lenin.

From the outset, the young American Communist movement began to take an active interest in the struggles of the Negro people. However, the Communist Party program, adopted in 1919, continued the traditional incorrect De Leon-Debs line that "The racial expression of the Negro is simply the expression of his economic bondage and oppression, each intensifying the other. This complicates the Negro problem but does not alter its proletarian character."[4]

It was not until the formation of the Workers Party at the end of 1921 that American Communists, by then more familiar with Lenin's historic writings, began to formulate the Negro question as a specific one within the general framework of Party policy. The resolution then adopted, after analyzing conditions in the South, declared: "The Workers Party will support the Negroes in their struggle for liberation, and will help them in their fight for economic, political, and social equality. It will point out to them that the interests of the Negro workers are identical with those of the whites. It will seek to end the policy of discrimination followed by organized labor. Its task will be to destroy altogether the barrier of race discrimination that has been used to keep apart the black and white workers, and weld them into a solid union of revolutionary forces for the overthrow of the common enemy."[5]

Although still bearing definite traces of the incorrect traditional Socialist line, this resolution does, in fact, single out the Negro question as a special one. In this respect it was a long step ahead. It was the most advanced resolution on the Negro question ever adopted, up to that time, by any Marxist Party in the United States. Succeeding conventions of the Workers (Communist) Party clarified the line, developing the theory of the Negro question as a special one with which organized labor had to concern itself, and expanding a program of specific Negro demands as an organic part of the general program.

THE C. P. AS THE PARTY OF THE NEGRO PEOPLE

With characteristic energy, devotion, and incisiveness, the Communists fought for their Negro program. Wherever the Negroes were attacked and oppressed, there, in the measure of their limited numbers and resources, were to be found the Communists. They encouraged the Negroes to fight back and strove to build a solid united front between them and the white workers against the common foe. Because of these activities, enemies of the Party characterized it as a Negro

Party, a title which the Communists proudly accepted. The election platform of 1928 said, "The Communist Party is the Party of the liberation of the Negro race from all oppression."

The period with which this chapter deals, roughly from 1919 to 1929, was a very difficult one for the Negro people. In the North there were race riots and widespread discrimination, socially and in jobs, housing, etc; and in the South, there was an orgy of lynching. As H. Snyder wrote: "Nowhere on earth among civilized nations are such atrocious outrages committed against human beings as are committed in the South against the Negro. Almost any day we can read of some benighted Negro peasant being hunted down with hounds, or shot by a posse of men, or burned at the stake amid the multitudinous cheers of a vast concourse of people."[6]

Here is a picture of a typical Southern lynching: "The sheriff along with the accused Negro was seized by the mob, and the two carried to the scene of the crime. Here quickly assembled a thousand or more men, women, and children. The accused Negro was hung up in a sweet-gum tree by his arms, just high enough to keep his feet off the ground. Members of the mob tortured him for more than an hour. A pole was jabbed in his mouth. His toes were cut off joint by joint. His fingers were similarly removed, and members of the mob extracted his teeth with wire pliers. After further unmentionable mutilations, the Negro's still living body was saturated with gasoline and a lighted match was applied. As the flames leaped up, hundreds of shots were fired into the dying victim. During the day, thousands of people from miles around rode out to see the sight. Not till nightfall did the officers remove the body and bury it."[7]

The A.F. of L. leadership was doing nothing to remedy the shocking situation. The N.A.A.C.P. directed an open letter to the 1924 convention of the A.F. of L., urging the adoption of a more intelligent policy toward Negroes, but nothing came of it. At about the same time, the Urban League also began to interest itself more in trade unionism, setting up a Department of Industrial Relations.[8] The Socialist Party ignored the Negro question, and its outstanding theoretician, Oneal, accused the Communists of exaggerating the extent of the persecution of the Negroes.[9]

The N.A.A.C.P. and the Urban League, conservatively led, were not responsive to the active struggle and united front offers of the Communists. But the Negro people were sympathetic in a rising degree. Negroes began to join the Party—never before had they shown extensive interest in a Marxist organization. Negro and white writers frequently expressed appreciation of the work of the Communists, an attitude which, especially in Negro circles, has largely continued through the years. Drake and Cayton stated the widespread Negro opinion thus: "We may not agree with the entire program of the Communist Party, but there is one item, with which we do agree wholeheartedly and that is the zealousness with which it guards the rights of the Race."[10] Spero and Harris commented on the line of the Party, "On the relationship of the Negro and white workers, the Party subscribed to full social equality. It advocated the right to work, the abolition of Jim Crowism in law and custom, including segregation and anti-intermarriage laws."[11] Meier said, "The Communist Party . . . is the only American group which has in practice offered Negroes full social equality."[12] Saposs summed up the work of the Party by saying that "With the notable exception of a few international unions, the Communists are the only labor element manifesting a sympathetic interest in the trials and tribulations of the colored workers."[13] And A. C. Powell, Jr., stated that "Today there is no group in America, including the Christian Churches, that practices racial brotherhood one-tenth as much as the Communist Party."[14]

The militant struggle of the Communist Party for and with the Negro people was characterized during the 1920's by its fight for the right of Negroes to work in industry and belong to unions; its tireless campaign against the infamous crime of lynching; it great stress upon the question of full social equality, something no other mixed organization had ever done; its fight against white chauvinism—the widespread expression of white supremacist ideology; its stress upon the basic fact that not only Negroes, but white workers also had a profound interest—a joint solidarity—in protecting all the rights of the Negro people; and its determined efforts to raise the Negro question to the status of an urgent national and international issue, with which not only the entire American people, but the world revolutionary movement should concern itself. In all these respects the Communists exerted an important influence from the outset.

The strong orientation of the Party toward active championship of the Negroes' cause did not come into being without considerable internal Party friction. Thus, the Lovestone group of leaders played down Negro activities and advanced the theory that the Negroes in the rural South constituted a "reserve of capitalist reaction." Against this the Party took the position that the workers are the leading force in the revolutionary movement, and that the Negro people are the best ally of the working class in both the daily struggles for immediate demands and the ultimate fight for Socialism. The Party supported the struggle of the Negro people not merely out of a sense of solidarity, but because the Negro masses were potentially a strong and constructive force in the class struggle. The Lovestone group were expelled from the Party in June 1929, because of their opportunistic attitude upon many aspects of Party policy including the Negro question.

THE PARTY AND THE T.U.E.L.

The Communist Party carried on much of its Negro work directly through its own Party apparatus. In the 1924, 1928, and 1932 elections, the Communist Party, with its national ticket headed by William Z. Foster, presented its program of Negro demands throughout the South. including the demand for full social equality. In the 1932, 1936, and 1940 campaigns the Party's vice-presidential candidate was James W. Ford, a well-known Negro leader. At all the Party conventions the Negro question was heavily emphasized, and Negro workers were systematically drawn into the Party's city, district, and national leadership, as well as into its press and office forces. At this time began the building up of the Party's present fine body of Negro Marxist-Leninist leaders. In March 1930, the Party had a total of about 1,500 Negro members.[15]

A vital part of the Communist Party's Negro work was to make internationally known the lynchings, Jim Crow, and other outrages perpetrated against the American Negro people. The Second International, with its American S. P. and S. L. P. affiliates, had never concerned itself in the slightest with the tragic situation of the Negroes in the United States; but the Communist International, under Lenin's leadership, made this subject a major issue from the outset. Lenin often specifically referred to Negro oppression in the United States. Consequently, the question was widely discussed in the Communist parties and Communist-led unions throughout the colonial and semi-colonial world. The Red International of Labór Unions, Communist-led, was also especially sensitive to this basic question and held a number of international conferences of Negro workers. The first of these was in Hamburg, Germany, in 1930, where an international Negro union committee was set up. This worldwide discussion of

American Negro grievances was to have profound effects years later in our own day, in shaping popular and governmental attitudes in the United States to the Negro people. Today sharp international condemnation is somewhat staying the hands of the lynch gangs in Mississippi, Georgia, and Alabama. What the Federal government has refused to do through an anti-lynch law, is being at least partially accomplished by Communist-cultivated world opinion.

The American Communists also raised the Negro question sharply in all the mass organizations in which they played a part. The Trade Union Educational League was very important in bringing the Negro issue forcefully before the trade union movement. The T.U.E.L., organized in November 1920, in Chicago, was a left-progressive organization of active workers throughout the labor movement. Its chief leaders were Communists. The group that launched it—William Z. Foster, Jack W. Johnstone, Joseph Manley, and others—had been responsible for leading the united campaign of a dozen A.F. of L. unions which organized the packinghouse workers nationally in 1917. This was the first mass production industry ever organized by the A.F. of L. Of the 200,000 workers unionized during the drive, some 20,000 were Negroes, about 12,000 of whom worked in Chicago. They constituted the largest organized body of Negro workers anywhere in the world. Under the leadership of Jack Johnstone, their general local organization, the Chicago Stockyards Labor Council, was a potent force in preventing the Chicago race riot of 1919 from getting altogether out of hand.

The T.U.E.L., with the full support of the Communist Party, became very influential in the labor movement. In 1922-23, at least three of its major slogans—for amalgamation of the craft unions into industrial unions, for a labor party, and for recognition of Soviet Russia—were formally endorsed by a majority of the trade union movement in the United States and Canada. The league also carried its Negro program into thousands of local unions and scores of city central bodies and international unions. It undoubtedly spread a great deal of enlightenment on this critical matter throughout the labor movement. The seeds thus sown were to blossom forth years later with the advent of the C.I.O. In harmony with the line of the Communist Party, the T.U.E.L. demanded that "Negroes be given the same social, political, and industrial rights as whites, including the right to work in all trades, equal wages, admission into all trade unions," etc.[16] In September 1929, the T.U.E.L. was reorganized into the Trade Union Unity League, which continued the trade union struggle for Negro rights.

THE A.N.L.C. AND THE I.L.D.

The American Negro Labor Congress was organized in Chicago, in November 1925, mainly upon the initiative of the Communists. It was a united front organization, accepting both Negroes and whites as members. It fought for a whole program of Negro demands in opposition to every form of discrimination and persecution of Negroes,[17] laying special stress upon the matter of trade unionism. The A.N.L.C. proposed to set up local branches, composed of representatives of Negro and white progressive organizations. The major purpose of this organization was to bring about the unionization of the Negro masses. It favored separate Negro organizations only in cases where the existing unions barred Negroes. The leader of the movement was Lovett Fort-Whiteman, and its journal was *The Champion*. Outstanding Communist Negro workers in it were James W. Ford, Harry Haywood, Maude White, and many others.

The A.N.L.C. had to combat strong opposition from such conservative forces as the A.F. of L. and the leadership of the N.A.A.C.P. and the Urban League. Its membership was eventually confined mainly to Communists. It did effective agitational work, however, enlightening Negro workers on the benefits of trade unionism and breaking down the lingering opposition of Negro intellectuals to the labor movement. Generally, however, it was handicapped by sectarianism—by writing too "left" a program for the masses. In 1930 the A.N.L.C. was merged into the League of Struggle for Negro Rights.

Another very important step in the development of the struggle for Negro rights was the formation of the International Labor Defense in Chicago, on June 23, 1925. This body was a united front organization of workers and middle class elements, of Negroes and whites of various political groupings. It had as its purpose the development of a mass political and legal defense in the many frame-up cases of fighters in the class struggle. The Communists took the initiative in the establishment of the I.L.D. It became an influential organization in many parts of the country and the major activity of such fighters as Elizabeth Gurley Flynn, J. Louis Engdahl, Anna Damon, Rose Baron, and others.

The I.L.D. devoted great attention to all labor cases and played a central part in the unsuccessful attempt to save Sacco and Vanzetti from the electric chair. From the outset it concerned itself especially with the legal and extra-legal attacks against the Negro people by K.K.K. elements, acting either as outright lynch mobs or as lynchers clothed with the garb of legal authority. In later years the I.L.D. was to lead in such historic fights as those to save the Scottsboro Boys and Angelo Herndon. It made these celebrated cases known all over the world. During its later years, its national secretary was William L. Patterson, the well-known Negro fighting leader. The I.L.D. was merged into the Civil Rights Congress in 1946 with Patterson as its present leader.

THE NEGRO QUESTION, A NATIONAL QUESTION

During 1928, a development occurred which was to have a profound and lasting effect upon the Negro work of the Communist Party. This was the adoption by the Party of a resolution which characterized the Negro people in the Black Belt as an oppressed nation, entitled to the right of self-determination. The fight of the Negro people against their planter-monopolist oppressors was characterized as fundamentally a struggle for national liberation. The resolution was worked out in October 1928,[18] in consultation between the American Communists and Marxist-Leninists from all over the world. It was amplified by another resolution in October 1930.[19]

The 1928 resolution declared, "While continuing and intensifying the struggle under the slogan of full social and political equality for the Negroes, which must remain the central slogan of our Party for work among the masses, the Party must come out openly and unreservedly for the right of Negroes to self-determination in the Southern states, where the Negroes form a majority of the population. . . . The Negro question in the United States must be treated in its relation to the Negro question and struggles in other parts of the world. The Negro race everywhere is an oppressed race. Whether it is a minority (U. S. A., etc.), majority (South Africa), or inhabits a so-called independent state (Liberia, etc.), the Negroes are oppressed by imperialism. Thus, a common tie of interest is established for the revolutionary struggle of race and national liberation from imperialist domination of the Negroes in various parts of the world."

The new political position—which considered the Negro people in the United States as an oppressed nation—constituted a big advance for the Communist Party of the United States. From the beginning, the Party had broken with the white chauvinist traditions of the S.P. and S.L.P. and recognized that the Negro question was a special one, requiring special demands and special methods of struggle. Nevertheless, it came to understand the true nature of this specific quality of the question only with the adoption of the 1928 resolution. This resolution was based on Lenin's famous colonial thesis of 1920, in which he characterized American Negroes as an oppressed people at the point in his resolution where it called upon the workers of the world "to render direct aid to the revolutionary movements in the dependent and subject nations (for example, in Ireland, the Negroes in America, etc.), and in the colonies."[20] In fact, as early as 1913, Lenin had said, "In the United States, 11.1 per cent of the population consists of Negroes (and also Mulattoes and Indians), who must be considered an oppressed nationality."[21] The 1928 resolution, which put this analysis into effect, corresponded basically with the economic and political situation in the United States. It was also fully in harmony with the historic trends of the American Negro people toward nationhood and self-determination.

43. The Negro People As an Oppressed Nation

Joseph Stalin, the greatest of all authorities on the national question, formulated the following classical Marxist definition of a nation: "A nation is an historically evolved stable community of language, territory, economic life, and psychological make-up manifested in a community of culture."[1] Stalin emphasizes that all four of these basic characteristics are necessary to a nation. If even one of them is missing, the people does not constitute a nation. On the basis of this scientific definition, clearly the Negro people in the Black Belt of the South comprise a nation, and those in the North and West constitute a national minority. Let us, therefore, in this general respect, consider Stalin's four elements of nationhood.

NATIONAL CHARACTERISTICS OF THE NEGRO PEOPLE

After three centuries in this area, the Negro people of the Black Belt definitely constitute "an historically evolved stable community of people." Their main concentration is in the so-called Black Belt,* 1,600 miles long and 300 miles deep, which stretches from Virginia to Arkansas through a dozen states, including the Carolinas, Maryland, Florida, Georgia, Alabama, Mississippi, Louisiana, Tennessee, and Eastern Texas.[2] According to the 1950 Census, in 169 counties in this broad area, Negroes form absolute majorities of from 50 to 85 percent of the total population, and in 263 adjoining counties their numbers run from 30 to 49 percent. In the Black Belt there are various areas of Negro majority, not one single area. In the twelve states as a whole, Negroes number 9,425,293 in comparison with 28,826,715 whites, or about 25 percent. Owing principally to Negro migration to the North and the more rapid increase of white population, there has been a steady decline in the number of counties of Negro majority—in 1900, 286; in 1910, 264; in 1920, 221; in 1930,

---

* Originally the term "Black Belt" signified the rich black earth of the area, but it has taken on an economic-political significance.

191; in 1940, 180; in 1950, 169. Nevertheless, the number of Negroes in the Black Belt as a whole is greater than the population of any one of 23 nations affiliated to the United Nations.

Obviously, the Negro people also have developed a community of language out of their original tribal tongues. That this common language is English, the language of the ruling nation, which the masters thrust upon them, in no sense vitiates Negro nationhood. The peoples of Scotland, Ireland, and Wales, who are manifestly nations, speak the language of the dominant country, England. The Negro people in the Black Belt also have a common economic life, which is expressed chiefly in their roles as farmers and workers in the plantation-industrial system of this whole area. And lastly, the Negro people also have a community of culture. The original diversity of the tribal cultures, which their forefathers brought over with them from Africa, was mostly stamped out under the fierce pressures of slavery, although some traces still persist.[3] The Negro took on a new culture which, although mainly that of the dominant nation, nevertheless has its own distinct Negro national characteristics in its music, songs, dances, painting, drama, literature, and historical works.

The Negro people of the South are not only a nation, but an oppressed nation. "National oppression," says Stalin, "is that system of exploitation and plunder of subject peoples, those measures of forcible restriction of the political rights of a subject people, which are resorted to by imperialist circles. These, taken together, present the policy generally known as a policy of national oppression."[4] The American Negro people have suffered such national oppression in extreme form, as our previous chapters have indicated. Besides the Southern lynch terror, Jim Crow system, and economic peonage, Negro representation in Southern legislative bodies—villages, cities, and states—is almost negligible. In the North, conditions are only slightly better, the great Negro populations of New York, Chicago, Philadelphia, Cleveland, Los Angeles, etc. having only a mere hand-ful of representatives in the local councils, state legislatures, and on the judicial bench.[5] In the U.S. Senate and House there are 531 members, among whom only two Negroes are in the House, although Negroes form about one-tenth of the national population. Bitter subjection, with its endless woes, has stunted, distorted, and confused the national development of the Negro people, and this is a basic factor that must always be borne in mind in considering their national characteristics.

CLASS DIFFERENTIATION

Despite almost insuperable obstacles, the Negro people, in their march to nationhood, have also been gradually developing the class differentiation characteristic of a nation. This process has been going on since long before the Civil War (see chapter 38). Davis thus characterizes this aspect of the Negro national development. "Before the Civil War," says he, the Negro people "had certain common characteristics, namely a common land, language, and psychological makeup growing out of their common oppression." And since the Civil War, "They have developed a strong proletariat, a petty bourgeoisie, professionals and middle class, and a distinct, although weak capitalist class, landowners and industrialists."[6]

The U.S. Census figures of 1950 give about 15,500,000 Negroes in a total population of 150,697,361. According to the same census, the general rate of increase, 1940-50, was whites 14.4 percent, Negroes 14.7 percent. The proportion of Negroes in the general population, some 10 percent, has remained almost constant since 1920. Of all Negroes, two-thirds live in the South, the bulk of the people remaining there despite all migrations. Of the Negroes in the North, 90 percent dwell in the cities, of which New York has 775,529, Chicago 600,000, Philadelphia 378,968, Detroit 303,721, St. Louis 154,448, Cleveland 149,-547, Los Angeles 100,000. These are heavily proletarian populations, with the largest percentage of actual workers of any national group in the United States. Some 63 percent of all Negroes are in the labor force, as against 57 percent of the whites. About 45 percent of all Negro workers are women, in contrast to 30 percent of the white workers in "gainful employment." The total Negro non-agricultural proletariat numbers about two million with concentrations in steel, coal mining, lumber, marine transport, railroads, automobiles, chemicals, meat-packing, and other basic industries.[7]

Negro farmers in 1950 are classified as follows: owners, 189,-232; tenants, 475,739; sharecroppers, 270,296; laborers, 425,000. Perlo states that "The number of Negroes in Southern agriculture declined from 1,449,000 in 1940 to 1,013,000 in 1950."[8] The Negro people are experiencing the urbanization also characteristic of white farmers.

The Negro people have also developed an intelligentsia typical of bourgeois society, with the usual strand of national oppression running all through it. An estimate of the 1950 Census gives an approximate number of 120,000 Negroes in the professions: 68,453 school and college teachers, 3,530 physicians and surgeons, 1,610 dentists, 1,063 lawyers and judges, 18,000 clergymen, and 376 journalists.[9] *American Men of Science* lists 77 Negroes, and *Who's Who in America,* 1941-45, contains 90 Negro names.[10] It is from this group that, traditionally, the leadership of the Negro people has come.

The Negro people likewise have a growing class of businessmen, with a few large capitalists and landowners. Selsam estimates these at 86,807, as follows: bankers, etc., 907; undertakers, 3,415; agents and salesmen, 24,571; restaurant keepers, 11,263; hotel keepers, 1,000; retail merchants, 17,422; barbers and hairdressers, 28,229. There are 14 Negro banks, with assets of $31,307,345 (1947); 240 insurance companies (1944 figures) and building and loan associations. There is practically no Negro manufacturing except on a small scale—mainly caskets and cosmetics. Among the few Negroes who may be listed as big capitalists are notably a number of Negro millionaires in Texas and Oklahoma, who struck it rich when oil was discovered on their lands. Thus, Major Kennedy of Overton, Texas, who has 4,000 acres of rich oil land, also "owns the all-Negro town of Easton, possesses large herds of thoroughbred cattle, and possesses fruit orchards in Mexico."[11] These wealthy Negroes, however, are unable to break through local Jim Crow restrictions. "Even for the educated or wealthy Negro the South is a prison."[12]

Negro industry (with its small capitalist class) is primarily a ghetto commerce of a service character, hedged about and limited by powerful white competition. Pierce says of it, "The Negro economy is essentially an isolated economy. It may be likened to a small economic area set off within the interior of the general economic system of the nation, surrounded by towering walls of racial segregation and discrimination." He calls it "an imprisoned economy." The Negro middle class proprietors of this industry have cultivated it by an intense appeal to the national, patriotic sentiments of Negro customers. Many Negro leaders, notably Booker T. Washington and W. E. B. Du Bois, once had illusions that Negro industry could become an all-satisfying economy for the Negro people, which it cannot do.

NATIONAL TRENDS IN NEGRO HISTORY

The history of the American Negro people is the history of the growth and development of a nation. The basic national trends of the Negro people are to be observed in every phase of their centuries-long fight against oppression. The generations of struggle against chattel slavery, with their many slave uprisings and the political activities of freedmen, were the early stages of the struggle for national liberation. The militant activities of the Negro people during the Civil War and Reconstruction periods represents this liberation struggle in its higher, revolutionary stages.

The convention movement, which played such a big role in the history of the Negro people, (and which we have dealt with extensively in previous chapters) was obviously a national movement, even though most of its leaders spoke in terms of "race." So, too, were the many migrations, either made or contemplated by the Negro people in their tragic history. In all such movements—as the early migrations, real or planned, to Africa, the West Indies, Canada, Kansas, Mississippi, the Far West, etc., the Negro leaders always had more or less definitely in mind the organization of a Negro state; that is, a Negro nation. Among examples of this were the Mississippi colonization movement of 1887, the plan to make a Negro state of Oklahoma in 1890, the Garvey movement, and following that, the 49th State movement. In their very nature, all such enterprises were directed toward the establishment of a Negro nation, and their leaders were quite conscious of the fact.[13] Aptheker cites many clear expressions of nationalism on the part of the moving spirits in these migrations.[14]

In their generations of struggle, the Negro people have created a whole series of specifically national organizations—among them churches, fraternal organizations, business institutions, newspapers, schools, colleges, and the all-Negro towns in various Southern cities. Jim Crow* segregation, enforced by the ruthless master nation, has helped to force the growth of all these organizations;[15] but we should fail to grasp the significance of such movements if we were to see only this element of oppression. Also to be considered is the element of national cultural affinity and solidarity, which has played a basic role in the creation of these organizations, even as it has in building the innumerable national institutions of many other national groups in this country. Even the Negro ghetto, the very symbol of the oppressive segregation and super-exploitation of the Negro, has its

* There is uncertainty as to the origin of the term "Jim Crow." It has been dated from a minstrel show of 1835. In 1841 it was first used in Mississippi, to designate a segregation car.

less barbarous counterparts in the national quarters of Germans, Jews, Italians, Poles, Finns, Scandinavians, and other national groups in many American cities.

For over a century also, the Negro people have expressed their growing national consciousness by seeking to link their struggle internationally with that of other peoples fighting for national liberation. Thus, a marked feature of Frederick Douglass' trips to Europe before the Civil War was the close co-operation that he established with the leaders of the Irish, Polish, Italian, and other peoples then battling for national freedom. The same general principle was involved in the several Pan-American Congresses organized by W. E. B. Du Bois in 1911, 1918, 1923, 1927, and 1945, and also in more recent years in the work of the Council on African Affairs, headed by Paul Robeson. An assertion of the national rights and existence of the American Negro people was the heart of the repeated appeals to the League of Nations and the United Nations by the American National Negro Congress, the N.A.A.C.P., the Garvey movement, and the Civil Rights Congress (see Chapter 40). Significant of the national character of these statements and protests was the passage in the N.A.A.C.P. "Appeal to the World" in 1947, which declared that "Prolonged policies of segregation and discrimination have involuntarily welded the mass almost into a nation within a nation with its own schools, churches, hospitals, newspapers, and many business enterprises." The document claimed for the Negro people the same right of appeal to the United Nations as "other nations."

An interesting and significant expression of nationalism among the Negro people has been their insistence that the word Negro be spelled with a capital N. This has long been a matter of national pride. Aptheker believes the demand was first made in 1878 by F. L. Barnet.[16] Washington, Du Bois, and other prominent national leaders of the Negro people have laid great stress on this matter, and the intense nationalist Garvey considered it important enough to be included as one of the demands in the U.N.I.A.'s Declaration of Rights.

NATIONAL NEGRO CULTURE

An important national characteristic of the Negro people is the specific quality of their culture, particularly in the field of writing. Practically all Negro writers—the very best of them—have devoted their major efforts to portraying the hardships, oppression, and exploitation, as well as the hopes, demands, and aspirations of the Negro people. This is entirely natural on the part of the true spokesmen of an oppressed nation, struggling under such barbarous exploitation and oppression as that which afflicts the Negro people in the United States. The Harlem Renaissance Movement, contemporaneous with Garvey but separate, was definitely bourgeois-nationalist.

Especially national in significance has been the great stress laid by the Negro intelligentsia on writing the history of their people. This trend has become steadily more marked since the Civil War. It took definite form in 1912 with the organization of the Negro Society for Historical Research, with John E. Bruce, president, and Arthur Schomburg, secretary, and further in 1915 with the establishment of the Association for the Study of Negro Life and History, headed by the noted Negro historian, the late Carter G. Woodson. In 1926, in the same spirit, Negro History Week was established, upon Woodson's initiative.

This Negro history movement has been accompanied by great research into every phase of the life of the Negro people in the United States and in their African background. The general purpose of such work has been to establish the historic past and achievements of the Negro people in such a way as to lay the basis for stronger national feeling among them. Negro historians have been quite conscious of the significance of this basic national task. As early as 1911, Reverend C. V. Roman (miscalling nationalism "race") pointed out that "a diffusion of such knowledge among the masses of the people will stimulate race pride, strengthen their consciousness of kin, without lessening their patriotism."[17] Among the outstanding leaders in this extensive movement to write the Negro nation's history have been the Marxist historians, Negro and white—H. Aptheker, H. Haywood, J. S. Allen, E. Lawson, J. W. Ford, P. S. Foner, P. Perry, and many others.

NEGRO-WHITE BIOLOGICAL EQUALITY

One of the major factors making for the growth of American Negro national consciousness has been the shattering, in both theory and practice, of the reactionary concept that Negroes are biologically inferior to whites. As Benedict points out, "The slave trade was originally justified on the grounds that the victims were lost souls and heathens."[18] But the idea of racial inferiority was eventually introduced, and Negroes were not considered human. It was given a big stimulus in 1853 by the publication of Count de Gobineau's *Essay on the Inequality of the Human Races.* Darwin's famous book, *The Origin of Species* published in 1859, was also seized upon as a justification of the white supremacist ideas of Gobineau and others—including, of course, the slaveholders in the South.

Darwin, it is true, made certain references to "inferior races of men," but this referred to their varying stages of social development rather than to degrees of biological capacity. The main trend in his analysis showed the biological unity of mankind. Darwin said, "Although the existing races of man differ in many respects, as in color, hair, shape of skull, proportions of the body, etc.; yet if their whole structure be taken into consideration they are found to resemble each other closely in a multitude of points. Many of these are so unimportant or of singular a nature, that it is extremely improbable that they should have been independently acquired by aboriginally distinct species."[19] On the famous voyage of the *Beagle,* Darwin was constantly struck by how similar the minds of primitive peoples "were to ours." Marx said of Darwin that his "book is very important and serves me as a basis in natural science for the class struggle in history."[20] And Engels, speaking at Marx's burial, said, "Just as Darwin discovered the law of evolution in organic nature, so Marx discovered the law of evolution in human history."[21]

The assumption that the Negro is inferior on biological grounds was soon turned into gospel truth in the propaganda of those capitalist elements financially interested in forcing the Negro people into a position of social inferiority, so that they could be the more effectively exploited. This white supremacist racism became widespread even in the so-called liberal circles, and has been used against the Negroes ever since. It eventually reached its apex with the development of fascism under Mussolini and Hitler. Directing their main attacks against the Jews, the Nazis built up, by means of their biological pseudo-sciences, a whole hierarchy of races, classes, and nations on the basis of their supposed degrees of biological rank, naturally with the white "Aryans" at the top and with Jews and Negroes at the bottom.

Negro leaders have fought a long and relentless battle against this monstrous racist distortion of science, of which they have been the special victims in the United States. For the past century, since the days of Henry H. Garnet and Frederick Douglass, a long line of

Negro scholars, artists, and political leaders have demonstrated in both theory and practice that the Negro is quite the equal of the white man or of any one else. In this growing struggle for equality as human beings, the Negroes have had on their side the best of contemporary science.

During the past generation enemies of the Negro people have sought to prove the biological inferiority of the Negro by statistics and by so-called intelligence tests. A pair of white chauvinist doctors even tried to show the comparative emotional instability of the Negro people by the mumbo-jumbo of Freudianism.[22] All such methods are absurd when used to "measure" the Negro in any respect. The lugubrious tables of statistics, government and otherwise, giving the Negro much the worst of it in terms of the prevalence of criminality, insanity, indolent habits, susceptibility to certain diseases, and an excessive death rate, are rendered absolutely worthless as guides because of the highly unfavorable economic and political conditions under which the Negro people live—not to mention the usual anti-Negro bias of the statisticians. Better the Negro's social conditions and the statistics about this oppressed people will also drastically improve.

The same can also be said of the numerous tables resulting from "intelligence tests." Such tests confuse intelligence with education and ignore the basic conditioning factor of environment. Thus, the famous U.S. Army intelligence tests of 1918 alleged that Northern Negroes were more "intelligent" than Southern Negroes and Southern whites, and that Northern whites were more "intelligent" than either Southern Negroes or Southern whites. These absurdities are based on a total disregard of educational and general environmental factors. Other tests have shown that urban children are more intelligent than those in rural communities. As Aptheker points out, "Uniformly the tests have resulted in lower scores for the poor and higher scores for the middle class and the rich."[23] The fact is that despite his abominable environment, the Negro makes a surprisingly good showing in these tests, and science indicates, that with equal conditions, he will not fall short of the whites. Klineberg and other serious investigators have discredited the intelligence tests regarding Negroes as almost valueless.[24] Ina C. Brown thus sums up scientific opinion on this score: "Few, if any, reputable psychologists now believe that the so-called intelligence tests prove anything at all about superior and inferior peoples."[25]

With the weight of science behind him, Franz Boas smashes into the racist slanders about the biological inferiority of Negroes. He says, "The existence of any pure race with special endowments is a myth, as is the belief that there are races all of whose members are foredoomed to eternal inferiority." He also says, "Negroes, Mongoloids and whites became isolated in times sufficiently remote to permit the development of far-reaching differences in certain bodily traits. . . . There is no scientific justification for classifying any one of these human types as more primitive in an evolutionary scale."[26] Freyre, the Brazilian scholar, agreeing with Boas and with reality, says, "The testimony of anthropologists reveals to us traits in the Negro showing a mental capacity in no wise inferior to that of other races."[27] Lipschutz, a noted anthropologist in Chile, states that "All the arguments of social anthropology, analytical psychology, and physical anthropology are in favor of the concept that the species of *homo sapiens* represents a biological unity very uniform from the point of view of cultural evolution, in spite of all its multifarious morphology."[28] Soviet anthropologists declare, too, that "Of overriding significance is the fact that the biological unity of all mankind is firmly established by science."[29]

In this field Negro scientists have made many outstanding contributions. This includes the work of such scholars as Dr. W. E. B. Du Bois, Dr. Montague Cobb, Mrs. Paul Robeson, Dr. T. M. Turner, and Dr. Ernest Everett Just. Dr. Just was especially noted in the sphere of biology. His last book (he died in 1941), *The Biology of the Cell Surface* (Philadelphia, 1939), was an attack upon the conservative biological theories of Weissmann and Morgan. Although an entirely independent product, it was basically along the lines developed by the Soviet scientists, Michurin and Lysenko.

These basic scientific conclusions are fully borne out by the splendid achievements of the Negro people in the fields of science, history, literature, politics, art, sport, etc., illuminated by such outstanding names as Phyllis Wheatley, H. H. Garnet, Frederick Douglass, Harriet Tubman, W. W. Brown, E. E. Just, M. R. Delany, B. T. Washington, P. L. Dunbar, W. E. B. Du Bois, George Washington Carver, C. W. Chesnutt, G. G. Woodson, Marcus Garvey, Claude McKay, Langston Hughes, C. H. Wesley, Paul Robeson, Benjamin J. Davis, and innumerable others. In every field of endeavor the Negro people, since emancipation, have made progress of which any nation might well be proud. During the past three centuries the Negro people have been terribly abused by their white conquerors; but obviously even this has not diminished their basic biological qualities.

RACIAL VERSUS NATIONAL SLOGANS

The development of the Negro people into nationhood has been especially marked since the beginning of the present century, with the rise of American imperialism and the intensified differentiation of the Negro people into definite classes—an intelligentsia, a bourgeoisie, and a proletariat. Marxist-Leninists have clearly recognized the nature of this national development and, consequently, have characterized the Negro people as a nation in the South and a national minority in the North. Many bourgeois Negro leaders in the past have also recognized their people as a nation, especially, but not always, in connection with the recurring migration movements. Most of the Negro leaders today, however, refuse to consider their people as a nation, and actively deny that they constitute one. Consequently, bourgeois Negro leaders are in considerable confusion over just how to characterize their people politically. They variously designate them as a race, a caste, a people, a minority group, etc. White commentators on Negro affairs are in similar confusion.

The Negro people are widely characterized as simply a "race." But obviously, this term is inadequate. A race is but a broad generalized biological concept, without specific political meaning. Benedict states, "Race is an abstraction even as it is defined by a geneticist; as it is defined statistically by a physical anthropologist it is even more of an abstraction."[30] Only in the most general sense can the people of the earth be classified under the head of three "races," or ethnic groups: Mongoloid, Negroid, and Caucasian. The Negro race is all the more tenuous as a concept in the United States, because, due to prevalent white supremacy, any person who has even the slightest percentage of Negro ancestry is characterized as a Negro.

There is no scientific definition of Negro, especially in the United States. Throughout the South the rule prevails, as in the Virginia law, that all those persons are Negroes "in whom there is ascertainable any Negro blood."[31] The U. S. government uses the same rule of thumb in characterizing predominantly white persons as Negroes. Thus, the Census enumerators were instructed that "A person of mixed white and Negro blood should be returned as a Negro, no matter how small the percentage of Negro blood."[32] This definition is essentially political, not biological. The purpose of such a crude white chauvinist, politically determined biological classification is to save the precious white master race from being "contaminated" by even the slightest Negro admixture.

The term "race" does not, in itself, express a political structure. "Race" lines vary and do run across national frontiers, and there may be several "races" in a given nation. Even peoples under primitive conditions do not live in "race" societies; their regimes are based on various forms of tribal communalism. And when a people acquires such institutions and culture as the Negro people have done in the United States, they cannot possibly be classified as a "race." They are becoming, or have become, a nation. In fact, the Negro people in this country have more qualities of nationhood than some of the peoples in the Far East who are now definitely fighting for national liberation.

Notwithstanding all this, the question of "race," as politically defined in the United States, is obviously a basic element in the oppression of the Negro people. For it is upon the basis of their color, or indicated African ancestry, that Negroes are marked out for special oppression and exploitation. Thus, "race" more or less sets the boundaries of the Negro nation. But as a definitive term this color designation is insufficient to describe the Negro's social status. As we have seen, the Negro people, besides the bonds of color or their element of common ancestry, are held together by a whole series of national institutions and habits, which they have developed in almost four centuries of life in this country. They have in the South a community of territory, a common economy, a common language, and a common culture, and these are what make them a nation. In the North, lacking some of these national attributes, they are but a national minority.

It is pertinent to ask: Why, then, do the Negro people generally use racial rather than national slogans? As far as the broad masses are concerned, this question may be answered on the ground that they have not yet fully attained national consciousness. Such a lag is not unusual on the part of young and undeveloped nations, such as the Negro people of the United States. Often, also, nations that have not acquired national consciousness carry on the struggle under religious slogans (as in Pakistan) or under racial slogans (as in the United States). It is not surprising that specific national consciousness develops slowly among the American Negro people, located as they are in the very heart of the biggest capitalist country in the world.

For the reformist bourgeois nationalist leaders of the Negro people, however, lack of knowledge does not suffice as an explantion. These leaders for the most part, comfortably situated under the influence of the big white bourgeoisie, systematically seek to stifle the growth of conscious national sentiment among the Negro people. They have their own narrow class interests to conserve at the expense of the mass of the Negro people. While supporting many lesser demands of the Negro people, they draw back before the prospect of putting forward the sharp and basic demands of an oppressed nation: such as, for proportional representation and for self-determination. They resemble the conservative leaders of the trade unions who, aligned in class collaboration with the employers, oppose the development of a fighting spirit and a Socialist consciousness among the masses of workers under their control.

During recent years the terms "people" and "minority group" are coming into wide usage among Negro writers and leaders generally. This is an indication that they find the vague term "race" unsatisfactory to define the status of their people. But these terms, too, are inadequate. "Minority group" is an offhand expression, which glibly equates the Negroes with such national groups as the Finns, Poles, Italians, etc., when obviously the situation of the Negroes is fundamentally different. The term "Negro people" is much more correct than "Negro race"; its expanding use definitely indicates a growth of national sentiment among Negroes, but it is limited and lacks the scientific accuracy and completeness of "nation" and "national minority."

ARE THE NEGRO PEOPLE A CASTE?

Many Negro writers and white commentators on the Negro question, dissatisfied with the term "race," designate the Negro people as a "caste." Myrdal, characteristic of this school, says, "When we say that Negroes form a lower caste in America, we mean that they are subject to certain disabilities solely because they are 'Negroes' in the rigid American definition and not because they are poor and ill-educated."[33] He uses the term specifically as a substitute for "race," "class," "minority group," "minority status," and also for "nation."

But Myrdal and his group are wrong; the Negro people are definitely not a caste. Castes are based essentially on class and occupation, and this definition in no sense fits the all-class, all-occupation Negro people. Introducing the concept of caste into the analysis of the status of the Negro people only further complicates and confuses an already complex situation.

India is the classical land of castes, which date back some three thousand years. Originally Indian society, emerging from a tribal system, was made up of four main classes, or castes, as follows: (a) Brahmans (priests and teachers); (b) Kshattryas (warriors); (c) Vaisyas (merchants, artisans and peasants); and (d) Sudras (primitive tribes, slaves, prisoners—the "untouchables").[34] "The Brahmans are not one caste, but a class, or rather an estate, comprising hundreds of castes, and this is likewise true for the Kshattryas, Vaisyas, and Sudras."[35]

During the centuries, the four original class-castes have subdivided into a great number of castes and subcastes, 3,000 at least. These have come to take on a religious significance and have developed their individual customs and etiquettes, involving inhibitions and discrimination against each other. These many subdivisions have occurred primarily along the lines of occupation. Caste differences are often minute: "Chungia Chamars smoke their pipes differently from other Chamars; Ekbaille and Kobaile are subcastes of Telis who yoke one and two bullocks respectively . . . the Goria are known to make white pots but not black ones," etc. Cox says that the "Hindus have never developed a method of identifying castes according to their physical variations," and that "the early Indo-Aryans could no more have thought in modern terms of race prejudice than they could have invented the airplane."[36]

Karl Marx indicated that "Modern industry . . . will dissolve the hereditary divisions of labor, upon which rest the Indian castes, those decisive impediments to Indian progress and Indian power."[37] What Marx forecast is now rapidly being realized under the pressure of the industrialization of India. Goshal states that "All that exists of the caste system today is intermarriage and inter-dining among the members of each caste."[38]

Obviously this primitive caste system has nothing in common with the position of the Negro people in the United States. The latter are suffering a national oppression at the hands of a modern imperialist capitalist class. It is absurd to argue that a highly industrialized America is creating castes, while in India industrialization is swiftly destroying them. The attempt by Myrdal and others to designate the Negro people as a caste confuses them and tends to prevent them from developing an effective struggle for national liberation.

THE QUESTION OF SELF-DETERMINATION

The right of self-determination is the right of every nation. Lenin says that this right "means only the right to independenc in a political sense, the right to be free, political secession from the oppressing nation."[39] And Stalin thus defines this basic attribute of nations: "The right of self-determination means that only the nation itself has the right to determine its destiny, that no one has the right forcibly to interfere in the life of the nation, to destroy its schools and other institutions, to violate its habits and customs, to repress its language, or curtail its rights. . . . The right of self-determination means that a nation can arrange its life according to its own will. . . . It has the right to enter into federal relations with other nations. It has the right to complete secession. Nations are sovereign and all nations are equal."[40]

This elementary right of self-determination belongs to all nations, as even the bourgeoisie itself, in the League of Nations and the United Nations, has been forced by rebellious peoples to admit. It is a right which must be conceded to the Negro nation in the Black Belt of the United States, to be used under such concrete forms as it so resolves. Many Negroes, however, and especially the conservative leaders, draw back from this proposition. They hold that the right of self-determination implies secession, the formation of a separate Negro state, and to this they are opposed. They wish to remain part of the United States and an integral segment of American life. In any event, they believe that the creation of a Negro state in the heart of this powerful capitalist country would be an economic and political impossibility.

But such fears are groundless. Whether or not, and how, the Negro people shall exercise their inherent right of self-determination will eventually be entirely up to them to decide.[41] When they determine to do so, they may exercise the right in various ways, as Haywood points out. "A nation may decide upon complete secession, that is, to set itself up as an independent state, or again it may decide upon federation with the former oppressing nation, or it may decide upon territorial autonomy within the borders of the former oppressing state, with a varying degree of sovereignty over its own internal affairs, viz., some form of local or regional self-government. There are, of course, varying degrees of autonomy within a state of mixed national composition, depending primarily upon the degree of unification of the respective autonomous people as a modern nation. Federation implies voluntary association between free and equal nations in the form of a federative state."[42] All these forms of self-determination have been widely developed in the relations among capitalist nations and, on a higher, Socialist scale, among the many peoples who compose the U.S.S.R.

Conservative Negro leaders affect to be shocked at the idea of self-determination as something alien to the wishes and experience of the American Negro people. But this hesitation is not borne out by Negro history. The fact is that many Negro leaders have advocated, and even attempted to practice, the right of self-determination for their people in one form or another. In 1919, Braselton, a Negro from Texas, wrote a book called *Self-Determination, the Only Remedy,* and in the same year, the *Amsterdam News* declared that the Negro people had as much right to self-determination as the Hungarians and Czechs.[43] The various petitions of Negro organizations to the League of Nations and United Nations (mentioned earlier) had in them the principle of the right of self-determination as expressed against the oppressor nation; and so did all the migration movements supported from time to time by sections of the Negro people throughout their history. Garvey in particular was conscious of the right of self-determination and demanded it for the Negro people.[44] He obviously had in mind some form of self-determination for the Negro people in the Southern part of the United States when he wrote: "We declare that Negroes, wheresoever they form a community among themselves, should be given the right to elect their own representatives to represent them in legislatures, courts of law, or such institutions as may exercise control over that particular community."[45]

The real issue that should concern the Negro people is not whether they possess the right of self-determination, but rather the concrete manner in which they should fight for and express this national right. More on this pertinent question will be said in the concluding chapter of this book.

44. The Economic Crisis and the New Deal

The decade from 1929 to 1939 was crowded with important events for the Negro people and for the American people in general. In October 1929, the hectic "prosperity" period—1923-29—blew up in a terrific explosion. The shattering economic breakdown, the worst in capitalist history, was a manifestation of the ever-deepening general crisis of the world capitalist system. The resounding crash came as the climax of a whole series of inner and outer contradictions of capitalism, manifesting themselves in a profound crisis of overproduction, industrial shutdown, and mass unemployment.

The great crisis of 1929-33 was worldwide in scope, but its starting point and storm center was in the economy of the United States, which capitalists and Social-Democrats had previously declared to be crisis-proof. In the United States, over $160 billion in stock-market values were wiped out, production in basic industry fell by 50 percent, 5,761 banks closed their doors, and the value of farm products collapsed from $8.5 billion to $4 billion.[1] On a world scale capitalist production fell 42 percent and foreign trade 65 percent.

THE RAVAGES OF THE CRISIS

The wages of the workers, on the average, were cut by at least 45 percent, and the total number of unemployed in the United States reached the monstrous figure of 17 million by March 1933. Starvation stalked the country, millions wandered about the nation hungry and jobless, while great masses of jobless workers in every city lived in shack towns called Hoovervilles. The Hoover Administration did nothing to relieve the distress but, through the Reconstruction Finance Corporation, handed out vast sums to the corporations. Hoover's theory was that the benefits of these monster doles to the capitalists would trickle down to the workers. Meanwhile, the people were deluged with lying propaganda that prosperity was "just around the corner."

The Negro masses—workers and sharecroppers—suffered most during the terrible crisis years. "In the industrial centers unemployment among them ran about twice as high as among the whites. Negro workers were laid off and whites given their jobs at lower wages. Wages for Negro workers averaged 30 percent less than for whites. Also in the matter of relief, the Negroes got much the worst of it, being either denied assistance altogther, given less of such aid, or discriminated against otherwise in the distribution process. Always the poorest paid in industry, the Negroes had few or no reserves with which to meet the crisis, and conditions among them beggared description. During the four crisis years 150 Negroes were lynched."[2]

The A. F. of L. leaders (and the Socialists) were demoralized by the crisis. Their beloved capitalist system was in a state of collapse, and all they knew how to do was to tail along after Hoover, hoping that his Pollyanna promises of returning prosperity might come true. The A. F. of L. top officials were even so reactionary as to oppose government unemployment insurance and relief up until July 1932, contending that these were the "dole" and would undermine the trade union movement and the American way of life.[3] The N.A.A.C.P. and Urban League leadership were likewise inactive.

In this situation the Communist Party and the Young Communist League, despite their small size, gave the lead to the unemployed. Along with the T.U.U.L., they established the National Unemployed Councils and organized hunger marches and demonstrations all over the country. At the great national demonstration of March 6, 1930, 1,250,000 workers turned out in cities all over the country—110,000 in New York, 100,000 in Detroit, etc. Several such gigantic national turn-outs were held. The national hunger marches to Washington of December 7, 1931, and December 6, 1932, attracted widespread attention. Under Communist leadership, several important strikes were waged against the sweeping wage cuts. This movement, led by the Communists, gave the impetus to the famous Bonus March of the hungry veterans to Washington in July 1932. Hundreds of militant workers were beaten and jailed during these years, and several were killed. In all these movements Negroes played a prominent part. The effect of this big struggle was to secure immediate relief for the unemployed, to make unemployment insurance a national issue, and to prepare the way for later New Deal legislation on this question.

THE COMMUNIST PARTY IN THE SOUTH

In the election campaigns of 1924 and 1928, the Communist Party carried its message militantly into the South. After the latter campaign it began systematic work there and, in August 1930, established the *Southern Worker* in Chattanooga, with James S. Allen as editor. The situation in the South was shocking, with mass unemployment, starvation in the cities and on the plantations, and the whole country overrun with K.K.K. and lynch-gang thugs. The entry of the Communists into the South was a bold challenge to the planter-monopolist masters, the first since the days of the Colored National Farmers Alliance in the 1890's—a challenge that neither the A. F. of L. nor the S.P. had ever dared to make.

This Southern work was stimulated by the formation in St. Louis, in October 1930, of the League of Struggle for Negro Rights, an outgrowth of the American Negro Labor Congress and also of the African Blood Brotherhood, the Equal Rights League, and the League of African Freedom. Its program declared, "We proclaim before the whole world that the American Negroes are a nation. . . . Land, freedom and equality . . . the watchword of the ex-slave during the period of Civil War and Reconstruction still remains the watchword of the embattled Negroes today."[4] This organization carried on vigorous agitational work all over the country, including the South. It was finally merged with the National Negro Congress in February 1936. Its general secretaries were Richard B. Moore and Harry Haywood; Langston Hughes was president.

The Communists in the South turned their attention first to the sharecroppers, who lived under conditions of poverty and oppression beggaring description. Since the breakdown of the Southern Alliance in the late 1890's (see Chapter 35), only desultory attempts had been made to organize the Negro tenants, sharecroppers, and laborers in the face of the reigning lynch terror, notably in 1919.[5] The national white farm organizations ignored them in their work in the South.

Under Communist leadership, in the spring of 1931, the Sharecroppers Union was organized in Tallapoosa and Lee Counties, Alabama. The conditions of struggle were savage. The Union carried on numerous strikes of cotton-pickers and exerted considerable political influence in neighboring states. One of its most serious battles with the planters' terrorist gangs was in Camp Hill, Tallapoosa County; in December 1932. The Negro sharecroppers resisted a raid upon their meeting, with the result that there were four known dead and a score wounded. Five Negroes got long prison sentences. It was in this vicinity that Ralph Grey, Negro sharecropper and union leader, had been murdered on July 15, 1931.[6] By 1936, the Sharecroppers Union reached some 12,000 members, with branches in Alabama, Mississippi, Louisiana, and North Carolina.[7] In the Lowndes County strike of 1935, six Negro strikers were killed. During the New Deal period, this pioneer organization finally merged with the A. F. of L. and C.I.O. farm organizations in the South.

During this period a significant event took place in New York, in March 1931, dramatizing the sincerity with which Communists take the fight for Negro equality in every field. A Finnish worker and Party member, A. Yokinen, accused of practicing social discrimination against a Negro, was charged with white chauvinism and given a public trial at the Finnish Club hall in Harlem, before a body made up of 211 delegates from 133 workers' mass organizations, and 1,500 spectators. Yokinen was found guilty and expelled from the Party. He agreed to mend his ways in the future. This trial illustrated the fight which the Communist Party relentlessly carries on against all evidences of the widespread poison of white chauvinism, within its own ranks as well as the mass organizations of which Communists are members.[8]

SCOTTSBORO

On March 21, 1931, nine Negro boys, the youngest but 13 years old, were jailed in Scottsboro, Alabama, charged with raping two white women on a freight train—a manifestly false charge which was later repudiated, especially by one of the girls, Ruby Bates.[9] The authorities at once proceeded to a legal lynching of the youths. All but one, the youngest, were sentenced to the electric chair after a kangaroo trial of only a few days.

The Communist Party, then very active in the South, promptly rallied to the defense of the Negro victims. The I.L.D. wired Governor Miller for a stay of execution and sent the veteran Communist lawyer, Joseph Brodsky, to defend the accused boys. Thus began one of the most famous battles against the frame-up system in American labor history. The case was fought back and forth in the courts for years. On March 25, 1932, the Alabama Supreme Court affirmed the verdict, but the United States Supreme Court, under heavy mass pressure, ordered a new trial on the ground that the accused had not had adequate counsel.

The Communist Party made a national and international issue of the case, which rivaled in public support the celebrated case of Tom Mooney. It was only long after the Communist Party and the I.L.D. had stayed the hand of the legal lynchers in Alabama that the hesitant N.A.A.C.P., Urban League, A. F. of L., and other liberal and labor organizations got into the historic struggle. In 1934, three years after the fight began, a big united front defense committee was set up, containing many of these organizations and headed by Judge Samuel Leibowitz. The following year a still larger committee, the Scottsboro Defense Committee, was organized. The great Scottsboro fight made the Communist Party known and respected everywhere by the Negro people.

The combined mass-legal fight saved the Scottsboro boys from the electric chair, but it was not strong enough to save them from prison. The savage Southern courts sentenced them to terms up to 99 years, and it was not until 1950 that the last of them was released. Nevertheless, the struggle was a great political victory for the Negro people. It exposed the terrible situation of the Negroes in the South as had not been done since the days of Reconstruction. Of the most vital importance was the great publicity given to the case internationally. It became especially known all over the colonial world. Thus, much of the anti-Jim Crow spirit, which has since become such a powerful force in restraining the Southern lynchers and modifying to some extent the ferocious Jim Crow system throughout the United States, was built up all over the world.

Another big struggle during these years was the one to save the young Negro Communist, Angelo Herndon. He was arrested in Atlanta, Georgia, on July 11, 1932. Because of his activities among the unemployed, he was sentenced under a law of 1861 to 18 to 20 years in prison. The I.L.D., with Benjamin J. Davis, Jr., as its attorney, fought and won this case after a five-year national struggle.

THE ELECTION OF FRANKLIN D. ROOSEVELT

In 1932, aroused by the disaster of the great economic crisis and enraged at Hoover's mass starvation policies, the American people elected the Democrat, Franklin D. Roosevelt, by a landslide, with a plurality of seven million votes. He carried all the states but six. In his campaign Roosevelt had presented a conservative program for government, a balanced budget, and sound currency, with vague promises of government relief for the unemployed. He gave hardly an inkling of his later elaborate reform program, the New Deal.

This election marked the first decisive break-away of the Negroes from the Republican Party, the party of Negro emancipation and also of Wall Street. During the Populist movement of the 1890's, many Negroes had voted independently. In 1896 Dr. Du Bois had voted for Bryan, and in 1916 he had supported Wilson—and many Negroes with him. In 1928, the *Pittsburgh Courier* was spokesman for the considerable body of Negroes who voted for Alfred E. Smith against Hoover.

But in 1932, about two million Negroes voted, the majority against the Republican ticket.[10] In the South, of course, Negroes were almost entirely voteless. In 1936, for the first time, there were Negro delegates at the national convention of the Democratic Party, the historic party of slavery and Jim Crow in the South. In the elections of that year, the Negro vote went even more heavily to Roosevelt; in Harlem, for example, the Negro vote for Roosevelt was four to one. Twenty-five Negroes were elected to state legislatures in the North.[11] On the basis of his liberal New Deal program, Roosevelt continued to hold the major Negro vote in the elections of 1940 and 1944. Their break-away from the Republican Party put the Negro people in a decisive political position in the elections in a number of Northern states—New York, Illinois, Ohio, Michigan, etc.

A striking example of independent, progressive Negro voting was the election in Harlem of the Communist Party leader, Benjamin J. Davis, in 1943, to the New York City Council. Davis remained there until 1950, making a splendid record. He was finally defeated by a Republican - Democratic - Liberal coalition, which had previously brought about the abolition of the municipal system of proportional representation in the drive to unseat him.

THE NEW DEAL

The New Deal, which President Roosevelt started in March 1933, was an attempt to fix up the prostrate capitalist system of the United States. Despite assertions to the contrary, there was nothing socialist about it. President Roosevelt, a wealthy liberal Democrat, and the capitalists behind him were entirely devoted to a restoration of the capitalist order of society, then badly broken down. The New Deal measures were mostly based upon the theories of the British economist, Sir John Maynard Keynes.

Summed up, the New Deal, by its many new laws rushed pell-mell through Congress, proposed, " (a) to reconstruct the shattered financial banking system; (b) to rescue tottering business with big loans and subsidies; (c) to stimulate private capital investment; (d) to raise depressed prices by setting inflationary tendencies into operation; (e) to overcome the agricultural overproduction through acreage reduction and crop destruction; (f) to protect farmers and home-owners against mortgage foreclosure; (g) to create employment and stimulate mass buying power through establishing public works; (h) to provide a minimum of relief for the starving unemployed."[12]

These reform measures relieved the crisis somewhat, but could not cure it. Despite $40 billion in government spending, the industries continued to limp along with 10 million unemployed as late as 1939. It was only on the outbreak of World War II, with its tremendous flood of munitions orders, that the industries, with this shot in the arm, began to go back into full operation. Under the Roosevelt regime, however, monopoly was linked more closely to the government—that is, there was a big expansion of state-monopoly capitalism.

THE GREAT MASS MOVEMENTS

The sweeping political upheaval, which elected Roosevelt in 1932 and reelected him in 1936, 1940, and 1944 in spite of powerful opposition, was accompanied by and based upon big, militant mass movements among the workers, farmers, youth, women, and Negro people. The Roosevelt coalition bore a distinct relationship to the anti-fascist people's front movements all over Europe. The workers did not head the Roosevelt coalition, but they were able to force concessions from the government. The Communists were a vital leading factor in this whole development, both here and abroad. One of Roosevelt's main objectives, besides patching up capitalism, was to prevent this great mass movement from getting out of hand, by making certain concessions to the workers—from pressing for drastic reform measures such as the nationalization of the banks and key industries, and forming a broad farmer-labor party.

The workers were in a militant mood, they joined the trade unions in masses and founded the C.I.O., of which we shall speak further in the next chapter. The farmers, also in a fighting mood, defended their farms from the money-grabbers who wanted to seize them for defaulted mortgages. They elected progressives to the state legislatures and congress and they built up their farmers' unions solidly throughout the North and West. During these years of intense struggle, the women, too, Negro and white, were on the march. They were on the picket lines, in the unemployed demonstrations, and active at the polls; several millions rallied around the Woman's Charter.

One of the biggest and most significant mass movements of the time was that of the youth, centered around the American Youth Congress.[13] This movement, organized in 1934, included the enormous total of 4,600,000 young people by the outbreak of the war in 1939. The government, which initiated the movement, hoped to keep it conservative, but the youth took hold of it themselves. Most of the youth organizations of the country were affiliated to it, and its program was militantly anti-fascist and progressive. The Young Communist League, whose head was Gilbert Green, was a leading, dynamic factor in this historic movement.

The Negro youth were very prominent in the whole A.Y.C. development. Most important was the united front Southern Negro Youth Congress, organized in Richmond, Virginia, in February 1937. Leaders in this organization were Edward Strong, James W. Ford, James Jackson, Henry Winston, Louis Burnham, and Esther Cooper. The S.N.Y.C. carried on a militant fight for their Negro program in many parts of the South. For over a decade (1937-1948), there was no battle of the Southern Negro masses in which this organization did not play a vital role. In 1946, when it held its seventh convention in the out-of-the-way Southern city of Columbia, South Carolina, 1,000 delegates were present. There were more white delegates in attendance than at the convention of the Southern Conference for Human Welfare, held the same year. The S.N.Y.C. was the most important movement ever conducted by Negro youth. It pioneered many of the constructive developments now taking place in the South—including the right-to-vote movement, the unionization of Southern industry, the fight for the right of education, and the general struggle against lynching and all forms of Jim Crow.

One of the most important mass movements of this period was the Southern Conference for Human Welfare, founded in Birmingham, Alabama, in November 1938.[14] President Roosevelt had called the South "the nation's economic problem number one," and his Administration gave active endorsement to the S.C.H.W. The Communist Party, a militant force throughout, was officially represented at the founding convention. The new organization brought together the leading liberals of the South, along with considerable representation from the not very strong Southern labor movement. Negroes were very active in the work of the S.C.H.W. They provided some 300 of the 1,250 delegates at the first convention, which met unsegregated— to the great shock of the Southern Jim Crowers and lynchers. Finally, the police ordered the convention to segregate its delegates on pain of their breaking up the big gathering. Negroes participated in the work of all the convention panels. They were given recognition in the official machinery set up by the S.C.H.W.; John P. Davis and Mary McLeod Bethune were elected as members to the Southern Council of 118.

Communist influence was strong in the S.C.H.W from the start and this was reflected in the advanced program it adopted. The organization condemned lynching, the poll tax, and the feudal-like system of sharecropping. It demanded civil rights, general suffrage, federal education, jobs, minimum wages, trade unions, as well as the industrialization of the area, and the removal of various monopolistic discriminations against the South. This program had double significance for the Negroes. During the several years of its existence, the S.C.H.W., the first extensive Negro-white movement in the South since the days of Populism in the 1890's, was a strong liberal influence throughout the whole area. Its greatest weakness was its lack of support from the white trade unions and poor white farmers.[15] The S.C.H.W. continued through World War II, but it held its last general convention in 1946.[16] Its death in 1948 was due primarily to sabotage and white chauvinism among its more conservative groups.

This, too, was the period of the so-called "panacea movements." During the crisis and throughout the early Roosevelt days, there sprang up a whole group of big mass movements, often led by reactionary demagogues like Senator Huey Long and Father Charles Coughlin. They offered various cure-all plans for the crisis situation; among them were "Technocracy," "End Poverty in California," "Utopians," "Townsend National Recovery Plan," "Ham and Eggs Movement," "National Union for Social Justice," and "Share the Wealth." These movements involved many millions of impoverished workers, farmers, professionals, the aged, etc. They eventually became absorbed in the broad Roosevelt reform movement.[17]

THE NATIONAL NEGRO CONGRESS

The Negro people played an important part in the great movement of the toiling masses during the years of the New Deal—in its political, trade union, youth, women's, and other activities. They also built up an important movement composed primarily of Negroes. This was the National Negro Congress, founded in Chicago, on February 14-16, 1936. At this convention there were 817 delegates from 28 states, representing 585 organizations. Present were Republicans, Democrats, Socialists, Liberals, Communists, churchmen, workers, professionals, businessmen—representing a "combined and unduplicated" membership of 1,200,000.

This broad movement, which operated in the tradition of the historic Negro people's conventions, had been suggested two years before by James W. Ford, in a debate with Oscar de Priest and Frank Crosswaith. With their strong concentration upon defending the rights of the Negro people, the Communists took a leading part in building the convention and were tirelessly active throughout the life of the N.N.C. Several Communists were members of the National Council elected by the congress.

The program of the National Negro Congress supported the growing struggle against fascism and war; endorsed an active defense of Ethiopia; condemned Jim Crow, lynching, and the poll tax; advocated trade union unity and the full inclusion of Negro workers into the labor movement; demanded adequate relief for unemployed Negro workers, insisted on the abolition of sharecropping; supported consumers' and producers' co-operatives; endorsed the Workers Alliance (of the unemployed); and favored the formation of a farmer-labor party. The congress did not raise the question of the Negro people as an oppressed nation.[18]

The N.N.C. was extremely active for the next few years in various parts of the country. Its national meeting of 1937 brought together 1,218 delegates, including such figures as Walter White, Norman Thomas, and Philip Murray. The organization built up branches in many cities and was a major factor in such political progress as the Negro people achieved during this period. Especially important was its great activity in recruiting Negro workers into the newly-formed C.I.O. It continued its work through the war, but on a diminishing scale. The liberal and reformist elements found its program too left and too militant for them. The N.N.C. was dissolved in 1947.

THE EARLY NEW DEAL AND THE NEGRO

Faced by the enormous mass movements of the 1933-39 period, the Roosevelt Administration was compelled to make certain concessions to the toiling masses, who were militantly protesting against the terrible conditions of the economic crisis. This was the only way to keep them from going left and forming a great political party of their own. The most important of these palliative concessions were the beginnings of a system of social insurance and the granting of a measure of legal recognition of the right of the workers to organize in trade unions. To the extent that they were workers, these reforms were also shared to a considerable extent by Negroes (despite discriminatory practices). But more on this vital question in the next chapter.

The government also made certain specific concessions to the Negro people as such. Perhaps the most valued among these meager benefits were those tending to stress, in however limited a way, the social equality of the Negro. These included a certain cordiality on the part of the liberal Roosevelt toward Negro delegations and others. He met with them socially and treated them as human beings—something Negroes were quite unaccustomed to in American political and social life. Very important was the intervention of Mrs. Roosevelt and Secretary of the Interior Harold L. Ickes in behalf of the great Negro singer, Marian Anderson, in 1939, after the ultra-reactionary Daughters of the American Revolution had denied her the right to sing in Constitution Hall, in Washington.

Another minor concession which Roosevelt made to the Negro people during these pre-war New Deal years was a minimum of political recognition. Thus, the number of Negro workers on the Federal payroll was increased from 50,000 in 1933 to over 200,000 during the war—although, characteristically, most of these workers were in the poorer-paid, unskilled categories. Roosevelt met freely with leaders of Negro organizations and also had what was called his "Black Cabinet." Previous presidents had occasionally condescended to listen to the advice of a Negro, but Roosevelt established a measure of real co-operation with Negro leaders, to the great outrage of the Southern wing of his party. Among the Negroes prominent in the New Deal Administration were Robert L. Vann, William L. Hastie, Robert C. Weaver, Eugene Kinckle Jones, L. A. Oxley, Mary McLeod Bethune, and others.[19] No Negro, however, was entrusted with major executive authority.

The Roosevelt Administration left untouched the bulk of the most burning grievances of the Negro people. Roosevelt did nothing to help put through the Federal anti-lynching legislation supported in Congress by Representative Vito Marcantonio and others. The same was true of the poll tax which was disfranchising many millions of Negroes and poor whites in the South. In the armed forces Jim Crow segregation prevailed, although Roosevelt personally could have ended it by an executive order. The gross inequality in the education of Negroes and whites in the South also went undisturbed during this whole period, as did many of the other deplorable conditions under which Negroes were forced to live.

The Harlem riot of March 19, 1935, dramatized the evil conditions under which Northern Negroes were living. The trouble began over an incident in a five-and-ten cent store. It rapidly spread along 125th Street, until several thousand people were involved; the people's anger was directed chiefly against the storekeepers, who were nearly all white and intensely chauvinistic. Before the affair was over four people were killed, thirty injured, and scores arrested. Behind this riot was a bitter accumulation of Negro grievances—unemployment, police brutality, job and relief discrimination, wretched housing, bad medical and educational facilities, and the rest of the tragic story of Harlem (See J. W. Ford, *Hunger and Terror in Harlem*).

Through the Agricultural Adjustment Act (A.A.A.), the New Deal applied the plow-under and crop-subsidy plan to the South; but the Negroes and poor white farmers got little benefit from it. Rapar thus pictures the "Sunny South" of the 1930's: "This most Democratic part of the nation is perhaps the least democratic; from six to sixty times as much public money is spent for the education of the white as for the Negro school child; Negro office holders are unknown, scarcely any Negroes register and vote in national presidential elections, almost none participate in local politics."[20] In Greene and Macon counties, Georgia, "only one out of every ten Negro farmers owns any land, and scarcely half of these have enough to make a living on."[21] "There are hundreds of rural white families in Greene and Macon counties who own no horse or mule, cow or calf, pig or chicken, farm implement or vehicle."[22] Johnson and Associates thus complete the dismal picture: The South presents "a miserable panorama of unpainted shacks, rain gullied fields, straggling fences, rattletrap Fords, dirt, poverty, disease, drudgery, and monotony that stretches for a thousand miles across the cotton belt."[23] And Kester adds that "malaria and pellagra are as common to many sharecroppers as their diet of meal, molasses and meat."[24]

The A.A.A. program took 10.5 million acres and 4.5 million bales of cotton out of production with price boosts of from 6 to 10 cents for cotton, which in 1933 doubled the cotton planters' income over 1932.[25] Bert indicates how the system operated: "Under the New Deal the federal relief organs became the instruments to sustain the croppers and other laborers at subsistence levels when the plantation landlords had no use for their labor, and to compel the laborers to work for the landlords during the cropping and planting seasons at less than relief standards. . . . The emergency crop and feed loans of the 30's served in the South primarily to finance the landlord . . . the landlord waived his right to the rent and appropriated the tenant's check. Sometimes the landlord distributed the proceeds of the loan to the tenants in cash and at such times and in such terms as he saw fit"—for which he charged eight or 10 percent, on top of the government's six percent.[26]

Raper thus describes how the A.A.A. worked in the South, chiefly regarding Negro tenants and sharecroppers: "When the money came [for plowing crops under] . . . practically all of it found its way into the hands of the landlord. One-half of it belonged to him for rent, while the other half was used to reduce the indebtedness to him for furnishings. . . . The A.A.A. has been generally satisfactory to the Black Belt's leaders—to the planters, to the business men, to the cotton factories, to the professional people."[27]

Over the whole tragic scene reigned the terrorists, the Jim Crowers, and the lynchers. The mealy-mouthed bourgeois moralists of the area saw nothing, heard nothing, and said nothing of the Negroes' terrible conditions. Raper says, "The white church just ignores the Negro. Nothing is said about him, no mention is made of his inadequate school facilities, of his physical disfranchisement, of his enforced landlessness."[28] This is the same church that once justified slavery, fought in the Civil War to protect it, and, through the succeeding decades, had no protest to make against the K.K.K. lynch mobs.

45. The Negro and the New Trade Unionism

The most important political development of the New Deal years in the United States was the trade union organization of the basic, trustified industries—steel, automobile, marine transport, metal mining, meat-packing, lumber, rubber, etc., particularly in the North. These major industries, the great open shop fortresses of monopoly capital, had long resisted successfully all attempts to organize them. And without these workers, the labor movement must remain largely impotent. Finally, during the decade between 1935 and 1945, this big job was largely done by the building of the Congress of Industrial Organizations.

This historic achievement laid a whole new basis for the American labor movement. Victory became possible because of the mass upheaval which got under way in the early New Deal years as a result of the unprecedented economic crisis of 1929-1933. Another basic cause was the vital political-war struggle of the American and other peoples against the deadly danger of fascism. The great industrial union movement was destined to have profound economic and political consequences in the life of the nation, and especially in that of the Negro people.

REACTIONARY A.F. OF L. POLICIES

Prior to the New Deal period, the American Federation of Labor had failed almost completely to organize the key sections of the working class, notably the workers in the basic industries. By 1934, the total membership of the A.F. of L. was 2,608,011, or only about 10 percent of the working class. This was a gain of but half a million in 20 years. The A.F. of L. contained mainly skilled workers in building, printing, railroads, the theater, etc. This situation represented virtual stagnation. The labor movement was stymied by the fundamental problem of the trustified industries, with the wages and working conditions of the great majority of the working class determined arbitrarily by the employers.

This long continued failure of the A.F. of L. had a number of elementary causes. The top union leaders, many of whom had been connected with the bootleggers and gangsters of the prohibition era, were personally thoroughly crooked and were tied up with the employers in many ways.[1] They refused to work out fighting policies to challenge the bosses' domination. They maintained a system of craft unionism more fitted to the needs of a century earlier than to the period of trustified industry. They followed the idiotic policy of keeping one group of unions in an industry at work while others were striking—a "union scabbery" which cost the loss of hundreds of strikes. They bitterly resisted the efforts of the workers toward independent political action and the establishment of a labor party. Small wonder, then, that the A.F. of L. remained unable to organize the monopoly-controlled industries.

One of the most disastrous of the policies of the A.F. of L. misleaders of labor was the systematic betrayal of the interests of the masses of women, youth, and unskilled for the benefit of the minority of skilled workers. The worst sufferers in this systematic betrayal by the reactionary union leaders were the Negro workers. They were deliberately kept out of the unions and the industries by the reactionary union leaders. As we have seen in earlier chapters, this old practice of the skilled workers' unions dated back to the days of the craft organizations in the National Labor Union and the Knights of Labor.

JIM CROW UNIONISM

This shameful exclusion reached its lowest depths in the A.F. of L. and Railroad Brotherhoods after the turn of the century. At the beginning of the New Deal period, 25 of the A. F. of L. organizations still excluded Negroes from membership, either by constitutional clause or in practice. Notable exceptions were the miners, longshoremen, and needle trades. The pressure of the labor officialdom was used not only to keep the Negroes from becoming union members, but also to keep them from getting jobs in industry, especially at skilled work.

In 1933, Lorwin said correctly, "The Federation is a white man's organization."[2] He estimated the number of Negro members in the A.F. of L. in 1928 "at between 40,000 and 60,000, out of a million or more Negro workers in American industry." At its convention in 1934, the A.F. of L. proved Lorwin was right by rejecting a motion, offered by Randolph, proposing to exclude "any union maintaining the color line." The convention decided that "the American Federation of Labor . . . cannot interfere with the autonomy of national and international unions." Even as late as 1941, the A.F. of L. bureaucrats justified their Jim Crow policies by arguing that "discrimination existed before the A.F. of L. was born, and human nature cannot be altered."[3]

The Railroad Brotherhoods—engineers, firemen, conductors, trainmen, and switchmen—were especially vicious in their anti-Negro policies. They succeeded in keeping the Negro workers almost entirely out of the operating and mechanical trades in the North, restricting them almost exclusively to the occupations of porters, waiters, and common laborers. It was as late as 1953 that the Pennsylvania Railroad hired its first Negro brakeman. In the South from pre-Civil War times on, Negroes had made their way in comparatively large numbers into all the railroad trades, a few even being engineers. The brotherhoods, therefore, started an active campaign to exclude them from these jobs, to make the Southern railroads as lily-white as those in the North.

While refusing membership to the Southern Negro railroad workers, the brotherhoods actually made agreements with the companies, designed gradually to squeeze the Negroes into the unskilled jobs. In March 1911, an exclusionist move led to a strike on the Queen and Crescent line (C.N.O. & T.P.) in which 10 workers were killed and many injured.[4] In 1944, the U.S. Supreme Court knocked out one such agreement (previously endorsed by the Alabama high court), which would have eliminated Negro firemen practically all over the South.[5]

These practices have drastically reduced the number of Negroes in skilled railroad work throughout the South. "Before World War I, 80 percent of the firemen on the Southern Railway were colored; by 1929 this number was reduced to 33⅓ percent. On the Atlantic Coast Line and Seaboard Air Line the percentages were reduced from 90 and 50 to 50 and 25 percent respectively, and so on."[6] At the 1926 convention of the Brotherhood of Locomotive Firemen and Engineers, President Robertson informed the delegates that he hoped to be able to tell the next convention that "not a single Negro remained on the left side of an engine cab."[7] The Negro railroad workers answered these segregation policies by attempting to form separate unions, but save in the case of the Pullman Porters (organized in 1925), they never succeeded. This organization has always been Jim Crowed and excluded from the joint wage negotiations carried on by the score of railroad unions. For years its leader, A. Philip Randolph, was insulted in A.F. of L. conventions when he demanded that Negroes be organized.

SUPPORTING NEGRO UNIONIZATION

During the crucial decades before the New Deal, the S.P. left wing and the Communists were by far and away the most outstanding and influential grouping demanding that Negroes have the right to work freely in industry and to join all trade unions. As for the decrepit Socialist Party itself, it either openly supported Jim Crow policies in the unions or failed to fight against them at A.F. of L. and other craft union conventions.

Among Negro intellectual leaders, too, there was anything but unity on the trade union question. While the Randolph group in New York and such men as Ralph Bunche agitated for the unionization of Negro workers, many other Negro intellectuals were quite cold to the matter. Even as late as September 2, 1937, when the big C.I.O. campaign was on and many Negro leaders were supporting it, the *Pittsburgh Courier* stated: "In the recent drive of the C.I.O. it was found that in almost every locality the Negro and professional groups opposed the participation of the Negro workers." According to Cayton and Mitchell, "In St. Louis, it was reported that only two preachers out of hundreds had taken any favorable interest in the unions."[8] Such nationalist opposition among the Negro petty-bourgeois elements (but not among the Negro workers) was intensified by the fruit of long years of Jim Crow policies on the part of the A.F. of L.

Throughout the pre-New Deal years, the Communist-led Trade Union Educational League agitated militantly for the unionization of Negro workers. It spread this message into many thousands of local unions where it had active connections. Originally the T.U.E.L. was a left-wing grouping in all trade unions, but eventually it began to organize industrial unions in industries where no solid unions existed. Consequently, in September 1929, in Cleveland it transformed itself into the Trade Union Unity League, which placed its major emphasis upon the organization of the unorganized, including the Negroes, into independent unions.

At this founding convention, 64 of the 690 delegates were Negroes —in contrast to A.F. of L. conventions, which usually had but two or three. The T.U.U.L. declared "for racial, social, and political equality for Negroes," and it devoted major attention to the organization of these workers. It made the following estimate of the Negro as a union member: "The Negro workers are good fighters. This they have proved in innumerable strikes in the coal, steel, packing, building, and other industries, despite systematic betrayal by the white trade union leaders and the presence of an all too prevalent race chauvinism among the masses of white workers. They are a tremendous source of potential revolutionary strength and vigor. They have a double oppression, as workers and as Negroes, to fill them with fighting spirit and resentment against capitalism."[9] It was in this understanding that the T.U.U.L. carried on its many organizing campaigns and strikes during the crisis and early New Deal years. In 1935, to facilitate trade union unity, it merged with the A.F. of L.

THE C.I.O. ORGANIZING CAMPAIGN

In 1935, the great pressure of the masses for unionization broke through the iron fence built around the labor movement by the reactionary leaders of the A.F. of L. Almost immediately after Roosevelt's election in 1932, workers began to come into the unions. The crisis was reached at the 1935 convention of the A.F. of L. in Atlantic City, when a resolution for industrial unionism was defeated by a vote of 18,025 to 10,924. Thereupon, a month later, under the growing mass pressure, eight unions formed the Committee for Industrial Organization with a program for unionizing the basic, trustified industries. The chief leaders of this historic movement were John L. Lewis, Sidney Hillman, and Philip Murray, and the pioneering unions were those in coal mining, textile, ladies' garment, men's clothing, typographical, oil, cap and millinery, and metal mining, with a combined membership of about one million workers.

The formation of the C.I.O. greatly alarmed the hidebound craft union bureaucrats dominating the A.F. of L. They feared the effect upon their preferred positions from millions of unskilled and semi-skilled workers streaming into their unions which were made up essentially of skilled workers. So they set out to sabotage and defeat the organizing drive. At their Tampa convention in 1936 they even went so far as to expel (suspend) the eight C.I.O. unions, 40 percent of the entire Federation, on charges of dual unionism.

Despite the King Canutes of the A.F. of L. Executive Council, however, the C.I.O. organizing campaign was a success from the start. During the immediate pre-war years before World War II, great masses of workers poured into the new industrial unions in steel, auto, maritime, textile, metal mining, meat-packing, and other key industries. A great wave of strikes swept the country. Many of them were "sit-down" strikes, notably in the automobile plants.[10] United States Steel, General Motors, General Electric, Armour & Co., and scores of other rabidly anti-union corporations were compelled to sign up with the new, militant unions. This broad C.I.O. organizing movement communicated itself to the A.F. of L. Many A.F. of L. unions threw down craft bars, became virtually industrial unions, and grew as rapidly as the C.I.O. organizations.

At their 1940 conventions, with World War II going on in Europe, the C.I.O. and A.F. of L. reported 3,810,318 and 4,247,443 members respectively. The total membership of the whole labor movement, including the Railroad Brotherhoods and other independent unions, was then about 10,000,000, representing a gain of some 7,000,000 members in four years. This union growth continued through the war, until, in 1946, the whole labor movement counted about 15,000,000 members, including approximately 6,000,000 in the C.I.O. and 7,151,-808 in the A.F. of L.

The huge and successful organizing campaign represented the greatest victory ever won by the working class in the United States. The strong unions in the basic industries enabled the workers, for the first time, to challenge the right of the trust barons arbitrarily to set their wages and working conditions, to terrorize and fire workers as they pleased, and to rule their lives tyrannically in the shops and in the towns. Building the new unions constituted the first real blow struck at the infamous system of spies, gunman control, and company towns, which had hitherto reigned supreme in the strongholds of open shop industry. The great new union movement also provided a solid mass base for the democratic coalition which re-elected Roosevelt in 1936, 1940, and 1944. It likewise laid the foundations for an eventual broad, independent political party of the workers and their allies.

This perspective, however, the workers have not yet been able to realize in the face of the opposition of their conservative union leaders.

THE NEGRO IN THE ORGANIZATION CAMPAIGN

The Negro workers in the basic industries joined wholeheartedly in the great organizing drive. They readily entered the unions everywhere, despite the outrageous way they had been betrayed and Jim Crowed for half a century by the A.F. of L. leadership, and notwithstanding the doubts, hesitations, and even opposition of many of the Negro petty-bourgeois intelligentsia. In the key area of Alabama the Negro workers took the lead in organizing the coal and steel unions. Statistics on the actual number of Negro workers in the A.F. of L. and C.I.O. are not too reliable, as many of the unions do not keep such records; but some figures are at hand. Dr. Ira De A. Reid estimated the number of Negro union members in 1930 at 110,000.[11] By 1935, this number had gone up to 180,000, and in 1948 the A.F. of L. claimed 650,000 Negro members, and the C.I.O., 500,000.[12] It has been calculated that, "Of the estimated 3,500,000 Negro men in the labor force in 1950 about 1,500,000 are in unions, probably evenly divided between A.F. of L. and C.I.O."[13] In 1945 the Labor Research Association compiled the following table on Negro union membership:[14]

C.I.O. UNIONS	Negro Members
Steelworkers of America, United	95,000
Automobile, Aircraft, Agricultural Implement Workers of America	90,000
Marine & Shipbuilding Workers of America, Industrial Union of	40,000
Electrical, Radio & Machine Workers of America, United	40,000
Packinghouse Workers of America, United	22,500
Mine, Mill & Smelter Workers, International Union of	20,000
Clothing Workers of America, Amalgamated	15,000
Federal Workers of America, United	10,000
Fur & Leather Workers Union, International	8,000·10,000
Transport Service Employees of America, United	10,000
Maritime Union of America National	8,500
Textile Workers Union of America	6,500
Food, Tobacco, Agricultural and Allied Workers Union of America	6,000
Longshoremen's and Warehousemen's Union, International	13,000
Retail, Wholesale and Department Store Employees of America	6,000
Furniture Workers of America, United	6,000
Woodworkers of America, International	3,000
Transport Workers Union of America	3,000
Farm Equipment and Metal Workers of America, United	3,000
State, County & Municipal Workers of America	2,800
Playthings, Jewelry & Novelty Workers Union	2,500
	412,800

A.F. OF L. UNIONS

Hodcarriers & Common Laborers	55,000
Hotel & Restaurant Employees, etc.	36,000-40,000
Building Service Employees	35,000
Maintenance of Way Employees, Brotherhood of	25,000
Meat Cutters & Butcher Workmen	25,000
Railway Clerks & Freight Handlers	12,000
Teamsters, Chauffeurs, etc.	15,000
Boilermakers & Iron Shipbuilders	14,000
Laundry Workers International Union	12,000
Longshoremen's Association, International	10,000
Garment Workers, International Ladies	10,000
Tobacco Workers International Union	9,100
Porters, Brotherhood of Sleeping Car	8,500
Musicians, American Federation of	4,500
Carmen of America, Brotherhood Railway	4,500
Carpenters & Joiners, United Brotherhood of	3,000
Bricklayers, Masons & Plasterers	3,000
Printing Pressmen, International	3,000
Cement, Lime & Gypsum Workers	3,000
Pulp, Sulphite & Paper Mill Workers	2,000
Painters of America, Brotherhood of	1,500
Cigar Makers International Union	500
Brick & Clay Workers, etc.	500
Glass Workers, American Flint	400
	296,500

INDEPENDENT

United Mine Workers	50,000
TOTAL	759,300

NEW DEAL LABOR LEGISLATION

The Roosevelt Administration passed several important labor laws, all of great importance to Negro workers. This legislation was not simply the product of Roosevelt's good will, as many conservative labor leaders tried to tell the workers, but of the surging mass movements of the New Deal period. One of the most basic of these laws was the Wagner Act of 1935. This law conceded to workers the right to organize, to bargain collectively, and to elect union representatives of their own choosing. The law was often called "Labor's Magna Carta." Another important labor law of the period was the Fair Labor Standards Act (wages and hours law), of 1938. This established the 40-hour week and a minimum national wage of 25 cents per hour. Among the workers covered, the law established minimum wages for about a million Negro workers in industry, but it excluded the great masses of those engaged in agriculture and domestic service.

The most important New Deal labor measure directly affecting Negroes, was the well-known F.E.P.C., the Fair Employment Practices Committee set up to implement President Roosevelt's Executive Order 8802 of June 25, 1941. This Order stated that it shall be the "policy of the United States that there shall be no discrimination in the employment of workers in defense industries or Government because of race, creed, color, or national origin." Several states later adopted F.E.P.C. laws.

On the eve of World War II, discrimination in industry against Negroes was almost universal. Practically everywhere, even in such "friendly" industries as Ford,[15] the portion of the Negro worker was the dirtiest, hardest, roughest, most unskilled, and most dangerous work, with wages to correspond. In this respect, Negro women were even worse off than the men. The Negro workers were walled off from the better jobs by employer policy, by white workers' prejudices, by trade union pressures, and even by law—in South Carolina there was a law forbidding Negroes to work at the same machines with whites.[16]

The Federal F.E.P.C. was patterned along the lines of a bill introduced into the House in 1940 by Vito Marcantonio, which prohibited discrimination in the hiring of Negroes in plants holding Federal munitions contracts. The F.E.P.C. was primarily the result of the great wartime demand for labor, plus the pressure of the Negro and progressive masses, notably the Communists. Many, however, have tried to hand the credit for the measure to A. Philip Randolph, who had threatened a Negro March on Washington.

The F.E.P.C. horrified the Southern bourbons, who claimed that it was virtually Socialism. While the C.I.O. supported the measure, the A.F. of L. leaders looked at it askance. The A.F. of L. convention of 1944 endorsed the F.E.P.C. but refused to discipline its affiliated unions which continued to discriminate against Negro workers. A.F. of L. and Railroad Brotherhood leaders also opposed national and state F.E.P.C. legislation on the ground that it was "an infringement upon the trade unions' right to regulate their own internal affairs."

The Negro worker has gained greatly as a result of the unionization of the basic industries. It has given him a better grip in industry, facilitated his passage to jobs of higher skills, provided him with some protection against boss persecution, and especially, it has tended to give him equality of pay rates for equal work. Something of the changed situation of the Negro in organized industry was illustrated by a recent strike of 3,200 mostly white workers at the Briggs Auto Works, Local 742, in Detroit, to force the Chrysler company to rehire Negro women who had been displaced by white women workers. A far cry this from the old days when white workers frequently struck against the hiring of Negro workers.[17]

ATTITUDES OF THE C.I.O. AND A.F. OF L. TOWARD NEGRO MEMBERS

From the outset the C.I.O., in the formation of which the Communists played a prominent part, took a friendly attitude toward the organization of Negro workers. This, largely influenced by the Communists, was also implicit in industrial unionism which, unlike craft unionism, does not confine itself to unionizing small minorities of the workers but includes all those in a given industry. The C.I.O. early wrote the following inclusive membership clause into its national constitution: it proposed, "To bring about the effective organization of the workingmen and women of America, regardless of race, creed, color, or nationality, and to unite them for common action into labor unions for their mutual aid." All the affiliated C.I.O. unions proceeded upon this general policy.[18]

Nevertheless, the present-day right-wing C.I.O. unions permit great discrimination against their Negro members. For example, although Negro workers are beginning to accumulate seniority rights of their own in industry, the seniority system in general has not decisively extracted the Negro worker from his traditional handicap of being "the last to be hired and the first to be fired." Negroes in industries controlled by these C.I.O. unions also fill a disproportionate percentage of the lower-paid, unskilled jobs, and efforts by the unions to upgrade and promote them to better jobs are altogether inadequate. The Negroes also get the worst of it with regard to holding official union posts; they are largely confined to the lesser offices. Negroes form at least 10 percent of the total membership of the C.I.O. unions, but they hold hardly one percent of the higher union posts, such as executive board members, organizers, etc. The big Auto and Steel Workers Unions, with a combined membership of 2,500,000, some 10 percent of whom are Negroes, have no Negroes at all on their national boards. Of the 23 leading C.I.O. unions, 12 have not a single Negro on their executive committees or among their international officers.[19] The C.I.O. and some of its unions have official anti-discrimination committees and sometimes write anti-discrimination clauses into union contracts; but their work is often "more honored in the breach than in the observance." All this in sharp contrast to the progressive independent unions, where Negroes workers play an increasingly important role in the top leadership.

The white chauvinist A.F. of L. leaders had to bend a bit before the mass demand for the organization of Negro workers, and they opened the doors partially at long last for the Negroes in industry. But in spite of F.E.P.C. laws and progressive measures, a number of A.F. of L. and independent unions continued to bar Negroes. In 1944, Northrup listed the following unions as the more flagrant examples of those that were keeping out Negroes, either formally or in practice: (*1*) Union which bars Negroes by ritual: machinists; (*2*) Unions which exclude Negroes by constitutional provisions: *A.F. of L.*—air line pilots; masters, mates and pilots; railroad telegraphers; railroad mail; switchmen; wire weavers; *Independent*—locomotive engineers; locomotive firemen; trainmen; yardmasters (two organizations); conductors; train dispatchers; (*3*) Unions which exclude Negroes by tacit consent: *A. F. of L.*—asbestos; electrical; flint glass; granite cutters; plumbers; seafarers; *Independent*—marine firemen; railroad shop crafts; (*4*) Unions which accord Negroes only segregated auxiliary status: *A. F. of L.*—blacksmiths; boilermakers; maintenance of way; railway carmen; railway and steamship clerks; rural letter carriers; sheet metal workers; *Independent*—railroad workers; rural letter carriers.[20]

Since the above list was compiled, a number of trade unions, under heavy pressure and often by court orders, have officially abandoned their Jim Crow clauses and practices, nationally or on a state-wide basis. These include the railway carmen; locomotive engineers; boilermakers; blacksmiths; telegraphers; maintenance of way; masters, mates and pilots; switchmen; machinists; flint glass; and rural letter carriers. But even though such unions are compelled by outside pressure officially to remove the bars against Negro workers, they frequently continue their policy of exclusion *sub rosa*.

Such segregation policies in the conservative trade unions dovetailed with those in effect in one form or another in many capitalist-controlled organizations, including the National Grange, Farm Bureau Federation, American Legion, Veterans of Foreign Wars, American Medical Association, American Bar Association, American Red Cross, Boy Scouts of America, National W.C.T.U., Y.M.C.A., General Federation of Women's Clubs, National Amateur Athletic Union, etc., etc. It was the great shame of the American labor movement that it ever allowed itself to be smeared with the Jim Crow slime, along with such bourgeois organizations.

THE COMMUNISTS IN THE GREAT ORGANIZING CAMPAIGN

To the Communists and other left-wingers belongs a great deal of the credit for the winning of the workers in the basic industries to the trade unions during 1936-45, and especially for the successful unionization of the Negro workers. For many years, the Communists were ardent fighters for industrial unionism, when most of the later-to-be C.I.O. conservative leaders were altogether cold to the matter. The Communists prepared the ground for the big drive. The Communists, too, were the most militant of all in supporting the organization of the Negro workers, and at every stage of the great campaign they were on hand to see that proper attention was paid to this hitherto crassly neglected body of workers. And most valuable to the campaign, the Communist Party had long carried on work among the unemployed and other groups throughout the trustified industries, and it had its branches in hundreds of major plants. When the great campaign began, the Communists Party put all these forces at work with its well-known militancy and devotion.

This was a period of the struggle against developing world fascism; and the Communist Party worked freely in formal or informal united front movements with John L. Lewis, Philip Murray, Sidney Hillman, and many other C.I.O. leaders, who were then following a progressive pro-union building, pro-Roosevelt, anti-fascist course. The Communists and other left-wing forces became a major factor in building the C.I.O. Alinsky, semi-official biographer of John L. Lewis, says that "Then, as is now commonly known, the Communists worked indefatigably. . . . They literally poured themselves completely into their assignments. . . . The fact is that the Communist Party made a major contribution to the organization of the unorganized for the C.I.O."[21] About one-third of the C.I.O. organizing staff in steel were Communists. The generally progressive position taken by the C.I.O. during these years was very largely due to the influence of Communists and other left-wing forces in its ranks.

Characteristic of the special attention paid by the Communists to the Negro workers was the conference, principally of Negro organizations, held in Pittsburgh on February 6, 1937, to stimulate the unionization of the Negro steel workers. This important gathering was organized by the well-known Negro Communist, Benjamin L. Careathers, then a paid organizer on the staff of the Steel Workers Organizing Committee. Present at the conference were 186 delegates, representing 110 organizations. Many leading national Negro figures attended. The conference was a potent factor in the successful organizing of this great industry. Similar activities were carried on in auto and the other industries involved in this historic organizing campaign.

In 1938, at the height of this movement, the Communist Party had some 75,000 members, a potent force under the circumstances. Of these 14 percent were Negroes. Such a large body of Negroes in a Marxist party was unique in United States history. The Party's prestige among the Negro masses may be gauged from the fact that in a recruiting campaign a few years later, in 1944, which brought in 24,000 members, about 7,000 of them were Negroes.[22]

46. Fascism and World War II

The growth of fascism in the aftermath of the first World War, and especially after the great economic crisis of 1929-33, was a manifestation of the deepening of the general crisis of world capitalism. The big monopolists, particularly those of Germany, Japan, and Italy, were confronted with an increasingly revolutionary working class and a decaying capitalist system. They sought to cut their way out of their multiplying difficulties by domestic terrorism and imperialist aggression. They set out to smash their class rivals at home, to crush their foreign imperialist rivals abroad, and, under the slogan of an anti-Communist crusade, to dominate the whole world.

The Seventh World Congress of the Communist International, in July 1935, following the action of its Executive Committee in December 1933, analyzed fascism as "the open terrorist dictatorship of the most reactionary, most chauvinistic and most imperialist elements of finance capital."[1] It characterized fascism as "rabid reaction and counter-revolution" and declared that its growth signified a weakening, not a strengthening of capitalism. This scientific Marxist-Leninist analysis shattered the current Social-Democratic nonsense about fascism being a middle class revolution.

Fascism first took definite shape in Italy in 1922, when Mussolini seized Rome and began to build up the "corporate state." Its next big advance came when Hitler grabbed power in Germany, on January 30, 1933, about six weeks before Roosevelt first became president of the United States. Rampant, reactionary militarism also took a firmer hold in Japan. And during the next few years, before the outbreak of World War II, many European countries went wholly or partially fascist—Poland, Hungary, Romania, Spain, Latvia, Lithuania, Finland, Bulgaria, Greece, Turkey, and others.

All the other major capitalist countries were also more or less infected with the fascist poison. The big monopolists of Great Britain, France, and other Western European countries were saturated with it; and through the League of Nations, they proceeded to "appease" the aggressive fascist bloc of states by one concession after another. Big monopoly capital in the United States also displayed strong fascist tendencies. Various fascist or near-fascist movements—the

American Liberty League, America First, Father Coughlin's, Huey Long's, and many others—sprang up and received heavy financial backing. Plans were even concocted in Wall Street for a fascist march on Washington, à la Mussolini, under General Smedley Butler.

That the United States, ruled by the biggest of big business, did not try outright the desperate expedient of fascism as an escape from the deep economic crisis, but turned instead to the reform program of the New Deal, was due to a number of important factors. Among these were the following: (a) This country was less deeply affected by the general crisis of capitalism than Germany. (b) Unlike Germany, it still had the financial means to carry out a reform program. (c) It did not fear an imminent proletarian revolution. (d) It belonged to the group of capitalist powers that temporarily favored the maintenance of the status quo in the relation of the world forces. (e) Of decisive importance, it faced a widespread democratic upheaval among the masses that it could only allay by a policy of concessions. "Although in less acute conditions of political struggle, the American workers, like those of France and other European countries, halted the advance of fascism in this country."[2]

THE FIGHT AGAINST FASCISM AND WAR

In the grave crisis presented by the drive of the fascist alliance (the anti-Comintern Axis) for war and international domination, the U.S.S.R. and the Communist International came forward with a practical program to save harassed humanity from bloodshed and slavery. In the League of Nations, in July 1936, the U.S.S.R. put forward a proposal that the peace-minded nations of the world form an international peace front against the fascist aggressor powers— Germany, Japan, and Italy. This was the program for "collective security," as Litvinov called it. Meanwhile, the Communist International at its Seventh Congress, proposed that anti-fascist people's fronts be formed to check and defeat the aggressors in the various nations. These national people's fronts were to be composed of all democratic elements—Communists, Socialists, trade unionists, farmers, professionals, and small businessmen.

If it had been applied, this program could have killed the fascist menace in its infancy. The fascist powers were still relatively weak, and the peace powers had vastly greater potential strength. But the Western governments, tainted with fascism, would have none of the international peace front, although Roosevelt favored it somewhat in words. They hoped that, in the end, Hitler would turn his guns against the U.S.S.R. International Social-Democracy proceeded to sabotage the whole anti-fascist peace program, nationally and internationally, tamely following its capitalist masters in the hope of an anti-Soviet war. Nevertheless, in Spain, and France in 1936, the Communist parties were able to initiate movements which won electoral majorities and set up people's front governments.

The treacherous appeasement policies of the Western democratic powers and the world Social-Democracy led to tragedy in the Spanish Civil War of 1936-39. Through their stooge, General Franco, Hitler and Musolini organized a counter-revolution in Spain against the People's Front government. From all over the world, Communists and other democratic forces rallied in the International Brigades to help the embattled Spanish people. The C.P. and other left-wingers in the United States sent 3,000 volunteers.

But the heroic Spanish Republican struggle was in vain. The Western powers took an attitude of "neutrality," and so did the Social-Democrats. They refused to sell arms to Spain while Germany and Italy continued to pour munitions and troops into that country. Consequently, the war was lost, and the fascist aggressors won a decisive victory. This deadly "appeasement" of Hitler was followed by a similar move, equally disastrous. At Munich, in May 1938, Chamberlain and Daladier, the heads of the British and French governments, sold out and surrendered Czechoslovakia to Hitler. They still hoped to avoid war themselves and to direct the fascists' blow to the East, against the Soviet Union. Roosevelt hailed Munich, and so did the the Social-Democrats everywhere; the Communists alone condemning it as a sell-out and a move toward war.

Meanwhile, for three years, the U.S.S.R. had been trying in vain to develop an anti-fascist front with Great Britain, France, and the United States. But these powers—especially the first two—were flagrantly working to develop Hitler's growing offensive into a war against the U.S.S.R. Aware of this open treachery, the U.S.S.R. finally abandoned its efforts to win them for a joint peace policy and signed a non-aggression pact with Germany. No longer held back by the restraining influence of the Soviet Union, the capitalist powers proceeded to fly at each other's throats like wolves. World War II began on September 1, 1939, with Hitler's armed invasion of Poland.

THE NEGRO PEOPLE IN THE FIGHT TO MAINTAIN PEACE

In the crucial pre-war struggle against fascism and for peace, the American Negro people played a characteristically active part. The Hitler propagandists freely maligned Negroes in general as "sub-human"—and the Negroes, familiar with such racist slander from their contact with white supremacists in the South and elsewhere, understood quite well that a fascist victory in the impending war would bode very ill for them. The whole Negro press was anti-fascist. As Franklin says, "Negroes were among the earliest and most energetic Americans to condemn the fascism that was rising in Europe."[3] They deeply resented it when Hitler publicly snubbed Jesse Owens and his fellow Negro members of the American team at the Olympic Games in Berlin in 1936; and they gloried in it as a victory over the conceited Hitlerite "Aryans," when Joe Louis, in the return match in 1938, knocked out the Nazi heavyweight champion, Max Schmeling.

Negroes took a very active part in the many anti-war, pro-peace activities and demonstrations of the pre-war period. They also gave enthusiastic support to the Republican cause in Spain. They set up the Negro People's Committee to Aid Spanish Democracy. Some hundreds of Negroes were included in the contingent of American volunteers in the International Brigades.[4] As usual they conducted themselves with high bravery on the field of battle. Many became officers, for, of course, in the Republican armies there was not the Jim Crow to which Negro sailors and soldiers were being subjected in the United States armed forces. About half of the Americans never returned from Spain, the rest being either killed in battle or massacred in Franco's prisons. Among the more widely known of the Negro fighters killed were Oliver Law, Milton Herndon, and Alonzo Watson.

The Negro people were especially aroused by the brutal conquest of Ethiopia by Mussolini's forces in 1935. Meetings and demonstrations of protest were held in all the more important Negro centers of the North. "Negro newspapers made banner headlines of the war and inveighed against 'the connivance of England and France' in blocking the sanctions against Italy proposed by Russia."[5] Several committees were set up to collect funds and other aid for Ethiopian refugees, and in their behalf, Dr. Willis N. Huggins protested to the League of Nations against the barbarous invasion of Ethiopia.

THE COURSE OF WORLD WAR II

The armies of Western Europe, whose political leaders and officer corps were saturated with fascist rottenness, offered only flimsy resistance to Hitler's on-rushing legions. Consequently, in a few weeks Hitler crushed Poland, and then, turning his forces to the West, he proceeded to smash the French, Dutch, Belgian, and British armies and to drive their remnants into the sea at Dunkirk, France, in May 1940. Hitler was now in full command of Europe. He would have invaded and conquered the British Isles at this moment, except that he dreaded a two-front war and feared the huge Red Army at his rear in the East.

Then Hitler made his fatal mistake. With the productive power of all Europe behind them, his armies invaded the Soviet Union on June 22, 1941. Six months later, on December 7, 1941, Japan made a similar error by its criminal attack upon the United States at Pearl Harbor. Hitler's "invincible" *Wehrmacht* stormed East, and the bourgeois military experts of the world agreed almost unanimously that in about six weeks it would destroy the Red Army. But the powerful Socialist Soviet people willed otherwise. In the terrible winter of 1941-42 Hitler was stopped dead at the gates of Leningrad and Moscow, with untold losses in manpower. Making a last desperate effort to win the war, the German Sixth Army was destroyed the following year at Stalingrad in the most decisive battle of all history. This finished Hitler's grandiose dreams of world conquest. Then, for almost two years, the Red Army drove the German Army before it, out of Russia, across Poland, and back into Germany, slashing it to pieces along the way. In the later stages of this heroic struggle, considerable amounts of American "lend-lease" munitions reached the Red Army.

Meanwhile, the United States went on piling up its armed forces in England, while the world cried out that they should cross the Channel and help finish off Hitler. But the tragic fact is that many reactionaries in the United States—Truman, Hoover, and innumerable others—wanted to see the U.S.S.R. ruined in its mortal struggle with Nazi Germany. This was the continuation of monopoly capital's long hatred of the Socialism of the Soviet Union. So the main strength of the United States was turned to defeating the lesser enemy, Japan, while the Soviet Army was destroying the main enemy, Germany. It was not until June 6, 1944, that the United States and its weakened ally, Great Britain, finally invaded Europe and opened up the long-awaited Western Front. This was after the Red Army had driven the shattered German Army back about 1,300 miles, had basically defeated it, and was in a position soon to occupy all of Nazi-controlled Europe. On April 12, 1945, the American and Soviet forces met on the Elbe River, and on May 2, the Russians captured Berlin.

In the meantime, the war was also being vigorously prosecuted against Japan. The United States smashed the Japanese Navy and Air Force and captured island after island on the way to Japan. The Chinese Red Army delivered mortal blows to the big Japanese armies in China; and finally, the Soviet Red Army, fulfilling its agreement, crossed the Siberian frontier and destroyed the Kwantung Army, Japan's best land force. Then, after two atom bombs were needlessly and brutally dropped by the U.S. military forces upon the cities of Hiroshima and Nagasaki, Japan gave up on August 14, 1945. The great war was over. By united action, the democratic and Socialist peoples had smashed the most terrible threat of fascist slavery that had ever confronted mankind.

THE AMERICAN NEGRO IN THE WAR

The American working class, the Negro people, the smaller farmers, and other democratic strata of the population gave whole-hearted support to the just and democratic World War II. While the big capitalists were busy profiteering on the war and seeking to turn it against the U.S.S.R., the toiling masses were doing all they could to win it. They adopted a no-strike pledge, speeded up production, gave of their meager funds to finance the war, and placed their military-age sons at the disposal of the Government. None were more ardent supporters of the war than the Communists.

The Negro people, in backing the war like all democratic Americans, also displayed their special concern as a Negro nation. They were very much interested in what happened to the oppressed colonial peoples around the world. There was a strong sentiment among them that this was a time for those peoples to advance their anti-imperialist interests. In some parts of the world, such as India, this sentiment was falsely applied and led to a neutral or even pro-Japanese attitude toward the war. This was a great mistake, for had the fascist Axis won the war, the colonial peoples would have faced more terrible national oppression than ever before. The first step toward breaking down the capitalist-imperialist system, as the course of events has shown, was to win the war against the fascist powers. Then would come the time to settle accounts with the traditional European imperialists.

More than three million Negroes registered for service in the armed forces. By the end of 1944, at the peak of the Army's strength, 701,678 Negroes were serving in it—with 165,000 in the Navy, 5,000 in the Coast Guard, and 17,000 in the Marine Corps. About 5,000 Negro women joined the services. All told, some 1,000,000 Negro men and women served during the war—a figure nearly in accordance with the ratio of Negroes to the general population. About 500,000 Negroes saw service overseas, of whom 200,000 were in the Pacific theater.[6]

At the beginning of the war, Jim Crow segregation policies prevailed in the armed forces pretty much as they had during the first World War. Under the influence of the democratic character of the war and the strong pressure of the masses, these Jim Crow regulations were slightly eased. But Negro soldiers, sailors, and airmen continued to suffer from a galling discrimination on every front throughout the war, all the propaganda to the contrary notwithstanding. Generals Eisenhower and McArthur were directly responsible for wholesale unjust arrests, courts martialling, and executions of Negro soldiers, and they did nothing to break down Jim Crow. Generally Negroes were kept in separate army units, up to regiments and divisions, but some mixed units were formed. Negroes succeeded in breaking their way into the Navy as other than the traditional messmen and officers' servants. There were also some 6,000 Negro officers all told, including one brigadier general (Benjamin O. Davis), 10 colonels, and 24 lieutenant colonels.

As in World War I, a disproportionate share of Negro troops were relegated to the Services of Supply. The famous Red Ball Express, the truck line in France which broke all hauling records, was operated almost exclusively by Negro drivers. Those Negro units assigned to combat duty acquitted themselves, of course, with great courage. Plenty of white Jim Crow officers were only to anxious to belittle the Negro soldiers, but many other officers were willing to do them honor. Thus, Major General Lanham told Negro soldiers, "I have never seen any soldiers who have performed better in combat than you."[7]

There were many Negro war heroes in the spirit of Dorie Miller, who, "without previous experience . . . manned a machine gun in the face of serious fire during the Japanese attack on Pearl Harbor, December 7, 1941, on the Battleship *Arizona*, shooting down four enemy planes"; five Negroes received the Distinguished Service Cross —Charles L. Thomas, V. L. Baker, E. A. Carter, J. Thomas, and G. Watson. Eighty-eight of the 600 Negro pilots got the Distinguished Flying Cross for outstanding achievements during their 3,500 missions flown in Europe before D-Day. No Negro got the Medal of Honor, however, although 21 Negroes won it during the Civil War and seven during the Spanish-American War. Franklin justly indicates that this highest medal, in Jim Crow fashion, is being reserved for whites only.[8]

DEMOCRATIC ADVANCES OF THE NEGRO PEOPLE

To some degree, the Negro people shared in the political achievements of the working class during the democratic, anti-fascist struggles of the New Deal-World War II period. They also made some progress in winning their own specific national demands. One of their greatest gains was the strengthening of their position in industry, especially in the North. The Northward migration from the oppressive South was particularly marked. Weaver estimates that the total number of Negroes who migrated North between 1915 and 1940, most of them going into industry, was about 1,750,000.[9] To this figure can be added several hundred thousand more in the decade 1940-50. During this period some 500,000 Negroes left the land for the cities, about half to the Southern munitions centers and the rest to the North. This growth of the Negro proletariat enormously strengthened the position of the whole Negro people. Not only did the Negroes succeed in getting into industry to a substantial extent; but they also became part of the great new trade union movement—a fact of vast importance not only to the Negro workers but to the entire body of workers. We have seen, too, that F.E.P.C. to some extent, introduced new principles of protection of the Negro workers in industry.

Another advance by the Negro people during this great period of democratic struggle was the partial breakdown of Jim Crow in the armed forces. This was an issue of great concern to the Negro people, since the bearing of arms in full equality in defense of one's country is a most elementary right of citizenship.

All through the period in question a constant struggle was also kept up against the discrimination in housing, education, and the right to vote, Jim Crow in hotels, trains, etc., but little progress was registered. The Supreme Court successfully evaded making clear-cut decisions on these questions. In 1944, it did declare the white Democratic primaries in Texas illegal; but, in the main, it still refused to kill the 1896 Plessy *vs.* Ferguson decision which hypocritically provided for "separate but equal facilities."

Throughout the period, a big struggle was carried on against lynching and the poll tax. In Congress this was led primarily by Representative Vito Marcantonio of New York City. From March 1933 until the end of World War II, no less than 149 anti-lynching bills were introduced into Congress (there were 30 between 1900 and 1933). These bills were all buried in the Committee on Judiciary, except the Gavagan Bill of 1937, which managed to pass the House, but was filibustered to death in the Senate.[10] The rulers of the South thus insisted successfully on their right to hang Negroes without trials or justice. The anti-poll tax bills, of which there were 18 between 1940 and 1945, fared no better. Three of them, those offered by Geyer in 1941 and Marcantonio in 1943 and 1945, passed the House but died in the Senate. The South thus reserved to itself the right to disfranchise 4,000,000 of its Negro and 6,820,000 of its white citizens in seven states. During 1942-45, 17 F.E.P.C. bills, introduced by Marcantonio and others, also died in committee.

The most important democratic advance made by the Negro people during this whole period was the better relationship established between Negro and white workers in industry and in the unions, especially those in the North. This was a development of the greatest significance not only for the New Deal-World War II period, but for the future. While scarred by numerous race clashes, directed especially against Negro soldiers in camps, the World War II years were not marked by the horrifying scope of the many bloody struggles that occurred at the time of World War I. Most serious riots were in Detroit, the city where, in 1925, Dr. O. H. Sweet had bravely defended his home, gun in hand, against white thugs. The first Detroit riot occurred in February 1942, when 38 persons were injured and 100 arrested in an unsuccessful attempt by white hooligans to bar Negroes from occupying the Sojourner Truth housing project. The second clash was a wild city-wide riot, on June 20, 1943. Twenty-five Negroes and nine whites were killed, and 500 persons were injured.[11] In Mobile, Alabama, a murderous clash took place in 1943, and in the same period half of the Negro section of Beaumont, Texas, was burned by a white mob.

The political advances made by the Negro people during this period and since, were not brought about by the working out of a metaphysical "American Creed" of democracy as Gunnar Myrdal puts forward in his book, *An American Dilemma,* nor were they conceded out of the goodness of heart of the white ruling class in this country. They were the result of hard struggle by the Negro people, shoulder to shoulder with their growing number of white worker allies. They were also due to the pressure of world democratic forces, which hate the American Jim Crow system.

World War II marked the termination of one period in the history of the Negro and the beginning of another, qualitatively higher, stage. The war registered fundamental changes in the development of the Negro liberation movement. Prior to World War II, the movement was dominated almost wholly by the bourgeoisie, but after the war there developed a joint (not necessarily united) leadership which included both bourgeois elements and workers. Many factors helped develop worker leaders, including the growth of the Negro proletariat, the intensified struggle for Negro rights, the nature of the war against fascism, the new expansion of the anti-colonial struggle in the world, etc. All of these factors were stimulated by World War II.

NATIONAL NEGRO CULTURE

After World War I, the national culture of the Negro people took a spurt forward in the 1920's, during the great northward migration and under the bitterly oppressive conditions of the period. This was the so-called Harlem Renaissance. Negro culture received another big impetus during the New Deal-World War II years, amid the general influences of the great democratic struggles of the times. This whole cultural development produced many outstanding artists, writers, and intellectual leaders.[12]

In the world of invention and science the Negro has come rapidly to the fore. Negroes are credited with nearly 5,000 patented inventions, some of them of major importance.[13] They have produced a number of well-known scientists, especially in the fields of biology, chemistry, and medicine. The most outstanding of these scholars were E. E. Just and the world-renowned George Washington Carver. The latter genius made fundamental industrial and agricultural researches into the potentialities of the sweet potato, peanut, and other agricultural products, which have added vastly to the wealth of the South. President Truman proclaimed January 5, 1946, as George Washington Carver Day, and a new three-cent stamp was issued in his honor.

The Negro people have also produced many noted historians (see Chapter 43), as well as a host of excellent writers of literature in all its forms. A few of the best known Negro writers are Paul Lawrence Dunbar, Countee Cullen, Langston Hughes, Claude McKay, Charles W. Chesnutt, Jean Toomer, Eric Walrond, Zora Neale Hurston, Frank Yerby, Arna Bontemps, William Stanley Braithwaite, W. E. B. Du Bois, James Weldon Johnson, Alain Locke, George S. Schuyler, and Carter G. Woodson.

In the fields of music, dancing, and the theater, Negroes have made basic contributions to American culture in general. Davie says, "These original contributions are, first, the Uncle Remus stories, collected by Joel Chandler Harris, and the folk rhymes and proverbs; second, the spirituals, whose beauty was first revealed to the world by the Fisk Jubilee Singers; third, ragtime, jazz, the blues and other forms of popular music; and fourth, the cakewalk, fox trot, Charleston, and numerous other dances. . . . It is perhaps not too much to say that the folk creations of the Negro are the only things artistic that have sprung from American soil and out of American life."[14] Innumerable are the brilliant Negro artists in these fields. Suffice it to mention only the unequaled singer, Marian Anderson, and the great singer, orator, and actor, Paul Robeson.

In the sphere of athletics, one of the few domains in which the Negro has had even half a chance to develop his capacities, he has long been known for his brilliant achievements. Joe Louis, Henry Armstrong, Jesse Owens, Eddie Tolan, Ralph Metcalfe, Paul Robeson, Ray Robinson, Jackie Robinson—to mention only a few—are known the world over as real champions. Little by little, the Negro has succeeded in breaking down the Jim Crow barriers that have barred him from participation in sports. The most important of his recent victories was his entry into major league baseball in 1947. Here, Robinson, Doby, Campanella, and other Negro stars at once leaped to fame.* Now almost half of the teams of the two big leagues have Negro players. And even more significant, Negroes are now playing professionally on baseball teams in Florida, Louisiana, North Carolina, Oklahoma and Texas.[15]

The Negro has had to surmount a mountain of white chauvinist

---

* The Communists pioneered in this fight. For 15 years, the Party, along with other fighters for Negro rights, kept up a steady pressure through leaflets, demonstrations, picket lines, and general agitation, for the admission of Negro players to the Major Leagues.

prejudice not only in sports, but in every other field of culture. As a writer, singer, actor, musician, he has had to be of the most outstanding quality in order to win recognition freely accorded to whites of greatly inferior caliber. One of the hardest jobs of Negro artists, particularly in the theater, motion pictures, radio, and television, is to break through the stereotypes, dating back to slavery times, which slanderously depict Negroes as clowns and disreputables.[16] Franklin says, "The greater portion of Negroes who secure parts in movie production are still servants, laborers, and criminals."[17] This caricature is designed primarily to satisfy the Jim Crow market in the South. The cultural front is one of the main scenes where the Negro has to fight for his most elementary rights as a human being. His progress to date has been made only in the face of the most heart-breaking discrimination and difficulty. Characteristically, the 635 TV jobs held by Negro performers constitute only one-half of one percent of total TV employment. Similar discrimination prevails in radio and motion pictures.

Especially during the past half century, the Negro people have greatly increased their educational facilities, the foundation for cultural development. In 1900, only 2,132 Negroes were enrolled in all the institutions of higher learning; in 1950, there were 116,190.[18] Today there are three times as many Negro professionals as there were at the turn of the century. "There are 91 Negro institutions of higher education which give four-year courses leading to degrees, including professional and graduate schools. In addition, there are 17 junior colleges and two-year normal schools, making a total of 107 institutions of higher education for Negroes."[19] Negroes are increasingly entering predominantly white colleges and universities. An extensive Negro press has been built up at the same time. The leading educational magazines are the *Journal of Negro History, Phylon,* and *Journal of Negro Education.* There are 15 Negro news-gathering agencies and some 183 Negro-owned newspapers and 98 magazines. The circulation of the following important publications is: the *Pittsburgh Courier* (281,708), the *Afro-American* papers (235,580), *Chicago Defender* (193,281), and the *Amsterdam News* (105,322).[20] *Our World* and *Color,* of New York and Charleston, each have circulations of 100,000 to 200,000. Especially notable are the big three Negro magazines published by the Johnson Publishing Company—*Ebony* (pictures, monthly, 500,000), *Jet* (news weekly, 250,528) and *Tan* (women, 300,000).[21]

Negro culture is essentially national in spirit. In this quality lies its strength and originality. The best Negro writers and artists of all kinds have always sought to express the needs and hopes and persecutions of their people, truly to reflect their life. This is fundamentally correct. But some Negro opportunists have looked askance at all this, considering it a shortcoming that Negro writers have so habitually "written Negro." They want them to write and speak simply as Americans, and nothing more. But this would be a mistake.[22] Negro intellectuals should, of course, concern themselves with the broad cultural currents and political struggles in America and the world; but this should not be done in terms of a formless and crass cosmopolitanism. The first and most basic task of Negro intellectuals and artists is to fight the cultural battles of their oppressed people against the entrenched and vicious forces of white chauvinism and white supremacy, and to link up these struggles with those of the whole working class and other democratic strata of the nation.

47. The Negro and
the Cold War

The post-World War II years have brought important developments for the American Negro people—both positive and negative. These can be understood only against the background of the great political struggle now going on in the world.

AMERICAN IMPERIALISM DRIVES FOR WORLD MASTERY

During World War II it was already evident that the Wall Street monopolists, who dictate the major policies of the United States government, were resolved upon setting out to dominate the world in the post-war period. This was the basic purpose behind the U.S. government's refusal to come promptly to the support of the Soviet Union with a second European front during the war. The monopolists wanted Germany and the U.S.S.R. to slash each other to pieces, so that neither of them could seriously resist the contemplated post-war drive of the United States for world mastery. Big business figured that this country, with its vast riches, huge armed forces, immense productive power, and sole control of the atom bomb, would be able swiftly to dominate the shattered post-war world.

This, of course, was not a plan ordinarily shouted from the housetops. Nevertheless, through the war and post-war years, many blowhards have openly expounded it. In 1940, Virgil Jordan, president of the National Industrial Conference Board, declared that "Whatever the outcome of the war, America has embarked on a career of imperialism in world affairs. . . . At best England will become a junior partner in a new Anglo-Saxon imperialism."[1] In 1941, Henry Luce of *Life* publications outspokenly proclaimed his doctrine of "The American Century" of world domination. Eric Johnston, a noted capitalist propagandist, stated in 1941: "We will organize the world or it will be organized against us."[2] Nowadays, it has become commonplace for American political leaders to sound off about the "world leadership" of the United States.

A number of basic motives drive American monopoly capitalists to strive to conquer the world: *(a)* as the most powerful group of capitalists in existence, controlling about 65 percent of all capitalist industrial production, they inevitably, by the very nature of imperialism, seek to dominate all other nations, as Great Britain, Germany, and Japan have each in turn tried to do; *(b)* The big capitalists figure they can maintain the vast flood of munitions orders bringing them in some $20 billions in net profits each year and they can achieve the main goal of modern capitalism, that of maximum profits, only by aggressive imperialist expansion and ultimate war; *(c)* They see the obsolete world capitalist system falling apart at the seams, and they foolishly believe that with their wealth, armed force, and "know-how" they can make it function effectively again; *(d)* They believe that only by wholesale munitions-making and war can they avoid an economic crisis far more devastating than that of 1929-33; *(e)* They are mortally afraid of Socialism and are convinced that it can be defeated only by an all-out capitalist war against the Soviet Union, People's China, and the European People's Democracies.

The liberal President Roosevelt, who in his later years had lost much of the support of monopoly capital, undoubtedly contemplated some sort of post-war co-existence between the U.S.A. and the U.S.S.R. But as soon as he became President, Truman, a long-time hater of the Soviet Union, began a campaign of active provocation against that country. President Eisenhower, with his big business government, has taken up where Truman left off and is prosecuting Wall Street's war line even more energetically. He and his firebrand Secretary of State, Dulles, put forth the aggressive slogan of "liberation," to succeed the "Contain Communism" slogan of President Truman.[3]

Post-war American policy, both foreign and domestic, has turned around the imperialist drive of Wall Street imperialism. It sums up to direct preparation for war and the instigation of an anti-Soviet war. To advance this policy has been the basic purpose of the Truman Doctrine, the Marshall Plan, NATO, the Japanese Treaty, the re-arming of Western Germany, A-bomb diplomacy, American domination of the United Nations, the building of hundreds of American bases all over the capitalist world, the present tremendous militarization of the United States on the basis of 50 billions yearly for Federal war preparations, the maintenance of American troops in 40 countries,[4] and, to cap it all, the tragic Korean war. It is also the meaning of the growing campaign to intimidate and fascize the American people through such reactionary measures as the Taft-

Hartley, Smith, and McCarran laws; the loyalty oaths in government, industry, schools, and colleges; the endless redbaiting and witch-hunting in all phases of American life; the growing, deadly plague of McCarthyism; the ceaseless attacks upon the Negro people and foreign-born; and the wholesale jailing of Communists on trumped-up charges.

These developments, on a national and international scale, are all co-ordinated parts of the Wall Street monopolists' master plan to establish world control through a great war. And this warlike imperialist aggression has been cunningly decked out with elaborate pretenses to make it appear necessary for the defense of world peace and democracy against a threatened Communist attack.

THE PEOPLE RESIST AMERICAN DOMINATION

Wall Street is not having the easy time it expected in its drive to conquer the world. On the contrary, it has run up against insuperable difficulties for its whole reactionary policy of self-aggrandizement and the subjugation of other peoples. The greatest obstacle in its path of conquest has been the sweeping revolution that has followed World War II. This upheaval has extended to many countries. Forced into war, slaughter and measureless poverty by the workings of the bankrupt capitalist system, they are striking out to build a new, free society—Socialism. The whole situation signifies a still further deepening of the general crisis of the world capitalist system.

During the course of this tremendous peoples' revolutionary movement, China broke the chains of the foreign imperialists and domestic landlords and set up a People's Republic. Czechoslovakia, Poland, Romania, Hungary, Eastern Germany, and Albania, which are People's Democracies, have also struck death blows to capitalism in their countries and are on the way to Socialism. Lithuania, Latvia, and Esthonia, adopting the Soviet form of government, reaffiliated with the U.S.S.R. Finally and most vital, the Soviet Union itself, instead of being ruined by the war as the Wall Street monopolists hoped and planned, emerged from the conflict far more powerful than ever and is now making economic progress that is astounding the world. "With a machine-tool capacity more than double that of 1944 and a steel production nearly three times as great, Soviet arms capacity must be at present at least twice as large as that of the last war years."[5] The post-war revolutionary wave also created powerful trade unions and Communist parties in many other countries, and it produced a vast and powerful people's peace movement throughout the world.

The 800 million people who are now building a new Socialist world are an insurmountable barrier to the imperialist plans of Wall Street. They will never submit to American domination. They possess vast potential economic-military strength, which is inspired by a profound revolutionary spirit. Any attempt to subjugate them on the part of the capitalist powers, led by the United States, could only result in a final, irretrievable military and political disaster for the world capitalist system.

Despite suicidal prospects, Wall Street and its obedient political agents—the Eisenhowers, McCarthys, Trumans, Stevensons, *et al*, together with the countless number of kept writers, docile professors, reactionary labor leaders, and controlled radio and television commentators—are eager to launch a desparate attack upon the peace-loving Socialist countries. But the masses in the capitalist world want none of this contemplated war. Despite the enormous flood of propaganda lies emanating from Wall Street and from Social Democratic misleaders of labor to the effect that there is a terrible Communist menace and that the U.S.S.R. is about to overrun the world, the peoples of the capitalist countries do not believe this Big Lie. Only with the greatest reluctance are they being induced, or rather forced, to make the sacrifices demanded of them by the warlike American military and political bosses. Time and again, they have demonstrated that they are resolutely opposed to war.

The American people, although deceived in large part by the propaganda lies of Wall Street, emphatically do not want war. Although betrayed by their bourgeois political and trade union leaders, they have nevertheless conducted an elementary resistance to the plans of the war-makers. This basic opposition to war is one of the major obstacles that Wall Street has to face on the world front. The Negro people have done their full share in these strivings of the American democratic masses for peace.

The Wall Street war-makers are finding it increasingly difficult, if not impossible, not only to war-propagandize the peoples, but also to line up the capitalist governments into an aggressive and effective anti-Soviet war alliance. The erstwhile powerful capitalist empires—Great Britain, France, Germany, Japan, Italy, etc.—have been gravely weakened by the havoc wrought during the war, by their idiotic post-war policy of cutting off East-West trade, and especially by their growing loss of overseas colonies. The whole capitalist colonial and semi-colonial world is shaking. India, Burma, Malaya, Indonesia, Indo-China, etc., together with many African colonies, are breaking loose from the old imperialist moorings and embarking upon courses of national independence. Since the end of the war, the United States has squandered $40 billion in attempting to rebuild and re-militarize the broken-backed European imperialist countries.[6] But if it came to the stress of war, these now bankrupt countries would be worth little or nothing as allies. Probably most of their peoples would then overthrow their capitalist masters and start along the inevitable road to Socialism. At the present writing the anti-Soviet war alliance is visibly cracking under the smashing strains of the antagonisms among the capitalist countries and in the face of the peace offensive of the Russians and Chinese, who are fighting Wall Street's war drive by their own policies of peace and democracy.

All of these developments sum up to a deep-going failure for American foreign policy. Wall Street capitalism cannot prosper as a system on munitions production and war, and it is having ever-greater difficulties, in the face of the growing popular resistance, in militarizing the peoples of the capitalist world and in forcing their countries into a useless slaughter. Above all, Wall Street cannot possibly defeat the Socialist world by war, and if it actually tries to do so, it will simply write its own death warrant. The two world wars did enormous damage to world capitalism; a third such war would wipe it out altogether. The U.S.S.R., People's China, and the People's Democracies stand on a policy of the peaceful coexistence of the capitalist and Socialist worlds. No other sane alternative is open to mankind.

Despite the difficulties of the war instigators, the danger of a new world war remains acute. The atomaniacs may be depended upon to use every desperate device in order to provoke the war that they are organizing. This calls for the utmost opposition and vigilance on the part of the peace-loving peoples of the world.

THE CORRUPTION OF THE NEGRO "ELITE"

It is a traditional policy of monopoly capitalists to corrupt and use for its own purposes the leaders of the people's organizations. The conservative top leaders of the labor movement, in the main, have long been labor lieutenants of the capitalists in the ranks of the working class.[7] When World War II ended and the Wall Street capitalists embarked upon their militant drive to dominate the world they immediately pressed into their campaign those loyal servitors of capitalism, the major leaders of the A.F. of L., C.I.O., and Railroad Brotherhoods. These misleaders, including the Meanys, Reuthers, Harrisons, Lewis', Dubinskys, *et al.*, became peddlers of the most blatant imperialism, the unquestioning supporters of every warlike move made by the Truman Administration. They endorsed the big war budget, supported atom-bomb diplomacy, yelled against the Soviet Union, and repeated all of Wall Street's pro-war slogans dolled up in labor language. They are labor imperialists. They even went so far as to split the labor movement on a national, hemispheric, and world scale in a desperate attempt to isolate the left wing from the masses and to overcome the peace will of the workers. Thus, they deliberately disrupted the Congress of Industrial Organizations, forcing out 11 progressive-led unions, with 900,000 members. They also split the Latin American Confederation of Labor and the World Federation of Trade Unions. All these were monstrous crimes against the working class and world peace.

The warmonger monopolists are now following a similar policy of corrupting the leadership of the Negro people. Their aim is to destroy the national solidarity and progressive orientation of the Negro people. Ralph Bunche, in his more progressive days, pointed out how the French imperialists in Africa systematically corrupted the Negro "elite"—the European-educated chieftains, professionals, etc.—in order better to control and exploit the masses.[8] American imperialism is now assiduously following a similar policy among the bourgeois Negro leaders in this country, and not without considerable success.

Outstanding Negroes are being flattered, cajoled, and politically promoted by the ruling class—but all, of course, within the narrowly prescribed limits of Jim Crow. In return, these leaders are expected to, and do, fight against all left forces among their people. As Du Bois says, "Today any Negro leader who is willing to testify to the 'free and equal' position of Negroes in America can get free travel to Asia, Europe, or Africa."[9] These opportunist elements have become shameless apologists for the Jim Crow system and the super-exploitation of the Negro people. They declare that the Negroes are rapidly being integrated into the American people as a whole, and that their grievances have almost evaporated. They propagate war slogans among the masses; but the Negro people have not been won to endorse and support the reactionary Korean war and the war program in general.

Touring the world recently, under the auspices of the notoriously reactionary "Town Meeting of the Air," Mrs. Edith Sampson tried in India to convince the people there that the reports they had heard about American Negroes being persecuted and mistreated were but Communist lies. In the same vein, Channing Tobias defended the Jim Crowers at a meeting of the United Nations in Paris by denouncing as an exaggeration the slashing attack of the Civil Rights Congress upon the lynch system in the South.[10] Jackie Robinson went to Washington and there, before the Dixiecrat-controlled Un-American Activities Committee, had the effrontery to denounce the brilliant Negro leader and fighter, Paul Robeson. And the redbaiting and warmongering of White, Randolph, Townsend, Granger, Wilkins, Schuyler, Yergan, and many other bourgeois nationalist Negro intellectuals, preachers, editors and businessmen is hardly to be distinguished from that of the worst white warmongers.[11]

Such activities have their roots far back in the history of the Negro people. There have long been those leaders who have believed that they had more to gain by appeasing the exploiters than by fighting them. Booker T. Washington was an outstanding exponent of this policy, and so, too, was Marcus M. Garvey. The Negro press, the N.A.A.C.P., the Urban League, and other Negro organizations have been heavily influenced by such elements and their ultra-rich white friends, who clutter up Negro organizations. A major step into reformism was taken when the great Negro leader, W. E. B. Du Bois, was ousted, first in 1934 and finally in 1948, from the leadership of the N.A.A.C.P.[12]

There is now an increasingly strong tendency to link up the Negro and white labor reformist elements. This develops especially through the labor committees of the N.A.A.C.P., which exist in many industries, and through the drawing of Negro union officials into the bureaucratic machines which are controlling the trade union movement.

In class terms, such appeasement policies by important sections of the reformist Negro intelligentsia signify a betrayal of the Negro people into the hands of the white big capitalists. And all for but a few crumbs from the rich man's table. Allen says, "The Negro middle class has made its own class aims the center of practically all social and reform programs that have been advanced during the past half century" (presumably in behalf of the Negro people).[13] In these days of American imperialist war aggression, the assumption of leadership by these elements of the middle class is largely translating itself into a sell-out of the Negro people to their exploiters and oppressors. To a greater or lesser extent, such betrayal as that of Tobias, Sampson, *et al.*, is to be found among oppressed peoples, all over the world, who are under the attacks of militant imperialism.

At the present time, under the pressure of Negro mass militancy and the pressing need of American imperialism in its foreign policies, to veil the face of Jim Crow in this country, the capitalists are being compelled to make some concessions to the Negro people. The Negro reformists go along with these reforms and they appear as the Negro people's official leaders, but their subservient attitude to big business slows up the movement and tends to prevent it from reaching its possible goals.

Meanwhile, the left and progressive leaders of the Negro people, expressing the true interests of these masses, have boldly fought for all the most urgent needs of the Negro people, notably against the hated and reactionary Korean war, and against the whole war campaign of Wall Street. During the 1948 and 1952 elections, they generally supported the Progresisve Party, whose vice-presidential candidate during the 1952 campaign was Mrs. Charlotta Bass, Negro editor of the *California Eagle*. In the fight against fascism and war, the veteran brilliant Negro scholar and political leader, W. E. B. Du Bois, although 83 years old, was arrested as head of the Peace Information Center and narrowly escaped a long prison sentence. The very symbol of the advancing, fighting spirit of the Negro people, the great cultural-political leader, Paul Robeson, was boycotted and denied a passport, because of his generally militant stand and because he dared to indicate that the American Negro people would never fight against the Soviet Union. William L. Patterson, head of the Civil Rights Congress, was indicted, but not convicted of contempt of Congress. Ferdinand Smith, pioneer and outstanding Negro trade union leader, was deported. Of the 87 Communists indicted and/or convicted (up until April 15, 1953), under the barbarous Smith Act, eight were Negroes, including Benjamin J. Davis Jr., Henry Winston, and B. Careathers, sentenced to five years each; Pettis Perry, three years; Claudia Jones, one year; four others, J. Jackson, T. Dennis, Paul M. Bowan, and M. Murphy, are under indictment.[14]

Negro women, during this general period, have displayed their characteristic energy as fighters. Approximately 2,500,000 of them are organized in various groupings. These include the National Association of Negro Women, the National Council of Negro Women, the National Federation of Women's Clubs, the Women's Division of the Elks Civil Liberties Committee, and many others. Of these, the first named, with 75,000 members, is the largest. Negro women are to be found on the firing line everywhere in the long front of the fight for Negro rights. Eslanda Goode Robeson, Ada B. Jackson, Rosa Lee Ingram, and Charlotta Bass are typical of these workers and fighters.[15]

JIM CROW IN THE INTERNATIONAL ARENA

One of the most outstanding developments in the post-war period has been the emergence of the Negro question in the United States as a sharp issue in international relations. That is, the Negro people in this country, in their fight against Jim Crow and lynching, have won the active sympathy and support not only of the colonial peoples and the nations of Socialism and People's Democracy, but also of the masses in the imperialist countries. This is a great fact, to which the United States must pay heed in its dealings with other nations. These world-wide allies represent an enormous strengthening of the position of the Negro people in this country.

For many years, the Communist parties of the world have been signalizing to their peoples the outrageous persecution to which the Negro people of the United States are subjected. Since the end of World War II, the huge World Federation of Trade Unions, with some 80 million members, is also pointing to this social crime as one of the gross evils against which it is fighting.[16] The Soviet Union has repeatedly raised this question in the United Nations and elsewhere. And the colonial peoples everywhere, themselves long-time sufferers under kindred injuries and indignities, have become quite aware of the American Jim Crow-lynch regime. They do not hesitate to speak out against it loudly, clearly, and persistently. American Negro political leaders, with a keen sense of internationalism and of the great importance of winning the world's democratic forces for their cause, have made repeated moves to bring the case of the Negro people to international attention. This was the substance of Marcus Garvey's international activities, of *An Appeal to the World* by the N.A.A.C.P. in 1947, addressed to the United Nations, and edited by Du Bois, and also of the blazing protest of the Civil Rights Congress, *We Charge Genocide,* addressed to the same body in Paris four years later. These actions were in the spirit of the repeated Pan-African Conferences initiated by Du Bois over the years. This, too, is the spirit of the current work of the Council on African Affairs, headed by Paul Robeson.[17] These activities have tended to give the American Negro people a sense of solidarity not only with the awakening Negro peoples of Kenya, Rhodesia, Nigeria, the Union of South Africa, and elsewhere in Africa, but also with the democratic peace camp of the entire world.

Militant American imperialists violently object to this world-wide opposition to Jim Crow. They consider it practically an infringement upon American national sovereignty that Southern mobs cannot freely burn, hang, and shoot Negroes without Indians, Chinese, Russians, various European peoples, and other outsiders intruding and complaining about it. Jim Crow thus turns out to be a real handicap in Wall Street's hypocritical attempt to portray itself as the champion of world democracy. The monopolists must cover up the foul mess somehow. So they call in their conciliators—Tobias, Sampson, Bunche, *et al.*—who play down the extent and significance of Negro persecution; they hand down a court decision or two stingily favoring the Negro, such as the insulting Supreme Court decision of June 2, 1953, which provides that Negroes may be served in Washington, D.C. restaurants "if they are well-behaved"; they put a ban on the Jim Crow term "gook" in Korea; they slacken Jim Crow practices among American troops in foreign services, while they maintain segregation in the camps in the United States;[18] and they get the United Nations to pass a Covenant of Human Rights, which is flagrantly violated daily throughout the United States. At the same time, wherever American imperialists go, all over the world they carry Jim Crow with them.

Jim Crow has become an international issue, one which greatly worries American white supremacists. Even the antediluvian heads of the A.F. of L., with a record of two generations of rank discrimination against the Negro, have to tip their hats to the world pressure against the Jim Crow system. In belatedly supporting F.E.P.C., the A.F. of L. convention of 1952 said, "America could not uphold the virtues of democracy in the family of nations while equal opportunity to work and to earn a living was denied to its own citizens because of race, creed, or color,"[19] And a U.S. Senate committee, complaining about Communist propaganda abroad, pertinently remarked: "It must be recognized that some of the effect of our magnificent efforts overseas has been offset by the loss of support traceable to the existence of domestic discrimination. . . . Discrimination is bad international relations."[20] *Time* says, "The U.S. has probably won more enemies by stories, true or false, about its treatment of Negroes than by any other propaganda."[21]

THE NEGRO QUESTION, A MAJOR NATIONAL ISSUE

For the first time since the Reconstruction Period following the Civil War, the Negro question has also become a major national political issue in the United States. This is a result of a number of important factors: the wide sympathy the Negro has won internationally, the increased political activity of the Negro people, the key political position they occupy in several Northern states, the progressive pressure of at least a million Negro trade unionists, and the growing insistence by Communists and other progressives, Negro and white, that an end must be made to the whole monstrous outrage of the Jim Crow-lynch system.

Characteristic of this increased Negro activity, 1,000 delegates of the Negro Phi Beta Sigma fraternity met in Richmond, Virginia, in December 1952, and adopted comprehensive demands for Negro economic, political, and social equality. Some 5,000 delegates of six national Greek letter fraternities and sororities met in Cleveland, Ohio, at the same time and adopted a similar program. The NAACP has become a coordinating center for all such specific activities, and is very active upon many fronts of the Negro struggles.

Because of the changed relation of forces after World War II, the Negro has not been subjected to the wild attacks directed against him after World War I. But while the hand of the lyncher and pogromist has been somewhat stayed, these elements have continued in various ways to terrorize and murder Negroes. Especially in the South, there has been an increase in individual and police terror against the Negro. "Once the classic method of lynching was the rope. Now it is the policeman's bullet."[22] The *Pittsburgh Courier* of January 10, 1953, hailed 1952 as a year without a lynching, but added, "There were during 1952 some disturbing instances of floggings, beatings, bombings, and police brutality." The Southern Regional Council reported that 40 Negro homes were bombed in 1951-52[23] One of the most known cases was the bombing to death, December 25, 1951, of Mr. and Mrs. H. T. Moore, at Sims, Florida—a crime for which no one was punished. "With the decline of lynching (none reported during 1952), it is plain that the bomb and other forms of secret terror have taken its place."[24]

The courts, too, have played their terrorist part—in the case of the "Martinsville Seven," all of whom were electrocuted on a fake charge of rape; of the "Trenton Six"; Willie McGee, Mrs. Rosa Lee Ingram, and scores of others. In each of these instances, the Communists and progressive forces made the cases known internationally to the great embarrassment of the Wall Street would-be masters of the world.

During this period the Negro and white progressive forces of the North and South were able to secure a number of important court decisions, which tended to relieve, at least to a minor degree, the handicaps Negroes have to face in connection with the right to vote, to secure a college education, to live outside of the ghettos, to serve on juries, to serve in the armed forces, and to travel without being insultingly segregated. Important among these was the breaking down legally of Jim Crow restrictions on the entrance of Negroes into the state-financed colleges of Missouri, Oklahoma, Texas, Arkansas, Louisiana, Tennessee, Kentucky, West Virginia, Maryland, Delaware, Virginia, Kansas, and North Carolina. But these concessions, although important, still only scratch the surface; the monstrous Jim Crow system is still substantially intact. Washington, the nation's capital, remains the symbol of Jim Crowism. "The capital of the free world still forcibly imposes on its many visitors from foreign shores the continuing force and virulence of racism in America."[25] Replying to those who would have us believe that the persecution of the Negro has been virtually ended, Gus Hall, prominent Communist leader, put the situation in a nutshell when he said: "Phrases about 'the progressive integration of Negroes in the total life of the United States are meaningless when the Negro people comprise 9.8 percent of the population but receive less than three percent of the national income."[26]

Two significant organizations were created by Negro progressive forces during the post-war period. The first was the United Negro and Allied Veterans of America, formed in Chicago, on April 5-6, 1946. The purpose of U.N.A.V.A. was to fight the gross segregation practices of the American Legion and the Veterans of Foreign Wars,[27] but it lasted only about a year. The second organization was the National Negro Labor Council, with William R. Hood as president, which was founded in Cincinnati on October 27, 1951. This organization, made up predominantly of Negro trade unionists, has the sound purpose of fighting for jobs for Negroes, for upgrading, for F.E.P.C. legislation, for Negro representation and leadership, and against all forms of discrimination, especially in the unions and the industries. From the outset, the N.L.C. has campaigned vigorously for the inclusion of anti-discrimination clauses in all union contracts. In 1952, both the A.F. of L. and C.I.O. set up national Negro committees, actions which indicate the growing influence of the Negro trade unionists and the need for special activities and organizations to protect their interests.

To capture the important Negro vote, the two capitalist parties are outbidding each other in demagogy. In some cases, too, they have made considerable concessions, as in the New York 1953 mayoralty elections when all four of the major parties put up Negro candidates for president of the borough of Manhattan. Mr. Hulan E. Jack was elected, the first Negro ever chosen for this office. President Truman, a master at making promises which he had no intention of fulfilling, appointed a committee, in December 1946, to work out a civil rights program. The resulting document attacked lynching and Jim Crow in its manifold forms.[28] Truman, however, obviously had no intention of making a fight for this program, and after it ran into strong Congressional opposition, he let it gather dust on the shelf. The Republicans have been hardly less glib in their promises to the Negro. No sooner was the new Republican Administration in office early in 1953, however, than it proceeded, in alliance with its friends, the Southern Dixiecrats, lineal political descendants of the slaveholding planters, to ditch the Negro program by preserving the filibuster in the Senate. Thus, the Negroes were given typical betrayal treatment by both parties.

48. Jim Crow System Today

Since the Civil War the Negro people have made much progress, educationally, organizationally, and politically, in the face of staggering difficulties. They have also made some economic gains. These are being grossly exaggerated by Negro and white opportunists, as indicating that the Negro question is just about solved. But held under barbarous Jim Crow persecutions and restrictions, the Negro people remain compressed into a category of second-class citizenship and live under conditions of ruinous deprivation. "It is difficult," says Gus Hall, "to speak about victory and progress when the dominant fact that stares us in the face is the continuation of a system of frame-up and lynching, when legal lynching in the electric chair is on the increase, when there is discrimination, segregation in every walk of life, in every corner of the land."[1]

The Negro people of the Black Belt and the minority in the North constitutes an oppressed nation within the American nation as a whole. They are deeply and systematically discriminated against economically, politically, and socially. The United States has a white supremacist government; national oppression, similar to that experienced by Negroes although much less sharp or extensive, is also practiced against Indians, Mexicans, Filipinos, Puerto Ricans, and various other non-European groups. In this chapter we shall deal with some of the present-day concrete expressions of the national oppression of the Negro people under the Jim Crow system and how to deal with them.

NEGRO INDUSTRIAL WORKERS

The Negro worker is becoming a very important factor in industry. This is emphasized by the fact that whereas in 1940 less than 50 percent of the Negro population lived in urban areas, in 1950 some 65 percent lived in towns and cities. In the rural South Negro population increased only three percent during 1940-50, but in the industrial Northeast it went up 50 percent, in the North Central states 57 percent, and in the West 275 percent. "In proportion to population, Negroes participate to a greater degree in the labor force than

whites because a larger ratio of Negro women must work to supple-
ment the family income."[2] Negroes now are estimated to comprise 11
percent of all industrial workers.[3] In the coal mines Negro workers
constitute about 25 percent, in steel mills and auto plants about 15
percent, and in meat-packing plants about 30 percent. These Negro
workers experience all the exploitation and suppression of workers
generally; in addition, they are subjected to many special national
oppressions, due to the fact that they are Negroes and that Jim Crow
prevails in America.

The new Negro proletariat remains located mainly in the North.
During the two wars and the succeeding "boom" periods, much industrialization has taken place in the South, but the extent of this has
been exaggerated. Many of the South's new industries relate directly
to munitions production—that is, chemicals, aircraft, shipbuilding,
aluminum, and the like. Regarding industry, as in so many other
respects, the South remains the nation's number-one problem. In
the new industries the Negro worker gets the lowest pay and does
the hardest, most unskilled work. In the South, where most Negro
workers live, the average weekly wage in manufacturing industries
in 1952 was $52, as against the national average of $70.80.

The most elementary injustice done to Negro workers is that they
are barred from many industries and callings. A recent survey showed
that 90 percent of the corporations in Pennsylvania discriminate
against hiring Negroes.[4] Practically all other states would show
similar rates of discrimination. Among the more glaring examples of
such exclusion may be cited the operating section of the railroads, the
more skilled building trades, the textile, aircraft, printing, and electrical industries; the telephone, telegraph, and other public utilities,
the movie, radio, and television industries; the general teaching staff;
the vast body of office, sales, and technical forces, and at least a
score of government services—all of which industries and vocations
are either completely or almost completely closed to Negroes. Usually
this is brought about by employer action, but frequently it is because
of resistance by the trade unions and the white workers. It is imperative that in all such cases the Jim Crow obstacles be broken down
and free access to all occupations be extended to Negro workers.
Especially, the government's contract compliance regulations must
be enforced against discriminating practices.

Another basic grievance of Negro workers is that even in those
industries where they are permitted to work, barriers are placed in

the way of their advancement to the more skilled and better-paid jobs. Perlo points out that three-fourths of male non-white workers are engaged in laboring and service occupations, as against one-third of the whites.[5] Thus, in 1950, under the census category of "craftsmen, foremen and kindred workers," 19.3 percent of all white industrial workers and only 7.6 percent of all Negro workers were in that category.[6] The unions generally are making but a poor fight against such gross discrimination. Characteristically, in steel Negro workers are almost exclusively confined to the lower, less-paid eight of the 32 classifications of workers. A common Southern pattern is that of the aircraft industry in Texas, which employs 10,000 workers, of whom only 300 are Negroes, and these are engaged in janitoring and other service jobs.[7] Obviously this situation must be drastically changed; the trade unions bear first responsibility for the systematic upgrading of Negro workers. It has been estimated that fair employment practices would shift 2,556,000 Negroes to higher-paid jobs.[8] In general, the upgrading of Negro workers is proceeding at a snail's pace.

Still another special grievance of Negro workers is excessive instability of employment. They are notoriously the worst sufferers from joblessness. At the start of World War II Negroes were hired in the booming industries only after the backlog of unemployed white workers had been pretty much absorbed, and at the war's end they were almost eliminated from many plants. The 1950 Census shows that current unemployment is twice as high among Negroes as among whites. In an economic crisis this ratio would be disastrous to Negro workers and it could also gravely rupture Negro-white worker solidarity. In the general interest of the working class, it is a basic task of the trade unions to demand proportional hiring of Negro workers and to see to it that when mass lay-offs come, Negro workers, through a proper division of available work, will not have to bear more than their proportionate share of unemployment. Seniority systems must be developed in this sense—a very serious problem, particularly in view of the current growing sag in industry.

Negro workers are also widely discriminated against in wage differentials, particularly as between North and South. A few examples: coremakers—Detroit $2.07 per hour, Birmingham $1.32; hand-shovelers in fertilizer plants—on the Pacific Coast $1.41 per hour, in Southern states 72 cents; workers in Southern sugar refineries 97 cents per hour, in the North $1.34;[9] Southern sawmill workers, mostly Negroes, $1.02

per hour as against $2.15 in the Northwest.[10] Such divergencies in pay rates are a major reason why "In 1950 the Negro wage and salary workers earned an average of about $1,300, 52 percent of the average for white workers."[11] The labor movement, if alert to the interests of the working class as a whole, must put an end to such rank and dangerous discrimination against Negro workers. Unionization, which seeks to establish equal pay in similar categories of work, is helping to reduce the wage gap between Negro and white workers.

Negro women are discriminated against worst of all. They are triply exploited and oppressed—as women, as workers, and as Negroes. Negro women received less than half the incomes of white women, and less than half the income of Negro men. Comparing the extremes, Negro women got one-fifth of what white men received.[12] They are overwhelmingly domestic workers, there being 45 percent of them engaged in such service, in contrast with 9.4 percent for all women.[13] Women are almost completely barred from clerical and sales jobs, the skilled trades, and many other of the better-paid occupations. Only 4 percent of Negro women work at clerical jobs, as against 29 percent for whites.[14] And worst of all, Negro women have to watch their children grow up deprived of the most elementary opportunities for education, health, jobs, and citizenship.

The abolition of the gross discrimination practiced against Negroes in industry, in respect to jobs, skills, wages, promotion, etc., should be a first concern of the trade union movement, far more so than at the present time. Organized labor needs to pay basic attention to this matter in the formulation of its contracts, and it should demand the establishment locally, state-wide, and nationally of a network of effective Fair Employment Practices Committees. At present the trade unions are grossly neglecting the improvement of the Negro worker, and the F.E.P.C.'s, which now exist in but 12 states and 25 cities (none of them in the South), are altogether inadequate to cope with the big problem.

Of decisive importance in improving the conditions of the Negro worker is the unionization of industrial workers in the South. The accomplishment of this fundamental task is also of immediate and basic importance to the strength of the whole labor movement. The recent C.I.O. "drive" to organize the South failed for the elementary reason, that the "Reds," the best of organizers, were excluded from the organizing staff; and that the organizers catered to the Jim Crow prejudices of Southern reactionaries.

THE NEGRO FARMER

Negro farmers are located almost exclusively in the South, mostly in the Black Belt. Like American farmers in general, they tend to decrease both proportionally and absolutely. In 1890, of the 7,500,-000 Negroes in the whole country, only 20 percent lived in urban communities; but in 1950, 65 percent of the 15,500,000 Negroes* dwelt in towns and cities. Negro farmers are moving to the North and into war-swollen Southern industry; they are also being squeezed off the farms by mechanization. During 1940-50, there has been a decline of half a million tenant farmers in the South, chiefly Negroes. In 1920 Negro farmers in the South operated 40,884,199 acres, but by 1950 this acreage had been reduced to 25,650,413 acres, or a loss of 37 percent.[15]

In general, Southern agriculture lags far behind the rest of the country in terms of mechanization. This has been caused chiefly by the presence historically of large masses of low-paid, oppressed Negro labor. But, under the recent pressure of the demand for workers, caused by the war and the post-war munitions boom, the tempo of mechanization has been considerably intensified. The number of tractors, cotton-pickers, and other farm machines is definitely on the increase. Raper asserts that "Mechanization is proceeding more rapidly in the South than in any other part of the country."[16] Nevertheless large numbers of even the biggest plantations, particularly in the Black Belt, still depend upon the primitive methods of hand-hoe and mule culture. The obsolete plantation system has by no means been destroyed by mechanization.

However, there are now some 750,000 tractors in the South. In Georgia alone, during 1940-50, the number rose from 9,000 to 60,000.[17] Cotton-pickers are also multiplying. Thus, "In 1946, the percentage of the cotton harvested by one-man mechanical pickers was about one-half of one percent, but in 1951 it was up to 17 percent."[18] In 1952 the figure went up to 25 percent. These machines are mostly in the western sections of the cotton area. The cotton-picker, operated by one man, does the work of about 30 adults. Welch and Miley estimate that with the perfection of the cotton-picker, 73 percent of the poorer farmers now in the Mississippi delta region—mostly Negroes

* There are probably up to 17,000,000 Negroes in the United States, many Negroes in the South being ignored by census takers.

—will not be needed.[19] Negroes are the least able to buy the costly tractors and cotton-pickers; hence, the marked tendency of mechanization is to squeeze them off the land or down into the lower categories of landless sharecroppers and agricultural laborers. The fight to get hold of tractors and cotton-pickers is of basic importance to the Southern Negro farmer. In the event of a major economic crisis, with serious cuts in cotton production, the Negro masses in the Black Belt, with their antiquated equipment, would face catastrophe.

Of the Southern Negro farm cultivators, 10 percent are owners and 71 percent tenants. This includes the 57 percent who are sharecroppers,[20] and pay up to one-half of their crop to the plantation owners. They are robbed by usurers, with interest rates of 25 percent or more on what they have to buy.[21] Besides, they are also mulcted by a complex series of other exploiters—railroads, elevator trusts, packing houses, fertilizer combines, rapacious cotton middlemen, etc. The major cash crop they produce—cotton—is in a chronically bankrupt condition. In 1952, despite the war boom and the reduction of cotton acreage by one-third, there was an overproduction of two million bales. To cap the climax, the Southern Negro farmers live largely voteless and Jim Crowed, under a regime of K.K.K. terrorism.

The basic land reform needed in the South, the carrying through of the agrarian revolution, is the break-up of the obsolete plantation system (which has not greatly changed since the Reconstruction Period) and the free distribution of the land to the poor Negro and white tenants and the agricultural laborers. This reform is theoretically posible within the framework of the capitalist system; but pending its accomplishment, many other vital reform measures are urgently needed. Among them are government limitation of rent rates for cash tenants and sharecroppers; national purchase of vast stretches of land to be given free to the landless sharecroppers and laborers; federal long-term, low interest loans to poor farmers for mechanization, electrification, etc.; full F.E.P.C. and social security legislation for all Southern workers of field and factory, especially for Negro women; the general extension of the school system and cultural activities of the South; the breaking down of Jim Crow policies in the national farm organizations and the complete organization of the small Southern farm-owners, tenants, and workers; and the national consideration of the South as the nation's number one economic problem, as Roosevelt called it.[22] The South is the heart of the national Negro question and of the liberation movement.

NEGRO PROFESSIONALS AND BUSINESSMEN

Negro doctors, lawyers, preachers, teachers, scientists, writers, and other intellectuals are all caught in the deadly embrace of the Jim Crow system. Their fields of opportunity, save in a minority of cases, are pretty much limited to Negro clienteles in the segregated Negro communities. In most cases these intellectuals are less integrated into the general body of American society than the Negro workers employed in industry. The doctor, with his patients chiefly limited to Negroes, is grossly discriminated against in white hospitals; the Negro lawyer is under a big handicap in the white-dominated courts; the Negro teacher finds it extremely difficult to get even a second-class job outside the Negro community; the Negro writer confronts a wall of prejudice among white publishers; and the Negro actor is restricted to certain limited roles. Of the 2,000,000 persons employed as chemists, architects, engineers, and other technical workers, only 400 are Negroes.[23] The proportion of Negroes in the nation's professional occupations is no higher than it was 50 years ago.[24]

The Negro businessman is even more limited than the professional by Jim Crow pressures. His business is confined almost exclusively to the Negro community, Negro business concerns being practically unheard of in white areas. Especially in the South is Negro industry and business stifled and crippled. By the same token, Negroes are almost completely barred from the sacred ranks of white business executives. Restricted for want of capital, denied a broad market, and faced by overwhelmingly powerful white competition, Negro business is not only tied to the Negro community, but it is also primarily of a marginal, service character (see Chapter 43.)[25]

The weak position of the Northern Negro bourgeoisie is thus indicated by Henderson: "On the South Side of Chicago, which is a predominantly Negro community, one-half of the businesses are owned by Negroes, but only one-tenth of the money income obtained from this community goes to these 50 percent of the businesses which are Negro."[26] The 90 percent goes to outside white businessmen. The situation of the Negro businessman in the South is, if anything, even worse. The dreams of some Negro leaders that they could build a rounded-out Negro economy have not come true, nor can they under an imperialist regime. To break the Jim Crow restrictions upon Negro professionals and Negro businessmen, the disbarment from professional associations, credit institutions, businessmen's organizations, etc., must, of course, be a concern of the Negro people and their white political allies. There is also a great need to build the co-operative movement among Negroes, in both the North and the South.[27]

The Jim Crowing of Negro professionals and businessmen goes to prove that the oppression under which the Negro people live is not simply of a "class," but of a "national" character. It also shows that, basically, these classes have a common interest in building one all-class national front with the Negro workers and farmers, and in joining with their white allies to smash the Jim Crow system. But politically these bourgeois forces cannot lead the struggle of the Negro people, although they constantly strive to do so and to exploit it in their own narrow class interests.

It was largely this policy of putting their own class interests above those of their people that led such bourgeois elements to oppose the unionization of the Negro workers for many years, and now leads them to support the warlike policies of Wall Street imperialism. This does not mean, however, that the whole Negro bourgeoisie, on all occasions, has entirely lost its progressivism. On the contrary, in its own way, the Negro bourgeoisie supports many of the immediate demands of the Negro people, as is now to be seen in the South and elsewhere. Nevertheless, the trustworthy political leadership of the Negro people devolves upon the Negro proletariat in close alliance with the Southern Negro farmers, since both classes have the most direct interest in developing a progressive policy for the United States in general and for smashing the entire Jim Crow regime. In the furtherance of these aims, however, they must seek the creation of an all-out national Negro front, involving as much as possible both the petty bourgeoisie and the bourgeoisie.

THE NEGRO AS A CITIZEN

In his general status as a citizen, the Negro is also burdened with a host of special Jim Crow discriminations and disadvantages. In every respect, his living standards are depressed by prevalent super-exploitation to levels far below those of whites. In 1950, 59 percent of Negro families received less than a $2,000 income, as against 27 percent of white families; percentage-wise, four times more white families than Negro families, had yearly incomes of $4,000 or over.[28] In the South, where two-thirds of the Negro people live, the typical income of a Southern white farm family is $1,200, or 40 percent below the poverty line; but the amount for an average Negro farm family is around $500, or less than half as much.

Negro housing conditions, North and South, are atrocious. Only one-half of the number of Negroes, compared to whites, own their own homes, and these are vastly inferior in quality. The N.A.A.C.P. says, "Negro citizens are held virtual prisoners in sub-standard housing all over America today."[29] In Baltimore Negroes form 20 percent of the population, but occupy only two percent of the housing. In Los Angeles, 30,000 Negroes are packed in an area formerly inhabited by 7,000 Japanese. In Chicago Negroes live 90,000 to the square mile, whites 20,000. In the Southern cities, Negroes are crowded three to four times as closely as whites.[30] Lacking running water, private toilets or baths, were 24 percent of Negro urban homes, as against 10 percent for all homes.[31] One of the worst features of Negro oppression is the mob violence that is so frequently used to prevent Negroes from occupying decent houses. Even as these lines are being written (August, 1953), a mob of thousands, for days past, has been violently attempting to oust a Negro couple from the Trumbull Park Homes in Chicago.

Negro health suffers accordingly from the existing conditions of poverty. Tuberculosis is five times more prevalent among Negroes than among whites, syphilis six times, and pneumonia two times. In 1940 there was one physician for every 743 persons in the United States, but only one for every 3,530 Negroes. Almost twice as many Negro children as white children die between the ages of one and four.[32] And when he dies, the Negro is buried in a segregated cemetery. A Washington animal cemetery even draws the color line on dogs.

Negro education is also sub-standard, especially in the South. Seventeen states and the District of Columbia enforce segregated schooling and two additional states permit it. About one-half as much is spent on educating a Negro child as on a white. The average amount of schooling for people of 25 years of age: whites, ten years; Negroes, seven. Almost seven percent of all white students are in institutions of higher learning, as against but three percent of Negroes. The income of 96 Negro colleges in 1938 was $14,697,712, or less than that of Harvard University alone. In New York City, with Negroes making up about ten percent of the population, less than two percent of the teachers are Negroes, and 90 percent of these work in Negro communities.[33] The stubborn opposition to equal education in the South is indicated by the threats of Governors Talmadge of Georgia and Byrnes of South Carolina that their states will abolish the public schools if the higher courts force upon them a policy of non-segregation.

While the Negro generally has the vote in the North, he is predominantly disfranchised in the South by means of educational tests, poll taxes, and sheer terrorism. Despite recent important successes of the right-to-vote movements, only 1,350,000 of the six million Negro citizens in the South were registered in 1952.[34] By the poll tax, some seven million Negroes and whites are disfranchised in the five remaining poll tax states—Alabama, Arkansas, Mississippi, Texas, and Virginia. In the elections of 1952, not one Negro reached Congress to represent the 10 million Negroes in the South; and in the North, only two were elected from the Negro districts of New York and Chicago, to represent five million Northern Negroes. In the state and city legislatures, especially in the South, Negro representation is almost equally negligible; a few local victories were won, however, in the early 1953 elections in Georgia, North Carolina, and Louisiana.

Notoriously, Negroes are Jim Crowed and insulted in hotels, restaurants, hospitals, and theaters, on beaches, in summer resorts, on trains, and busses, and in public places all over the country. In the South this segregation is largely enforced by legal statute, in the North by custom and white chauvinist pressures. In the armed forces Jim Crowism still persists, although, under the pressure of hostile foreign opinion, some reforms have been instituted in this respect. In 30 states racial intermarriage is prohibited, often with barbaric penalties.[35] The outrageous American Jim Crow system is unequaled anywhere in the world, save in the Union of South Africa and African colonial areas.

The segregation and oppression of the Negro people is particularly evident in the whole system of justice, both North and South. Negro lawyers are few and seriously handicapped, and Negro judges are few and far between. Negroes facing capitalist courts are usually railroaded to jail with a minimum of ceremony and with little regard for the facts and circumstances. Innumerable tragic cases bear witness to this deadly fact. In the North, Negro prisoners are especially subjected to savage police brutality, which Perry calls "the chief and modern form of lynching."[36] In the South, the dread threat of mob violence, legal and extra-legal, still hangs over the whole Negro community.

Obviously, it is indispensable to smash and eradicate the entire Jim Crow system, root and branch, North and South. The evil must be especially attacked by national political action—the Dixiecrat Jim Crowers, like their slaveholding forebears of a century ago, must not be allowed to hide behind the tricky doctrine of states' rights. Together with the elementary measures already mentioned above, the need is especially urgent for drastic Federal laws on a national scale against lynching, poll taxes, and Jim Crow practices in general, and also for the extension of the school system, and the economic protection of poor Negro and white farmers.

THE PROFITS OF JIM CROW

Jim Crow in the United States is not simply a matter of white chauvinist prejudices, it is an organic part of Negro national oppression and will not completely vanish until Negro national liberation is achieved. It boils down to a system of super-exploitation of the Negro people, and it is highly profitable to the capitalist-planter exploiters. Figuring on the basis of the difference in the median wage of Negro and white productive workers, Perlo estimates that a total super-profit of almost four billion dollars is filched yearly from Negroes.[37] This is a minimum estimate and does not include such big items as the low pay of Negro women domestics or the depressed conditions of white Southern sharecroppers, all of which are tied in with the super-exploitation of the Negro workers. Major beneficiaries of this wholesale robbery are the gigantic corporations which now dominate the South like colonial masters—U.S. Steel, General Motors, Morgan, du Pont, Rockefeller, Armour, Firestone, etc.[38]

During the past 14 years of war and preparations for war with the consequent artificial national expansion of industry and production, the Negro made some meager economic gains. In many cases the unions knocked out wage differentials for similar work, frequently before the National War Labor Board. Perlo states: "During World War II the Negro people achieved absolute economic and social gains and made advances relative to the population as a whole. Since World War II they have suffered serious losses in both respects . . . there has been a sharp widening of the income differentials against Negro workers both in the North and the South. By 1949 most of the wartime gains in the South had been lost, while the situation in the North was no better than before World War II."[39]

Negro and white opportunists have greeted the limited industrialization of the South, and the war-produced improvements in the
economic and political position of the Negro people as an indication
of the automatic liquidation of Jim Crow and of the Negro question
in general. This was the line of the renegade Communist, Jay Lovestone, in the 1920's and it was the essential position of Earl Browder,
renegade of the past decade. On this basis, the latter undertook to
halt Communist efforts in support of the Negroes' fight and also to
liquidate the Communist Party in the South. Such opportunist illusions are highly dangerous. The Negro cannot depend upon the
industrialization of the South, or war booms, automatically to solve
his problems. He has had to fight desperately for all the real gains he
has made—emancipation, the franchise, the right to work in industry,
etc.—and his need for struggle is still most pressing. In 1953, ninety
years after the signing of the Emancipation Proclamation, the
N.A.A.C.P., at its St. Louis convention, still finds it necessary to put
out the slogan "We want to be free by Sixty-three."

Actually, the position of the Negro people and of their recent
limited economic and political gains is very precarious, because the
drive of American imperialism for world mastery is fraught with
catastrophe, for the American people in general and for the Negro
people in particular. It has resulted in most dangerous war policies
abroad, it has released virulent fascist tendencies at home, and it is
leading the American economy straight into a major economic crisis.
Obviously, the Negro people would be the worst sufferers from such
a crisis, and such economic and political gains as they have made
during the great demand for labor caused by wartime production
would be gravely jeopardized. These social gains are also dangerously
threatened by growing McCarthyism, which is budding fascism. Hence,
the Negro people have the profoundest interest in all efforts in defense of American democracy and maintaining world peace. For them,
the war campaign carries with it the most dangerous menace to their
entire economic and political status.

49. The Road Ahead

It is of vital importance to white workers and progressive forces generally to fight side by side with the Negro people for the destruction of the Jim Crow system. For that system injures not only the Negroes but also the white toiling masses. If Negroes are compelled to work for sub-standard wages, this inevitably harms the wages of the great mass of white workers, as the South drastically demonstrates. Stone's theory that "every white man" profits from the Negroes' suppression is a monstrous perversion of the truth.[1] If Negroes are barred from industry and from skilled jobs, this has a definite reaction against the unity and solidarity of the working class. If Negroes are Jim Crowed and denied civil rights, this is a victory for every fascist in the country. If Negroes in the South are stripped of the right to vote, the white workers in the North pay for it dearly in the reactionary activities of the Dixiecrat bloc in Congress, the rotten political front of the Jim Crow political system. No truer political words were ever spoken than Karl Marx's famous dictum that the white workers can never free themselves while Negro workers remain in bondage. The Jim Crow system is a menace to every prospect of freedom and democracy in the United States.[2]

WHITE CHAUVINISM AND NEGRO BOURGEOIS NATIONALISM

The building of the indispensable alliance of Negro and white democratic and progressive forces requires a constant fight against white chauvinism, the bourgeois ideology of white supremacy. The purpose of this political poison is to facilitate the super-exploitation of the Negro toilers and therewith to weaken the whole anti-capitalist struggle of the working class and its political allies. White supremacy, the false theory of the inferiority of the Negro, was evolved by the Southern planters to justify chattel slavery. Taken over by the capitalists in general as an important weapon in their scheme of exploitation, it has become a basic element of predatory Wall Street monopoly capital in its drive for Anglo-Saxon world domination. White chauvinism tends to spread abroad with the expansion of the aggressive role of American imperialism.

American history is crowded with tragic examples of the operation of white chauvinism. This was the principal means by which the planters were able in the main to keep the poor whites of the South alienated from the Negroes, before, during, and after the Civil War, despite their common economic interests. Every lynch mob, every race riot that has disgraced our nation has had white chauvinism as its ideological driving force. Race hatred, injected among the toilers by the exploiters, saturates the government, industries, churches, schools, theaters, movies, press, radio, television, and all other capitalist-controlled institutions. From long propagation it also subtly permeates our national language, customs, and habits. White chauvinism is a cancerous disease in American culture. Large sections of the working class, constantly subjected to this flood of intellectual filth, are also more or less afflicted with it. It is white chauvinism that lies behind tendencies to bar Negro workers from jobs, from union membership and leadership, from friendly social relationships.

One of the most important services of the Communist Party is its long and relentless fight against this deadly, divisive force. Whereas other organizations, although speaking in the name of the working class, practically ignore the whole question of white chauvinism, the Communist Party not only fights it without let-up among the broad masses, but also fights against such manifestations as may crop up in the Party itself. The Party works endlessly for a free, frank, friendly relationship between Negro and white workers on the basis of complete economic, political, and social equality.[3]

Despite the assertions of reactionaries, white chauvinism is not a natural phenomenon. It is definitely propagated by those who benefit financially from it. Young children have no racial prejudices—it is only after they are half-grown that they begin to learn them from their elders. This poison is less common than here in many capitalist nations, especially the Latin nations of Europe and the nations of Latin America. The peoples of Socialism and People's Democracy not only have no white chauvinism, but they militantly educate and campaign against it.

The experience of the Soviet Union emphatically demonstrates that despite differences in color, religion, and national background, nations can live in complete equality and harmony. The Constitution of the Communist Party of the U.S.A. also states in Article IV, Section

11: "It shall be the obligation of all Party members to struggle against all forms of national oppression, national chauvinism, discrimination and segregation; against all ideological influences and practices of barbarous 'racial' theories such as white chauvinism and anti-Semitism." The thoroughgoing Marxist-Leninist analysis of white chauvinism made by Communist writers stands in the front rank of American political writing.

While the Communist Party militantly combats white chauvinism as the worst ideological menace to Negro-white co-operation and solidarity, it does not ignore the lesser danger of Negro bourgeois nationalism as a divisive force. It fights on both fronts. Bourgeois-nationalist ideology "is the instrument through which the Negro petty bourgeois leaders, posing as champions of general 'race' interests, *i.e.*, the interests of the whole Negro people, seek to rally them in support of the narrow class interests of the Negro bourgeoisie."[4] It manifests itself in a two-fold way: in reformist illusions of automatic integration into white institutions and, consequently, in the idea that there is no need to struggle against the white oppressors; or in sectarian, isolationist policies of segregationism. In both cases it is a surrender to white supremacy.

Such Negro nationalism, seeping down from the petty bourgeoisie into the ranks of Negro workers, tends to create suspicions against friendly white workers and to make co-operation with them more difficult. This plays right into the hands of the big white capitalist exploiters. It also enables the Negro bourgeoisie to sell out the Negro people to the white ruling class whenever it sees fit to do so. Bourgeois nationalism was at the bottom of the Negro intelligentsia's long opposition to Negro workers joining trade unions, and it now operates through such figures as Tobias, Sampson, Bunche, White, *et al.*, to tie the Negro people to the war chariots of American imperialism (see Chapter 47).

THE BROAD PEACE COALITION

The present situation in the United States insistently demands the formation of a broad Farmer-Labor party as the basis of a wider political coalition of all the democratic forces of this country. Such unity must include the Negro people in close alliance with the white workers. In their ruthless drive for world mastery, the Wall Street monopolists are confronting the masses of the people with the imperative need to unite in defense of their most elementary rights and interests. The warmongers, with their mad munitions race, are lowering the living standards, bankrupting the people and hastening the country into an eventual economic crisis far more devastating than that of 1929-33. With their ruthless attempts to militarize the fundamentally peace-loving American people, they are trampling upon the Bill of Rights; they are cultivating the deadly fascist menace of McCarthyism, of which the Negro people are a special target. With their aggressive foreign policies, they are driving the world toward the precipice of a frightful atomic war which would reduce civilization to ruins.

To halt and defeat this world surge toward fascism and war is the task not only of the working class, but of all democratic groups: the Negro people, the farmers, professionals, and small businessmen. Eugene Dennis, general secretary of the Communist Party (now in Federal prison because of his fight for peace), thus states this policy: "The most decisive immediate task confronting all progressive workers —non-Communists and Communists alike—*is to bring about the unity of action of the entire labor movement in alliance with all anti-fascist and democratic forces.* It is to forge a broader and more militant labor-democratic coalition which can rally all anti-monopoly and anti-war elements and groups, irrespective of political, trade union and religious affiliations. It is to unite the democratic camp around a common program of struggle for jobs, security, and equal rights for all, for progress, democracy, and peace, moving toward a new progressive political alignment under labor leadership."[5]

All the democratic forces have the most fundamental interest in the maintenance of peace and democracy. It was the people who brought about the end of the Korean war, despite stubborn efforts of Wall Street and its government to expand the war into China. They also have the power to halt war altogether by abolishing imperialism. But if they do not act together the great cause of peace will be lost and the world forced into measureless disaster by the atomaniacs of Wall Street. The monopolists are wedded to the fascist-war program, and, they can be turned from it only by decisive political defeat.

The general purpose of such a great political combination of trade unions, workers' parties, Negro organizations, farmers' associations, women's clubs, youth groupings, veterans' organizations, etc., would be to defend the immediate urgent interests of the masses of the people. Its ultimate aim would be the election of a people's government. But such a government would be firmly committed to the maintenance of democracy and peace and based upon the acceptance of the principle that the Socialist and capitalist worlds can and must co-exist in peaceful competition. This broad anti-fascist, pro-peace alliance (akin to the plan originally projected by the Communists to fight the Hitler menace, for which see Chapter 46) is fully in the tradition of the repeated joint movements of workers, Negroes, farmers, etc., throughout United States history in the hard struggles against the planter and monopolist enemies of democracy.

The political basis of the peace coalition must be the defense not only of the general interests of the people as a whole, but also of the specific group, class, and national interests of its component elements. These are harmonious, in the main, and they lend themselves to an all-inclusive program. This means that the national demands of the Negro liberation movement for jobs, the franchise, civil rights, and land reform would receive expression in the coalition program and activities. Of basic importance to the success of the coalition will be a relentless fight against the whole Jim Crow system in all its ramifications, along the lines indicated in the previous chapter.

The leading force in the peace coalition is the working class, of which the Communist Party is the best spokesman and leader. It is a historic necessity that the main forces of this coalition unite definitely into a broad, mass labor or farmer-labor party. The workers must break, at long last, from the political tutelage of the capitalists, exerted especially through the Democratic Party—a tutelage cultivated by the A.F. of L.-C.I.O. top leaders' policy of political dependence on that party. The workers must become the leaders of the people. The strongest element, the most clearly and resolutely anti-capitalist, and eventually pro-Socialist, they must assert this political leadership and class independence. Upon them falls the historic task, as Stalin has so often stressed, of leading the nation through this crucial period, since the bourgeoisie has largely abdicated its once progressive role of national leadership and become the enemy of the nation. In this anti-imperialist peace coalition, the best and most reliable ally of the working class is the Negro people as such, steeled by their bitter national persecution and armed by their long and heroic record of domestic struggle.

PEOPLE'S FRONT AND PEOPLE'S DEMOCRACY

The peace coalition, or People's Front government, elected by a majority of the people under the Constitution, would be established within the framework of the capitalist system. Such a government would have as a central task to take vigorous measures against economic crisis, by increasing wages, shortening work hours, developing public works, opening up East-West trade, etc. It would restore, preserve and develop the people's civil rights and living standards. It would put a halt to the war danger, or end the war if one were going on. Naturally, one of its first concerns would be to protect the welfare of the Negro people.

Such a government, standing in the path of the main drive of American imperialism toward fascism and war, would certainly have to face the most vigorous, even violent opposition of the big monopoly interests and their multitudinous hangers-on. The history of American capitalism leaves no other conclusion. In order to be elected by the workers and their allies in the first place, and then to function as a government, a People's Front would have to be strong enough to defeat and repress all capitalist resistance and to keep democratic processes in action. Daily the capitalists move toward fascism, and daily the threat becomes greater that they would try to put down by force any political movement basically attacking their entrenched interests.

In order to cope with this aggressive capitalist opposition and to deal effectively with the critical economic and political situation confronting it, a People's Front government would eventually have to adopt a number of far-reaching measures, in addition to the steps already mentioned, including the nationalization of the banks, railroads, and key industries; the elimination of reactionaries from control of the armed forces; the placing of reliable elements at the head of the industries, etc. The people's government would have the legal right to take these steps, since it would be backed by the mandate of the great majority of the people. It would also be compelled to adopt them or face destruction from capitalist attacks from within or without. Failure to take this general course was the reason why the prewar Spanish People's Front government was crushed from without by the Franco rebellion, and also why the French People's Front of the same period was betrayed from within by the Social-Democrat Léon Blum.

This policy would take the coalition government in the direction of a People's Democracy. Such a government would be no mere copy of existing People's Democracies in other countries, but would have its distinct American features. This type of government eventually undertakes the building of Socialism. It is a form of the dictatorship of the proletariat, or the rule of the working class in alliance with the laboring farmers and the Negro people. A People's Front government would curb the trusts; a People's Democracy would break their power. A government of the People's Democracy type might come into existence either by a reorganization of the forces within the People's Front government or by the formation of a new government. This course would be the victorious revolution. How peaceful this transition would be would depend upon the extent to which the workers and their allies were able by democratic action, to curb, stifle, and repress attempts at violence by the forces of capitalism. The Communist Party holds that despite the growing threat of fascism, a relatively peaceful establishment of Socialism in this country is within the realm of political possibility, and it orients itself upon this basis. The Government's charge, by which many Communists have been railroaded to jail under the Smith Act, that the Communist Party "teaches and advocates the violent overthrow of the United States Government," is a deliberate lie and frame-up.

THE GENERAL CRISIS OF CAPITALISM

The most significant political development of our times is the fact that 800 million people are building Socialism in their countries. The U.S.S.R. has already traveled so far along this path that it is now on the verge of establishing Communism, a still higher form of society. The difference between Socialism and Communism is this: Under Socialism the guiding social principle is "From each according to his ability, to each according to his work"; under Communism the motto is "From each according to his ability, to each according to his needs." In both forms of society all the means of social production are owned by the people, and there is no exploitation of man by man.

Behind this great reality of the rapid spread of world Socialism is the basic fact of the decay and decline of the world capitalist system. This is the general crisis of the capitalist system, manifestations of which we have remarked earlier in passing. By the very nature of its private ownership of the means of production or distribution, by its exploitation of the toiling masses for the benefit of the capitalist owners and rulers, by its chaotic, competitive manner of operation, capitalism has many internal and external tensions and contradictions—between workers and capitalists, between capitalists and farmers, among the capitalists themselves, between capitalist countries and colonial peoples, among rival capitalist empires, and between world capitalism and world Socialism.

With the maturing of capitalism into imperialism, these contradictions have become so accentuated and acute that society is being now thrown into one crisis after another, and life under capitalism grows more and more unendurable for the masses of the people. World Wars I and II, the Russian Revolution, the Chinese Revolution, the People's Democratic Revolutions in Eastern Europe, the growth of fascism, the great economic crisis of 1929-33, the division of the international economy into two world markets, and the present critical world situation regarding peace, all manifest the decay of the capitalist system, its sinking into incurable general crisis. The position of world capitalism becomes all the more impossible with the growth of many Socialist countries and with the break-up of the capitalist empires, both of which are now taking place.

The American economy is capitalist and is therefore subject to all the internal and external contradictions characteristic of the world capitalist system summing up to its deepening general crisis. This was dramatically illustrated by the great economic smash-up of 1929-33, and it is daily being demonstrated by the whole course of American capitalist society. During the past 15 years, the United States has experienced much growth and industrial activity, but this has been due basically to the industrial stimulus given by the great demands for munitions during the war, by the expenditures of vast sums for repairing the war's damages, and now by the insane re-armament race. United States capitalism, cannibal-like, is profiting from the disasters that have fallen upon the rest of the capitalist world.

Those who believe that the present American (and European) "prosperity," based on munitions production, will last indefinitely, are living in a fool's paradise. Unless its course is reversed by the progressive pressure of the masses along lines previously indicated, the United States is headed for a major economic disaster, if not for the even worse catastrophe of world war. Signs of economic crisis are already multiplying, both in this country and in Western Europe. With imperialism dominant, there is no basis in the normal world capitalist markets for the war-swollen and lop-sided economy (with double the production of 1929) which the United States now possesses. The workers can protect themselves from the developing crisis only by the economic and political measures proposed by the peace coalition.

Bourgeois economists, proceeding upon the theories of John Maynard Keynes, believe that they can keep this country from an economic smash-up by their so-called managed economy. They declare that they can repair the broken-down capitalist countries which clutter up the world landscape and make them going concerns again. These bourgeois illusions have been absorbed by the top trade union leadership, who have made them into the official policies of the labor movement. But all this is mere wishful thinking. The world capitalist system is doomed, and it cannot possibly be rescued from the workings of its own fatal internal contradictions. It must be superseded by Socialism. And any attempt to cut the Gordian knot of world capitalism's difficulties by world war, as Wall Street is contemplating, would only hasten the downfall of that system. As Lenin pointed out, we are living in the era of the transition from world capitalism to world Socialism. The path now being taken by the peoples of the Soviet Union, China, Czechoslovakia, Poland, Hungary, Romania, Bulgaria, Eastern Germany, and Albania, is the one which, before long, all the peoples of the world will be following. The everyday fight of the workers and their allies for peace, democracy, and better living conditions inevitably grows, under the leadership of the Communist Party, into the fight for Socialism.

The time lag in the acceptance of Socialism by the American working class is due principally to the historic factors that have temporarily facilitated relatively higher wage standards in this country than in other capitalist lands. Besides, the American bourgeoisie, wealthy beyond any other capitalist class, has, with its imperialist super-profits, been able to corrupt, with special wage concessions, the skilled workers, and during the post-war boom, also some sections of the semi-skilled. This is what Engels called the "bourgeoisification" of the workers. But this is only a temporary situation; inexorably capitalism works for the worsening of the economic conditions of the toiling masses to the point of unbearability.

THE QUESTION OF SOCIALISM

Socialism eliminates the internal contradictions sentencing the world capitalist system to historic death. Under Socialism the grip of the monopolists and big landowners upon the nation's life processes is finally broken, and political power rests in the hands of the workers and their allies. For the first time there is truly a government of, by, and for the people, and the peril of fascist reaction is forever liquidated. The major means of social production—the industries and the land, the banks, the transportation systems, and the main media of social culture—are owned and managed by the people. Exploitation of man by man is abolished, and with it the deep poverty for the many and the immense wealth for a few that have cursed the world for centuries. Mass living standards drastically improve. The oppressed peoples of the earth, freed of every trace of colonialism, march swiftly to new independence, freedom, and prosperity. The great evil, war, will finally be brought to an end, for free Socialist peoples have no reason to wage war upon each other.

Planned production under Socialism puts an end to the recurring economic crises and to the chronic competitive chaos of capitalism; it breaks all the shackles that monopoly capitalism has riveted upon production. Socialism is a new era of unparalleled freedom for women and youth, of security for the sick and aged. Education and culture are at last at the disposal of the masses, and mankind rapidly proceeds to new heights of mental, physical and cultural development. Although obscured from the capitalist world by a thick curtain of bourgeois lies, this great social advance is now marching ahead with seven-league boots in the Soviet Union, People's China, and the European People's Democracies.

The American people will eventually establish Socialism. They will do this when, by the relentless workings of the general crisis of capitalism in which the United States is enmeshed, a majority of them come to realize the impossibility of continuing under that obsolete system. Their present capitalist illusions will collapse in the face of this growing reality, and they will surely take steps to abolish capitalism and to initiate Socialism. The Socialism they will build will not follow some long-planned blueprint, but it will be in line with American traditions and with concrete American economic and political conditions.

The masses of the people of the United States will gain immensely when they establish Socialism in this country. At present the capitalists are robbing the American people of at least $100 billion a year, in the manifold forms of interest, rent, and profit. They perform no useful role, reaping their fabulous incomes merely for owning—a parasitic function. Under Socialism these sums would be used to improve living and cultural standards. Defenders of the capitalist system allege that these billions find their way back into the pockets of the people, not into those of the capitalists. They emphatically declare that the people, in fact, own the industrial system of the United States. But all this is a brazen lie; capitalism is organized robbery of the producing masses, and the people own little or nothing. In reality, only one individual in 16 (and hardly any Negroes whatever) owns any industrial stocks at all,[6] and the three percent of the people with incomes of $10,000 or more per year "may own as much as four-fifths of the total. . . . The 79 percent in the under $5,000 earnings class own next to nothing."[7] According to the Bureau of Labor Statistics, the annual cost of living for an average family was about $4,160, but the income of 64 percent of all families fell below this figure.[8]

Besides putting a halt to this gigantic capitalist robbery of the people, Socialism in the United States will also cancel out the reactionary political domination exercised by the big monopolists of this country. The United States has the form of a democracy, but through their ownership and control of the industries, the press, the schools, the armed forces, the churches, and all other key institutions, the capitalists are able in election after election to fill up the national, state, and local governments with their agents. Our government is a dictatorship of monopoly capital, of Wall Street.

The undemocratic character of the Federal government stands out like a mountain. Congress is made up chiefly of capitalists, corporation lawyers, big farmers, and upper middle class people. The workers and poor farmers, who comprise the majority of the American people, have only a handful of representatives. Women, who constitute 52 percent of the population, are represented by only a baker's dozen of their number, and the Negro people, forming 10 percent of the entire population, have but two congressmen. The state and city governments throughout the country represent a similar undemocratic picture. Socialism will radically change all this by placing the power in the hands of the democratic masses—the working class, the Negro people, the poor farmers, and the professionals.

Socialism, by abolishing economic crises, will also forever wipe out mass unemployment, that deadly menace in the life of the working class. It will do away, too, with the economic uncertainty of the sick and aged, which is now a never-ending worry to the toiling masses. It will open new fields of cultural development to the people. A Socialist United States, with its tremendous resources and productive power, will develop new high levels of freedom, prosperity, and culture such as are now hardly dreamed of by the American toiling millions.

The Negro people will be the greatest gainers under Socialism, by the very token that they are the worst sufferers under capitalism. This fact is amply demonstrated by the wonderful progress made in the Soviet Union by the many peoples who were once deeply oppressed under tsarism. Lynching, Jim Crow, job discrimination, and all the other bitter abuses that the Negro people have had to contend with for so long, will be quite impossible in a Socialist regime. Negro women especially, the most exploited and oppressed group in our country, will truly be emancipated. The Negro people will be free in a free country for the first time in their long and tragic history in the Western hemisphere.

50. Negro National Liberation

The national question, as it applies to oppressed peoples, is always a complex one, presenting many different aspects and facets in different countries. But nowhere is it so unique and complicated as in the case of the American Negro people. The situation of the Negroes of this country, who are fighting against national oppression, is obviously very different from that of the peoples of Korea, Indo-China, Malaya, and many other oppressed peoples who are battling their way toward national liberation and independence. Therefore, in analyzing the position of any oppressed nation, in proceeding within the framework of Leninist-Stalinist principles on the national question, it is of basic importance to give full consideration to the specific national characteristics of the people involved—in this instance the American Negro people.

In the United States the national liberation movement of the Negro people displays many special features in its history, its composition, and its general social relationships. Among these specific characteristics are the following facts: Originally the Negro people were forcibly transported to this country from Africa; they experienced chattel slavery for two and a half centuries; the great revolutionary Civil War was fought to free them; they speak the same language as their oppressors; white chauvinism is notoriously virulent in the United States; the Negro people are situated in the midst of the oppressor nation—not thousands of miles away, as is often the case; and this oppressor nation, which has extensive democratic traditions, is the most powerful capitalist state in the world. Hence, in order to understand the character and course of the national liberation movement of the Negro people of the United States, it is indispensable that these and other specifically American conditions be borne carefully and constantly in mind.

THE REALIZATION OF NEGRO NATIONAL LIBERATION

Theoretically, it is possible for the Negro people to win national liberation, including the right of self-determination and secession, within the framework of the American capitalist system. Theirs is a revolutionary bourgeois-democratic movement. Historically, national liberation revolutions have not generally been anti-capitalist. During the past two centuries many oppressed peoples, including our own, have succeeded in breaking loose from oppressing nations and in setting up independent states, without themselves abolishing capitalism as such. Indeed, such revolutions have formed a basic part of the building of the world capitalist system.[1]

However, in this period of imperialism and of the deepening crisis of the world capitalist system, the historic nation-making process is being fundamentally modified. Newly born nations during these years —such as India, Burma, Ceylon, etc.—are able, in the face of aggressive imperialism, to win only a degree of real national independence. Indeed, the national independence of old established nations, as in Latin America, and even of great capitalist empires, as Britain, France, Germany, and Japan, is being seriously infringed upon and limited by super-aggressive Wall Street imperialism. More and more, therefore, the matter of the national liberation of oppressed peoples is becoming bound up with the general question of Socialism, in the shape of either their domestic orientation, or close collaboration with the Socialist nations of the world, or both. All this emphasizes Lenin's statement that "It is impossible, under capitalism, to abolish national (or any political) oppression."[2] This elementary fact has basic importance for the liberation struggle of the American Negro people.

The American Negro people are faced by very powerful oppressors who are determined to keep them deep under super-exploitation. They have to fight stubbornly and with all possible outside aid to win even the most elementary human rights, such as the right to work in industry, to be paid equal wages, to vote, to get an education, to enjoy bodily safety from lynching, and to avoid being insulted at every turn by outrageous Jim Crow restrictions. Hence, it requires but little imagination to conceive of the stubborn resistance they will encounter, and their consequent urgent need of allies, when the Negro national liberation movement tackles the more fundamental aspects of the problem, including the securing of land in the South, the systematic unfoldment of a Negro national economy, and the establishment of the Negro people's political rights as a nation.

It is one of the specific American conditions that, because of the geographical location of the Negro people and their deep integration in American life, they have very powerful white working class and other allies at hand.

Negro national liberation cannot be the work of the Negro people alone; it can be achieved only in close collaboration with the broad labor and progressive movement and with the support of world democratic forces. By the same token, the white workers and other democratic strata of the country imperatively require the co-operation of the broad masses of the Negro people, who constitute one of the most powerful progressive currents in our national life, in the fight for both their immediate and ultimate objectives. All this emphasizes the basic need for Negro-white unity and combatting white chauvinism and all other forces tending to impair or prevent this unity.

Experience has amply demonstrated that to carry on a successful struggle against even such glaring evils as lynching, disfranchisement, and the indignities of Jim Crow, the Negro people require a high degree of organization, militancy, and consciousness on their own part and also on that of their white allies.. Although the national liberation movement does not, as such, fight for Socialism, it is pretty safe to conclude that when it comes to the breaking up of the big Southern plantations, to the free distribution of the land to the Negroes and poor whites, and to the establishment of the Negro people's right to self-determination, these basic demands can be won only by a Negro-white coalition movement which has either established a People's Front government or a People's Democracy, or at least is developing a definite orientation toward Socialism. Certain it is, in any event, that the Negro people can achieve national liberation in the fullest sense of the word—with the complete obliteration of every form of Jim Crow—solely under a Socialist regime. The complete solution of the national question is possible only under Socialism.[3]

ON THE RIGHT OF NATIONAL SELF-DETERMINATION

In chapter 43 and elsewhere, we have indicated the fact that the right of self-determination belongs to all oppressed nations, including the American Negro nation. We have also pointed out that the slogan of self-determination has not yet come to be widely accepted by the American Negro people for a variety of reasons, among which are the relative youth of the Negro nation, confusions regarding such concepts as "race" and "caste," illusions about automatic absorption into the American people as a whole, belief that in any event an organized American Negro state would be impossible. As Davis says, "The Negro people would have reached a higher level of maturity as a nation, had their growth not been partially stunted by the extreme rigors and double oppression of the Jim Crow system."[4] The Negro people will surely gain a clearer national consciousness and a definite perspective of national development during the course of this struggle.

As we have said earlier, one of the most deep-seated objections to the concept of nation as applied to the American Negro people is the notion that self-determination necessarily implies secession. But Stalin long ago clarified this misconception: "A nation has the right to arrange its life on autonomous lines. It even has the right to secede. But this does not mean that it should do so under all circumstances, that autonomy, or separation, will everywhere and always be advantageous for a nation, for the majority of its population, for the toiling strata."[5] It is within the province of the nation in question, therefore, to decide for itself whether or not it wants actual independence, autonomy, federation or some other relationship with other nations. The basic thing to understand in the matter is that, with the advance of the class struggle and the growth of domestic and world democracy, the right to make such a decision, if it so chooses, will be conceded to the Negro people. It is a practical certainty that under Socialism, if not before, the Negro people as such will freely arrange their national contacts with surrounding peoples. For the right of national self-determination will extend far into the period of Socialism, as the U.S.S.R. demonstrates.

Then there is the false argument that the very concept of an organized Negro nation is impossible, because of the practical problems involved in winning the legal right of self-determination, in establishing the nation's boundaries, in building a self-sustaining industry, and in financing the regime.[6] Under present monopoly capitalist rule, these specific American difficulties are indeed formidable. But with a powerful, advancing People's Front or People's Democracy movement and with the Negro people demanding self-determination, such difficulties would rapidly fade in importance, and under Socialism they would have no validity whatever. In the long run, the national status of the Negro people is not going to be determined by bourgeois legalism and political reaction, but by the Negro people themselves in agreement with their white allies.

In assaying the substance and forms of self-determination, the significance of the steadily declining area of Negro majority in the Black Belt of the South (see Chapter 43) must also be considered. This decline is caused by the influx of whites into these regions and by the migration of Negroes northward and into Southern urban communities. The conclusion to be drawn from this situation is not that the right of self-determination for the Negro nation is thereby invalidated, as opponents assert, but that more extensive territorial reorganization will be necessary when the time comes and the Negro people determine to exercise this basic right. With the development of a powerful democratic coalition movement in this country and the rise of national sentiment among the Negro people, it may well be that there will be tendencies to reverse the current migrations and to reassemble in the South, which has been their homeland for so many generations, much as happened, under special conditions, in Pakistan. As Stalin says sagely, it is not the task of the proletariat to gather dispersed peoples together into nations,[7] but this does not mean that the Communist Party would oppose such a possible eventual regrouping movement on the part of the American Negro people.

The present Negro migration northward and toward the Southern cities, with the consequent loss of majority status in many Black Belt counties, confronts the Negro people and their political allies with the urgent necessity of raising and stressing the demand for political proportional representation for Negroes. This may develop into forms of self-determination. There is far too much of a tendency now to accept mere token representation for Negroes, whereas the Negro people are obviously entitled to representation in all elective and appointive political bodies according to their numerical strength in the community, North as well as South. Sometimes this demand for proportional representation may be advanced in concrete proposals, and sometimes only as a general principle to be applied. But whatever the form in which it is to be achieved, political proportional representation for Negroes should be vigorously insisted upon.

NATIONAL INTEGRATION

The national liberation movement fights for the full integration of the Negro people into American life.[8] This means that the Negro must be accorded citizenship in the most complete sense of the word, with full economic, political, social, and cultural equality. Every Jim Crow barrier, however brutal or subtle, direct or implied, must be completely broken down and penalties established for the practice of white chauvinism. Negroes must be given the most complete freedom and equality with regard to education, residence, marriage, the vote, jobs in industry, leadership in trade unions, the government services, sports, the arts, business and industrial activities, the professions, veterans' organizations, scientific societies, and every other grouping and form of activity in the United States. For the first time in their long and tragic history, the Negro people must receive the full protection of the Bill of Rights.

This complete integration of the Negro people into the broad stream of American life in no way contradicts their developing nationhood, or the principle of self-determination as applied to them. On the contrary, full Negro national development, under specific American conditions, demands such integration. The actual integration of the Negro masses into all American rights, activities, and institutions on the basis of full equality, is different in principle from the snail-pace gradualist, phony "integration" being achieved by the Negro petty bourgeois "elite" favored by the ruling white capitalist class. Such false integration, beneficial to only a few individuals, cannot pass beyond the walls of the Jim Crow system, and it is designed to keep the Negro masses locked within that social prison. What is needed is not the semi-integration of a few compromising leaders, but the destruction, root and branch, of the whole Jim Crow system and the integration socially of the entire Negro people.

The history of the Negro people proves that such rights and integration as they have achieved—emancipation, limited franchise, entry into industry, etc.—have been won only after the hardest struggle. So it will continue to be. On their way to complete emancipation from the chains and fetters of the Jim Crow system, the Negro people will need all their own strength as well as that of their white allies. This fact clearly implies that while militantly insisting upon the right to participate in all the predominantly white organizations, they must maintain and strengthen all their own national organizations, which they have built so laboriously through decades of struggle—the Negro press, the N.A.A.C.P., the Negro National Labor Council, fraternal organizations, business institutions,* and others. Those elements, Negro and white—the Whites, Schuylers, Tobiases, Browders, Reuthers, *et al.*—who preach to the Negro masses that their integration is now taking place automatically and that there is no need for real

---

* This is a question primarily of demanding the removal of all restrictions on Negro business. The Negro workers have no obligation, however, to support the "Buy Black" movement, at the expense of paying higher prices and getting poorer goods and services.

struggle, are doing the greatest harm to the cause of the Negro people.

Although the Negro masses, in their long political struggle, have found it necessary to build many national organizations—the Negro church, press, fraternal organizations—this trend must be modified in certain situations. When, for example, the working class and its allies organize a broad mass political party in this country, the Negro people should form one of the great foundation pillars of this party rather than establish a separate party of their own. This course is determined by specific American conditions. Such a mass party, however, should have Negro Commissions and activities, from top to bottom, to reflect the special problems of the Negro people. There would still be a definite place, however, for such independent organizations as the N.A.A.C.P. (and those of a more progressive character) to carry on general political work for the specific national demands of the Negro people.

In this respect the Communist Party gives a correct lead for labor and the coalition movement. In line with the principles of proletarian internationalism, the Party is composed of a joint membership of Negroes and whites, with Negroes freely occupying posts of the highest leadership and responsibility. At the same time, throughout its structure, it has Negro commissions to attend to specific Negro issues and problems. "To organize a Party only of Negroes would divide the Negro and white working class and defeat the fight for national liberation."[9]

In the trade union field there is now also relatively little need for building separate Negro unions, as there was, for instance, in the days of the Colored National Labor Union and during the later periods of the grossest Jim Crow and segregation in the A.F. of L. craft unions. Now the main requirement is full Negro participation in the existing unions. This line also is determined by the specific American situation. The unions, however, must necessarily pay direct attention to specific Negro problems in their general political activities, and in their contracts with employers, through a network of Negro commissions—local, state, and national. Some unions, notably the progressive independent unions, have gone far in this direction, although they still have many shortcomings.

There is also a distinct need for such an organization as the National Negro Labor Council in the realm of trade unionism, even as there is for a more progressive N.A.A.C.P. in the field of politics. The N.L.C., better than any official body could do, serves to keep the Negro question, in all its national and class significance, squarely before the whole labor and progressive movement. This is an indispensable function. It is also a strong factor in the struggle for Negro rights and for working class leadership in this fight.

The imperative need for joint Negro-white unity in the political and trade union fields raises sharply the question of Negro leadership. In view of the wide prevalence of white chauvinist moods among the masses and their white leaders, this matter cannot be left to chance. If so, the Negro will get very much the worst of it, as is now the case. In the mass unions and parties, therefore, special concern must be shown for this matter of leadership, both by Negroes themselves and by the most advanced white workers. There must be insistence that Negroes be accorded their full measure of leadership. Here the principle of proportional representation, although not put forward formally, must be kept in mind. Token leadership for Negroes, as is now the rule, is entirely inadequate. Those opportunists—Walter Reuther, for example—who claim that specific insistence upon Negro leadership as such is "Jim Crow in reverse," are only using this tricky sophistry to keep Negroes altogether out of the top leadership, as is done in the Auto Workers Union and in scores of other labor organizations.

On this question, a genuine fraternal spirit of equality and mutual confidence must be cultivated among Negro and white workers. All bourgeois nonsense to the effect that whites cannot lead Negroes, and vice versa, must be given short shrift. The white worker must accept his Negro brother in the fullest understanding that he is quite as capable and eligible as himself, or as any other white, to stand at the head of the Communist Party, of the A.F. of L., the C.I.O., or the United States Government.

Historically, the Negro people have placed varying stress and hopes upon the question of integration. In the Reconstruction period after the Civil War, Frederick Douglass and other Negro leaders were strong advocates of complete integration, on the basis that the Negro people had won the Emancipation Proclamation and the Thirteenth, Fourteenth, and Fifteenth Amendments. But after the sell-out of the Negro by the Republican Party in 1876 and during the next half century of lynch terror and deep oppression, Negro hopes waned in this respect and separatist ideas flourished, as strikingly represented by the activities of Booker T. Washington and Marcus M. Garvey. However, under the impact of the New Deal, the fight against fascism in World War II, the pressure of revolutionary international forces, Communist Party influence, and an awakening working class in this country, the process of mass integration, pushed militantly by the Negro people, has now taken on greater vigor with better prospects of success than ever before. The integration now beginning to be achieved will not be merely the "integration" of a small, favored petty-bourgeois group of Negro "elite," but of the broad Negro masses, whose true spokesmen are such left-wing and Communist leaders as W. E. B. Du Bois, Paul Robeson, Benjamin J. Davis, Jr., Henry Winston, Pettis Perry, Claudia Jones, W. L. Patterson, and others.

NATIONAL AMALGAMATION

The allegation that there is a natural sexual antipathy between Negroes and whites is a hypocritical lie. The fact is that, despite all the blue-nose preaching and taboos to the contrary, the three great ethnic groups, or races of Indians, Negroes, and whites, have widely intermingled ever since Columbus landed on San Salvador. The living proof of this racial amalgamation is the large number of people of mixed descent throughout the hemisphere. In several countries of Latin America, *mestizos* (part Indian, part white) form the majority of the population; in Panama there are 61 percent; Chile, 65 percent; Nicaragua, 70 percent; Venezuela, 70 percent; El Salvador, 77 percent; Honduras, 85 percent; and Paraguay 92 percent.[10] Mulattoes (part Negro, part white) also form large percentages of the populations of Brazil and various of the West Indian islands.

Widespread racial intermixture of whites and Negroes has also gone on in the United States ever since the earliest colonial times, despite ferocious prohibitions against intermarriage. One of the most disgraceful of all the aspects of race relations in this country has been that white fathers in slavery times left their children in bondage and since "emancipation" have exposed them to the whips and scorpions of the savage Jim Crow system. Du Bois says that less than 25 percent[11] of the Negro people are of unmixed African descent, and Herskovits pinpoints the figure at 22 percent.[12]

In many countries where the Negroes are in large majority, the small minority of white rulers, to broaden out their very narrow base, give a somewhat favored status to Mulattoes. This scheme of building the Mulattoes into a barricade against the great mass of Negroes was applied in various islands of the West Indies, in French Africa, and in early days, in the Union of South Africa. But in the United States, where the Negroes never commanded large population majorities over wide areas, the planters did not feel the same urgent need to widen their social base. Hence they never cultivated the Mulattoes, politically. They did, however, tend to favor them to a certain extent as house servants and mechanics under slavery, and in some cases made it somewhat easier for them to buy their way out of slavery.[13] Today the Mulatto, although still relatively favored by capitalism, is essentially held in the iron clasp of the Jim Crow system—a situation which makes for powerful solidarity among the widest ranks of the Negro people.

As Lenin points out many times, the ultimate revolutionary course of national development leads to the amalgamation of nations. He speaks of the "amalgamation of all nations."[14] This amalgamation of nations can take place fully only under Socialism. The sole "amalgamation" which capitalism can attempt is conquering, enslaving, and crippling colonial peoples. Says Stalin, "National distrust, national segregation, national enmity, and national conflict are, of course, stimulated and fostered not by some 'innate' sentiment of national animosity, but by the striving of imperialism to subjugate other nations and by the fear inspired in these nations by the menace of national enslavement."[15] Imperialism, says Kammari, "can 'unite' nations only by annexations and colonial conquests, which inevitably leads to a struggle of the oppressed nations against the violent forms of imperialist 'amalgamation' of nations, leads to the break-up of multi-national colonial powers."[16]

National amalgamation is one of the basic social tasks to be accomplished by Socialism. Lenin thus describes it in principle: "The aim of Socialism is not only to abolish the present division of mankind into small states and all national isolation; not only to bring the nations closer to each other, but also to merge them." And he goes on to explain that this can happen only after Socialism has been established: "Just as mankind can achieve the abolition of classes only by passing through the transition period of the dictatorship of the oppressed class, so mankind can achieve the inevitable merging of nations only by passing through the transition period of complete liberation of all the oppressed nations, i.e., of their freedom to secede."[17]

Under specific American conditions, the ultimate amalgamation of the Negro nation with the American nation as a whole—an eventuality greatly stimulated by the processes of national integration and self-determination described above—would imply the breaking down of all racial barriers. A Socialism with taboos and bans against racial intermarriage is unthinkable. Freedom would be established in this respect, as in all others. Bourgeois contentions that racial mixtures constitute social retrogression are utter nonsense. The reality is that one of the great dynamic forces in human evolution has been precisely the intermingling of nations, with their rich variety of institutions, cultures, and peoples.

Thus we come to the end of our story, with the Negro people now battling to win even the most elementary human rights. Their history in this country is that of three and a half centuries of heart-breaking struggle against the worst forms of chattel slavery, peonage, capitalist exploitation, social ostracism, and lynch terror. They have made splendid headway in the face of desperate difficulties. And now the whole horizon begins to brighten before them. The complete victory of the Negro national liberation movement is on the agenda of history. Nor will it be long, as measured against their bitter centuries of persecution, before Negro men and women will walk in our country, free in every sense of the word. This perspective of ultimate emancipation now still has to be courageously fought for, shoulder to shoulder with the white workers, who are also fighting to defend peace, democracy, and living standards and for their own ultimate emancipation. The fate of both groups is inseparably bound together. Victory is historically assured. The breaking down of the capitalist system and the growth of Socialism, which constitute the decisive political processes now taking place in the world, will bring final emancipation to all the oppressed of the earth.

REFERENCES

Chapter 1

1 *Encyclopedia Britannica,* 1952, Vol. 1, pp. 292-99, Chicago
2 John Hope Franklin, *From Slavery to Freedom,* p. 36, New York, 1947
3 Maurice Delafosse, *The Negroes in Africa,* p. 280, Washington, D. C., 1931
4 Diedrich Herman Westermann, *The African Today and Tomorrow,* p. 21, London, 1939
5 Franklin, *From Slavery to Freedom,* p. 8
6 W. E. Burghardt Du Bois, *The World and Africa,* p. 106, New York, 1947
7 A. Meier, *The Emergence of Negro Nationalism,* p. 54, MS.
8 John Howard Lawson, *The Hidden Heritage,* p. 206, New York, 1950
9 Carter G. Woodson, *The Negro in our History,* p. 8, Washington, D. C., 1947
10 *Encyclopedia Britannica,* Vol. 1, p. 305
11 Franklin, *From Slavery to Freedom,* p. 16
12 Woodson, *The Negro in Our History,* pp. 39-40
13 Delafosse, *The Negroes in Africa,* p. 260
14 Du Bois, *The World and Africa,* p. 155
15 *New York Times,* May 17, 1953
16 Lewis H. Morgan, *Ancient Society,* Chicago, 1907
17 Du Bois, *The World and Africa,* p. 163
18 M. F. Ashley Montagu, *Man's Most Dangerous Myth: The Fallacy of Race,* p. 62, New York, 1942
19 Delafosse, *The Negroes in Africa,* p. 162
20 *Ibid.,* p. 146
21 *New York Times,* May 24, 1953
22 W. E. Burghardt Du Bois, *Black Folk, Then and Now,* p. 106, New York, 1939
23 Frederick Engels, *Anti-Duehring,* p. 202, New York, 1939
24 *Encyclopedia Britannica,* Vol. 4, No. 745
25 Parker Thomas Moon, *Imperialism and World Politics,* p. 76, New York, 1928
26 V. I. Lenin, *Imperialism, The Highest Stage of Capitalism,* pp. 80, 63, New York, 1933
27 Moon, *Imperialism and World Politics,* p. 148
28 Du Bois, *The World and Africa,* p. 161
29 Walter Miller Macmillan, *Africa Emergent,* pp. 156-63, London, 1938
30 Raymond Leslie Buell, *The Native Problem in Africa,* Vol. I, pp. 163-69, New York, 1928
31 Lamar Middleton, *The Rape of Africa,* p. 167, New York, 1936
32 Douglas G. Wolton, *Whither South Africa,* pp. 13-27, London, 1947

Chapter 2

1 Maurice R. Davie, *Negroes in American Society,* pp. 3-4, New York, 1949
2 John La Farge, *The Race Question and the Negro,* p. 292, New York, 1943
3 Franklin, *From Slavery to Freedom,* p. 49
4 Davie, *Negroes in American History,* p. 7
5 Katherine Coman, *The Industrial History of the United States,* p. 78, New York, 1918
6 Royal Institute of International Affairs, *The Republics of South America,* Oxford, 1937
7 Du Bois, *The World and Africa,* p. 54
8 Ralph Korngold, *Citizen Toussaint,* p. 11, Boston, 1944

568 REFERENCES

9 Theodore Canot, *Adventures of an African Slaver*, p. 107, New York, 1928
10 Elizabeth Donnan, *Documents Illustrative of the History of the Slave Trade in America*, Vol. 2, p. 642, Washington, D. C., 1931
11 C. A. Macinnes, *England and Slavery*, p. 136, Bristol, 1934
12 Karl Marx, *Capital*, Vol. I, p. 775, New York, 1947
13 Karl Marx, *Poverty of Philosophy*, p. 94, New York, 1935
14 Marx, *Capital*, Vol. I, pp. 784-85
15 Melville J. Herskovits, *The Myth of the Negro Past*, p. 38, New York, 1941
16 Franklin, *From Slavery to Freedom*, p. 54
17 *Ibid.*, p. 58
18 Donnan, *Documents Illustrative of the History of the Slave Trade in America*, Vol. 2, p. 592
19 Ulrich Bonnell Phillips, *American Negro Slavery*, p. 34, New York, 1918
20 Canot, *Adventures of an African Slaver*, p. XV
21 George Francis Dow, *Slave Ships and Slaving*, p. 212, Salem, 1927
22 *Ibid.*, pp. XXVIII-XXXV
23 Donnan, *Documents Illustrative of the History of the Slave Trade in America*, Vol. 2, p. 555
24 *Ibid.*, Vol. I, p. 406
25 *Journal of Negro History*, July, 1937, Washington, D. C.

Chapter 3

1 Edward C. Kirkland, *A History of American Economic Life*, p. 68, New York, 1933
2 Emory Q. Hawk, *Economic History of the South*, p. 75, New York, 1934
3 Carrol D. Wright, *Industrial Evolution of the United States*, p. 52, New York, 1895
4 Hawk, *Economic History of the South*, p. 263
5 *Ibid.*, p. 81
6 Macinnes, *England and Slavery*, p. 21
7 Kirkland, *A History of American Economic Life*, p. 73
8 Charles A. and Mary R. Beard, *The Rise of American Civilization*, Vol. I, pp. 44-45, New York, 1942
9 Richard Brandon Morris, *Government and Labor in Early America*, p. 321, New York, 1946
10 Lawson, *Our Hidden Heritage*, p. 200
11 J. Saunders Redding, *They Came in Chains*, p. 24, New York, 1950
12 Herbert M. Morais, *The Struggle for American Freedom*, p. 101, New York, 1949
13 Anthony Bimba, *History of the American Working Class*, p. 115, New York, 1927
14 Lorenzo Johnson Greene, *The Negro in Colonial New England*, p. 74, New York, 1942
15 Phillips, *American Negro Slavery*, p. 33
16 Greene, *The Negro in Colonial New England*, pp. 316-17
17 W. E. Burghardt Du Bois, *Suppression of the African Slave Trade*, p. 4, New York, 1896
18 Elizabeth Lawson, *History of the American Negro People*, mimeo, pp. 8-9, New York, 1939
19 Du Bois, *Suppression of the African Slave Trade*, p. 6
20 Woodson, *The Negro in Our History*, p. 87
21 Joseph Dorfman, *The Economic Mind in American Civilization*, Vol. 1, p. 86, New York, 1946
22 Greene, *The Negro in Colonial New England*, p. 260
23 Karl Marx, *Capital*, Vol. III, p. 934, Chicago, 1909

24 Karl Marx, *Theories of Surplus Value*, Vol. II (German edition), p. 72

25 Marx, *Capital*, Vol. I, p. 785

26 Eric Burt, *MS.*

27 Morais, *The Struggle for American Freedom*, p. 135

28 Benjamin Brawley, *A Short History of the American Negro*, p. 18, New York, 1944

29 Herskovits, *The Myth of the Negro Past*, p. 87

30 Herbert Aptheker, *American Negro Slave Revolts*, pp. 162-208, New York, 1943

31 Du Bois, *The World and Africa*, pp. 61-62

32 William Z. Foster, *Outline Political History of the Americas*, p. 85, New York, 1951

33 Korngold, *Citizen Toussaint*

Chapter 4

1 Morais, *The Struggle for American Freedom*, p. 179

2 Louis M. Hacker, *The Triumph of American Capitalism*, pp. 145-58, New York, 1940

3 (The) Beards, *The Rise of American Civilization*, Vol. I, p. 233

4 Lawson, *History of the American Negro People*, pp. 12-13

5 Franklin, *From Slavery to Freedom*, p. 131

6 Herbert Aptheker, *The Negro in the American Revolution*, p. 20, New York, 1940

7 Jack Hardy, *The First American Revolution*, pp. 43-44, New York, 1937

8 Franklin, *From Slavery to Freedom*, p. 132

9 Redding, *They Came in Chains*, p. 42

10 Aptheker, *The Negro in the American Revolution*, pp. 27-42

11 Lawson, *History of the American Negro People*, p. 10

12 Morais, *The Struggle for American Freedom*, p. 229

13 Herbert Aptheker, *A Documentary History of the Negro People in the United States*, p. 11, New York, 1951

14 Monroe N. Work, ed., *The Negro Year Book, 1931-1932*, Tuskegee; Thomas E. Drake, *Quakers and Slavery in America*, New Haven, 1950

15 John A. Schuts, *Journal of Negro History*, October, 1945

16 Work, *The Negro Year Book, 1931-1932*

17 Philip S. Foner, *The Life and Writings of Frederick Douglass*, Vol. II, p. 423, New York, 1950

18 James Ford Rhodes, *History of the United States*, Vol. I, p. 21, New York, 1907

19 Dorfman, *The Economic Mind in American Civilization*, Vol. 1, pp. 182-83

20 V. I. Lenin, *A Letter to American Workers*, p. 9, New York, 1934

21 Hacker, *The Triumph of American Capitalism*, p. 186

22 Vernon Louis Parrington, *Main Currents in American Thought*, Vol. I, p. 300, New York, 1927

23 *The Federalist*, Feb. 12, 1788, New York, 1937

24 (The) Beards, *The Rise of American Civilization*, Vol. I, p. 320

25 J. B. McMaster, *History of the People of the United States*, Vol. II, p. 356, New York, 1895

Chapter 5

1 (The) Beards, *The Rise of American Civilization*, Vol. I, p. 380

2 Parrington, *Main Currents in American Thought*, Vol. I, p. 322

3 Phillips, *American Negro Slavery*, pp. 118-20

4 Horace Greeley, *The American Conflict*, Vol. I, p. 39, Hartford, 1869

5 Henry Steele Commager, *Documents of American History*, Vol. I, p. 132, New York, 1948

6 W. E. Burghardt Du Bois, *Black Reconstruction*, pp. 7-8, New York, 1935
7 McMaster, *History of the People of the United States*, Vol. V, p. 184
8 Morris, *Government and Labor in Early America*, p. 183
9 Henry Wilson, *The Rise and Fall of the Slave Power in America*, Vol. I, pp. 24-25, New York, 1872
10 Drake, *Quakers and Slavery in America*, p. 79
11 Brawley, *A Short History of the American Negro*, p. 43
12 Aptheker, *Documentary History*, p, 17
13 *Ibid.*, pp. 32-35
14 Shirley Graham, *Your Most Humble Servant*, New York, 1947
15 Wilson, *The Rise and Fall of the Slave Power in America*, Vol. I, p. 29
16 Aptheker, *American Negro Slave Revolts*, p. 24 *ff*
17 Korngold, *Citizen Toussaint*; Foster, *Outline Political History of the Americas*, pp. 134-37

Chapter 6

1 Commager, *Documents of American History*, Vol. I, p. 197
2 Morais, *The Struggle for American Freedom*, p. 229
3 Ernest Ludlow Bogart, *Economic History of the United States*, p. 118, New York, 1908
4 Helen D. Hill, *George Mason, Constitutionalist*, pp. 230-31, Cambridge, 1938
5 McMaster, *History of the People of the United States*, Vol. III, p. 515
6 *Ibid.*, p. 521
7 *Encyclopedia Brittanica*, Vol. 20, pp. 778 *ff*
8 Eric Williams, *Capitalism and Slavery*, p. 182, Chapel Hill, 1944
9 Macinnes, *England and Slavery*
10 Dow, *Slave Ships and Slaving*, p. 273
11 Du Bois, *Suppression of the African Slave Trade*, p. 162
12 Walter W. Jennings, *History of Economic Progress in the United States*, p. 334, New York, 1926
13 *Encyclopedia Britannica*, Vol. 20, p. 782
14 Rhodes, *History of the United States*, Vol. I, p. 29
15 McMaster, *History of the People of the United States*, Vol. VII, p. 279
16 Aptheker, *American Negro Slave Revolts*, p. 91
17 Redding, *They Came in Chains*, p. 63
18 Woodson, *The Negro in Our History*, p. 200
19 *Ibid.*, p. 201

Chapter 7

1 Jennings, *History of Economic Progress in the United States*, p. 140
2 Phillips, *American Negro Slavery*, p. 157
3 Aptheker, *American Negro Slave Revolts*, p. 238
4 U.S. Department of Commerce, *Historical Statistics of the United States, 1789-1945*, pp. 108-109, Washington, D. C., 1949
5 U.S. Department of Agriculture, *Statistics on Cotton and Related Data*, p. 5, Washington, D. C., 1951
6 Herbert Aptheker, *Negro Slave Revolts in the United States, 1521-1860*, p. 4, New York, 1939
7 Wright, *Industrial Evolution of the United States*, p. 147
8 J. A. Cairnes, *The Slave Power*, p. 55, New York, 1862
9 Redding, *They Came in Chains*, p. 64
10 Marquis James, *The Life of Andrew Jackson*, p. 177, New York, 1940

11 Harold Underwood Faulkner, *Economic History of the United States*, p. 88, New York
12 Jennings, *History of Economic Progress in the United States*, p. 242

Chapter 8

1 Faulkner, *Economic History of the United States*, p. 137
2 Dorfman, *The Economic Mind in American Civilization*, Vol. I, p. 373
3 McMaster, *History of the People of the United States*, Vol. V, p. 188
4 Dorfman, *The Economic Mind in American Civilization*, Vol. I, p. 399
5 Commager, *Documents of American History*, Vol. I, p. 226
6 McMaster, *History of the People of the United States*, Vol. IV, p. 561
7 Brawley, *A Short History of the American Negro*, pp. 74-75
8 Woodson, *The Negro in Our History*, p. 286
9 Aptheker, *Documentary History*, p. 70
10 Woodson, *The Negro in Our History*, p. 283
11 Federal Edition, *The Works of Thomas Jefferson*, Vol. XII, p. 189, New York, 1904
12 Redding, *They Came in Chains*, p. 76
13 Korngold, *Citizen Toussaint*, p. 211
14 Brawley, *A Short History of the American Negro*, p. 75
15 Woodson, *The Negro in Our History*, p. 293

Chapter 9

1 Woodson, *The Negro in Our History*, p. 290
2 Aptheker, *Documentary History*; Bella Gross, *The Historical Development of the Negro People's Movement in the United States from 1817 to 1840*, p. 5 ff, New York, 1947
3 John W. Cromwell, *The Early Negro Convention Movement*, Washington, D. C., 1904
4 Redding, *They Came in Chains*, p. 144
5 Aptheker, *Masses and Mainstream*, February, 1952
6 Foner, *The Life and Writings of Frederick Douglass*, 4 Vols., New York, 1950-54
7 Gross, *The Historical Development of the Negro People's Movement*, p. 8
8 Frederick G. Detwiler, *The Negro Press in the United States*, Chicago, 1922
9 Redding, *They Came in Chains*, p. 91
10 Gross, *The Historical Development of the Negro People's Movement*, p. 45
11 Redding, *They Came in Chains*, p. 91
12 McMaster, *History of the People of the United States*, Vol. VI, p. 72
13 Aptheker, *Documentary History*, p. 90
14 Aptheker, *American Negro Slave Revolts*
15 Du Bois, *Black Folk, Then and Now*, p. 202
16 Herbert Aptheker, *To Be Free*, p. 16, New York, 1948
17 Brawley, *A Short History of the American Negro*, p. 57
18 McMaster, *History of the People of the United States*, Vol. IV, pp. 432-33
19 Aptheker, *American Negro Slave Revolts*, p. 266; see also pp. 264-65
20 Aptheker, *American Negro Slave Revolts*, pp. 268-72; Woodson, *The Negro in Our History*, pp. 178-80; McMaster, *History of the People of the United States*, Vol. V, pp. 199-202
21 Aptheker, *Documentary History*, pp. 119-25
22 Aptheker, *American Negro Slave Revolts*, p. 304
23 McMaster, *History of the People of the United States*, Vol. VI, p. 73
24 *Ibid.*, p. 74
25 J. Winston Coleman, *Slavery Times in Kentucky*, pp. 86-87, Chapel Hill, 1940
26 Aptheker, *American Negro Slave Revolts*, pp. 291-92; Woodson, *Negro in Our*

History, pp. 180-87; *Journal of Negro History*, Vol. 20, pp. 208-34, 1920

Chapter 10

1 Aptheker, *American Negro Slave Revolts*, p. 265
2 McMaster, *History of the People of the United States*, Vol. V, pp. 209-11
3 *Negro Year Book*, 1931-1932
4 Commager, *Documents of American History*, Vol. I, pp. 278-81
5 *The Liberator* (January 1, 1831), *Old South Leaflets*, Vol. IV, pp. 3-4, Boston
6 Foner, *The Life and Writings of Frederick Douglass*, Vol. II, p. 339
7 Herbert Aptheker, *The Negro in the Abolitionist Movement*, New York, 1941
8 Foner, *The Life and Writings of Frederick Douglass*, Vol. I, p. 33, New York, 1950
9 Aptheker, *Documentary History*, p. 108
10 John Jay Chapman, *William Lloyd Garrison*, p. 31, New York, 1913
11 Kirkland, *A History of American Economic Life*, p. 327
12 Herman Schlueter, *Lincoln, Labor and Slavery*, p. 38, New York, 1913
13 *Ibid.*, p. 39
14 *Old South Leaflets*, Vol. IV, p. 18
15 Ralph Korngold, *Two Firends of Man*, p. 362, Boston, 1950
16 Williams, *Capitalism and Slavery*, pp. 181-82
17 George D. H. Cole and Raymond Postgate, *The British People, 1746-1946*, New York, 1947

Chapter 11

1 U.S. Department of Commerce, *Historical Statistics of the United States*, p. 109
2 U.S. Census Bureau, *A Century of Population Growth, 1790-1900*, p. 133, Washington, D. C., 1909
3 Jennings, *History of Economic Progress in the United States*, p. 259
4 Dorfman, *The Economic Mind in American Civilization*, Vol. II, p. 629
5 (The) Beards, *The Rise of American Civilization*, Vol. I, p. 673
6 Jennings, *History of Economic Progress in the United States*, p. 286
7 David Duncan Wallace, *South Carolina, A Short History*, p. 408, Chapel Hill, 1951
8 James, *The Life of Andrew Jackson*, p. 703
9 (The) Beards, *The Rise of American Civilization*, Vol. I, p. 602
10 *Ibid.*, p. 606
11 Foner, *The Life and Writings of Frederick Douglass*, Vol. I, p. 292
12 Lawson, *History of the American Negro People*, pp. 20-21
13 Foster, *Outline Political History of the Americas*
14 (The) Beards, *The Rise of American Civilization*, Vol. I, p. 609

Chapter 12

1 Aptheker, *American Negro Slave Revolts*, pp. 325-39
2 Redding, *They Came in Chains*, p. 113
3 Aptheker, *Masses and Mainstream*, February, 1950
4 Lawson, *History of the American Negro People*, pp. 35-36
5 J. Albert Woodburn, *Political Parties and Party Problems in the United States*, p. 61, New York, 1914
6 Greeley, *The American Conflict*, Vol. I, p. 122
7 Korngold, *Two Friends of Man*, p. 92
8 W. S. Savage, *The Controversy Over the Delivery of Abolitionist Literature*, Washington, D. C., 1938

9 McMaster, *History of the People of the United States*, Vol. VI, pp. 291-96

10 *Ibid.*, p. 383

11 Foner, *The Life and Writings of Frederick Douglass*, Vol. I, pp. 35-38

12 E. Delorus Preston, "Genesis of the Underground Railroad," *Journal of Negro History*, p. 147, April, 1933

13 *Columbia Encyclopedia*, p. 1807, New York, 1947

14 Henrietta Buckmaster, *Let My People Go*, p. 108, New York, 1941

15 Redding, *They Came in Chains*, p. 98

16 William Still, *The Underground Railroad*, Philadelphia, 1872

17 Aptheker, *The Negro in the Abolitionist Movement*, p. 15

18 Earl Conrad, *Harriet Tubman*, New York, 1942

19 Elizabeth Cady Stanton, Susan B. Anthony, Matilda Joslyn Gage, *History of Women's Suffrage*, p. 52, Rochester, 1889

20 *William Lloyd Garrison*, By His Children, Vol. I, p. 413, New York, 1885

21 *Ibid.*, Vol. II, pp. 230-31

22 Foner, *The Life and Writings of Frederick Douglass*, Vol. II, p. 347

23 Jennings, *History of Economic Progress in the United States*, p. 244

24 *William Lloyd Garrison*, By His Children, Vol. II, p. 350

25 Foner, *The Life and Writings of Frederick Douglass*, Vol. I, p. 42

26 *Ibid.*, Vol. I, pp. 42-43; Wilson, *The History of the Rise and Fall of the Slave Power in America*, Vol. I, pp. 407-20

27 Aptheker, *Documentary History*, p. 192

28 Foner, *The Life and Writings of Frederick Douglass*, Vol. II, p. 416

29 *Ibid.*, p. 380

30 Aptheker, *To Be Free*, pp. 55-59

31 Herbert Aptheker, "Militant Abolitionism," *Journal of Negro History*, p. 463, October, 1941

32 Gross, *The Historical Development of the Negro People's Convention Movement*

Chapter 13

1 Charles Buxton Going, *David Wilmot, Free Soiler*, p. 98, New York, 1924

2 Greeley, *The American Conflict*, Vol. I, pp. 187-89

3 (The) Beards, *The Rise of American Civilization*, Vol. I, pp. 713-17

4 Commager, *Documents of American History*, Vol. I, pp. 319-23

5 Greeley, *The American Conflict*, Vol. I, pp. 208-209

6 (The) Beards, *The Rise of American Civilization*, Vol. II, p. 20

7 Elizabeth Lawson, *Lincoln's Third Party*, p. 18, New York, 1948

8 *Ibid.*, p. 19

9 Greeley, *The American Conflict*, Vol. I, p. 192

10 Foner, *The Life and Writings of Frederick Douglass*, Vol. I, pp. 368-69

11 Elizabeth Lawson, *Thaddeus Stevens*, New York, 1942

12 Thomas F. Woodly, *Thaddeus Stevens*, p. 217, Harrisburg, 1934

13 James Truslow Adams, *The Epic of America*, p. 275, Boston, 1932

Chapter 14

1 *Journal of Negro History*, p. 355, July, 1922

2 Marx, *Capital*, Vol. I, p. 219

3 Lawson, *History of the American Negro People*, p. 18

4 Rhodes, *History of the United States*, Vol. I, p. 308

5 Frederick Law Olmstead, *The Cotton Kingdom*, Vol. II, pp. 185-86, New York, 1861

6 Ulrich Bennell Phillips, *Life and Labor in the Old South*, p. 310, Boston, 1929

7 Gunnar Myrdal, *An American Dilemma*, Vol. I, p. 222, New York, 1944

8 Faulkner, *Economic History of the United States*, p. 24

9 Phillips, *American Negro Slavery*, p. 284

10 Aptheker, *American Negro Slave Revolts*, p. 123

11 James, *The Life of Andrew Jackson*, p. 349

12 Rhodes, *History of the United States*, Vol. I, p. 318

13 By Himself, *Life and Times of Frederick Douglass*, p. 45, Hartford, 1881

14 McMaster, *History of the People of the United States*, Vol. VII, p. 240

15 Lawson, *History of the American Negro People*, p. 18

16 Sterling A. Brown, Arthur P. Davis and Ulysses Lee, *ed.*, *The Negro Caravan*, p. 859, New York, 1941

17 Rhodes, *History of the United States*, Vol. I, p. 307

18 Kirkland, *A History of American Economic Life*, p. 188

19 Aptheker, *American Negro Slave Revolts*, pp. 120-24

20 Wilson, *The History of the Rise and Fall of the Slave Power in America*, Vol. II, p. 61

21 Aptheker, *Documentary History*, p. 86

22 Phillips, *American Negro Slavery*, p. 462

23 Wilson, *The History of the Rise and Fall of the Slave Power in America*, Vol. III, pp. 258-59

24 E. Franklin Frazier, *The Negro in the United States*, p. 310, New York, 1949

25 Phillips, *Life and Labor in the Old South*, p. 162

26 Olmstead, *The Cotton Kingdom*, Vol. I, p. 57

27 Frazier, *The Negro in the United States*, p. 307

28 Aptheker, *Masses and Mainstream*, February, 1949

29 V. I. Lenin, *Religion*, p. 7, New York, 1933

30 Aptheker, *American Negro Slave Revolts*, p. 56

31 *Ibid.*, p. 58

32 Woodson, *The Negro in Our History*, p. 227

33 McMaster, *History of the People of the United States*, Vol. VI, p. 272

34 Morris U. Schappes, *A Documentary History of the Jews in the United States*, p. 446, New York, 1950

35 Jacob Rader Marcus, *Early American Jewry*, p. 64, Philadelphia, 1951

36 Bogart, *Economic History of the United States*, p. 253

37 Arthur Charles Cole, *The Irrepressible Conflict*, p. 76, New York, 1934

38 Charles H. Wesley, *Negro Labor in the United States*, p. 23, New York, 1927

39 McMaster, *History of the People of the United States*, Vol. VII, p. 243

40 Coleman, *Slavery Times in Kentucky*, p. 184

41 Redding, *They Came in Chains*, p. 147

Chapter 15

1 Aptheker, *American Negro Slave Revolts*, p. 340

2 U.S. Department of Commerce, *Historical Statistics of the United States*, p. 109

3 Aptheker, *American Negro Slave Revolts*, pp. 340-58

4 *Journal of Negro History*, October, 1950, p. 418

5 Coleman, *Slavery Times in Kentucky*, p. 107

6 *Annual Report of the American Anti-Slavery Society*, 1857-1858, p. 77, New York, 1859

7 Carl Sandburg, *Abraham Lincoln*, Vol. II, p. 27, New York, 1939

8 James Hugo Johnston, *Journal of Negro History*, April, 1931, p. 160

9 H. Biel, *The Communist*, February, 1939

10 Greeley, *The American Conflict*, Vol. I, p. 216

11 *Ibid.*, p. 216

12 Aptheker, *Documentary History*, p. 334

13 Brawley, *A Short History of the Negro People*, p. 88

14 Aptheker, *The Negro in the Abolitionist Movement*, p. 23

15 Wilson, *The History of the Rise and Fall of the Slave Power in America*, Vol. II, p. 358

16 Commager, *Documents of American History*, Vol. I, p. 335

17 Woodson, *The Negro in Our History*, p. 262

18 (The) Beards, *The Rise of American Civilization*, Vol. I, p. 656, 1927

19 Aptheker, *Documentary History*, pp. 327-28

20 Commager, *Documents of American History*, Vol. I, p. 345

21 (The) Beards, *The Rise of American Civilization*, Vol. II, p. 16

22 Foner, *The Life and Writings of Frederick Douglass*, Vol. II, p. 412

Chapter 16

1 Commager, *Documents of American History*, Vol. I, p. 331

2 *Ibid.*, p. 331

3 McMaster, *History of the People of the United States*, Vol. VIII, p. 208

4 *Ibid.*, p. 201

5 Foner, *The Life and Writings of Frederick Douglass*, Vol. II, p. 279

6 McMaster, *History of the People of the United States*, Vol. III, p. 215

7 *Ibid.*, p. 223

8 *Ibid.*, Vol. VIII, p. 259

9 Greeley, *The American Conflict*, Vol. 1, pp. 287-88

10 Redding, *They Came in Chains*, p. 126.

11 Oswald Garrison Villard, *John Brown*, p. 487, New York, 1943

12 *Ibid.*, p. 498

13 Commager, *Documents of American History*, Vol. I, p. 361

14 Villard, *John Brown*, p. 523

15 McMaster, *History of the People of the United States*, Vol. VIII, p. 425

16 Villard, *John Brown*, p. 560

Chapter 17

1 Lawson, *Lincoln's Third Party*

2 Ray Allen Billington, *The Protestant Crusade, 1800-1860*, New York, 1938

3 Wilson, *The Rise and Fall of the Slave Power in America*, Vol. II, p. 420

4 William Starr Myers, *The Republican Party, A History*, p. 41, New York, 1928

5 *Ibid.*, p. 66

6 Woodburne, *Political Parties and Party Problems in the United States*, p. 92

7 Philip S. Foner, *Business and Slavery*, Chapel Hill, 1941

8 Foner, *The Life and Writings of Frederick Douglass*, Vol. II, p. 65

9 *Ibid.*, p. 333 *ff*

10 *Annual Report of the American Anti-Slavery Society*, 1859, p. 144, New York, 1860

11 Philip S. Foner, *History of the Labor Movement of the United States*, Vol. I, pp. 249-96, New York, 1947

12 Schlueter, *Lincoln, Labor and Slavery*, pp. 67-68

13 Marx, *Capital*, Vol. I, p. 287

14 Wesley, *Negro Labor in the United States*, p. 74

15 Schlueter, *Lincoln, Labor and Slavery*, p. 61

16 *Ibid.*, p. 72

17 Karl Marx and Frederick Engels, *Letters to Americans, 1848-1895*, New York, 1953

18 Foner, *History of the Labor Movement in the United States*, Vol. I, pp. 282 *ff*

19 *Ibid.*, p. 287

20 Karl Obermann, *Joseph Weydemeyer*, New York, 1947

21 Wood Gray, *The Hidden Civil War*, p. 25, New York, 1942

22 Karl Marx and Frederick Engels, *The Communist Manifesto*, p. 43, New York, 1948

Chapter *18*

1 Aptheker, *Masses and Mainstream*, February, 1950

2 Foner, *The Life and Writings of Frederick Douglass*, Vol. II, pp. 289-309

3 Parrington, *Main Currents in American Thought*, Vol. II, p. 80

4 Schlueter, *Lincoln, Labor and Slavery*, pp. 114-15

5 *Ibid.*, p. 118

6 Samuel Sillen, *Masses and Mainstream*, March, 1952

7 Harriet Beecher Stowe, *Uncle Tom's Cabin*, p. 439, New York, 1932

8 H. R. Helper, *The Impending Crisis of the South*, New York, 1857

9 A. M. Simons, *Social Forces in American History*, p. 230, New York, 1918

10 Carl Sandburg, *Abraham Lincoln: The Prairie Years*, New York, 1926

11 Korngold, *Two Friends of Man*, p. 266

12 *Ibid.*, p. 268

Chapter *19*

1 Commager, *Documents of American History*, Vol. I, p. 337

2 Greeley, *The American Conflict*, Vol. I, p. 319

3 Commager, *Documents of American History*, Vol. I, p. 365

4 Foner, *History of the Labor Movement in the United States*, Vol. I, p. 290

5 Greeley, *The American Conflict*, Vol. I, pp. 309-19

6 *Ibid.*, pp. 309-19

7 Commager, *Documents of American History*, Vol. I, pp. 365-66

8 Harold Underwood Faulkner, *American Political and Social History*, p. 329, New York, 1937

9 Foner, *Business and Slavery*, p. 204

10 Hawk, *Economic History of the South*, p. 388

11 Gray, *The Hidden Civil War*, p. 21

12 Schlueter, *Lincoln, Labor and Slavery*, pp. 176-77

13 Foner, *History of the Labor Movement in the United States*, Vol. I, p. 293

14 Foner, *The Life and Writings of Frederick Douglass*, Vol. II, p. 515

15 Carlos Martyn, *Wendell Phillips*, p. 303, New York, 1890

16 Lawson, *Lincoln's Third Party*, pp. 40-41

Chapter *20*

1 Greeley, *The American Conflict*, Vol. I, p. 239

2 Karl Marx and Frederick Engels, *The Civil War in the United States*, p. 80, New York, 1937

3 McMaster, *History of the People of the United States*, Vol. VIII, p. 487

4 R. B. Nye, *Science and Society*, Summer, 1946

5 Redding, *They Came in Chains*, p. 149

6 Wilson, *The History of the Rise and Fall of the Slave Power in America*, Vol. II, pp. 548-49

7 Rhodes, *History of the United States*, Vol. III, p. 117
8 Commager, *Documents of American History*, Vol. I, p. 379
9 Aptheker, *Masses and Mainstream*, November, 1951
10 Greeley, *The American Conflict*, Vol. I, pp. 344 *ff*
11 Commager, *Documents of American History*, Vol. I, p. 376
12 *Ibid.*, p. 370
13 Rhodes, *History of the United States*, Vol. III, p. 301
14 Joseph Stalin, *Marxism versus Liberalism*, p. 18, New York, 1935
15 Philip S. Foner, *The Life and Writings of Frederick Douglass*, Vol. III, pp. 59, 61, New York, 1952
16 Commager, *Documents of American History*, Vol. I, pp. 385-88
17 Foner, *The Life and Writings of Frederick Douglass*, Vol. III, p. 73

Chapter 21

1 *World Almanac*, 1951, p. 512, New York
2 (The) Beards, *The Rise of American Civilization*, Vol. II, p. 55
3 Jennings, *History of Economic Progress in the United States*, pp. 274 *ff*
4 Bogart, *Economic History of the United States*, pp. 161 *ff*
5 Wallace, *South Carolina, A Short History*, p. 457
6 Wesley, *Negro Labor in the United States*, p. 14
7 Jennings, *History of Economic Progress in the United States*, p. 241
8 Cole, *The Irrepressible Conflict*, pp. 63-64
9 Adam Smith, *The Wealth of Nations*, p. 81, New York, 1937
10 Marx, *Capital*, Vol. I, p. 178
11 Bogart, *Economic History of the United States*, pp. 255-56
12 Wesley, *Negro Labor in the United States*, p. 3
13 Hawks, *The Economic History of the South*, p. 278
14 Wright, *The Industrial Evolution of the United States*, p. 151
15 Bogart, *Economic History of the United States*, p. 258
16 Cole, *The Irrepressible Conflict*, p. 49
17 *United States Census*, 1850
18 Marx and Engels, *The Civil War in the United States*, p. 65
19 Simons, *Social Forces in American History*, pp. 232, 233, 237
20 Frederick Engels, *Herr Eugen Duehring's Revolution in Science*, *(Anti-Duehring)*, p. 200
21 Marx, *The Poverty of Philosophy*, p. 94
22 Aptheker, *American Negro Slave Revolts*

Chapter 22

1 Lenin, *A Letter to American Workers*, p. 16
2 Stalin, *Marxism versus Liberalism*, p. 22
3 (The) Beards, *The Rise of American Civilization*, Vol. II, p. 50
4 Marx and Engels, *The Civil War in the United States*, p. 281
5 *Ibid.*, p. 81
6 *Ibid.*, p. 155
7 *Ibid.*, pp. 81-82
8 *Ibid.*, pp. 252-53
9 Foner, *The Life and Writings of Frederick Douglass*, Vol. III, p. 15
10 Adam Lapin, *The People's World*, April 4, 1952
11 Myers, *The Republican Party, A History*
12 Korngold, *Two Friends of Man*, p. 285

13 Marx and Engels, *The Civil War in the United States*, p. 186
14 Wilson, *The History of the Rise and Fall of the Slave Power in America*, Vol. III, p. 304
15 Foner, *The Life and Writings of Frederick Douglass*, Vol. III, p. 317
16 Marx and Engels, *The Civil War in the United States*, p. 253
17 Herbert Aptheker, *The Negro in the Civil War*, p. 30, New York, 1938
18 Bramferd Dyer, *Journal of Negro History*, p. 276, July, 1935
19 Aptheker, *To Be Free*, p. 94 ff
20 Gustavus Myers, *History of the Great American Fortunes*, p. 406, New York, 1936
21 Simons, *Social Forces in American History*, p. 280
22 Charlotte Todes, *William H. Sylvis and the National Labor Union*, p. 31, New York, 1942
23 Simons, *Social Forces in American History*, p. 282
24 Myers, *History of the Great American Fortunes*, pp. 291-92

Chapter 23

1 Davie, *Negroes in American Society*, p. 45
2 Commager, *Documents of American History*, Vol. I, p. 396
3 *Ibid.*, p. 398
4 Redding, *They Came in Chains*, p. 154
5 Foner, *The Life and Writings of Frederick Douglass*, Vol. III, p. 14
6 Lawson, *Thaddeus Stevens*, p. 16
7 Foner, *The Life and Writings of Frederick Douglass*, Vol. III, p. 21
8 Rhodes, *History of the United States*, Vol. IV, p. 61
9 T. Harry Williams, *Lincoln and the Radicals*, p. 166, Madison, 1941
10 Commager, *Documents of American History*, Vol. I, p. 403
11 *Ibid.*, p. 403
12 Rhodes, *History of the United States*, Vol. III, p. 592
13 John G. Nicolay and John Hay, *ed., Complete Works of Abraham Lincoln*, Vol. IV, pp. 89-90, New York, 1894
14 Wesley, *Negro Labor in the United States*, p. 105
15 Woodson, *The Negro in Our History*, p. 380
16 Foner, *The Life and Writings of Frederick Douglass*, Vol. III, p. 261
17 James Bryce, *The American Commonwealth*, p. 534, New York, 1941
18 Marx and Engels, *The Civil War in the United States*, pp. 252-53
19 Commager, *Documents of American History*, Vol. I, p. 420
20 Foner, *The Life and Writings of Frederick Douglass*, Vol. III, p. 15
21 *Ibid.*, p. 273
22 Wilson, *The History of the Rise and Fall of the Slave Power in America*, Vol. III, p. 700
23 Commager, *Documents of American History*, Vol. I, pp. 418-20
24 *Founding of the First International*, A Documentary Record, p. 38, New York, 1947
25 Samuel Bernstein, *Science and Society*, Spring, 1953

Chapter 24

1 Lawson, *History of the American Negro People*, p. 54
2 Schlueter, *Lincoln, Labor and Slavery*, p. 209
3 (The) Beards, *The Rise of American Civilization*, Vol. II, p. 80
4 *Ibid.*, p. 81
5 Gray, *The Hidden Civil War*, p. 145

6 Commager, *Documents of American History*, Vol. I, pp. 429-31

7 *Ibid.*, p. 440

8 Rhodes, *History of the United States*, Vol. IV, p. 517

9 Carl Sandburg, *Abraham Lincoln, The War Years*, Vol. III, p. 246, New York, 1939

10 Greeley, *The American Conflict*, Vol. II, pp. 657-68

11 Foner, *The Life and Writings of Frederick Douglass*, Vol. III, pp. 48-51

12 Williams, *Lincoln and the Radicals*, p. 331

13 Greeley, *The American Conflict*, Vol. II, p. 672

14 Marx and Engels, *The Civil War in the United States*, p. 256

15 Carter G. Woodson, *Negro Orators and Their Orations*, pp. 519, 521, Washington, D. C., 1925

Chapter 25

1 Woodson, *The Negro in Our History*, p. 373

2 Aptheker, *To Be Free*, p. 120

3 Woodson, *The Negro in the United States*, p. 374

4 Wexley, *Negro Labor in the United States*, p. 108

5 Aptheker, *The Negro in the Civil War*, p. 43

6 Marx and Engels, *The Civil War in the United States*, p. XXII.

7 Brawley, *A Short History of the American Negro*, p. 118

8 Foner, *History of the Labor Movement in the United States*, Vol. I, p. 317

9 Aptheker, *To Be Free*, p. 78

10 Sandburg, *Abraham Lincoln, The War Years*, Vol. III, p. 210

11 Foner, *The Life and Writings of Frederick Douglass*, Vol. III, p. 403

12 By Himself, *Life and Times of Frederick Douglass*, p. 463

13 Foner, *History of the Labor Movement in the United States*, Vol. I, pp. 302-303

14 Schlueter, *Lincoln, Labor and Slavery*, p. 138

15 Foner, *History of the Labor Movement in the United States*, Vol. I, p. 306

16 *Ibid.*, p. 307

17 Terrence V. Powderly, *Thirty Years of Labor*, p. 58, Columbus, 1889

18 Schlueter, *Lincoln, Labor and Slavery*, p. 140

19 John R. Commons and Associates, *History of Labor in the United States*, Vol. II, p. 15, New York, 1918

20 Todes, *William H. Sylvis and the National Labor Union*, pp. 42-43

21 Marx, *Capital*, Vol. I, p. 287

22 Foner, *History of the Labor Movement in the United States*, Vol. I, p. 310

23 Obermann, *Joseph Weydemeyer*

24 Schlueter, *Lincoln, Labor and Slavery*, pp. 188-91

25 Marx and Engels, *The Civil War in the United States*, p. 284

Chapter 26

1 Adam Lapin, *The Worker*, April 4, 1952, New York

2 James S. Allen, *Reconstruction*, pp. 73-78, Appendices, 2, 5, New York, 1937

3 Korngold, *Two Friends of Man*, p. 341

4 Aptheker, *Masses and Mainstream*, February, 1950, p. 48

5 Williams, *Lincoln and the Radicals*, p. 373 *ff*

6 Marx and Engels, *The Civil War in the United States*, p. 315

Chapter 27

1 Commager, *Documents of American History*, Vol. II, pp. 7-8

2 *Ibid.*, pp. 8-10

3 Morais, *Science and Society*, p. 13, Winter, 1948
4 Du Bois, *Black Reconstruction*, pp. 166-80
5 *Ibid.*, p. 261
6 *Ibid.*, p. 292
7 Hacker, *The Triumph of American Capitalism*, p. 377
8 Du Bois, *Black Reconstruction*, p. 265
9 *Ibid.*, p. 261
10 *The World Almanac*, 1953, p. 636
11 Hacker, *The Triumph of American Capitalism*, pp. 376-77
12 Allen, *Reconstruction*, p. 69
13 Du Bois, *Black Reconstruction*, pp. 265-66
14 Foner, *The Life and Writings of Frederick Douglass*, Vol. IV, New York, 1954
15 Henderson H. Donald, *The Negro Freedman*, p. 5, New York, 1952
16 Aptheker, *To Be Free*, pp. 144-75
17 Allen, *Science and Society*, p. 378, Spring, 1937
18 Allen, *Reconstruction*, p. 48
19 M. Gottlieb, *Science and Society*, p. 356, Summer, 1939
20 Allen, *Reconstruction*, pp. 49-51
21 Allen, *Science and Society*, p. 401, Spring, 1937

Chapter 28

1 Schlueter, *Lincoln, Labor and Slavery*, p. 200
2 William H. Skaggs, *The Southern Oligarchy*, p. 41, New York, 1924
3 Du Bois, *Black Reconstruction*, p. 319
4 Commager, *Documents of American History*, Vol. II, p. 22-28
5 Rhodes, *History of the United States*, Vol. VI, pp. 12-13
6 Commager, *Documents of American History*, Vol. II, pp. 30-49
7 *Ibid.*, pp. 43-48
8 Rhodes, *History of the United States*, Vol. VI, pp. 98-157
9 Lawson, *Thaddeus Stevens*

Chapter 29

1 Allen, *Reconstruction;* Du Bois, *Black Reconstruction*
2 Du Bois, *Black Reconstruction*, p. 372
3 *Ibid.*, p. 627
4 James S. Allen, *The Negro Question in the United States*, p. 182, New York, 1936
5 Allen, *Reconstruction*, p. 130
6 *Ibid.*, pp. 116-31
7 Du Bois, *Black Reconstruction*, pp. 597-98
8 Hacker, *The Triumph of American Capitalism*, p. 343
9 John R. Lynch, *Some Historical Errors of James Ford Rhodes*, p. 4, New York, 1922
10 Carter G. Woodson, *The History of the Negro Church*, p. 233, Washington, D. C., 1921
11 *First Annual Meeting of the National Equal Rights League*, Cleveland, Ohio, October 19-21, 1865, Philadelphia, 1865
12 *Proceedings of the National Convention of the Colored Men of America*, January 13-16, 1869, Washington, D. C., 1869
13 W. E. Burghardt Du Bois, *The Souls of Black Folk*, p. 27, Chicago, 1903
14 Wilson, *The Rise and Fall of the Slave Power in America*, Vol. III, p. 501
15 Donald, *The Freedman*, p. 98
16 Allen, *Reconstruction*, p. 93

17 Franklin, *From Slavery to Freedom*, p. 322
18 Walter L. Fleming, *Civil War and Reconstruction in Alabama*, p. 553 *ff*, New York, 1905
19 "The Union League in North Carolina," *Suwanee River Quarterly*, 1912
20 Aptheker, *To Be Free*, pp. 163-87

Chapter 30

1 Allen, *Reconstruction*, p. 182
2 Donald, *The Negro Freedman*, p. 221
3 Allen, *Reconstruction*, p. 184
4 E. Merton Coulter, *The South During Reconstruction*, 1865-1877, p. 169, Baton Rouge, 1947; Walter L. Fleming, *Documentary History of Reconstruction*, Vol. II, p. 327, Cleveland, 1907
5 Commager, *Documents of American History*, Vol. II, pp. 49-50
6 Redding, *They Came in Chains*, p. 181
7 Du Bois, *Black Reconstruction*, p. 483
8 Aptheker, *Documentary History*, pp. 572-606
9 Rhodes, *History of the United States*, Vol. VI, pp. 311-13
10 Commager, *Documents of American History*, Vol. II, p. 52
11 Allen, *Reconstruction*, p. 197
12 Rhodes, *History of the United States*, Vol. VI, p. 412
13 Commager, *Documents of American History*, Vol. II, p. 71
14 Commons, *History of Labor in the United States*, Vol. II, p. 155
15 Rhodes, *History of the United States*, Vol. VI, p. 438
16 Du Bois, *Black Reconstruction*, pp. 381-525; Allen, *Reconstruction*, pp. 197-206
17 Woodson, *The Negro in Our History*, p. 414
18 Allen, *Reconstruction*, p. 190
19 Du Bois, *Black Reconstruction*, p. 674
20 Commager, *Documents of American History*, Vol. II, p. 86

Chapter 31

1 Myers, *The Republican Party, A History*, p. 239
2 Foner, *The Life and Writings of Frederick Douglass*, Vol. IV, 1954
3 Allen, *Reconstruction*, pp. 205-206
4 Marx and Engels, *The Civil War in the United States*, p. 245
5 C. Vann Woodward, *Origins of the New South*, 1879-1913, pp. 456-57, New Orleans, 1951
6 Parrington, *Main Currents in American Thought*, Vol. II, p. 3
7 Francis Butler Simkins, *Journal of Southern History*, p. 53, February, 1939
8 Allen, *Reconstruction*, p. 194
9 Woodward, *Origins of the New South*, p. 14
10 *Ibid.*, pp. 19, 20, 21
11 Allen, *Reconstruction*, p. 194
12 Foner, *The Life and Writings of Frederick Douglass*, Vol. IV
13 Brown, Davis and Lee, *The Negro Caravan*, pp. 1066-69

Chapter 32

1 Foner, *History of the Labor Movement in the United States*, Vol. I, p. 376
2 Allen, *Reconstruction*, p. 151
3 S. E. Matison, *Journal of Negro History*, October, 1948
4 James C. Sylvis, *The Life, Speeches, Labors and Essays of William E. Sylvis*, p. 235, Philadelphia, 1872

5 Todes, *William H. Sylvis and the National Labor Union*, p. 62

6 *Ibid.*, p. 73

7 Aptheker, *Documentary History*, pp. 626-33

8 *Ibid.*, p. 633

9 Foner, *History of the Labor Movement in the United States*, Vol. I, p. 397

10 Wesley, *Negro Labor in the United States*, p. 171

11 *Proceedings of the Colored National Labor Convention*, Washington, D. C., December 6-10, 1869, Washington, D. C., 1870; Aptheker, *Documentary History*, pp. 628-36

12 Foner, *History of the Labor Movement in the United States*, Vol. I, p. 405

13 Allen, *Reconstruction*, p. 174

14 Wesley, *Negro Labor in the United States*, p. 164

15 Foner, *History of the Labor Movement in the United States*, Vol. I, p. 429

16 *Journal of Negro History*, October, 1948

17 Wesley, *Negro Labor in the United States*, p. 188

18 *Ibid.*, p. 186

19 Allen, *Reconstruction*, p. 177

20 *Ibid.*, p. 178

21 *Ibid.*, p. 179

Chapter 33

1 V. I. Lenin, *Selected Works*, Vol. XII, p. 198, New York, 1943

2 *Ibid.*, p. 200

3 Jennings, *History of Economic Progress*, p. 396

4 Coman, *The Industrial History of the United States*, p. 310

5 Coulter, *The South During Reconstruction*, p. 213

6 Robert Selph Henry, *The Story of Reconstruction*, p. 428, New York, 1938

7 Lenin, *Selected Works*, Vol. XII, p. 199

8 Woodward, *Origins of the New South*, p. 196

9 *Ibid.*, p. 179

10 *Ibid.*, p. 6

11 U.S. Department of Commerce, *Historical Statistics of the United States*, 1789-1945, p. 108

12 Hawk, *Economic History of the South*, p. 457

13 Woodward, *Origins of the New South*, p. 118

14 Wesley, *Negro Labor in the United States*, p. 132

15 Woodward, *Origins of the New South*, pp. 213, 214-15

16 Du Bois, *Black Reconstruction*, p. 699

17 Eric Burt, *MS.*

18 Paul H. Buck, *The Road to Reunion*, 1865-1900, p. 284, Boston, 1937

19 Aptheker, *Documentary History*, pp. 727-34

20 Aptheker, *Jewish Life*, July, 1950

21 Helen M. Blackburn, *The Populist Party in the South*, p. 113, Washington, D. C., 1941

22 George Brown Tindall, *South Carolina Negroes*, pp. 309-10, Columbia, 1952

23 Aptheker, *Masses and Mainstream*, February, 1949

24 Du Bois, *Black Reconstruction*, p. 136

25 Tindall, *South Carolina Negroes*, pp. 154-58

26 Wesley, *Negro Labor in the United States*, p. 214

27 Roy Garvin, *Journal of Negro History*, January, 1948

28 Aptheker, *Documentary History*, pp. 713-26

29 Carter G. Woodson, *Negro Orators and their Orations*, pp. 453 ff

Chapter 34

1 U.S. Department of Commerce, *Historical Statistics of the United States, 1789-1945,* p. 179

2 Hawk, *Economic History of the South,* p. 476

3 Jennings, *History of Economic Progress,* p. 394

4 Bogart, *Economic History of the United States,* p. 532

5 Foner, *History of the Labor Movement in the United States,* Vol. II, MS.

6 Wesley, *Negro Labor in the United States,* p. 237

7 Foner, *History of the Labor Movement in the United States,* Vol. II, MS.

8 Wesley, *Negro Labor in the United States,* p. 254; Richard T. Ely, *The Labor Movement in America,* p. 83, New York, 1886

9 Foner, *History of the Labor Movement in the United States,* Vol. II, MS.

10 *Ibid.*

11 Powderly, *Thirty Years of Labor,* p. 662

12 Lewis L. Lorwin, *The American Federation of Labor,* pp. 10-18, Washington, D. C., 1933

13 Wesley, *Negro Labor in the United States,* pp. 257-58

14 *Constitution of the American Railway Union,* Terre Haute, 1895

15 *American Federation of Labor History, Encyclopedia Reference Book,* pp. 300-301, Washington, D. C., 1919

16 Wesley, *Negro Labor in the United States,* p. 259

17 *American Federation of Labor History, Encyclopedia Reference Book,* p. 300

18 Aptheker, *Documentary History,* pp. 838-45

Chapter 35

1 (The) Beards, *The Rise of American Cîilization,* Vol. II, p. 275

2 Foner, *History of the Labor Movement in the United States,* Vol. II, MS.

3 Woodward, *Origins of the New South,* pp. 81-84

4 Anna Rochester, *The Populist Movement in the United States,* p. 40, New York, 1943

5 Woodward, *Origins of the New South,* p. 188

6 *Ibid.,* p. 195

7 Rochester, *The Populist Movement in the United States,* p. 41

8 John D. Hicks, *The Populist Revolt,* p. 115, Minneapolis, 1931

9 F. M. Drew, *Political Science Quarterly,* Vol. VI, 1891

10 Woodward, *Origins of the New South,* p. 192

11 J. Abramowitz, "The Negro in the Populist Movement," *Journal of Negro History,* July, 1953

12 Aptheker, *Documentary History,* pp. 804-11

13 Abramowitz, "The Negro in the Populist Movement," *Journal of Negro History,* July, 1953

14 M. Ross, *The Third Party Tradition in North Carolina,* p. 7, Greensboro, 1947

15 Rochester, *The Populist Movement in the United States,* p. 59

16 Ross, *The Third Party Tradition in North Carolina,* p. 16; C. Vann Woodward, *Tom Watson, Agrarian Rebel,* New York, 1938

17 Woodward, *Origins of the New South,* p. 257

18 *Ibid.,* pp. 256-57

19 Hicks, *The Populist Revolt,* p. 120

20 J. L. Reddick, *The Negro and the Populist Movement in Georgia,* MS.

21 Rochester, *The Populist Movement in the United States,* p. 51

22 Robert F. Hall, *The Communist*, August, 1940
23 Francis Butler Simkins, *The Tillman Movement in South Carolina*, p. 137, Durham, 1926
24 Woodward, *Tom Watson, Agrarian Rebel*, p. 402
25 Rochester, *The Populist Movement in the United States*, p. 69
26 Aptheker, *Documentary, History*, pp. 736-43, 792-95

Chapter 36

1 V. I. Lenin, *Imperialism: The Highest Stage of Capitalism*, New York, 1939
2 John Moody, *The Truth About the Trusts*, p. 477, New York, 1904
3 Jürgen Kuczynski, *A Short History of Labor Conditions in the United States*, p. 105, London, 1943
4 Woodward, *Origins of the New South*, p. 7
5 *Ibid.*, p. 300
6 Aptheker, *Jewish Life*, July, 1950
7 Victor Perlo, *American Imperialism*, p. 82, New York, 1951
8 *Ibid.*, p. 83
9 Tindall, *South Carolina Negroes*, p. 291
10 Buck, *The Road to Reunion*, p. 288
11 Aptheker, *Documentary History*, p. 792
12 Woodward, *Origins of the New South*, p. 344
13 Buck, *The Road to Reunion*, p. 286
14 Woodward, *Origins of the New South*, p. 462

Chapter 37

1 Marx and Engels, *Letters to Americans*, 1848-1895, p. 258
2 Rudolph Schwab, Henry Kuhn, Olive M. Johnson, and others, *Daniel De Leon: A Symposium*, New York, 1920
3 Eric Hass, *Socialism: World Without Prejudice*, pp. 19, 28, New York
4 Daniel De Leon, *A Decadent Jeffersonian on the Socialist Griddle*, New York, 1935
5 Ira Kipnis, *The American Socialist Movement*, 1897-1912, p. 130, New York, 1952
6 Arthur M. Schlesinger Jr., *Writings and Speeches of Eugene V. Debs*, p. 68, New York, 1948
7 James Oneal, *The Next Emancipation*, p. 12, New York, 1929
8 Socialist Party, *A Political Guide for the Workers*, p. 30
9 Socialist Party, *National Platform, Socialist Party*, 1932, Chicago
10 *International Socialist Review*, November, 1903
11 Ray Ginger, *The Bending Cross*, p. 260, New Brunswick, 1949
12 Eugene V. Debs, *International Socialist Review*, November, 1903
13 *Ibid.*, January, 1904
14 C. H. Vail, *Socialism and the Negro Problem*, p. 8, New York, 1902
15 Max Hayes, *International Socialist Review*, August, 1903
16 Paul F. Brissenden, *The Industrial Workers of the World*, p. 84, New York, 1920
17 Charlotte Todes, *Labor and Lumber*, pp. 171-79, New York, 1931
18 William D. Haywood and Frank Bohn, *Industrial Socialism*, Chicago, 1911
19 Clarence S. Darrow, "The Problem of the Negro," *International Socialist Review*, November, 1901
20 W. E. Burghardt Du Bois, *The New Review*, February 1, 1913
21 Morris Hillquit, *History of Socialism in the United States*, New York, 1903; Hillquit, *Socialism in Theory and Practice*, New York, 1917; Harry W. Laidler, *Socialism in Thought and Action*, New York, 1920

22 Sterling D. Spero and Abram L. Harris, *The Black Worker*, p. 407, New York, 1931
23 Ginger, *The Bending Cross*, p. 259
24 *International Socialist Review*, December, 1901
25 Socialist Party, *Proceedings of First National Congress of the Socialist Party of the United States*, pp. 75-77, Chicago
26 William English Walling, *American Socialism and the Race Problem*
27 Kipnis, *The American Socialist Movement*, p. 132

Chapter 38

1 Booker T. Washington, *Up From Slavery*, p. 155, New York, 1929
2 *Report to the Fifth Annual Convention of the National Negro Business League*, p. 45, Chicago, 1905
3 Aptheker, *Documentary History*, pp. 747-48, 781-84
4 Washington, *Up From Slavery*, pp. 221-22
5 Woodward, *Origins of the New South*, p. 364
6 Aptheker, *Documentary History*, p. 755
7 W. E. Burghardt Du Bois, *Dusk of Dawn*, p. 72, New York, 1940
8 Woodward, *Origins of the New South*, p. 358
9 *Ibid.*, p. 359
10 Redding, *They Came in Chains*, p. 197
11 *Ibid.*, pp. 197-98
12 Abram L. Harris, *The Negro as Capitalist*, p. 4, Philadelphia, 1936
13 Woodson, *The Negro in Our History*, pp. 246-48
14 J. A. Pierce, *Negro Business and Negro Education*, p. 9, New York, 1947
15 Harris, *The Negro as Capitalist*, p. 9
16 Redding, *They Came in Chains*, p. 191
17 Harris, *The Negro as Capitalist*, p. 46
18 Haywood, *Negro Liberation*, p. 172
19 Aptheker, *Documentary History*, pp. 765, 768, 820-26
20 Redding, *They Came in Chains*, p. 214
21 Commager, *Documents of American History*, Vol. II, p. 193
22 Aptheker, *Documentary History*, p. 825
23 *The Midwest Journal*, Winter, 1951-1952
24 W. E. Burghardt Du Bois, *In Battle for Peace*, p. 173, New York, 1952
25 Aptheker, *Documentary History*, pp. 901-904
26 Du Bois, *Dusk of Dawn*, p. 90
27 Redding, *They Came in Chains*, p. 200
28 Haywood, *Negro Liberation*, p. 176
29 Brown, Davis, and Lee, *The Negro Caravan*, p. 764
30 Redding, *They Came in Chains*, pp. 233-34

Chapter 39

1 *Final Report of the Commission on Industrial Relations*, p. 298, Washington, D. C., 1915
2 *Ibid.*, pp. 127-29
3 Aptheker, *Documentary History*, p. 813
4 Franklin, *From Slavery to Freedom*, p. 435
5 Florence Murray, *ed.*, *The Negro Handbook*, 1949, p. 99, New York, 1949
6 Du Bois, *Dusk of Dawn*, p. 241
7 Myrdal, *An American Dilemma*, Vol. I, p. 563
8 Mary White Ovington, *How the National Association for the Advancement of Col-*

ored People Began, New York, 1945

9 R. L. Jack, *History of the National Association for the Advancement of Colored People,* p. 7, Boston, 1943

10 Redding, *They Came in Chains,* p. 228

11 Haywood, *Negro Liberation,* p. 181

12 L. H. Wood, *Journal of Negro History,* April, 1924, p. 121

13 Frank R. Crosswaith, Norman Thomas, Alfred Baker Lewis, *True Freedom for Negro and White Labor,* p. 34, New York

14 Aptheker, *Documentary History,* pp. 838-45

15 *Ibid.,* p. 853

16 Franklin, *From Slavery to Freedom,* p. 445

17 Henry Lee Moon, *Balance of Power: The Negro Vote,* p. 91, New York, 1948

Chapter 40

1 Aptheker, *New Masses,* April, 22, 1941

2 A. Philip Randolph, *The Messenger,* November, 1917

3 *The Crisis,* June, 1917, New York

4 Brawley, *A Short History of the American Negro,* p. 189

5 Woodson, *The Negro in Our History,* p. 516

6 Redding, *They Came in Chains,* p. 242

7 Woodson, *The Negro in Our History,* pp. 524-25

8 *Ibid.,* pp. 527-28

9 (The) Beards, *The Rise of American Civilization,* Vol. II, p. 747

10 *Final Report of the Commission on Industrial Relations,* p. 28, Washington, D. C., 1915

11 Faulkner, *Economic History of the United States,* p. 205

12 The National Council of American-Soviet Friendship, *Constitution of the U.S.S.R.,* p. 35, New York, 1947

13 Du Bois, *Dusk of Dawn,* p. 287

14 E. Franklin Frazier, *The Negro in the United States,* p. 702, New York, 1949

15 Paul Robeson, *The Negro People and the Soviet Union,* p. 15, New York, 1950

16 Franklin, *From Slavery to Freedom,* p. 465; Carter G. Woodson, *A Century of Negro Migration,* Washington, D. C., 1918

17 Allen, *The Negro Question in the United States,* p. 136

18 Wesley, *Negro Labor in the United States,* p. 266

19 Jack, *History of the National Association for the Advancement of Colored People,* p. 18

20 Moon, *Balance of Power: The Negro Vote,* p. 10

21 Franklin, *From Slavery to Freedom,* p. 472

22 *The Negro Year Book,* 1949, p. 99

23 Alexander Trachtenberg, *ed., The American Labor Year Book,* 1921-1922, p. 100, New York

Chapter 41

1 Haywood, *Negro Liberation,* p. 197

2 *The Crusader,* October, 1921, New York

3 *The Crisis,* June, 1923, New York

4 *Journal of Negro History,* October, 1940

5 Eric D. Walrod, *The Independent,* January 3, 1925

6 Amy Jacques Garvey, *ed., Philosophy and Opinions of Marcus Garvey,* pp. 135-42, New York, 1926

7 Haywood, *Negro Liberation,* p. 200

8 *The Messenger,* August, 1920

9 *The Negro World,* August 27, 1927, Chicago

10 *Current History,* September, 1923, New York

11 *The Daily Worker,* June 14, 1930

12 Garvey, *Philosophy and Opinions of Marcus Garvey,* pp. 69, 70, 72

13 Marcus Garvey, *An Appeal to the Soul of White America,* New York, 1924

14 *The Workers Monthly,* April, 1926, New York

15 *The Communist,* June, 1930, p. 549, New York

16 *The Liberator,* October, 1924, New York

17 *The Century,* February, 1923, New York

18 *Congressional Record,* May 24, 1938

19 A. Jacques Garvey, *Memorandum to the United Nations,* British West Indies, 1944

20 Myrdal, *An American Dilemma,* Vol. II, p. 746

21 *The Crisis,* February, 1928

22 *The Messenger,* March, 1923

23 *The Liberator,* October, 1924

24 *The Daily Worker,* August 5, 1924

25 Garvey, *An Appeal to the Soul of White America*

26 Mary White Ovington, *Portraits in Color,* p. 30, New York, 1927

27 Marcus Garvey, *The Black Man,* September-October, 1926

28 Haywood, *Negro Liberation,* p. 198

Chapter 42

1 J. Lenz, *The Rise and Fall of the Second International,* New York, 1932

2 Lenin, *Selected Works,* Vol. V, pp. 269-70

3 *Ibid.,* Vol. X, pp. 231-38

4 Trachtenberg, *ed., American Labor Year Book,* 1919-1920, p. 419

5 William Z. Foster, *History of the Communist Party of the United States,* p. 192, New York, 1952

6 *North American Review,* January, 1924

7 Southern Commission on the Study of Lynching, *Lynchings and What They Mean,* Atlanta, 1931

8 Wesley, *Negro Labor in the United States,* p. 277

9 James Oneal and G. A. Werner, *American Communism,* p. 335, New York, 1947

10 St. Claire Drake and Horace R. Cayton, *Black Metropolis,* p. 401, New York, 1945

11 Spero and Harris, *The Black Worker,* p. 418

12 Meier, *Emergence of Negro Nationalism,* p. 4, MS.

13 David J. Saposs, *Left Wing Unionism,* p. 165, New York, 1926

14 Oliver Cromwell Cox, *Caste, Class and Race,* p. 574, New York, 1948

15 Foster, *History of the Communist Party of the United States,* p. 269

16 *The Labor Herald,* July, 1924, Chicago

17 *Constitution and Program of the American Negro Labor Congress,* New York, 1925

18 *The Communist,* January, 1930

19 *Communist International,* January 15, 1931; *The Communist,* February, 1931

20 Lenin, *Selected Works,* Vol. X, p. 235

21 Claudia Jones, *Political Affairs,* January, 1946, New York

Chapter 43

1 Joseph Stalin, *Marxism and the National Question,* p. 12, New York, 1942

2 Haywood, *Negro Liberation,* pp. 11-20

3 Herskovits, *The Myth of the Negro Past;* Aptheker, *Masses and Mainstream,* December, 1949

4 Stalin, *Marxism and the National Question,* p. 69

5 Abner Berry, *The Worker,* May 3, 10, 1953

6 Benjamin J. Davis, *The Path of Negro Liberation,* p. 9, New York, 1947

7 U.S. Department of Labor, Bureau of Labor Statistics, *Negroes in the United States,* December, 1952

8 Victor Perlo, *Trends in the Economic Status of the Negro People,* p. 121, New York, 1952

9 Selsam, *The Negro People in the United States,* p. 10

10 Florence Murray, *ed., The Negro Handbook,* 1946-1947, New York

11 *Ebony,* August, 1952, New York

12 Harry J. Laski, *The American Democracy,* p. 467, New York, 1948

13 Oscar C. Brown, *The Crisis,* May, 1935

14 *Political Affairs,* June, 1949

15 G. T. Stephenson, *Race Distinctions in American Law,* p. 208, New York, 1910

16 Aptheker, *Documentary History,* pp. 744, 746

17 Meier, *Emergence of Negro Nationalism, MS.*

18 Ruth Benedict, *Race, Science, and Politics,* p. 108, New York, 1945

19 Charles R. Darwin, *The Origin of Species and the Descent of Man,* p. 539, New York, 1936

20 Karl Marx and Frederick Engels, *Selected Correspondence,* p. 125, New York, 1942

21 J. D. Bernal, *Marx and Science,* p. 46, New York, 1952

22 Abram Kardiner and Lionel Ovesey, *The Mark of Oppression,* New York, 1951; Lloyd L. Brown, *Masses and Mainstream,* October, 1951

23 Herbert Aptheker, *The Negro People in America,* p. 60, New York, 1946

24 Otto Klineberg, *Characteristics of the American Negro,* p. 402, New York, 1944

25 Ina Corinne Brown, *Race Relations in a Democracy,* p. 14, New York, 1949

26 Franz Boas, *Race and Democratic Society,* p. 20, New York, 1945

27 Gilberto Freyre, *The Masters and the Slaves,* p. 295, New York, 1946

28 A. Lipschutz, *El Indoamericanismo,* p. 164, Santiago, Chile

29 Doxey Wilkerson, *Political Affairs,* August, 1952

30 Benedict, *Race, Science, and Politics,* p. 56

31 Pauli Murray, *States' Laws on Race and Color,* p. 462, Cincinnati, 1950

32 Murray, *The Negro Handbook,* 1946-1947, p. 1

33 Myrdal, *An American Dilemma,* Vol. I, p. 54

34 Kumar Goshal, *The People of India,* p. 55, New York, 1944

35 *Science and Society,* Spring, 1943

36 Cox, *Caste, Class and Race,* pp. 12, 13, 91

37 R. Palme Dutt, *India Today,* pp. 103-104, London, 1940

38 Goshal, *The People of India,* p. 348, New York, 1944

39 Lenin, *Selected Works,* Vol. V, p. 270

40 Stalin, *Marxism and the National Question,* pp. 22-23

41 *Communist Party Resolution,* February, 1931

42 Heywood, *Negro Liberation,* p. 159

43 Aptheker, *Political Affairs,* June, 1949

44 Universal Negro Improvement Association, *Declaration of Rights,* Article 27

45 *Ibid.,* Article 4

Chapter 44

1 Labor Research Association, *Labor Fact Book 2,* New York, 1934

2 Foster, *History of the Communist Party of the United States*, pp. 279-80
3 Lorwin, *The American Federation of Labor*, p. 292
4 M. W. Jackson, *MS.: Equality, Land and Freedom*, pp. 7-9
5 U.S. Department of Labor, *Unionism in American Agriculture*, Bulletin 836, Washington, D. C., 1945
6 Labor Research Association, *Labor Fact Book* 6, p. 142
7 *Ibid.*
8 Communist Party, United States of America, *Race Hatred on Trial*, New York, 1931
9 *Daily Worker*, April 6, 1935
10 Elbert Lee Tatum, *The Changed Political Thought of the Negro*, 1915-1940, p. 138, New York, 1951
11 James W. Ford, *The Negro and the Democratic Front*, p. 50, New York, 1938
12 Foster, *History of the Communist Party of the United States*, p. 293
13 Labor Research Association, *Labor Fact Book* 3, pp. 70-71, New York, 1936
14 Foster, *History of the Communist Party of the United States*, pp. 314-17
15 Robert Hall, *The Communist*, January, 1939
16 *Phylon*, Second Quarter, 1951, Atlanta
17 *The Southern Patriot*, 1949
18 *Official Proceedings of the National Negro Congress*, New York, 1936
19 Franklin, *From Slavery to Freedom*, pp. 519-22
20 Arthur F. Raper, *Preface to Peasantry*, p. 5, Chapel Hill, 1936
21 *Ibid.*, p. 21
22 *Ibid.*, p. 76
23 C. S. Johnson, E. R. Embree and W. W. Alexander, *The Collapse of Cotton Tenantcy*, p. 14, Chapel Hill, 1935
24 Howard Kester, *Revolt Among the Sharecroppers*, p. 41, New York, 1936
25 Johnson, Embree and Alexander, *The Collapse of Cotton Tenantcy*, p. 48
26 Burt, *MS.*
27 Raper, *Preface to Peasantry*, p. 245
28 *Ibid.*, p. 371

Chapter 45

1 William Z. Foster, *Misleaders of Labor*, New York, 1927
2 Lorwin, *The American Federation of Labor*, p. 304
3 H. R. Northrup, *Organized Labor and the Negro*, pp. 11-13, New York, 1944
4 Spero, Harris, *The Black Worker*, p. 291
5 Raymond Pace Alexander, *Journal of Negro History*, April, 1945, pp. 144-48
6 Northrup, *Organized Labor and the Negro*, p. 52
7 Spero and Harris, *The Black Worker*, p. 307
8 Horace R. Cayton and George S. Mitchell, *Black Workers and the New Unions*, p. 381, Chapel Hill, 1939
9 William Z. Foster, *American Trade Unionism*, p. 183, New York, 1947
10 William W. Weinstone, *The Great Sit-Down Strike*, New York, 1937
11 Ira DeA. Reid, *Negro Membership in American Labor Unions*, New York, 1930
12 *The Negro Handbook*, 1947, pp. 146-48
13 American Jewish Congress and National Association for Advancement of Colored People, *Civil Rights in the United States*, p. 48, New York, 1952
14 Labor Research Association, *Labor Fact Book VII*, pp. 73-74, New York, 1945
15 Robert W. Dunn, *Labor and Automobiles*, New York, 1929
16 Robert W. Dunn and Jack Hardy, *Labor and Textiles*, New York, 1931
17 *Daily Worker*, November 6, 1952

18 Congress for Industrial Organization, *Working and Fighting Together*
19 John Williamson, *Political Affairs*, November, 1947
20 Northrup, *Organized Labor and the Negro*, pp. 3-5
21 Saul Alinsky, *John L. Lewis*, p. 153, New York, 1949
22 Foster, *History of the Communist Party of the United States*, p. 421

Chapter 46

1 Georgi Dimitrov, *The United Front*, p. 10, New York, 1938
2 Foster, *History of the Communist Party of the United States*, p. 296
3 Franklin, *From Slavery to Freedom*, p. 558
4 *Volunteer for Liberty*, 1937-1938
5 Redding, *They Came in Chains*, p. 290
6 Florence Murray, *The Negro Handbook*, 1949, pp. 242-79
7 Redding, *They Came in Chains*, p. 294
8 Franklin, *From Slavery to Freedom*, p. 572
9 Robert C. Weaver, *The Negro Ghetto*, p. 25, New York, 1948
10 The Library of Congress, Legislative Reference Service, *Lynching*, H. V. 6435, Washington, D. C., 1937
11 Weaver, *The Negro Ghetto*, p. 94
12 Davie, *Negroes in American Society*, pp. 374-83
13 Franklin, *From Slavery to Freedom*, pp. 393-94
14 Davie, *Negroes in American Society*, p. 377
15 A.J.C. and N.A.A.C.P., *Civil Rights in the United States*, 1952, p. 133
16 V. J. Jerome, *The Negro in Hollywood Films*, New York, 1950
17 Franklin, *From Slavery to Freedom*, pp. 508-9
18 *Pittsburgh Courier*, "Fifty Years of Progress," Pittsburgh, 1950
19 Murray, *The Negro Handbook*, 1949, p. 122
20 *Ibid.*, pp. 310, 316
21 *New York Times*, May 11, 1953
22 Lloyd L. Brown, *Masses and Mainstream*, March-April, 1951

Chapter 47

1 Perlo, *American Imperialism*, p. 122
2 Eric Johnson, *We Are All In It*, p. 37, New York, 1941
3 *U.S. News and World Report*, June 12, 1953
4 George Marion, *Bases and Empire*, New York, 1948
5 *The Reporter*, May 26, 1953
6 Labor Research Association, *Economic Notes*, April, 1953
7 Foster, *Misleaders of Labor*
8 Ralph J. Bunche, *A World View of Race*, p. 50, Washington, D. C., 1936
9 *Monthly Review*, April, 1953
10 Civil Rights Congress, William Patterson, *ed.*, *We Charge Genocide*, New York, 1952
11 Howard Johnson, *Political Affairs*, February, 1951
12 Du Bois, *Dusk of Dawn*, p. 313; *Battle for Peace*
13 Allen, *The Negro Question in the United States*, p. 160
14 *Families Committee*, New York, 1952
15 Claudia Jones, *An End to the Neglect of the Problem of the Negro Woman*, p. 9, New York, 1949
16 World Federation of Trade Unions, *World Trade Union Movement*, Paris, 1950
17 Alphaeus Hunton, *Africa Fights for Freedom*, New York, 1950
18 A.J.C. and N.A.A.C.P., *Civil Rights in the United States*

19 *Proceedings of the 71st A.F. of L. Convention*, New York, 1952
20 *Report of Committee on Labor and Public Welfare* (S. 3368), July 3, 1952, Washington, D. C.
21 *Time*, May 11, 1953
22 Civil Rights Congress, *We Charge Genocide*, p. 8
23 The *Daily Worker*, December 9, 1952
24 A.J.C. and N.A.A.C.P., *Civil Rights in the United States*, p. 12
25 *Ibid.*, p. 116
26 Hall, *Marxism and Negro Liberation*, p. 5
27 Justin Gray, *The Inside Story of the Legion*, New York, 1948
28 Civil Rights Commission, The Report of the President's Committee on Civil Rights, *To Secure These Rights*, Washington, D. C., 1947

Chapter 48

1 Gus Hall, *Marxism and Negro Liberation*, p. 11, New York, 1951
2 The President's Committee on Government Contract Compliace, *Equal Economic Opportunity*, p. 55
3 *Time*, May 11, 1953
4 *Daily Worker*, May 19, 1953
5 Perlo, *American Imperialism*, p. 84
6 Senate Sub-Committee on Labor and Managament Relations, *Employment Status of Negroes in the United States*, 1952, p. 14, Washington, D. C.
7 Berry, *Sunday Worker*, August 31, 1952
8 Union Research and Information Service, *Facts and Figures*, February, 1952
9 *Ibid.*, March, 1952; *Final Report*, Fair Employment Practices Committee, June, 1946, p. XI
10 *Labor Fact Book* 11, p. 34, New York, 1953
11 U.S. Senate Sub-Committee on Labor and Management Relations, *Employment Status of Negroes in the United States*, 1952
12 Perlo, *Science and Society*, Spring, 1952, p. 136
13 Jones, *An End to the Neglect of the Problems of Negro Women*
14 Grace Hutchins, *Women Who Work*, p. 13, New York, 1952
15 *Journal of Negro Education*, p. 324, Summer, 1953
16 Arthur F. Raper, in *Proceedings of Tuskegee Rural Life Conference*, June 18-20, 1950, Tuskegee, 1950
17 U.S. Census of Agriculture, *General Report*, Vol. II, p. 226, Washington, D. C., 1950
18 *Life*, January 5, 1953
19 Burt, *MS.*
20 C. C. Taylor, *Proceedings of Tuskegee Rural Life Conference*, p. 60
21 W.P.A. Division of Social Research, T. J. Woofter, *Landlord and Tenant on the Cotton Plantation*, Washington, D. C., 1936
22 Communist Party, *The Southern People's Common Program for Democracy, Prosperity and Peace*, New York, 1953
23 Robert H. Kinzer, and Edward Sagarin, *The Negro in American Business*, p. 120, New York, 1950
24 *Journal of Negro Education*, Summer, 1953
25 Harris, *The Negro as Capitalist*
26 S. T. Henderson, *Political Affairs*, December, 1952
27 Mann, *Stalin's Thought Illuminates Problems of Negro Freedom Struggle*, p. 37
28 *Federal Reserve Bulletin*, August, 1951

29 National Association for the Advancement of Colored People, *An Appeal to the World*, p. 79, New York, 1947
30 Housing and Home Finance Agency, *Housing of the Non-White Population*, Washington, D. C., July, 1952
31 Labor Research Association, *Labor Fact Book 11*, p. 39, New York, 1953
32 Selsam, *The Negro People in the United States*, pp. 11-15
33 *Ibid.*, pp. 11-16
34 A.J.C. and N.A.A.C.P., *Civil Rights in the United States*, p. 11
35 Herbert Aptheker, *America's Racist Laws*, p. 8, New York, 1952
36 Pettis Perry, *Political Affairs*, June, 1949
37 Perlo, *American Imperialism*, p. 89
38 Haywood, *Negro Liberation*, pp. 233-38
39 Perlo, *Science and Society*, Spring, 1952

Chapter 49

1 I. F. Stone, *New York Compass*, February 17, 1952
2 Charles P. Mann, *Political Affairs*, March, 1952
3 Pettis Perry, *Political Affairs*, June, 1949
4 Harry Haywood, *Negro Affairs Quarterly*, Vol. I, No. 1, p. 3, Spring, 1953
5 Eugene Dennis, *The People Against the Trusts*, p. 21, New York, 1946
6 *New York Times*, September 21, 1952
7 Sylvia Porter, *New York Post*, November 13, 1952
8 Labor Research Association, *Labor Fact Book 11*, p. 36

Chapter 50

1 Charles P. Mann, *Stalin's Thought Illuminates Problems of Negro Freedom Struggle*, p. 16, New York, 1953
2 V. I. Lenin, *Collected Works*, Vol. XIX, p. 271, New York, 1942
3 M. D. Kammari, *The Development by J. V. Stalin of the Marxist-Leninist Theory of the National Question*, p. 18, Moscow, 1952
4 Benjamin J. Davis, *The Path of Negro Liberation*, p. 9, New York, 1947
5 Stalin, *Marxism and the National Question*, p. 24
6 George S. Schuyler, *The Crisis*, May, 1935
7 Stalin, *Marxism and the National Question*, pp. 62-68
8 John Pittman, *Masses and Mainstream*, February, 1951
9 Robert Thompson, *Questions and Answers, Communist Party*, New York, 1947
10 International Labor Office, *Report No. 2*, April, 1949, p. 17
11 Du Bois, *Black Folk, Then and Now*, p. 197
12 Melville J. Herskowits, *The Anthropometry of the American Negro*, p. 177, New York, 1930
13 Edward Byron Reuter, *The Mulatto in the United States*, Boston, 1918
14 Lenin, *Collected Works*, Vol. XIX, p. 292
15 Joseph Stalin, *Marxism and Linguistics*, p. 49, New York, 1951
16 Kammari, *The Development by J. V. Stalin of the Marxist-Leninist Theory of the National Question*, p. 30
17 Lenin, *Collected Works*, Vol. XIX, p. 50

INDEX

Abolitionists, after American Revolution, 59; anti-union bias, 115-16; and case of Anthony Burns, 169-70; in Constitutional Convention (1787), 53; and Emancipation Proclamation, 255; in England, 69-71; and Free Soilers, 137; ideological struggle against slavery, 203-211; and Kansas-Nebraska Bill, 178-79; literature barred in mails, 128, 129; and Mexican War, 124; and Negro colonization, 91; Negro-white unity, 110-11; and Negro women, 114; and non-resistane, 166; persecution of, 112, 128; and slave revolts, 127; Southern, 111; vanguard of capitalist class, 111; vote for Lincoln (1860), 218; and women's rights movement, 132; see American Anti-Slavery Society; Douglass; Garrison; Phillips; Sumner

Abolitionists, Negro, 111; demands, 203; and liberation movement, 113-14; ideological defense of Negro people, 204; on slave revolts, 127

Act to Prohibit the Importation of Slaves (1807), 67

Actors, Negro, restricted roles, 537

Africa, agriculture, 17; alphabet worked out, 17; ancient art, 18; awakening of Negro peoples, 527; British economic penetration, 70; Christians in, 20; civilization's debt to, 17; colonial revolt, 522; cradle of mankind, 16; craftsmanship, 18; cultural influence, 17; division of, 21; Douglass, on, 204; ethnic groups, 15; Europeans in, 15; explorers' ignorance of institutions, 20; fetishism in, 20; folk tales, 18; Garvey program, 444; geographical conditions, 16; gold and diamond mines, 15; kinship system, 19; Labor Supply Association, 162; land held in common, 19; Methodist Church, 102; plans of Colonization Society, 89-90; primitive accumulation, 27; seizure of by imperialist powers, 21; slavery in, 24; smuggling of slaves, 162; stripped of population, 26; struggle to defend homeland, 22

African Labor Supply Association, 162

Agriculture (U.S.), Adjustment Act (AAA), 490; after American Revolution, 56; growth in West, 84; mechanization and Negro farmers, 535, 536; Negroes in (1950), 465; plantation retards, 232, 233; production increase, 365; reorganization in post-Civil War South, 358; slave and free compared, 235; and slavery, 35, 152, 231; see Cotton production; Negro farmers; Plantations; Sharecropping; Tobacco

Alien and Sedition Acts (1798), 57

American Anti-Slavery Society, agitation, 110; anti-political, 135; Declaration of Sentiments, 107-09, 111, 117; formed,

105; leaders, 110; membership, 129; on Negro emancipation, 109; split in, 136, 137, 289, 290; see Abolitionists

American colonies, anti-slavery sentiment, 48-49; commerce, 44; economic systems, 38, 39; slavery issue, 85; slave codes, 37, 38; slave revolts, 42; slave trade, 25; "solving" land problem, 32

American Colonization Society, deportation program, 93, 109; scant results, 91; schemes opposed by Negroes, 90; supporters, 89

American Federation of Labor, anti-Negro policies, 372-74, 426, 498, 502; craft organization, 370-72, 459; crisis of 1929-33, 480; on F.E.P.C., 502, 527; growth (1900-1914), 422; Jim Crow clauses, 502; labor aristocracy, 372; letter from Negro organizations (1918), 438; membership (1920-23), 440, (1934) 492, (1940) 497, (1945) 499; Negro members (1928), 493, (1948), 498; Negro officials, 524; white chauvinism, 372, 438-39, 502

American fortunes, origin of in Civil War, 246-47

American League of Colored Laborers (1850), 348

American Negro Labor Congress (1925), 460, 481

American Party; see Know-Nothing Party

American Revolution (1776), causes of, 44; and chattel slavery, 48; class forces in, 43; Lenin on, 50; reason for victory, 45

American Society for the Colonization of the Free People of Color of the United States (1816); see American Colonization Society

Amistad revolt, 127

Anderson, Marian, 489, 515

Anglican Church on slavery, 38

Angolese, slaves to U.S., 28

Anti-Imperialist League (1899), 415

Anti-lynching bills, introduced in Congress, 513; and Roosevelt Administration, 490

Anti-Masonic Party, 147

Anti-secessionist sentiment in Border states, 245

Anti-slavery journals, 106-07

Anti-slavery sentiment, among poor whites, 78; in colonial America, 48-49; in early South, 68; in England, 70; in woman's rights movement, 114, 132; in working class, 199-200

Anti-slavery societies, in early 1800's, 62; first formed, 49; influenced by slave insurrections in Spanish-American colonies, 106; tasks of, in 1850's, 201; see Abolitionists, American Anti-Slavery Society

Arabs, overrunning North Africa, 20; slave trade in women, 24